The Mistress-Knowledge

Sir Philip Sidney's *Defence of Poesie*
and Literary Architectonics in the
English Renaissance

The
Mistress-Knowledge

Sir Philip Sidney's *Defence of Poesie*
and Literary Architectonics in the
English Renaissance

M. J. Doherty

VANDERBILT UNIVERSITY PRESS
Nashville 1991

Published 1991 by Vanderbilt University Press
Printed in the United States of America

Library of Congress Cataloging-in-Publication Data

Doherty, M. J. (Mary Jane), 1945–
    The Mistress-knowledge: Sir Philip Sidney's Defence of poesie and literary
architectonics in the English Renaissance / M.J. Doherty.
        p.   cm.
Book began as author's dissertation at the University of Wisconsin in Madison.
Includes bibliographical references (p.   ) and index.
    ISBN 0–8265–1241–0 :
    1. Sidney, Philip, Sir, 1554–1586—Knowledge and learning.   2.English poetry—
Early modern, 1500–1700—History and criticism—Theory etc.   3. Sidney, Philip, Sir,
1554–1586. Apologie for poetrie.   4. Knowledge, Theory of, in literature.
5. Self-knowledge in literature.   6. Rhetoric—1500–1800.   7. Allegory.   8. Poetry.
I. Title.
PR2343.D57   1991
821'.3—dc20   90–23176
                                                                                CIP

For my French mother and Irish father

In paradísum dedúcant te Angeli:
in tuo advéntu suscípiant te Martyres,
et perdúcant te in civitátem sanctam Jerúsalem

Contents

Acknowledgments

The researching and the writing of this book have drawn two universities in my scholarly life together, full circle, and require more expressions of gratitude than I can properly make.

The Mistress-Knowledge began as a dissertation many years ago at the University of Wisconsin in Madison where Professors Madeleine Doran and Alex B. Chambers codirected it and Professor William Courtenay oversaw its medieval intellectual history. I would like to think that the resultant book contributes to the definition of merely one of the aesthetic terms Miss Doran's *Endeavors of Art* taught generations about, and I hope I have caught some aspect of the wisdom my teacher's friendship has steadily demonstrated in the living, too. Besides giving of his polymathy to save me from many errors of judgment, Alex Chambers has faithfully watched over my career in teaching, personifying for me the bond between traditions of learning at Wisconsin and at Vanderbilt University, his alma mater. If my work possesses some symmetry with his humane scholarship, I shall be happy. William Courtenay, who advised me long ago to look at Sophia and to judge historical continuities between medieval thought and the Reformation, will recognize, I trust, *scintillae rationis* here, flying between Cambridge and Nashville. The dissertation was written at the Folger Shakespeare Library in Washington, D.C., the book at Vanderbilt University while I was teaching there.

At Vanderbilt the University Research Council funded summer trips to the Houghton Library, Harvard, and a substantial sabbatical grant, which I used during 1983 and 1984 at the University Library, Cambridge, England, the Bodleian Library, Oxford, and the British Library, London. To all of these research institutions and to two department chairpersons, James F. Kilroy and Vereen M. Bell, I say thanks.

Individually, and for lending their lights in various ways to this effort, I want to thank Professors Jane Donawerth, Phyllis Frus, S. K. Heninger, Jr., Robert Kimbrough, Arthur Kinney, Laurence Lerner, Leonard Nathanson, Barbara Nolan, Jack Prostko, Thomas P. Roche, Jr., Richard Schoeck, John T. Shawcross, and Harold Weatherby. Elizabeth Cawley, C.S.J., corrected my Latin translations and Greek paraphrases. As I prepared the manuscript

ix

for publication, Professors Don E. Wayne and Andrew D. Weiner generously provided critical perceptions that helped me bring the aggregate of historical evidence I had collected to bear on contemporary literary theory and interpretive argument. I am in debt to them for understanding the significance of the lost image I have attempted to recover. Mr. John Poindexter is the kindly godfather of this book's publication and the able Director of Vanderbilt University Press. Mr. Bard Young, his assistant, and copy editor Mrs. Dimples Kellogg have given the manuscript unstinting care.

Any errors that remain after all this help surely belong to an ungraceful division in me between "Nature's child," "Studie," and the unseen Image in the heart. But I dare hope that readers will make up what is lacking with their own most literate self-knowledge.

The edition of *The Defence of Poetry* cited throughout is that of Katherine Duncan-Jones and Jan van Dorsten, eds., in *Miscellaneous Prose of Sir Philip Sidney* (Oxford: Clarendon, 1973), pp. 73–121. The title of the treatise I uniformly use because of the feminine allegory that is my subject, however, is *The Defence of Poesie,* which is William Ponsonby's in the 1595 edition, deriving *poesie* from the Italian *poesia.* Any citations of the *Arcadia* are to the Countess of Pembroke's 1590 edition in Albert Feuillerat, ed., *The Complete Works of Sir Philip Sidney,* 4 vols. (Cambridge: Cambridge Univ. Press, 1912), vol. 1, unless another version, volume, or edition of the *Arcadia* is indicated. For *Astrophil and Stella* I cite the edition of William A. Ringler, *The Poems of Sir Philip Sidney* (Oxford: Clarendon, 1962). Citations of *The Bible and Holy Scriptures Conteyned in the Olde and Newe Testament* (Geneva: Rouland Hall, 1560) are taken from *The Geneva Bible, A Facsimile of the 1560 Edition,* introduced by Lloyd E. Berry (Madison: Univ. of Wisconsin Press, 1969).

Unless otherwise noted, translations are my own; in presenting Latin sources I have left the text unedited, not changing the *u* and *v* or *i* and *j*. I have, however, often filled in *que* for *q,* and supplied an *n* or *m* where the copy had an abbreviation. Where Greek is involved, I have done my best to interpret the ligatures of early printed Greek and have transcribed the word or phrase in modern characters. Wishing to acknowledge the French influence and some Sidneian resistance to it in the burgeoning nationalisms of the sixteenth century, I have regularly alluded to Jean de Serres or de Serres, keeping the particle and neither Anglicizing (Serres) nor Latinizing (Johannes Serranus) the name of the Huguenot humanist whose gift of *Plato* to the bright young Sidney was part of an intellectual, political, and religious appeal to British and Scottish monarchs to look kindly on the Reformed Church.

Madison, Wisconsin
Pentecost 1990

Preface

Dig deepe with learning's spade. . . .

—*Astrophil and Stella* 21

Unlike Thales of Miletus, the ancient astronomer who looked up at the skies and fell into a ditch, the readers of—and, indeed, the characters *in*—renaissance writing often stumble over metaphors that carry us into the heavens only to drop us back to earth with a jolt. Having visions of heavenly beauty is not a problem; what one does with the knowledge so gained and how one expresses it with the "remnant" of one's wit in a Babel's tongue usually are (*A & S* 2). Metaphors abound in Sir Philip Sidney's writing, both heavenly and earthly ones, and the case for metaphor comes home to Sidney and his personifications in the *Defence*. Playing the roles of the poet-captain and the heroic reader, both of whom Sidney names "Cyrus," he looks within himself, interrelating all these visions and problems in an experience of a third persona, "the mistress-knowledge," that is, an idea of poesie as self-knowledge. Looking within makes the connections necessary to thinking and to acting.

Readers of Sidney have met "the mistress-knowledge" before, more in name than in meaning. In *The Countesse of Pembrokes Arcadia* published for the first time four hundred years ago, Strephon and Claius have seen Urania and remember her in the mind's eye:

And, alas, who can better witness that then we, whose experience is grounded upon feeling? hath not the onely love of her made us (being silly ignorant shepheards) raise up our thoughts above the ordinary levell of the worlde, so as great clearkes do not disdaine our conferences? hath not the desire to seem worthie in her eyes made us when others were sleeping, to sit vewing the course of the heavens? when others were running at base, to runne over learned writings? when others marke their sheepe, we to marke our selves? hathe not shee throwne reason upon our desires, and, as it were given eyes to *Cupid*? hath in any, but in her love-fellowship maintained fellowship between rivals, and beautie taught the beholders chastitie? (1:1.1, 7–8)

In the case of Sidney's *Astrophil and Stella*, the extended metaphor of poet-soldier and the inspiring lady produces an entirely different effect. Astrophil's mind's eye is quite a muddy one; his desire to seem worthy is mixed thoroughly with a base longing to possess a self-carved, idolatrous image. The thing made with Cupid's dart is adored "in temple of our hart, / Till that good God make Church and Churchman slaive" (*A & S* 5). As Astrophil records the moral disjuncture within him, readers change uni-verses from that of the apparently good Stella, Simplicity and Claire who look an absent presence, to that of a bad Christian. "For though she passe all things, yet what is all / That unto me, who fare like him that both / Lookes to the skies, and in a ditch doth fall?" (*A & S* 19). Stella may be the "fairest book of Nature" in which Astrophil may know "How Vertue may best lodg'd in beautie be," for her self "doest strive all minds that way to move," but Astrophil fallen in a fallen world will not be so moved in love to the good. " 'But ah,' Desire still cries, 'give me some food' " (*A & S* 71).

One problem for man is woman, and vice versa. Another is the mind and the degree to which learning itself is useless or even corrupted; and a third is action, the ethical and political decision-making one must bring to practice in the world. All pertain to religious faith or the lack of faith. As Philippe du Plessis Mornay put it in the Protestant apologetic whose translation was partially credited to Sidney, atheists "offend not through reasoning, but for want of reasoning." Those who believe the Gospel and profess the Christian religion offend by living "as though we beleeved it not" and by preaching the kingdom of heaven but scarcely thinking about it in earnest "once in a whole yeare."[1]

In *The Defence of Poesie*, however, Sidney gave his audience a way of reasoning, believing, and thinking about heaven and earth. This way is named "the mistress-knowledge," the art not of poetry but of *poesie*:

> But when by the balance of experience it was found that the astronomer, looking to the stars, might fall in a ditch, that the inquiring philosopher might be blind in himself, and the mathematician might draw forth a straight line with a crooked heart, then lo, did proof, the overruler of opinions, make manifest that all these are but serving sciences, which as they have each a private end in themselves, so yet are they all directed to the highest end of the mistress-knowledge, by the Greeks called ἀρχιτεκτονική, which stands (as I think) in the knowledge of a man's self, in the ethic and politic consideration, with the end of well-doing and not of well-knowing only. (*Def.*, pp. 82–83)

Because Sidney's poesie is the art that discerns visionary reality from illusory images and turns earthly learning into virtuous action, this book, which began as a gloss on one aesthetic metaphor in Sidney's critical lexicon, has grown in face of accumulating historical data into a consideration of the whole of English renaissance poetic theory and practice through the perspective glass of the *Defence*.

Likewise, this preface—which is a preview of the history and significance of Sidney's metaphor in the contents of the book—parts ways with the

linear, patriarchal fashions of deconstruction and its criticism of prefatory
efforts to unify and totalize. For the sake of clarity, this introductory discourse circles through the contents of the entire manuscript; for the sake of
the recovery of Sidney's feminized allegory of self-knowledge, these remarks briefly preview the questions of epistemology and criticism, the
definition of "literary architectonics," the reassessment of Protestant poetics, and the Sidneian assertion of theological and feminine presences of
grace that have been suppressed in the celebration of the male poet's
sprezzatura or the male critic's dissemination of ideas.

The Renaissance Context and Sidneian Self-Knowledge

This book is about a concept of universal knowledge that was allegorized
as a feminine persona in an English renaissance definition of a philosophical
poetics. When, however, Sir Philip Sidney coined his complex figure of
speech in *The Defence of Poesie*—"the mistress-knowledge, by the Greeks
called ἀρχιτεκτονική"—the critical metaphor at the center of his allegory of
poesie stood for a masculine self-knowledge associated with the powers of
language to move action. Architectonics "stands (as I think) in the knowledge of a man's self, . . . with the end of well-doing and not of well-knowing
only," Sidney explains.

In the history of Western thought the philosophical concept of architectonic knowledge was, indeed, called *master*craftsmanship after the architect's ability to coordinate several disciplines in the art of building. From
antiquity onward, the name signified less the literal praise of the master-
builder and more, by analogy, the ethical and political building of the state
out of the superior knowledge of all the arts and sciences described in
classical metaphysics. Renaissance humanists applied the architectural
analogy in rhetoric to the organization of speculative, practical, and linguistic arts and sciences and to the mechanical crafts. In this manner they
recorded a cultural response to perceived changes in epistemology, especially in the structure of knowledge received from Platonic and Aristotelian
traditions and transformed by medieval Augustinianism.

One revision particularly affected Sidney. In 1578 the French historian
and theologian Jean de Serres produced his syncretic defence of classical
philosophy on the religious grounds of an irenic and learned Calvinism in
Estienne's *belle-édition* of the *Platonis Opera Quae Extant Omnia*; in his
dialogue commentaries the concept of an architectonic knowledge was
further transformed into a Protestant humanist statement of "the true and
well-grounded philosophy" of Christian learning, language, and life. At-
tempting the reconciliation of Plato and Aristotle through his historical and
theological knowledge of Augustinian, scholastic, and Calvinistic doctrines,
Jean de Serres especially turned his philosophical syncretism toward an

architectonic philosophy of language. His commentaries were a version of
the *philosophia Christi* of antiquity, and he developed in them an awareness
of the gifts of God—reason, learning, conscience, speech, statesmanship
that seeks the "golden world"—and an idea of love and its allegory that is
more Solomonic than Socratic. Seeing a providential design in the universe,
de Serres extended Erasmian humanism into a Protestant political program
for the building of godly kingdoms. His intention was pragmatic: he wanted
architectonic principles expressed in the powerful speech and statesmanlike
actions of regenerate minds to infuse ethical force into political reality, and
he especially addressed his architectonic philosophy in dedications to
Queen Elizabeth of England, King James of Scotland, her successor-to-be,
and the citizens of the theocracy of Berne. Sir Philip Sidney was sent a gift
copy of this edition of *Plato* along with a request, which came through his
mentor Hubert Languet, that he commend the edition to the Queen.[2]

Already mightily intrigued by the *dispute dell'arti* of his age, Sidney used
Jean de Serres's conflation of classical and Christian architectonic philosophies for his own historical purpose. He imaginatively fulfilled Languet's request by directing his reading of this *Plato* specifically toward the
historical defence of the poetic art in England—the poesie that surpasses
both philosophy and history. By doing so Sidney contributed a further
revision of classical and medieval traditions to the Protestant humanist
enterprise.

From our modern vantage, one may say that Sidney anticipated philosophers of history such as Hegel and Heidegger but in his own fashion
and according to his own sixteenth-century operative beliefs.[3] Writing in the
ripeness of the medieval vision but distinctly as a Protestant *and* English
thinker, Sidney appropriated the force and scope of classical ideas of architectonics for poesie by placing all knowledge under the allegorical model
of its unity, which he found theologically authorized by the change in
history of thought brought about by the coming of "the light of Christ" and
biblically imaged in the feminine figure of Sophia or Solomonic "wisdom."
In the context of the English Reformation, poesie, therefore, not philosophy
or history per se, was the divinely blessed knowledge that mediated between the human limits of the arts and sciences and the Wisdom of God, and
this ἀρχιτεκτονική "stood" in a man's self-knowledge. By taking on the
allegorical veil of the mistress-knowledge, Sidney took on as well her intellectual and moral superiority as the sovereign gift of God and metamorphosed her intermediate power of conscience into the wisdom possible in a
man in history. If one man could be so generated (or regenerated) in
self-knowledge, then other men could be re-created by his "Adamic" power
of language to name things and to increase and multiply.

Obviously such appropriation of a feminized power is another version of
containing "Eve" or of capturing the Spirit, and Sidney's invention of a

feminized allegorical figure to unify the many strands of architectonic philosophical tradition resonates on one level with the demands of his immediate
political context, that is, the rule of Queen Elizabeth. The differential,
androgynous figure of the mistress-knowledge constitutes in renaissance
poetics the appropriation of a power gendered as feminine, and Sidney's
Defence of Poesie is, among other things, an imaginative defence of aristocratic male power in an historically specific form.

The argument of this book is the recovery from history of the side of
Sidney's allegory of poesie that has not been articulated in literary criticism,
namely, the image of the mistress-knowledge in whose name Sidney reconstructed the myth of Platonic inspiration into a renaissance Protestant doctrine of gnosis. The recovery of this sort of rhapsody is tantamount to the
remembering of Sidney's epistemology.[4] Scholarship has been fixed on a
reified image of the poem as a verbal artifact and has been unable to assess
adequately the influence of the *Defence* in the formation of an English
literary culture from the Renaissance to the present because it has denied
Sidney's epistemological and feminine figure for an integrative, mediating,
and sovereign knowledge of human conscience. Although the figure of the
mistress-knowledge has been excised from literary study as if it were merely
an accidental trope based on the grammatical gender of Aristotle's Greek
grammar in the *Nicomachean Ethics,* it should be restored as the organizing
metaphor par excellence of the *Defence.*[5] Only when we do restore it will the
Defence be free of its historical treatment as a rhetorically brilliant miscellany
of ideas (but little more than that) and be known as a wellspring of English
poetic authority for centuries.

Epistemology and Criticism

Three questions emerge from Sidney's vivid metaphor in *The Defence of
Poesie,* and this book aims to ask and to answer them as much as possible.
First is the question of the influence of the *Defence.* Literary history has
constantly asserted the *Defence*'s influence while refusing to acknowledge
the epistemological link between the universal knowledge inherent in an
Aristotelian-Platonic and architectonic art of poesie on one side and the
feminized metaphor of religious, political power in the mistress-knowledge
on the other.

Second is the major set of epistemological questions that result from
establishing such a link. Does Sidney put knowledge aside in favor of a
religiously inspired moral force? Or does he apprehend the rehabilitation of
all the knowledges in a foolish world by means of the conscientious art of
poesie? If so, does Sidney see in poesie the principle of analogy that discovers some deeply embedded formal unity in the arts and sciences? Does
the mixture of disciplines and subject matters in the content of renaissance

poetry imply the poet's true polymathy, or is it the poet's rhetorical specialty
or methodology that allows him to order the various knowledges in words?
Is poesie a special knowledge like dialectic or geometry, grammar or music,
or rhetoric? We know that Sidney performs an Aristotelian anatomy of the
forms of knowledge according to their objects, ends, and scopus and then
distinguishes poesie from the revealed truth of religion in Holy Scripture in
itself and from *all* other types of knowledge, which have their ends in nature
and are "actors and players" of nature—even the metaphysics that ordinarily would organize the arts and sciences into a philosophical unity. We also
know that in posing the *intermediacy* of poesie between divine and human
knowledge Sidney answers the charges made by Plato against poetry with
Aristotelian, Stoic, and Judeo-Christian arguments. That is, he argues the
final integrity of human knowledge in poetic discourse *because* poesie teleologically achieves the "ending end" of learning, which is to lift the soul out
of its dungeon and toward heaven.

The comparison of poesie as "the highest point of man's wit" with "the
maker" (*natura naturans*) of the world (*natura naturata*) puts the poet as
maker into a triangular analogy with the heavenly Maker and focuses the
third question. In the epistemology of the mistress-knowledge what kind of
power and how much of it does Sidney give to the poet's verbal making?
How does poesie, the art of thinking and making, really differ from the poet
as maker and from the poem as a thing made, an artifact?

Insofar as Sidney's participation in the arts disputes of the Renaissance
redirected his knowledge of philosophy and history into an allegory of
poesie, numerous epistemological questions raised by his treatise continue
to affect our modern arts disputes as well. The fact that Sidney lived out the
masculine, "heroic" side of his allegory of poesie gave his poetics and its
apparent focus on praxis that status of an aristocratic standard of letters in
many, if not all, quarters in the 1590s and, by reputation, confirmed him well
beyond the middle of the seventeenth century as the icon of the learned
poet's soldierly statesmanship.[6] Sidney's poetics, which is a microcosm of
the culture of the English Renaissance according to C. S. Lewis, thus became
formative of that culture's later development and, through its great literature, of our literary culture, too.[7] For centuries the *Defence* has informed the
master-building of England by being the critic's poem of himself, the reified
image of the witty but nonetheless brave and active literary man whose
character has been built in his own education and whose writing and
example contribute to the construction of his times.

Although suppressed during the rise of eighteenth-century textual
scholarship, Sidney's view of poetic imagination, ethical power, politics,
and inward light was transposed into nineteenth-century thought by Coleridge, Lamb, Shelley, and Arnold, until J. A. Symonds could say in his
biography published on the tercentenary of Sidney's death that his character

established the historical analogy between two centuries of rule by English Queens. The "kindly blending of many qualities" in Sidney, Symonds stated, is a lesson bequeathed from Elizabethan to Victorian England, "which can never lose its value for Greater Britain also, and for that confederated empire which shall, if fate defeat not the high aspiration of the Anglo-Saxon race, arise to the grandest birth of future time."[8] Thus critics alluding to Sidney's Defence often place it in the context of Shelley's Defence of Poetry published in 1821 or of Coleridgean aesthetics, following I. A. Richards, to speak about modern literary knowledge. Kenneth Myrick demonstrated that Sidney was a "literary craftsman," and William K. Wimsatt and Cleanth Brooks credited the Defence as an early statement of literary self-consciousness in English literary criticism, continuing the argument of Sidney's modeling of the gentleman of letters. This approach has fed twentieth-century "ideologies" on both sides, pro and con New Criticism, as theorists routinely allude to Sidney's poetics as a silent touchstone or ground of reference and rarely explore the Defence of Poesie in its own historical dimension and documentation. Yet we should take greater care today not to confuse Sidney's moral-theological sense of the "balance of experience" (Def., p. 82) with the post-Kantian efforts of New Criticism and its kind of balance and presence in stabilizing the sublime in the harmony, unity, and order of the beautiful object.[9] If we must use eighteenth- or nineteenth- or twentieth-century philosophy, better Hegel, history, Husserl, and phenomenology than Kant and his eternal, "pure" reason, as I shall try to explain in the Epilogue.

In large measure, our contemporary theories risk misinterpretation of Sidney because they are tacitly based on his poetics. English literary criticism is, in this respect, like a repetition compulsion operating until the unconscious becomes conscious. Twentieth-century critics have striven to dissociate literary pursuits from the religious and political premises that formalism affirmed and denied as it developed in England and America in our early decades, notably in New Criticism. As we open up this unconsciousness, "ideologies" multiply and "truth" has become, for a time, elusive. Older style historical scholarship has been finding documentation well enough, but often without intervening in our modern discussion of literary theory to track the implications. For students of Sidney the intellectual danger of continuing to underwrite the premises of New Criticism has been matched in recent years, therefore, by the intellectual danger of falsified analyses from quarters trying to defrock it—namely, the projection of modern historical judgments on the sixteenth-century English context in the Marxist critique or in some expressions of New Historicism.

In the most general terms, the recovery of the mistress-knowledge and of Sidney's ideas of literary architectonics should enable us to observe the so-called rise of literary study in the university in the nineteenth century, which Terry Eagleton has discussed, as an event having longer and more complicated historical roots. Evangelical minister Thomas Dale called literary study a "mental culture connected with moral instruction," both of which were "enlisted in the service of Religion" in his inaugural lecture as professor of literature at University College in 1828. I follow D. J. Palmer's history in this respect more than Eagleton's assignation of responsibility to New Criticism for associating the poem with "an absolute mystical authority" which brooked no rational argument" and which cultivated its tie to "religious dogma." Palmer recognized "a natural point of departure" in the rise of English consciousness of a national literature in the sixteenth, not the nineteenth, century, and specifically in the renaissance awareness of rhetoric and of belles lettres. We come still closer to the mark, perhaps, in the remark of Jerome J. McGann, a well-known exponent of New Historicism, who has recently called Sidney's *Defence* "the most influential text on poetics in English" because Sidney distinguished poetic discourse from historical and philosophical kinds and indicated the mimetic rather than the predicative and propositional nature of poetry. "Poetry therefore delivers a kind of virtual reality wherein nothing is affirmed and nothing is denied," McGann says in *Social Values and Poetic Acts.* [10]

But we can, and must, go further. We must also recognize the widening gap between readers who see poems as technical contrivances (artifacts, microcosms, verbal machines, the mimetic thing projecting man's identity and praxis) and those who hear poems in human voices through the numinosity of history. This gap is essentially a modern and patriarchal division, and the poets of the Renaissance insisted on our seeing and hearing to cross it. So poesie, the art of inspired *thinking*, freely crosses all sorts of epistemological boundaries with her spoken words, including those of written poetry—the specific, historically limited products of her craftsman's mimesis. For poesie transcends all arts and sciences epistemologically by being their integrative moral purpose, their gnosis.

Since Sidney's transformation of epistemology took an emphatically literary, gendered, and religious expression and since those very features have been dramatically suppressed in modern discussions of Sidney's poetics and renaissance aesthetics, this book necessarily presents a triple theme: an historical elucidation of the tradition of philosophical and literary architectonics; a reading of the metaphors and oratorical patterns of the *Defence* in the sixteenth-century context; and an intervention in current debates concerning the status of the literary subject or so-called central self of the humanists and their theological grounding of some determinate meaning. Long before Nietzsche, Sidney the Protestant humanist questioned the constructions of historiography, and well before Derrida the philosopher despaired at tracing an elusive presence, Sidney the poet remembered a revealed Wisdom.[11] If the influence of *The Defence of Poesie* on English letters is a literary-historical commonplace that can hardly be questioned, its effect on our cultural efforts to justify literary knowledge in the practice of criticism has, nonetheless, hardly begun to be documented in all of its ramifications.

To my rewriting of this history, Professor Margaret W. Ferguson provided a brilliant prelude, the essay on criticism and Sidney's "pleas for power" in her book *Trials of Desire*.[12] Ferguson listens to the voices in Sidney's arts treatise, using the dialogic method of Bakhtin to measure the speaker's apology for himself and his art. Many of my interpretive insights finally concur critically with Ferguson's analysis, but I arrive at them having worked through history on different premises. In substance we explore ultimately divergent spheres and follow different methods of inquiry in our studies of Sidney.

Beginning with Socrates's apology in a quasi-Derridean approach from the ground of Platonic discourse, Ferguson cogently argues that Sidney's *Defence* represents an historical stage in the defense of the speaking subject, and she follows this trial into Freud's defense of psychoanalysis. Essentially she analyzes the generic patterns of attack and courtship inherent in literary criticism in Sidney's speech according to the rhetorical definition of allegory as a courtly figure promoting duplicity. Historically, as we shall see, this definition is more Puttenham's than Sidney's, although both implement the figure. The phenomenological allegorical presence of the mistress-knowledge remains unacknowledged and unarticulated in Ferguson's "Pleas for Power." But Sidney's figure is a theological and scriptural personification, not merely the duplicitous mask of Sidney's "knowledge of a man's self" on which Ferguson bases her sense of his aesthetic retreat and political search for power—that is, his inner division as a speaking subject. In quoting the passage of the *Defence* in which Sidney alludes to self-knowledge, for instance, Ferguson actually elides the text so as to *omit* both the word ἀρχιτεκτονική and Sidney's figurative translation, the mistress-knowledge. Yet she rightly supplies the sense with the word "wisdom" (p. 142). The elision is charged—either with the potential for undermining Ferguson's argument about the "epistemological barrier" in Sidney's *Defence* and how he does or does not overcome it or, more likely, with the implication that Ferguson's intent in this essay is to clear the field of numerous defenses (all the way to Freud's defense of psychoanalysis) so as to enter it with a feminist critique. Meantime, though, the modern dialogue that permeates Ferguson's study exercises a censoring function; this serves criticism but not historical documentation or argument.

The part of wisdom's defense has fallen, appropriately, not to the male speaking subject's plea for power, but to the epistemological story of the mistress-knowledge. In her trial, like that of another slandered woman,

Shakespeare's Hermione in *The Winter's Tale*, she must begin by hoping for "clearer knowledge" in those who banish her, but she ends as an image that moves and lives to speak about her self-preservation.[13]

Although our contemporary dissolution or division of the speaking subject possesses its own modern energy, we can learn something about its best application in gender studies by articulating images before we try to dissolve them. To a great degree the humanistic idea of a central self is more a topos of modernists trying to account for their own sense of fragmentation than it is an idea of the Renaissance or the Reformation. In twentieth-century parlance the conceptual dissolution of such a central self or Kantian transcendent ego serves the good purpose of breaking down certain illusions of cultural integrity, including that of the masculine and heroic speaking subject. Yet the same critical dismantling of the proposition of the central self can sometimes import historical distortions into the literary study of medieval and renaissance texts precisely because the lack of or even denial of a properly theological ground imposes either a false rationality or an amorphous mysticism on poems spoken by selves that had a strongly documented theological and spiritual basis.

In this respect the intertextuality one finds in the *Defence* actually expresses the Protestant icon of the self who is and is not. The process of self-knowing invariably works out the true self, bringing the false self or selves to the light.[14] In biblical terms, Sidney's architectonic selves in the *Defence*—his "notable *prosopopoeias*" (*Def.*, p. 77)—perform exactly this function. In them he has built masks of personality to demonstrate the necessity of having a self before losing the self in order to regain the true image of God in the soul, which is the purpose of the human experience of time. In Freudian terms one must have an ego to lose the ego. The mistress-knowledge is one such personification, and in Sidney's *Defence* she signifies more than a fleeting allegory of universal knowledge. Sidney's Sophia actually affords a glimpse of something transcendently "other," and that is why the speaker experiences some urgency in making her immanently his own "knowledge of a man's self."[15]

To say so I have borrowed and qualified Julia Kristeva's study of developments in language that "structured in" masculine forms of presence and apparently erased the feminine forms. Although drawing on Husserl, Kristeva does not reestablish Kant's transcendent ego. She thinks over Saint Augustine's philosophy of language, the "mother tongue," and the feminization of the City of God as a mother to whom every son returns, recovering the Augustinian notion of the "magister" within the inner man who governs the truth of language, by way of her intention, as a woman, to carry out the desire for language "to the outer borders of the signifying venture of men."[16] In so doing, Kristeva in *Polylogue* actually undertakes a negative form of inquiry into architectonic construction. Her epistemological interrogation of the relations among various kinds of knowledge and expression through types of analogy appears in the discussion of the truth of language and her discourse about language; she examines not a common *truth* in those analogies but a common *illusion*—"la constitution de quelques illusions communes; la Langue, le Discours, la Linguistique, la Peinture, la Littérature" (p. 7)—and her examination proceeds by way of modern sciences of symbolization overlapping with psychoanalytic disciplines. In this negative approach to architectonics, which is a concept but not a word that Kristeva uses, she dismantles the truth of the analogy of the Word in Augustinian, medieval, and renaissance philosophies of language. Without saying so, Kristeva also opposes, I think, the Kantian sense of architectonic unity phrased in Werner Jaeger's *Paideia*, German scholarship of World War II vintage.[17] Jaeger's historical approach and Kristeva's distinctly postwar–French sensibility further contextualize the statement of renaissance literary architectonics in this book, which searches out an early modern view.

In my reading of the mistress-knowledge, the erotic dimension and the displacement of desire in Augustine's thought coexist with the recovery of a feminine image and with its transformation into the very inquiry into God, that is, theology, when Augustine had reached the boundary of his intellect in the probing of his memory. This desire is finally theological love. Augustine saw a divine Providence operating in history, and so did the Calvinist Sir Philip Sidney whose poetics may be named "literary architectonics" not because it validates the signifying and "making" venture of men, but because it challenges the constructions of reality men do, indeed, make.

Literary Architectonics

The first chapter of this book locates Sidney's ἀρχιτεκτονικὴ at the center of the *Defence* as one of three "notable *prosopopoeias*" he invents (the mistress-knowledge, the poet-soldier-prince, and Cyrus the reader) and places the figure in the cultural context of the renaissance usage of the word *architectonic*.

Historical data and the reading of the *Defence* in their context, however, immediately require consideration of the implications of Sidney's allegory of poesie for our contemporary critical theories, particularly phenomenology, structuralism, deconstruction, historicism, Marxism, and feminism. But I have deliberately delayed this consideration until chapter 2 in order to place Sidney's text and renaissance historical data before us more clearly before weighing the significance of Sidney's allegory of self-knowledge and its relation to Sophia.

Since the three prosopopoeias of the *Defence* actually structure its argument as a story of thought, the third chapter looks at Sidney's invention of prosopopoeias as an expression of a practical wisdom shared between author and reader. These images constitute the *rhetorical intertextuality* of the *Defence* since Sidney fashions his "voices" and "masks" out of his wide learning and practical knowledge.

The fourth chapter primarily demonstrates the philosophical influence of Jean de Serres's *Plato* on Sidney's treatise. The intertextualization of this "philosopher's book" almost uniquely accounts for the treatment of architectonic knowledge in the *Defence* simply because de Serres's commentaries are a French compendium of renaissance thought; but because Sidney's use of the book is so singularly English, it is also the source of some parody in Sidney's rehabilitation of the Plato who exiled poets from the good republic and of Sidney's own working definition of literary architectonics.

The fifth chapter examines renaissance arts treatises written both before and after the *Defence,* especially noting their use of a gender analogy of knowledge that finally opposes the feminine figure to an architectural construction of male character. This chapter also examines philosophical poems by John Davies and Fulke Greville, Sidney's biographer, in which Sidney's allegory of poesie was recapitulated—in the first case including the feminine figure and in the second case reducing or expunging it.

The Epilogue actually picks up the threads of chapter 2 with regard to the implications of the image of the mistress-knowledge for contemporary literary history and criticism. In this conclusion I strive to sort out the differences between Sidney's poetics and Kantian aesthetics in view of the fact that much modern criticism regularly confuses Sidney's ἀρχιτεκτονική with the "Architectonic of Pure Reason" of Kant's *Critique of Pure Reason.*

The truest demonstration of an English renaissance transformation of architectonic knowledge first into poetry and then into the "true Poems" of character inspired by this mistress is the actual metaphor-making of renaissance poems. Poesie *is* Sidney's literary theory, for the high philosophizing of the English Renaissance was not primarily a scientific or a systematic speculation or a practical revolution in history. It was poetry. Sidney's *Defence* justifies the folly of poesie in the terms of the folly of its "sister," religious belief, who is a type of wisdom, and Milton's designation of his Urania as the sister of that eternal Wisdom in the invocation to Book 7 of *Paradise Lost* follows suit.

Throughout this book I have named Sidney's definition of poetic discourse "literary architectonics" and generally described its features in chapter 2 in relation to several kinds of modern theory. Literary architectonics reflects a particularly renaissance model of poetic language committed to the negotiation of complex analogies, antitheses, and paradoxes so that its balances are peculiarly open, not closed, and its unity-in-multiplicity volatile, not fixed. In operating the structures of the encyclopedia and intellectual decorum, of teaching and delighting, of building and unbuilding, of masculine and feminine genders, and of earthly *techne* with heavenly purpose, English renaissance poets usually implied that closure and fixity were forms of illusion or idolatry. Poetry resulted from the paradoxical effort to contain and to order the growing scope of knowledge in language while vividly registering dissatisfaction with epistemological and cognitive structures that claimed to do so—even those of one's own poem. Thus poems present the secret work of conscience to society in the form of the poet's ethical and political, not architectural, master-building. Poesie achieves a "presencing" of conscience to the mind, the judgments of which *do* affirm and deny at the same moment in which the poet's fiction explicitly does not affirm or deny.

Intellectually, literary architectonics expresses the poet's Horatian *ingenium* as the genius informing many distinct knowledges through vivid analogies and moral contraries that bear all of the attendant tensions, elusive significations, and pleasures of language. This *ingenium* moves toward an "engineering" of language but also resists it and is in this respect different from modernism. That is, literary architectonics conducts a teleological dismantling of its engines and building through the *voicing* of the mistress-knowledge between the lines, in the interludes, because of the juxtaposition of tropes, characters, passages and events, and in the more visible metaphors, metonymies, and adjuncts that continue to inscribe and disclose her presence.

Such poetic discourse is epistemological, technical, and prudential all at once. All three functions occur with an oratorical simultaneity so forceful as to require personification. Thus literary architectonics is characteristically the balance of experience in which the prosopopoeia of the mistress-knowledge coordinates the multiple movements of the work. As a quasi-scriptural allegory of the teleology of knowledge and the knowing self, the mistress-knowledge enacts a presencing that may relate literary architectonics to the phenomenology developed from the thinking of Hegel, Husserl, and Heidegger, for example. The major problem in making such an association is the problem of the historical statement of theological truth in *experience*.

Protestant Poetics Once More

Theologically, Sidney was able to authorize poetry, the product of the art of poesie, both in relation to Holy Scripture and in response to the ancient Western injunction, "Know thyself," by modeling the Aristotelian concept of architectonic knowledge on the Solomonic figure of Sophia as a type for prudential wisdom. Sidney's syncretic revision of the concept allowed the poet to claim universal knowledge at the historical moment when the arts and sciences were radically expanding and when a new religious orthodoxy

demanded the justification of intellectual pursuits. Composing under the
political mastery of a Queen, this poet elevated himself by taking the ethical
role of conscience as his own.[18] In Judeo-Christian tradition conscience had
long been defined as the summit of human consciousness, the apex of the
mind. The prudential mastercraft of good and evil was allegorized in
Sophia, who played before God in the morning of the world, who built her
house of wisdom and did not destroy it, who set her table full of good things,
including knowledge. Thus the mistress-knowledge is the poet's oracular
guide to action and courses of action because she possesses the classical
knowledge of philosophy, history, science, art, and craft *and* the Socratic
awareness of limitation, the self-knowledge that knows when it does not
know, and because she gives the poet "some divine force" without diviniz-
ing him. She allows him to mediate between pagan ideas of poetic
learning—which Plato associated with daemonic possession and which
Sidney's continental contemporaries developed into a cult of *poeticus furor*
that Sidney the English Protestant had to reject—and new ideas of strictly
human genius—which ran the risks either of completely deifying the poet or
of leaving the poet and the poem utterly ineffectual.

In the historical context of reformation anthropology and Protestant
humanism, I think Sidney's poesie asks not for the dismissal of the products
of an intellect hurt in the Fall but for a transformation of knowledge in the
imagination. Thus the mistress-knowledge enables the poet to achieve the
teleology of knowledge. Sidney, we must recall, was not only the exemplar
of action; he was Oxford's glory and the favorite of the Muses, the desirable
figure of Adonis and the paradoxical union of Mercury and Mars, "our
Scipio, Cicero, and Petrarch."[19] He fulfilled the Erasmian notion of the *miles
Christianus*—the model layman presented in the *Enchiridion* as a man free to
undertake the classical and Christian learning of antiquity and to translate it
into his life and times insofar as he knew himself in his division as an
"inward" and "outward" man and sought his integrity.

In classical terms alone, Sidney could have made an argument for the
epistemological status of the allegory of poesie on the basis of the frequent
confusion in renaissance arts debates between prudence and a supreme
sapience, as defined in Aristotle's hierarchy of intellectual virtues. But
Sidney knew better. His allegory engages other dimensions. If the
mistress-knowledge is a personation whose image begins in the kind of folly
inherent in the very human desire to know, she ends, ultimately, as the wise
folly of an unfolding history of human experience and types divine Wisdom,
the paradox of the Word made flesh.

For this reason the theological paradoxes that underwrote many of the
linguistic expressions of division and single-mindedness in reformation
anthropology lead also to the questioning of Protestant poetics as a
twentieth-century "ideology" in criticism and to the questions of modern

gender studies. Critically we cannot address the questions of woman, man, gender difference, gender hierarchy, and gender constructs without addressing renaissance ideas of divinity, too. Not intending to underwrite Sidney's theology, I think it is absolutely necessary to understand that Sidney's Protestant humanism would never logically identify the pagan with the Christian. Sidney himself could never have supported, for instance, the verbal effort to divinize the self. He was compelled instead to lose the self to gain a subjectivity and a community known only in the mystery of Christ and the Church, which the Reformers usually envisioned as a union of head and body, bridegroom and bride, in the establishment of a new household of faith. The failure to participate in this transformation is the tragedy of Astrophil: for Astrophil strives mightily to constitute the mask of his integrity in language, but ends in despairing self-knowledge, unmasked and longing for the light in sonnet 108.[20] Yet his conviction of sin may be salutary in a Calvinistic framework, insofar as self-knowledge can be the prelude to the reception of grace. So, too, the arts of discourse through which he has exhausted his masks in verbal posturing may be said to be salutary because, in the end, they do not manufacture sustained idols but iconoclastically wear out Astrophil's willingness to make such illusions in poetry.

What I am describing as a feature of Sidney's Protestant humanism carried out in poetic practice takes us to the heart of reformation polemicism, namely, the connection between revealed scriptural truth, which has primacy, and the doctrinal discussion of Scripture in classical philosophical literary forms such as patristic treatises on true religion, apologetics, epistles, disputations of mythology, and hagiography. In aiming to distinguish the literature developed out of renaissance biblicism from the literature developed through a medieval hermeneutic, we have, perhaps, taken the differences of Protestant poetics too far and neglected some of the continuities with both ancient and medieval theological traditions. Historians of religion are now reevaluating the connections, not the differences.[21]

First of all, historians no longer feel obliged to dissociate the recovery of patristic thought, which was part of the rebirth of ancient learning in the Renaissance, from the assertion of the primacy of the revealed Word of God. In the sixteenth century in England, Scripture and tradition are polemically yoked.[22] In poets like Sidney, Spenser, and Milton, quoting Scripture often signifies a vociferous silencing of the Fathers, but their echoes ring nevertheless in either the debate or the descant since the Fathers taught the difference between the myths and the Word. Thus it is useful to place Sidney's integrative image of the mistress-knowledge and his oratorical performance of his own self-knowledge in the context of the refashioning of certain aspects of patristic anthropology in Protestant humanism. Even if Sidney read no Fathers directly, du Plessis Mornay's treatise, *Trewnesse of the*

Christian Religion, is formally designed, for example, as a patristic treatise on "true religion" and contains numerous allusions to Augustine, Cyprian, and Lactantius; Sidney would have absorbed some patristic thought—and a lot of Plotinus—in the mere reading.

Although patristic ethics uniformly struggled with sin, that is, the shameful discrepancy between the human vocation and the human promise, patristic anthropology emphasized potential human dignity. In the Renaissance, Scripture and tradition affirmed that men and women were divine icons, creatures made in the image of God. The category of divine likeness was, however, lost to reformation theology, which saw likeness itself lost to human nature in the Fall. [23] In the multiple portraits of Adam and Eve in renaissance art one may find the simple visual declaration of that prelapsarian dignity and that postlapsarian diminishment and shame. Interestingly, the Reformers drew from patristic scriptural commentary and Christian doctrine the notion of the self-authenticating authority of Holy Scripture as a revealed truth transcending historical culture. Simultaneously, the Renaissance that loved literacy found in the Fathers the explicit use of structures of classical thought, literature, and language. Funded by the principles of translation and interpretation put down by the great patrologist Erasmus in, for example, the *Antibarbarorum*, Christian humanists of the Renaissance were free to take their knowledge of classical learning and literature seriously as the propaedeutic to revealed truth in Scripture. Well into the seventeenth century, the grand moral *contentio* between the just practice of religion and the right use of learning, between the love of God and the desire for letters, filtered into the theory and practice of the Christian use of secular literature and the Christian arts of reading, writing, and making poems.

Sidney's poesie is a species of this literary understanding or "humanism" whose center is less a conceived and fixed self than the incarnate person of Christ the Word seen through the "notable *prosopopoeias*" of human character the poet invents, "when he maketh you, as it were, see God coming in His majesty" (*Def.*, p. 77). Sidney's Protestant humanism may be defined, perhaps, as the scriptural dismay in and hope for human nature that pursues the knowledge of God and charity toward the neighbor by using learning and the written word to see through illusions and to help recover the memory of the divine image. The psychology of such a literary art is focused on rhetorical technique and on the interpretation of irony and analogy as didactic methods for removing the obstacles to recovery, such as false constructions of the self. The combination of the aesthetic and the didactic in poesie makes it to this extent a therapeutic. The theology of Protestant humanism finds a literary approach to the truth, especially the truth of revelation in the scriptural Word; its poetics takes the body and the mind as well as the heart and the will as the arenas of spiritual combat, the classrooms of spiritual nurturance, and the courtrooms of judgment or the wedding chambers of spiritual union. In the living poems of human character, verbal formulas regularly break down, then, giving way to a surpassing understanding. We should expect that such a poetics would raise gender constructs and take them down in searching out the truth of men and women.[24]

Imagination and the Temple of the Heart

On Sidney's Protestant poetics my thinking has been instructed by that of Professor Andrew D. Weiner, although we differ on the grace of the imagination. Weiner examines how Sidney was influenced by Philippe du Plessis Mornay and his Christian polemic, *Trewnesse of the Christian Religion*, against "impious" (that is, non-Calvinistic) Christians and Jews. Weiner's book *Sir Philip Sidney and the Poetics of Protestantism* is the unique statement to date of Sidney's deeply religious privileging of the irrational—of grace and faith based on the revealed truth of Scripture—and reduction of human knowledge, including poetry, to the status of instrumentality.[25] Where Weiner sees Sidney's radical Protestantism and assumes lines of difference between medieval and renaissance theologies, however, I see Sidney's intellectual participation in a long-evolving theology of knowledge and poetry and find historical continuities in his recapitulation of a wisdom tradition. Our different approaches to the question of Sidney's poetics result finally in our different assessments of the power of poesie, not the techniques of poetry.

Du Plessis Mornay turned his Hebraic studies under Emmanuel Tremellius toward the defense of a Calvinism that already varied on the Continent from severe to irenic attitudes. From my perspective Sidney's link to Tremellius is historically quite important because it is biblico-literary. Tremellius was, of course, a learned Italian Jew who converted to Catholicism and then became a Calvinist. He translated the Old Testament into Latin between 1575 and 1579 while at Heidelberg, and it was published in Frankfurt. Sidney visited both cities several times, notably for the Frankfurt Book Fair in 1573 or 1574 and on diplomatic missions to Heidelberg in the late 1570s. In the *Defence* Sidney singles out Tremellius's biblical scholarship, along with that of Junius, to comment on the "poetical part of Scripture," which includes David's Psalms and Solomon's Song of Songs, Ecclesiastes, and Proverbs—a significant representation, in short, of the wisdom tradition. Calling this aspect of Scripture a "divine poem," Sidney clearly aims to define poesie, but not all poetry, in relation to the standard of biblical *truth*. Since a good Protestant knows the self-authentication of the Word of God, poetic art defined in relation to Scripture in any respect testifies intellectually to the ways in which poetic speech does and does not partake of the vatic qualities of such a measure of truth.

The recorded images of poetry may be reduced to instrumentality, but a transcendent and imminent poesie may not. If anything, the wisdom of the mistress-knowledge poesie is the figure of grace in the operations of conscience and is, therefore, both in her affirming and denying functions, a gift of God and a source of assurance. So, as Weiner himself once observed, "the force of a divine breath" with which Sidney's poet brings forth forms different from and better than nature is more than a merely "natural" gift.[26]

As a poetic type of wisdom in the conscience, the mistress-knowledge overcomes the apparent boundary Calvin put between the usefulness of strictly human knowledge in the social and political sphere and the gnosis and praxis of the regenerate human mind that is free, as Sidney put it, to range within "the zodiac of his own wit" and to "make" poems almost as God created out of nothing. The dark side of Calvinism promoted a sense of human ruin and depravity that extends even to modern critical perceptions of fragmentation, empty centers, and divided selves. There is much truth to the recognition of this darkness. But juxtaposed to it was a lightsome side in English Calvinism of the late sixteenth century—a conviction that almost anything is possible to the elect who have been graced with the hope of the recovery of the divine image within themselves. The coexistence of these dark and light sides is frustrating to modern desires to synthesize or to analyze completely, but such juxtaposition is precisely the antithetical art that Sidney proposes in his setting of the "oblique" and the "right" side by side in actual poems.

This juxtaposition in language is also the proper locus for the theological and historical consideration of the speaking subject and the English renaissance Protestant formulation of the problem of the divided self and the centering or true self. In the patristic humanism of the Renaissance as the rebirth of Christian as well as of classical antiquity, renaissance poets saw the discovery of psychological fragmentation and the recovery of an originally whole image of God in the soul as simultaneous events in time. Exploring images—some *eikastic*, some *phantastic*—in their articulation of their different voices, poets learned that the icons of their own making were, at worst, idols to be brought down by an orthodox iconoclasm and, at best, merely working models for the exercise of the mind in pursuit of truth until the imagination is exhausted in its usefulness and the image can be discarded. The aim of the imagination is not the making of the poem, but the making of the character.

By neglecting the feminine personification of the art of poesie in Sidney's Christian-Platonic-Aristotelian epistemology, scholarship has skewed the sense of moral force with which Sidney, like other renaissance theorists, counterbalanced the architecture of knowledge in poetic imitation with the experiential power of imagination to invent character—not merely *in* the mimetic text but *through* the text in the lives of the poet composing and the reader interpreting it. The balancing of character-making with intellectual and verbal architecture is crucial because thinkers of Sidney's time were surrounded by the old ruins of classical and medieval civilization and the building of the constructs of new nationalisms. The emphasis on character-making is the focus of critical debates over imitation in renaissance theories of architectonic art, particularly with regard to drama. It pushes imitation beyond the vision of ideas in constructed verisimilitudes in the "visual epistemology" that Forrest Robinson described almost twenty years ago and into the practical work of applied conscience on the stage of history itself—until the poetic "house of intellect" becomes the apocalyptic expression of the visionary word *and* deed.[27] The recovery of the figure of the mistress-knowledge in Sidney's historical context exposes in sixteenth-century arts treatises and in English renaissance culture in general the temple-building aesthetics that Professor Barbara K. Lewalski saw realized in the English religious lyrics of the seventeenth century in her book *Protestant Poetics*.[28] By examining the earlier sources that contributed to the evolution of such a poetic theory and practice, I hope to demonstrate that Sidney's *Defence* was a major renaissance synthesis of the English Protestant identification with the Hellenized wisdom of Solomon's books and that it aesthetically informed many of the great poems of the late sixteenth and early seventeenth centuries.

Thus the very consideration of the mistress-knowledge discloses how concerns of the sacred and the secular and gender issues inevitably cross in poetic images and may not be dissevered. Since secular derives, after all, from *saeculum*, or procession of the ages, to interpret the boundaries of the sacred and the secular is to interpret history. Although Eugene Rice once argued the neat severance of a medieval emphasis on grace from the so-called renaissance secularization, "which humanized the object of wisdom and guaranteed the natural autonomy of its acquisition," Antonio V. Romualdez has successfully argued the opposite case. Renaissance thinkers consistently drew on *two* operative ideas of wisdom in tension with each other: wisdom as an acquired virtue and wisdom as an infused gift of God.[29]

The mistress-knowledge is categorically intermediate between these two kinds of wisdom and obviously a feminized figure, too. What erases some aspects of the divine from past centuries has also erased some aspects of the feminine. Consequently, in the strange boomerang of history, I must make every effort in this study to follow the genesis and efflorescence of Sidney's figure even where she may seem to violate the boundaries of definition on which literary criticism thrives because doing so is a resistance to modern censorship. Ultimately, we may have to view those very boundaries of law, politics, and society—which Annabel Patterson has studied in the bonds between author and reader and writing and interpretation—as the constructs of a masculinized culture. This asserts ownership of authority and language, as Patricia Parker has explained, but women readers must reclaim copia.[30]

Beyond the Poet As Maker

Teleology contends with *techne* in this fashion, and metaphorically, the mistress contends with the captain, Eve with Adam in our criticism. A masculinized literary culture insists either on the *agon* or on the projection of poems as things, as verbal artifacts, into time and space. Where Stanley Fish recognized the self-consuming power of these artifacts in "affective stylistics," S. K. Heninger, Jr., concludes that renaissance artifice is verbal mimesis, "the poetics of making."[31] Indeed, "the poet as maker" *is* our literary tradition as it has been formed, handed down, and received. Historically and quite literally, however, such a tradition does not speak the whole truth as Sidney spoke it, writing it down as an oration to be read and heard.[32] The literary culture of the English Renaissance was, apparently, much more daringly androgynous—whether we laugh at Bottom's dream, which "man's hand is not able to taste, his tongue to conceive," or admire Milton's Muse. Thus even in the imaginative speech of manly, heroic, and witty Sidney, the mistress-knowledge of the *Defence* testifies to another idea in a different voice. In this vision the characters of the letters composed by the poet serve the characters of the spirited men and women who know themselves.

It is true, though, that very soon what follows in the production of actual poems in the English Renaissance is the effort of poets to mediate virtue in a Sidneian vein by *shifting* the feminine figure of Judeo-Christian wisdom toward the masculine Logos who is the Word, with whom they thought they shared a masculine likeness. What follows, then, in the history of criticism for four hundred years after Sidney's writings first appeared in print is also a selective construction of those features of the *Defence* that finally validate a Kantian architectonics and the suppression of those visitations bespeaking presences between men's words.

The selection and suppression started before the sixteenth century was over and before Sir Francis Bacon turned poetic to scientific invention, for the problems of nature, knowledge, and the products of knowledge were inherent in the epistemology Sidney conceived in poesie and gave to the poet as maker. In the encyclopedic products of the poetic art—the poems that were "speaking pictures," "ground-plots," anamorphoses, optical illusions, castles, engines, characters, emblems, labyrinths, temples, songs, fables, and mirrors of the poet's idea—the poets themselves tried to empty their devices of the presence of the mistress-knowledge. More precisely, they gradually transformed the memory of her presence and its judgments of conscience within them into the God within them as men and, later, into their own image. Horace had said that a poem was like a painting; English writers allowed that a poem might also be like a cosmos, a calendar, a telescope, a mathematical instrument, a musical machine, an encyclopedia, a church, a human body, a mythology of words, and almost any mimesis the poet wanted, as long as he could "engineer" his poetic invention through the inspiration of an enlightened conscience that elevated his erotic, aesthetic, political, and religious desire. For the *ingenium* that Horace gave renaissance poets as their "genius" or native wit they would also understand as the "engine" of their minds when they tried, for better or for worse, to name their balance of experience and to fix it in words.

This book is about the Sidneian mind that did not come to rest in such things, even if they rhymed. For such rhyme, as one of Sidney's elegists put it, is "the sonne of rage, which art no kin to skill"; but the mistress-knowledge is a vision of grace that enables history to remember Saint Orpheus in Sir Philip, or the English Petrarch, or the Phoenix, and therefore to "Salute the stones, that keep the lims, that held so good a minde."[33] So the *ethos* of Sidney as a Protestant icon in the following pages is not his rhetorical brilliance or aesthetic retreat or his politics, his reputation, his manhood, his desire, his religion, or even his poems per se. I have tried to search out, instead, the intellectual prowess he demonstrated in the *Defence*, the book knowledge he loved, and the *good* will, I think, his character revealed there. Sidney's learning and faith seem to have led him through beautiful illusions and ugly truths to the understanding of Augustine's deepest desire, which was a lovely Love. Sidney gave its spirit a feminine name and form. And the spirit of Sidney's thought should occasion some reconciliation between early modern perceptions of art and our late twentieth-century theoretical discoveries, if we can see the forest through the trees and keep the skill of a sonnet. The critical timber of patriarchy is not the whole truth.

1

The Mistress-Knowledge

Therefore, it may be understood which one of the arts and sciences has the greatest power and is in the highest degree, as it were, the queen of all the rest. The civil faculty is seen to be such a one; for it determines what knowledge is necessary in civilized states and what sort each person learns and to what extent.

    —Pietro Vettori,
       Commentarii in X Libros Aristotelis, De Moribus ad Nicomachum

Lady Poesie and Her Princely Poet

Sir Philip Sidney claimed in *The Defence of Poesie* that the *energia* of the rhetorical poet was the source of his imaginative power.[1] We should expect that the sixteenth-century writer who advocated poetic liveliness of speech as a standard would exhibit it in the persuasive metaphors and antitheses of his own arts treatise, and he does. We need to return and reread the metaphors of the *Defence,* asking not merely the questions of systematic argument and rigid formal structure and style independent of significance but also the question of some central, organizing image. The presence of such an image, if sustained throughout, constitutes a rhetorical allegory, an argument for poetry in the context of the renaissance arts disputes, and the reading of the language and historical context of the *Defence* in this chapter recovers such an argument.

Sidney's allegory of poesie is, in this respect, an allegory of literary knowledge and its value. The *Defence* is an intertextual construction of Sidney's readings advocating the poetic art partly on the strength of the fact that Aristotle assigned no specific place to poetry in his scheme of the arts and sciences; the *Poetics* lacks the usual prefatory remarks defining the object, end, and scope of poetry.[2] Thus Sidney was free to invent a figure of his own, using other Aristotelian and Platonic texts to do so.

Vettori's comment on Aristotle's *Nicomachean Ethics,* cited in the epigraph, is roughly contemporaneous with Sidney's composition a few years earlier of the *Defence.* Praising the "civil faculty" as the *regina reliquarum,* Vettori immediately proceeds to link military generalship and the art of public speaking to her "rule."[3] So, too, Sidney's mistress-knowledge develops out of the Aristotelian structure of the intellectual virtues in the *Ethics* into a renaissance vision of epistemology distinct from but in sustained

1

tension with the architectural organization of knowledge. Renaissance thinkers apparently envisioned the lively ordering of different kinds of knowledge around a central principle so powerfully present as to require personification. In Sidney's case, the reading of the *Defence* for its implications discloses the presence of the mistress-knowledge mediating between Sidney's use of *energia* in the "building" of his words and his rhetorical aim to persuade the reader to undertake, in another sense of the phrase, the moral building of history in his or her own life and in society. Such building is tantamount to the construction of a particular culture.

Sidney went further than Vettori, though, for Sidney also attached his figure of the mistress-knowledge specifically to language. He presents her as Lady Poesie. In general terms, language exposes culture to begin with, and culture informs events, persons, places, and things with significance as much as words. But Sidney's central image is one of the control of the dissemination of language and learning, so his metaphoric text portrays especially the aristocratic *literate* culture of the Protestant English Renaissance.

Sidney identifies poesie with the integrative gathering of knowledges and calls its reading and writing not an "architectural" unity but an "architectonic" power of self-knowledge (*Def.*, pp. 82–83). He thus opposes the Italian artists' adulation of the "learned architect" with an English appreciation for the *ars legendi*. Our modern critical confusion of the word *architectonic* with *architecture* led to the wrong notion of *architectonic* form as a critical metaphor for describing the verbal structure of a text.[4] This, in turn, is strangely parodied in the reversals of deconstruction as a type of analysis seeking precisely to undo the text as a supposed unity, an "ideology of totality," and to find the differences within it, that is, the differences of meaning the text itself betrays against itself. In linking the value of poetry to the practice of an *ars legendi*, Sidney has, in the vocabulary of deconstruction, "staged" the possibilities and modes for misreading his treatise within the treatise, which he presents as a poem at the same time he constructs a critical theory.[5] But I would argue that exactly on the topic of Sidney's *ars legendi* must the modern dialectic between the binary oppositions of Western logic and deconstruction and between unity and fragmentation be sidestepped as a cultural problem in late twentieth-century criticism. This modern debate distorts the communication of renaissance texts when it is imposed on their dialectic. The radical difference we must seek in Sidney's pronunciation of his speech about poesie requires listening to his architectonic analogies, not merely seeing his or any other poet's verbal architecture.

Early in the *Defence* Sidney revises the old idea of poetry as the "treasure-house" of learning, of poesie as the "lady" who lives there, and of the poet as the mastercraftsman who "builds" the place. Personification is a distinct figure that may be regarded generally under the topic of metaphor or particularly in relation to metonymy. It may be seen as the image-making producing a presence or as the voice of an absent presence. In Sidney's case, both external and internal sources offer guidance on how to regard the figure.

Externally we ought to look at Scaliger's definition and at an example in Erasmus's writings. Scaliger explains that prosopopoeia is "duplex." The first mode is the introduction of a fictive persona, like Fame in Virgil or Ovid or, we may add, like Lady Poesie at points in Sidney's *Defence*. Scaliger sees this mode of personification as a production of poetic argument useful for teaching. The other mode of personification, he says, discloses an attribute of speech. Quintilian calls the first mode or "fiction" ιδεῶν and the second mode something that pertains to the division of the speech; properly called sermocination, it appears, for example, in a rhetorician's posing of a question that he then answers or making of a remark to which he then responds.[6] This kind of prosopopoeia, whether it appears in one's conversation alone with oneself or in company, is a dialogue.[7] Sidney uses both modes in giving us the mistress-knowledge as a fictive persona and simultaneously talking aloud with himself and with us—sometimes in the voice of the poet, sometimes in the voice of the reader, sometimes in the voice of the critic, and sometimes in the voice of the mistress-knowledge. We have seen such behavior in a renaissance speech before, most certainly in Erasmus's *Praise of Folly* in which Dame Folly is Erasmus's "female talker," his persona and sermocinatrix.

Reserving the discussion of this example of female impersonation in the Renaissance until chapter 3, we may identify another Erasmian text as a potential external guide in reading Sidney's use of personification. Not only a treatise apologizing for poetry, the *Defence* is a vigorous statement on the nature and purpose of a decidedly *English* poesie proposed to the English and, we may reasonably assume, to continental observers of English life and of the young humanist who wrote the text. The political dimension of the *Defence*, in other words, possesses both domestic and foreign aspects. It is not impossible that Sidney knew Erasmus's *Prosopopoeia Britanniae Majoris*—"The Personification of Great Britain"—that Erasmus dedicated to the future King Henry VIII in 1499. In it Erasmus particularly discusses the propriety of dedications and of praise from a poet to a person of eminence. The prefatory letter alludes to Midas disfigured by the ass's ears as a comment on the lack of judgment in modern princes, as does Sidney in the *Defence* (p. 121) but without explicit reference to any recent or contemporary prince. To the extent that Sidney's *Defence* proposes the literary cultivation of Britain at home and abroad, however, it may be seen as a personification of England; likewise, to the extent that the text echoes some of the vocabulary in Sidney's *Letter written . . . to Queen Elizabeth* on her proposed marriage to Alençon and carries out Hubert Languet's request to commend Jean de Serre's edition of Plato to the Queen, we may find in Erasmus's address to Henry VIII, Elizabeth's father, a model for the critical and yet decorous discourses of piety in the Enchiridion as his discovery the image of the mistress knowledge, which is, on one plane of the allegory, a type of queen.[8]

Internally, Sidney invents personae and wittily gives them names. The argument from etymology, which begins with a survey of the Greek, Latin, and English names of the poetic art and of the poet, permeates the treatise in scriptural example and in comparison to nature, art, and imitation before Sidney actually discloses the name of poesie. Sidney's argument is the image of a gendered architectonics of a man's self-knowledge; this image presents renaissance epistemology of a certain sort, the sort to be practiced in the national English household of faith:

> But when by the balance of experience it was found that the astronomer, looking to the stars, might fall in a ditch, that the inquiring philosopher might be blind in himself, and the mathematician might draw forth a straight line with a crooked heart, then lo, did proof, the overruler of opinions, make manifest that all these are but serving sciences, which, as they have each a private end in themselves, so yet are they all directed to the highest end of the mistress-knowledge, by the Greeks called ἀρχιτεκτονική, which stands (as I think) in the knowledge of a man's self, in the ethic and politic consideration, with the end of well-doing and not of well-knowing only—even as the saddler's next end is to make a good saddle, but his further end to serve a nobler faculty, which is horsemanship, so the horseman's to soldiery, and the soldier not only to have the skill, but to perform the practice of a soldier. (Pp. 82–83)

By holding this gendered figure of the mistress-knowledge at the center of the thinking of the *Defence*, Sidney metaphorically brings history and philosophy under the aegis of poesie and "builds" his house of intellect. Recognizing this center, we may go further and argue that the *Defence*, therefore, represents an early declaration of what English literature was to be about, and it also contributed to the direction that English renaissance literature took in practice. The *Defence* is a critical resource for the culture, particularly in the poet's cultivation of intellectual universality and moral productivity.

How, in technical terms, did Sidney accomplish so much? He did so, again, through etymology, which was a linguistic tactic renaissance grammarians had firmly established as a procedure of inquiry. And he did so wittily and fortuitously, in the way Shakespeare would begin to do in the late 1580s, that is, through punning. Borrowing liberally from Aristotle's definition of the architectonic knowledge in the *Nicomachean Ethics* (1.1 [1094a]; cf. 1.3 [1095a], 1.6 [1097a]), Sidney made a new metaphor as he translated the grammatically feminine Greek adjectival form ἀρχιτεκτονική into the image of a sovereign English character. All other knowledge serves this mistress-knowledge that liberates the mind most effectively by promoting virtuous action just as, one surmises metaphorically, the English Queen receives the service of citizens and promotes virtue in them. The Greek roots of the word suggest Sidney's vivid personification, for ἀρχή signifies "first principle," "cause," "rule," "ruler" or, in renaissance idiom, "prince," and τέκτων signifies "builder," "maker," "craftsman," "maker of an art." Together they refer literally to the architect or practitioner of master-building, but Aristotle had already used them to refer to the superior philosophical knowledge and to the political mastercraftsman of the state.

This may seem to make much of a grammatically feminine adjective based on Aristotle's text, but Sidney was not alone in that feminization, nor was he willing to sacrifice the hierarchy of knowledge that Aristotle inscribed in the passage in question, in which the craft of bridle-making, the skill of horsemanship, and the art of military strategy rise from the bottom of that hierarchy and move upward in service to the top, to the true mastercraft that includes, by definition, the ends of all the other crafts, arts, and sciences.[9] Sidney the critic has satisfactorily combined old grammatical competencies, not the insights of modern structuralism, with an experienced awareness of historical potential and political reality to obtain through etymology and punning the effect in composition that a deconstructive reading seeks in the play of language. Moreover, Sidney does not discard *archia* in the process, but follows Aristotle to interrelate them with *scientia*, *artes*, and *techne* in a specific arrangement to suit his definition of poesie. In effect, Sidney has translated his whole culture into his own articulated vision of Englishness; for him, it is no accident that the name of metaphor in the Latin rhetorical handbooks on which renaissance writers relied was *translatio*. Sidney's further identification of self-knowledge as the philosophical significance of his *translatio* from Aristotle's *Ethics* shows that he has followed his humanistic rule for devouring ancient texts whole to make them wholly one's own. The mistress-knowledge is an "attentive translation" of Aristotle's idea, not merely a copying of it (*Def.*, p. 117).

This Sidneian metaphor is generative and controlling in Sidney's treatise with regard to structure, as I shall explain in chapter 3, and also to style. The feminization of the word *architectonic* had occurred in John Shute's book, *The First & Chief Groundes of Architecture*, a practical treatise that enjoyed several publications between 1563 and 1584, including one in 1579 or 1580, shortly before Sidney composed the *Defence*. Sidney plays his Greek off Shute's, I think, showing how the Aristotelian doctrine of *political* mastercraftsmanship is much higher in the ranking of knowledge than the technical craft of architecture, no matter what the theory of the "learned architect" coming up to England from Italy says. Shute praises his newfound study and then allegorizes it as a type of the "prudent ladye *Scientia*" in "lerned men." Nothing deserves more praise, he says, "then that whiche is of the grekes named Architectonica, and of the Latines Architectura (I thinke not altogither unfite nor unaptlie by me termed in Englishe, the arte and trade to rayne up and make excellent edificen and buildinguu),"[10] The philological similarity between Shute's phrase, "of the grekes named Architectonica,"[11] and Sidney's phrase, "by the Greeks called ἀρχιτεκτονική," constitutes a major semantic difference as Sidney feminizes not the Latin name of the technical craft "architecture" but the Greek philosophical name of the "prudent ladye *Scientia*" whom Shute, in a more or less Ficinian version of architectonic knowledge, has associated with the literal master-building of material structures by the learned architect. Sidney, though, follows a different and truer Plato who criticized material building, as we shall see, and identifies "architectonica" with the statesman's "living" speech, not the architect's plastic craft. The poet is the master-builder who practices the supremely philosophical mastercraftsmanship of moving all knowledge into virtue, and he must be distinguished from the mere "architector" of words (*Def.*, pp. 85–86). From the very ground of the significance of the word, Sidney's case for poesie resists the architectural interpretation of architectonic form that twentieth-century readings of renaissance texts have observed in a modern obsession with structure and technique.

In another case throughout the *Defence* as well, Sidney's remodeling of Aristotelian mastercraftsmanship to suit a sixteenth-century English political situation carefully observes the Aristotelian hierarchy of knowledges. The writer of the *Defence* is a horseman and soldier and an orator—the two categories of special service that Vettori had attached to the political "queen of the arts." The decided topic, though, on which the orator of the *Defence* speaks is the mistress-knowledge. Much has been made in recent studies of Sidney's verbal play on the themes of horsemanship and speech-making throughout the treatise, beginning with the little story of Pugliano.[11] But this thread of the *Defence*, which is sustained from start to finish, is *not* the stylistically integrative center of the treatise; it is, rather, the proper and decorous declaration of the position of subordination from which Sidney the soldier-orator must speak in his move toward the place occupied by the mistress-knowledge.[12] The allegorical issue here is that of *ménage*, the classical allegory of the will that Fulke Greville singled out as Sidney's special talent, his "Architectonical art" of centering:

But the truth is: his end was not writing, even while he wrote; nor his Knowledge moulded for tables, or schooles; but both his wit, and understanding bent upon his heart, to make himself and others, not in words or opinion, but in life and action, good and great. In which Architectonical art he was such a Master, with so comending and yet equal waies amongst men, that wheresoever he went, he was beloved, and obeyed: yea, into what Action so ever he came last at the first, he became first at the last: the whole managing of the business, not by usurpation, or violence but (as it were) by right and acknowledgment, falling into his hands, as into a naturall Center.[13]

Greville knew his Aristotle, too, for Aristotle explains that the end of the political science of mastercraftsmanship is action, not knowledge (*Nic. Ethics* 1.3.7). The proper manner in which to read Sidney's textual play with the figure of horsemanship and its connection to oratory, then, is in their definition of the speaker's special arts. Sidney will climb from them and the identity they give him in a hierarchy of power to the identity that the practice of poesie gives him. Greville implies that Sidney centers in such a fashion, managing the whole business "not by usurpation, or violence but (as it were) by right and acknowledgment." We shall have to judge on the political plane of Sidney's allegory whether his gradual appropriation of central power in the name of the poet is "by right" or is a form of "usurpation" in which a man *must* dominate a woman while a Queen must be allowed to exercise sovereignty over her subjects, including her wise and courtly counselors. Behind the story of Pugliano, in other words, stands Sidney on the delicate boundary between Daedalean craftsmanship of words and Icarean overreaching. Like a woven fabric, the text of the *Defence* stylistically begins with, sustains, and ends in exposition of the architectonic idea or one of its adjuncts. Does Sidney himself not play Hercules "spinning at Omphale's commandment" in his style (*Def.*, p. 115)?

Sidney starts his speech with the apparently light touch of the story of Pugliano's horsemanship only to draw the immediate comparison that the art of poesie—which Sidney sees as his "unelected vocation"—also demands exercise.[14] But if Sidney is implying that his elected vocation is that of the soldier and orator, or courtier, then his very dialectic at the start of the *Defence* reveals his intention to center on the mistress-knowledge, that is, to climb in power as a poet from the mere exercise of a verbal craft (a kind of architecture) to the exercise of ethical and political considerations of self-knowledge.

Thus the art of government, one surmises, is also a *pedanteria* in comparison to poesie (*Def.*, p. 73), and one must remember Plato's discussion in the *Republic* of the roles of men and women, of the engendering and education of children, and of the breeding of horses when Socrates explains the skills required in rulers (5.458–59). In the *Utopia*, too, More gave a certain Platonic twist to the construction of society when he compared the premarital examination of naked spouses to the procedure used in purchasing a healthy colt. Thus the opening analogy of *ménage* actually introduces the main subject of education and civilization. It is not some peripheral rhetorical appeal to the attention of the audience, nor does its status as a metaphoric scaffolding in the *Defence* deny the presence at the center of the house. Sidney's definition of the mistress-knowledge ten pages later appropriates the Aristotelian definition of political mastercraftsmanship in the *Nicomachean Ethics* almost literally, as we have seen, and that definition begins at the bottom with bridle- or saddle-making, moves through horsemanship to other arts and, finally, arrives at government. By the end of the

Defence, the metaphoric networking of figures of horsemanship can take an ironic and critical turn because Sidney has, indeed, centered his allegory of poesie. Sidney does not present as horsemen those who would "hear the planet like music of poetry" to the fate of Midas, whose abuse of his wit and his hearing gave him "ass's ears," but the implication in that the man or woman who lacks self knowledge can rule neither horse nor poem and is condemned to lovelessness and mortality (p. 121)—even a Queen who should rule her state and her speech. Horsemanship is Sidney the cavalier's metaphor throughout the *Defence* for the way poetry teaches management of one's infected will. As a speaking subject, Sidney starts with the management of his own will and its potential for Icarean overreaching; but at least one contemporary read the 1595 publication of the *Defence* in a way that satirized the Faerie Queene Titania for falling in love with an ass.

Sidney's argument for poesie as the mistress-knowledge that surpasses all the arts and sciences in the quest of the renaissance mind for intellectual and moral *virtù* is logical and metaphorical, metaphysical and political, verbally exact and racy all at once. Since Sidney lived and wrote under the rule of a monarch who was a woman, and since he served Queen Elizabeth, finally, in various enterprises of statesmanship for which he was educated, his effort to define poetic mastercraftsmanship in relation to the political master-building of his country by his sovereign necessarily falls into the rhetorical form of juxtaposed definitions of a word, or allegory. The recovery of the image of Sidney's figure from a literary history that has marginalized it produces this reading: if poesie is a lady and an English prince, a queen of all the other arts and sciences in the way the mistress-knowledge Elizabeth practices some philosophy in her kingdom, then the poet-maker is an architect of the society insofar as he makes a fit consort to her in the generative art of making character by producing well-doing out of well-knowing.[15] The workmanship involved was the poetic and political task of Christian humanism peculiar to the Renaissance. Politically Sidney had the imagination to name the task with a chief metaphor that joined the Virgin Queen and the statesman, the mistress-knowledge and the knowledge of a man's self, in a moral coupling based on the sexualized decorum of language. On one side the metaphor bestows the compliment of high philosophy on the Queen; on the other side the metaphor confirms the statesmanship of the poet and the poetic task of the statesman.

Critical evaluations of the *Defence* have been strangely blind to the metaphoric quality of Sidney's critical diction with respect to the mistress-knowledge. She has been rendered invisible, and her invisibility has hampered literary assessment of the centrality of the architectonic argument in the *Defence*. The metaphorical definition of the mistress-knowledge is not merely one phase of Sidney's rhetorical confirmation of the poetic art; this prosopopoeia is the essence of the confirmation, the point that unifies all other subordinate arguments. Most editors of the text in recent times have glossed the word *architectonic* in accord with Aristotle's *Ethics* but stopped at that. A. E. Malloch went further in "Architectonic Knowledge in Sidney's *Apologie*," an essay that identified the ethical aspect of self-knowledge but retreated from the equally important rule of the hierarchy of the arts and sciences that Sidney—and Aristotle—had incorporated in the metaphor.[16] Only a late nineteenth-century editor, Albert S. Cook, showed some receptivity to the epistemological and metaphysical implications of Sidney's choice of words. Cook observed long ago that Sidney considered poesie itself to *be* the architectonic art par excellence and that he linked it to religion "almost as sisters."[17] The critical difficulty in receiving the femininity of Sidney's metaphor has extended into the interpretation of his use of Plato as well, touching the subject of the good character of the poet and the goodness of the poem. Sidney disputes the idea of *furor poeticus* and its enthusiasm, as we shall see, while nevertheless upholding an idea of the poet-maker's likeness in his art to the divine Maker's "maker," or *natura naturans,* and the divergence of the poem from mere imitation of *natura naturata.* In the renaissance imagination, *Natura* is feminine.[18] In the *Defence*, the feminine focuses the poet's experience of inspiration.

The language of the *Defence* proceeds, then, with ample evidence of Sidney's delight in the persuasive play of words. Through this play, though, far from beating an aesthetic retreat, Sidney builds his own multileveled political philosophy of poetry and gives us his image of the poet, too. The crucial passage of definition in which he pictures the mistress-knowledge and the self-knowing poet *is* Sidney's statement of literary architectonics, and it revises, as I shall demonstrate by the end of this chapter, the ladders of love, rule, and being. The passage concludes with the highly teleological declaration, "So that, the ending end of all earthly learning being virtuous action, those skills that most serve to bring forth that have a most just title to be princes over all the rest" (p. 83). Sidney has personified mastercraftsmanship as a female type of ἄρχων, a ruler or first principle who dominates scientific knowledge with moral superiority.

In his very next breath, he takes on the moral philosopher and the historian—the two pillars of renaissance ethical superiority—to argue the metaphoric identification of poesie as the ruling knowledge just as the poet is her princely workman. This speaking subject is, indeed, showing his *ménage,* for the pace of the *Defence* picks up in Sidney's swift cross-referencing of various definitions of terms. Thus the efficient cause (the poet) moves up to the rank of final cause (the mistress-knowledge) in Sidney's vocabulary. To follow this shift, the reader must first accept Sidney's lead and distinguish the art of poesie from the poet who practices it and from the poem, the product of the art; in the atmosphere of the renaissance arts debates, Sidney asks his reader to concur with the statement that "poetry" is the most familiar to teach virtue and the "most princely" to move toward it and is, therefore, of all worldly learnings, "the most excellent workman" in "the most excellent work" (p. 94). But then the reader must recall what Sidney has already said "poesie, according to Aristotle's authority, is not only a "workman" but also a universal or philosophical consideration above the particulars of history (p. 88). At this point Sidney is ready to mix his definitions of poet and poesie and poem, and he does. The *poet* of whom Sidney speaks moves downward in the hierarchy toward an association with *techne*: the word *poet* suddenly signifies the "art" in its capacity to teach and to delight and not the "artificer" (p. 89).

But the whole argument is an elevation of the technical or mechanical arts in the Aristotelian scheme of knowledge. So the poet also moves up the hierarchy as a "monarch" of all human sciences when Sidney gives him the "laurel crown" over the moral philosopher, the historian, and every sort of learned person (pp. 90–91). Finally his "poesie" mounts to the level of a comparison with Scripture itself (p. 99). In the activity of the poetic art, the ascent and descent of Sidney's discourse have successfully merged the technical craft of making poems with the serving sciences of liberal knowledge *and* with the mistress-knowledge of master-building the society. As in Pico della Mirandola's vision of human dignity, the mobility matters. One cannot critically put this line of reasoning in the *Defence* aside as merely a passing allusion to the mastercraftsmanship defined in Aristotle's *Ethics* as the civil faculty of statesmanship, for the outcome of Sidney's thought is the relating of poesie not to a "natural" metaphysics but to faith.

He compares the inventive poet's "divine consideration of what may be and should be" with the divine poetic word, and he does so by letting the tensions of metaphor carry his hierarchical, sexual, and religious allusions (pp. 80–81). The work of the poetic art is the actual poetry composed in words by the poet *and* the ethical and political composition of all things and all words in the realities of living human character that is the image of God. Near the start of the *Defence* Sidney proposed, with Aristotle, that poetry is an imitation, a "representing, counterfeiting, or figuring forth—to speak metaphorically, a speaking picture" (pp. 79–80). But the metaphoric discourse of the *Defence* moves beyond the proposition to the demonstration as Sidney reinterprets the axiom from the *Poetics* and appropriates ancient philosophy in particular and history in general under the auspices of the poetic art in his speaking picture.

The speaking picture of the *Defence* is the image of the mistress-knowledge and the poet-mastercraftsman joined in morally fruitful union and balance of power. In their power to re-create human character, these divine icons may refashion nature, knowledge, and love. The authority of the Word reconstructs the epistemologies of the word. The two figures of poesie and poet politically make a "brave new world" indeed.

They, too, are the central and organizing metaphor of Sidney's critical theory because it works both causally and figuratively through the treatise as a whole. The poetry that is a serving science *becomes* a princely knowledge of first principles in the exercise of the invention promoting virtue. By serving well its immediate end of poetic craftsmanship, the art rises up the ladder of the hierarchy of knowledge to accomplish the final end of learning, too. Thus the material object, the poem, best performs its function as an imaginative agent of moral truth when it participates in the final ruling cause of architectonics and contributes to the formation of the hero in the poet and in the reader. The metaphor distinctly works figuratively because the poet-master-builder who is consort to the queenly mistress-knowledge relates metonymically to her powers; he shares in them, or as we say today, he appropriates her powers as his own. [19]

The *Defence* pictures the poet as the male sexual adjunct of a female ruling power. The true ethos of the poet is the *coupling* of the craftsman and the mistress-knowledge when the "erected wit" of the poet is "lifted up with the vigour of his own invention" (p. 78). Together they produce poems, and the poems reproduce good citizens. The "balance of experience" teaches the moral limitations of merely intellectual knowledge; the balance of metaphor generates moral re-creation through writing and reading for poet, citizen, and Queen alike. The appropriation of power is operative in the male poet's treatment of the royal mistress poesie in Sidney's gendered metaphors of the *Defence*; consequently, the subject and the structure of the text politically engage the reader in the subject-sovereign relationship of Sidney and the Queen. The *Defence* allows no division among theory, practice, and pleasure.

It is critically insufficient, therefore, to say that the central argument of the *Defence* is the case for poesie as the *analogue* of philosophy and history. The reading of metaphor produces, rather, a superior identification of a presence on the strength of which the speaker, another presence, articulates and does not demolish his oratorical house. The central argument of the *Defence* is alive and well in the experiential personification of the meaning of the mistress-knowledge as the male poet appropriates her power by exercising it, by figuring it forth or fleshing it out. The poet, "moderator" of the debate between the historian and the moral philosopher, is "the man who ought to carry the title from them both" (*Def.*, p. 84), that is, the title of Plato's "prince" or "monarch" of all kinds of learning (*Def.*, pp. 91–92, 94). The poet is the "monarch" for two reasons. His verbal images compose general philosophical precept and particular historical example in the poetic picture of heroic characters. The poet's method of invention, meantime, engenders in the reader *how* and *why* his or her literacy may become heroic in a godly kingdom. Sidneian poesie entices and seduces for the good. It yokes pleasure to the desire for virtue: "Now therein of all sciences (I speak still of human, and according to the human conceit) is our poet the monarch.

For he doth not only show the way but giveth so sweet a prospect into the way as will entice any man to enter into it" (pp. 91–92).

In sum, the main apology for Sidney's powerful poetic art is the integra tion of all knowledges in moving images of human character that promote ethical and political self-knowledge, and this is the function of desire on one level of Sidney's allegory. In reading the language of the *Defence* as Sidney's oratorical composition, one is being persuaded to agree to make corrective connections in the knowledge of the arts and sciences represented in poetry so that the living knowledge of those two prosopopoeias may serve its final end. Sidney has received the teachings of the philosophers not as "thorny arguments" (p. 85) but as vivid metaphors, the "masking raiment" that Lady Philosophy borrowed from Lady Poesie, as Boethius and Plato well knew (p. 93).

Thus Sidney engages the reader of his treatise in the exercise of the very art of reading metaphor that he proposes, and this art of reading is aimed, in turn, at the reformation of the English mind and English nation through poetic self-knowledge. In the treatise, the figures of Sidney's mistress-knowledge and poet-*architector* enable him to connect all arts and sciences in causal chains linking what one reads to what one knows and what one knows to what one does in the private and public government of action in one's life. The argument contained "in little" in the pairing of two icons, therefore, condenses a highly learned reading theory. A similar affirmation of the strength of a good reading program in education informs at least two of Sidney's letters, one to his brother Robert and the other to his friend Ned Denny, as well as several letters from Hubert Languet, Sidney's mentor.[20] The prosopopoeias of the Queen and the poet-statesman logically turn the reader toward the prosopopoeia of the literate and self-knowing man whose generative name is Cyrus. Through the characterization of Cyrus in the *Defence*, Sidney speaks his way up a Protestant Platonic ladder *from* the plane of rhetorical allegory in which power struggle occurs *to* the vision in the mistress-knowledge of a superior wisdom of self-knowledge.

Reading, Politics, and the English Protestant *Cyropaedia*

In the Renaissance at large, classical philosophy and history gave images of the hero in abundance to renaissance readers. Plutarch's *Lives*, Xenophon's *Cyropaedia*, and the epics of Homer and Virgil populated contemporary minds with ideal characters, and the writers of renaissance fable increased the population. So, too, Sidney's gendered metaphors reinterpret the classical nature of heroism. The *Defence* lists repeated references to Achilles, Aeneas, Alexander, Hercules, Rinaldo, Turnus, Tydeus, Ulysses, and their poet-makers with almost no discrimination of philosophers, historians, mythographers, and poets, or of ancients and moderns. All writers by virtue of writing create the image of their heroes poetically. At least this seems to be the assumption in Sidney's catalogue of cultural stars. The allusions culturally appropriate classical characters of excellence in the manner in which Sidney's poet-architect appropriates the sphere of power of the mistress-knowledge.

No classical hero appears with greater frequency in the *Defence*, however, than Cyrus (pp. 79–103). Cyrus is the name of the particular hero on whose education Sidney pins his version of poetic invention and the right sort of *ars legendi*. Cyrus is Sidney's ideal reader; through his many appearances in the *Defence*, one may see further into Sidney's metaphoric networking of argument in that treatise to define the poet as a good soldier and ruler, too. For Sidney, the *Cyropaedia* is less a classical historical text than a metaphor for an inventive process he wishes to claim for poetry as an ethical and political force. Moreover, Xenophon's Cyrus doubles in Sidney's imagination, as in history, with the pagan mentioned in the Bible who authorizes the rebuilding of the Temple in Jerusalem after the Babylonian captivity.[21] Composition and reading—literacy—constitute the new heroism of Elizabeth's Christian noblemen in Sidney's estimation, but not without an awareness of the difficulties of interpretation, and not without an assertion of a biblical faith.[22] One character—Cyrus seen from the different perspectives of two texts, Xenophon's fiction and Scripture's truth— exemplifies the encounter of two cultures in the reading Elizabethan, the mind being educated in the Renaissance.

Plato had actually challenged Xenophon's Cyrus and *Cyropaedia* on the grounds that the Persians possessed no true cultural training, no *paideia*, any more than the early Athenians did. In the *Laws*, Plato's Athenian remarks that Cyrus was a good general and patriot, but he was untouched by right education. Since he was always campaigning, he never gave a thought to the disciplining of his household, including the upbringing of his son Cambyses, who was reared as if he were a special creature, fortune's favorite, by women (694–96). The result was a character full of pride and pomposity. Cambyses was a poor governor, and his fate in the sixteenth century was to be made the type of the tyrant on the Elizabethan stage in Thomas Preston's play *A Lamentable Tragedy, Mixed Full of Pleasant Mirth, Containing the Life of Cambises, King of Persia*. The play was entered in the Stationers' Register in 1569–70 and published soon afterward, with a second edition appearing in 1584, and it is not impossible that Sidney knew it. If he did know it, he studiously avoided mentioning Cambyses, tyrant or play, in the *Defence*; he does mention another Persian, Darius, whose son Xerxes was considered by Plato to be as uneducated by his father as Cambyses was by Cyrus (*Def.*, pp. 89–95; Plato's *Laws* 694–96).

The point of the Platonic discussion of Persian rule and its successes portrayed by Xenophon is, of course, that any success was an effect of

serendipity, not rational thought or governance transmitted from generation to generation. In this sense, as a literary judgment of images of rule, the
play *Cambises* implicitly shows up in Sidney's *Defence* in the condemnation
of the mixed, irrational form of drama that defies the rules of genre—the
"mongrel tragi-comedy" that joins admiration and murder (*Def.*, pp. 141-42).
This criticism Shakespeare will turn into the "tragical mirth" of his Athenian
artisans in *A Midsummer Night's Dream*.

The Cyrus of Holy Scripture, however, offers a way to account for
Persian successes different from the Persian fairy tale of the princes of
Serendip. However accidental and short-lived and despite the lack of a
proper cultural training to pass from father to son, Persian rule served divine
Providence. Beyond both Plato's rational ideal and Persian empire-building
stands the larger divine purpose of the restoration of Israel and the reconstruction of the Temple. This paradox of divine Providence—that the ir-
rationalities, paganism, and fortune of the Persians might serve the upbuild-
ing of God's chosen nation by divine design—Sidney means to evoke as a
model for Elizabethan England.

England under Elizabeth seems to have arrived at the moment of history
when it can move in the direction of Athenian culture, Persian power, or
divine destiny. The Tudor dynasty progresses toward the British Empire,
and by 1590 Edmund Spenser will dedicate his *Faerie Queene* to an Elizabeth
he calls "magnificent empresse" over England, France, Ireland, and Virginia. Not surprisingly, in Spenser's *Letter . . . expounding his whole intention* in that poem, he returns to the dispute over culture between the
philosophical Platonists and the historical Xenophonians, and the dispute
over culture constitutes an argument over forms of discourse. Plato's *Republic* provides an image of the commonwealth that "should" be; Xenophon's
Cyropaedia presents the government of Cyrus and the Persians as one "such
as might best be." Neither one matters much, Spenser suggests to Sir Walter
Raleigh, because both Athenian and Persian images of rule must be read
from the vantage of the new standard of literacy and the true *paideia* of
scriptural revelation. On the foundation of this Christian historiography
alone does the Protestant poet form his theory and practice of poesie.

A decade earlier, however, as Sidney composes the *Defence* at the start of
the 1580s, the significance of the Elizabethan potential has to be judged
precisely and its imperial promise entered carefully. In the character of a
Cyrus seen from both classical and Christian perspectives, Sidney primarily
finds a way to assert metaphorically the difference between right and wrong
use of the imagination. Wrong use of the poetic art makes a travesty of
learning and its final end by producing merely phantasy; abusive poetry can
only "build castles in the air" (*Def.*, p. 79). Good poetry constructs an ideal
image of the hero in its verbal imitation, but the construction does not
necessarily move the reader to imitate the heroic behavior. The best

poetry—the poetry of the mistress-knowledge and the poet-architect—surpasses history, philosophy, science, and the fine arts because it works "not only to make a Cyrus, which had been a particular excellency as nature might have done, but to bestow a Cyrus upon the world to make many Cyruses, if they will learn aright why and how that maker made him" (*Def.*, p. 79). The ethical principle of a universal knowledge generates heroes in the audience if, indeed, contemporary readers will only grasp the inventive point of Sidney's master-building poetic theory for rebuilding the temple of the mind in England. The poet's presentation of "champions" in the analogues of his poetic fiction can teach and move to the "most high and excellent truth," which is the practical realization of the heroic in the actions of the reader's life. For "the lofty image of such worthies most inflameth the mind with the desire to be worthy" (p. 98), Sidney says, again presenting his version of ethical desire. The truest mastery of architectonic poetic art, therefore, will appear in the poet's ability not just to imitate heroic images but also to present even *villainous* or *merely ordinary* flawed characters in verbal proportions that still teach, delight, and move.

Such a learned proportionality constructs Sidney's *Defence* as his English Christian "cyropaedia," or "leading out" of the hero who *is* the temple of God. The real hero—perhaps protagonist is a better word to use—of an architectonic poem or treatise is the human being who writes it or reads it as vigorously as a valiant captain might wage war for the Queen and for God. Both the writer and the reader, no matter what their social status or moral condition, providentially share in poetic triumph of some sort as Sidney perorates on the sum of his argument:

Since therein (namely in moral doctrine, the chief of all knowledges) he doth not only far pass the historian, but for instructing, is well nigh comparable to the philosopher, for moving leaves him behind him; since the Holy Scripture (wherein there is no uncleanness) hath whole parts in it poetical, and that even our Saviour Christ vouchsafed to use the flowers of it; since all his kinds are not only in their united forms but in their severed dissections fully commendable: I think (and think I think rightly) the laurel crown appointed for triumphant captains doth worthily (of all other learnings) honour the poet's triumph. (P. 99)

Earlier in the *Defence* Sidney had claimed that the "feigned example" of Herodotus and the "fiction" of Xenophon teach as forcefully as true examples and that the narrative "stratagem" of the historian is truly a poetic power (*Def.*, p. 89). The "triumphant captain" of the *Defence* seems related to the "valiant capitaine" of a midcentury English translation of Xenophon, William Bercker's *Institution, Schole, and Education of Cyrus*.[23] In the translation Bercker intensified the comparison of poets and historians by adulating the writer himself as a hero. He retells the well-known story of Alexander's approval of Homer. Alexander extended the praise of the heroic Achilles to the writer who immortalized him, Bercker comments, observing the origin of the great debate between contemplative and active types of knowledge—whether "the valiant capitaine, that by corage and policie attaineth to fame, or y skillful writer, that by learninge and cunning maketh report thereof, is worthy more commendation" (sig. A.ij). Sidney, too, uses this tale when he points out that Alexander left "living Aristotle" behind him but took "dead Homer" with him into the field, to receive from him "more bravery of mind by the pattern of Achilles than by hearing the definition of fortitude" (p. 106).

One way to interpret Sidney's language here is self-referentiality. That is, Sidney, the young Elizabethan nobleman known for his intellectual precocity, argues his own longing for the political chance to demonstrate his power practically in actions authorized by the Queen. I do not find this autobiographical reading incompatible with the didactic one proposed by Sidney's assertion that poetry aims to make many Cyruses of the audience. Another way is to recognize the brilliance of Sidney's Protestant view of the political ambivalence of history.

What is interesting in the study of Sidney's epistemological hierarchy is *how* he authorizes himself. Having established the standard of the experiential knowledge of a man's self in relation to literacy, Sidney presses forward the identification of the poet and captain, giving him a laurel crown, partly because of the authority of Christ the Savior, the supreme Word. We find that Philip Sidney's idea of poetic invention suitably expands the realm of the mistress-knowledge, therefore, beyond the fallen nature known by science and art and beyond the intellectual and moral limitations of classical thought to juxtapose the ethics of poetry to theological truth. Autobiographically Sidney argues his case as a divine call, an "unelected vocation" (*Def.*, p. 73) he did not choose for himself but one on which his salvation may nevertheless depend. This is an appeal to high authority indeed as the source of Sidney's rhetorical pleas. Culturally, though, Sidney justifies reading; he relates poetry to theological truth by proposing a Christian art of reading.

Coincidentally, the same translator of Xenophon, William Bercker, also translated Saint Basil's treatise on the usefulness of secular letters: *An exhortation of holy Basilius Magnus, to hys younge kynsemen, sturrynge theym to the studie of humaine lernynge, that they might thereby be the more apt to attayne to the knowledge of divine litterature. Translated out of Greke into Englysshe* (London, 1557). Basil, of course, had baptized Plutarch's art of reading. If Sidney is following suit in his handling of the scriptural Cyrus with Xenophon's Cyrus, as I think he is, Sidney has set in the scales with Persian serendipity and Greek culture the national and providential program of English Protestant humanist education. This is the true *paideia*—the English answer, as I shall demonstrate by the end of chapter 2, to the Cyrus of the Italian Machiavelli.

To examine Sidney's *ars legendi*, we may first profit from remembering his hierarchical definitions of the different kinds of poets. This set of definitions interrelates with Sidney's central metaphor of architectonic knowledge along one radius, and the *ars legendi* that promotes the making of many Cyruses radiates out on other references to the reader. A humanistic sense of literary order helped Sidney devise three levels of poetry and encompass all of them within his central image of architectonics as a teleological proposition. Indeed, Sidney's ἀρχιτεκτονική mediates between "earthly" or "worldly" learning and the divine science he acknowledges as the immeasurable outer limit of the inventive poetic art. He establishes the intellectual recognition of the limit not because he utterly separates sacred knowledge from profane in the scope of poetry but because, like justice in the Aristotelian scheme of virtue, divine knowledge expressed poetically has no deficiency, no excess, and no mean. It is *the* center without circumference, the circumference according to whose measure everything else is to be ordered and judged.[24] The divine poem of creation is the work of the Word of God as much as the poem of Holy Scripture and both are the most excellent (*Def.*, p. 80). The human poetry that expresses theological truth directly, such as the poetry of du Bartas, is not divine poetry properly speaking and is not too different from the second kind in Sidney's estimation, the philosophical poetry that expresses ideas in verse.[25] Architectonic poems, the third kind, are poetry properly speaking, for they are the work of the human mind "making" or inventing.

Thus Sidney sustains a certain proportionality in his definition of three kinds of poetry according to three kinds of makers and three kinds of knowledge. Divine poetry exists in the provenance of divine workmanship and divine revelation. Philosophical poetry exists within the cosmological or natural realm; it merely mirrors the thinking of metaphysics, or the human ordering of the arts and sciences, mimetically, and has a subspecies in human verse that represents or "copies" either religious doctrine or the truth of science. The inventive exists in the "zodiac" of the poet's and the reader's wits, which are meant to recover their image and likeness to God by exercising it. The proportionality among these three kinds of poetry appears in Sidney's reasoning as a relational or an analogical chain of degrees of truth. The inventive kind, he says, is poetry properly speaking—the mistress-knowledge who exercises sovereignty over philosophy and history and all the arts and sciences that have nature along as their object because nature now is fallen, and poesie makes things quite other than the products of that "maker." In so doing, poesie is like the divine Maker. The rule of the mistress-knowledge fulfills, in effect, the expectations that the Renaissance placed on literary education from her position of intermediacy between earth and heaven. She may use the knowledge of philosophy; yet she does so not as an exemplar of imitation alone but as the force of divine imagining that constructs the renaissance arts of inventive composition and inventive interpretation.

Sidney's Protestant humanistic handling of the levels of poetry was underwritten by Aristotle, who comes to the foreground of the *Defence* in its proposal of an end *gradi*. With Aristotle in the classical authorization of Sidney's personification of the poesie that moves men "to take goodness in hand" (*Def.*, p. 81) are Cicero, Plutarch, and Saint Basil. The business of reading or interpretation takes our consideration of the text of the *Defence* into the arena of philosophy just as Sidney's treatment of history brilliantly engages the exegete of the *Defence* in a confrontation with fiction, politics, and theology.

First of all, Sidney extends the poet's rule of rhetorical composition to the reader's active invention of analogies among language, learning, and life. The argument of final cause that establishes Sidney's *gradatio* on reading, knowledge, and the government of action, for instance, continues to reflect the significance of Aristotle's *Ethics* and *Rhetoric* (*Def.*, p. 105). Sidney argues the poetic inspiration of noble deeds in practice, not merely in literary phantasy. Like Aristotle, he recognizes that knowledge alone does not make a man or a woman good; rhetoric, whether political or poetic, was needed in society precisely as a moving force corollary to law to teach those citizens who were neither intelligent enough nor docile enough to grasp the connection between truth and goodness and implement it. Better still, poetic persuasion can move those already learned minds who find themselves morally unable to translate sound doctrine into deeds. For the Ciceronian in Sidney, likewise, the point of rhetoric is success at persuading; the intellectual power of poetry is proportionate to its delightful manner of drawing men by the ears to virtue, leading them across the gap between well-knowing and well-doing.[26] The revised ladder of the gradated argument for the interrelationship of reading, knowledge, and action in the *Defence* focuses Sidney's English understanding on the relationship of poetry to the civil faculty.

Poetry is a re-creative political ability in the state because the poet demonstrates the mastercraftsmanship of knowledge and virtue in writing it and because the reader demonstrates mastercraftsmanship in discovering the invention of the poet. As learned men took their first light of knowledge from Homer the poet, so active men, Sidney says, received "their first motions of courage" from poetry, too (p. 106). Invention allows the reader to parallel his discovery of knowledge and virtue to the poet's fashioning of metaphors and images. Thus Sidney philosophically appropriates the whole of analogy—the intellectual, moral, and verbal making of connections under the overseeing eye of one's self-knowledge—for the work of writing and reading poetry. Thinking is "poeticizing," Heidegger has said. But from one historical vantage, as Sidney rewrites the "metaphysics" of poesie,

Sidney thought so first, and on the authority of moral philosophy: "Aristotle writes the Art of Poesy; and why, if it should not be written? Plutarch teacheth the use to be gathered of them; and how, if they should not be read?" (*Def.*, p. 109).[27]

In the reach from metaphysics to ethics and politics through rhetoric, Sidney arrives at the practical and technical questions, *how* and *why*, once more. This is the point of entry of Plutarch and Saint Basil into Sidney's metaphoric discourse. The same Plutarch who advocated the communication of learning in the images of heroic lives trimmed the writing of his philosophical statements with "the guard of poesy" according to Sidney (*Def.*, p. 109). He understands that Plutarch practically founded the classical theoretical awareness of the process of reading as a moral act of thinking. In the essay on hearing, Plutarch explained that one "hears" a poem better if one works to exercise one's wit, "to invent something of our owne, as well as to comprehende that whiche we heare of others" (trans. Holland, p. 63). Indeed, through the reader's exercise of inventive connection-making, the reading of poems provides an education in liberal arts and much moral profit. Plutarch wants readers, therefore, to search into the reasons of the discourse before them, "to draw in the end a deeper sense and higher meaning, reaching even to Morall Philosophie, and the gentle framing of the mind unto the love of vertue" (trans. Holland, pp. 17–18). Plutarch's *ars legendi* illuminates Sidney's rhetorical strategy in the *Defence* fully enough to tempt the modern scholar to stop at the acknowledgment of Plutarch's influence on reading theories.[28] But we cannot stop there if we are tracing an English Christian humanist substratum in Sidney's metaphoric discourse, nor should we in face of the evidence of Sidney's text. Plutarch's *ars legendi* leads directly to Saint Basil's in the epistle on the usefulness of secular letters, the "Address to Young Men," *Ad Adolescentes*.[29] Whatever else may be going on in the posture of defense and apology that Sidney strikes, a response to religious attacks on knowledge in general and poetry in particular is a main feature of his argument, and on this point Sidney authorizes his defense on patristic sources as much as on Scripture and Apocrypha.

Saint Basil's epistle to his nephews was a patristic handbook promulgated by renaissance humanists as *the norm* for the Christian literary education of the young.[30] Saint Basil's rule for reading effectively standardized analogy-making between secular texts and sacred doctrine or Holy Scripture. In England, Thomas Elyot adopted Saint Basil's and Plutarch's notion of reading for moral profit. Bercker translated the exhortation to humane learning in 1557. In essence, Basil simply presents the model of accommodation: the Christian reader, like a bee, "gathers" knowledge toward sweetness and light by judging it in reference to the truth of scriptural revelation. What does not meet the accommodation falls aside, but almost everything

can be brought into such a relationship in some way. English schoolboys—
and aristocratic and royal English women—were well practiced in the exercise of this rule of reading.[31] The Sidney of Shrewsbury and Oxford too
asks his reader to discover the poet's "imaginative ground-plot of a profitable invention" in poems that seem merely to be "fiction" (Def., p. 103).
Reading is the "gathering" of many knowledges (Def., p. 105). A good poem
or a good oration represents the composer's gathering of his knowledge
according to the unifying principle of one idea that the imagery of the poetic
artifice evokes in the reader's mind. For the poet, poeticizing is thinking; and
for the reader, reading is thinking. In the measurement of such a purpose in
reading, mere statement of the idea in images is as inferior to the poetic art as
carpentry is to philosophy. The inventiveness of the poet and of the reader
reigns supreme. Thus, on humanistic grounds, Sidney's *Defence* collects
numerous Greek and Latin literary conventions and presents poesie as the
architectonic art of composition and interpretation. As an oration the *Defence* thereby redefines inspiration and demands the active practice of moral
judgment on the part of knowing minds in the audience.[32]

Insofar as this English Christian humanist program of education is the
thrust of Sidney's view of poetic invention and its relationship to the government of action through reading and knowing, Sidney has surely unmasked himself in the middle of his persuasion. He almost *preaches* the
value of poesie. For its portrayal of inspiration, Sidney's poetic theory
recapitulates the ethos of classical texts and the scope of learning in the
statement of a Christian principle of moral engagement with politics. It
appears that he extends the rhetorical and poetic expectation of verisimilitude—sufficient likeness to the scientific and artistic knowledge of reality to
make the poetic text credible—to the invention of an ethical realization in the
characters of poet and reader precisely because he *can* assert a theological
link among inventive, philosophical, and divine kinds of poetry. Intellectual
pursuits undertaken on their own merit lead to stumbling one way or
another, Sidney has informed us; but philosophical eloquence taken together with the knowledge of revealed truth—learning that sets forth doctrine in a goodly frame of order or in verse—undergirds the inventive poet's
ability to make his analogies. This by itself is the statement of a Protestant
poetics.

The making of analogies that generates heroes in the audience, similarly,
shows how the poet's exercise of *two* powers at once—his "masculine" wit
and his "feminine" self-knowledge in the ethic and politic consideration—
makes the poet godlike in creating out of nothing. Thus Sidney's Protestant
poetics moves into the territory of grace in the kind of appropriation that
faith alone allows: in poetry, the grace is in no one thing, but in the
combination.[33] The making of those analogies implies a giftedness. The
poetic vocation remains an "unelected" one (*Def.*, p. 73). A man does not

choose it as his art; she chooses or elects him by virtue of his birth and calling. *Orator fit, poeta nascitur*, Sidney says (p. 111), bringing to the defense of the poetic art the sense of vocation that the Christian religion—and a Calvinist doctrine of *sola Scriptura* and divine election—demanded of him. Certainly Sidney's recognition of this giftedness allows poetry and oratory "affinity in the wordish consideration" (p. 119), that is, in technique. But poetic invention differs as certainly from the gorgeous descriptions of the sophists in teleology. The fundamental gift of the poet is his native wit. No *furor poeticus* can compare with this, for the gift marks the apex of the regenerate and graced mind touched from within, not from without, by the supreme truth of revelation in the Word.

The optimism with which Sidney describes the inventive poet lifted up in the vigor of his mind parallels the hopefulness of the reader delighted by parallel discoveries. This sense of joyful affirmation and play is a universe away from the aestheticism of deconstruction. Sidney does not detach himself from the knowledge of grief and guilt in order to assert the knowledge of wise pleasure. He balances both. On the side of human limitation, for example, Sidney seriously evaluates the actual poetic struggle through literary labyrinths in order to see and to express freely a truth. The "erected wit" stands primarily for uprightness as a moral philosophical assertion of the "highest point" of human consciousness and only secondarily operates as a sexual pun in Sidney's twofold definition of love. Yet Sidney's metaphor addresses specifically the problem of the uses of pleasure in the literary imagination, and he does not negate pleasure in favor of moral severity. His humanism, although definitely of a Protestant type, prevents that imbalance, which came to characterize a later Puritan aesthetic developed in colonial America more than in sixteenth-century England. A Protestant recognition of the warp inherent both in human nature and in products of the imagination affected the English renaissance poet's awareness of the need to portray honestly his own distortion and to try to correct the warp in conscience. With respect to his poetic practice, therefore, Sidney identifies himself as a mind that is as "sick" and "awry" with the "common infection" of writers as the next poet. All, therefore, must "bend to the right use of matter and manner" by practicing the rule of poetic invention (p. 119). That rule fulfills the moral purpose of the geometry of words by means of effective thoughts; what is more, the corrective proportion-making of literary architectonics uses pleasure to reveal the moral measure of the writing and reading man or woman in the very self-knowledge of "infected will."

Plutarch had aptly explained the architectonic principle of analogy or proportion in his *Philosophie* with a citation of Pindar:

Neither were he a good musician or poet . . . who should sing against measures: nor the magistrate righteous who in favour of any person doth ought against the laws. . . . Also that an architect or master builder knoweth how to chuse those workemen and laborers under him, who will in no case hurt his worke, but set it forward   and a Statesman or governour, who as Pindarus saith well,

  Of justice is the architect

  And policy ought to direct,

not knowe at the very first to chuse friends of the same zeale and affection that he is himselfe, to second and to assist him in his enterprises, and to be as it were the spirits to inspire him with a desire of well doing. (Trans. Holland, p. 359)

Sidney's sense of proportion in the direction of policy is a supreme balancing act within a complex gender hierarchy. "Neither let it be deemed too saucy a comparison to balance the highest point of man's wit with the efficacy of nature," Sidney says, and the wit of which he speaks is the regenerate mind of the poet who displays most his special knowing of the mistress-knowledge, who plays before God in creative activity, when together with her he re-creates a fallen nature (*Def.*, p. 79).

To the degree that Sidney's central metaphor is sexualized, the arguments on history and philosophy that radiate out from it and back to it are as well. Sidney's central metaphor of the coupling of the mistress-knowledge and the self-knowing man certainly appears to be logocentric and phallocentric in the establishment of Cyrus as the heroic model of literacy by the reader. The poet, too, as a "valiant capitaine," might fall under that criticism from a feminist perspective. But neither logocentrism nor phallocentrism completely triumphs simply because Sidney's statement of his metaphor is androgynous and hierarchical. The mistress-knowledge remains present; the poet does not completely absorb or appropriate her. On the literary plane, which is in this text also the philosophical or metaphysical plane, the mistress-knowledge is saved by her own mystery from a total disappearance. On the political plane, the fact of Queen Elizabeth's sovereignty imposes a sufficient boundary on Sidney's efforts to teach his royal audience how to treat poets, including himself. It is true that Sidney's metaphorical drive into this center is bold. But throughout the *Defence* he asserts the centrality of the architectonic metaphor without ever totally claiming the logocentrism that would have dominated the figure he decidedly wants to present in its superiority, its role of intermediate between earth and heaven.

A major reason for this sort of balancing in the *Defence*, in which we meet that other, historically providential Cyrus, is Sidney's subordination of his logocentrism to the centrality of the Word of God in Holy Scripture and, correlatively, to the sovereignty of the English Queen, which was understood to be divinely authorized. The Bible promoted architectural analogies for Christian life in the many prophetic images of building the Temple (or seeing it destroyed and abandoned) and also in the New Testament narratives that envisioned Christ's body as a temple to be "razed" and "raised up." Saint Paul had extended this piece of typology to the "edification" of the Church in Ephesians in particular and to the spiritual pattern of death to the "old" man and regeneration of the "new creation" that fills the Pauline epistles in general. The building metaphor of temple-body-church struck the Genevan translators of the Bible with enough force to have them borrow it in their prefatory letter to Queen Elizabeth.[34] The prophecy of Ezekiel described the vision of God's chariot-throne and the measurements of the Temple; the prophecy of Isaiah called Cyrus to a statesmanship congruent with divine ministry, for Cyrus was specially elect to build up and to destroy according to God's will. The prefatory letter, exhorting the Queen to her princely duties in the state, applies the imagery of prophetic vision, architecture, and heroism to her work while drawing liberally on the Pauline doctrine of edification, too. The Queen is exhorted to the great charge God has laid on her in making her "a builder of his spiritual Temple" by means of the erection and maintenance of God's Word in England. Zerubbabel went about building "the material Temple," but the Queen is to build the spiritual and "moste excellent Temple," the "house of God" (sig. ∴.ii'). Opposing the workmanship of "rule" and "Word" are both the weakness of human nature and the devilish enemies who would destroy true religion. The Queen, laying a sure foundation of a godly kingdom, must remove those impediments that would hurt, deface, or even ruin the building, and one way she can do so is by choosing wise workmen to do her bidding (sig. ∴.ii'). The "manner" of this building activity is that of the Spirit and the Word of God, not the flesh, and the advancement of this theocracy depends clearly on the Queen's faith and wisdom. She "builds up the ruines of Gods house to his glorie" in the discharge of her conscience (sig. ∴.iii). Imaged as an architect or a mastercraftswoman—or, in Sidney's later metaphor, a mistress-knowledge who supervises and commands subordinate workmen—the Queen bids various political, military, and clerical agents to do her will in church and state.

The statesmanship of Cyrus described by Isaiah, similarly, cannot have been severed in English minds from the hero whom Xenophon celebrated in the *Cyropaedia*. Characterized in the glosses of the Geneva Bible as God's delivery of his people, Cyrus's statesmanship compelled him as a military leader "to come vpon princes as vpon claye, and as the potter treadeth myre vnder the fote" (Isaiah 41:25). God says to Cyrus about the rebuilding of the ruined Temple, "Thou art my shepherd: & he shal reforme all my desire, saying also to Ierusalem, Thou shalt be buylt: and to the Temple, Thy fundacion shalbe surely laied" (Isaiah 44:28). As the divine election calls Cyrus, so, too, election compels prophets to announce the work of Cyrus in the fact that Jerusalem shall, indeed, be "inhabited" and "buylt vp" with its "decaied places" repaired (Isaiah 44:26). When Sidney selects the "feigned Cyrus" of Xenophon as the major heroic image of the *Defence* (p. 86) and

links his education program to Christian humanist literacy, classical statesmanship and an English Protestant model of mastercraftsmanship merge to
serve Sidney's idea of the poetic making of the nation.

Besides the prophetic and Pauline idea of edifying the English church,
the translation of the Genevan Bible selected the sixth pimmillenium as the richer
image expressing doctrines of faith to the English Queen.[35] The English
Calvinists who promoted the Genevan translation had made the interpretation of Jacob's ladder generally available in their glosses on the pertinent
passages in Holy Scripture. The image of Christ the Ladder is an image of
mediation, and the ladder is also a *crux dissimulata*, a cross in disguise; it
signals the achievement of spiritual victory not in theological sophistication
but in moral simplicity.[36] John Calvin had gathered traditional interpretations of Christian humility, Christ's descent in the Incarnation, and the
ladder of the cross into a uniform vision of Christian spiritual progress.
Suppressing the monastic elaborations of the image, Calvin stressed devotional and exegetical sources.[37] The humility of the Ladder that is Christ
descending into human nature is the powerful delivery of the Word of God,
the proclamation of the Gospel that enables man's humble ascent to the
divine Truth. In Calvin's view, therefore, Christ in John 1:51 only seems to
allude to the ladder seen in a vision by the patriarch Jacob; Calvin says in *The
Institutes of the Christian Religion* that Christ is actually marking the excellence of his own advent, for he has opened by it the closed gate of heaven
"that each of us may enter there."[38] The Genevan translators point out for
Genesis 28:12 and John 1:51 that by Christ men "ascende into heauen" and
in Christ they have "access to God," becoming "felowes to the Angels"
(pp. 13ʳ, 43ʳ). The letter dedicatory to Queen Elizabeth states the identification of Christ the Ladder "that reacheth from the earth to heauen: he lifteth
up his Church and setteth it in the heauenly places." In Christ the good
works of faith allow "our godly conuersation [conversion]" to be a confirmation of divine election so that the elect may be good examples of those
who walk "as apperteyneth to the vocation whereunto thei are called."
Thus the Queen must know the cross in her *conversatio morum* and royal
vocation and, we may surmise, the poet know the cross *in the very construction of mediating ladders in his art*, particularly if his art is a Christian
courtier's counseling of his monarch.[39]

In Sidney's speech both in the *Defence* and in *Astrophil and Stella* (1 and 2)
the imitation of the ladder of Christ the Word appears, I think, in a stylistic
preference for the figure called *gradatio* or *climax*, "the ladder," which
Sidney often combines with antithesis. Poets and readers are, on this high
authority, the wise workmen who help Elizabeth build up her temple-
kingdom at the same time they are the living stones whom she alone sets up
and takes down according to her sovereign disposition of the divine plan for
England.[40] Otherwise they are its antithesis, its enemies. Both Queen and
citizens are, however, subject to the divine will.

Along with varieties of antithesis, the presence of such a stylistic device as *gradatio* qualifies Alan Sinfield's otherwise superbly succinct analysis of the effect on discourse of the shift from a medieval Christian to a renaissance Protestant viewpoint in *Literature in Protestant England 1560–1660*. Sinfield remarks that the ladder of love described in Plato's *Symposium* and adapted both in Petrarchism and in social theories of the Italian Renaissance met with increased resistance to human sexual expression in Protestantism. Finding the Petrarchan movement from earth to heaven impossible, Sinfield says,

The Reformation set up a further barrier against one resolution which had seemed possible: the notion that one may ascend through love of a person to love of God. . . . Protestants found this accommodation unhelpful because it proposes a continuity between human and divine—a series of steps—where they insisted upon disjunction. The whole argument of the Reformation was that one is either in the devil's kingdom or in God's: there is no compromise. Divine grace may raise sinners from one to the other, but they cannot work their way up. The spiritual realm is absolutely distinct from the human and there are no mediators—neither blessed virgins nor priests nor Beatrices. (Pp. 49–50)

The qualification comes in the emphasis; for the Reformation that radically perceived the disjuncture between earth and heaven and ruled out the ascent from a human person to God just as radically envisioned God's descent from above to human beings. The issue, again, is the issue of grace, which modern criticism tends to censor. Protestantism emphasizes a divinely human mediator who is Christ the Ladder connecting heaven and earth. The Genevan translators addressing themselves to Queen Elizabeth and Sir Philip Sidney devising the stylistic ladders of his poetic discourse imagine the tumbling down of illusory human efforts to reach heaven and the establishment of the coming of the Word. This is a transformation of the mediation proposed in Plato's *Symposium* and by Petrarch. Edmund Spenser, of course, will confirm Red Crosse Knight's conversion with a vision of such a ladder of angels both ascending and descending.

Moreover, renaissance Protestantism saw the mediation—the advent of Christ—as a dynamic one. I say dynamic because, as Calvin put it in the *Institutes*, quoting Saint Paul, the Scriptures proclaim "the triumph Christ obtained for himself on the cross, as if the cross, which was full of shame, had been changed into a triumphal chariot" (*Institutes* 1:2.16.6, p. 511). From this paradoxical triumph comes the transmutation of nature that grace is all about. The metamorphosis of a static cross into the dynamic historical motions of a triumphal chariot is extremely significant in the *fin de siècle* literature of the sixteenth century as it gathers up the entire significance of Christ's life in one figure—Incarnation, death, resurrection, triumphal judgment—of advent. This moving Ladder ties the doctrine of the cross to the vehicle John Milton will later call "the Chariot of Paternal Deity" on which the Word rides out to defeat the rebel angels at the end of Book 6 of

Paradise Lost and to create the world in Book 7. Following Sidney, we may surmise, Milton, too, requires his reader to practice the *ars legendi* of a Protestant *paideia* as the narrator descends into hell and rises up to heaven.

By the same reasoning, also, the biblical narrator behind Sidney's English Christian "cyropaedia" expresses a male privilege in envisioning the heavenly city being built on earth as a feminine thing. Sidney goes further, parodically modeling his speech on Solomon's allegory of love. By indirection he lets the Word in the words of English poets dominate the Queen who heads the English church and state as the Christian husband dominates the wife who must be obedient to him and as Christ dominates his spouse, the Church, in a union that constitutes the heavenly Jerusalem.

In the Hellenized Book of Proverbs, "Wisdom" is feminine, and she plays a mediating role between the one divine Creator who knew how to build the universe and the minds of the sons of men. "When he prepared the heauens I was there, when he set the compas vpon the depe," she says. "Blessed is the man that heareth me, watching daily at my gates, & giuing attendance at the postes of my dores" (Prouerbes 8:27–33, Geneva). It is her image that Sidney praises in his Urania of the *Arcadia* and that Edmund Spenser praises in "An Hymne of Heavenly Beautie" as the "Sapience" who "rules the house of God on hy" (1.194, p. 598). The first piece of English prose fiction written by a woman—and one related to Sidney—was entitled *Urania*. Milton's Urania in the invocation to Book 7 of *Paradise Lost* is the sisterly power of the eternal Wisdom with whom she "didst play / In presence of th'almighty Father," and Milton emphasizes her voice and her conversation with Wisdom.[41]

On one level of Sidney's construction of his chief figure of Logos, this feminine Wisdom *is* the divine mastercrafts*woman* who is the natural archetype of the poet's mistress-knowledge. She is the superior source of the art through which the poet mediates wisdom in words. She is a teleologically mysterious and divine figure. Sidney does not destroy the scaffolding of this level of significance in his *Defence*, even though there is another level of appropriation of power going on at the same time. On this other level, in shaping the play of the divinely re-creative thought of *his* "erected wit" when it makes a second nature and "with the force of a divine breath . . . bringeth things forth surpassing her doings," the mistress-knowledge figures merely the poet's *techne*. She contains *his* generative power and gives the material form of things to *his* superior knowledge of a man's self. The division in Sidney's use of the image accrues to unresolved gender division in scriptural, apocryphal, kabbalistic, and philosophical statement. Self-knowledge, according to an Augustinian Platonism, is the inner word or "idea" in which *he*, the poet, *must* be most like the uncreated Wisdom, the Word who is Christ (*Def.*, pp. 78–79, 82). Sidney's poet has the godlike force of generation that proves in poetic products how he "knows" the mistress-knowledge and orders her power.

The balancing of hierarchies, then, requires us to read in Sidney's aspirations and autobiography an aspect of his culture. Yet there is a limit of reality that the speaker of the *Defence* acknowledges: the real existence of a powerful female monarch. So Sidney's expression of the mistress-knowledge in face of this model of power balances the poet's erected wit not merely with infected will but also with the forceful presence of a transcendent integrity or unity. The *regina reliquarum* is one—that is, single and monarchical. The *regina reliquarum* is, in cultural archetype if not in *real politik*, a special virgin, and Sidney positively credits that aspect of power. The whole text of his story of himself reaches beyond autobiography to present a cultural paradigm in which Sidney both praises and limits the two powers of nature and of the Queen.

In his fashioning of analogies that serve double purposes, he may have observed to some extent the gender inquiry of Saint Augustine and of Genevan translators of the Bible. As I shall explain later, Sidney reconciles his apparent contradictions on the femininity of Wisdom in an Augustinian and perhaps kabbalistic fashion. But Genevan translators are historically a little closer to his making of the image: they actually gloss the feminine Wisdom of Scripture as an allegory for the masculine and "eternal Sonne of God . . . whome S. Iohn calleth the worde that was in the beginning" (Prouerbes 8:22, gloss k, p. 269ᵛ).[42] Modern editors of the Revised Standard Version term Lady Wisdom a "master workman" who was beside God when he marked out the foundations of the earth (Proverbs 8:30) and gloss the difficulty of translating an ancient word that may mean "coordinator." The Genevan translators, in comparison, distinguish genders but avoid the image of a feminine architect or "chief worker" saying, "When he appointed the fundacions of the earth, Then was I with him as a nourisher" (Prouerbes 8:29–30). Their gloss dutifully records the alternative translation, however, even though the gender-typed word "nourisher" appears in the biblical text, and the gloss also provides some theological justification of the gender difference in interpreting the allegory of Wisdom: "Some read a chief worker: signifying that this Wisedome, euen Christ Iesus, was equal with God his Father, and created, preserued and stil worketh with him, as Ioh.5.17" (gloss m, p. 269ᵛ).[43] The absent presence in this language surrounding Lady Wisdom is, of course, the name of the third person of the Trinity, the Spirit coequal with the Father and the Son.

In sum, Sidney's metaphoric definition of the mistress-knowledge and of the poet's erected wit allows him to negotiate sovereignty to a goodly degree and to appropriate the force of a queenly maker for the statesmanlike poet by means of a culturally sanctioned gender hierarchy in the structures of religion, society, and knowledge. In every sense of the word *virtù*, the mistress-knowledge is the knowledge of a man's self. Yet there is a sphere, and Sidney's metaphoric networking of his chief image throughout the *Defence* inscribes it, in which the power of the mistress-knowledge is untouched by man because it is superior; it touches his conscience as she will, whether dominating him much in fellowship with her in serving his divine image-making of himself by nourishing him.

A Culture for Building

As wonderfully original as Sidney's strategies of translation and appropriation make his metaphoric revision of the architectonic concept, the lively synthesis of the *Defence* does not occur in the sixteenth century in a cultural void. Sidney's is an integral and uniquely English achievement of criticism in the midst of numerous, well-published expressions of the architectonic concept. Many sixteenth- and seventeenth-century thinkers especially developed a Christian-classical theory of architectonics out of these commonplaces to argue the congruence of the divine architecture of the world known by science with both the master-building of the Word in Scripture and the mastercraftsmanship of human thought in the arts intended to help build history toward its completion in the divine temple of the City of God. However, until readers of the *Defence* recognize the epistemological commonplaces that Sidney synthesized with his imagination, they will not grasp how the poetic doctrine of Sidney's preference for the production of character mirrors the logical doctrine that in this City there would actually be no building, no temple, for "the Lord God almightie and the Lambe are the Temple of it" (Revelation 21:22, Geneva).

Historically, the communication of the architectonic metaphor to the reading and writing of poetry in Sidney's definition of poetic theory took place in the Renaissance through Latin rhetoric, Aristotelian ethics and politics, and the Vitruvian analogy of the physical universe, of architectural construction, and of the human body and character. But the motivating and integrating power of this architectonic metaphor was the Pauline understanding of the evangelist "as a skilful master buylder" who has "laid the fundacion . . . which is Iesus Christ" of a people who are "the Temple of God" (1 Corinthians 3:10–11; 2 Corinthians 6:16, Geneva).

Primarily, the rhetorical concept of the poetic fiction extended the metaphysical and ethical capacity of the architectonic metaphor to the structural capacity of the poetic art. Cicero had compared the order and arrangement of ideas in an oration to the parts of a building, saying that the "foundation" is memory, but delivery brings thought into the light of day.[44] Delivery or pronunciation is, of course, what readers of the *Defence* need to "hear" in the voice of its writer as he networks a series of metaphors emanating from a central image. Our difficulty in hearing such a voice reflects not only our own division between the spoken and the written word but also a division historically rooted in the origins of textuality. Centuries after he proposed his oratorical conception of a voiced building in the fifth part of rhetoric, oral pronunciation, Cicero's use of the architectural metaphor was not lost on the medieval poetic theorist Geoffrey de Vinsauf. But this Englishman, who explained in *Poetria Nova* the rhetorical idea that composing a poem was like building a house, was already shifting the dynamism of speech toward the rigidified linearity of visual structures.[45] The crisis of difference and similarity between oral and written forms occurred a fortiori in the Renaissance after the invention of the printing press. In the sixteenth century Johannes Sturm fully developed the architectural analogy for rhetoric in his *Scholae in Libros IIII Hermogenis de Inventione* (sig. a.iij^v), an edition of Hermogenes' *De Ratione Inveniendi*, a primary source of renaissance concepts of the art of persuasion (Strasbourg, 1570). When, then, Edmund Spenser's sometimes mentor, Gabriel Harvey, produced a Ramist rhetoric in 1577, it was not surprising that he elaborated an architectural comparison, too. Harvey argued the universality of rhetorical invention because it exercised parts of dialectic, ethics, and politics and even performed some of the functions of mathematics. Treating the organization of a speech in an architectural order, Harvey telescoped invention and disposition together; he considered the orator's combination of "genesis" and "analysis," composition and reading, to be as necessary to the speaker as arms to a soldier or a measuring "rule" to an architect.[46]

In an English translation of Francesco Patrizi's *De Institutione Reipublicae* (1519), the combined analogies of architecture and military science, of eloquence and poetry, and of moral philosophy and religion establish a definition of civic virtue. Richarde Robinson's *A Morall Methode of Ciuile Policie* (London: Thomas Marsh, 1576) links the renaissance idea of the learned architect to the Aristotelian organization of all the arts and sciences under the master art, political science:

For in euery Cytye there ought to bee a speciall care for the mayntenaunce of good artes & scyences. . . . It shal therfore behoue them (which beare rule in a common weale) to be careful ȳ there want no deuisers or chief workmaisters in a citty: for when the sacred or publique buildings are by euill measure & proportion framed, yt ministreth occasion to straungers to thinke, that the chief princes and rulers of that comon weale are cleane voyd of elegancy. . . . Let the chief master of the worke therfore respect and loke wel to the form and fashion of houses in the city . . . in time of peace and quietnes: but in time of warres an Architecte or chief deuiser of workes shall stande in so good steede for engines, gonnes, and other municions, that hee cannot but be worthy of great preferment, honour, & publique offices: for we reade of some cityes that have bene delyvered from the siege of their enemies, only by the skilfull dylygence of the chiefe deuiser or workemaister. (1.7^v, 10)

Besides explaining the role of the architect as a master of the work, a military engineer, and a politician who makes walls, fortifications, and churches (8.71ᵛ–74ᵛ), Robinson compares him to the "fyrste workemaister of the universall worlde" who invented musie (2.11ʳ) and prefers the "liuelye instructor" on the use of a contradiction in a "deal that be" in some cultivation of precepts. "For," Robinson explains, "mans diligence & long consideration . . . surpasseth the deuise and skill of the Artificer" (8.74ᵛ). Earlier Robinson presented Patrizi's view that all men should be learned and that eloquence is the "Medicine or Physicke for the mind" just as the practice of the poets is profitable to a nation (2.15ʳ–16ʳ). Epistemology, didactic persuasion, and literary decorum undergird the making of a good city in Robinson's feminized idea of eloquence:

Auncient wryters saye that Eloquence was the ladye and Mistris of matters, nether is it only accoumpted profitable in peace and quietnes, but also in warres and tumultes excellethe all other strengthe and force. . . . Poetes are to be mayntayned in a Cyttye, and to bee made famous as well wyth honour, as wyth prayse: whiche Persons surelye oughte to bee most cheryshed and welcomed vnto all men, as well for the rarety of theym, (for nothing in all ages of man can be found more rare than a good Poet) as also for the abundaunce of their wit, and theyr deuine Nature, neyther shall Poets be exiled from a good Cyttye, whatsoeuer *Plato* shall saye, sithens they are well knowen to bee verye profitable vnto theyr Countrye: For, what learninge hathe Grammar in ye contayned, wythout the pertractation of Poetes? The Elegancye or Fynenesse of words, the proprietye of the Tounge, the sweete translations of Metaphors, the lybertye of Speache and Sentences, whyche doe beautyfye the Oracions as it were with certain starres were they not invented onelye by Poetes, and aptlye placed and dystynguyshed by theym, in theyr ryghte places. (2.15ʳ–16ʳ)

As Robinson's version of Patrizi's argument augments the value of learning, the text climbs toward the Socratic assertion that it is better to know one's own mind than to penetrate the secrets of nature:

The Oracle at *Delphos* (whych they saye was fixed before the dores of the Temple) ought to be prefixed before all mennes eyes, which desire to be right wyse: which is *knowe thy selfe*: for he knoweth not himselfe which dothe not know how to use the vertue of his mynde. . . . To this philosophie will euery good Cytizen endeuour himselfe, that desireth to profite not onlye himselfe and his, but hys natiue countrye also. (2.16)

The profitable "philosophie" of self-knowledge unifies the commonweal and the architecture of the arts and sciences. This Platonic idea is hardly new in Patrizi, for the twelfth-century John of Salisbury had stated it a fortiori in his Augustinian description of the primacy of self-knowledge in the *Metalogicon* and had related reason to faith with an architectural analogy for his architectonic argument in his political treatise, the *Polycraticus*.[47]

Peter Ramus, too, would make the architectural comparison to the organic arts and would extend the architectural analogy through his revision of the structure of knowledge.[48] He took the analogy further when, in the *Commentariorum de Religione Christiana*, he applied his method to sacred letters and discussed the architecture of the Word of God in creation and in Holy Scripture.[49] The text, which was published posthumously with a life of Ramus appended to it by Theophile de Banos (Banosius), was dedicated to Sir Philip Sidney in 1576 by de Banos, four years after Ramus died in the Saint Bartholomew's Day Massacre in Paris. Because of the degree to which both biography and text use the architectural analogy to express the significance of the architectonic metaphor for knowledge, the *Commentariorum* uniquely illustrates the complexity of the idea.

First of all, in the dedication to Sidney, de Banos praises Sidney's learning as a kind of architecture; the young Englishman ought to receive this praise in the same way Lucullus received commendation for his buildings, pyramids, arches, and other constructions (sig. a.2).[50] Later de Banos compares Ramus to Cicero; Ramus's dialectical invention and disposition, the first two parts of rhetoric, are like the architect's gathering of materials and ordering of them in the production of his building of thought (sig. b.4ʳ).

In the *Commentariorum* proper, Ramus applied his method of organization to the divine science not by dividing questions into alphabetical categories or precepts, examples, and arguments as, he says, had been done by scholastic thinkers, but by arranging them in constructive order and referring all Christian doctrines to a single head (Intro. 1.5). Before seventeenth-century divines would make much of the axiom that God is a circle whose center is everywhere and circumference nowhere, Ramus appropriated the geometric comparison with reference to Menander and Virgil (1.3, p. 13). Then Ramus expressed a many-faceted metaphor of "architectural" unity in the world, the human mind, and the power of God. Creation is a "machine" that reveals the work of the omnipotent Architect (1.5, p. 18), and creation may be compared to the image of God—the human being or rational and immortal soul who participates in divine justice and holiness according to Ephesians 4 and Colossians 3:10 (1.5, pp. 21–22). Finally, Ramus multiplied his correspondences by comparing creation and the mind of man to the chariot-throne described by the prophet Ezekiel in his vision of the temple. This "circle of creatures," this "amphitheater" like the wheels-within-wheels of the theophany that revealed the faces of the four beasts and the many flashing eyes of the watchful cherubim, declares to all the nations the immense majesty and triumphant glory of God (1.5, pp. 21–22).[51] As in other contemporary sources, the architect often does the work of an engineer, and architecture signifies a moving invention as often as it does a static construction. Discussing a phrase in the Lord's Prayer, "hallowed be thy name," Ramus refers again to Ezekiel's vision of the chariot-throne, remarking that few have grasped the wondrous architecture of this machine and fewer understood this "philosophy" (3.5, pp. 218–19).

Ramus's use of what rabbinic scholars call the *merkavah* reflects exegetical and esoteric significance while extending it. Saint John had borrowed the figure in Revelation. Saint Jerome had composed the four creatures and the many-eyed angelic wheels into an allegory of the four evangelists and the four powers of the human soul with particular reference to Saint John and to the sparks of a burning conscience in the breast of Cain.[52] Calvin compared the cross to a triumphal chariot (*Institutes* 1:2.16.6, p. 511). In Book 4 of the *Commentariorum* Ramus relates the "machine" of creation and the Word of God to the idea of a sacred "Logic" that is not only "learned" but "built" on the cornerstone of the Christ who brings all things into congruence and agreement (4.13, p. 315). Ramus finishes his essay by citing Saint Augustine's open attitude to science; the power of God is not a subject of geometry and physics, not even Euclid's geometry and Aristotle's physics, but the truth of arts and sciences is justified by the truth of God (4.15, p. 325). The universe is rhetorically made and scientifically established, in other words, as Scripture is written and the mind of man rectified.[53]

In the dedication to Sidney, de Banos also comments on the dialectical nature of Scripture in architectural terms; echoing Saint Augustine, de Banos says that dialectic is almost the very soul of wisdom, and the eloquence of Scripture contains the knowledge of all things (sig. e.2^v). Such religion aims morally to cultivate human character through the knowledge of the Word in Christian speech; Ramistic unity of doctrine applied in practice to faith. As Gaspar Trevir put it in the *Expositio Symboli Apostolici, siue Articulorum Fidei* (1576), multitudes of doctrines unified by the "rule" of the Word of God "build up" a true and solid piety that best consoles the conscience (*Epistola* 4). Word, world, and mind are God's engine, and Protestantism argues the new coming of the Word.

From the structure of an oration to the application of the rule of faith in scientific and philosophical discourse, these few examples show how some thinkers in the late sixteenth century used the architectural analogy of rhetoric to develop one complex image: an architectonic vision of the knowledge of creation, the Book, and the soul. On the strength of this vision, polymathic Christian poets could similarly compose their universal knowledge in the spoken or written word for the sake of articulating not so much an architecture of the truth as an architectonics of the mind. The dominant fact that Plato had banished poets from the ideal republic presented no immovable obstacle to the reinstatement of the renaissance poet in the Christian commonwealth. That Aristotle did not assign a specific place to poetry in his organization of the arts and sciences left open the *Poetics*, a treatise lacking the usual prefatory statement on the position of a given art in the structure of knowledge, to renaissance commentators who increasingly identified the poetic art with the freedom of the mind to draw knowingly on all arts and sciences.[54] In the rhetorical concept of the architecture of the poetic fiction we obviously find the origin of modern critical problems in structuralism, poststructuralism, and deconstruction.

At the same time that rhetorical tradition presented the architectural analogy for language to renaissance minds, readers recovered the Greek word *architectonic* from Aristotle. Aristotle was the chief publicist of the idea of an architectonic knowledge, properly so called; he gave renaissance humanists trained in scholastic thought the necessary principle for reorganizing the scheme of the arts and sciences to include new disciplines and subject matters. The *Nicomachean Ethics* is the *locus classicus* for the idea of a master science. The *Ethics* includes some useful standards for distinguishing the intellectual virtues of sapience, science, prudence, art, and craft and a rule for cross-referencing them and rearranging their hierarchy. Aristotle explains, "The ends of the master arts are things more to be desired than the ends of the arts subordinate to them, since the latter ends are only pursued for the sake of the former" (1.2 [1094a]).[55] Final cause is a general Aristotelian principle for ordering any hierarchy. Thus science, which is a knowledge of the necessary and eternal, has a higher status than art, which knows how to produce things (6.3.1), and whatever is an end in itself, like a certain activity, has a higher status than anything that has its end in something other than itself. The supreme end of all activities, sciences, and arts must be the supreme good that, in turn, "must be the object of the most authoritative of the sciences—some science which is pre-eminently a master craft. But such is manifestly the science of politics" (1.2 [1094a]). In the *Physics* Aristotle explained further that the user of a product of an architectonic knowledge may be considered a mastercraftsman with respect to the knowledge of its form just as the maker is with respect to the knowledge of its manufacture (194b).[56]

While northern renaissance writers committed to the Protestant movement imagined the building to be effected by the rhetorical and dialectical arts of invention and disposition, Italian arts theorists borrowed Aristotle's architectural analogy and his definition of architectonic knowledge in moral philosophy in their discussion of poetry throughout the sixteenth century. Minturno, for example, in his *L'Arte Poetica*—a treatise subtitled "the rules for heroic, tragic, comic, satiric, and other kinds of poetry, with the doctrine of sonnets, canzoni, and Tuscan rhymes, a consideration of the Petrarchan mode, and a discussion of Aristotle, Horace, and other Greek and Latin writers on the poetic art"—argued for the truth of Homeric poetry on the grounds that the art of imitation always has a rationale, like the rule with which an architect builds variety into unity ([Venice, 1564], p. 33). He began the treatise with the remark that poetry is the "overseer" or "ruler" of all knowledges, their "mother" and the "muse" both of the excellent arts of invention and of the art of government (p. 1). Battista Guarini generally followed Castelvetro, however, to reject the architectonics of moral philosophy in the poetic art in favor of imitation; when Guarini disputed with Denores, who strongly advocated the ethics of architectonics, the moral philosophical status of poetry appeared again with some qualifications. In his treatise *Il Verrato ovvero difesa di quanto ha scritto M. Giason Denores* (Ferrara: Alfonso Carassa, 1588), Guarini emphasized the rhetorical aspect of the architectural analogy and the idea of the unity of poetic construction commensurate with that idea of imitation. Even Guarini finally borrowed Aristotle's expression of the first principle or final cause of architectonic knowledge from the *Nicomachean Ethics* to distinguish clearly the architectonic ends of tragedy, comedy, and tragicomedy. Drama is the production of character much as Aristotle's moral philosophy produces character in the name of happiness (pp. 19–27).[57] Thus Guarini supplied what to him were missing features of Aristotle's *Poetics* with conclusions based on the *Ethics* in order to explain the aesthetic and moral integrity of the poetic artifact.

By 1595 the English word for the ethical organization of knowledge appeared in a "Sermon for Queen's Day" by one J. King, who mentioned the art that was "architectonical . . . and commander of all other functions."[58] That is the year of publication of both versions of Sidney's poetic treatise, the *Apologie* and the *Defence*. In 1596, the translator of Ariosto's *Orlando Furioso*, Sir John Harington, felt free enough with Aristotle's idea of an "Architectonicall" knowledge to make a joke out of it in *The Metamorphosis of Ajax*. Here Harington reduces the principle for the organization of knowledge to a scurrilous distinction between the "house" itself and the "businesse" done in the house; he makes the joke at the expense of the seven wise men— probably mocking the way Sidney, who used the Greek word in his *Defence*, was compared to them—but rightly grasps Aristotle's sense of the order of things.[59] Harington glances at the courtly folly of Sidney's wisdom and the futility to which it leads in the "jakes."

Shakespeare seems to have picked up and used the entire point of architectonical art in this courtly skirmish in *The Tragedy of Richard the Second*, which was entered in the Stationers' Register in 1597 but probably composed in 1595. *Richard the Second* pivots on the rhetorical tension between palaces and castles—Richard's palace, Lancaster's palace, Ely House, Windsor, Pomfret, Bristol, Barkloughly, Flint—and the poetic character of the king. The play is an architecturally well-constructed piece of drama; rhetorically and philosophically, though, the play is a state metaphor for Shakespeare's imagination of rule and misrule, regicide, and the moral structure of an entire nation reflected in the "mirror" of the king's identity. "This other Eden, demi-paradise, / This fortress built by Nature for herself" (2.1.42–43), as John of Gaunt names England, has become the natural scene

for politically "empty lodgings and unfurnish'd walls" (1.2.68–69), an "un-
ruly" garden (3.4). Richard is Shakespeare's speaking picture of a ruling
character who tragically comes to know himself and in whom a rhetorical
poetics gradually organizes fantasies into an architectonic consolation of
philosophy. The poet-king works on the word *comfort* and its parallels, for
instance, until a truly royal speech emerges from several architecturally
balanced scenes in the form of the drama (2.1; 3.1; 4.1; 5.1).[60] Shakespeare's
Richard even passes on to his Queen the rhetorical *ars poetica* of Orpheus
and Amphion, the musical builders of cities, which Sidney had described in
the poet's tale "that holdeth children from play, and old men from the
chimney corner" (*Def.*, pp. 74, 91–92). She is to listen to the "mirrors" of
magistrates—

> In winter's tedious nights sit by the fire
> With good old folks and let them tell thee tales
> Of woeful ages long ago betid—

but then go on to tell "the lamentable tale of me / And send the hearers
weeping to their beds" (5.1.40–50). The passing on of an architectonic
poetic, enabling hearer or reader to exercise it, is its essence.

At the turn of the century the architectonic idea and its link to conscience
were commonplace references in treatises in the arts and education, in devotional books and biographies, and in poems. The product of poetically
architectonic reasoning was some image intended to move the heart while it
expressed the scope of human knowledge of the arts and sciences and
helped produce a new creation out of a fallen world. In the seventeenth
century the rhetorical idea of architectonic knowledge was well enough
known—and, no doubt, so dramatically influenced by the temple-building
analogies of Protestantism—that it reappeared in a form that neglected the
inherently intellectual emphasis of the architectonic metaphor on the encyclopedia and directly evoked the moral application.[61] For example, William
Gilbert's devotional treatise *Architectonice Consolationis; or, the Art of Building Comfort: occasioned by the death of that religious gentle woman, Jane Gilbert*
(London, 1640) simply presents the necessity of the construction of spiritual
comfort in the Christian commonwealth as the latest product of a long
tradition of consolation literature. In fact, though, an appropriately full
development of the philosophical and literary significance of the architectonic metaphor appeared in the early seventeenth century in the rhetorical
flourishing of the architectural analogy in polymathic or "metaphysical"
poetry. John Donne's control of scientific and philosophical ideas, George
Herbert's *The Temple*, with its integral recapitulation of Christian truth,
Henry Vaughan's prophetic vision of conscience in poems that, like
Ezekiel's heart of stone turned to a heart of flesh, are "sparks from the flint,"
and John Milton's metaphoric treatment both of the encyclopedia and of the
operations of God's chariot-throne in the verbal intricacies of the fables and

speeches of *Paradise Lost* obviously resist literal interpretation of the rhetorical building metaphor or one of its aspects.

Most English writers who used the architectonic idea emphasized its metaphoric value and teased the tension between architectural building of words and the intellectual and moral architectonics of a ruling, theoretical knowledge; wisely, they sustained the sense of difference that logically accompanies true similitude. The architectonic metaphor in its proper name expressed several ideas, and interpretation could move in the direction of one or all of them. For example, Topsell's mixture of architecture and architectonics combined natural and moral philosophies in the use of the word in 1608 to comment on the way bees "build their combes with such an architectonic prudence." Topsell may have been dressing up Pliny's view of the bees in the *Natural History*, but John Lyly had already compared their architectural order to a Daedalean poetic art in *Euphues and His England* in 1580, and seventeenth-century writers would variously develop their own rhetorical and intellectual mazes. The famous concluding simile of Book 1 of *Paradise Lost* similarly combines architectural craft with natural and moral philosophical significance, for instance. Milton satirizes the construction of Saint Peter's in Rome by reducing the building of Pandemonium to a form of insect architecture. Pandemonium is a "Straw-built Citadel" for the state affairs of fallen angels who are now like swarming bees—giants reduced to "less than the smallest Dwarfs" (*PL* 1.768–79).[62] The apian metaphor predicts Milton's criticism of the devilish rhetoric of Book 2 and prefigures his inversion of the moral philosophical organization of knowledge in the encyclopedic poem as a whole; exposing the moral ambivalence of knowledge, Milton's Pandemonium is the kind of architecture that images the demonic metaphysics, politics, history, and speech that hellish minds produce and that the Word of God will demolish in the battle in heaven and does demolish in the course of human history.

Yet, on the architectonic side of conscience, perhaps the fullest poetic expression of the presence of the mistress-knowledge came in her *compression*, not suppression, in Milton's Eve. Milton imagined the disrupted moral coupling of history in his conflated myths of Noah, Deucalion, and Janus. History is a process of building up and tearing down and building up. We live "Betwixt the world destroy'd and world restor'd" (*PL* 12.3) and try to say all of it through the measure of our characters. Thus Eve speaks her "dream" and Adam tells the story of himself historically. Adam has to narrate "My Story" (8.205) not only in juxtaposition to the great myths of creation and the battle in heaven but particularly in reference to the story of his seeing and loving Eve. To him, she is a creature,

> Manlike, but different sex, so lovely fair,
> That what seem'd fair in all the World, seem'd now
> Mean, or in her summ'd up, in her contain'd.
>
> (8.470–73)

His story, then, like the story of knowledge in the poet's architectonic language, is the story of desire to possess and to contain *her*. Only when *her* story is told—and in Milton it is the story of the Fall, of the self, and of the Incarnation, the loss and regaining of Paradise—does Adam experience in his story the beginnings of a self-knowledge of intellectual, moral, and gender boundaries. The loss of a balance of power between the two genders appears characteristically then as a power struggle between containment and freedom; but at the same time the struggle communicates a moral lesson that Adam identifies with self-knowledge. This he expresses to Michael in a statement of humility offering the lesson to be grasped immediately by the reader of renaissance poems shaped by literary architectonics:

> Greatly instructed I shall hence depart,
> Greatly in peace of thought, and have my fill
> Of knowledge, what this Vessel can contain;
> Beyond which was my folly to aspire.
>
> (12.557–60)

In contemporary feminist discourse there have been many puns on "history" to distinguish the story of man from "her story," or the suppressed cultural record of women and of woman's contribution to civilization. Recapitulating Sidney's architectonic poetics, however, John Milton actually constructed the problem of knowledge *as* a problem of gender appropriation and definition. In the context of renaissance aesthetics, in the literary sphere of influence of Sidney's mistress-knowledge and the self-knowing poet, it was inevitable that he do so. And it was inevitable that Milton would make two characters, two icons, two prosopopoeias figuring the self and the other, the knowing and the unknown, present.

Distinct from Milton's poetic world—whether that of Eve or that of the intellectual order of hell—is the purer, enlightened order of the Word, the Logos whom Ralph Cudworth, one of the Cambridge Platonists and one associated with Christ's College, Milton's college, identified as "the Demiurgus or Architectonick Framer of the Whole World" in 1678—one hundred years after Jean de Serres's Christian Platonism had compared the Word of God in history to man's philosophical knowledge of architectonic first principles.[63]

Sir Philip Sidney named poetry an architectonic art, the mistress-knowledge, on the strength of rhetorical and poetic tradition and Aristotle's *Ethics*, and he did so in the context of renaissance arts disputes that opposed the pictorial and plastic arts (painting, sculpture, architecture) to poetry. Sidney's use of de Serres's philosophical view of the power of conscience when expressed by the burning words of the elect linked an architectonic poesie to the moving chariot of the Word of God and made the verbal motions of poetry far more than a building.

Beyond the well-developed cultural context in which Latin rhetoric and Aristotelian thought contributed to the sixteenth-century idea of architec-
ture, the Vitruvian analogy also helped Sidney cultivate his metaphor of the mistress-knowledge. In his first-century treatise on architecture, Vitru vius had simply analogized the proportions of a building and the propor tions of the human body. In the Italian Renaissance Leon Battista Alberti borrowed many aspects of Vitruvian proportion and extended them with his consideration of the hierarchy of knowledges necessary to the "learned" architect. The English scientist Doctor John Dee followed suit in "The very fruitfull preface . . . specifying the chiefe mathematicall sciences" preceding Billingsley's edition of *The Elements of Euclid* (London, 1570), and Dee alludes both to Vitruvius and to the Italians. When Dee discusses the architect's knowledge of painting and geometry, he comments on the use of "Groundplats" as the means of producing the descriptions of buildings. Sidney appropriates Dee's explanation of the architect's geometric "dispatches" and poeticizes it as he transfers the learned architect's universal knowledge of the arts and sciences into the hands of the poet. He argues that a fictional composition or poem is an "imaginative ground-plot of a profitable invention" (*Def.*, p. 103).[64] Dee's passage addresses the making of patterns:

Secondly, it is behofefull for an Architect to have the knowledge of Painting: that he may the more easily fashion out, in patternes painted, the forme of what worke he liketh. And Geometrie, geveth to Architecture many helpes: and first teacheth the Use of the Rule, and the Cumpasse: whereby (chiefly and easilie) the descriptions of Buildinges, are despatched in Groundplats; and the directions of Squires, Levells, and Lines. (Sig. d.iij^v)

The renaissance discussion of Vitruvius encompasses a theory of knowledge, a theory of proportion, and a mathematical appreciation of what we today call an architect's blueprint. Dee is characteristically interested in the mathematical knowledge that informs the making of such proportions. When Sidney makes a metaphor out of the word "ground-plot" in reference to rhetorical invention, he creates, so to speak, the notion of a poetic geometry or rule that is at once scientifically exact, artistically delightful, and morally effective—but distinctly verbal.

Dee's version of the tradition of the learned architect presented it to England in English with the scientist's interest in working out the organization of knowledge, and I shall pursue it further in chapter 4. There was, however, also in English, an earlier treatise on the practice of architecture that also cultivated the tradition of the learned architect in the more literal terms of the mastercraftsmanship of architecture. We must return, therefore, to John Shute's treatise, *The First & Chief Groundes of Architecture*, reprinted in 1579 or 1580, and examine more closely what Shute did with the tradition of the learned architect in relation to *his* feminized allegorical figure, "the prudent ladye *Scientia*." Here is Shute's passage in full:

And amongst all other studies there is none in my simple iudgement of this sorte that diserveth greater prayse, then that whiche is of the grekes named Architectonica, and of the Latines Architectura (I thinke not altogither unfite nor unaptlie by me termed in Englishe, the arte and trade to rayse up and make excellent edifices and buildinges) the whiche like as in all other ages before hath bene in mervelous accoumpte and estimation, as ful well appereth by diuers learned Philosophers and famous princes that imbraced ȳ same, as l'lato, Aristotel, l'lini, who were excellent therin as their workes will witnesse. . . . And surely such is the amplitude and largnes (I may well say perfection) of this facultie, that without sum acquaintance with many other artes ye shall not enter into ȳ depe secretes: for it hath a naturall societie and as it were by a sertaine [*sic*] kind & affinitie is knit unto all the Mathematicalles which sciences and knowledges are frendes and a maintayner of diuers rationall artes. . . . Notwithstanding I know well there hath bene a multitude and at this time be very many lerned men who hath (throughe trauile receiued) the ful perfection of the prudent ladye *Scientia*.[65]

Shute's treatise was first published in 1563, seven years before John Dee's preface to Billingsley's *Euclid*, but in it Shute, too, links the primacy of architecture to the deep secrets of mathematics as the archetype of rational arts.

We should remember that Sidney's mentor Languet notes that geometry is "an excellent study, and one particularly worthy of a liberal mind" but urges Sidney to consider his "position in life" and to assign his rare leisure time for reading to "the most necessary studies." "To be sure," Languet says, "geometry can be of great service to highborn man for fortifying and attacking cities, for setting up camps, and for all kinds of architecture," but studying it well enough to benefit from it takes too much time; Languet thinks it "absurd to learn the elements of many skills for the sake of display rather than use." Besides, "that study will make you more melancholy still." Thus Languet advises Sidney on the guidance of one's intellectual appetite as well as any other and goes on to encourage the "necessary" studies of Latin, Greek, and the modern European languages, placing all of them under the rule of the primary knowledge of religion and, after that, moral philosophy and history:

The knowledge most necessary for us is that of our salvation, which Holy Scripture teaches us. After this study, I consider nothing more beneficial to you than that branch of moral philosophy which teaches right and wrong. As for reading history, there is no need for me to try to convince you, since you incline towards it of your own accord, and have already made great progress in it.[66]

By the time Sidney composes the *Defence* he seems to have put Languet's advice into effect. He opposes Shute's praise of the universality of the knowledge of architecture, based in mathematics, to the moral philosophical reading of "architectonica" in Aristotle's *Ethics*, and he constructs his argument for poetry out of elements from philosophy and history. Indeed Sidney's first challenge is to the mathematician who draws straight lines with a crooked heart, and the final standard of judgment is an ethics based on Holy Scripture.

Stating his own theory of foundations, Sidney revises cognitive psychology:

For as in outward things, to a man that had never seen an elephant or rhinoceros, who should tell him most exquisitely all their shapes, colour, bigness, and particular marks, or of a gorgeous palace, an *architector*, with declaring the full beauties, might well make the hearer able to repeat, as it were by rote, all he had heard, yet should never satisfy his inward conceit with being witness to itself of a true lively knowledge; but the same man, as soon as he might see those beasts well painted, or the house well in model, should straightways grow, without need of any description to a judicial comprehending of them: so no doubt the philosopher with his learned definitions—be it of virtue, vices, matters of public policy or private government—replenisheth the memory with many infallible grounds of wisdom, which, notwithstanding, lie dark before the imaginative and judging power, if they be not illuminated or figured forth by the speaking picture of poesy. (Pp. 85–86)

The "visual epistemology" of this passage is clear, but Sidney's use of it does not imply a collapsing of the pictorial and philosophical terms of the architectonic metaphor to give the fine arts, after all, the victory over poetry.[67] On the contrary, this same passage is loaded with philosophical references establishing the demonstrative, verbal geometry of thought within the image, a technique that is the essential strength of Sidney's intertextual argument in the *Defence*.[68] Geometry itself is taken into Sidney's literary modeling of illumination.

When we analyze the allusions in this version of the arts debates, in which Sidney imagines painters, architects, and poets arguing the instantaneous cognitive and moral effects of their image through the perceiving eye, we see first that Sidney echoes the philosophical influence of Plato's dismissal of the verbal architecture of gorgeousness in the *Gorgias*.[69] Cicero's architectural analogy for the way oratorical delivery gives light to the invention that one has discovered in memory also plays a part in Sidney's view of the illumination of poetry.[70] The parallel between the "living speech" of Plato's statesman (*Phaedrus* 276a) and Sidney's "true lively knowledge" is similarly obvious. As Plato's statesman speaks according to the truth of his dichotomous dialectic, he succeeds in making citizens in his audience good at knowing how to make yet other men good at knowing in order to *be* good in the living; in the same way Sidney claims a forceful intellectual clarity for poetic images that vividly present moral truths.[71] Sidney's poet challenges the moral philosophers who plainly set down how virtue "extendeth itself out of the limits of a man's own little world to the government of families and maintaining of public societies" (*Def.*, p. 83). As in other passages in the *Defence* and in letters to Robert Sidney and to Hubert Languet, Sidney here reveals his awareness of an Aristotelian organization of knowledge, especially the bonds among ethics, economics, and politics—moral philosophy—and rhetoric, or "public policy and private government" reflected in one's discourse.[72]

By implying a comparison of the mere "architector" of words to the architectonic poet who produces in life what he signifies through his words, likewise, Sidney echoes a well-known little parable in Plutarch, the philosopher who advocated the teaching of philosophy in the images of heroic lives: of two architects in competition with each other, the first lengthily described in gorgeous words what he would build; the second, finally getting his turn to speak, demonstrated his mastercraftsmanship by pointing and saying, "This have I done."[73] So, too, Sidney rejects the idea of poetry as merely an "architector's" recitation of a pictorial philosophy and history. He describes a poetry that produces the things themselves—the human character and the house of civilization—by *giving the reader* the blueprint for building them.

Thus Sidney's view of the nature of the poetic image in this passage vividly recapitulates the work of Julius Scaliger who had similarly argued the philosophical status of poetry on the grounds of rhetoric, dialectic, and history. Scaliger explained in a prefatory epistle to the *Poetices* that oratory, dialectic, and other knowledges are all drawn in principle from philosophy and that all sciences are inferior to it.[74] Beyond grammatical matters and matters of jurisprudence, the significant business of correcting evil and imitating what is good involves moral precepts that make the reading of poetry philosophically better than reading history—which, if properly understood, is poetic anyway. Typical of other poetic treatises, Scaliger's discourse regularly mixes Horatian and Aristotelian theories. In writing his history of poetry Scaliger also self-consciously weighs Platonic "ideas" with Aristotle's view of the subject matter of poetry (1.1, p. 4; 2.1, p. 55) and treats the forms of poetic thought under the title "Idea" in categories of invention and disposition.

Commenting on *tractatio*, for example, Scaliger cites Greek and Latin opinions before explaining it as the "drawing out" of the lines and dimensions of the reason of a piece; because of its likeness to the *modulum* or "little measure" of the architect, the Italians have familiarly named the structural disposition of an idea *modellum* or "model" (3.33, p. 122).[75] Scaliger's handling of *translatio*, *exemplum*, *imago*, *collatio*, and *comparatio* with the Greek *paradigmae* similarly cross-references linguistic counters as he asserts that *imago* stands frequently in *translatio*, the former being called "icon" and the latter "metaphor" by the Greeks (3.50, pp. 127ff.).[76] Scaliger weaves

through etymology a parallel definition of idea and image, of thought and metaphor, of logical disposition and architectural model. His critical judgment of poetry both ancient and modern includes allusions to contem-
poraries such as Melanchthon, Fracastoro, and Languet (6.2, pp. 308 10),
and he praised the ancients, Scaliger and T millions of Italia, whose certi
epistles effectively stated one of the first versions of an *ars poetica Christiana*.[77]

Scaliger's favorite poet, however, is the philosophical and divine Virgil, and on the strength of his example Scaliger can say that history really is *poesis historica* and that the poet practices the right reasoning of philosophy by teaching moral precepts in ways that move men to action (7.1–3, pp. 345–47).[78] The power of poetry to teach and to delight makes it a force either of perdition or of beatitude, but properly of beatitude, if it is used correctly; for as nothing shows the perfection of a blessing better than action, so the deduction of moral precepts from a poem ought to lead to the performance in an ethical way of the deeds the poem portrays (7.3, p. 348).

The argument of Scaliger's treatise obviously touches the argument of Sidney's *Defence*, and Sidney refers to it repeatedly for its learned philosophy of poetry, for its view of verse, for the understanding that Plato criticized only the poetry portraying false images of the Deity, and for the praise of Virgil (pp. 100, 108, 110, 121). Many of the contemporary European poets and theorists whom Sidney lists in order to contrast the harsh treatment of poetry in England to ancient and modern celebration of it in other nations (*Def.*, p. 110) appear also on Scaliger's list (6.2, pp. 295ff.). The central influence of Scaliger's treatise on the *Defence* was, I think, the example of a literary history and aesthetics that helped to Christianize in a Protestant way points of view that other Italians had elaborated.[79] In the ethical, political, and theological defence of poesie as a mastercraft, Sidney argues a Virgilian case for how *not* to build Rome as well as the Augustinian and historical case for building England's household of faith.

The "house well in model" and "beasts well painted" indeed draw on the architectural and pictorial arts to illustrate a poetic structure. But the truly architectonic sense of form in Sidney's idea of poetic art manifests itself in the experience of illumination in the poet's and reader's minds. Plato explained metaphorically that the soul exercises the functions of the "painter" and the "scribe" in such a way that the devising of images serves the articulation of truth (*Philebus* 39a–d). Augustine described the intellectual life as the search for the uncreated Light of the Word of God. Sidney in the *Defence* similarly subordinates the pictorial arts to the primacy of thought and the efficacy of its expression in words. The *Defence* revels in a bias toward the ethics of language, and the probable source of Sidney's image of the "beasts" and "house" helps confirm the point.

One testimony to the written word and then the printed word was the

Frankfurt Book Fair visited by bookmakers, booksellers, learned printers, scholars, and political figures alike. In the 1570s Henri Estienne, du Plessis Mornay, Hubert Languet, and the Sidney brothers all visited the Fair to pay tribute to the book as the treasure-house of learning. One year the Fair included a live elephant in the garden of the Gallus-Gasse, and the life-sized image of this "beast" was later painted on the wall of a nearby house that was afterward called "Zum Elefanten."[80] Sidney records his version of "beasts well painted" and the "house well in model" in the *Defence* as figures of speech for the poet's realization of general truths in vivid images like that of the elephant, whose memory made it a renaissance type for wisdom. The great significance of those images is the intellectual excitement of knowledge, of thinking epistemology through by making analogies. Estienne's description of the Fair reveals the quality of that excitement; the description should balance in our critical perception the way the encyclopedia informed visual epistemology:

For here may all enjoy the living voice of many honored persons who gather here from many different academies. Here very often right in the shops of the book-sellers you can hear them discussing philosophy no less seriously than once the Socrateses and the Platos discussed it in the Lyceum. And not only the philosophers; those celebrated universities [of the world] . . . send to the Fair not only their philosophers, but also poets, representatives of oratory, of history, of the mathematical sciences, some even skilled in all these branches at once—those, in short, who profess to encompass the whole circle of knowledge, which the Greeks call *encyclopoedia* or *encycliopoedia*.[81]

So, too, Sidney's aim for the poet was to be skilled in all the branches of knowledge at once and to have succeeded in integrating them in morally effective verbal images.

Sidney closes the *Defence* with Clauserus's opinion "that it pleased the heavenly Deity, by Hesiod and Homer, under the veil of fables, to give us all knowledge, logic, rhetoric, philosophy natural and moral, and *quid non*."[82] The next remark presses the metaphoric quality of poetic discourse: "There are many mysteries contained in poetry, which of purpose were written darkly, lest by profane wits it be abused" (*Def.*, p. 121). The mystery of building a fable characterizes Sidney's architectonics as the ethical invention of living characters in history.

The liveliest image that renaissance poems must reveal according to the poetic theory of the *Defence*, therefore, is *not* a pictorial or an architectural structure but an architectonic proportion of the mind itself in its character-making operations. Sidney proposes a literary civilization founded on aristocratic moral pleasure and productivity. The poetic invention he praises distinctly compares composition and reading to the work of an androgynous generative power. The sexuality embedded in the *Defence* is the chief way of moralizing Sidney's political purpose: to build up and extend the national household, to make the houses or family lines of England integral around their Queen.

Understanding this historical version of the architectonic concept illuminates the reading of renaissance poems by confirming the balance of words and things, of male and female genders, of rhetorical invention and scientific inventions, of thought-filled verbal art in visual images and the art of the human life striving to become, as Milton would put it, a "true Poem." Sidney personified the architectonic concept in his metaphoric idea of poesie as the mistress-knowledge and the knowledge of a man's self. Milton, too, expressed the agency of architectonic poetic structure in the creation of character and society when he insisted that the poet be "a composition and patterne of the best and honourablest things," not presuming "to sing high praises of heroick men, or famous Cities, unless he have in himself the experience and the practice of all that is praise-worthy."[83] Both writers followed Aristotle, but through Ciceronian rhetoric, Horatian doctrine, and Platonic values, when they connected the genetic argument for the moral quality of the life of the poet to the teleological argument for the end of learning in virtuous action and linked both to the material argument for the intellectual content of poetry so that the reader, too, is the discoverer of architectonic form. An architectonic poetic thrived on the moral tensions of the ancient philosophical analogy: it balanced the encyclopedic structure of knowledge with the actively knowing minds of characters who lived out the discovery of truths in virtuous action.

Art Working "Euen As Nature Her Selfe"

Having begun with the reading of metaphor in order to find the centrally organizing metaphor of Sidney's *Defence* in its historical context, this chapter may profitably conclude with a few self-referential images from other renaissance texts. These images parallel the aesthetic Sidney expressed out of the vitality of his mind when he manipulated the balancing of correspondences and antitheses throughout the *Defence*. His arguments are grounded in the knowledge of renaissance rhetoric and its cultivation of similarities, contraries, and variations on a theme. Rhetorical writing and reading, consequently, as regularly tore down edifices of thought as built up images of it. The critical danger in too easily applying the methods of deconstructive criticism to renaissance texts written out of this rhetorical knowledge is the imposition of our modern sense of subversion of significance on a language that operated by its own elaborate codes for altering, contesting, confirming, or refuting a given verbal predication. Typically, the awareness of this potential in language surfaces in images of building up and tearing down in renaissance texts. These images are applied, moreover, to verbal realities as detailed as syntax and as large as the definition of the culture of antiquity. An historical reading argues that the production of such self-referential images in renaissance texts was, indeed, a cultural mirror, but of the culture of the Renaissance, not ours. In general, it seems true to say that renaissance poets used the architectural analogy of rhetoric to articulate the architectonic moral power of affirmation and negation in history. From their vantage such images were tantamount to the judgment of conscience.

In the middle of the sixteenth century, for example, the French diplomat Joachim du Bellay imagined his poetic task in the architectural analogy of the city of Rome, which lay both in old ruins and in new scaffolding around him. It was "L'antique orgueil," the image of ancient pride that menaced the heavens like a tower of Babel and through which a fatal hand moved to resuscitate the dusty smithereens.[84] Edmund Spenser's translation of the "Ruines of Rome" clearly expressed his meditative version of this architectonic truth when the poet sought beyond the "paterne of great Virgils spirit diuine" to try what was within his very self, "To builde with leuell of my loftie style, / That which no hands can euermore compyle" (25.347–49). Spenser surpassed the act of translation of du Bellay's architectonic declaration, furthermore, when he created his own English composition on the theme. This time, through the allegory of history in "The Ruines of Time," Spenser mourns the ancient Roman foundation in his native Britain in order to comment on the present historical moment. "The Ruines of Time" is primarily a moral philosophical critique of the English nation in Spenser's century. The monuments are now all "turned to dust" (11.92–98) while an integrating and supervisory type of knowledge—here cast as Camden's ancient art of history (11.169–75)—serves the poet's practice of historiographical poetry—"wise wordes taught in numbers for to runne" (1.402). These words will outlast the vanity of pyramids, colossi, pillars, shrines, and other architectural constructions built by "earthly Princes" (11.407–13). In the name of history and philosophy together, one cannot redact the intentionality of an architectonic poetic better than that, for Spenser's optimistic assertion of a lasting significance in wise language is accompanied by the realistic perception of the potential vanity of words as well, even of poetic words.[85]

There is no question that the architectonic concept gripped history through various images of presence. In the way of metaphor, Aristotle's inquiry into the nature of human happiness in the *Nicomachean Ethics* had lent this image of architectonic power to history while simultaneously suggesting the destructibility of thought that is like a building. Renaissance poets, including Sidney in the *Defence*, kept this sense of ambivalence before their eyes when they imagined the hazardous project of building their own lives and the characters of their civilization into a culture. These poets worked in the allegorical context of Saint Augustine's building of the chaste mind that is by definition, also his feminized view of the City of God, "our mother."[86] In the fifteenth century Christine de Pizan tried to appropriate this authoritatively male cultural building task, for herself as a writer. In effect, she constructed a city of ladies and deconstructed patristic antifeminism.[87] In the seventeenth century, when Descartes's *cogito* envisioned man as the measure of all things in a philosophical doctrine of the self, Descartes, too, used an architectural parable of destruction and buildings to say as much. The historical construction, dismantling, and rebuilding of an entire "city" was his metaphor for the mind and for thinking.[88] The Cartesian version of a simultaneously destroying and re-creating architectonic metaphor influenced the development of modern science and French literary criticism through the *Discourse on Method* and through Descartes's new geometry.

But the poets had already said as much in their vivid English images. In *Paradise Lost*, two divine icons architectonically center the architecture of the poem even though they have fallen from "nak'd majesty" (4.290) to "guilty shame" (9.1058). Michael's pause in the narrative of prophetic history is a pause "Betwixt the world destroy'd and world restor'd" (12.3), and both worlds gravitate centripetally around Adam and Eve whose inner speech, finally, compels them (as the narrator's compels us readers) to go in search of the Paradise located *within* character. So, too, the expression of the architectonic metaphor as an antithesis—a gendered destruction and reconstruction of thought—shows up again and again in subsequent texts, beyond those of the Renaissance. Freud produces his version of self-knowledge of human character when, interrogating religion and sexuality in *Civilization and Its Discontents*, he reverses Aristotle's question. Aristotle had asked the ethical question of human nature, "What makes man happy?" Freud asks the medical question, rather, why man is so unhappy.[89] Once again, as in Aristotle, Augustine, du Bellay, Spenser, and Descartes, the analogy Freud uses for the memory of the mind is the archaeology of the Eternal City, in this case Rome, in its many layers of historical ruin.

Such a pattern of architectural images and images of ruin in renaissance art was not unconscious or mystifying. The architecture did not subvert the ruin or vice versa because renaissance poets intended to pose both figures. Renaissance theories of language explain why renaissance poems were so metaphorically productive in the balancing of architecture and character, buildings and ruins, and how that productivity uses but resists resolution to critical constructs or to critical deconstruction. "Second nature" (*Def.*, p. 79) and a poetic art working "euen as nature her selfe" were exactly what Sidney and Puttenham unconditionally affirmed as the definition of metaphoric speech in English poetry.[90] The combination of genesis and analysis, composition and reading, found expression historically in an allegorical gender hierarchy because it figured the productivity or generative purpose the poets were aiming to fulfill. At the same time, the power of poetic invention did not represent a magical grasp of some transcendent moral principle; the moral principle of poesie was imaged because it was accessibly concrete. Far from illustrating a contempt for learning and knowledge, the figure of the mistress-knowledge personified their power.

There are, no doubt, different ways to read her, even on renaissance terms. Using a classical pagan allegory, for example, and the ambivalence the Renaissance saw in it, one may see in Sidney's poet-mastercraftsman the Promethean thief of a divine moral fire for the formation of all kinds of knowledge. In Christian terms one may see the male poet's Augustinian appropriation of a feminine Wisdom's power in order to identify himself with a masculine Word. Or one may see both in the terms of patristic and medieval feminist and antifeminist debates, and consider the androcentric appropriation of woman's power to make judgments or to read and write.[91] None of these interpretations is far from Sidney's somewhat Pauline text, in which the poets steal not from Zeus but from poesie herself, who gives it all away: she is the "first nurse, whose milk by little and by little enabled them to feed afterwards of tougher knowledges" (*Def.*, p. 74). Somehow, in defining the ethically re-creative power of the poet, English theorists assigned his self-knowledge the productive virtue of the mistress-knowledge's polymathy and *techne* and conscience, too. They wanted, like her, to be able to be pregnant wits. All other kinds of thinkers—the astronomer, arithmetician, musician, natural philosopher, moral philosopher, lawyer, grammarian, rhetorician, logician, historian, physician, and metaphysician—work as "actors and players . . . of what nature will have set forth. . . . Only the poet, disdaining to be tied to any such subjection, lifted up with the vigour of his own invention, doth grow in effect another nature, in making things either better than nature bringeth forth, or, quite anew" (*Def.*, p. 78). The mistress-knowledge Sidney imagined appeared in her creative powers as Wisdom, the true mediatrix between the earthly and heavenly cities, the true agent of the only Ladder who is Christ the Word.[92] These were high compliments indeed for Elizabeth—if she could deserve them—and high powers for the poet who, articulating them, might share in their exercise without exactly overreaching. For the mistress-knowledge made *her* men, "when others were running at base, to runne ouer learned writings" and to "marke" or watch themselves, and she threw reason upon desire (*Arcadia* 1:1.1, 7–8).

In reading Sidney's *Defence*, we read the book of the mistress-knowledge, which is, in turn, the book of Sidney's soul. Whether we approach Sidney's view of this sort of living book of the soul from the earlier perspective of du Bartas, who saw the world as "a Book in Folio" in which "Each

Creature is a Page; and each Effect, / A faire Character," or from the later, more subjective perspective of John Donne, we must recognize the subordi-nation of structural, architectural concerns to intellectual and spiritual ones. As Donne would put it in his *Devotions upon Emergent Occasions*, published in 1624, a constant God processes "manifoldly by the mind, and this book of concentric books the book of life, the book of nature, the book of Holy Scripture, the book of just laws, the books of individual conscience and of particular sins, and the book of the seven seals opened by the Lamb—is one in which Donne hopes to find his meaning in agreement with that of the Holy Spirit. Donne's God refers him "to that which is written," and Donne himself is a book written for "a new reading, a new trial" by all these other books; he is saved not by the book of his own conscience, but by the first book, the book of life decreeing his election, and the last book, the book of the Lamb who shed his blood. From such an elaborately metonymic con-junction of the writing subject and the text written, it is not far at all to John Milton's assertion in *Areopagitica* that books are not dead things but contain a potency of life in them as active as the soul whose progeny they are, since "a good Booke is the pretious life-blood of a master-spirit."[93] But Sidney's figure of the mistress-knowledge personified for English literature the au-thority of this subjective wisdom in his ink-wasting toy, his little book, the *Defence of Poesie*.

2

Poesie and History, or the Allegory of Self-Knowledge in Time

Wherefore I praied, and vnderstanding was giuen me: I called & the Spirit of wisdome came vnto me. . . . All good things therefore came to me together with her. . . . So I was glad in all: for wisdome was the autor thereof, & I knew not that she was the mother of these things. . . . For she is an infinite treasure vnto men, which whoso vse, become partakers of the loue of God, & are accepted for the gifts of knowledge. God hathe granted me to speake according to my minde, and to iudge worthely of the things, that are giuen me: for he is the leader vnto wisdome, and the director of the wise. For in his hand are bothe we and our wordes, and all wisdome, & the knowledge of the workes. For he hathe giuen me the true knowledge of the things that are. . . . The beginning and the end, and the middes of the times. . . . The nature of liuing things . . . and the imaginacions of men. . . . And all things bothe secret and knowen do I knowe: for wisdome the worker of all things, hathe taught me it. . . . For she is the brightnes of the euerlasting light, the vndefiled mirroure of the maiestie of God, and the image of his goodnes. And being one, she can do all things, and remaining in her self, reneueth all, and according to the ages she entreth into the holie soules, and maketh them the friends of God and Prophetes. For God loueth none, if he dwell not with wisdome.
—Wisdome of Solomon 7:7–28, Geneva

The Presencing of Sophia

The mistress-knowledge confronts readers with an early modern appropriation of Sophia, the personified wisdom of Solomon, in the Christian temple-building aesthetics of sixteenth-century English Protestant culture. The historical and contextual resources of the image are complex, but Sidney's biblicized personification already represents a declared simplicity beyond the multiplicities of classical philosophical architectonics and scholastic notions of conscience. Specifically, this personification asks readers to discover their subjective experience of thought as they read Sidney's statement of his. In the unfolding of "truth" within time and history, Sidneian self-knowledge is analogous to writing and reading from moment to moment. That Sidney works out an interlinking of poesie, history, and self-knowledge in the particularly gendered form of Sophia while giving her multiple references in the story he constructs means that the experience of subjectivity is largely a judgment of conscience in which one sorts through selves more or less true to the matter at hand as one hears Sidney's voices doing the same thing. The writer of the *Defence* is not a central self or centered authority but a *centering* self whose poesie is the medium of self-knowing in time, and so must the reader engage in a similar inner discourse in response.

From our late twentieth-century vantage, therefore, the figure of a feminized poesie confronts us, again, with the very nature of allegory, of image-making, and of the interpretation of allegorical images. The highly kinetic allegorizing of self-knowledge in the *Defence* is not what Rosemond Tuve once called "bad allegory"—that is, "a set of concretions to mean nothing more or less than some set of concepts we would write out, and to which they are 'equal' "—but something much closer to the old Aristotelian definition of metaphysics as thought thinking itself.[1] Ἀρχιτεκτονική is Sidney's "both-and" figure for thought thinking the self and the self thinking the other, which is implied in the etymology of the word *allegory* whose roots are *allos* and *agora*. As such, to apply Maureen Quilligan's description of allegory as a genre to Sidney's figure, the mistress-knowledge is inherent in the words Sidney has written on the pages of his *Defence*, not as disjuncture or as a series of names, but as multiple signification, and she also hovers above the text and through its disjunctures, hierarchies, and equivocations in the name of a biblically archetypal other, Sophia.[2] Sidney claims from the mistress-knowledge as a constructed other what Solomon claims from Sophia—that she taught him the beginning, the end, and the course of history, the nature of living things, and the imaginations of men (Wisdome of Solomon 7:18–20, Geneva). He makes the claim not without mocking the presumption of his own desire, like Solomon's, "to marye her" who is loved of the Lord, "for she is the scholemastres of the knowledge of God" (Wisdome of Solomon 8:2–4, Geneva). By making the mistress-knowledge not only a persona but also his own sermocination, however, Sidney draws Sophia down into the marketplace of everyday life, composing her into the narrative of his inherent and dynamically developing self-knowledge and, in the way of allegory, ours. The question of Sidney's imagination of the copular relation between the poet and poesie thus becomes the reader's question of the marriage of words and meanings in everyday life and their relation, similarly, to the love of God, "For God loueth none, if he dwell not with wisdome" (Wisdome of Solomon 7:28, Geneva).

This is potentially quite a profound topic to consider since, at its deepest, the Sidneian allegory of self-knowledge touches, in effect, the reality of salvation. But in this chapter I shall take more ordinary paths of consideration in a form of discursive analysis. To the extent that gender appropriation and cross-gendering, political power, and religious belief are at the heart of the making of Sidney's subjectivity and ours in the writing and reading of the literary mirrors of poesie, we must undo the strands of Sidney's sources of this image of Sophia to understand the activity of his allegorizing of the mistress-knowledge within the bounds of contemporary critical discourse. In this way we have a better critical chance of perceiving a very good allegory at work in Sidney's *Defence*; for we will have *used* all of the images presented, according to Tuve's "safeguarding" principles, and not abused them by suppressing some images in the interest of others, and we will have allowed "the principal drift" of meaning—the dominant figure of the mistress-knowledge—to govern other meanings "attributable to the incidents borne upon the stream" (*Allegorical Imagery*, pp. 234–35). The first strand to be taken up is the relation among Sidney's feminine personification, feminism, and modern views of renaissance allegory and its theological interests in the context of Elizabethan politics. A second strand is Sidney's attachment of his feminine allegory to a knowledge of a man's self, and a third is his engineering of experience in literary architectonics. All three lead to a discussion of historicism.

Some of the strongest statements of feminist critical theory come from imaginations formed by and responding to rigidly patriarchal institutions of the synagogue, the Church, and the academy and their cultural oppression of women. The literary critical dismantling of this oppression occurs in the reconstruction of woman's "heresy" and, better yet, the construction of woman's orthodoxy, which history has tended to deny.[3] In particular, the recovery and liberation of feminine images of divine power must accompany the reading of the literature of the Middle Ages and the Renaissance because that literature demands acknowledgment of religious mystery, however distorted the expression of mystery may be in the actual gender hierarchies of its historical forms.[4] Avoiding the theological perspectives of this literature in the propositions of supposedly more "ideology-free" theories simply perpetrates a dialectic with a masculinized culture and continues to marginalize or deny some forms of the feminine.[5] Properly communicated, theological knowledge—or the inquiry into the nature of the divine—should provide the tools for distinguishing presence from illusion, for discerning the difference between an icon and an idol, including the idols of privileged gender. The literature of the English Renaissance borders on an obsession with such a distinction as renaissance writers recapitulate the patristic humanism that envisioned the divine *in* the human as a matter of "image" and "likeness." In its joint iconological and iconoclastic practices, this literature actually produced heterogeneous images of the divine.[6] Woman, the androgyne, the hermaphrodite, a gendered *natura*, and a feminized text-body appeared from Skelton's time to Milton's despite efforts to eradicate all alternatives to the anthropocentric primacy of "man."

As Murray Krieger has observed in his study of metaphor, *Poetic Presence and Illusion*, the renaissance poet and theorist asserted "presence" and upon mankind ~~to common the fullness presence~~ in face of the unholy human alternative, which was the divinity's intolerably complete transcendence of language, leaving it full only of deferral and deference and therefore empty.[7] Krieger cites the example of Sidney's praise of prosopopoeia in David's psalms as an illustration of words invoking "invisible presence." He remarks, again astutely, "This equivocal importation of God into the poem raises serious questions about the entire nature of Renaissance symbolism, what it permitted and forbade" (p. 8). Yet Krieger strangely misses Sidney's metaphors; he presses forward the rhetorical definition of metaphor as a verbal structure of duplicity by neglecting the force of allegory as a symbolic mode (pp. 3–27 passim). The problem of definition is not easy to negotiate, especially if one is aware of the historical research of Michael Murrin in *The Veil of Allegory*, in which he describes aspects of a sixteenth-century shift from the divinely symbolic to the humanly rhetorical mode. That is, both modes operate in the imagination of someone like Sidney, and the scholar's task is deciding where and to what degree. Murrin makes some interesting distinctions on precisely this kind of doubling of symbolic allegory and rhetorical allegory.[8]

The earlier study of Angus Fletcher, *Allegory*, contributed greatly to the phenomenological definition of a metonymic allegorical presence articulated in personification, but did so without reference to biblical paradigms, historical documentation, or Sidney. The later study of John M. Steadman, *The Lamb and the Elephant*, expresses the scholar's grief at a necessary conflict: we need large-scale generalizations about renaissance aesthetics at the same time "the complexity of the subject constantly reminds one of one's limitations" and of the falsity in even suggesting a renaissance "uniformity of approach that did not and could not exist in fact."[9]

Of all of these modern assessments of renaissance allegory, probably Fletcher's phenomenological approach is the most useful in recovering a sense of the mistress-knowledge as Sidney conceived and expressed it. Fletcher states, "The various analogies that can be drawn between religious, literary and psychoanalytically observed phenomena all point to the oldest idea about allegory, that it is a human reconstitution of divinely inspired messages, a revealed transcendental language which tries to preserve the remoteness of a properly veiled godhead" (*Allegory*, p. 21). Thus the mistress-knowledge is an image testifying, in Fletcher's general terms, not to a "dull" systems-making that rigidifies thought but to a "symbolic power struggle" that elicits self-criticism in the audience (p. 23). As a Sidneian poetic principle, consequently, the mistress-knowledge exemplifies Fletcher's idea of a "teleologically controlled trope or figure," and it presides over the production of a language that consistently registers the poet's and the reader's experience of "doubt, double meaning, and ironic detachment" (p. 84). Sidney's invention of the phrase "the mistress-knowledge" to signify "the knowledge of a man's self" gives the concept of architectonic knowledge the status of an archetypal or a pure allegory—what Fletcher explains as the kind of metonymy that surfaces in a prosopopoeia, a personification depending on the sustained interplay of tenor and vehicle in a power struggle in a given metaphor (pp. 84–85). One may easily see and identify that with which the personification struggles. In her connection to the cosmos, the figure of the mistress-knowledge exposes various kinds of hierarchy, including those of epistemology, gender, social order, and language.

She is a fable of the human effort to contain and order knowledge; the power struggle figured in this dynamic personification of mistress and man *is* on one level the epistemological impulse to systematize and rigidify the structure of thought. The genders split and the genders join because Sidney's allegory of poesie is less a critical "idea" to be spun out in linear argumentation on one side, the masculine side of self-knowledge and master-building, than it is a poetic image of inherent tensions in the ways of knowing and being. Sidney's literary critical "theory," articulated in a figure that is both symbolically allegorical and persuasively oratorical, distinctly conveys its burden of knowledge as a matter of true equivocation on sixteenth-century grounds, not twentieth. The text is united on those philosophical and political grounds because philosophy in the sixteenth century often relied on the invention of images to carry the force of argumentation. Tracing the allegory contributes, in other words, to a necessary redefinition of renaissance epistemology.

It is critically curious that even Fletcher, whose study of allegory as a symbolic mode is thoroughly informed by renaissance lore and to whose terminology this book is obviously indebted, omits consideration of Sidney's *Defence* entirely and does not observe the power with which Sidney has invested prosopopoeia. Sidney underscores the figure as the *proof* of the poetry of Holy Scripture and the authority in the style of the psalms of David:

For what else is the awaking his musical instruments, the often and free changing of persons, his notable *prosopopoeias,* when he maketh you, as it were, see God coming in His majesty . . . but a heavenly poesy, wherein almost he showeth himself a passionate lover of that unspeakable and everlasting beauty to be seen by the eyes of the mind, only cleared by faith? (*Def.,* p. 77)

Perhaps Fletcher's omission illustrates not only a scholar's effort to limit the scope of his book, with which we all must sympathize, but also an historical problem with the critical enterprise that he acknowledges. Fletcher says that "no comprehensive historical treatment" of the protean device that is allegory exists; his book has outlined "a theoretical, mainly non-historical analysis of literary elements" in order to get at "the essence of the mode" (p. 1).

Later Fletcher clarifies further. To reach the traditional conclusion that allegory is "a human reconstitution of divinely inspired messages," he has taken the nontraditional route, among others, of the "psychoanalytic view" and chosen a "non-metaphysical line of argument" as the best course to follow. "I have stayed away from the metaphysics of the subject. I have also stayed away from the history and theory of biblical exegesis," Fletcher says, because it aims at the defense of the Bible as the revealed Word of God. Even considered as "a non-metaphysical semantic device . . . allegory likewise appears to express conflict between rival authorities" (pp. 21–22). In a post-Kantian attitude, then, Fletcher produces a theoretical account of allegory while reducing potential critical conflicts that would arise if metaphysics, biblical revelation, and religion were brought into the "pure reason" of philosophical reflection. The problem is that Sidney's idea of prosopopoeia, with its scripturally validated poetic value, engages historical rivalries in religion while articulating some biblical exegesis in practice as his defence of the divinity of poesie itself. The particular personification that Sidney invents in the mistress-knowledge draws in traditional metaphysics at the historical moment of its application and revision in the Reformation, and Sidney does not flinch from the task of expressing his poetics to the point of theological faith.[10] The longer history of the word *architectonic*, which appeared so frequently in texts of the sixteenth and seventeenth centuries, is a context for his expression.

From antiquity through the Renaissance to the present, the word *architectonic* has testified to the genius of metaphor to create other metaphors. The history of the word is a history of amplification, accretion, alteration, allegorization, deletion, and denial of signification. The idea of architectonic knowledge emerged primarily in classical moral philosophy; it emphasized the knowledge of character by subordinating metaphysics to ethics and by constructing intelligent arguments in pleasing words to persuade the audience to the good.[11] Historically the architectonic knowledge of knowing and doing the good established by Plato and Aristotle in their definitions of statesmanship was recapitulated, with some shift in nuance, in the philosophical eloquence through which Cicero defined wisdom in relation to justice.[12] Meanwhile, in the Hellenized Book of Proverbs in the Hebrew Bible, such wisdom was already a female allegorical figure, a master-craftswoman who played before God in creation (8:22). Saint Augustine radically transformed the classical idea into the visionary practice of "hearing and doing" the Word of God through salvation history. He described history as a journey through time not to the classical republic but to the City of God, which was feminine, the "mother" of men. Boethius, too, envisioned the integration of knowledge and virtue in his figure of Lady Philosophy, who consoled him in the difficulties of his statesmanship.[13]

Thus men seem first to have intuited the idea of a transcendent wisdom—the mysterious wisdom of myth, the Hebraic wisdom of revelation, the Greek wisdom of absolute adherence to the good, the Stoic and Roman knowledge of things divine and human, or the Wisdom who is Christ of the Fathers of the Church—and then to have developed the notion of a supervisory, intermediate knowledge that is best under wisdom, or most useful in attaining it, or most like it, but somehow above other ways of knowing and yet immanent. At different times in the West through the Renaissance, prophecy, dialectic, mathematics, statesmanship, ethics and politics, astronomy, theology, philosophical eloquence, painting, poetry, or some other knowledge propaedeutic to wisdom reigned as a "master" or a "mistress" of those who know.[14] The relation of a designated architectonic knowledge to a transcendent wisdom is a fascinating problem in intellectual history because changing definitions of the two terms reveal the values of a given culture.[15] As the building metaphor in Western thought, the architectural analogy for architectonic knowledge contributed to constructions as diverse as the imagination of the state, the schematization of knowledge, the disposition of an oration, the design of a cathedral, the shape of a scholastic argument, the conversion of classical philosophy to Protestant norms for building a godly kingdom, and the moral re-creation of human beings through literary persuasion. Inevitably, the building analogy was linked to the ruling power of men to "make" things happen. As a feminine persona, however, the allegorical figure simultaneously oversaw many of those constructions as the very myth—or symbolic narrative—of their inspiration and production. The word *architectonic*, once recovered in the Renaissance, thus promoted multiple meanings and metaphoric tensions in the sixteenth-century imagination. The following chapters transcribe and categorize as many as possible with a view toward further defining both the political culture out of which *The Defence of Poesie* emerged with Sidney's architectonic concept of the poetic word and the literary culture that emerged from Sidney's influence.

Besides presenting the figure of the mistress-knowledge, Sidney coupled her with a consort, the poet-statesman, as we have seen. Together, she and the poet figured the royal making of men in their time, their history. In the *Defence* the figure of Cyrus, the destined general and good reader whose education was made historically famous by Xenophon and whose action prepared the way for the liberation of the Jews and the rebuilding of the Temple in Jerusalem according to Isaiah, is the measure of the successful operations of the mistress-knowledge and her self-knowing man. "Cyrus" is the moral product in England of the "delivering forth" of their art, and his *virtú* was praised by Machiavelli before Sidney.

Which delivering forth also is not wholly imaginative, as we are wont to say by them that build castles in the air; but so far substantially it worketh, not only to make a Cyrus, which had been but a particular excellency as nature might have done, but to bestow a Cyrus upon the world to make many Cyruses, if they will learn aright why and how that maker made him. (*Def.*, p. 79)

Indeed, Sidney saw history less as a methodology or a chronology or an objectified content of the past than as a fictive activity by means of which knowledge was made present and powerful. That is, history is a form of *poesis*, a "making." His own "making" in the *Defence* operates as a triangulation of these three prosopopoeias—the mistress-knowledge, the poet-statesman, and the "reading and doing" Cyrus—in history.

When we confront the historical ambivalence of Sidney's characterization of Cyrus, however, in relation to the gendered epistemology and politics of the mistress-knowledge, the androgynous allegory of poesie in the *Defence* not only references the power of Queen Elizabeth and the culture formed around her but also illuminates the putative integrity of Sidney's text. In Xenophon's *Cyropaedia* the development of the hero is partly fictive; Xenophon constructs the image of the character building of a powerful man in history. In Machiavelli's *The Prince*, composed around 1513, Cyrus appears as the very type of the hero who acquired power through his own arms and ability and not by means of fortune, and Machiavelli both compares him to Moses in the liberation of the Jews from Egypt and contrasts him, since Moses was carrying out God's orders (*The Prince*, chap. 6). Sidney addresses both views; he uses his Augustinian view of a providential history to appropriate both and to structure his ambivalent image. Thus Sidney's Cyrus is a fiction and a generative model for the making of other heroic images in poetic fiction; but at the same time Cyrus is the model of divine agency in human history, for he is the hero of the second liberation of the Jews recorded in the First Book of Esdras, which appears among the apocryphal texts in the Geneva Bible: "The Lord raised vp the spirit of Cyrus King of the Persians . . . Saying . . . The Lord of Israel, euen the moste high Lord, hathe made me King ouer the whole worlde, And he hathe commanded me to buylde him an House in Jerusalem" (1 Esdras 2:2–4). Sidney's ambivalent identification with this figure of historical action and divine Providence enables him to balance his power with that of the Queen.

Certainly, therefore, the image of the mistress-knowledge in Sidney's treatise binds epistemology to politics in the historically immediate "presencing" of Elizabeth, Queen of England, to herself and her subjects. Since Sidney reconstructs his life and times as a subject under an ironically corrective and allegorical veil *and* through the agency of "the knowledge of a man's self," however, it would be a critical mistake to read his allegory merely on the level of historical reference as if it were simply an expression of his courtly participation in the political cult of Elizabeth. The ethical dimension, which directly communicates a theological dimension in English Protestantism, also requires interpretation. In poesie the potential for the politically immediate allegory of the *Defence*, which modern criticism tends to emphasize, coexists with Sidney's merger of history, philosophy, religion, pictorial arts, and literature on the epistemological plane, and all of these are mediated through conscience, too.[16]

On the epistemological plane the Protestant Sidney recognizes the Queen as God's vicegerent in the same way that William Perkins, a decade later, would see conscience as the divine vicegerent and would counsel against regicide.[17] The apparent power struggle between types of allegory in Sidney's speech is as much a struggle of conscience within him as it is his special pleading for political power. But Sidney's was a learned Calvinism skeptical of all human powers, including those of the Queen, unless they could be shown to be graced. Even in face of her sovereignty, then, he could argue the demonstration of his conscience in the effects of a higher power within him—higher than Elizabeth's political power—but available to her in conscience as to any reader or writer in the poet's success at teaching, delighting, and moving him or her to well-doing.

At the beginning of the *Arcadia*, Sidney reenacted the demonstration of the effects of such an operative figure of conscience. Associating Urania with sovereign knowledge and with biblical Apocrypha, he gave his mistress-knowledge a mythological name and a narrative purpose in his fiction. Urania is quasi-scriptural and, as such, could be truly particular and historical in application as well. Thus Spenser will call Sidney's sister Mary, the Countess of Pembroke, by the name of Urania in his poem *Colin Clouts Come Home Againe* when he is discussing particularly Elizabeth's court and her ladies-in-waiting.[18] Yet Solomon associated this figure of conscientious wisdom with light itself: "I loued her . . . & purposed to take her for my light: for her light can not be quenched" (Wisdome of Solomon 7:10, Geneva).[19] Calvinists placed Solomon's Book of Wisdom among the Apocrypha, and it is suitable that Sidney draws on such material to situate the *intermediacy* of poesie between the divine and the human. Apocryphal books followed the Prophets of the Old Testament not as books to be "expounded publikely in the Church" or "to prove any point of Christian religion . . . but as bokes proceding from godlie men." They were to be well received and to be read "for the aduancement and furtherance of the knowledge of the historie, & for the instruction of godlie manners, which bokes declare that at all times God had an especial care of his Church and left them not vtterly destitute of teachers and meanes to confirme them in the hope of the promised Messiah" (Geneva Bible, p. 386ʳ). Indeed, from this headnote to the Apocrypha in the Geneva Bible of 1560, it is a short step to the mistress-knowledge poesie of Sir Philip Sidney, and not a much longer one to the Muse of Milton, Puritan theodidact of the seventeenth century.[20] It has long been recognized, although often in provisional fashion, that Sidney uses Herodotus, Xenophon, Aristotle, Cicero, Horace, Ovid, Plutarch, Augustine, Boethius, Erasmus, and others to reconstruct Plato the adversary of poetry into its patron. The question of the definition of allegory in the *Defence*, which is the corollary of the suppression of the allegorical figure of the mistress-knowledge, has inhibited a synthetic recognition of the manner in which Sidney accomplishes that reconstruction. In parodying Plato and all other critics of poesie—the "μισόμουσοι" or "mis-musers," a phrase that Sidney translates as "poet-haters" as if poets and Muses were the same thing in order to condemn those who treat the good use of poetry like abuse—Sidney transfers a universal knowledge to the poet's domain. This ousts the philosopher from Sidney's vision both of Xenophon's republic that "might best be" and of Plato's republic that "should be," to borrow the analysis of Spenser in the *Letter* to Raleigh. In reclaiming the Muses for the patronage of poetry, Sidney takes them back from history and uses an historian's kind of thinking to curtail philosophy.[21] Sidney replaces the rhapsodic inspiration of the poet—which Socrates had criticized in the *Ion* as a daemonic seizure from without rather than a dialectical thinking from within the mind—with a "high flying liberty of conceit" and "some divine force" (*Def.*, p. 77). The "liberty" and "force" are Christian, and Sidney identifies them historically insofar as he testifies that "the light of Christ" has come and makes a difference in the practice of poesie. Poesie, or the mistress-knowledge, bears the power of a Protestant conscience that affirms and denies words and deeds from *within* a man's character even though poetry itself is primarily a mimetic discourse.

Like Sophia, the mistress-knowledge can be a consolation as well as a penetrating critique, and one of the uses of Sidney's *poesie* is the work of assurance in the very same breath in which his *poetry* seems to produce only the verbal proportions of *eikastic* and *phantastic* images. Drawing on the philosophical authority of Aristotle, whose architectonic rhetoric, moral philosophy, and metaphysics Sidney assimilates, the *Defence* justifies the master of those who know through Sidney's own historical mimesis of Solomon, whom he subordinates, in turn, to the new temple-builder, the Christ who presides over all. In this way, Sidney's transfer of universal knowledge to poetry and his appropriation of the wisdom of poesie will not be undone by paganism, libidinousness, madness, or ordinary Elizabethan ambition. The transfer is analogical and communicates power: Sidney's poet appropriates the feminized powers of the mistress-knowledge as the "new" myth of inspiration, the superior gnosis that out-Platos Plato.

The Knowledge of a Man's Self

When we let Sidney's metaphors speak for themselves, we can see that a balance of power expressed in the allegorical figure of the mistress-knowledge parallels Sidney's description of the didactic, aesthetic, and moral functions of poesie. Borrowed from Aristotle and Cicero, the Sidneian formula of teaching, delighting, and moving is an *oratorical simultaneity* as Sidney conceives poesie, and it evokes personification. The feminine figure of the intellectual architecture and moral building up of the self-knowing man conveys a certain sexualized balance of power. Thus Sidney portrays a poesie suspended between two genders, a poesie of gender intermediacy, and the second strand of our consideration must be Sidney's attachment of this feminine allegory to the knowledge of a man's self. The metaphoric coupling of the mistress-knowledge and her self-knowing man operates integrally in the *Defence* through "Cyrus" to represent the cultural values of a masculine, aristocratic construction of language, learning, and life. Yet in the figurative presentation of *two* genders, the Sidneian allegory for architectonic knowledge advocates a poesie most literally "androgynous."[22]

One must speak to the fact historically, therefore, that the prosopopoeia of the mistress-knowledge calls attention to the numinosity of the feminine figure and to the gender hierarchy that has allowed "masculine" master-building to flourish for centuries in cultural assessments of architectonic knowledge—all the way into Kant's "Architectonic" and Hegel's reaction and modern critical theories—and has neglected the "feminine" value of the mistress-knowledge. The vestiges of her cultural appearance and disappearance as the very spirit of integration of "the man's self" in Sidney's embodied balancing of poetic powers identify her, as C. S. Lewis might have said, as one of the "discarded" images of history. Indeed, Lewis did say so indirectly when he discussed the mysterious oneness of the seven liberal arts in the medieval and renaissance imagination.[23] A question addressed in chapter 5 of this book is the degree to which the historical status of the mistress-knowledge and her parallels in other gendered metaphors of epistemology in other renaissance texts argues a male cultural bias leading to an "absent presence" in four centuries of English literary criticism—not the bias of the Petrarchists, who formed the paradox in literature and cultivated its rhetorical development, but that of the New Critics and the deconstructionists.

Despite the denial of her image, however, the parallel life in time of the mistress-knowledge has not been completely suppressed. Her voice echoes in numerous textual elaborations of man's image of himself. So literary history is able to make the effort to recover the textual life of a feminine personification for knowledge that has coexisted with a masculinized and architectural power of language. The figure enjoyed many points of origin and reception in antiquity and the Middle Ages. It flourished briefly in tension with its architectural counterpart through the renaissance amplification of the Vitruvian analogy of bodies, buildings, and poems. For a time during the sixteenth and seventeenth centuries, the feminized image of a power of voiced thought not only balanced the architectural structures of thought that fixed the architectonic concept in the Western mind with so much solidity, but actually countered the metaphysics of the Aristotelian architecture of knowledge with the moral significance of the Platonic criticism of merely materialistic constructions of reality—whether the "making" was composed of stones, ideas, words, or actions in time, that is, history. The mistress-knowledge underwent negation in the second half of the seventeenth century and, later, suppression in the philosophy of the late eighteenth century and of the nineteenth and twentieth, although for a time the romantic poets revived her under other names. We need to return to original sources to see why. Almost all early studies of the *Defence* locate its importance in its own metaphoric integration of renaissance aesthetic theories but without satisfactorily explaining *why* and *how*. The critical trend in recent years has been, rather, the exploration of *why not*, of the divisive elements that leave Sidney's speech in the state of contesting and unresolved convictions and rhetorical strategies.

Sidney was not exactly the philosophical begetter of English renaissance poetics in his appropriation of the power of this feminine personification, but he was the influential genius of a gendered and generative poetic speech, including that of the *Defence* itself, in which the "feminine" and "masculine" tensions of the architectonic metaphor openly worked. What Sidney named in his analogy of the arts and sciences in the *Defence* was a developing aesthetic in the Renaissance at large and an operative critical assumption for many poets from Skelton to Milton. In the 1590s Spenser and Shakespeare certainly responded creatively to various aspects of Sidney's poetic theory. Davies would restate it at the turn of the century, and Donne, Jonson, Herbert, Vaughan, and Milton would modify and reformulate in their poetic and critical practice a concept of universal learning that Sidney had so well "Englished." In the usual Hellenistic and medieval division of the subject into *poesis, poema,* and *poeta,* the renaissance poetic art acted the part of the "queen" of the arts and sciences, ruling them all; the poem was the building or the body of their analogical unity, the house of intellect; and the poet who devised verbal fictions saw himself as an inventive statesman-architect who knew how to use both mistress and poem to produce civilized characters in the audience.[24] But Sidney took all of that into a new philosophical dimension with his synthesizing wit. Our wits tend to respect analytical proofs more, and that is why the tools of modern critical methods are so often better at opening up the possibilities of textual significance than at finding in the closure of metaphor a still lively contemplation of some truth glimpsed but not contained. Only now is modern feminist criticism reentering and reclaiming some of those cultural spaces.

Sir Philip Sidney's immediate historical context repeatedly qualifies the significance of the mistress-knowledge. One reads his literate culture, therefore, with a sense of really drawn but flexible boundaries of interpretation because, as the saying goes, the fish is in the water and the water is in the fish. We cannot keep pursuing an extreme literary-critical emphasis on the architecture of Sidney's speech, in other words; nor can we react against the presence of forms we have not yet understood by examining semantic structures only to undo the text, as if it were so much scaffolding. Metaphor especially is the domain of both-and thinking, and the allegory of self and universal knowledge reinforces the need to read images, not merely ideas.

Two of Sidney's countrymen will illustrate. At the turn of the sixteenth century, when John Skelton's poetic persona, Parott, defended himself, he argued the case for metaphor by borrowing the psalmist's praise of divine rampart and shield. In Parott's opinion, metaphor by definition was one of the poetic engines of war; it simultaneously revealed and concealed its meaning. "No matter pretendyd, nor nothyng enterprysed, / But that *metaphora, alegoria* withall" shall be the poet's "protectyon, his pavys and his wall."[25] The passage indicates Skelton's technical or architectural poetic theory. The theory is complex because he sees the nothingness of substance implied in the fictive expression at the same time he poses for poetry the work of an ironic balancing of fictive expression with hidden truth. So the passage exposes Skelton behind the voice of Parott on exactly the opposite point; that is, Skelton rejoices in saying something and getting away with it. The thrust of the passage, then, is the acute perception of the political need to phrase one's truth *in* duplicity, in the art of dissembling in words. For the renaissance poet, disguise goes hand in hand with the metaphysical force of the truth that metaphor presents through a verbal fiction. A few decades after Skelton penned his theory poetically, Sir Thomas Elyot would urge on Englishmen the wisdom needed for eloquence and politics. His program showed the influence of Cicero, but his method in *The Boke Nam'd the Governour* was distinctly Tudor as Elyot used a flow of metaphors to present oratory as the "heap of all manner of learning," the "world of science," and the "circle of doctrine" that the Greeks called *encyclopedia*. Without blinking, Elyot extended the scope of this kind of oratory to poetry, "the first philosophy that was ever known."[26]

As we approach Sidney's *Defence of Poesie* historically and contextually, then, it is hardly surprising that Sidney juxtaposes the metaphor-making of an architectural or a master-building poetic theory to the encyclopedic knowledge needed in statesmen whose words would help to realize national ethical and political goals. But Sidney's juxtaposition does more; it creates a league between technique and teleology. With a series of appositives that amplify even Elyot's vision of the primacy of understanding in *The Boke Nam'd the Governour*, Sidney explains learning as a "purifying of wit," an "enriching of memory, enabling of judgment, and enlarging of conceit" that may have different immediate ends but has only one final end: to lead and draw us to as high a perfection as our degenerate souls, made worse by their clayey lodgings, can be capable of" (*Def.*, p. 82). The entire epistemological structure of poetic learning, in other words, aims at the reformation of our architecturally embodied souls.[27]

The expression of such a league of means and ends was not entirely new. Boethius had used the architectural analogy to contrast the prison of history to the philosophical tradition of the liberally educated or free mind in the Christian vision of the *Philosophiae Consolationis*. Sidney anatomizes the good use of learning as a renaissance Protestant who wants to "English" the idea of the intellectual universality of poetry: all knowledges have the purpose "to know, and by knowledge to lift up the mind from the dungeon of the body to the enjoying of his own divine essence" (*Def.*, p. 82). But in modern criticism such an architectural analogy has produced a crisis of interpretation, and the crisis has to do with conflict over deconstruction, which is, in turn, a conflict over belief and over the logically apprehended truth that Ramistic revisions of the structure of knowledge had already addressed in the sixteenth century.[28]

Properly read in its historical context, Sidney's metaphor for the purpose of learning in the human mind and body is complex. Its psychological longing and ethical skepticism coexist with a Protestant conviction about knowledge and a vision of religious faith. The "dungeon" of the body living in historical time and space and the "divine essence" of the mind enjoying the pleasure of its eternal truth go together in the here and now. Deconstructive analysis does not allow such coexistence but throws the equilibrium of Sidney's balance of flesh and spirit, however contradictory and tense in itself, away from his assertion of a bond between human and divine things and toward the experience of contradiction. Thus a deconstructive interpretation of this particular passage in the *Defence* emphasizes imprisonment and the desire to escape. The deconstructive reading isolates Sidney's metaphor and its obvious theological significance from the metaphysical foundations of Sidney's renaissance, Protestant, and English culture in which the discovery of the truth of the spirit through the letter was the biblical model of interpretation.[29]

A deconstructive reader may affirm the "dungeon" experience of Sidney's written language as a confinement of thought, but only by denying the other side of the metaphor, the assertion of a knowledge that lifts up the mind to "the enjoying of his own divine essence." For deconstructionists look for "difference" or "traces of traces" of an absent presence. "The

absence of the transcendental signified," says Derrida, "extends the domain
and the play of signification infinitely." In *Of Grammatology* he takes the
point further: "One could call *play* the absence of the transcendental signified as limitlessness of play, that is to say, as the destruction of ontotheology and the metaphysics of presence." But if essences, divinity, and
sure knowledge of first principles are seen merely as the "play" of a "dream"
of "full presence," one can interpret Sidney's language only according to a
psychoanalytic idea of wishes and desires. Linguistically, no matter how
much we trace Derrida's grammatology back to Saussure's departure from
grammar and philology to develop linguistics systematically as a science,
this modern projection into a renaissance text effectively abolishes the
signifying power of metaphor, reducing it to the status of "ornament." In
terms of renaissance rhetoric, deconstruction recapitulates the old debate
between image and idea in renaissance theory and splits the two.[30] When
we use the methods of deconstruction in the interpretation of the metaphors
of renaissance poets, therefore, we must take care not to import with us a
hall of critical mirrors obfuscating so metaphoric a treatise as Sidney's
Defence and the credit it gives to moral essences.[31]

A similar architectural analogy between divine essences of the mind
imprisoned in the body or in history receives complex treatment in Sidney's
handling of the Daedalus myth, Virgil's *Aeneid*, and Saint Augustine's
Confessions. Here, too, teleology finds yet another technical development
later in the *Defence*. Sidney uses the myth of Daedalus to express again a
sense of uplifting purpose. When Sidney says that he wants English "high-
flying wits" to have a Daedalus to guide them in their use of the three wings
of art, imitation, and exercise, he further rewrites the myth of Daedalean
craft and the relationship between technological skill and politics. Virgil had
pictured the architect of the Cretan labyrinth giving thanks for his winged
escape from the tyrant Minos and building a temple to Apollo on Cumae's
heights not far from the spot where Aeneas would enter the underworld
(*Aeneid* 6.1–40). Saint Augustine had rewritten the Virgilian descent into the
underworld in the *Confessions*. Augustine constructed it as a descent within
the memory in which one might find the presence of God, and when
Augustine's own depths exceed his intellectual capacity to know them, he
progresses by means of desire, which is a lover's kind of knowledge in his
view, a kind already infused with the presence it seeks (1.13; 10.8). Sidney's
allusions to these ancient sources are embedded in his emphasis on a
favorite renaissance theme, the overreaching of Icarus, who died in abusing
the invention by means of which he took flight. Thus Sidney's statement is a
metaphoric admonishment to English writers about the use of their poetic
craft in a political context informed by the propositions of their first "philosophy," that is, religion.[32]

We may dispute the meaning of Virgil and Ovid, Augustine and Sidney.

But we cannot dispute the fact that Sidney's perception of the condition of the poet-statesman in his political world poses a certain experience of the value of knowledge and the power of religious faith in tension with the experience of human limitation, frustrating boundaries, oppression, and even death. The control of Sidney's metaphors is not empty, and Sidney's speech does not betray Derrida's "absence of a center or origin" (*Writing and Difference*, p. 280). Sidney's architectural analogies are, in short, architectonic. They redefine poetic imitation and inspiration by subordinating human thought, including allegorical mythology, technical skill, and the literate knowledge of ancient classical and Christian texts, to the inventive experience of grace in the temple of the mind that sees through Apollo to the light of Christ (*Def.*, pp. 108, 111–12). Sidney's friend Fulke Greville summarized the point in his use of the Daedalean myth to praise the integration of knowledge and power in Sidney. As Greville put it, Sidney used his great learning to compose moral examples and images as "directing threds" to guide every man "through the confused *labyrinth* of his own desires, and life" (*Life of Sidney*, p. 223), and that guidance *was* his "Architectonical art" (*Life*, pp. 20–21). Neither technique nor teleology alone is at the core of Sidney's metaphoric discourse, but a superior kind of knowing that binds both together in the act of speech.

If we inquire more fully into Sidney's methodology for extending this kind of knowledge to his audience, we find it frankly, if parenthetically, stated in the *Defence* as an *ars legendi*. Sidney articulates his chain of causal links as a self-evident truth not to be bothered by "the ordinary doctrine of ignorance," which, in attacking poetry, attacks learning itself. "It is manifest," Sidney says, "that all government of action is to be gotten by knowledge, and knowledge best by gathering many knowledges, which is reading" (*Def.*, p. 105). The argument of the *Defence*, we may profitably conjecture, is an intertextual construction of classical and contemporary readings advocating a Christian art of poesie. Sidney identifies this *ars legendi* with the "gathering" of knowledges and calls its writing and reading not an "architectural" unity but an "architectonic" power of self-knowledge (*Def.*, pp. 82–83). That power is as open in signification of the self as that unity is closed and self-contained. Insofar as Sidney produces an *ars legendi*, his treatise should provide a way to judge the lasting effects of a renaissance architectonic concept on English literary standards for composition and interpretation. Perhaps the recovery of the figure of the mistress-knowledge at the center of this art of reading will help dismantle cultural stereotypes and establish the status of the poem—*verbum et res*, open-ended word and articulated thing—more androgynously in critical imaginations. It is not difficult to follow the passage of the architectonic concept from the classical philosophers through medieval thinkers to renaissance poets such as Sidney. In the midst of historical shifts of emphasis, there was a continuity reaching into the humanist's perception of a unified knowledge of science, art, natural and moral philosophy, technology, and civil prudence in *practice*, even though such unity was difficult to sustain in compact theories as new knowledge was harvested from libraries, travels, scientific research, and political experience.

The occupational hazard of literacy in the context of an allegory of universal knowledge that *is* poesie, of course, is the one Sidney represents in his implicit allegorical-mythological critique of Icarus. Stephen Greenblatt has reminded us how the Augustinian vision of a character-building rhetoric also warns against "self-fashioning" in language: " 'Try to build up yourself, and you build a ruin.' "[33] The social and political counterpart to this ethical difficulty appears everywhere in the "aspiring mind" that Anthony Esler has marked as the significant feature of the younger Elizabethan generation for whom Sir Philip Sidney was, in his courtliness, intelligence, and heroic death, the patron saint.[34] But Sidney stressed the need for Daedalean guidance through such aspirations in a down-to-earth passage of the *Defence*:

> Yet confess I always that as the fertilest ground must be manured, so must the highest-flying wit have a Daedalus to guide him. That Daedalus, they say . . . hath three wings to bear itself up into the air of due commendation: that is, art, imitation, and exercise. But these, neither artificial rules nor imitative patterns, we much cumber ourselves withal. Exercise indeed we do, but that very forebackwardly: for where we should exercise to know, we exercise as having known; and so is our brain delivered of much matter that was never begotten by knowledge. (*Def.*, pp. 112–13)

This passage is the supreme statement of the balancing act inherent in Sidney's affirmation of the balance of experience in the *Defence*.[35] It is also one of his original contributions to the sorting out of the critical mirror-images of *his* time, the arts disputes over definitions of inspiration, invention, imitation, imagination, genius, craft, skill, and so forth. The definition of invention implied in the passage is largely Stoic and can be traced back to Hermogenes through Johannes Sturm and forward to Peter Ramus through Sturm as well.[36]

This definition is compatible, as I have already suggested, with Saint Augustine's rewriting of Virgil's version of the story of Daedalus at the gateway of Aeneas's journey to the underworld in his own descent into memory through language, reason, and desire. "The ordinary way back to paradise is memory," Augustine says. Sidney's superior craftsman knew how to build prisons for monsters and to escape political oppression—to fly free and to put his talent to use in the construction of a temple of thanksgiving. The image of Daedalus is verbally expressed in the *Defence* while the related image of Icarus and artistic and political overreaching is implied critically. We may expect, therefore, that in the *Defence* Sidney would put the language crafted by art into relationship with a hierarchy of truths providing the needed guidance, and he does.

The tensions Sidney finds in the poetic art are ordered in his construction of a set of definitions of the different kinds of poets. The first Poet for Sidney is the Divine Poet who knows and speaks all things him relating. The second or philosophical kind of poet merely copies these realities, like "the meaner sort of painters" who counterfeit faces. But the third or inventive kind of poet has "no law but wit" and imitates in order "to teach and to delight" (*Def.*, pp. 80–81). The humanly inventive poet, as Sidney explains elsewhere in the *Defence*, is a maker equal to the Nature that makes things at God's verbal behest *and* like the Maker whose wit speaks things into existence. Sidney's construction of these definitions is obviously analogical; hierarchy allows correspondences between levels in principle and even invites them. To say as much, Sidney has drawn on the authority of Italian arts treatises in which other poetic theorists also claimed a master-building epistemology.[37] They defined poems by analogy to the rule of architectural production but identified the philosophical rhetoric of poetic imagination as the supreme intellectual act *because* it paralleled a divine kind of knowledge and speech. Essentially, the poet's expression of the "idea" he has found in his act of invention invites the reader to practice an *ars legendi* of discovery, too. One must make a leap of intuition from the poetic image to the vision of intellectual and moral truth—not just any truth, but the moving truth of that poet's "idea" in a given poem and the didactic truth of one's self-knowledge of character at that moment.

Beyond rhetorical structure, therefore, the Sidneian poet argues for a presence that is knowable and essential, although mysterious. This truth cannot finally be destroyed (or deconstructed) because it was never constructed. In the poet's and reader's use of the rhetorical structure that is a platform for such discovery, however, poet and reader may perform as wisely as Daedalus or as wittily and foolishly as Icarus. The charm of the "high-flying wits" of the Renaissance is that they write as wisely as Daedalus by presenting themselves in the self-knowledge of their likeness to Icarus. In other words, Sidney has taken the architectural proposition of unity in the renaissance rhetorical tradition and developed it into the architectonic metaphor of a philosophical poesie by establishing the proportion-making of poetry as an ethical and political art of spoken words, a verbal art of moral vision, not merely a written trace or a pictorial art of sight.[38]

The attachment of a feminine allegory for the self and universal knowledge precisely to the knowledge of a man's self is as much a narrative as it is an argument. The *Defence* presents, as it were, the story of the soul, sometimes the "degenerate" soul made worse by its "clayey" lodging and sometimes the high-flying mind lifted by knowledge "from the dungeon of the body to the enjoying of his own divine essence" (*Def.*, p. 82). As Aeneas encountered Dido in his descent into the underworld to receive his father's confirmation of his destiny, and as Augustine found his rational mind giving way to the power of the will in his descent within, his exploration into God in the soul, so Sidney's articulation of the knowledge of a man's self brings him to the borders of something *other*, something feminine, something quasi-divine, whose presence somehow engages the body and the soul in time. By inscribing the feminine allegory of the mistress-knowledge with the knowledge of a man's self, Sidney made *both* poesie and history Daedalean arts, that is, dynamic disciplines of invention, not static reifications of ideas or events.

This story of the soul, similarly, is not simply a representation of a known truth; the fashioning of allegorical images to typify the process of self-knowledge is, rather, a story-telling principle analogous in the early Renaissance to commonplace books that traced the development of a boy's mind and, at the end of the English Renaissance, to Adam's need to tell his story to Raphael in Milton's *Paradise Lost* (8.205ff.) as evidence of his intellectual prowess. Inevitably, such a subtext of narrative approximates a verbal portrait of the thinker or artist as a young man, and the feminine appears in representative form in the story not only as the pleasant inquiry into the zodiac but also as the painful problem of the speaker's sexuality in its projective identification with a mistress. Like portraits in renaissance tapestries telling a story to the eye that knows the allegory, Sidney's *Defence* communicates a whole if unfinished story of himself knowing himself under the aegis of the mistress-knowledge.

If we are going to look critically at Sidney's metaphor for master-building a society politically through the architectural technique of language *and* the architectonic teleology of thought thinking itself, we may have to adjust our modern critical vocabulary to the nuances of Sidney's diction. For Sidney, the knowledge of a man's self is not merely a matter of autobiography; autobiography itself is a matter of "making" history.

Here the capacity of structural analysis to produce what Jonathan Culler calls a "reversal" of interpretive or critical perspective is useful.[39] The major reversal the *Defence of Poesie* rhetorically demands from the audience of modern readers may, however, be the humble recognition that Sidney actually stated "ideas" about poetry, history, and philosophy that we, in the position of dwarfs standing on giants' shoulders, think we have "invented." Politics for Sidney is an active discipline of moral philosophy, a *practical* art, for example, while history starts as something else—exemplum or chronology—and becomes practical when it is honest about its own fictional construction of supposedly existent realities.[40] As something constructed, historical narrative is "made" as a poetic fiction is made. In the *Defence*,

Sidney directly asserts the fictive nature of writing history and moralizes the assertion: the historian's affirmation of many things "in the cloudy knowledge of mankind" makes him unable to escape "many lies" (*Def.*, p. 102).[41] Thus a question that the advocate of structuralist poetics might ask of Sidney's text, here applied specifically to the claims of New Historical promises, actually produces the critical recognition of Sidney the writer engaged in a rhetorical reversal, a rebuttal of the historian's claim to truth. Again, analogy comes into play, for Sidney makes the rebuttal in order to argue the moral superiority of poetry, which does not claim truth statements and therefore does not lie. So, too, history at its best is a form of *poesis*, which is practical.

The further probing of Sidney's text in this one respect by means of still other modern critical approaches brings to light other "mirrors" in our aesthetic definition of terms. The Marxist critic of the *Defence*, for instance, confronts history itself in the evaluation of Sidney's politics and polemicism. Here the relation between Sidney's criticism of history and the defence of a master-building poetics clearly establishes our debate in renaissance context. What is the meaning of literature in making and changing society? One finds out that Sidney appropriates *historia* as the poet's domain. Like other renaissance theorists, Sidney also saw the building of poetic fictions as a prudential integration of the arts and sciences, an encyclopedia of knowledge. With his combination of universal learning and the specialty of imagination, the poet did not build an essentialist history out of the data of the past, like the record of chronology claimed by historiography, but composed stories through verisimilitude to that data for the sake of reconstructing the present and the future in an act of prophetic moral vision. It is the inventive poet who "may justly be termed *vates*" (*Def.*, p. 81), Sidney remarks.[42] The Latin reference reminds us once again how much the Virgilian theme, which poses the artist's reconstruction of history in the presentation of the image of the hero who rebuilds lost Troy in the new city, resonates in the English imagination. But Virgil's *Aeneid* echoes with the critique of the civilization that moves from burning city to burning city as well, and Sidney, like Saint Augustine, looks toward another vision of the republic in the City of God.[43]

Renaissance proponents of poetry found in the consideration of history a ready-made argument against the proponents of painting. Leonardo and others claimed that pictorial artists took all of natural philosophy as the source of their visually convincing geometric demonstration of truth—the art of geometric perspective that delivered instantaneous knowledge to the viewer.[44] The defenders of poetry saw in their art not the documentation merely of the details of history in some representational fashion, but the remaking of the moral significance of time itself in the poet's fables. Such *historia* belonged to a superior moral philosophy; in the poet's distinguished art of making, the higher moral perspective of prophetic production of regenerate characters and Edenic society fulfilled actively the pursuit of wisdom, the philosophy that translates the knowledge of the mind into the virtue of the art of living.[45] Sidney practices a structuralist's kind of reversal by taking the historian's claim to truth as his claim to an honest fiction, which the historian does not make as well because the historian falsifies. The reversal is not structuralist in our sense, of course; it does not have to be insofar as it is a normative rhetorical strategy of debate well known in the cultivation of antithetical reasoning in the Renaissance. So, too, Sidney's interrogation of letters implies not a Marxist but a moral philosophical praxis. But both views of praxis direct the historical building of words toward the construction of society. As Sidney explained, the poets' "naming of men is but to make their picture more lively, and not to build any history" in a literal sense (*Def.*, p. 103). Bodin's *Methodus*, which Sidney recommended to his brother Robert, presented views of history and the writing of it; as historiography, it counterpointed moral exemplum and scientific record. Writers of history and of historiographical poetry, however, called history itself a type of poem, as Saint Augustine had, and gave rhetorical invention a secure place in its composition.[46] Sidney's history is thus an imaginative act and neither the scientific pursuit of chronological veracity nor the critical pursuit of one rigorous methodology. History is "story."

In the writing of history, Samuel Daniel remarked, one may invent speeches and actions for historical characters in just proportion to the nature of men, and the course of affairs, for doing so does not distort the truth.[47] That remark reflects the political atmosphere in England in the 1590s. Daniel undertook the writing of his poetic history, *The Civil Wars*, for the moral purpose of encouraging national self-knowledge, and his poetic method, interestingly, was the same kind of rhetorical antithesis Sidney recommended (*Def.*, p. 96). Daniel wanted "to shewe the deformities of civil Dissension and the miserable events of Rebellions . . . and thereby to make the blessings of Peace and the happiness of an established Gouernment (in a direct line) the better to appear" (*Civil Wars* 1:67). Daniel's argument in the last decade of Queen Elizabeth's reign expresses the civilizing power of an architectonic philosophy and of an architectonic poetic; it does so at least partially under the influence of Sidney's articulation of an architectonic art that transcends history and philosophy by making an "imaginative ground-plot of a profitable invention" (*Def.*, p. 103).

Is the rhetorical structuring of antitheses for the sake of perspicuity in moral and political teaching of history remotely related to the large philosophical design of a Marxist view of historical change? By analogy, it may indeed be so related; by chronology and by conviction, however, the entire renaissance proposition of the activity of historiographical poetry differs from the nineteenth-century model of a history progressing by means of thesis, antithesis, synthesis in revolutionary fashion. Poetic history in the

Renaissance, it is true, is like any other kind of poem and philosophically encourages the wise re-creation of present historical moments into something else, something ostensibly better; in this, renaissance poetic history is similar in aim to the Marxist critique of culture. But finally the renaissance thinker's confrontation of historiographical poetry (witness Spenser in the *Letter* to Raleigh) conflates a moral allegorization of historical events with the apocalyptic message of religious prophecy.[48] Historiographical poetry, or poetic history, or poetry that appropriates both the aggregate and the moral force of history in the Renaissance responds to the religious and political goals of the Reformation by emphasizing the integrating power of self-knowledge, even when the first phase of such self-knowledge was the dismantling of false (that is, narcissistic or Icarean) conceptions of oneself. Such religious doctrines Hegel tried to distinguish from his philosophical project, and the nineteenth century tried to supplant with scientific prophecy.[49]

In the name of history, therefore, the rhetoric of metaphor permeates Sidney's definitions of poetry. The balances of metaphor expose his verbal structures on the large scale of a reversal traditionally called debate, in this case with the historians. So we hear in the interstices of words and structures the speaking subject, the voice defending poesie. And the voice returns us to the grounds of philosophy since Sidney engages ex tempore in thinking aloud. The return to that voice, which is the obviously consistent force of integration throughout the *Defence*, is a reader's experience analogous to the listener's hearing of the orator's pronunciation. Of necessity such a voice speaks in time, in a particular time, and resists suppression by other voices of other times.[50] One returns to it by rhetorically echoing it, by repronouncing it the way a Platonic rhapsodist might recite what the divine *furor* dictates. Sidney's poesie exercises a similarly rhetorical manipulation of words and images to control the reader's mind, but through a similarly autobiographical and historical Christian possession from within.

Literary Architectonics and the "Engineering" of Experience

A third strand of our consideration of Sidney's poetics obviously has to be some working definition of his "theory" vis-à-vis our critical constructs. Sidney's poesie almost "engineers" distinct knowledges—as long as we understand the etymological root of "engine" in Horace's sense of *ingenium* or native wit in the *Ars Poetica* and do not take it in the Newtonian and Kantian senses of mechanized system that influenced New Critical organicism—through vivid analogies and moral contraries in all of the attendant tensions, elusive significations, and pleasures of language. It is thus epistemological, prudential, and technical all at once. Sidney formulated this balancing of poetic powers in the *Defence* as the interplay of teaching, delighting, and moving. This interplay is a rhetorical simultaneity, a voicing of the prosopopoeia, the mistress-knowledge, who speaks the judgments of conscience between the lines, within the interludes, because of the juxtaposing of characters or passages or events, and so forth. But as an essentially metonymic and teleological allegorical figure, the usually invisible mistress-knowledge is sometimes quite visible in her own persona and almost always visible in various adjuncts in which poesie is historically recorded.

The expression of literary architectonics in the English Renaissance turns on a core set of specific metaphors, or adjuncts, drawn from the metonymic subject of the mistress-knowledge that allegorize, in turn, an architectonic philosophy of arts and sciences. These metaphors constitute a system of mutually linked and often interchangeable correspondences. Where one of these metaphors is present in a text, it is likely that some feature of literary architectonics, if not all, has informed the composition of that text. Chief among these metaphors are the geometric rule of the architectural analogy; the definition of ethical and political mastercraftsmanship; the prophetic vision of the chariot-throne of God; the analogy of the Word of God and the "sparks" of conscience; the apocalyptic revelation of divine judgment in the human character; the building of the temple in the universe of nature and of human history; the coming and going of the uncreated Light in the created light; the historical journey to the chaste mind of the City of God; the hunt of invention; the evolution of techniques of language to express the ency-clopedia of all things and to provide a correspondent art of reading characters and signatures in the cosmos; and, first and last, the summary expression of these multiplicities in the personification of the mistress-knowledge, the feminine spirit of wisdom that mediates knowledge and virtue.

Sidney's articulation of literary architectonics began to undergo change in the seventeenth century, and some of poesie's adjuncts have accumulated changed values since then. Primarily, ways of saying the architectonic metaphor ripened, intensified, and separated. Certain of the core analogies became more dominant. We find, for example, an increased hardening of the vehicle and tenor of metaphoric discourse so that stylistic architecture overtakes and suppresses several other adjuncts of this poetic expression. At the same time, though, an engineering of words in verbal machines that produce the illumination of conscience also coalesced several adjuncts. Similarly, as the moral coupling of the poet's image surrendered the an-drogyny that Sidney posed in the pairing of the mistress-knowledge with her self-knowing man, the poetry of statement seems to overtake the poetry of intellectual and moral discovery. In place of the Sidneian androgyny, which was charged with power *because* the mistress ranked hierarchically higher than the poet for whom she figured the divinely moral superiority within himself, a gender leveling or reduction of the feminine contributed to new gender distinctions and imbalances. These may have contributed to the advancement of women on one hand, but only by introducing other versions of interiority on the other, often in guises much more invisible than the visible force of allegory.

Ideas of invention, already complex in the sixteenth century, changed radically, too. In the self-conscious competition of poetry with the fine arts, with science, and with the invention of technological devices, the structural analogy for thought gradually broke from the poetic voice and experienced, so to speak, a cultural dehiscence that made it visible. There is a gradual subordination of philosophical architecture to character as a determinant of poetic form in the poetry of the late sixteenth and early seventeenth centuries. Critically, this development has historical roots reaching back further than "metaphysical wit" and reaching forward more than modernism's appropriation of it; the emphasis on character reappears, in fact, in contemporary criticism's strong sense of the loss of the central self and speaking subject and the perception of fragmented voices and, finally, of linguistic indeterminacy. But in character and in culture, as in buildings and in poems, the tensions of the architectonic metaphor of the sixteenth century implied the possibility of structures that neither God nor human being would want to inhabit while, almost in the same breath, the metaphor uttered the hope of discovering the living temple of the heart. The hope is not the same as the psychoanalytic or deconstructive "dream," for these poems were "ground-plots" for mediating wisdom to the human beings who spoke them and read them, by and large, in a cultural context of belief.

The aesthetic features that the theory of an architectonical art produced in renaissance poems are clear and consistent enough to be described. First of all, in literary architectonics a sharp sense of *intellectual* decorum controls the poet's analogies. The poet means to know, and learning informs his search for a moral fit between subject and style and ways of knowing. There is a rational balance between poetic fiction taken as a whole and the act of thoughtful invention the fiction is supposed to stimulate through several kinds of knowledge.

Second, literary architectonics presumes the poet's self-conscious exercise of the gender analogy of the arts and sciences. He works not so much to build a unified poetic structure out of the multiformities of words as to practice an androgynous poetic power in an effort to integrate himself. From discrete figures of speech in given poems, this androgynous style reaches toward the most complex metaphor of all: the generative myth of paradise and the hope that poetic analogy might help rebuild a fallen world of man, woman, and nature in the sight of God.

Third, literary architectonics is a Protestant poetics in which the poet questions the "making" of his imaginary paradise as he makes it. He balances the veracity of his *eikastic* images with the distortions of *phantastic* images and connects both to the discovery of an idea in fiction; but the moral success that proves the truth of the poetic fiction hangs in the balance of the correspondences that the reader, like the poet, makes in self-knowledge. The recovery of paradise is inherently ambivalent on the moral plane of composition and interpretation; it requires the corollary discovery of a divine similitude in human character.

These three features—intellectual decorum, gender analogy, and a style of contraries that counterbalances fiction-making with a revealed standard of truth—inevitably center architectonic poems on the discovery of an inner word and the criticism of master-building. Fourth, then, many renaissance poets use images of architecture in structural ways while denigrating their own verbal construction, or vice versa: sometimes the criticism of architecture is direct. This constitutes a self-conscious criticism of the master-building done in language itself, but as I shall explain throughout this book and in the notes, such criticism is not the same as the despair of deconstruction. It is, rather, an aspect of the exhortation to "know thyself," which takes the shape of "little models" of thought as Scaliger explained them, and of little "icons" of human character in various figures of speech.[51] Insofar as literary architectonics is a Protestant poetics, those who practice it compose their critique of the master-building of knowledge, language, and selves *between* the attraction of iconology and the necessity of iconoclasm. Their mastery is a centering process.

As a *renaissance* critical theorist, Sidney historically practiced the semiotic model for building and unbuilding, and for Christian Platonic reasons, before modern criticism thought to develop the dialectical and centrifugal possibilities within a text. Since the *Defence* enacts the intermediacy of Sidney's poetics, this book will examine the rhetorical intertextuality of his treatise with regard to three prosopopoeias of human character he presents. Around his three icons Sidney constructs the richly intellectual references, the self-conscious gender analogizing, the developing of contraries in style and in structure, and the ironic and often parodic attitude with which he makes a case for poesie. The critical demand that the *Defence*, one of the earliest models of English literary criticism, puts on modern criticism, in various ways its descendant, is the recognition of similarity and difference, which is the domain of metaphor. Historically there can be little doubt that Sidney's poetics are similar to and different from our own. His is a poem.

Sidney was not alone in devising compelling rhetorical images on the basis of the real knowledge of optics, perspective, dialectic, music, history, or philosophy. Such images consistently demonstrate in renaissance poetry the wide learning that renaissance poets in general brought to the making of the moral lessons and the aesthetic delight of their poems. It is as if the mistress-knowledge taught poets from Skelton to Milton that moral, social,

and poetic integrity could no more be gained by intellectual means alone—
yet knowledge there was and had to be—than heavenly salvation could be
gained by human effort alone, yet good actions had to be practiced. By no
means, though, is Sidney Kantian.

The balancing of teaching, delighting, and moving that Sidney formulated in his voicing of the mistress-knowledge clearly precedes historically
the sense of "system" and rational "systems-making" to which Immanuel
Kant assigned his "Architectonic of Pure Reason" in the eighteenth century.
Such precedence insists on our critical recognition of an English renaissance
poetics independent of this or that aspect of Kantian metaphysics and
aesthetics and modern critical reactions for or against Kant and Hegel's
response to Kant. Modern British and American literary theories tend to
originate in this nineteenth-century debate, and modern French critical
theories have tended to amplify the same terms.[52] Sidney is as different from
Kant as the Renaissance is different from antiquity. Applied to Sidney's
Defence and to the aesthetic terminology of the Renaissance with which
Sidney works out *his* architectonic concept of poesie, our modern theories
tend to tip the balance of *archia, techne,* and *teleologia* that Sidney explicitly
intended to sustain through his notion of "the balance of experience" (*Def.,*
p. 82).[53] If theorists are likely to privilege the didactic function of teaching,
formalists are likely to privilege aesthetic pleasure, and moralists the pragmatic power of persuasion. In Sidney's poetics, though, the prosopopoeia of
the mistress-knowledge directs significance, learning, usefulness, delight,
purpose, intention, stylistic technique, desire, and effectiveness along centripetal lines of metaphoric force in his racy Elizabethan translations of ideas.

I see three kinds of critical misperception implicated in the blindness to
the mistress-knowledge. The first is the retreat from the balancing of powers
I have just mentioned because of multiple problems of definition. Our
critical difficulties here are compounded by (or originate in) our use of
certain critical terms that Sidney and other renaissance theorists used. Thus
in the voiced poetics of the *Defence* Sidney formulates speculative knowledge of several types (*gnosis, theoria, scientia, ars, sapientia*) with delight
(pleasure, desire, will, love), and with prudential and practical knowledge
(praxis, exercise, virtue, demonstration, skill, power). The last feature includes aspects of technical knowledge, or craft, because of the arguments
used in renaissance epistemology to elevate mechanical knowledge on the
scale of the Aristotelian hierarchy of the intellectual virtues while revising
the scheme of knowledge.

The critical effort to do a taxonomy of renaissance critical terms has been
an important contribution to our understanding of Sidney's *Defence* and of
renaissance literary works in general, particularly because Sidney nimbly
synthesizes renaissance epistemology and political and religious purpose.

So this century has also seen the emergence of self-consciously methodological phases of criticism. Early in the century critics pursued systematically the elaboration of the form, genre, and style of the *Defence*; this work may be associated with I. A. Richards's *Principles of Literary Criticism* and with the development of New Criticism.[54] Late in the century a highly diversified but uniformly severe critical inquiry has reformulated renaissance poetics according to new "rules" of art. Texts are now read in a refined systematic analysis not of the whole but of some part. Modern criticism tends to receive something like Sidney's theory, practice, and desire as powers already split apart and to approach their joint expression through methods of division and classification. These methods may sometimes be analogical to those of some science or art.

For example, a structuralist poetics seeks to establish the "science" of literary criticism on the model of the "system" of linguistics.[55] A Marxist critique, meanwhile, insists historically on assessing economic structures evidenced in a text and moving the work of literary professions toward practical revolution in the academy and in society. Psychoanalytic criticism leads to the conclusion that all of culture, including language, literature, and literary criticism, is a construction of the ego extended from the narcissistic desire for the self experienced in the "mirror stage" of infancy. From another historical perspective, these theoretically intensive approaches effect singularly insightful but imbalanced emphases when applied to a poetic arts treatise such as *The Defence of Poesie*. Often our crediting of these approaches reflects a New Critical judgment that Sidney's poetics is purely Aristotelian, and then we discredit New Criticism because Aristotelian metaphysics no longer works for moderns.[56] Aristotelian architectonics, however, worked well into the Renaissance and in Sidney's *Defence*.

This leads to the second way modern readers may alter Sidney's critical vocabulary and example: not by retreating from the Sidneian balance of powers but by intuiting the spiritual phenomenon it metaphorically discloses and then expressing the conviction that the presence escapes either into the irretrievable past or into the unknowably eternal, which may be the same as our present moment.

Kant and Hegel begin to cross-reference here.[57] Hegel's descendant, Heidegger, held that thinking is not necessarily argumentation and certainly not the stimulating of an audience to convictions, but a "presencing."[58] He takes Hegel's "phenomenology of spirit" into his eschatology of Being.[59] This is fine; it may actually work in reading Sidney's kind of poeticizing, too. With some modification both structuralist and phenomenological readings of renaissance texts contribute to our understanding—structuralism because of its revelation of *patterns* of signification in language and phenomenology because of its engagement with *historical consciousness*. But the path from Kant and Hegel leads through Nietzsche to Husserl, Heidegger, and Jacques

Derrida and his reaction against "the metaphysics of presence."[60] So we now reconsider history while observing in a Kantian manner Heidegger's handling of it. Heidegger wanted to put aside the accumulation of "philological and historical facts" as "surveys of sediment" to the degree that they prevent thinking and promote arbitrariness. If there is to be interpretation, it should stay close to the "language of the saying" and the "mother tongue." Heidegger allows some historiography—"Perhaps the discipline of history is still for us an indispensable tool for making the historical contemporary"—though with a strong qualification: "This does not mean however that historiography, taken by itself, enables us to form within our history a truly adequate, far-reaching relation to history."[61] Phenomenology has great importance in the understanding of allegory as a symbolic mode, which has a direct bearing on the reading of medieval and renaissance texts. So, too, the Heideggerean questioning of the relation of history to thought may contribute to the kind of New Historicism it is useful to practice with regard to the renaissance interrogation of history and lead us back to an Augustinian, not a Nietzschean, examination of time, philology, and will.

The third way in which modern critical approaches may alter Sidney's statement of a philosophical poetics and produce misperceptions is the turning from teleological significance and toward the technical games of words. This turn most especially marks the Derridean movement away from the metaphysics of presence in the confrontation of metaphor and away from structuralism in the development of deconstruction; Derrida eschews metaphysics and logocentrism.[62] Why, then, would a critic use this deconstruction to read Sidney or any other renaissance writer? Sidney distinguished poesie from metaphysics, too (*Def.*, p. 78), but also authorized poetic knowing and writing with reference to the revealed truth of the Word of God. Deconstruction poses a dilemma—an opposition between a presencing that seems to work and the felt need to "know" that presence and the experience of *différance* enabling one merely to trace an absence because metaphor operates without specific referentiality that can be determined. Language and significance are indeterminate. Thus deconstructive analysis of a text occurs as a form of play—a brave or sadly defiant play, depending on one's point of view—without reference to a metaphysical ground. This dilemma can be most acute in the modern reading of Sidney because he almost always plays in rapidly differentiating and multiplying analogical connections, all of which he sustains in a rigorously rhetorical, logocentric speech.

Obviously, in the content of his witty speech, Sidney has undertaken *not* the demolishing of metaphysics and the modernist shoring of its fragments against his ruin, but something closer to its metamorphosis in his appropriation of it for the poetic act of thinking. Sidney first constructs his defense of poetry as a craft in the midst of renaissance arts debates so as to define it as a legitimate type of knowledge participating validly in a recognizable scheme of the arts and sciences. He thus grounds poesie as a type of metaknowledge—as an architectonic knowledge in the Aristotelian sense—by associating it with rhetoric, then moral philosophy or ethics and politics, and finally epistemology. Sidney accomplishes this game of metamorphosing poesie, furthermore, with the seriously humanistic intention of convincing members of his audience of the paradoxes of serious play and playful seriousness in the exercise of *their* literacy. His own speech, meantime, demonstrates these definitions of the significance of the mistress-knowledge and of mastercraftsmanship by means of an informed practical knowledge of renaissance rhetoric, which he has here mastercrafted into a multitude of similarities and differences, or metaphors. These he regularly builds and unbuilds in his disputation toward its several ends, including the demonstrations of some cognitive link between poesie (reading), epistemology (the gathering of knowledge), and the government of one's actions. Next to this Sidneian play, *serio ludere*, Derridean or deconstructive play is Johnny-come-lately.

The mirror-question of our aesthetics is not *whether* Sidney gives himself and his text to deconstruction in this building and unbuilding, which is *his* architectonics, for he clearly does not, but *how much* early twentieth-century literary formalism, from which deconstruction descends, "privileged" Sidney's *Defence* as an early landmark in English literary criticism and a model of the very process of critical definition and argument *according to Kantian norms.*[63] Historically it is useful to inquire into the degree to which nineteenth-century romantic and Victorian cultural perceptions—themselves in reaction against eighteenth-century historiography—influenced formal judgments that have established a certain continuity in "the Yale school."[64] Can we now see through modernism, romanticism, and the Enlightenment to renaissance statements *as* renaissance statements? To the degree that we can, what is the relationship between Sidney's critical theory and poetic practice in certain renaissance texts? Both René Wellek and John Steadman have commented, for instance, that there is very little relationship between renaissance aesthetic theories and the manner in which poets actually composed, and this is no small argument to overcome regarding Sidney's influence.[65]

From different perspectives, both Jonathan Culler in *Structuralist Poetics* and Jerome McGann in *Social Values and Poetic Acts* have helped to establish some guidelines in answering the first question. Culler's linguistic analogy allows his definition of forms of convention and of literary competence particular to a given language—in this case, for example, the language of renaissance England, its arts treatises, and its literary education and practice. McGann sorts out nonnormative from normative truth and "the scandal of referentiality." Insofar as Saussure's *General Linguistics* is the bible of structuralism, however, and Saussure openly moves from "grammar" and "philology" to his (Kantian?) system of signs, renaissance scholars have to be cautious in relying on structuralist analyses when historical research might actually disclose renaissance grammar and renaissance philosophies of language that more usefully explain renaissance texts; many studies have already provided such materials to contemporary scholars and students.[66] Likewise, McGann's intellectual origins in nineteenth-century studies may qualify his perspective on renaissance texts somewhat; but I have seen a refinement of that perspective developing in his books. The last one makes very careful distinctions, for example, when McGann observes Sidney's use of an Aristotelian argument to defend poetry from Platonic criticism; confirms the theological nature of Sidney's "ideological ground"; compares Sidney's "light of Christ" to Coleridge's "sacramentalism" but not without contrasting them as historical documents as well; and contrasts both Sidney and Coleridge not to Kant's assertion of values but to Kant's placement of the "fundament of the aesthetic moment" in metaphysics and not theology (*Social Values and Poetic Acts*, pp. 73–74). I find in this book no unconscious vestige of the New Critical singling out of Sidney's treatise; rather, McGann offers an opinion now informed by our many theoretical debates, which have anatomized the problem of historicism. In *Social Values and Poetic Acts*, McGann also returns directly to Herodotus and his version of Cyrus (pp. 64–72) and to Plato (pp. 17–31); in so doing he comes closer to Sidney, the renaissance reader of classics. Nevertheless, the proper aesthetic and historical context in which to read Sidney's version of the metaphoric identification of poesie as a "divine science," or his analogical hierarchy of three kinds of poets, or his triangulation of the inventive poet, *Natura*, and God as "makers" is the Renaissance and its treatises.[67]

Feminism and Historicity

Since the mistress-knowledge is the centering metaphor of Sidney's *Defence*, her story must somehow articulate the overview of literary architectonics and our contemporary critical discourses. The knowledge of a man's self is an allegory of universal knowledge is the allegory of poesie is the mistress-knowledge is literary architectonics. And the balance of experience is an historical pursuit of Wisdom and of wisdom, Sophia, in the new English temple of mind and nation. Sidney's experience of the balancing of poetic powers, of gender, of various kinds of knowledge, and of a multiplicity of texts in a shared culture places his triangle of woman, man, and their engendered reader in an Elizabethan culture that adulated marriage. This household of faith, economics, and politics ordinarily makes the man the head, the woman the body, and the child the obedient subject as the Epistle to the Ephesians says.[68] Sidney's balances in this respect are consistent with the Protestantism of his effort to articulate the character of the poet. The feminism in my reading of this aspect of Sidney includes his awareness of theological questions, therefore, but must operate dialectically with his quest for a divinely authorized social justification of this gender hierarchy as if it were natural and complementary. Yet another aspect of Sidney's balancing of ethical and political considerations shows that he could not, in fact, completely assimilate "the other"—and ultimately the other was the cognitive infinity of knowledge and the epistemological archetype of the unknown, the feminine sign of the divine.[69] I suppose I have identified with this feminine form in his text more than the oppressed form, and I argue that Sidney the poet actually testifies to a certain revelation of this "otherness" in his text. In a way he has saved the mistress-knowledge from destruction, though not from the subsequent marginalization of literary scholars.

In *Rewriting the Renaissance,* Margaret Ferguson, Maureen Quilligan, and Nancy J. Vickers define feminist scholarship as a scholarship of discovery and recovery.[70] It foregrounds phenomena "completely overlooked or relegated to the margins of scholarly discourse" (p. xxi). Some feminists challenge the very notion of a canonical tradition; others read canonical texts, usually by men, "in heretical ways" (p. xxi), among which Marxist, deconstructive, and psychoanalytic methodologies are especially acknowledged as feminist forms of skepticism or "suspicion" (pp. xxii–xxiii). Likewise, historical inquiry is "heretical" when it looks at what women read or wrote, or how women worked, and so forth (p. xxii). To the extent that this scholarship is feminist, it is "heretical" in some of these ways, especially with regard to the recovery of a lost history. To the extent that "her" story is a rewriting of the English Renaissance about a particular topic, furthermore, it must engage the feminist editors' metaphor of religious heresy, like Elaine Showalter's, with literary and cultural studies using some degree of self-consciousness regarding stated or implied "orthodoxy."

On the one hand, the scholarship of discovery in this book appears in print only because some feminist challenge to the canon and to established literary or historical methods has already occurred. On the other hand, the particular recovery and discovery of literary architectonics in this book may qualify the implication that a single feminist orthodoxy does, indeed, exist. These chapters pay some political tributes while the history recovered requires the denial of others. That is, this book ethically and politically observes a recognition of a shared cause in several kinds of feminist critique. But in bringing to light previously unacknowledged data, this book goes "beyond" a simple politics because the "presencing" of lost images in gynocriticism is qualitatively even more political than dialectical argument against oppression. In presencing this mistress to history, which is a form of collective memory, Sidney gave audiences a specific figure that makes the feminist metaphor of heresy and orthodoxy literal and real. Whether we approach her strictly figuratively or read the political allegory of Elizabeth in her, the image has a positive power. She is not simply the object of a Marxist-feminist study of the manner in which women were historically advanced in the Renaissance by social institutions and artistic productions (*Rewriting the Renaissance*, pp. xvii xxi).[71] She is the subject, rather, of the learning of women who are discovering the tools of learning as well as their own paths as they inquire into the evidence. The power of this image comes neither from the authority of the patriarchy nor from opposition to it, but from her own numinosity in time.

The mistress-knowledge validates the knowledge of a self that need not always be cast into guilt or error because of the phallocentrism of male culture. Rather, she can know herself in the demonstration of her freedom as an equally regenerated mind. No, more than that, she can identify with the very power of regeneration, the source that renaissance poets and critics envisioned in feminine form before a later age dismantled the honest struggle for androgyny—"honest" because the coupling of *two* different forces in language and in society bespoke the cultural glimpse of an integrity *beyond* gender. The old-fashioned, masculine, and moral-theological name for this numinosity is "chastity," for this integrity, "virginity," and it applied to male as well as female. As we begin to grasp the sexualized constitutions of textuality and the "fetishing" of the literary object, we may, indeed, find "virgin text-bodies" vulnerable to violation.[72] But we also encounter a textual virginity that constitutes an authentic power of language, a "living flame" found as much in Milton's "Lycidas" as in Spenser's *Faerie Queene* and contesting gender boundaries. Where poets and critics compose in it, they have been the most themselves and the most powerful. Women scholars and critics are at the juncture where such a composition in historical studies and in literary criticism has begun to become possible.[73] The possibility accounts, perhaps, for our scrutiny of Lacan and our passion for Kristeva as women and men alike try to grasp the motion of desire in language insofar as such a motion has determined the construction of our culture.[74]

Roland Barthes said in *Critique et vérité*, "To read is to desire the work, it is to wish to be the work, it is to refuse to double the work in any other vocabulary than the same speech of the work. . . . To pass from reading to criticism is to change desire, it is to desire no more the work, but one's own language."[75] Barthes made the observation two decades ago, and the treatise practically launched structuralism. Structuralism, Jonathan Culler remarked, did for French literary theory and criticism many of the same things New Criticism did for the English variety.[76] What if we press further back, though, than Barthes's interrelationship of writing (*l'écriture*, *l'oeuvre*), reading (*la lecture*), and criticism (*la critique*) and find out that four centuries ago Sir Philip Sidney interrelated language, learning, and life in his vision of poesie? Sidney's desire for many works of literature and their promise of the power of an heroic identity for the English could be said, then, to have motivated his construction of his own critical language on the subjects of reading, writing, making the poem and, in turn, being re-created by it. Like American and English critics of this century, Sidney came to the writing of his critical language in the confrontation of classical, Italian, and French criticism and philosophy, which provoked in him an intense awareness of the social and political enterprise intertwined with poesie. Asking the question—of Barthes, of Sidney, of ourselves—confronts us with history. If, in Barthes's sense, the literary history of the word *architectonic* mirrors the model of linguistics and the history of a language, this book is somewhat structuralist because it is primarily a "reading" that refuses to double Sidney's vocabulary, at least until scholarship has recorded still more of the wordlist in Sidney and in his contemporaries. But where this book clearly passes from "reading" to "criticism," engaging me in the desire for a self-referentially constructed language, is also in its historical emphasis. A scholarly identity inclines me in that direction, and so does feminism, since my gender makes me, as Mary Jacobus has put it, a "reading woman (reading)."[77] Thus the respect for Sidney's diction inevitably interlaces with the manner in which his articulation of an androgynous image has sexualized his text.

Sidney speaks of history as an informed party who asserts views of history rooted in earlier centuries than his own, and certainly earlier than the nineteenth century, which is often the source of our contemporary evaluation of historicism. The additional fact that the historical context of almost all of Sidney's lifetime was filled by the royal presence of a woman, not a man, further qualifies Sidney's allegorical image for architectonic knowledge, his motives and strategies in presenting the androgynous figure, and our reception of his text. The theoretical question asked by the New Historicism in this regard as in others is what the proper discourse and the limitations and potentialities of historical interpretation are.

In reading the metaphor of the mistress-knowledge through many of its correlatives in the Renaissance, I have been reading history as a metaphor. The process itself produced one of those reversals that structuralists mention; I also began to read metaphor in order to understand the history that excluded this major image of feminine power. In scholarly activity, the study of a renaissance critical vocabulary in its historical context has gradually produced the awareness of certain convictions. The first premise to be acknowledged in the historical methods of this book, obviously, is the conviction that the Renaissance still provides testimonies about itself. Literary historical scholarship does not yet claim to have found and mined all the resources or to have asked all the interpretive questions of familiar sources.

Any historical research at all privileges the idea that *some* historical referentiality can yet be discovered and known. Specifically, the architectonic concept in Sidney's poetic theory witnesses to a Renaissance that self-consciously refused to keep the hard facts of an architectural principle of multiplicity in unity separate from the personified "first mover" of knowledge. Renaissance minds coordinated thinking in several directions at once, even contradictory ones. Thus the modern imposition of rigid philosophical categories or strict critical codes or precise time boundaries on the age (resulting in the capitalization of the words *Middle Ages, Renaissance,* and *Enlightenment,* for example) or on the architectonic concept risks continuing to falsify the evidence.[78] For such methods especially participate in the structural blind spot of merely *one* of the concept's metaphoric counters and abstract references architecturally or structurally or deconstructively. Historical study of literature benefits from a certain tentativeness, an openness in inquiry. While deconstruction can provide some such openness and tentativeness, its own methodological evolution is too weighted, I think, to provide the kind of rhapsody and aggregation that may, in the long run, be as felicitous to the intellectual historian as the scientist's dream of the benzene ring. It seems historically truer to identify as many versions of the architectonic metaphor as possible and to try to describe them. The description can be done in an open manner while acknowledging how the aggregate of architectonic metaphors in the Renaissance reveals the analogical elusiveness of renaissance concepts of universal knowledge, including "history" and "story," "image" and "idea," "building" and "poem," imitation and invention, poet and reader, male and female, fiction and "true Poem."

A second premise is that qualification of referentiality is a renaissance activity to begin with and not Nietzsche's discovery.[79] By establishing historical perspective as the preeminent discipline to organize knowledge, the Renaissance stimulated the self-reflexive interrogation of history that produced first its exalted value and then its modern critique. For some literary scholars, the extreme development of the historical perspective of renaissance thought has led beyond antiquity to the vanishing point at which the meaningfulness of the age called Renaissance recedes from critical view, taking an objectively knowable history—or text—with it. My perspective does not extend to this extreme. I see a certain Western current in the many historical references of the architectonic metaphor.

At face value the architectonics of Herodotus's praise of the master-builder and of Cicero's philosophical eloquence, for example, does not seem to have much bearing on R. G. Collingwood's twentieth-century effort to achieve a rapprochement between philosophy and history in *The Idea of History.*[80] But Collingwood's work became the history of his own thought, a self-examined life reflecting the argument from ethos that Herodotus had praised as the core of historical narration, that Cicero—and Sidney, Ibsen, and Auden, for that matter—appreciated. The implications of the architectonic idea in any Western person's struggle toward moral and intellectual integration on the basis of self-knowledge connect Cicero to Collingwood and both to Sir Philip Sidney, whose intensive intertextuality in the *Defence* established the art of "making" above history and philosophy alike. Just as the study of history requires the intellectual effort to dismantle rigid forms when they can be seen as such (the difference *between* Sidney's architectonics and Kant's, for example), so should the study of history recognize the analogues produced in words and in deeds when they are articulated, even across centuries.

Recognizing how the challenging of history can proceed only from an historically self-conscious vantage, one must concur with the proponents of the New Historicism on reformulating the finished past into forms answerable to the present. At the same time, working *with* extant texts and *with* referentialities proposed by the Renaissance speaking for and about itself in the architectonic metaphor that is the subject of this book, I find renaissance, medieval, and antique reasons for such reformulation contained in the metaphor as Sidney coined it. This metaphor occasions interpretive breakthroughs on reified concepts of the recent and distant past, of the self, and of society. As Edward Pechter has observed in his essay, "The New Historicism and Its Discontents," the value of the New Historicism is not so much its exposure of the will to power, *libido dominandis*, but the rehistoricization of literary studies in the poststructuralist period.[81] This rehistoricization refuses "to isolate the literary text from other discursive practices"; as a "less specialized" critical activity, it may be called "culture criticism" or "just criticism" (p. 302). C. S. Lewis recognized over thirty years ago that the greatness of Sidney's theory is its status as the form into which the actual taste, ethics, religion, and poetic practice of his time and class fell when reflected upon.[82] Literary architectonics should qualify our hypertrophied interest in systematic critical theory, precisely because Sidney's metaphoric poetic theory communicated the culture of his time.

A third premise asks all of us critics and historicists to defend against modern critical terminologies where they obscure rather than disclose significances in renaissance texts. For reasons Victoria Kahn has generally explained in her essay "Humanism and the Resistance to Theory," descriptive critical metaphors clearly presented as metaphors may be preferable in the discussion of humanistic texts to the verbal tools of critical analyses that appear neutral but are, in fact, disguised analogues to other knowledge systems.[83] On their own terms and in our own day, various knowledge systems are contesting the title of mastercraftsmanship.

Finally, an historical approach presents the traces of a presence. As a gendered allegory, the theme of the mistress-knowledge may be peculiarly haunting and ghostly. It seems always to be getting lost in the critical assessment of the architecture of thought and the systems of words. But men have recorded their glimpses of her in substantial ways. The Italian humanist, Coluccio Salutati, for example, frankly stated the intellectual universality of poetic knowledge in his treatise *De Laboribus Herculis:* poetry is composed out of both the trivium and the quadrivium (1.4). C. S. Lewis identified this idea in his fundamental analogy of the arts and sciences, "the liberal arts." The multifold integrity of the liberal arts possesses, he remarked, the numinosity of a fact in nature. Numinosity—and its inclination to articulate philosophical truths in mythic images—is central to the shifting significances of the renaissance architectonic metaphor. It is the veil that gave the appearance of the unity of the truth to the allegory of the mistress-knowledge long before Kantian philosophy converted it into the clouds of the sublime. From yet another vantage on the integrity of the arts and sciences, Mario Praz in *Mnemosyne* appropriately described the shared features of the arts instead of trying to put a deceptive set of classifications upon them; he saw the effort to define a precise morphology of the arts as a temptation to seek the source of a sevenfold Nile.[84] So, too, Paul Oskar Kristeller has brought to light the sources of renaissance learning in the balancing of philosophical statement and allegorical mythology; he has distinguished this learning from the system of the arts expressed in the eighteenth century and from modern categories.[85] Sidney placed his lively personification of architectonics on a vertical plane *between* the divinely creative and the humanly poetic, that is, technical. The intermediacy of poesie as the mistress-knowledge conveys a numinous power, and that placement has been most suppressed or jeopardized in the reduction of this elusive allegory to manageable, if masculinized, structures or in her elevation to a metaphysical divinity irrelevant to modern man. In the final analysis, then, the allegorical existence of the mistress-knowledge on the same plane of intermediacy as the self-knowing man matters historically. On that plane, history is politics and philosophy is poesie.

Not surprisingly, the *reduction* to the merely technical and technological appears in modern reception of the sixteenth-century metaphor, for modern literary imaginations have affected a structural fascination with architecture and engineering in the cultural domains of the post-Renaissance. Twentieth-century poets have frequently turned to the architectural analogy to express their longing for an architectonic philosophy that is no more. In *The Art of Poetry*, translated by Denise Folliot, the French poet Paul Valéry called the poem not a "building" but a "machine" for building the mind, "for producing the poetic state of mind by means of words." The poet is "the architect of poems."[86] Rosemond Tuve made much the same remark about the "slot-machine quality" of rhetoric in renaissance poems designed to produce effects in the reader.[87] Cecelia Tichi, drawing on Henry Adams's perception of medieval architecture and the tension of likeness between "the virgin and the dynamo," has recently demonstrated how technological constructions and the heroic idea of the engineer affected early twentieth-century American letters. She argues that the dynamo does not displace but actually absorbs and replaces the old feminine center of the cathedral.[88]

W. H. Auden retained some of the resonances of renaissance literary architectonics in his evaluation of poetry, perhaps because he was so informed with his own literary tradition. Auden saw poetry as the difficult making of intellectual and moral standards of judgment. He pressed his architectural figure of speech in "The Birth of Architecture," the prologue to *Thanksgiving for a Habitat* in the volume entitled *About the House*, until it yielded the point: poetry is a moral game of knowledge in which the poet re-creates human nature—or tries to—by constructing a "second nature of tomb and temple." Since Auden's view of the aesthetic game has a teleology, it is not deconstructive. For him, metaphor was a conditional mode of thought that asserted logical identity between what we could be as a civilization and what we actually are by virtue of what we do. Yes, that conditional mode is necessarily moral and ironic. Auden called the person of creative imagination an "architect" and mourned the fact that our world is composed, instead, of so many "masons" and "carpenters" and so few poets who can make metaphor.[89] In the suppression of the intermediacy of the feminine allegory for architectonic knowledge, it appears that the post-Renaissance centuries have gradually lost the older vision of the master-builder, too. "I want a hero," Byron had said, commenting on the lack before Auden.

The femininity of Sidney's mistress-knowledge is rooted in the grammatical gender of a word. Of that piece of grammar, Sidney made a metaphor that pulled the complexity of the intellectual past into a mediating position for a literary future that she would help generate. Sidney did not, however, elevate his mistress-knowledge to the full status of divinity, mystifying her, even though his expression of the concept of an architectonic knowledge in a feminine allegory has theological, historical, and literary implications for our understanding of the poetic language of the Renaissance. Rather, in her cultural appearances and disappearances, the mistress-knowledge poses the problem of masculine desire to contain knowledge, to control the feminine—which is in itself a figure of containment in the way metaphoric language also contains thought—and to apprehend the divine mystery, bringing it within human scope.

But the Reformation taught a fortiori that human intellectual and moral efforts could not by themselves constitute Christ. Exponents of the Protestant poetics of renaissance texts agree that those texts argue the necessity of grace, of that which is neither controlled nor contained by man.[90] While Reformers wanted the self to be metaphysically remade as a divine image and society re-created as the City of God, the poets articulated not the recovery of the hidden unity of the arts and sciences which is the Christ, the Truth of medieval visions, but the fallen language resulting from the very fact of fallen men writing in a fallen world. In general, renaissance literary architectonics observes this condition; it is neither a statement of ideas nor an imitation of ideals but a *preference for an ironic mode of failing the struggle to attain to and to contain the truth of things;* and this ironic mode works through the balancing of variegated, discrepant, and often contradictory images. Sidney described it when he alluded to the difference between *eikastic* and *phantastic* images, but other renaissance poets found as well that the multiplicity of knowledges and of words bespoke the necessity of grace at the same time it marked the human effort "to know" (*Def.,* p. 112). When renaissance poets struggled to speak the "word" of their poems in relation to the Word of God, consequently, they communicated a complex balance of experience. The poems themselves were occasions of self-knowledge in which a superior creative Word spoke the truth of the characters of the poets as the poets composed written characters of letters in the truths of their fictions.

As a complex wisdom within renaissance poets moved their speech, the struggle with God was not unlike the struggle with woman. This wisdom was initially feminized, maternal, and queenly, and cast as the Muse or the beloved or the elusive presence, but finally masculinized as the saving Word originating the poets' own image. Peter Stallybrass has observed that woman was the emblem for "the perfect and impermeable container" and that the virgin, like the state, was a *hortus conclusus* reflecting both the Garden of Solomon's erotic Song of Songs and the "body" of the Church.[91] Indeed, when this extension of the Vitruvian analogy is taken into the realm of epistemology and theology, the *double* images of the house of all knowledge and the feminine aspect of wisdom reveal the complexity of the renaissance imagination of power struggle. For one image seems balanced in its building and unbuilding, which the poet's craft can control, and the other image is balanced in appearing and disappearing at will, but not necessarily that of the poet. In this respect Jonathan Crewe's effort to define "historical" in terms of "the rigor of any single discipline or method" and to deny validity to a "historicism" that uses several methods at once is simplistic.[92]

In the Renaissance, the idea of the mistress-knowledge as a type of Sophia generated the great fable of the poetic word as an engine of creation and destruction, of love and knowledge, of the cosmos and technology, of conscience and science, and then was displaced by shifts in those very dialectics. *Both* her feminine godliness and the masculine virtue of the poet should be understood in gender studies as allegorical images or icons, the little "temples" in human bodily form for what could be imagined but not contained—the unattainable divine Reality that, renaissance poets constantly asserted, nevertheless indwelled Solomon's Temple and the developing Protestant sense of "the temple of the heart." The allegorical articulation of the architectonic poet in the English Renaissance—especially the mythos of learning and love in the gendered character of the relationship *between* the two sexes, the two divine icons of man and woman who together type the living temple—necessarily presents to our minds the disjunction as well as the communion of the mistress-knowledge and her consort, the poet-statesman. Learning finds "the true philosophy" with difficulty, the polymaths say. But love has to find it gracefully or be doomed. When Sophia appears and emblematizes the human quest for the wisdom of justice, which is the true philosophy, learning begins to feel its wisdom and the poet takes pleasure in his light.

I do not think such an illumination had much in common with the so-called Enlightenment in which the solitary Immanuel Kant performed *Critiques* of all kinds. It was, rather, some "faire beames" that touched poets like Spenser, who felt weakness in their vision, who were humble, who struggled with an "afflicted stile," and it enabled them to be poets of the light.[93] The criticism of renaissance texts properly begins not in the desire for one's own modern language but in the desire for a stroke of that light. The regeneration of the mind, where it was thought to occur, was like Aristotle's definition of happiness: no more than a single swallow can make the spring can a single day define what takes a lifetime. Poesie is historically regenerative because poesie is the allegory of self-knowledge in time.

3

Notable Prosopopoeias and the Rhetorical Intertextuality of the *Defence*

> Adam could have stood if he wished, seeing that he fell solely by his own will. But it was because his will was capable of being bent to one side or the other, and was not given the constancy to preserve, that he fell so easily . . . [and] in destroying himself he corrupted his own blessings. Hence the great obscurity faced by the philosophers, for they were seeking in a ruin for a building, and in scattered fragments for a well-knit structure.
>
> —John Calvin, *The Institutes of the Christian Religion* 1.15.8

Ethos, or the Confirmation of the Poet's Character

Ever since William Temple, Sidney's secretary between 1584 and 1586, attempted to analyze the argument of the *Defence* and to apply it, the text has elicited the investigation of the way Sidney reread and rewrote ancient and contemporary materials to compose his own poetics.[1] Sidney's message is quite clear when he compares poetic fiction to so-called historical truth: readers will find the moral synthesis of the arts and sciences—the integration of antique learning and contemporary reality—in the poet's fable insofar as the fable presents *character*. The poet labors not "to tell you what is or is not, but what should or should not be" (*Def.*, pp. 102–3). Within the *Defence* itself, however, there is a fashioning of character going on, too, in the fictive iconology of the three notable prosopopoeias of Sidney's making—the mistress-knowledge, the poet-statesman, and the "product" of their art of poesie, Cyrus the "good" reader.

This fashioning of character within the text pulls in the reader insofar as Cyrus is a mirror who relates Sidney, usually typed by the poet-statesman and here the orator of the *Defence*, with other Cyruses. One may read the shifting voice among these three—and the "shared knowledge" of Sidney's culture resonating in his allusions to numerous works of classical and contemporary thought—as an intertextuality that is also intersubjective. Thus Sidney's speaking self is lost in many echoes, as Kristeva's *vraisemblance* suggests. Or one may read Sidney's voice in the *Defence* as self-conscious yet divided—that is, duplicitous—for political reasons. But the best reading, I think, attends to Sidney the speaker consciously shifting among the three masks and appropriating in their roles *all* the other resonances of his view of culture as a clear definition of *his* subjective identity as a poet. Sidney marks his text in this manner: now he speaks with the "art"; now as the "artificer"; now the poet-statesman "lifted up" into the zodiac of his wit and united in voice with the power of judgment in the mistress-knowledge; now a type of Cyrus the military man and reader of the classics, and governor, and so forth through the voices of Plato, Aristotle, Plutarch, and others. The Sidneian definition of the poetic fable as an "imaginative ground-plot of a profitable invention" asks that the *Defence* be "heard" through his articulation of directives coordinating all its elements; that is, the *Defence* ought to be read "oratorically" with Sidney's own iconology of himself as a speaking subject very much present and controlling the complex movement of the treatise (*Def.*, p. 103).[2]

The oratorical reading of the *Defence* gives us a Sidney, although intelligent and witty, who is passionately engaged with and not rationally detached from the crisis of his manhood. For this reason, interpretations of the *Defence* limiting it to the gentleman's literary essay, a miscellany of opinions from the well-read Englishman, have seriously obscured the evidence of the psychological, political, and religious struggle of the good son, the lover, the heroic soldier and citizen, and the new, artistic man in Sidney's statement. Initially, this may be seen as the struggle of the son with the father and all patriarchal authority, and modern Freudian analysis illuminates the rule of the father in the age of Elizabeth in Sidney's case. But Sidney's politics in the *Defence* inevitably appears in his choice of myths taking us into a deeper past than modern psychoanalysis, and I shall argue that he develops his character by subordinating the Troy legend of Britain to the story of England's conversion along Augustinian lines.

This means that Sidney appropriates classical literate culture in the philosophies of Plato, Aristotle, and Cicero, for instance, and in the fables of Homer, Xenophon, Herodotus, Plutarch, and Virgil, by interpreting it through the eyes of Boethius and Saint Augustine. The politics in which freedom contests tyranny finally comes home to the life of the Protestant artist or poet. So Sidney's *Defence*, as a character of emerging manhood, a "portrait of the artist as a young man," presents his resolution of certain aesthetic alternatives as an answer to the problem of his identity. Having read Virgil well, and through the eyes of Saint Augustine's self-critique in the *Confessions*, Sidney subordinates the fictive story of Aeneas to the historical and biblical story of Cyrus. Virgil had faulted his hero for not understanding the relation between politics and art either in the story of Daedalus and Icarus engraved on the doors of the Temple of Apollo Daedalus built to give thanks for his escape from the tyranny of Minos

(*Aeneid* 6.14–35) or in the scenes of Roman history on Vulcan's shield (8.625–731). Artistically Sidney turns to the Daedalean type—the craftsman, inventor, and temple-builder—as well as the Virgilian type of the visionary poet, and the counterpointing of the two transforms the crisis of manhood into the crisis of the poet who must both fulfill and usurp from the role of the father.

Acting the part of a son united to his father's cause is the challenge of Sidney's faith, which he meets in the confession of the *Defence*. The Virgilian poet is a seer—*vates*—who bears witness to the divine destiny of fathers and sons and whose vision of history may be Christianized in the image of the incarnate Son of God who is sacrificed to produce the City of God. The Daedalean poet is a maker, a craftsman, whose guidance comes from the inward possession of the genius of the mistress-knowledge. In her he escapes the patriarchy, its tyrannies, and the futility of human sacrifice not merely negatively, by means of witty flight from the prison of history, but positively, by means of the freedom to range in the zodiac of his wit and to re-create the world as the Word spoke it and *Natura* made it. Sidney the Protestant poet thus marks in the ambivalent androgynous portrayal of different powers of the artist the two faces of knowledge, politics, and poetry that will later inform the writing of John Milton on the grand scale: reason and faith, death and regeneration, destruction and deliverance, sinful making and graceful re-creation in the image of the Son of God.

The declaration of this historical ambivalence is already apparent in Sidney's own *Arcadia* and in *Astrophil and Stella*. The quasi-fictional history of thought in the intertextuality of the *Defence* is the correlative of the romance and antiromance. To recognize the declaration of Sidney's Protestant poetics of history in the *Defence*, we may begin by hearing the oratory in which Sidney rewrites the philosophical eloquence of the Roman and Stoic Cicero into English Augustinian desire.

The *Defence* is not merely a "feigned example" of literary criticism. It is an epistemological fable, a poem about knowledge and its purpose, which Sidney locates in ethos. His allegory of poesie narrates the story of English renaissance culture, which finds in this distinct spokesperson an oral presence that integrates the many voices in the text within his own. Emphasizing the significance of delivery or pronunciation, Sidney develops Scaliger's definition of the two kinds of prosopopoeia as a conscious rhetorical strategy. The choice is supported by Saint Augustine's famous answer to a question on the most important part of rhetoric: "Delivery, delivery, delivery," he said, and Calvin in the *Institutes* appropriated the emphasis in religion, saying that "humility, humility, humility" is the foundation of necessary self-knowledge.[3] Sidney is, at it were, speaking to know himself in the *Defence*, and the primacy of this teleological purpose organizes the form of the treatise.

Sidney's preference for delivery is a pragmatic preference for liveliness in speech; it is also a means of self-presentation, an *appearance* of the truth of the self. Only a simplistic history thinks *all* iconology and construction of fiction forbidden by the Puritan mentality; rather, Calvin and others urged the avoidance of fashioning any idols of God and the discovery of the disaster within oneself that inhibited the religious realization of the true icon of God in need of restoration within the self. Without humility, Calvin explained, self-knowledge is proud and underwrites all the errors in philosophy, all the ruins; with humility, self-knowledge is a Calvinist's kind of good faith (*Institutes* 1:1.1.1, p. 37 n.4). In his good faith Sidney uses and does not abuse the little icons or prosopopoeias that he sets up as masks. He validates them in his allusion to David's use of similar masks to speak of the true beauty of God. Instead of establishing idols of the self, therefore, Sidney slips in and out of his masks to confirm his own ethos, the more elusive icon or speaking picture of himself as a good character, while he dismantles and corrects images that, left to themselves or taken too seriously, might become idolatrous or proud. The proof of his good use of such masks is that he *does* shift them, always gravitating toward centering a truth, however mixed, of his own identity, his own recognizable voice, no matter its limitations.

In this respect, therefore, we should understand that the *Defence* is not formed by an adherence to an architecture of the classical seven-part oration, the linearity of which editors have routinely sought to impose upon it. Rather, the structure of the *Defence* follows the end and purpose of its speaker and adheres to the rhetorical forms used for the construction of character. Specifically, Sidney speaks the *Defence* oratorically according to the rule for confirmation of character provided by Cicero. As an integrating oral presence, Sidney approaches his audience with an effort to impress us with his trustworthiness, his learned and witty ethos of self-knowledge. In triangulating himself with his three prosopopoeias, Sidney uses them to make us "see" what he means about "poetry in England" in much the same way David's psalms show "the unspeakable and everlasting beauty" of God to the eyes of the mind cleared by faith (*Def.*, p. 77). Writing as a Protestant humanist, Sidney begins his arts treatise carefully defining himself as an "elected" male aristocrat and military man and an "unelected" poet; the latter role is tantamount to a "call" beyond the ordinary social and political sphere, and he gradually moves through its authority to a position of poet-statesman that authorizes his speaking *for* the best interests of the mistress-knowledge, whom he masks as the art of poesie. As an orator, Sidney does not wash out his own identity in the sounding of voices of other texts, such as Erasmus's *Prosopopoeia* of Great Britain and *The Praise of Folly*, or Boethius's *Consolation of Philosophy* and Sidney's *Letter* to the Queen opposing her proposed marriage to Alençon. His soundings of moral philosophy lead him, rather, all the way through echoes of a Christian culture to the injunctions of the divine Word as well. Instead of wanting away Sidney's "I," this triangle reveals his effort to center himself in his discourse and to show the theological justification of his speech.

First of all, to see how Sidney structurally advocated the poet in the *Defence* as a whole, we should look at the treatise as an oration formed according to his knowledge of Cicero's recommendations in the *De Inventione* on the confirmation of character. As an oration, the *Defence* is divided almost equally into two parts—confirmation and refutation. The first contains Sidney's metaphoric redefinition of Plato's philosophy of the statesman and of Aristotle's hierarchy of knowledge in which Sidney uses Aristotle to counter Plato (pp. 73–99).[4] This section incorporates the bit on Pugliano that opens the *Defence*, as I have explained in chapter 1, because Sidney develops it as a parody of the lowest ranking on Aristotle's hierarchy in contrast to the highest ranking, which is architectonic knowledge.[5] The second part unravels both foreign and domestic arguments against English poetry with respect to true doctrine, political master-building, and national defense (pp. 99–121). It really applies the theory of the first part and moves theory toward practice and therefore fulfills Sidney's poetic standard of literary architectonics. As if answering the French "philosophers" of poetry, such as du Bellay in his famous *Défense et illustration de la langue française*, the text is a poetic application of the general principles of a moral poetic theory to the particular case of English writing, religion, and politics.[6] Sidney seeks to manifest the oratorical imagination of a converted Plato whose patronage of the poetic art concurs with English Protestant Christianity and nationality, not with the poetic *furor* of the Pléiade.

In the *De Inventione* Cicero examined the orator's thought—his finding of ideas and arguments according to the topics or categories of ideas and his bringing forth of those arguments by way of speech. The core of a good speech is its positive evidence for the idea being presented, its confirmation, with regard to the mode of argumentation undertaken. Among the three modes proposed—*logos, ethos,* and *pathos*—*ethos* had great appeal to the moral English. Cicero gives some precise advice to the orator on how to construct an argument of confirmation of character: one ought to list the person's name, nature, manner of life, fortune, habit, purposes, achievements, and speeches made (1.24.34–36).[7] The *Defence* falls right into this order as Sidney's consistent argument for the mastercraftsmanship of poesie engages philosophy, history, and theology.

After the opening on Pugliano, with whom Sidney contrasts himself (p. 73), we meet Sidney's character in the explication of his persona, poesie. Poesie contains the theory and the causes of all knowledge, as Aristotelian metaphysics must by definition; but Sidney's definitions of an architectonic metaphysics are here stated as metaphors. Poesie is "the first light-giver to ignorance," the "treasure-house of science" (p. 74). The philosophers of Greece were poets or wore the masks of poets, including Solon the wise and Plato. The body of their work, he says, "though the inside and strength were philosophy, the skin, as it were, and beauty depended most on poetry" (p. 75). Herodotus, who entitled his history with the names of the nine Muses, appropriated them, Sidney remarks, and usurped poetry in the passionate descriptions of human feelings and the particularities of battle (p. 75). Then, in conclusion, Sidney affirms Aristotle's view that poets were "the ancient treasurers of the Grecians' divinity" (p. 121). Hesiod and Homer testify that all knowledge, in the form of fables, is given by God to man (p. 121).

Sidney's interweaving of classical and Christian antiquity with his definition of architectonic poesie leads him to pay tribute to the *philosophia Christi* that John Calvin had defined essentially as the exposition of the Word of God. "Holy David's Psalms," Sidney says, "are a divine poem" full of "notable *prosopopoeias*" (p. 77). "Our Saviour Christ" is Sidney's prototype for the making of *eikastic* images and architectonic poetic fables out of our *phantastic* selves, for Christ could have spoken in "moral commonplaces" instead of "divine narrations" and "instructing parables" (p. 87). Since poetry is "comparable" to philosophy in moral doctrine, "the chief of all knowledges," and better at moving the accomplishment of its truth, and "since the Holy Scripture (wherein there is no uncleanness) hath whole parts in it poetical, and that even our Saviour Christ vouchsafed to use the flowers of it," poetry experientially triumphs over mere knowledge (p. 99). The dismissal of the architectonic mistress-knowledge from the English church and commonwealth as if poetry were merely the gorgeous architecture of a false rhetoric would be a denial of the greatest truth. The exercise of a philosophical poesie with its knowledge of the first, "golden" principles of the architectonic consideration will, however, bring the exercise of all other knowledges into line with the end of making a godly kingdom. Thus the *Defence* moves gracefully from Pugliano to Plato, from Aristotle to Elizabeth in telling the story of the character of poesie. If poesie is a prince of learning in the achievement of its greatest end, she is distinctly a female prince, a mistress-knowledge, and the poet who practices her art is a "triumphant captain," a war hero who is the agent of a Queen (p. 99). The poet and captain tend to merge with the mistress.[8]

Readers discover, therefore, that the rhetorical balance, the integrity, of the *Defence* relies on Sidney's image of three notable prosopopoeias. The architectonic poesie in the structure of the *Defence* stems from the ethos of the mistress-knowledge and her poet-consort. In the mistress-knowledge and poet-mastercraftsman Sidney revises, first of all, the long-standing analogy of the arts and sciences in the marriage of Mercury and Philology.[9] Sidney's imagination of the character of the poet as the statesman, soldier, and lover of the queenly art of public metamorphoses philosophical historiography into an Augustinian-Protestant image of the English statesman's moral union with the unmarried Queen to whom he offers the "body" of his military skills and the mind of his knowledge and governing power. The oratorical structure of the *Defence* includes the extension of this little love-fable to the reader's imagination, for the discovery of the character of the English poet enables the reader, too, to bring well-knowing to well-doing and so "bring in civility" (p. 121).

The text of the *Defence* (or of the *Apology*) has never completely fulfilled editorial expectations of the structure of a neat, sevenfold division of the classical oration because it was not composed as such.[10] Instead, the intertextuality of the *Defence* elaborates a metaphoric character of the poetic art in theory and in practice, abroad and at home, in the past and in the present as a political statement.[11] A binary dialectic of sustained confirmation and refutation also helps to generate the *Defence* in the formal disposition of Sidney's figures of antithesis, juxtaposition, and similitude so that style, subject, and structure merge.

The first half of the *Defence* (pp. 73–99) confirms the mistress-knowledge in Sidney's speaking picture of Plato's statesman-architect; the second half (pp. 99–121) refutes the charges made everywhere against poetry but especially details the state of the art in England. A Platonic philosophy dominates the *Defence* as Sidney weaves his twofold Aristotelian argument for the queenly poesie and princely poet around the conversion of Plato from an adversary to a patron of poetry in theory and in practice for the sake of reinstating the poet in the good republic of England. Part one of the *Defence* speaks of the "art," and part two of the "artificer" (p. 89), and Sidney rhetorically subordinates the texture of his argument in two modes—*logos* and *pathos*—to the third mode, *ethos*. This feature of the *Defence* reinforces its disposition into confirmation and refutation, or the appropriately antithetical structure of a disputation, while presenting the analogical images of the art and the artificer, the personifications of the mistress-knowledge and the statesman-poet. Cyrus is present between them as their "product," the changed reader.

Sidney's *argument* reflects the logical tasks of affirming and denying; his *method* mixes a bifocal rhetoric of general principles and particular images and of analogy and antithesis with Cicero's recommendations for the rhetorical confirmation of a character in the *De Inventione*. He fleshes out the dialectical process experientially, as it were, in the coupling of the two prosopopoeias whose characters fulfill the rhetorical expectations of Cicero's recommendation of a person's attributes, and the *Defence* itself exemplifies one of the speeches of this new English poetic characterization being made. Since the attributes of a person rhetorically define the adjuncts of a subject, the metaphors of the *Defence* confirm an elaborately metonymic speaking subject in Sidney's voice. Together poet-statesman and lady poesie constitute his *eikastic* proportion of the national character of the poetic art. The eloquence of the *Defence* turns on their mythic personifica-tion as one couple, and Sidney probably would not have conceived this apology for poetry without a woman on the throne of England—a woman who was considering matrimony to a French prince whom many En-glishmen considered an unsuitable match.

Thus, to begin with, Sidney follows the Ciceronian pattern and names his masks "the mistress-knowledge" and the "maker." Their English names lead to recognition of their nature and origin in an ancient, noble line of the learned; the testimonies of every nation and of antiquity acknowledge the good manner of life encouraged by the poetic art. Poesie has had good fortune in every nation, similarly, because of her habit of persuasion; with a "heart-ravishing knowledge" she moves human feeling. Her interests re-veal intellectual universality, for she is "the treasure-house of science" who transcends mere nature. The reason for her existence is the practice of divine sovereignty over all the other knowledges, for she achieves proximately what all the others seek ultimately—the architectonic end of self-knowledge in the ethic and politic consideration. She is the economy, the union of private and public purposes, in England. The achievement of poesie may be seen in several categories—divine, philosophical, and inventive—and in many parts. Nevertheless, because of the accidents of verse, the falsification of poetic truth, and the abuses of poor writers, poesie has met with slander. She is accused of temporizing, deceitfulness, phantasy, and bad politics; she has made few speeches in England, and fewer still have been well attended. The product of her art in England, "like an unmannerly daughter showing a bad education, causeth her mother Poesy's honesty to be called in question" (p. 116). What poesie obviously needs to set her household right is the "right" poet-statesman to make her art fruitful again, and the proof of her regeneration lies in the production of heroes to make other heroes and not "castles in the air."

Sidney's argument confirms poesie, for the most part, in the portion of the *Defence* that editors designate *narratio*. In fact, though, the argument from etymology, the argument from comparison of the arts and sciences, and the argument of the analogies of nature and second nature, zodiac and wit, maker and Maker cannot belong to a conventional *narratio*. Thomas Wilson defined narration as "an euident setting forth of all things" in "a breefe rehersall," that is, a general description of contents. Confirmation is, rather, a complete development of thought, "a declaration of our owne reasons, with assured and constant proofes" (*Arte of Rhetorique*, p. 7). Sidney's confirming arguments lead directly, moreover, to the refuting arguments in which he answers the charges made against poesie and her practitioner, the poet, by way of educating the English reader on the nature of the art of poesie and the uses and limitations of genres, conventions, allegory, and style.

Obviously, the likely literary model for Sidney's organization of the *Defence* according to the Ciceronian attributes for invention of ethos was, in the sixteenth century, Erasmus's *Praise of Folly*—a text teasing the Platonic flattery that uses pleasure to bait folly (*Gorgias* 464d) and exemplifying the ironic character invention and transformation Sidney praises. The antitype of the feminine Wisdom of Proverbs who builds her house and sets her table, human folly literally destroys "hers" (Proverbs 9:1; 14:1) while Erasmus's allegorical Folly actually destroys to good purpose the rhetorical building of her own speech through irony. Sidney honors Erasmus early in the refutation because the "commending of folly" as a kind of wisdom discloses in Erasmus's contraries, in the doubling of his ironies, the seriousness of the "foundation" of his argument (*Def.*, p. 100).[12] Erasmus's Folly gradually dismantles her own false self-love and human traditions in order to preach truly the Word of God. Folly is Erasmus's version of Plato's ladder in the *Symposium*; she begins in mockery and rises to the mystical status of the wise folly of the love of Christ of First Corinthians.

Textually, Erasmus's splendid rhetoric begins in contraries he develops in ironic doubling but ends in the sublime contradiction that is nevertheless true—the paradox of incarnation and redemption, which is a "stoumbling blocke" to the Jews who want signs and miracles and "foolishness" to the Greeks who want wisdom (1 Corinthians 1:22–24, Geneva). In this way Erasmus's Folly follows the foolishness of Saint Paul, which was "preaching" (1 Corinthians 1:21). So, too, the poet Sidney, in the speaking of the *Defence*, preaches the folly of poetry—as if poets were the inheritors of fools—into the praise of its "sacred mystery" with the same aplomb with which his ironies, his *sprezzatura*, toss off this "ink-wasting toy" in Calvinist good faith (*Def.*, pp. 120–21). The oratorical attitude of the sixteenth century appears in Erasmus's shift *away* from the dialogic nature of the classical treatise, in which characters spoke out to one another, and toward a voiced persona that spoke out of the text to an audience. Erasmus's oration gets more credit from Sidney than Saint Thomas More's dialogue, *Utopia*, and for this reason modern critics ought to take care not to confuse our contemporary interest in dialogic forms with the rhetorical emphasis on speech-making in Sidney's effort to center himself in the pitch of an authoritative voice. Erasmus was the great renaissance exponent of the *philosophia Christi*, the author of *The Institutions of the Christian Prince* and the *Enchiridion*, the image of the good Christian soldier, in which he proposed a rule for reading the pagan classics.[13] Sidney composes his *Defence* to suit this rhetorical model and contemporary authority. Thus the verbal architecture of the seven-part oration, and even that of the five-part speech of judicial rhetoric used in defense, recedes formally in Sidney's treatise as the architectonic prosopopoeias who together represent the English ethos of a master-building poetic advance in Sidney's counterpoint.

The folly of the *Defence* analogizes cleverly to that of the wooing courtier, and we should wonder whether Sidney prefers the appearance of spontaneous and sincere pronunciation to the architecture of the seven-part oration for explicit historical reasons. In 1579 the author of *The Arte of Rhetorique*, Thomas Wilson, was secretary of state; in 1576 he had been ambassador to the Netherlands engaged in negotiations for the projected marriage of Elizabeth (*Arte of Rhetorique*, p. xii), which Sidney and his family opposed. Wilson had explained in his *Arte of Rhetorique* that unless an orator had "vtterance" or pronunciation to "speake his minde" and frame his voice, gesture, and countenance in a comely way, his finding out of "good matter and good wordes," his "handsomely" setting of them together and carrying of them "very well awaie in his minde," was to no purpose (p. 6). But Sidney's "vtterance" turns the folly of the wooing courtier to such a good purpose. The apparently light tone that the soldierly speaker adopts in his treatment of the poetic art, especially in the conclusion of the *Defence*, conceals in metaphor the serious wisdom of his arguments. The remarkable unity of the text is demonstrated in Sidney's merging of his recommended style of antithesis—setting off the right by the oblique, the even by the odd, the virtuous by the vicious, and the wisdom of learning by good fooling—and the analogies that "make" images and dismantle them with the larger, bipartite structure of confirmation and refutation, general principle and particular application, theory and practice (*Def.*, p. 96).

Where other orators give the audience a single speaker, Sidney gives his single speaker a multiplicity of authoritative voices in one harmony. He especially presents the binary pair of man and woman, statesman-architect and queenly art, ethical knowledge and political power, in the intertwining of confirmation and refutation. This is Sidney's "feeling proof," in Astrophil's phrase (*A & S* 102), his courtly persuasion in which both his love and his desire for useful power and purpose are revealed. Speaking for himself and his family, the oratorical Sidney also dares to speak for the nation.

Just as Sidney's composition in the *Defence* eschews the modern fragmentation of voices in dialogism, whether conscious or unconscious, for the sake of a ladder of gradual approximation to the "truth" of poesie, so does the dominant genre of the *Defence* resist the realization of his characters to the point of turning his treatise into theater. Sidney's mistress-knowledge remains a prosopopoeia, a figure of similitude in an oration. She is not, like

Erasmus's Folly, distinctly separate from Sidney in characterization; nor is she, in Sidney's political parallels, exactly the Queen—although she comes perilously close to that reference and such proximity controls the allusion to Boethius who was, in prison, comforted by Lady Philosophy. Much has been made in social history of late about Sidney's troubles at court; in literary focus, however, the personal, historical tensions of his structurally architectonic metaphor in the *Defence* are contained by it; Sidney establishes poesie as a moral force of judgment that falls precisely *between* the visions of the golden world, on one hand, and the shadows of this brazen one. In Sidney's speech the feminine poesie *is* a "character" of the poet when he is "lifted up in the vigour of his own invention" and able to "grow in effect another nature" that makes things "either better than nature bringeth forth, or, quite anew" (*Def.*, p. 79).

The moral coupling of the erected wit of the poet with the mistress-knowledge produces characters for the godly kingdom, including the character of the speaker—namely, those true lovers, constant friends, valiant men, right princes, and excellent human beings that invention *delivers* into the light of this foolish world:

> For any understanding knoweth the skill of each artificer standeth in that *idea* or fore-conceit of the work, and not in the work itself. . . . Which delivering forth is not wholly imaginative, as we are wont to say by them that build castles in the air; but so far substantially it worketh, not only to make Cyrus . . . but to bestow a Cyrus upon the world to make many Cyruses. (P. 79)

As Fulke Greville would later say, "In all these creatures of his [Sidney's] making, his intent, and scope was, to turn the barren Philosophy precepts into pregnant images of life" (*Life of Sidney*, p. 18). When we consider the particular historical circumstances in which Sidney composed his vision of the poetic art, therefore, we can see the boldness of his effort to influence the brazen world of late sixteenth-century England—and why he might seek comfort from a Queen. Politically Sidney aims to persuade the Queen to see herself and her best national interests in the character of this poetic Cyrus; while Sidney argues her advocacy of him, he also argues her superiority in herself in a "marriage" to the English people.

The metaphoric diction of the *Defence* shares numerous parallels with the language of Sidney's *Letter written . . . to Queen Elizabeth* against her proposed marriage to Alençon.[14] This letter defends the particular interests of a Protestant church and nation by arguing that the English people are the true lovers and legitimate children of the unmarried Queen. The only "fortress" of the Queen's plan to marry the Frenchman is a "private affection" that is "too incident" to her person. Thus Sidney appeals to her statesmanship on the grounds of her already established English household. His courtly wooing enters the realm of moral counsel:

Your inward force (for as your treasures, indeede the sinews of your crown, your Majesty doth best and only know) consisteth in your subjects. . . . Virtue and justice are the only bands of the people's love. . . . Not that I deny the bliss of children, but only mean to show religion and equity to be of themselves sufficient stays. . . . I leave it in you, to the sincereness of your own conscience, and wisdom of your judgement in the world. . . . Let those in whom you find trust, and to whom you have committed trust in your weighty affairs, be held up in the eyes of your subjects. Lastly doing as you do, you shall be as you be: the example of princes . . . and the perfect mirror to your posterity. (*Letter,* passim)

In the process of appealing to the Queen's "conscience" and "wisdom" of self-knowing, Sidney also appeals to his own "imagination" (p. 53) and to the "love" that forms the likeness of the Queen in her people's hearts. He writes, "No, no, most excellent lady, do not raze out the impression you have made in such a multitude of hearts" (pp. 55–56). The propagation of the image of the Queen's "virtue" constitutes the fruitfulness of her reign; but her true partners in this generative power are those trustworthy statesmen to whom she has committed her weighty affairs. The Queen must stand alone, but with her will stand the people, the nation, and the church that will fall if she marries the Duke: "I do with most humble heart say unto your Majesty that, laying aside this dangerous help, for your standing alone, you must take it as a singular honour God hath done unto you, to be indeed the only protector of his church" (p. 56).

The *Defence* differs from the *Letter* in intention, certainly, but Sidney's idea of the poet corresponds to the English statesmanship he practiced in his advice to Queen Elizabeth. If the *Defence* was written shortly after the *Letter,* while Sidney was in voluntary "banishment" from court during Elizabeth's weighing of the matter, the Boethian model of discourse that seeks comfort from Lady Philosophy and the Erasmian model of oratory that seeks to transform Folly into Wisdom together help explain the tone of Sidney's *Defence.* The *Letter* appeals to the Queen *not* to flesh out in behavior the contemptible image of her that her slanderers speak (pp. 53, 55). The *Defence,* using an architectonic philosophy of religion, conscience, knowledge, and illuminating speech, describes the true sovereignty of poesie in her production of virtuous characters—beginning with the transformation of a "courtesan-like painted affectation" back into the "honey-flowing matron Eloquence" in poetry itself (*Def.,* p. 117). So, too, in the *Letter,* Sidney had asked the Queen not to go about in a disguise in the souls of her subjects where love has impressed her image, "so if anything can stain so true a form it must be the bringing yourself not in your own likeness, but in new colours unto them" (*Letter,* p. 56). "The mistress-knowledge," Sidney explains, "stands in" the self-knowledge of the "erected wit" of the poet-statesman who overcomes with his ethical and political considerations in images and measures the "infected will" (*Def.,* pp. 82–83). In practice, the architectonic art of love by means of which her Majesty and English statesmen can generate a heroic citizenry through the "poetic" reproduction of a stable and godly rule is an economy that transcends the building of a "fortress" and the protection of "Ajax's shield" that Monsieur offers to "stead" Elizabeth. Ajax's shield "weighed down" rather than defended those that bore it (*Letter*, pp. 53 56). Thus Sidney's application of an architectonic philosophy interprets moral and political precepts in the actual historical moment.[15]

In *The Life of the Renowned Sr Philip Sidney*, Fulke Greville, Lord Brooke, identified the Protestant League and the *Letter* to the Queen as the first two significant actions of Sidney's public service. In them Sidney "so sweetly yoaked fame and conscience together in his large heart" (p. 47). The "league of Religion" intended to associate several Protestant nations "by an uniform bond of conscience, for the protection . . . of Religion and Liberty," and it was "the first prize which did enfranchise this Master Spirit into the mysteries, and affairs of State" (p. 53). Of two other public actions—"the Heroicall design of invading, and possessing America" and the encounter with Spain "at the specially vulnerable spot of Flanders" (*Life of Sidney*, pp. 90–91)—the first did not, in the end, include Sidney, and the second took his life. By Greville's testimony, however, conscience centered both Sidney's knowledge and his action. Whatever else the *Defence* may be as a text—a reading list, a *ratio studiorum*, an exposition of rhetorical theory and literary criticism, an arts debate—it is the historical definition of the politically architectonic art of poesie as the art of conscientious judgment. Greville calls such art "this Characteristicall kind of Poesie. . . . For that this representing of vertues, vices, humours, counsells, and actions of men unfeigned and in scandalous Images, is an inabling of freeborn spirits to the greatest affaires of States" (p. 2). If the poet Sidney made an Augustinian effort to re-create characters embroiled in history, and if such an effort daringly took him to the task of instructing the conscience of the Queen herself, so much the better. Presenting a moral mirror to the Prince is an old tradition in Sidney's book, even if the courtier's accomplishment of his duty in this literary unity of truth might well be his own heroic life and death.

Lady Philosophy and the Chaste City of God

Besides the literary conventions of the *speculum principis* expressed in Sidney's *Letter*, recognition of the binary interplay of Sidney's personifications with the rhetorical confirmation and refutation of his cultural fable links the *Defence* to two ancient Christian images that thrived in the Middle Ages. Sidney's mistress-knowledge is the cultural descendant of Boethius's Lady Philosophy, whom he transforms into a mirror of the Elizabeth who translated Boethius, and of Saint Augustine's more complex, biblical, and feminine metaphor of the City of God and man's inward journey home to her. Augustine's created wisdom is "the rationall mind and an intellectuall

[one] of that chast City . . . our mother which is above and free," the lightsome house and "place of habitation" of the Lord, her "builder and owner," the uncreated Wisdom (*Conf.* 12.15).[16] Augustine's created wisdom and Boethius's Lady Philosophy, besides personifying for their authors— exiles and prisoners on earth—the subordination of classical thought to divine revelation, represented versions of the feminine wisdom that existed before creation, playing before God as God's own mastercraftsman in the dawn of the world. She is kept allegorically distinct from the person of divine Wisdom in the Word, the Christ, but relates to him as the mediate image between divine and human knowledge. Augustine's idea of created wisdom embodied a Christian concept of the liberal arts and supported a Boethian view of Lady Philosophy's architectonic speech in the medieval educational program and in renaissance humanism.[17] Both, similarly, helped renaissance thinkers, including Sidney, to develop the ambivalence of an architectonic poetic: the balancing of poetic structure and form that parallels, in turn, the tension between human efforts to build truly an earthly city of man and to edify or illuminate the human mind on its journey home to the maternal City of God.[18] A feminized *Natura* imprisons while an androgynized art liberates.

In function if not in explicit definition, the voice that brought Boethius the visionary comfort of truth in the *Philosophiae Consolationis* was the voice of a philosophical poesie. In her speeches, Lady Philosophy actually integrates the arts and sciences in the structure of her argument; she gathers up their knowledge to console Boethius through self-knowledge. The consolation effects a moral liberation of Boethius's mind while he languishes in the prison that architecturally limits the movements of his body. As she interweaves the principles of grammar and number, rhetoric and music, Lady Philosophy enlightens Boethius's mind; her organization of knowledge simultaneously constitutes a whole greater than the sum of its parts, for her illumination of his mind aims also at the catharsis of his grief and at the moral effect of a change of heart. Sometimes Lady Philosophy speaks in verse, sometimes in prose. Her own attitude toward poetry is bifocal. Initially she dismisses the Muses of poetry from Boethius's chamber because they are *scenicas meretriculas*, prostitutions of truth.[19] However, when she herself practices poetry, whether in verse or in prose, the poetic act of composition—analogous both to grammar and to music—produces exactly the intellectual and moral congruence she desires in order to teach, comfort, and move her audience. Her reordering of thought according to the Christian doctrine of divine providence makes her linguistic activity poetically architectonic—that is, illuminating and re-creational—for the mind and character of Boethius.[20]

In medieval thought Lady Philosophy inexhaustibly imaged the prudential wisdom that served divine sapience while arranging all other knowledges under her dominion. The *Philosophiae Consolationis* allegorically sustained in this fashion a vivid personification of philosophy that the fourteenth-century poet Geoffrey Chaucer and the seventeenth century poet Henry Vaughan could reinterpret and that Sidney did reimagine in the *Defence*. Centurion approved the link between learning and language and Christian wisdom that her image presented, and the translation of Boethius by Queen Elizabeth, in which she took great pride, would give English writers of the 1590s a special reason to appeal to the Queen's Boethian learning.[21] As Sidney had called poetry "the first nurse" of learning and challenged the harlotry of her mother, Eloquence (*Def.*, pp. 74, 117), the Queen's Lady Philosophy severely criticizes whoever let the Muses—"these stagis harlots"—approach Boethius, and she firmly interrogates him: " 'Art thou the same,' quoth she, / 'Who ons nourriched with my milke, fed with our foode art growen to strength of manly mynd?' " (pp. 3, 5). In a Platonic fashion Lady Philosophy's image implied an allegorical conflict between the architecture of a civilization that encloses the human spirit and the statesmanlike architectonics, the learned speaking that might illumine human understanding and liberate moral character.

If anybody loved this maternal Lady Philosophy, the "renaissance Plato" did, for a philosophical *poesis* dramatically communicated Plato's contrast of edifices and human beings in her enlightened stimulation of character-building. Lady Philosophy, Sidney explains, often borrows the "masking raiment" of Lady Poesie, "as Plato and Boethius well knew" (*Def.*, p. 93). Thus his mistress-knowledge will also play the queenly consort of the poet and help him to build in thoughts a lively, encyclopedic representation of civic liberty or wisdom or justice. The androcentric poems produced, in turn, provoke the reader's desire to know the truth and lead to the visionary realization of liberty in the reader's character.[22] Shakespeare's Prince Hamlet would later explain what happens when one does *not* follow her lead. With Lady Philosophy, one could be "bounded in a nutshell" and consider oneself "a king of infinite space"; without her, thinking and dreaming go morally awry, and even a prince can be prisoner of conscience in his mind or a whole country function as a prison.[23]

How a philosophical mistress-knowledge might liberate from prisons of the body and mind and lead freely to wisdom seems largely attributable to Saint Augustine. Standing above all ancient texts for renaissance poets were the fables and characters of Holy Scripture, now in the vernacular. But threading through the legacy of medieval literature was the knowledge, too, of Augustinian classics—the *Confessions*, the *De Civitate Dei*, and the *De Doctrina Christiana*—that helped renaissance readers recognize and imitate what Dante, Chaucer, and Langland had begun to define in poetry: the rule of Christian history. Augustine was not the only Father of the Church whose works were reedited and translated in the renaissance textual recovery of the *philosophia Christi*, but his strong presence in the Middle Ages and his strong influence in the Reformation lent weight and familiarity to the appearance of his doctrines in renaissance garb.[24] In the long history of significant revisions of the architectonic metaphor, his thought is singularly representative.[25] If Augustine's *Confessions* is the autobiographical record of one soul's return from exile, the *De Civitate Dei* is a blueprint of the City built not stone by stone but soul by soul. Similarly, the essay *De Doctrina Christiana*, a treatise on exegesis, is Augustine's handbook for Christianizing civilization by incorporating the arts into the hearing and doing of the Word of God. These three texts alone show how Augustine transformed the classical architectonic concept by shifting the ethical and political weight of knowing and doing the good to the inner event of moral and intellectual wayfaring in the Word. Augustinian architectonics is the hearing and doing of the Word in the earthly city for the sake of union with God in the mind of wisdom that is God's City—or society ideally imaged, to some extent, in the Church or, in the case of the godly kingdom of renaissance England, in the theocracy. "Let them [the ministers of God] be a pattern to the faithful by living before them and by arousing them to imitation. For thus do men truly hear, not merely to hear, but also to do" (*Conf.* 13.21, trans. Ryan, pp. 353–54).

Augustine longed to reenter the "rationall and intellectual mind" of the City of God, the mind which he saw as the "mother" of human nature and the dwelling-place of the divine Builder from whom he keenly felt exiled (*Conf.* 12.15). In his discovery of self-knowledge, Augustine cried out for congruence between the created wisdom—biblically envisioned playing before God in the morning of the world and implementing the divine architecture of all things—and the human mind that could know things.[26] The significance of Augustine's earthly pilgrimage rested in the successful discovery of the analogy between human knowledge and the person of divine Truth, the Word, who could be met in this mediate "place," the mind of the City of God. The moral recovery in Augustine's life of the vision of wisdom that allowed the congruence of his mind with the mind of the chaste City of God, similarly, depended on grace and love, not merely the efforts of human reason.[27]

The medieval Augustine touched learning, monasticism, statesmanship, and the arts to a degree that allowed one version of his thought to be debated by another. The renaissance Augustine provoked similarly diverse interpretations. Juan Luis Vives, the Spanish humanist, applied Augustine's view of wisdom to education and glossed the *De Civitate Dei*. Saint Thomas More, future chancellor of England, lectured on the *De Civitate Dei* in a parish church in London, composed the *Utopia*, and cultivated self-knowledge as a principle of moral and political integrity that led him to his death. Thomas

Cranmer, Archbishop of Canterbury, possessed the standard renaissance edition of Augustine's writings in ten volumes and selectively made marginal notes on, for example, the treatment of heretics and the suffering of persecution.[28]

In the Renaissance at large, one has to recognize the great influence of Saint Augustine on Ficino in the very way Ficino promoted Plato. Ficino sustained a Platonic-Augustinian emphasis on spiritual discovery and practical application when he imagined the physical construction of city monuments and the earthly city. Evoking the favorite renaissance commonplace of contemplation and action, Ficino's comments on Plato's *Republic* and other political dialogues include a series of similes drawn from Aristotelian and scholastic philosophy to say that the contemplative discovery of the "ideal" city is preferable to the active production of cities in the here and now. But the manner in which his vivid imagery presents the hierarchy of value almost subverts it in the midst of the actual building program of civic humanism in Italy. Ficino balances the building of "ideal" and "actual" cities:

For which reason our Plato is more excellent, at least, than the other founders of cities and laws, because the rest of mankind builds the city for great action but he, himself truly like God, carries through the action of the city in everything public and private for the sake of the most powerful contemplation; and he establishes the ideal city before he sets up the rule of his own actual world not because he fears public opinion but because he respects all nations and forms a heavenly Jerusalem for men on earth.[29]

Although Ficino gives contemplation priority by defining it as the highest action of the human being, his recognition that Plato's ideal act of thought in the *Republic* can help generate an image of "heaven on earth" reveals a practical renaissance application of the Augustinian idea that the City of God is being built in human history and that those who build it in thought and language are like God. Contemplation is indeed the highest action of the mind, which mounts on its wings to the vision of the new Jerusalem; but then the mind necessarily returns to the actual world with a visionary pattern to model the "rule" of men for "great action." Ficino's philosophy, in short, supports both the intellectual renovation of a lost Eden and the poetic shaping of a visionary Jerusalem as types of earthly paradise revealing a glimpse of the City of God. His philosophy confirmed the building projects of architects and statesmen who sought to "copy" the idea by constructing models of the types; it undergirded the verbal patterning of philosophical vision in the fables of renaissance poets. What is more, in his commentary on the *Symposium* Ficino wrote a Christian praise of chaste male bonding in the character of the androgyne to personify justice in ways that echo Augustine's long search for chastity. The balancing of the powers of contemplation and action, theory and practice, appears in the Ficinian effort to equalize or even neutralize sexual powers, too.[30]

The later renaissance edition of *Plato* by Jean de Serres explicitly acknowledged Saint Augustine in the interpretation of the same philosophy as de Serres seeks an even more combinatory synthesis. Headnoting the text of the *Platonis Opera Quae Extant Omnia* of 1578 is the passage from the *De Civitate Dei* that explains why Plato's philosophy is perfect: the study or pursuit of wisdom is *both* active and contemplative. To Plato is given the praise of having perfected philosophy by combining the two into one (*De Civ. Dei* 8.4; *Platonis Opera* sig. ***.iii*). The quotation by de Serres apparently counters Ficino's scholastic emphasis on the superiority of contemplation by highlighting the Augustinian experience of the philosophical quest as a pilgrimage during which the mind brings knowledge to virtue, well-knowing to well-doing. Both translators, however, arrange contemplation and action in hierarchical orders that require, at some point, the exercise of contemplation and action. Where Ficino gives contemplation a metaphysical priority of time and place, de Serres prefers action for historical and moral-philosophical reasons. All of de Serres's argument leads from the defense of contemplation to the philosophical activity of the graced mind that strives to realize the discovered truth in a present historical moment. For this reason de Serres subordinates his scholarly achievement to the persuasion of two living monarchs, Queen Elizabeth of England and James VI of Scotland, the builders and philosopher-princes of a true Christian commonwealth, and to the citizenry of Berne, and he sends a copy of the *Plato* to Sidney. De Serres's triple dedication reflects his sense of the delicate political gender balance in England and his vision of the production or generation of good citizens. In his English character, as I shall explain in the next chapter, Sidney will reinterpret both the French philosophy and the Protestant heroism of the martyred Coligny presented by de Serres.

In the commentary on the *Symposium*, as we might expect, de Serres tips the gender balancing of love toward patriarchy and counters Ficino's praise of the chaste androgyne with a moral condemnation of the pederast and of the "man-woman" as Egyptian corruptions that had crept into Greek thought. He also exonerates the maleness of Socrates and Plato, blaming Aristophanes for the corruption (3:171). For him, the ladder of love inscribes the orthodox hierarchy of the productive Calvinist household and township and certainly not the celibate priesthood of religion, knowledge, and art that Ficino praised. In Augustine the verbal sojourn of philosophy changed the classical vision of a supreme self-knowledge engaged in knowing and doing the good in the building of the state to the rhetorical ethic of building an inner paradise of the mind by hearing the Word of God and then performing it in one's public and private life according to one's vocation. But Augustine imaged that vocation as a journey of integration in which one rejected "effeminate" carnality and was assimilated into the feminine City of God. If one's call was that of a poet and one read de Serres's synthesis of philosophy, the vocation itself enforced an intellectual compulsion to seek the light in one's chaste words and just deeds.[31]

Sidney's *Defence of Poesie* is permeated with Augustinian assumptions that he has rewritten and condensed into an English version of the treatise on the liberal arts or the Christian doctrine of poesie. First of all, Sidney assumes the Augustinian as well as the Basilian commonplace for reading and interpreting. Scripture is the divine poem in which the Author has used similitudes the way a teacher does with children, playing with us and powerfully healing our "inward eyes" by smearing them, as it were, with "clay."[32] By reading the similitudes or analogies correctly, both in the world of things and in books, we may make our way back to the clear vision of God. That "unspeakable and everlasting beauty," Sidney also says, is "to be seen by the eyes of the mind, only cleared by faith" (*Def.*, p. 77). For him, Augustinian thought required the philosopher-poet-reader to read through the allegorical mystery of things to the very truth of God in the way the reader of a poem interprets its fiction as a "profitable invention" (*Def.*, p. 103). Since learning, like everything else but God, was not to be gained for its own sake but was to be "used" for the sake of understanding the invisible things of God through visible things in order to "enjoy" God alone, Augustinian judgment also influenced Sidney's idea of the "ending end of all earthly learning" (*Def.*, p. 83). The cleansing of the visionary mind was not so much a possession of wisdom as it was a "voyage home" advanced by good endeavors and habits (*De Doct. Christ.* 1.10, trans. Robertson, p. 13). Without the aid of Christ the Teacher, the return home would be impossible; but the same Christ—Wisdom, Word, and Way—justified learning if it corresponded to his truth, the truth of the incarnate Word. This truth of Christianity drives out the "wrong opinions of the Deity" and the "hurtful belief" and superstition that once justified the condemnation of poetry (*Def.*, p. 108).[33]

It is by the power of the Word in the Augustinian-Christian *rhetor*'s experience of the good life that eloquence brings moral victory to human nature on its journey home to Wisdom (*De Doct. Christ.* 4.12–13). In Sidney's terms, the architectonic proof of a moving poesie must assert self-knowledge most when the "balance of experience" shows that "the mathematician might draw forth a straight line with a crooked heart" (*Def.*, p. 82). The poet with his images of experience is preferable to the philosophers who, "shaking off superstition, brought in atheism" (*Def.*, p. 108).[34]

Thus Sidney also follows the Augustinian lead on the limited status of knowledge. Like Plato in the *Republic* and *Philebus* and Aristotle in the

Metaphysics, Augustine implies that there is an order among the kinds of knowledge reflecting the unified order of the world. Yet Augustine's orientation of the body of knowledge toward the exercise of the arts of discourse because of the primacy of love and for the sake of the kingdom of God changes the significance of that order.[35] Augustine praises Pythagoras, the exponent of cosmic parallels to rational order, for having taught government last, after all the other liberal arts, to disciples already educated.[36] For Augustine, however, government is not a master science, as it was for Plato's statesman-architect, for Aristotle's politician, or for Cicero's civic leader. Rather, statesmanship is, in theory, one more study to aid the mind in its ascent to God and, in practice, one more demonstration of the success of Christian justification in an individual who happens to be a "governor."[37] Augustine's master science has much more to do with journeying in love through the consciousness of time—both the time of the individual life and the history of the ages—and the ethical *rhetor* displaces the classical states-man.[38] Sidney's list of arts and sciences similarly revises a conventional and classical metaphysics to subordinate all knowledge to the Augustinian-Calvinist ethics of self-knowledge and the knowledge of God (*Def.,* pp. 82–83). The best politics is right speech.[39]

To explain this ethical priority, Sidney's Platonic-Augustinian theory of language and its images emphasizes the power of the poetic word to help distinguish truth from falsehood. The Socratic doctrine of *eikastic* and *phantastic* images in the *Defence* parallels the Augustinian description of the mind's discovery of the "inward" word. The work of the Augustinian master science begins with the injunction, "Know thyself," for self-knowledge embodies the likeness between the outward and the inward words of man in conjunction with the incarnate Word and Wisdom of God. Ultimately Sidney's idea of the "inward light" and the imagination (*Def.,* pp. 91, 85–86) reflects an Augustinian idea of verbal illumination. Created wisdom, the rational and intellectual mind of God's City, visually represents the Person of the Word and the Wisdom whom Augustine loves, but her personification *is* the house to which her architectonic art of journeying seeks to return him in memory.[40] The return to this wisdom of a true human likeness to God is the way the Augustinian-Christian poet participates in the building of the City of God in his own life and times because, as Sidney implies, he now has "the light of Christ" that pagan poets lacked.[41]

Finally, Sidney's idea of poetic power implies Augustine's doctrine of the two cities. Plato and Aristotle had turned the architectonic metaphor into a supervisory principle of knowledge and virtue; Cicero had shown that philosophical eloquence implemented that principle, and the orators were mastercraftsmen of civil order.[42] Augustine, however, turns the architectonic metaphor—already a contrast of architectural buildings to philosophical ones—into an antithesis of earthly and heavenly cities that dominates medieval and renaissance interpretations of the architectonic metaphor.[43] He then puts the antithesis at the service of a divinely ordained end: redemption, or the work of justification and sanctification in human history in which the city of man is not, theologically speaking, a city, but a zone of disaster, a ruin.[44] In Sidney's phrasing, the poet "builds" by ranging through the zodiac of his wit to correct the brazen world and to discover the golden world (*Def.*, p. 78). The two cities make a metaphor of contrast, an antithesis, for Augustine's architectonic metaphor is as much an antithesis as it is a comparison, and so are Sidney's metaphors of nature and art and of the brazen and golden worlds.

The lesson of the *De Civitate Dei* is that the triune God incarnated in the Word is the divine Architect who creates heaven and earth ex nihilo, who teaches human nature wisdom, who builds the City of true justice, and who dwells with humanity in time to give directions to each human being who must use history to fulfill appointed tasks.[45] Because of the Fall from paradise, human nature forfeited the integrity of its original architectonic prerogative to fill the earth and subdue it. Because of the Fall, therefore, no human architectonic art can develop education and statesmanship in the exercise of speech with any success, except with the aid of grace. Only in the Word of God might divine Wisdom and the architectonic knowledge of created wisdom produce for human beings a proper proportion, or analogue, between the worship of God and the ability to be good at knowing how to make yet other people good at knowing, *ad indefinitum*.

The Augustinian transformation of the classical ideal man produced, of course, a different concept of the hero, for Augustine's Christ is the unique Hero of human history and the saints are people who imitate him. In this perspective, the fruit of human knowledge in the city of man—both intellectual and moral constructions and the physical, architectural, and technological constructions that demonstrate knowledge of arts and sciences—is actually a by-product of the important architectonic art of raising up the soul. Human beings do not help build the heavenly City by erecting one stone upon another or by devising philosophies or by producing poetic structures but by obeying the divine Architect and by living the Word in exemplary patterns that other men and women are architectonically inspired to imitate (*Conf.* 13.21). By drawing the Wisdom who is Christ the Architect, the Word of God, into the operations of human life, learning, and history, Augustine synthesizes a philosophy of history based on ethical priority and makes the manufacture of Christian history the vocation of every Christian. Salvation history determines the analogical and antithetical relations of the two cities in time. In the proximate reality of one's historical moment, the Christian who strives to build up an earthly city according to his knowledge of Christian principles must remember that the true and lasting City he imitates is neither a republic of law and order nor a republic like Rome, but God's own temple (*De Civ. Dei* 10.3).

For this reason, as well as the historical one, the cities, republics, and societies of many renaissance poems compatible with Sidney's Augustinian aesthetics are imaged as ruins or works-in-progress or both. The Christian "workman" who is a poet knows that he does not know everything about the Architect's design of history. In this temple there is finally neither human buildings nor human wisdom but only godliness, "which offers due worship to the true God, and looks for its reward in the society of the saints, of holy angels as well as holy men" (14.28, trans. Dods, p. 477). This temple is the "living temple" of a holy society; its scriptural and patristic definition overthrows the balance of the classical architectonic metaphor and urges renaissance poems toward the disappearance of buildings of all kinds in the divine plenitude that invites poetic creation to participate in the fact that God is "all in all." The Christian poet, truly "like" God, may fashion an imitative temple in exemplary verbal and ethical patterns in his speech or, better yet, picture the failures in his quest for truth in his life. To read poetry was to do through unfinished texts and imperfectly realized or even comically distorted characters—one's cultural intersubjectivities—what one was supposed to do anyway in the living of history: read the signs set up *"between* the folly of man and the pure truth of God." Poets and readers alike need to interpret signs, and the external patterns of the poem can be distinctly composed as a fiction that enkindles the internal traces (in Augustine's sense, not Derrida's) of the Word in the reader who reads between ruin and re-creation.[46]

The poetry of architectural epistemology and the masking raiment of Lady Poesie as an English stateswoman in the *Defence* gradually expose a fine relationship between the Augustinian view of the inward light and Sidney's literary architectonics. Recognition of the feminine models of the mistress-knowledge in Christian antiquity, likewise, requires a rereading of the cultural materials out of which Sidney composed his vision of the heroism of the poet. Many of these materials have already been recognized in Sidneian scholarship; at issue here are their reinterpretation from a new perspective and the addition to them of several new sources. At the center of Sidney's intertextuality is a willingness to do *vraisemblance,* to think analogically, to condense complex philosophical statements in vivid images, and to draw significant parallels between the classical past and the sixteenth-century present in the name of self-knowledge. Other texts besides those of Cicero, Boethius, Augustine, and Erasmus cluster around Sidney's figure of the mistress-knowledge.

Philosophy, Fable, and Living Speech

To begin with, Plato's analogy of seeing and knowing in the *Republic* and Aristotle's law of contradiction in the *Metaphysics* undergird Sidney's trust in analogy and contribute to a renaissance sense of allegorical shadowing and figuring.[47] Sidney's version of the organic point of view of Greek thought is a philosophical principle of the relatedness of things to a knowing self. To say that one thing is like another but is not the other—to know who I am and to name as "other" all else that may exist and be named by me—is to think, to penetrate the darkness that clouds the mind and inhibits its decision to act. Between Plato's hypothesis, or leap of intuition, and Aristotle's hierarchy of intellectual virtues, Western thought has generally supposed a higher wisdom that, in turn, promotes a governing knowledge whose activity links all other, lesser knowledges to the good.[48] The higher knowledge of Boethius's Lady Philosophy and the Augustinian personification of the City of God describe hierarchical approaches to feminized versions of the highest consciousness. Such thinking encouraged the proliferation of images through its very elusiveness. How else could one articulate the idea of an intermediate knowledge, a knowledge most like supreme wisdom or most useful in attaining it through the quest, the pursuit of wisdom called philosophy?

Both classical and early Christian associations of Plato with Egyptian knowledge put an allegorical cast on the unity of truth that declared the workmanship of the world to the renaissance imagination.[49] The fact that King Solomon, the author of the grand allegory of divine and human love in the Song of Songs, was infamously libidinous perplexed those who wanted a simple and moral authority to control the relationship of a writer or a reader to a text. The Word of truth had taken an allegorical cast, which made a reifying closure on its unity almost impossible. The idea of unity was recapitulated in syncretic renaissance interpretations of myth, philosophy, history, and sacred Scripture as a matter of allegorical principle, moreover, and the allegory often took the form of personification.[50] Plato thought Prometheus possessed this intermediate knowledge that linked the arts and sciences (*Philebus* 16c). Erasmus compared Socrates to Christ much as Plato was compared to the Moses "most wise" from whom he learned everything.[51] Saint Justin Martyr, exemplar of the philosophical quest, explained the unity of truth in his idea of the *logos spermatikos*, and his *First* and *Second Apologies*, along with other samples of early Christian apologetical literature, informed reformation polemicism with a doctrine of the Word.[52] Arthur Golding, who translated Ovid's *Metamorphoses*, called it a "dark philosophy of changed shapes" and sought to demonstrate the origin of all the chief fables and characters of the poets in Moses' writing.[53] As personifications, Sidney's mistress-knowledge and poet-statesman belong to this long line of allegorical descent.

The great fable-maker of the Greeks, of course, was Homer. Homer's verb ποιειν, "to make," as often means "to build" in the *Iliad* and the *Odyssey* as "to compose poems," according to Liddell-Scott. Sidney rejoiced in the fact, "whether by luck or wisdom, we Englishmen have met with the Greeks in calling him [the poet] a maker" (*Def.*, p. 77). Appropriately, therefore, Sidney made Greek the natural language of the characters of his heroic poem, the *Arcadia*.[54] The poetic decorum of having the Greek language "spoken" in a "Greek" place and the invention of Greek names observe more than verisimilitude, for Sidney wanted his political fable to express the more significant issue raised by a Christian writer's imitation of the classics. May English poets, too, "make" men and "build" a kingdom now, and if so, how? The architectonic metaphor informed Homer's poetic images with a mythic declaration of the ambivalent human potential for destruction and edification, for war and education. Both the *Iliad* and the *Odyssey* originated the literary exposition of the full circle of knowledge, similarly, by using oral formulas to store and to retrieve the encyclopedia in narrative. But Sidney's interest in the *Arcadia* and in the *Defence* was in the moral peopling of a kingdom. He wanted to turn the architectonics of the past into a renaissance Christian civilization by building the moral history of the present in the image of imperfect characters who need to spend time becoming better men and women through contemplation *and* action.[55]

Sidney could have constructed texts so pleasantly provoking the English imagination to the building of a godly Christian nation instead of a Stoic empire only if he had thought through the classical models of such literature and re-created them according to renaissance Christian differences. The *Defence* represents such a thinking through. In the *Defence*, history touched moral philosophy in his imagination, and both were transcended by the intertextuality of his poetic fable-making. The integrity of the *Defence* in its pronunciation of speech is precisely Sidney's articulation of myriad learned textual references and literary allusions in the apparently unified, simple "intersubjectivity" of his own voice. Critically, what has been the delight of the philologist in reading the *Defence* is really the art of the poet telling his "story." This narrator is less a divided or decentralized self than he is a Daedalean craftsman, a most self-conscious great deceiver of tyranny, which ought to be deceived. In Sidney's oratorical utterance in the *Defence*, we hear the soundings of a transcending ego who simultaneously records the dangers of such self-elevation. Sidney flies high through human knowledge but does not sever his duplicity of self-knowledge from the superior standard of truth in the Word.

Yet even Krieger says that Sidney merely gracefully compiles Italian literary criticism and fails to construct for these commonplaces an original philosophical framework.[56] On the contrary, the economy of metaphor *is the structural economy of the literary house of intellect that Sidney's inter textuality builds as his argument in the Defence*. Metaphor operates by sustaining the tension of similitude, by appearing to identify significance with one side, only to reverse direction suddenly, and by generating other similitudes that reinforce, deny, or qualify the original perception of sameness with an awareness of difference. The architectonic metaphor of self-knowledge extended allegorically through the personifications of the *Defence* reveals Sidney's composing power and integrates various metaphoric subtexts in his discourse. He writes with an epistemological sense of science and art and their limits as accurate as the alchemist's experimental measuring of substances, on the one hand, and as deftly combinatory as nature's ability to generate, on the other. This "bravery of mind" in his practice of genesis and analysis, composition and reading, constitutes the intertextual and imaginative philosophical integrity of the *Defence*.

Perhaps it is exaggerating to say that Sidney "reformed" Homer in the *Arcadia*, but his mythos of moral philosophy, historical narrative, and poetic invention in the *Defence* certainly refashioned the histories of Herodotus and Xenophon. Herodotus used history to explore ideas and to make an encyclopedic record of civilization as it was then known. Documenting the status of various arts and sciences, including architecture, in the larger work of history, Herodotus effectively presented the expression of all knowledge in the image of the hero and in the representation of his life and times.[57] The Renaissance rewarded his idea by considering his historical writing the habitation of the Muses. Henri Estienne, the famous scholar-publisher who made gifts of books to the young Philip Sidney and whom Sidney met, wrote an *Apologia pro Herodoto* in which ancient historians and poets were compared with one another and then with the authorship of Holy Scripture—another kind of historical poem—to defend fables and the fabulous.[58] The introduction to the *Apologia*, an antipapist treatise, advertised "the conformities of ancient and modern wonders"; Estienne turned Herodotus's fables to contemporary political use.[59] Another arts debate emerged in the English translation of Herodotus in 1584 that was attributed to Barnabe Rich. The letter dedicatory to Robert Dormer marked the "counterfeiting" ability of history with a pictorial analogy:

Such were the dayes, then, and the people so farre enamored with the Arte of Paynting, that to have skyll in the draught of shadowes, and the apt framing of pictures, was deemed the best quality that could rest in a Gentleman. . . . [Yet] so lyuely in many things and so evident in all things is the pleasaunt discourse of hystories, that a better counterfayte may be drawne wyth two pen full of inckes in

Herodotus tale, then with two potfull of colours in Apelles table. (*The Famous Hystory of Herodotus*, sig. Aij)

The written form of verbal "characters"—letters on a page—accompanied the moral development of human character in the image of heroic lives and lent writing an artistic superiority. Sidney endorsed such a view in his handling of Xenophon's Cyrus and Homer's Achilles, whose image Alexander carried into the field.

In the pattern of Alexander recorded in "dead Homer,"or in any other heroic comparison, Sidney found something better than the definition of fortitude by the "living Aristotle" (*Def.*, p. 106). Even in such a pattern, however, metaphor remains an implied proportioning of two different things; disguised as a logical identity, it may never truly attain to one and remain a metaphor.[60] Especially in the representation of character, the architectonic metaphor, as the analogy for the making of analogy, implies the union of various types of knowledge in the perceivable image of some persona; this character proportions the ways of knowing in his or her mind's eye, showing the reader how or how not to do so, too.

In his English translation of Plutarch's *Lives* in 1579, Sir Thomas North eloquently expressed the preference for tales of living icons of knowledge over philosophical definition. North's translation advertised itself as the stories of heroes that ought to be read as an illustration of the doctrine of Plutarch's *Philosophy*, or *Morals*. The architectonic philosophy of the *Lives* depends on its combination of literary decorum and universal learning in the narration of biography:

All other learning is private, fitter for Universities then cities, fuller of contemplacion than experience, more comendable in the students themselves, then profitable unto others. Wheras stories are fit for euery place, reache to all persons, serve for all tymes, teach the liuing, revive the dead, so farre excelling all other bookes, as it is better to see learning in noble mens liues, then to reade it in Philosophers writing. (Sig. *iiij^r)

The argument for the value of heroic "lives" was that they brought well-knowing of all sorts into the kind of living unity that might, by example, better effect well-doing in the readers who could "see" learning in the actions of noble men and judge ignorance in villains. Moral integration represented the felt proof of the unity of truth.

Sidney's and North's preference for storytelling should remind us of the reason renaissance thinkers *could* reshape the Greek message of Herodotus, Xenophon, and Plutarch to make the poet himself a type of hero. The reason was Plato, the prime philosopher of the "new age." The love of language and Plato's icon of the philosopher-king and statesman-educator peculiarly engaged renaissance minds. For Plato's development of the architectonic metaphor had emphasized not the hard-edged stones of architecture or the

structural building of knowledge or the fiction of heroic lives but the statesmanlike discourse that, joining those things in the tension of metaphor,
inspired good character and the moral building of the just society. This
connecting or analogizing ability constitutes the integrity of Sidney's inter
textuality in the *Defence* through its "oral" delivery of voices.

Exposition of the architectonic metaphor occurs throughout Plato's
Dialogues. It appears dramatically in the *Gorgias*, the dialogue named for the
rhetorician who claimed that his speeches inspired the production of major
buildings in the city. Socrates observes that the "building" of good men is
indeed like the making of good buildings, but more exalted, so he challenges
Gorgias's ignorant claim of universality for rhetoric (*Gorg.* 503e–504e). He
also disputes Gorgias's use of speech. The architectural speech of sophistic
rhetoric compares unfavorably with the architectonic speech of dialectic in
the *Gorgias* much as the *phantastic* sculptural images based on false proportions fail to express the true measure of the frame of reality that *eikastic*
images can convey (*Sophist* 235d–236d). Similarly, the "living speech" of the
true statesman rejects gorgeous verbal patterns and distorted sculptures
alike (*Phaedrus* 276a). The statesman eschews these warped imitations and
prefers to form human character truly (in imitations that are proportional)
and really (in actual thought and life). Only when an orator possesses
self-knowledge and, unlike Gorgias, is a just man who knows what is just
should he publicly signify by speech his statesmanship or his ability to form
others in proportionally right ways (*Gorg.* 508c; cf. *Phaedrus* 230a; 275a).
Architecture, far from making the city great, has filled it with garbage and
made it into a disease. The statesmen of old who preferred architectural
construction to architectonic education of the citizenry have paid "no heed
to discipline and justice, but have filled our city with harbors and dockyards
and walls and revenues and similar rubbish" (*Gorg.* 517–19; cf. 465c).
    In the *Republic* Socrates again uses the architectural analogy to point out
the superiority of the architectonic science, the true statesmanship. But the
very exercise of thought that he invites in the imagination of this science is
already a practical demonstration of its significance. Socrates wants to build
his ideal city in wise thoughts, not in stones, and recognize its source of
justice. Not on account of architects and carpenters is a city to be called wise;
they make her "mistress of the arts of building." But because of the guardians and creators of civic liberty is the city made wise; and because of the
justice of the people is she made just (4.428–35). The implied gender hierarchy of the Platonic view—in which material production makes the city a
mistress of the building arts while masculine guardianship creates civic
liberty, wisdom, and justice in the citizenry—surfaces in Book 5 of the
Republic in the questions whether the male and female sexes have distinct
qualifications for any arts or pursuits (5.454d) and whether women may be

guardians. This line of interrogation of strength and weakness contributed to the political practice of English renaissance thought and art under the Tudor Queen and helped to shift it away from feminine power in politics and away from the mistress-knowledge in art in the seventeenth century.[61]

On its own terms such Platonism focuses political and poetic power on language. In the *Philebus,* the mental effort to create an ideal republic is explicitly bound to speech in the discourse on whether wisdom or pleasure is the greatest good: "Then here, one may say, we have at hand the ingredients, intelligence and pleasure, ready to be mixed, the material in which, or out of which, we as builders are to build our structure—that would not be a bad metaphor" (*Philebus* 59e). Socrates makes a verbal proportion, a metaphor, to explain the supreme knowledge of mastercraftsmanship. The joining force, the cause of coherence and intelligibility, in discourse is dialectic—the science of the philosophers, the art of the true orator, and the wise speech of the statesman who builds the feminized city. Dialectic—the art of collecting all that is like and dividing all that is unlike—takes precedence over all other studies to be, as it were, the "coping stone" (*Repub.* 7.534e). This truly proportion-making or analogical science characterizes the supreme knowledge of the statesman-architect whom Plato presents in the *Politicus.* The duty of the mastercraftsman is to initiate and to sustain the building of the state, to guide the work of those arts and sciences instructing men in methods of action, and to master many arts and sciences, including public speaking, in order to produce good men. The statesman-architect exercises the most vital knowledge of knowing how to make men good at knowing how to make yet other men good at knowing, *ad indefinitum.* Dichotomous dialectic is the chief instrument of statecraft, and the statesman is learned, supervisory, and generative.[62] Plato turned the architectural analogy inside out to make men seek the moral and intellectual kingdom within them—the City that Saint Augustine would call chaste.

In the Renaissance, Plato's metaphor for the ruling knowledge and its exercise centered on the character of the one who performed it—the masculine character of the statesman-architect. Plato worked the architectural analogy through the *Dialogues* as a proportion that challenged Greek literalism; in the renaissance translations of Plato by Ficino and Jean de Serres, the idea of statesmanship eventually moved renaissance interpretation of the architectonic metaphor away from the civic humanism that produced architectural works and toward the more difficult production of good human beings by means of dialectical speech.

Yet the philosophical source of the architectonic metaphor in Aristotle was as well known in the Renaissance as the image of the heroic lives of epic and history and of the Platonic statesman. Because of the scholastic tradition, the Aristotelian metaphor of the edifice of thought primarily shaped renaissance ideas of mastercraftsmanship. In the *Metaphysics*, Aristotle's hierarchical arrangement of knowledge paralleled his discussion of the intellectual virtues in the *Nicomachean Ethics* Aristotle held the man of experience to be wiser than anybody who merely possesses sensation; the artist to be wiser than the man of experience, the mastercraftsman to be wiser than the artisan; and the speculative scientist to be wiser than the productive scientist; at the top, the wise mind master-built the structure of knowledge because wisdom is the sure knowledge of principles and causes (*Met.* 1.1.17 [981b–982a]; cf. *Nic. Ethics* 6.3–8 [1139b–1142b]). In the process of saying so much about the human practitioners of different levels of knowledge, Aristotle did not hesitate to use numerous geometric examples to illustrate his points. Sometimes he actually spoke of the distinction between substance and accident with reference to the way one builds a house (*Met.* 6.1[1026b]) or imagined character-building as an art that has its end in itself with regard to architectural construction (*Magna Moralia* 1211b).

Aristotle built his own edifice of knowledge through his analysis of speculative, productive, and practical types, with one architectonic art for each kind of knowledge and each one defined according to object, end, and scope. For knowledge itself the theoretical or speculative architectonic science is metaphysics because it builds the structure of the arts and sciences as a unity, a truth about being. With regard to the practice of knowledge Aristotle joined Plato in judging politics or statesmanship to be preeminently architectonic because it directs all human activity in the arts and sciences toward the happiness of the supreme good. Rhetoric, too, is architectonic, because it supervises subordinate arts and draws on the knowledge of all arts and sciences to produce all available means of persuasion. Metaphysics teaches knowledge of the one true good; politics employs knowledge in the practice of the good; and rhetoric, properly used as a division of both politics and logic, effects persuasion to the good by producing arguments.[63]

The clustering of so many geometric and architectural correspondences around Aristotle's idea of building thought and the complexity of the scholastic transmission of his intellectual hierarchy to the Renaissance gave amplitude to the architectonic metaphor. It was significantly Aristotle's thinking that Leonardo da Vinci and, later, Bacon revised in their praise of the man of experimental knowledge, for example. So, too, it was clearly Aristotle's *Ethics* that Sidney paraphrased in his inventive translation of the mistress-knowledge in the *Defence* to redefine the heroic concept. A survey of Italian and English examples will show how Plato's version of the architectonic metaphor overlapped with Aristotle's in the renaissance imagination and then supported a critique of the material construction of civilization. The converted Plato of the Fathers of the Church also distinctly contributed to renaissance views of the art of building life in words.

When medieval thinkers defined architecture as a carpenter's skill or craft, they reflected an Aristotelian sense of the hierarchy of the intellectual virtues and placed mechanical skills outside the scheme of the liberal arts.[64] In the Renaissance, though, architecture gradually rose on that scale to the status of an art, a rational skill concerned with making or producing, and then to the status of a geometric science, a knowledge of the necessary and eternal. The process gradually brought architecture to the elevated plane of a master science practiced by "the learned architect."[65] Renaissance buildings, in turn, were the physical analogues of new intellectual and cultural achievements, and the art of architecture that produced such buildings was decidedly a mastercraft suited to political realities. The Italian argument for the primacy of architecture and for the metaknowledge, the *virtú*, of the architect rendered the Aristotelian emphasis on building a structure of thought both visual and actual.[66]

Benedetto Varchi, for example, had noted the significance of the derivation of the word *architettoniche* from *architettura* in his 1546 treatise on the pictorial and plastic arts in relation to verbal knowledge, the *Lezzioni* (1.21). However, as he extended his theorizing to poetry, the demonstrability of scientific knowledge increasingly made it superior in his judgment to the variability or fortune-bound quality of artistic knowledge. Later, inquiring into the differences between science as knowledge and art as "making" in the preface to his lecture to the Florentine Academy in the *Lezzioni* of 1590, Varchi argued that art, too, was also demonstrative (Florence, pp. 191–92). His change of heart incorporated Aristotelian standards and Horatian values into a Platonic sense of the value of the leap of intuition. Thus Varchi examined the scientific quality of painting and explained away the Aristotelian distinction between science and art by appealing to the higher knowledge of "l'Artifice," the craftsman, the "buono Maestro," who practices *virtú* (*Lezzioni* [1590], pp. 204–12). *Virtú* translates a renaissance version of Horatian *ingenium*, or the gift of the native wit, into the exercise, the activity of the mind at its best.[67] *Ingenium* also belongs to the category of the variable in art, but it becomes worthy of the status of a metaknowledge, a master science, when it is coupled with the doctrines of mathematical science in the mind of the mastercraftsman who demonstrates what he knows in the products of his imagination. Varchi's driving interest was the desire to establish mechanical crafts such as painting, sculpture, and architecture within the scheme of the liberal arts and to explain the superior knowledge of artist and poet on the basis of a transformation of Aristotle's definition of speculative and practical arts.

Earlier in the Italian Renaissance, however, the great Florentine translator of Plato had already argued much the same point by joining, in the spirit of civic humanism, politics and metaphysics. Instead of arguing the case of the superiority of the artist, Ficino alludes to the power of the artist to argue the superiority of the statesman. Ficino pays special attention to Plato's metaphor of the statesman as an architect; in the introduction to the dialogue on statesmanship, the *Politicus*, he extends an interpretative renaissance commentary on Socrates' idea of the statesman architect to the literal praise of Federigo de Montefeltro, Duke of Urbino, as an architect of buildings and of thought.[68] In other words, Ficino's use of the architectonic metaphor insists on a balance of powers, a dynamic equilibrium between the active and the contemplative realms; the Florentine does not merely read one side of the metaphor in terms of the other but crosses back and forth between them.

Castiglione, similarly, in his Platonic book of manners *Il Cortegiano*, acknowledged the same Duke Federigo literally as the architect of a splendid building, a library where the monuments of learning were preserved, and also metaphorically as an "architect of thought," a statesman of the arts and sciences in practice.[69] Already, though, the Italian treatment of the architectonic metaphor had increased its tension and found a new direction in the Platonic emphasis on language. Castiglione dedicated the greater portion of his text not to the praise of architects and their buildings, as Vasari had, but to the exposition of that more mysterious and complex architecture, the codes of language representing the codes of conduct in society. Castiglione adapted Plato's verbally geometric proportion-making in the ideal republic to analysis of the ways of speaking decorously in order to form morally an ideal court. As good geometric demonstration in the art of architecture produces buildings that can represent civilization in visual space and in history, so the demonstrated decorum of speech may wisely produce the best courtly society. Architecture can illustrate the truth; but in the Platonic scheme of knowledge, architectonics is practically one and the same with lived wisdom that is spoken. Indeed, a delicate debate emerges in *Il Cortegiano:* whether the courtier who advises his prince does not, in fact, possess a greater knowledge of the truth because, in effect, his statesmanship knows how to use language to move the prince to a vision of wisdom in practice.[70] Of course, history is the record of princes who did not take the advice of wise counselors and of poets who tried to influence noblemen. The comparison of statesmen-architects to the "edifice of learning" that they both practiced and built more safely stated a commonplace in the Renaissance with regard to the construction of libraries.[71] Books began to bear title pages mounted in the design of architectural facades.

In the sixteenth century in England, literature exhibited a clearly Platonic and patristic influence on the subject of language. A major example of the manner in which patristic knowledge of the Platonic architectonic metaphor amplified the theme of proportion-making was Saint Thomas More's treatment of Plato's *Republic* and Saint Augustine's two cities in his rewriting of the genre of the classical political treatise in the *Utopia*. To the extent that Sidney considers More's style in the *Utopia*, Sidney, too, recomposes the classical political treatise in his *Defence*.

More's ironic contrast of the ideal earthly city and the ultimate City of God implicitly formulates a proportion, and the proportion—or disproportion, in this case—expresses his criticism of real European society. One reason More's "philosopher," Raphael Hythloday, brings Plato to the Utopians is probably the argument of proportion stated in the *Philebus*. Socrates had taught that the truly philosophical prince did not prefer either wisdom or pleasure to the other but sought a greater good in the just proportion of them.[72] By sanctifying pleasure in a verbal description of the goodness of nature, More simultaneously praises the pursuit of wisdom, "philosophy," as a high pleasure in its own right and ironically records the patent discrepancy between accepted truth and moral and political practice in European society. The *disproportions* of the elegantly ironic speech of the *Utopia* satirize the society that ought to know rationally how to produce the justice of which it speaks but fails to produce it. The text of *Utopia* as a whole promotes the making of better proportions between knowledge and action by humanist-statesmen who envision a better model for their patterning of a commonwealth than Raphael's lovely foolish rationalistic island—that is, a model informed by the knowledge of the City of God as a proportion of truths learned in divine revelation. In More's imagination, a Platonic-Augustinian strain gave the architectonic metaphor a moral philosophical bent and a central focus on the manipulation of language. Like Socrates' voice, or Lucian's, More's tone is ironic and subtle and is meant to compel intellectual recognition of a problem in society.

Another version of how a city gets built—whether with stones or with intelligent and verbal human characters—was the popular renaissance recounting of the myths of persuasion in Amphion and Orpheus; they had been well developed by the Latin rhetoricians and in the medieval tradition.[73] In the mythological tale of Amphion's music, the famous musician actually moved stones in the building of Thebes. Orpheus's poetry, similarly, charmed beasts. Horace alluded to those myths to articulate his idea of dichotomous dialectic; the poet builds civilization by separating right and wrong, the sacred from the profane.[74] One of the Fathers of the Church whose Greek text was recovered in the mid-sixteenth century, Saint Clement of Alexandria, had dramatically revised the myths by transforming their image of tearing down and building up civilization. Clement mixes the story of Deucalion with the tales of Amphion and Orpheus to speak of the "new Song," the person of the Word of God who brings to life a God-fearing seed sensitive to virtue from the very stones, the stone-worshiping nations.[75]

Not surprisingly, a sanctified Plato, a Utopian Thomas More, a poetical

Amphion and Orpheus, and a Word who builds the Church show up at different points in Sidney's *Defence*, marking it as a political treatise for Protestant England. Sidney asserts, first of all, that the poet has the power to move stones and to charm beasts, "indeed, stony and brutally people," by stimulating them to virtue (p. 74).[76] A combination of myth and philosophy contributes to Sidney's discussion of Platonic *furor* and of More's *Utopia*.

Discussing the role of the poet-*vates*, Sidney turns Plato's challenge to the idea of inspiration in the *Ion* into a praise of the poetic nature of the real truth of revelation in Holy Scripture.[77] Since the Word of God in Holy Scripture is poetic, Sidney may rightly conclude, by analogy, that poetry "rightly" applied ought not to be banished or "scourged out of the Church of God" any more, his reasoning implies, than the true poet ought to have been driven out of Plato's republic (p. 77). David's prophecy is "merely poetical"—but a "heavenly poesy" in which he shows himself the "passionate lover of that unspeakable and everlasting beauty to be seen by the eyes of the mind, only cleared by faith" (p. 77). Thus Sidney praises David the statesman and poet according to an Augustinian standard of the beauty ever ancient and ever new, the beauty that transcends even Plato's imagination in the *Symposium*. Going further, Sidney says that Christ "vouchsafed to use the flowers" of poetry (p. 99), and if "flowers" conventionally referred to rhetorical tropes and figures, they referred also to the natural objects that Plutarch, Saint Basil, and other Christian writers encouraged readers to "use" like bees gathering honey. Readers ought to read the poems that good poets—divine and human—have composed of "flowers" in the light of their composers' standard of poetic invention.

The standard for the poet-*vates*' composition of notable images of virtue and vice is, in Sidney's estimation, the truth of the Word revealed to the Christian Renaissance. For this reason the poet may not be scourged out of the Church of God. Moreover, to the extent that Sidney's Christian poet fulfills the greatest hopes of Plato's statesman-architect, the poet may not be exiled from the Christian commonwealth. In this line of argumentation, Sidney discloses his radical application of the making, building, and teaching functions of Plato's statesman-architect to the role of the Christian poet in a new English theocracy or church-state. Although the sixteenth century saw a general renaissance absorption of the doctrines of Plato in ways that suited contemporary history, Sidney's particular application shows radical optimism about the powers of poetry in the operations of the human mind. He thinks poetry to be an expression of the "erected wit" that can, somehow, overcome in human nature the dire effects of an "infected will" (p. 79). To the extent that Sidney's poet practices the compelling persuasion of an Augustinian *rhetor*, poetic "prophecy" implements teaching and preaching in the proportion of wisdom and pleasure that ravishes the heart of the audience. The society that the renaissance Christian poet builds is more than the stones of Thebes, and the people to whom this poet addresses himself in imitation of the "new Song" are meant to be the citizens of the City of God.

Sidney praises, therefore, the metaphor-making of Sir Thomas More's *Utopia*. The success of the *Utopia*, the characteristic that makes it a poetically absolute way of "patterning a commonwealth," is More's "feigned image." Yet Sidney blames More the man for the faults and limitations of his metaphor. Metaphor-making is a "most absolute" way to determine goodness and to direct a prince though More "perchance hath not so absolutely performed it" (*Def.*, pp. 85–86). The distinction between More the poet and More the man echoes the Socratic evaluation of the orator as one who should not publicly signify his statesmanship in speech until he is a just man who knows what is just and possesses self-knowledge (*Gorg.* 508c). From Sidney's Protesant vantage, Thomas More could well build his words into the pattern of a whole commonwealth, but because his idea did not sufficiently arise from the mind of a man who had been justified, the truth that should be at the heart of the poem of the *Utopia* remains merely a well-constructed fiction. Thus *Utopia*, in Sidney's opinion, fails to communicate the spark of ethical action to the reader that truth, made known by a Daedalean craftsman, would convey. More's proportions remain intelligently ironic in Sidney's view; they teach and delight but cannot rhetorically move the reader to well-doing.

Sidney parts ways with More's ironic image of the ideal republic, moreover, by reinterpreting some of More's sources in Plato, Augustine, and Boethius from a Protestant Christian perspective. He also appears to judge the historical results of More's thinking in More's death as a form of Icarean overreaching. Sidney prefers to it Erasmus's "ladder" of Christian folly. The greatest irony of all, of course, is that Sidney will obey his sovereign's orders to go to the Netherlands, fight, and die in the Protestant cause, and in the *encomium moriae* produced by the subsequent Sidney legend the Catholic humanist and martyr Sir Thomas and the Protestant humanist and hero Sir Philip are paradoxically yoked by history and Tudor politics.

The New Poet's Auto-da-fé

Further probing of Sidney's intertextuality in the *Defence* regularly confirms his affirmation of architectonic philosophizing over architectural literalism. The moral coupling of the two prosopopoeias coordinates the multiple intersubjectivities within the *Defence* and also links it to the masks of other characters in the *Arcadia* and in *Astrophil and Stella*. Thus the rhetorical pronunciation of Sidney's arts treatise leads back to the psychological, political, and poetic integrity of the character making the speech and centering himself. Having gathered various knowledges in *his* reading,

Sidney makes his poetic confession of faith in the allegories of his romance and his sonnet sequence and in the allegorical mythology of the *Defence*.

We see within the *Arcadia*, for example filling its landscape and architecture, inaugurating the tale, and touching the characters in their interactions no other structural principle than a reigning figure of the mistress-knowledge I began this book by noting that it is Urania whose remembrance, a philosophical history of her heavenly beauty, motivates the action of Strephon and Claius in helping the shipwrecked Pyrocles and Musidorus (1:1.1, 7–8). Where the *Defence* defines the operations of poesie, the *Arcadia* portrays a society struggling to remember her spirit and its ethical and political meaning. Indeed, under Urania's eye the *Arcadia* is a fiction working less by those Xenophonian and Platonic standards of the commonwealth that might best be or should be and more by the contrast of images of human life among Stoics to images of secular—that is, merely historical—life as it is. In various betrayals, confusions, accidents, and irresponsible choices, all of the difficulties of love, friendship, thought, and political rule come into focus. In genre, this is the necessary wandering along paths of error particular to romance; but in Sidney's hands the romance plot is also a tool for the judgment of the worse kind of serendipity or irrationality masking as reason in human affairs. The *Arcadia* is a book about an absent presence. Thus Sidney's careful construction of antitheses of character and episode in the *Arcadia* patterns his so-called Arcadian picture of nature and art into a self-knowledge that must finally reflect judgment on his contemporary society, if one reads rightly. This does not bring well-knowing to well-doing within the politics and love affairs of *Arcadia* because Sidney portrays a natural, that is, fallen, unconverted, and ungraced society. Yet such a scene is exactly the quasi-Calvinistic scene of recognition in which the vision and the voice of the mistress-knowledge may be remembered.[78] For without such self-knowledge, Calvin had remarked at the beginning of his *Institutes*, there is no·knowledge of God; but with self-knowledge, even pagans perceiving their own unhappiness grasp the existence of divine majesty (1:1.1–3, 35–43, ed. McNeill).

For this reason, too, the landscape of the place called Arcadia recedes behind the dominance of the characters. The place, identified by a "singular reputation" of the "well-tempered minds" of its people, is as much a no-place as More's *Utopia*, with the difference that More portrays the rule of reason in his *eu-topos*, or pleasant island, to challenge his home island, while Sidney portrays the irrationality and artifice of the pastoral state of mind in contention with the heroic character caught in the failure of its ideals. In a book in which Musidorus claims Palladius as one of his fictive names, this contention is the struggle of reason, passion, and grace in Sidney's fictive characters (1:1.2, 12–15).

On the grand scale of the Arcadian story, the pastoral motif sharpens the philosophical contrast of the works of nature and the works of the mind in vivid images. So Basilius, the prince who has made a trip to the oracle at Delphos, and the father of Pamela and Philoclea, has returned home to practice self-knowledge by giving up his rule and retiring into the forest as into a desert (1:1.3, 19–22).[79] The choice to withdraw may or may not mistakenly execute Delphic gnosis. From the Stoic perspective of Roman standards, the choice violates the public duty of a ruler, and one hardly needs the support of Cicero's *De Officiis*, Virgil's *Aeneid*, or the *Dream of Scipio* to recognize as much. From a radically Protestant perspective on the vanity of the works of nature in a fallen world, Basilius's withdrawal makes a certain sense. What would make the most sense, however, is the idea of rule Sidney does *not* explicitly state, namely, the conversion of the king who would then take up his duties informed by a Christian sense of historical destiny. But this problem of election, sovereignty, and historical destiny is precisely the problem of ethical interpretation and moral action that Sidney explores in the *Arcadia*, asking his readers to do likewise. It is also the problem of ethics and politics, love and war, posed by the *Aeneid*. The false withdrawal of the Protestant from the work of the world and the false building of empire by so-called Christians who think they know who they are undergo Sidney's interrogation in his fiction, and our reading as much as Basilius's Stoic failure undergoes the poet's judgment in the text as written. Basilius's withdrawal is the negative example of the mistress-knowledge's absence. Quite suitably, then, Sidney's use of architectural description in the *Arcadia* subordinates both place and the designs of Palladius the architect to the revelation of virtue or vice in the human character. Kalendar's house of stone is not extraordinary; it is an "honorable representing of a firme statelines" in which the appointments are directed to the use of the guest, not to the "eye of the Artificer" (1:1.2, 15). The virtue of the character who is the genius of the house dominates it.

So, too, Sidney's text is a structurally well-devised fiction that offers true hospitality to the reader not by painting pictures of characters comfortably taking refuge from the demands of ethics and politics but by speaking speeches that encourage the reader's exercise of his or her mind under the reading rule of the mistress-knowledge. This is especially true in the Arcadian stories of love. For instance, Sidney's Pyrocles in the *Arcadia* falls in love with Philoclea through her portrait. He pretends, first, that he wants to see the place where she actually lives because "the *Architecture* of the lodges" will contribute to his learning and, second, because he wants to judge better "the painters cūning" (1:1.13, 85). In order to get to her, Pyrocles experiments with gender roles and disguises, too, and—once caught in the indecorous imitation of an Amazon named Zelmane—finally admits to Musidorus the truth of his far greater desire "to see her selfe" (pp. 85–91). The person in flesh and blood indisputably ranks higher than all learning and all the pictorial arts.

In the original *Arcadia*, of course, the vitality of the human body as the castle and fortress of the beautiful soul overcomes Prince Musidorus with desire for Pamela. Having nimbly mounted Pamela upon the horse he provided for her, Musidorus rides with her into the wildest part of the desert, and Pamela, full of desire and fear, calms down enough to consider her situation with some degree of self knowledge: "Nowe that the pange of Desyer with evident hope was quyted, & moste parte of the feare passed, Reason began to Renew his shyning in her harte, and make her see her self in her self, and weighe with what wynges shee flewe oute of her Native Contry and upon what grounde shee buylt her Determinatyon" (*Prose Works* 4:185, ed. Feuillerat). Finding an orderly and spacious pine grove in which to rest, Musidorus and Pamela perform the "vertuous wantonyes" (p. 189) of a musical duet until Pamela falls asleep in Musidorus's lap. Then, in the face of Pamela's beauty, which is described as more than "the Picture of some excellent Artificer" because she breathes, Musidorus is tyrannized with the desire to enter that "Mansyon," "that well closed Paradyse," and to "wynn the Bullwarke before tymely help mighte come" (p. 190). The architecture of the body itself contends with the ground of reason on which Pamela built her determination to remain virtuous.

In the poems of *Astrophil and Stella,* as in the ground-plot in the prose of the *Defence*, we find that Sidney's favorite metaphor for the mind of a character comes from the cartography that maps out new discoveries. For him the *locus classicus* of poetic invention is the zodiac of the wit, the cosmology of exploration of an intellectual and moral sort (*Def.*, pp. 78–79). Likewise, when Sidney's Astrophil reviews current poetic theories in sonnet 6 in order to contrast his ability to speak what he feels to the limitations and artificialities of other poets, he asserts that everything within him condenses to one metaphor—"that all the Map of my state I display, / When trembling voice brings forth that I do Stella love" (6.13–14). The sum of poetic eloquence is also a chart of one's inmost self insofar as it androgynously pictures the effeminate, carnal image of Astrophil's love for Stella and the masculine force of his verbal testimony. But these two powers, ideally joined in the *Defence*, are in a state of caricature and disjunction in the sonnet sequence. Sidney's lovely conceit on the totality of love argues that four commonplace words do, in fact, say everything in their psychological disclosure of an entire "state" of mind. The "map" of the mind that reaches up to the heavens and down into psychological depths—even Astrophil's picture of his hell—is the kind of ground-plot, or intellectual and moral organization of collected data, that bears upon a central, architectonic point of moral interpretation in the mind's eye of conscience: the conviction of sin. From an Augustinian vantage, *Astrophil and Stella* is about a failed quest to come home—a journey to hell, not heaven.

Thomas P. Roche, Jr., has already brought to light the antiheroic nature of Astrophil's journey; presenting a negative example of the wanderings of Odysseus in Astrophil's exploration of the inner world of his desire, Sidney leads Astrophil to despair, not homecoming, because Astrophil refuses to learn from his experience. "We the readers," Roche remarks, "are meant to supply the Christian context that will make sense of the insufficiencies of Astrophil's insights into his predicament."[80] Aside from the manner in which Sidney's sonnet sequence revises Homer in this respect, Sidney's *Defence* revises Virgil according to Augustinian standards. These standards may very well be the dominantly Christian context of Sidney's composition, and he presents them by contrasting the labyrinth—whether that of the political tyrant, the errors of romance, the equivocations of language, or the devious heart—and the temple.

The antithesis of the architectonic ordering of the mind that the *Defence* presents is the verbal labyrinth, the naturely chaotic or perversely artificial construction of the world and of the mind, from which Astrophil and the lovers of Arcadia suffer. In the maze of the fallen mind, young men like "Zelmane" the Amazon, Dorus the rapist and prince, and Astrophil get lost by making false turns in falsely imagined places and in the name of falsely conceived personal masks. However, in their necessary quest for self-knowledge *because* they are stricken with some knowledge of love, they are verbally able to find themselves, too, to come to some awakening of the truth about themselves, even through the disguises of the warrior-maiden, the shepherd, and the Cupid who typified for them the lust they projected.[81] Self-knowledge envisions poetically the moral chart of judgment that, in a flash of recognition, may take one's mind and mortal nature into the desire to navigate in true freedom. In Spenser's *Faerie Queene*, too, the verbal architecture of the labyrinth repeats in descriptions of sea and land, amplifying the poet's vision of the many ways people can get lost in time, space, and language.[82] Yet the quest of Red Crosse Knight in Book 1 illustrates as well an architectonic illumination of words gradually liberating the conscience from its variously imprisoning coils precisely because of the poet's control of his "afflicted stile" (Stanza 4, Proem, *FQ* 1).

Psychological ambivalence about persons and places and the desire to resolve it are the necessary corollaries to the antithetical poetic art, which Sidney's prosopopoeias analogically coordinate. The profound ambivalences of Sidney's poems appear in English renaissance poetry in general in the self-conscious tension of the poets' analogical methods and in given metaphors. This is the balancing of male and female powers and the mediation of brazen and golden worlds, as Sidney put it, and the hierarchy of Cleopolis, Eden, and the new Jerusalem in Spenser's vision of English history. For George Herbert and for John Milton the ambivalence results in the contrast between the historical Church and the living temple of the heart and mind. The poetic character who inhabits these poems, voicing them, is ambivalent and conflicted, too; he holds dual citizenship in the city of man and the City of God. When the characters of renaissance fictions speak and act in the imagined universe of a poem, they articulate, in turn, a plethora of other metaphors besides their own personification of the poet to trouble the reader's interpretation. Trouble is the point: in Sidneian intertextuality, ambivalence, like the sexualized tension of metaphor sustained between the mistress and the man, is essential to the moral coupling of the architectonic art. Not for nothing did renaissance poets constantly return to the mythic paradox of Venus and Mars and the Judeo-Christian one of Adam and Eve.

The proposition of a moral coupling in an "inward light" of truth could not have appeared at all possible for Sidney, Spenser, Herbert, or Milton without a broad cultural commitment to mastercraftsmanship and without the strong influence of a particularly biblical authorization of poesie as the architectonic rebuilding of the temple of the Protestant mind and heart in England. Yet by no means did the standard of *sola Scriptura* encourage ignorance of classical or contemporary knowledge or medieval constructions of Christian truth. On the contrary, in Sidney's case in the *Defence*, at least, the reading of Boethius, Augustine, More, and Erasmus properly contextualized the reading of classical philosophers, historians, and poets. Revealed knowledge, however, gave the Protestant thinker or poet the freedom to roam among the ruins of all previous writers, especially the philosophers—among which the unbeliever encounters only scattered fragments or truth or mere fantasies, as Calvin explained in the passage from the *Institutes* cited as the epigraph to this chapter—because the resources of a transcendent truth helped him to see in those fragments and fantasies the potential for a well-knit structure of thought blessed by the Word.

Cicero instructed Sidney on the way to arrange his rhetorical invention of the confirmation of the poet's character, but it was Saint Augustine, finally, who directed Sidney's shaping of the peculiarities of his speaking character in the Augustinian discourse of faith brought to understanding, the confession of a faith that justifies and therefore makes the Puritan icon of the self.[83] In discussing renaissance "self-fashioning," Stephen Greenblatt did not say much about Sir Philip Sidney, perhaps because Sidney's work does not fit very well into a critical scheme of self-representation in Greenblatt's sense. Greenblatt argues that Petrarch and others developed a poetics of self-representation, an anthropocentric concept of the creative human self, that consciously parodies Augustinian autobiography "now idolatrously severed from a belief in the origin of human discourse in the creative Logos."[84] But such a phrase describes the self-absorption of us moderns, not the iconology and iconoclasm of the English Renaissance. Sidney certainly makes a contribution to modernity that is literary, psychological, and parodic in its intertextuality, but it remains theological, too. The Sidneian imitation of the Augustinian *Confessions* in the *Defence* is less a parody of the fourth-century Christian philosopher than it is an inventive recapitulation of the Augustinian treatment of Virgil and the Petrarchan observance of inwardness. The center of Sidney's auto-da-fé as a poet is, in this respect, a son's declaration of himself before his father and a Protestant Englishman's rewriting of the Troy legend of the *Aeneid,* which Augustine had previously rewritten, to accommodate Sidney's biblical standard. In the story of Dido and Aeneas, we find yet another variant of the story of Adam and Eve—or, for that matter, of Penelope and Odysseus, Theseus and Ariadne, Venus and Mars, Astrophil and Stella. Behind the struggles and joys of the couple stands the presence of some patriarchal rule, whether that of the family or of a divine majesty. The way through the cultural labyrinth for Sidney was identification with the creative Word, the Son of God made manifest in the Wisdom of the mistress-knowledge poesie.

As close in time to the medieval view of the "comedy of salvation" as he was, Sidney the Calvinist did not find it difficult to bring ironic wit to bear on the serious doctrines with which his poetic character made him struggle. Long after the *Defence* was composed, well into his active political life, and shortly before he heard of his father's death, Sidney expressed the serious doctrine of his saving faith simply as his reliance on a higher power in a letter to Walsingham dated March 24, 1586. Little could he have known that he, too, would be dead in less than a year. Already in the *Defence,* however, in the speaker's triangulation with the three prosopopoeias he invents oratorically, we should see the pattern of an English Protestant family and hear the voice of one coming into his manhood in Sidney's "cyropaedia."

After Freud we inevitably read the Oedipal triangle in this one as Sidney alternately makes himself the consort of the mistress-knowledge and the good child, the product of her art of moral coupling with the statesman.[85] Yet the psychology of the Renaissance expressed itself through the great myths of antiquity and of the Bible, unmediated by modern psychoanalysis, and the methods of allegorical mythology encouraged the reader's cross-referencing of the stories of the poets with the histories of religion not as infantile submergence in the ocean of feeling but as a matter of faith that breaks through the prisons of history and culture. Augustine emerges as an important model for Sidney because Augustine presents himself as a reader of classics in the *Confessions* and as a philosopher whose conversion enabled him completely to reinterpret the ethics and politics of antiquity. Sidney does more than copy Augustine. What Sidney brings to his appropriation of the Augustinian model of the reader and writer is a new recognition of the significance of the myth of Daedalus and his son Icarus in Virgil's composition of the *Aeneid.* Sidney's definition of a fictive Daedalean master-craftsmanship articulates an alternative poetics placed beside Virgil's or any pagan's, and the alternative balances Sidney's confession of desire for power with his confession of faith.

The great classical model of a hero who kept to the ways of his father by abandoning a woman who succored him is Aeneas abandoning Dido, the Queen of Carthage, to follow his manifest destiny as the founder of "new Troy."[86] In the *Aeneid*, Virgil tells the story of the Minotaur, Daedalus, and Icarus just before Aeneas is to descend into the underworld to consult with his father. The story of the labyrinth is inscribed on the doors of the "awe some shrine" that Daedalus built on Apollo's hill near the cave of the Cumaean Sibyl. The doors portray the Minotaur as the "monument to love profaned" and the labyrinth as the "winding, wearying, hopeless house" whose "riddle" and "puzzle" Daedalus solved out of pity for a "princess lost for love" by providing a "thread to guide blind feet." Grief prevents Daedalus from picturing the story of Icarus in this masterpiece, Virgil tells us: "Twice Daedalus tried to carve your fate in gold, / twice fell a father's hands."[87] When Aeneas arrives and inspects the doors before praying to enter the underworld, he promises Apollo that he will imitate Daedalus and will also build a shrine to honor Apollo and the Trojan gods in his new realm (6.71).

But Aeneas's reading of the details of the doors is as interrupted as the doors themselves are artistically unfinished, and in this Virgilian note lies the future Sidneian perception of conflict between politics and art—a conflict he locates in erotic desire, which is often the subject of the genealogy of the gods and goddesses. Aeneas relentlessly carries out his purpose; he enters "hell" primarily to speak with his dead father and validate his trip to Latium, although he does see Dido there and again claims that the law of God drove him away from her unwillingly (6.458–64). Later, Virgil presents a second scene of aesthetic criticism for the soldier-hero: Aeneas does not grasp the significance of the artwork on the shield of Vulcan, which his mother Venus has requested for him. Vulcan undertakes the making of the armor needed by a brave man as the labor of mastercraftsmanship (*Aeneid* 8.441–42, *magistra arte*), and the shield will prophetically reveal the future of Rome. But Aeneas, exulting in the military usefulness and beauty of the shield, sees in its scenes "only art, not history" (8.730). He admires the gift of his mother and takes pleasure in the representation of things of which he is ignorant, Virgil explains. In bearing this shield, the hero bears on his shoulder as well the fame and fate of his offspring (8.731). Joining his mother's brother in the military and political battle for the Netherlands, the legendary Sidney will fatefully cast off his armor and be wounded, like Adonis, in the thigh.

In the *Defence* Sidney addresses the poet's historical naming of heroes like Aeneas and Cyrus as part of the patriarchal construction of civilization from father to son, generation to generation, having a moral purpose. The purported education of Cyrus tells of maturation to manhood and its powers and responsibilities; the conduct of the "hero" in public life tells of his elevation to the status of his father in exemplary ways in Aeneas's case. "The poet nameth Cyrus or Aeneas no other way than to show what men of their fames, fortunes, and estates should do" (*Def.*, p. 103), Sidney says, answering the charge that poets lie with a defense of his whole aristocratic and literate culture. Likewise, the heroic image is supposed to inflame the reader's mind (*Def.*, p. 98). Behind the presentation of Daedalus in the *Defence*, however, we may perceive Sidney's understanding of the Virgilian artist's questioning of the political hero, of his aesthetic blindness, and we may hear his Protestant questioning of himself and his art. In the context of the English historical appropriation of the matter of Troy and the legends of King Arthur to identify the nation, Sidney contrarily prefers the biblical-historical Cyrus and the mythic Daedalus as models of moral discrimination to the military politics of Aeneas and the unbaptized visions of human success and doom of Virgil.

Just as the Daedalus to whom Sidney refers in the *Defence* as the chief guide to high-flying wits may nonetheless be a Virgilian Daedalus who possesses *pietas*, so, too, the Aeneas whom Sidney embraces is an Aeneas revised by Saint Augustine's voice in his *Confessions*—that is, Augustine himself, or some other fideistically or scripturally authorized character such as Cyrus. In articulating and limiting the capacity of heroic images to effect moral change in the reader, Sidney chooses to speak *not* in the voice of the classically destined Aeneas's self-justification to Dido, the abandoned woman, but in a voice echoing Augustine's self-accusation on his obsessive love of literature, specifically Virgil's poem, in the *Confessions*. This reverberates, in turn, with the identification of the Cyrus who was divinely chosen to prepare the way for the rebuilding of the Temple.

In the opening chapters of the *Confessions*, Augustine reviews his literary education and criticizes it, with special mention of the *Aeneid*. He accuses himself of being fascinated by the wanderings of Aeneas and overcome with tears over the death of Dido when he was far away from God, dying in the fornication he committed in learning and in life. "And this sort of madness is considered a superior and richer form of learning than learning how to read and write!" Augustine exclaims. So much for literature, one might concur if we were to stop here and prefer grammar or grammatology.[88] Neither Augustine nor Sidney did stop here, however. Augustine rewrote Virgil's fiction in the theology of the founding of the City of God, and Sidney testifies throughout the *Defence* to the appeal of literary knowledge in the light of Christ. In conflating the classical myths of Daedalus's successful escape from tyranny, Icarus's overreaching and tragic fall, and Aeneas's combined journey within himself or into the underworld and out to the new world of building the new nation with Scripture and allegorical mythology, Sidney rewrites the Virgilian heroism of the founding father Aeneas and the intellectual confession of Augustine's erotic and spiritual desire in the poet's confession of faith. Augustine's only Architect is the Word of God who builds the City of God, and Sidney's Cyrus is the historically designated servant of that Word according to divine revelation, just as Daedalus is the fictive persona of the gifted mastercraftsman.

In his figurative use of the characters of Cyrus and Daedalus, Sidney aims to bring literary studies away from moral uselessness and toward moral profit. As much as the Augustine who loved literary knowledge also condemned the romances and "fancies dreamed up by the poets" (*Conf.* 1.13 [34], trans. Pine-Coffin), Augustine himself tells the story of his sinful past in the first nine books of the *Confessions* as a story of grace. This autobiography establishes the rhetorical as well as the historical context for his entrance into his "underworld"—that is, into memory—in Book 10 in order to know himself. Aeneas at the threshold of the underworld in which he knows himself in the eyes of his father promises to build a shrine of thanksgiving to Apollo in imitation of Daedalus's good example. Augustine at the threshold of his own psychological and spiritual depths discovers another truth and changes the myth. He discovers in the limits of his cognition that his memory is endless because he *is* a shrine for the indwelling of divine mystery, and he cannot know all that he is (10.8). The statement immediately precedes the passage justifying the self-examined life, the life of self-knowledge, the life particularly of man as a creature made a little less than the angels, which is the passage Petrarch consulted like an oracle on the top of Mount Ventoux, asking men to wonder more at themselves as images and likenesses of God than at mountains, seas, and stars.

Petrarch had his own copy of the *Aeneid,* as Thomas M. Greene has reminded us, and it was accompanied by the apparatus of centuries of hermeneutics.[89] The English Petrarch was the young Sidney who took on the hermeneutical task. Sidney makes the necessary qualifications of the ancient Virgil and Augustine and the renaissance Petrarch through a Calvinistic faith. The politics of Cyrus has a divine sanction more than a patriarchal one, and Daedalean invention leaves the realm of gnosis and becomes praxis. For the same reasons the Cyrus destined by God in Holy Scripture represents in Sidney's *Defence* not merely a wise military leader and political builder of a civilization but also a living critique of those generals and governors who think their success is due to their own efforts. Likewise, Daedalean *ingenium* is a divine gift not to be abused by high-flying and Icarean wits.

To the extent that a Protestant poet like Sidney had to reconstruct Petrarchan hermeneutics, Sidney renounces falsely centered selves and embraces the imagination of a speaking subject whose centering voice unifies multiple allusions by steadfastly clinging to the grace and authority of a higher power. The speech of the *Defence* is, in this respect, the revelation not of the foolish *philautia* of Folly but of the proper self-love of Wisdom. The many allusions in the *Defence* produce an intertextuality and intersubjectivity that may be read, to be sure, through the duplicity or doubling of rhetorical allegory for political reasons. But flowing within and alongside that current in Sidney's discourse is a complexity greater than merely duplicitous or dualistic masking. Sidney writes out of a rich cultural foundation; as a renaissance Protestant he refuses to be narrowed down to a simple antithesis by the very dialectic of a living speech. The foundation includes the history of the Troy legend refashioned into Christian salvation history by Augustine. It supports the strongly Protestant assertion that human nature *is* dual, and that one should expect to find the ruins of a man coexisting with the vestiges of an integral beauty and the potential for an ethos that would re-create him as a divine icon.

Finally, this foundation is the strength of the Protestantism of the Sidney family—the father who was a dedicated public servant able to oppose the Queen on some matters as he supported her in others; the mother who was closely related to the Queen; the uncle who carried out many of her wishes; and, soon enough, the father-in-law whose Calvinism was highly self-conscious and developed. In all of the events touching Sidney's family in the late 1570s and early 1580s, and in all of his own efforts to achieve a position of power in which he could bring his gnosis to fruition in praxis, the Sidney who composed the *Defence* had to have been aware of the need to work out his ethos with great care.[90] As a result, the learned orator who rewrites his classical and Christian education into an *ars poetica Christiana* for Protestant England is primarily a man practicing self-knowledge, and a Cyrus poised on the threshold of a departure from his books to act, like his father and uncle, in the world. The metaphorical unity of the *Defence* is its oratorical success, its pronunciation and delivery of a new and poetic man. This success is more Sidney's than the *Letter written . . . to Queen Elizabeth*, in which the son spoke for his uncle and father, home from Ireland in the late 1570s and active in his opposition to the Queen's match with Alençon. Already beginning to know social and political contests and rebuffs, the Sidney of the *Defence* presents poesie as his thinking through of a history that shapes his life and death in the long-range building of England according to the model of another Son, the only Architect of the City of God.

Sidney moves classical myths of all kinds out of the hermeneutical labyrinth and toward the histories of scriptural characters such as Cyrus and, especially, the passionate poet, lover, and prince David, and the wise, if libidinous, temple-builder Solomon, and through them to Christ.[91] One paradigm of father and son evokes another, and in the shift from the classical to the Judeo-Christian Sidney registers his own arrival in manhood and his acceptance of the responsibility to shape his culture. He had good classical, Christian, and patriarchal reasons to know himself in the construction of the ethos of his speaking voice in the prosopopoeias of the *Defence*. So, too, it was not necessarily English xenophobia but the desire to assert an English

Christian character among various French Protestant influences that may have determined the particular shape Sidney gave the "shared knowledge" of his culture. Finally, Sidney's exposition of the mistress-knowledge culturally reflects the Protestantization of Plato encouraged by a learned Calvinism. For his conversion of Plato, Sidney found in Jean du Serres's 1578 edition of Plato's extant works all the material he needed. De Serres's philosophical syncretism and his Augustinian, architectonic philosophy of language were ready to be translated into Sidney's definition of the poet's art. So Sidney "Englished" the French "philosopher's book" (*Def.*, p. 91) sent to him as a gift, holding up to Elizabeth the mirror not of philosophy but of learning seeking virtue, faith seeking understanding, that is connatural to poesie.

4

Lover and Statesman:
The Reformed English Poet
Between Two Cities

In short, I have referred to that class of *scintillae* all disciplines that
honestly and rightly make for the self-examined life and that ought to be
assigned to the ἀρχιτεκτονικην and first consideration as its subordinates and serving members, as our Plato also says.
—Jean de Serres,
   "Verae Solidaeque Philosophia," *Platonis Opera Quae Extant Omnia*

The English Pursuit of Justification

The historical moment that saw Sidney's writing of the *Defence* was
preceded by more than a decade of temple-building analogies in, for
example, the Geneva Bible of 1560, John Shute's treatise on architecture, and Doctor John Dee's arts treatise the "Mathematicall Preface" to
Billingsley's *Euclid*, published in 1570. Shute's treatise was reprinted around
1579 or 1580, and Thomas Twyne translated Lambert Daneau's Calvinistic
tract *The wonderfull workmanship of the world* in 1578. Sir Thomas North's
translation of Plutarch's *Lives* also appeared in 1579, as did Edmund
Spenser's *The Shepheardes Calendar*, dedicated to Sidney and mentioned in
the *Defence*. John Lyly's *Euphues and His England* was available in 1580, and
Sidney's *Letter* to the Queen touching her marriage to "Monsieur" is also
dated to 1579 or 1580.

All these texts share an interest in "justification," whether it refers to a
theology of salvation or a fitting of words to the subject, of knowledge to
moral purpose, of classical figures to ethical examples in history as lived, or
of numbers to causes and principles. A good number of these books reveal
an English receptivity to a certain French cultural standard, whether in
Amyot's preface to Plutarch or Daneau's Huguenot scholasticism. Two
other texts appearing in print between 1578 and 1580 also addressed this
cultural theme and the potential alliance between French and English forms
of Protestantism: Jean de Serres's edition of *Plato* (1578) and his biblical
commentary *In Ecclesiasten Solomonis* (1579). Apart from S. K. Heninger,
Jr.'s thorough article, these sources have received hardly any mention in

critical studies of Sidney's shaping of the *Defence* when, in fact, they may pose the most direct influence of all. In these and in de Serres's histories of France and his biography of Coligny as the Protestant martyr par excellence of the Saint Bartholomew's Day Massacre on August 24, 1572, literary history possesses an angle of vision to document Sir Philip Sidney's intellectual appreciation of and resistance to the French connection in the name of an English identity.[1]

This chapter will examine in detail Jean de Serres's philological and religio-political appearances—sometimes ideal, sometimes parodic—in the *Defence*, but not without considering first the broader cultural context of other documents expressing the ideal building of a holy, learned, and powerful Britain. In particular, the *Plato* of 1578 and its political and religious significance informed Sidney's "conversion" of the philosopher from an adversary to a patron of poesie. De Serres especially developed a philosophy of language in his commentaries on three language dialogues of Plato, which the French historian and theologian groups together in a pattern of gradation ranging from the "logic" of the *Cratylus* through the "duplex" rhetoric of the *Gorgias* to the poetics of the *Ion*. In the commentary on the *Cratylus*, de Serres draws on some biblical and kabbalistic views of Hebrew language to "justify" Greek philosophical principles. In glossing the *Sophist* 236, de Serres appropriates the distinction between *eikastic* and *phantastic* images as the model for discussing true and false rhetorics in the commentary on the *Gorgias*. Those contrasting images must have appealed to him because they appear also in the Prefatory Letter, in the commentary on the *Ion*, and in the commentary on the *Symposium*. The distinction between *eikastic* and *phantastic* images is the dominant avenue of verbal justification, and it is the avenue of style that Sidney also takes for poesie.

De Serres's commentary on a wisdom book of Holy Scripture, *In Ecclesiasten Solomonis*, was published in Geneva in 1579 by Peter Santandreanus and translated into English by John Stockwood in 1585 as *A godlie and learned commentarie upon the excellent book of Solomon called Ecclesiastes, or the Preacher* with a preface by William Fulke. Sidney used its commonplace contrast of true and false philosophies, of Circean enchantment and moral profit, most probably, to order the relationship of pagan learning and Christian truth in the literary architectonics of the *Defence*. Those categories were, after all, commonplaces in the Christian humanist handling of allegorical mythology and of classical texts vis-à-vis revealed and absolute truth. The English pursuit of justification registered in Sidney's poetics in relation to this text among others, however, inevitably departs from mere book knowledge and production to bespeak those other, analogical texts: the book of the living and literate English Protestant soul engaged in the religious conversion of the nation and the book of English political action in the internal and external affairs of the Old World and the New.[2] Poesie was to mark the difference between the ungodly and the godly kingdoms. De Serres's work allows us to discern a highly structured, if partial frame of reference for Sir Philip Sidney's articulation of an English poesie's epiphany in the world; the mistress-knowledge has dominance over philosophy and history *because* she is a political handmaiden of a true religion.

Finally, when we realize that de Serres played multiple parts as a writer of philosophy and biblical commentary and of history (in the *Commentaries* on the civil wars of France attributed to him), we must approach his condensation of all of these matters into the biography of a great man, Coligny, as another cultural influence on Sidney. This political hagiography gives us another slant on the heroic Sidney, who may have met Coligny when he was recuperating from a failed assassination attempt shortly before the Massacre in Paris. The drama of this historical event and the later political support of Robert Dudley, Earl of Leicester, Sidney's uncle, for the alliance of England with France—but not the marriage of Elizabeth to Alençon—reveal cultural ambivalences that Sidney apparently needed to resolve.

In its most acute manifestation, therefore, the singular French expression of Jean de Serres may have served more than any other influence to reinforce Sidney's insistently *English* view of the poet's character. Both priest and victim of an ethical and political Love, Sidney's reformed English poet is a self seeking its center and working to constitute the poetic word as an instrument for the light of Christ, "the Desire of the nations." The Sidney who devised an architectonic poetics on the basis of de Serres's Augustinian Platonism would later preside with "Architectonical art," in Fulke Greville's phrase, at his own self-sacrifice in the Protestant cause on the field of Zutphen in the Netherlands.[3]

Clearly, the historical argument I outline here is political, and as such it directly touches our debates in modern literary criticism. It is not difficult to place Sidney's composition of the *Defence* in our modern critical context once we recognize its demonstrable authorization of an English literary culture. Not only did Sidney address a ready-made audience on the themes of national self-knowledge and self-esteem in his historical era, but his very approach to the subject reaches across the centuries to speak to the boundary-making efforts of modern Europe.

Behind Sidney's justification of things English one must perceive, for example, the political events in Ireland treated as internal affairs and the political events in France treated as external affairs. The two are related. In October 1577, a year before he resigned his office as Lord Governor of Ireland, Sir Henry Sidney recommended a "cess" of land tax in the support of which his son Philip wrote "A Discourse on Irish Affairs." Duncan-Jones and van Dorsten remark that Sidney was more willing to pursue a severe course of action in the subjugation and reformation of Ireland than either his father or the Queen, who avoided financial expenditure and strong military intervention when she could. They also comment on the similarity of style in the "Discourse" and the *Defence*, since both employ irony, colloquialisms, and parenthetical remarks.[4]

Taken as a microcosm of the domestic English debate of the Irish question, the Sidney family evidently had differences of opinion on the subject, not least because the English were also embroiled in foreign events. Thus Sir Henry Sidney prayed Psalm 114, which celebrated the Mosaic liberation of the Jews from Egypt, a barbarian nation, when he left Ireland in September 1578. That was more or less at the same time that his brother-in-law Robert Dudley, Earl of Leicester, urged alliance with France and that the edition of the Protestant *Plato* was conceived, executed, dedicated in its first two volumes to Queen Elizabeth of England and King James of Scotland, and sent as gifts to Sir Philip Sidney and George Buchanan in those countries so they could publicize it.[5] Such a presentation was, of course, an aspect of the French Protestant effort to influence English politics.

Not surprisingly, Sir Philip Sidney appears to have directed his political energy eastward, toward the Continent and toward a response to French arguments. In the violence of the English effort to dominate Ireland in the sixteenth and seventeenth centuries, one may find the measure of the cost of English expansion of its boundaries in the direction of the Continent, however veiled the price has been by English writers when they have tried to speak, as Sidney did, both as "an Irish advocate" and "a true English subject" ("Discourse," *Miscellaneous Prose*, ed. Duncan-Jones and van Dorsten, p. 9). The Eastern front was perceived to be more complex culturally than that of the wild Irish, and in the years immediately following Sir Henry Sidney's return from Ireland, his son was called upon by his family to write the *Letter* to Elizabeth against her liaison with Alençon and by his own English soul to defend national interests at home and abroad in the composition of the *Defence*. But Hubert Languet, a mentor if not exactly a father figure, may have had more to do with the composition of the *Defence* than we have recognized insofar as he wrote to Sidney from Cologne on September 24, 1579, to ask him to inquire into the Queen's reception and opinion of de Serres's *belle-édition* of *Plato*. Because the first volume is dedicated to her, Languet even suggests that the Queen ought to reward the Huguenot scholar with some monetary gift.[6]

The English literary debate with French poetic sensibility, genres, and purpose was an old and intimate one, and it is likely that the presentation of the intellectual and political values of a reformed Christianity in the French Protestant thought of Jean de Serres in his commentaries on Plato constituted a particular historical model of courses of action to be both embraced and avoided in Sidney's adumbration of English poetics and politics in the *Defence*. The *Defence* emerges as an English treatise in this European context specifically because it expresses the nationality of a Protestant culture *differ-*

ent from the barbarism of Ireland and the Catholicism of the Spanish Empire and *related to* but also *different from* the division of Catholics and Protestants in France. That Sidney made the focus of this declaration of an English national character a treatise on poesie, inventing her in the allegorical form of the personified mistress-knowledge, is a stroke of witty English genius. As the Latin language reached its peak of usefulness in the establishment of the universal European discourse of humanism and continued to thrive politically into the next century, Sidney put his force in another humanistic tenet. He helped to establish the new wave, so to speak, by using the vernacular language to express *all* of the cultural differences between England and other nations, whether they spoke classical Greek, Virgil's Latin, renaissance Italian, reformation German, or modern French. And he established the native tongue and its cultural power in his assertion of a specially English literary architectonics.

To the extent that the *Defence* reveals a peculiarly Anglo-French cultural competition, it is not surprising that discussion of it today resonates with the articulation of such competition in other periods of history. Anglo-French literary debate has continued to resound throughout modern history, most recently in the debate of critical theory in the late twentieth century. The English literature of F. R. Leavis and of New Criticism has clashed with Saussurian linguistics, Lacanian psychoanalysis, Derridean deconstruction, and French feminism. To argue the importance of a French source of influence on English thought in general and Sidney (who went to German book fairs) in particular in the 1570s and 1580s does not minimize other continental influences, including the one that Terry Eagleton has caricatured as the "ponderous Teutonic nonsense" of philology, which produced a Germanic flavor in debates about the rise of English literature as a course of study in the late nineteenth century. The French-source argument concurs with Eagleton so far as to point out that events and memories of events taking place across the Channel have often moved the English to speak their difference. This is true not merely in the case of the French Revolution and its effects on romanticism, or that of the First World War and the response of Leavis and T. S. Eliot, as Eagleton observes, but surely in the case of the Norman invasion, too, "1066 and all that," and, I shall argue, in the late sixteenth-century beginnings of England's cultural revolution.[7]

From Sidney's vantage, the building of the temple of the new Protestant England was, among other things, a making of the English poem of character on the continental scene and in America—ultimately, if not proximately. Jean de Serres's writings give us a case study of Sidney's effort to define an English literary identity in the broader context of cultural justification.

The quest for moral and intellectual justification in late sixteenth-century England was fierce, and Sidney participates fully. In the explicit architectural images of Holy Scripture in new translation, in English art, science, and mathematics, and in a new Protestant scholasticism that sought the collaboration of science and religion, a process of setting things right seems to have taken center stage as a metaphor for English culture in the last decades of the sixteenth century. Whether building a nation or a temple of the mind, a cell or a poem, renaissance Englishmen were finishing or dismantling something.

I have already suggested that the *Defence* is a creative synthesis that far exceeds a learned collation of Sidney's reading. In a political context, the construction of the *Defence* is a cultural directive to an English imagination already called to cross the gap between this nation and the one that might be and to acknowledge in the process the warp of character inherent in the nature of language and the engendering of texts. In this cultural context, Sidney celebrates poetic invention as the authentic mental act, the means by which the statesman—now a poet, too—moves from well-knowing to well-doing. When, then, Sidney ponders why England, "the mother of excellent minds, should be grown so hard a stepmother to poets, who certainly in wit ought to pass all other, since all only proceedeth from their wit, being indeed makers of themselves, not takers of others," he has set up the mythic couple of Nature and Art, of the poetic mistress-knowledge and her poetic mastercraftsman, on a renovated ladder of love (p. 110). Together they are the imaginative force that brings an inward justice or rightness—in the Pauline sense—to all other arts in Christian England, and all for Love.

The central philosophical question behind this corrective kind of master-craftsmanship comes, of course, from Plato. Socrates had challenged Protagoras's view that there must be something citizens shared—not the art of building or making pottery but a form of virtue that poetry taught best—if there was to be a state at all (*Protagoras* 325a). Using a verse from Simonides—"Foursquare, wrought without blame"—Socrates showed how difficult it was to interpret a poetic text; how much harder it must be, therefore, to "know thyself" and to become the just character Simonides' verse described (*Protagoras* 339–44). Yet the idea of man as the measure of all things flourished in the Renaissance, and in the arts debates it surfaced with similar Platonic ambivalence toward proportion-making.[8] Knowledge filtered through the judgment of character was only as true as the particular man who named reality in relation to himself was good (*Crat.* 386a). Whether the intellectual proportion was expressed in Leon Battista Alberti's combination of architecture and *istoria*, in Dolce's Platonic analogy for nature and moral philosophy, in Copernicus's synthesis of religion and mathematical astronomy, or in Spenser's and Milton's expression of learned poetic speech and the conduct of government service, the proof of knowledge was measured by a man's practice of it in living.[9]

The cultural demand for integrity that the rule of character put on knowledge—on theology, on social decorum, on picture and word, on contraptions and inventions—regularly exposed in the analogy of the arts a demonstrable warp between truth and falsehood. In character the warp testified to the difference between an idol and a divine icon at the very moment when Puritanism pursued the iconoclasm of exterior things for the sake of an image within. Theologians faced with the human inclination toward evil pointed to the duplex status of history as a life lived in two cities, and they valued the self-authenticating testimony of scriptural faith as their standard of truth, not human effort; scientists made experimentality their proof; and painters and poets, too, disputed the judgment of an informed "eye" in the measurable moral effects of seeing a painting or reading a poem.

By the end of the sixteenth century, for example, Paolo Lomazzo set color up as the "virtue" of painting, signifying by the term both the agency and the effect of artistic power. Sidney praised the inventive poet's use of "colours . . . fittest for the eye to see" (*Def.*, p. 80). In Richard Haydocke's translation of Lomazzo's *Trattato dell'arte de la pittura*, entitled *A Tracte Containing the Artes of Curious Paintinge, Caruinge, Building*, painting emerges in the glory of a universal, supervisory art—an architectonic art. For painting works "by the helpe of the Eie . . . , the principall sense," and it not only expresses the outward form of things but also discovers certain inward passions.[10] By doing so painting makes itself available as an instrument of moral reform to civil discipline; painting represents worthy and famous men and virtue itself. Painting, in short, is "a rule and direction to all other arts," and the artist is the wise man, the exponent of wisdom.

Wherfore it is worthy to be embraced and reverenced of all as an especiall gift of God, for the increase of Morall and Civile behaviour, as also for the glory of Painters, whose rare workes make knowne the power and force of the Arte, which is so manifold, that it is a rule and direction to all other arts insomuch as it ministreth them examples of fair and beautiful works. (3.1, pp. 94–95)

Haydocke's translation in 1598 included a prefatory epistle by John Case who, having issued a caveat against the conventionally immoral "coloring" of ladies' cosmetics, confirms the universality and morality of painting. Case bravely praises the usefulness of this treatise to those seeking knowledge—any kind of knowledge, for Lomazzo examines anatomy, botany (herbs, fruit, and plants), geometry, architecture, and cosmography and gives illustrations of history, of the construction of engines of war and ornaments of peace, of moral wisdom, and even of the works of God:

One shadow of man, one image of his partes, in this Booke, sheweth us better use. For if Hippocreates will read an Anatomie, heere-hence he may learn exact and true proportion of humane Bodies; if Dioscordies will make an Herball, here he may haue skill to set forth hearbes, plantes and fruites, in most liuely colours. Geometritians heere-hence for Buylding may take their perfect Modelles, Cosmographers may finde good arte to make their Mappes and Tables. Historians cannot heere want a pencell to over-shaddow mens famous Actes, Persons and Moral pictures. Princes may heere learne to builde Engines of warre, and ornamentes of peace. For (Vitruvius who writeth of Building to Augustus the Emperour) saith, that all kind of warlike Engines were first invented by Kings and Captaines, who were skilfull in the Arte of Painting and Carving. One thing more I adde aboue all the rest (my good friend M. Haydocke) that in reading your booke I finde therein two notable images of Naturall and Moral Philosophie, the one so shaddowed with preceptes of Nature, the other so garnished with the best colours of Vertues; that in mine opinion I never found more use of Philosophie, in any booke I ever read of the like theame and subject. And truely had I not read this your Auctor and Translation, I had not fully understoode what Aristotle meant in the sixth booke of his Ethikes, to call Phidias and Polycletus most wise men; as though any part of wisedome did consist in Carving and Painting; which now I see to be true; and more-ouer must needs confesse the same, because God himselfe filled Bezaleel the sonne of Uri, with an excellent spirit of Wisedome and understanding, to find out curious workes, to worke in Golde, Silver, and Brasse and in Graving stones to set them, and in Carving of wood, even to make any manner of fine woorke. In like manner hee indued the heart of Aholiah with Wisedome (as the Texte saith) to worke all manner of cunning in embrodred and needle-worke. And thus he did for the making of his Arke, his Tabernacle, his Mercy-seate, his glorious Temple, which were the wonders of the Worlde, and only rare monuments of this Arte. (Sig. *j.ʳ)

Case's highest praise for Haydocke's translation of Lomazzo's treatise is the "use" made of philosophy—the production of things out of the knowledge of natural and moral truths, the making of invisibles visible—even to the religious manufacture of the ark and the Temple.

But the English arts theorist could not have claimed so much for painting, I think, had Sir Philip Sidney not already worked out the architectonic philosophy of poesie. Metaphors of mediation and proportion-making for the production of good character filled contemporary discussion of the arts and sciences. Case reads the invisible "spirit of Wisedome" in the products of art, while Sidney sustained the relation between the visible and personified wisdom of the mistress-knowledge and both the products of her art and the moral effects evident in human behavior.

In the Preface to Billingsley's *Euclid* of 1570, for example, Doctor John Dee stated his version of architectonic character-making. He met the advancement of learning with equanimity of spirit because of his combination of self-knowledge and Christian hope.

NOSCE TEIPSUM: (Knowe thy selfe) so long agoe pronounced. . . . And then you will perceave, how long agoe you have bene called to the Schole, where this Art might be learned. Well. I am nothing affrayde, of the disdayne of some such as thinke Sciences and Artes, to be but Seven. Perhaps those Such, may with ignorance, and shame enough, come short of them Seven, also; and yet nevethelesse they can not prescribe a certain number of Artes: and in eche, certain unpassable boundes, to God, to Nature, and mans Industrie. New Artes dayly rise up: and there was no such order taken, that All Artes, should in one age or in one land, or of one man, be made knowen to the world. Let us embrace the giftes of God, and wayes to wisedome, in this time of grace, from above, continually bestowed on them, who thankefully will receive them: *Et bonis Omnia Cooperabuntur in Bonum.* (Sig. C.iiij)

Dee's search for a flexible moral knowledge that might integrate the multiplication of the arts and sciences lets go of a fixed structure of knowledge, a prescribed number of arts, and motivates his invention of an analogy-making master art—the "anthropographie" by means of which a man may engrave or "write" his own character by constantly growing in knowledge and by assimilating discoveries of things unknown to things known. This master art, in turn, depends on another new knowledge that Dee calls "archemastery," a science closely related to optical perspective and etymologically related to the analogy of architecture. "Archemastery" can "bryng to actuall experience sensible, all worthy conclusions by all the Artes Mathematicall purposed, & by true Naturall Philosophie concluded" (sig. A.ij). Both "anthropographie" and "archemastery" constitute working solutions to problems raised by skepticism.

The "Mathematicall Preface" falls into the category of a treatise on Vitruvius, the classical author whose explanation of architecture strongly influenced renaissance thinking. Vitruvius had proportioned human anatomy to the structure of buildings and parts of buildings, thus giving architecture an anthropormorphic aspect and the body an architectural symmetry by analogy. But Dee's combined interest in "anthropographie" and "archemastery" applies mathematical measure well beyond buildings and bodies to a Christian Platonic realm of the mind where, as Saint Paul testified, all things will cooperate for the good of those who love God. Dame Frances Yates has rightly commented that Dee's Vitruvian exploration of knowledge does not, in fact, actually contain a discussion of ancient buildings or of architectural designs for anatomy. What interested him was not architecture but the analogical power of "the basic theory of proportion in its mathematical and symbolic aspects . . . and the relationship of the arts and sciences to one another."[11] If I may extend Dame Frances's argument, Dee's interest was not in architecture but in architectonics, the bringing of knowledge to power not merely in physical products of the inventive and imaginative mind but even in that supreme example of divine workmanship, the embodied moral character of the human being, or what he calls "absolute *Architecture*."

I have preferred *Architecture*, to be bred and fostered up in the Dominion of the pereles *Princesse, Mathematica*: and to be naturall Subject of hers. And the name of *Architecture*, is of the principalitie, which the Science hath, aboue all other Artes. And *Plato* affirmeth, the *Architect* to be *Master* over all, that make any worke. Wheruppon, he is neither Smith, nor Builder: nor separately, any Artificer: but the Hed, the Provost, the Director and Iudge of all Artificiall workes, and all Artificers.

For, the true Architect, is hable to teache, Demonstrate, distribute, describe, and Iudge all workes wrought. And he, onely, searcheth out the causes and resone of all Artificiall thynges Thus excellent, is Architecture though few (in our dayes) atteyne thertoi yot may not the Arte, he otherwise thought on, then in very ded it is worthy. Nor we may not, of auncient Artes, make new and imperfect Definitions in our dayes: for scarsitie of Artificers: no more, than we may pynche in, the Definitions of *Wisedome*, of *Honeste*, or of *Frendeshyp* oi of *Iustice*. No more will I consent, to Diminish any whit, of the perfection and dignities (by iust cause) allowed to absolute *Architecture*. ("Mathematicall Preface," sig. d.iiij.ʳ)

On the basis of the Vitruvian analogue of buildings and bodies, an analogical shift toward a metaphysical ethics and mathematical morality was easy. The translators of the Geneva Bible argued for an integration of religion and politics in a wise and morally upright nation; Dee makes scientific application of a similarly integral knowledge to the moral and psychological invention of human nature. The key to his highly Platonic view of proportion-making is the propagation of light, for "seeing" guaranteed a certain experiential validity in knowing if one moves appropriately from visibles to invisibles.

Dee's organization of knowledge in his "Mathematicall Preface" illustrates a cognitive hierarchy based on the laws of optics. "Archemastery" has "Mastership" over "so many and so mighty Artes and Sciences" because it certifies the truth of conclusions "by Experience complete and absolute" while verbal arts can merely persuade or prove. Dee's interest in optics as a mathematical division of geometry came not only from his desire to account for the marvels of optical illusion and to correct anamorphoses but also from his appreciation of the mediate status of mathematical knowledge between things supernatural and things natural: "A meruaylous newtralitie haue these things Mathematicall and also a straunge participation between thinges supernaturall . . . and thynges naturall" (sig. *.j). Geometry reveals the light of eternity in newly understood and demonstrable natural laws. For Dee the highest points of perspective belong to the art of "anthropographie" that orders the number, weight, and measure of "euerie diuerse thing conteyned" in the body of man to the universe and orders the symmetry of the universe to man. Perspective is the chief science as architecture is the chief practical art, but next to the proportional knowledge of "anthropographie," architecture takes a subordinate place. Although esteemed for learning, it is merely one of the "outward images" of this superior "Art of Artes" of self-knowledge in the microcosm made to the image and likeness of God, for "anthropographie" establishes the principles that undergird all the pictorial arts and sciences ("Mathematicall Preface," sig. c.iiijʳ).

Beyond "anthropographie," however, stands "archemastery," the art that brings to "experience sensible, all worthy conclusions by all the Artes Mathematicall purposed, & by true Naturall Philosophie concluded" (sig.

A.iij^r). Above human anthropographers and architects alike, Christ is the "Divine Archemaster" (sig. d.iij–d.iij^v), and the "chief Science, of the Archemaster, (in this world) as yet knowen, is an other (as it were) OPTI-CAL Science" (sig. A.iij^v). Almost all of Dee's "Mathematicall Preface" turns on the Platonic doctrine of the One and on the emanation of light as a state of revelation in the analogy of the arts and sciences; the multiplication of light is another type of ladder:

> Well, well, It is time for some to lay hold on wisedome, and to Iudge truly of thinges: and not so to expound the Holy words, all by Allegories: as to Neglect the wisedome powre, and Goodnes of God, in, and by his Creatures, and Creation to be seen and learned. By parables and Analogies of whose natures and properties, the course of the Holy Scripture, also, declareth to us very many Mysteries. The whole Frame of Gods Creatures, (which is the whole world,) is to us, a bright glasse: from which, by reflexion, reboundeth to our knowledge and perceiverance, Beames, and Radiations: representing the Image of his Infinite goodnes, Omnipotency, and wisedome. (Sig. b.ij^r)

We have seen, though, that Sidney steals the visual and experimental fire from artists and scientists to define a poetic art whose "delightful proportions" create not only verbal images but moral realizations of the invisible in the visible and of human character in the light of conscience, for "there are many mysteries contained in poetry, which of purpose were written darkly," that is, allegorically (*Def.*, pp. 92, 121). Where Dee analogizes the infusion of grace and the genesis and propagation of light in the created universe—"the true Sonne of rightwiseness is risen aboue the Horizon, of our temporall Hemisphaerie, and hath so abundantly streamed into our hartes, the direct beames of his goodnes, mercy, and grace: Whose heat All Creatures feele: Spirituall and Corporall: Visible and Invisible" (sig. b.ij^v)—Sidney, in effect, appropriates for poetry the "archemastery" of the Word of God and the "anthropographie" of re-creating human characters in just proportions. Sidney "expounds" the Word by making his allegorical figure of wisdom, the mistress-knowledge, quite visible to imagination.

Henry Peacham had explained the value of visual metaphors

> because the sight is a sure sence, and sildome deceyued, for that which we see, we beleeye it to be so, therefore, when we understand a thing very well, we may say we see it, sygnifying thereby, that we doe as wel perceaue it, as if it were a thing visible, which oure eyes doe perfectlye beholde, from the sight diuers signifycations be taken. (*Garden of Eloquence* [1577], sig. B.ij^v)

Sidney, too, subscribed to the visual model of cognition and its experiential validation of knowledge, for he understood that the poetic idea had to be illuminated by the poet's imaginative figures sensibly and experientially before they could communicate the light of conscience to the reader (*Def.*, pp. 85–86). But the poetic making of apt proportions or characters to express all things principally extended the analogy of the arts and sciences into optics to state the sure moral superiority of the poetic enlightenment of conscience to the philosopher "blind in himself" (*Def.*, p. 82).

New knowledge of optics was revealing the deceptions of sight. The Neoplatonic aesthetic of the *velo*, or corrective frame of glass, had already taught artists the ambivalence of the rules of perspective, and writers were quick to imitate the possibilities of illusion in their references to Friar Bacon's "optic glass," to "natural perspective," and to games of perception.[12] The skeptical philosophy of Agrippa von Nettesheim, whose essay *Of the vanitie and uncertaintie of artes and sciences* had influenced Sidney's *Defence*, expressed the insecurity of the geometric eye in all the pictorial arts and sciences.[13] Agrippa satirizes the Daedalean "builder" of engines and mazes:

The doubtfull Geometricians, laiynge on me Triangles, rownde, and square figures, will take me prysoner, being as it were entangled in Gordions Knot. The vayne woorker in the arte Perspectiue, will engraue and depainte me more bruitishe and deformed, than an Ape or *Thersites*. . . . The Dedalean builder, with his moste mightie Injins, will priuely undermine me, and compel me to wander in confuse Laberinthes. (Sig. A.ij)

His purpose is to attack the arts and sciences as if they were the castles of giants and to declare how great human blindness is (sig. A.iij).

Although the analogy of reason and light was antique and the multiplication of light had been Christianized in the Middle Ages to signify the infusion of grace, renaissance optics made thinkers cope with the fact that the sure sense of sight was not so sure after all.[14] Learned Protestants applied their divine science to knowledge as a corrective and an expression of faith in an Augustinian and scholastic fashion, consequently, using infused Light to redirect the acquired light of the mind.

The Calvinist Lambert Daneau developed new versions of the intellectual architecture of scholasticism to promulgate Aristotelian and Platonic doctrines according to the self-authenticating primacy of Scripture.[15] Daneau's renovation of intellectual history and tradition in the Church actually depended on a prior judgment: that the mind of the elect was regenerated by grace. When he comments on the harmony of creation, knowledge, and human character, Daneau lays a foundation for a new collaboration of religion and science.

In the treatise that appeared in England in translation by Thomas Twyne in 1578 as *The wonderfull workmanship of the world; wherein is conteined an excellent discourse of Christian naturall Philosophie concernyng the fourme, knowledge, and use of all things created*, Daneau expressed the fundamental theological difference between human creation out of "stuff" and divine creation ex nihilo: "Take away yron from the Smith, timber from the Carpendour, yearne from the Weauer, what other good can they doe but stand still gaping in their shoppes . . . ? But hee that is the true creatour, hee maketh his matter and stuffe in whiche and of which he woorketh, of nothing" (sig. 40ʳ). In a letter to William of Orange, the proposed leader of a new Protestant League in Europe, though, Daneau revealed his intellectual purpose as a rule of production analogous to the divine creation out of nothing because congruent to its truth, and he posed it in relation to the Protestant church in the Netherlands in the early 1580s. Presenting the creation of a Christian physics, a Christian ethics, and a Christian politics, he proclaimed, *Nihil Pulchrius Ordine,* "Nothing is more beautiful than order."[16] The central principle of this Calvinist restructuring of knowledge was not, however, the finished product merely of philosophical thought; Daneau wanted to see the active historical exercise of "order" in the enlightenment of living men. Like Dee's "archemastery," Daneau's "spiritual" knowledge of the arts and sciences pursued the forms and use of all things created for the sake of remaking man himself. Daneau's work joined the efforts of many irenic Calvinists in the 1570s and 1580s to plead the cause of their religion in England.[17] Sir Philip Sidney's learning, social status, character, and religious sympathy suited their argument, and both Sidney and Puttenham would envision the poet creating out of nothing but his own "stuff." When Sidney defined the poetic art by using but redirecting Jean de Serres's architectonic philosophy of language, his rationale in the *Defence* showed a cultural cross-pollination with the moral and visionary "geometry" of late sixteenth-century English Calvinism and its justification, and he would later give his life to establish such a spiritual order in the Netherlands.

The True and Well-Grounded Philosophy of Jean de Serres's 1578 *Plato*

Jean de Serres's elaboration of the architectonic philosophy in the 1578 *Plato* undergirds Sidney's poetic idea. The philological study of de Serres's commentaries and the recognition of the politics of religion contributing to Sidney's fiercely English intertextualization, or even parody, of classical and continental sources put the *Defence*, in turn, in a new historical light. Although numerous renaissance sources absorbed and transformed notions of the architectural God, the descent and ascent of Love, and the golden world, none put them together with classical and Christian thought in quite the consistent and sustained synthesis that de Serres's commentaries do. The evidence for Sidney's appropriation and transformation of de Serres's reasoning is overwhelming; he must have written the *Defence* with the *Plato* either open before him or so well assimilated from de Serres's consistent rationale that the young Englishman could style the rhetorical uniformity of multiple ideas in the *Defence* with a flash of his pen.[18]

Specifically, Jean de Serres composed in the 1578 edition of Plato's extant

works an architectonic philosophy of language that gave Sidney exactly the
compendium of classical and Christian thought to justify his definition of the
mistress-knowledge as the "inward light"—the poetics of conscience and
architectonic wit. The northern renaissance revival of the *philosophia Christi*
that guides de Serres's synthesis of Plato and Aristotle is largely a patristic
argument—and that mostly Augustinian and Calvinistic—although elements of scholasticism enter into the discussion. [19] De Serres's explicit use of
the architectonic idea throughout his commentaries justifies philosophy as a
useful source of ethical knowledge correspondent to Protestant faith and
doctrine. Thus the 1578 Protestant *Plato* presents a philosophy in which
ethics and politics determine the value of physics and metaphysics, and its
architectonic philosophy of the Word in human thought and speech gives
Protestant humanists, statesmen, churchmen, and poets an elegant integration of various traditions. This edition of Plato probably contributed also to
Spenser's idea of Christian poetic historiography in the *Letter* to Raleigh and
to Milton's encyclopedic architecture of prophetic fables. Literary history
supports the argument that de Serres's version of Platonism affected other
poets not only through the work and reputation of Sidney but also directly.
According to Sandys, de Serres's *Plato* was *the* edition of Plato's works to be
consulted in the late sixteenth through the eighteenth centuries. [20]

The ethos of the renaissance Christian scholar shelters the ethos of the
classical pagan philosopher as de Serres teases the scholastic concept of the
intellectual architect. If Plato were to be "hissed off the stage" of history as
"the architect of monstrous opinions," de Serres says, then all of the ancients and all of the Christians of old, even those ignorant of philosophy, are
also damned:

Damned is Cicero, damned is Plutarch, Galen, and the most learned of the Gentiles.
Damned are our own—Augustine, truly the most eminent theologian, and Jerome,
Justin, Basil, Gregory, and Clement; in short, damned are all of the Greek and Latin
ancients who have called Plato, out of the crowd of other philosophers, their chief,
and named Homer the ocean of philosophers, and Moses the wisest, the best, the
most useful, the holiest, the most august and, finally, the divine philosopher.
(1:sig. **v^r)

This defence of Plato denigrates the material role of the architect and praises
the spiritual role of the philosopher. The Fathers whom de Serres names are
the patristic writers whose thought he uses to connect philosophy to religion. De Serres acknowledges the Platonism of patristic theology, similarly,
with an enthusiasm unusual in a Protestant divine for whom the principle of
sola Scriptura was absolute and the work of the Fathers in theology relative.
However, as the Prefatory Letter, the commentaries, and the summary
axioms show, de Serres does not, in fact, depart from a commitment to the

self-authentication of Scripture; he builds up an historical vision of human reason, speech, and action in a corrected philosophy, a philosophy made complete and solid in the mind regenerated by knowledge of the Word.[21]

Early in the letter de Serres alludes to Saint Paul's comment in Acts 17 on the Athenian recognition of an "unknown" God—as Sidney would later credit the same passage to show the scriptural acknowledgment of a kind of truth in poetry (*Def.*, p. 108). The scriptural passage—besides asserting that the true God who made heaven and earth "dwelleth not in temples made with hands" (Acts 17:23–24, Geneva)—places de Serres's philosophizing in the context of John Calvin's emphasis on the knowledge of God and self-knowledge.[22] De Serres does not explicitly allude to Tertullian, but Tertullian's well-known condemnation of classical philosophy and his questioning of the relationship between Jerusalem and Athens, the Church and the academy, the holy City and the city of man in chapter 7 of *The Prescription against Heretics* inform the logic of de Serres's rebuttal of the claim that philosophy is idolatrous.[23] De Serres's reasoning suggests great familiarity with doctrines of the Logos, the Word, in the Christian apologetic of Justin Martyr, who argues the measure or proportion of human participation in the fullness of the truth.[24] To reconcile the patristic doctrine of the image with Calvinist theological emphases, de Serres's interpretation seems to turn to the *locus classicus* in Irenaeus on the divine election of the "spiritual man" who walks according to the light of reason.[25] De Serres, no doubt, was familiar with the work of his fellow Calvinist scholar, Nicholas des Gallars (Gallasius), the editor of Irenaeus's works and the former minister to the "strangers' church" in London; des Gallars's letter dedicatory to Archbishop Grindal strengthens the association of Calvinist patristic scholarship with English religion.[26]

Especially convincing for de Serres, however, is the Augustinian vision: a man who does not know himself can hardly be expected to know God. This view, affirmed by Calvin, inspires de Serres to make an Augustinian statement on the obvious connection between wisdom and the love of wisdom, that is, philosophy:

For whatever philosophy itself is (as Augustine has said), who does not recognize that it is absurd in human affairs for Philosophers to prefer the study of wisdom to wisdom itself? Indeed, what that wisdom may be and how much of it remains in men, and what use it may be to them, is to be seen; and so philosophy itself is described according to the laws of true demonstration. (1:sig. **ii^r)

Following Augustine in this fashion, de Serres links the pursuit of wisdom to dialectic (cf. *De Doct. Christ.* 2.39) and summarizes the positive view of philosophy. For the regenerate or spiritual man, he says—following Paul and qualifying the negative assertions of Tertullian and Jerome—as for the pure, all things are indeed pure. If one knows Christ the Word in a true philosophy, one may enter the realm of philosophical reasoning and prove what is good (1:sig. **iii^v–**iiii^r). A regenerate philosophical architecture of thought produced by the spiritual man reclaims the mind for Protestant Christianity in the great debate called Reformation.

When Jean de Serres's patristic concepts join Plato's first principles and Aristotle's architectonic knowledge, the central argument for the architectonic philosophy has been forged. De Serres is free, then, to acknowledge the presence of the seeds or "sparks" of truth and virtue in men in different ways at different points in history.[27] This central argument establishes the moderation of de Serres's Calvinism without destroying the crucial difference between Christian revelation and human thought. Thus de Serres refers to Saint Basil and Eusebius among the ancients and to Bessarion and Sturm among the moderns to distinguish the truth of Plato's philosophy from various philosophical falsehoods. He explains how Platonic thought upholds what useful doctrines there are among the Stoics and determines what is useful in Aristotle. De Serres even discusses how Platonic allegory ought to be understood. The truth of Christian doctrine, similarly, is the right measure to use in reconciling the contradictions in Platonic and Aristotelian teachings. After echoing several renaissance commonplaces on the subject of Platonism, de Serres discusses the question of Plato's having gained his best lights from Moses and the Egyptians; comments on the various Platonisms expressed by Iamblichus, Proclus, and Porphyry; develops correspondences between the Plato who teaches and the Aristotle who proves; and refers, finally, to Ficino.

The Prefatory Letter closes with a Greek epigram, the Latin title of which is "De Platone et Aristotele Coniungendis" (1:sig. ***ii^v), and several other epideictic epigrams. De Serres headnotes the text proper, as I have already mentioned, with Saint Augustine's comment in the *De Civitate Dei* (8.4) on the perfection of philosophy accomplished by Plato's having united its contemplative and active kinds. A striking illustration of renaissance scholarship, the text of the 1578 *Plato* testifies to the union of contemplative wisdom and active virtue—well-knowing and well-doing. For de Serres has rhetorically used his defense of philosophy to persuade his readers, especially Queen Elizabeth and King James, to the intelligent building of the godly kingdom on earth. The letter to Elizabeth compares her rule to those of Solomon and Augustus and proudly reiterates de Serres's elegant yoking of religious, philosophical, and political issues of the day: when Plato says that the happy republic is the one where the ruler philosophizes or the philosopher rules, the kind of philosophy meant is not merely the earthly knowledge of the arts and sciences but the greatest wisdom that has its origin in the knowledge of God (1:sig. ii^v). Later, in the commentary on *Theages, siue De Sapientia, Obstetricius,* in the volume dedicated to Elizabeth, de Serres remarks, "Wisdom [*Sapientia*] is of all sciences the Lady and Queen" (1:120). The letter to James, more epideictic and less didactic, also allegorizes wisdom as the "Lady and Queen" whom James should seek. It is not difficult to see how Sidney's imagination changed that picture of wisdom to the Solomonic allegory of poesie as the mistress-knowledge.

The measure of de Serres's influence on the *Defence* is great. Sidney borrows the thrust of the letter to the reader defending the ethos of philosophy and uses it to create the ethos of poesie. In describing the poet's exploration of his own mental zodiac as a version of the true philosophy, Sidney has obviously relied on Cicero's sense of the teaching, delighting, and moving powers of oratory and Horace's sense of the wise wit whose poetry is both sweet and useful. Both Latin writers advance Sidney's effort to refashion Plato's view of the poetic mind in the same way de Serres has rehabilitated Plato, and Sidney injects a racy Elizabethan tone.

Almost as soon as Sidney praises the poet for ranging freely in the zodiac of his wit, for example, the *Defence* presents a sexual pun to center the theological distinction between the "erected wit" and the "infected will" (p. 79). From the vantage of Christian thought, not classical, Sidney sounds out the character of the poet, the integrity of his art. Permeating the discourse of Sidney's oration, as he cross-references "wit," "invention," "imitation," and imagination, is an argument that explains away divine inspiration but asserts that something *like* "the force of a divine breath" allows the poet's erected wit to overcome the infected will in the fine utterance of his poetic fictions. "Our erected wit maketh us know what perfection is," he says, "and yet our infected will keepeth us from reaching unto it" (p. 79). Nevertheless, the creative power of poesie—the art that rules over a "second nature" in the way nature rules over hers—can "with the force of a divine breath" bring forth those heroic characters who overcome the breach in fallen human nature between knowledge and virtuous action. Wit is man's mental universe; the knowledge that engages the wit and erects it is less a static body of facts than a penetrating habit of knowing—a wide-ranging invention exploring all facets of knowledge and gathering them up in instructive and delightful combinations that move the inner "inspiration" of virtue. "Wit" and "invention" describe the specialized activity of knowing the good and then, by the art of measure and proportion-making, motivating its achievement. Thus Sidney urges the Queen and nation, as it were, to become pregnant and deliver.

A most Platonic leap of intuition is made here over the serious gap called "infected will." But Sidney explains the poet's springboard of pleasure as the well-ordered verbal music and imaginative proportions of eloquence, the delightful proportions of words. For this reason, Sidney asserts later in the *Defence*, it is not poetry in the "lovely name of Love" that abuses man's wit, but man's wit improperly used that abuses poetry (p. 104). Poesie purifies the wit and is the corrective, educative agent of statesmanship.

Through the power of language one may know the universe and—what is better—know God in the universe and return to him with a renewed mind. The purpose of Sidney's architectonic poesie, like the purpose of de Serres's architectonic philosophy, is the production of living men who bear within them that inborn speech or spark of truth that corresponds to Saint Augustine's chaste mind of the City of God. Sidney's poesie best accomplishes this purpose because the inventive activity of poet and reader moves them from knowledge to virtue.

Jean de Serres essentially combined three strains of the theological concept of the sparks of conscience: Augustine's connection between moral judgment and the knowledge of the arts and sciences in the *scintilla rationis*; Jerome's scriptural correspondence between the apocalyptic visions of Ezekiel and John and the Platonic powers of the soul in the *synderesis scintilla*; and Bonaventure's metaphysics of the *apex mentis*, the highest point of man's mind illumined by grace.[28] Sir Philip Sidney's appropriation from "learned men" of the definition of the "inward light" of nature that determines ethical judgment (Augustine et al.) and of the "highest point of man's wit" (Bonaventure) reveals his transformation of de Serres's architectonic philosophy into the "English" theological erection of the moving power of poesie (*Def.*, pp. 91, 79).[29]

To justify philosophy, de Serres constructed a ladder pointing to the shared truths of religion, the movement of the conscience from knowing the good to doing the good, and the influence of architectonic knowledge in speech.[30] Attributing his argument to Plato, de Serres established the self-examined life as the ultimate mastercraftsmanship, the art of living that rules over other disciplines and other arts and sciences as its subordinates and serving members (1:sig. **iii'). By defining *scintillae* as the intellectual means by which men discern good and evil and by including the operations of dialectic and speech in mastercraftsmanship, de Serres certainly recapitulated a Platonic-Augustinian line of reasoning. But by associating the sparks with Ezekiel's and Saint John's apocalypticism (1:sig. **ii'), he indicated that the Lamb who alone is worthy to open and read "the Book" is the type of the new, spiritual man who eats "the little book" and teaches the truth (Revelation 5:9; 10:9). Because de Serres's spiritual men possess the true and well-grounded philosophy of an architectonic Word of God and because the Light penetrates the darkness of the world and illuminates knowledge and action, a certain optimism addresses precisely the human activity in which humanism and skepticism most clashed—that is, speech and language—when conscience makes words of light combat words of darkness.[31] The attribution of moral efficacy to architectonic speech implies a radically optimistic view of the intellectual endeavors of those who accept the truths of religion and the work of conscience as their graced intellectual foundation—the inspiration for the building of an earthly city like the heavenly

City.[32] Sidney specifically transforms this argument into the essence of poesie.

As a child of the Renaissance, Jean de Serres understands that the disposition of all knowledges by an architectonic principle that, in turn, is the *synderesis scintilla*—the moving of knowledge to virtue—notably appears in language as the cognate of reason.[33] Parallels between God's eternal Word and man's invented word depend on the fact that speech is a special signature of the Wisdom that creates in the wisdom that is created. God's Word and man's word are distinct; yet they are related in a complex analogy of cause and effect.[34] Although the seeds of ethical knowledge are in every person, and in the elect more, in those who are able to speak well the seeds are evidently very powerful. In speech the sparks may become flames to virtue. Thus in de Serres's hierarchy of the gifts of God, speech follows religion, conscience, and knowledge:

Also among the good gifts of God I count brightly burning and wise speech; that is, the conduct of speaking, arguing, and proclaiming well. For that faculty of speech is a cognate of and has affinity to reason. (1:sig. **ii^v)

The proportion of man's word to God's Word appears in a relation of effect to cause in de Serres's treatment of the characters of spiritual men:

Besides, [God] has aroused some men from the common crowd in whom these *scintillae* are more illustrious and more efficacious little flames to virtue and integrity: the services and helps of these men are brought to light in the sciences and arts, for the human community of learning is held together within the bounds of integrity. . . . Have these *scintillae* not been efficacious in pagans? To what extent they may be powerful the divine Word teaches (which Plato truly desired but he had no knowledge of it). . . . Without doubt, the first spark of this truth is the sense of religion, which is contained in men so far as these words of the same man tell: τὸ γνωςτὸν τοῦ Θεοῦ ἐν αὐτοῖς ἐφανερώθη [the knowledge of God has shone forth in men]. Similarly, such knowledge about God has been hidden in the intimate, most hidden rooms of the mind; it progresses out of the contemplation of the created things themselves and from the interior source of the immortal soul to the extent that it grasps in itself the eternal power of God. . . . In short, I have referred to that class of *scintillae* all disciplines that honestly and rightly make for the self-examined life and that ought to be assigned to the ἀρχιτεκτονικην and first consideration as its subordinates and serving members, as our Plato also says. (1:sig. **ii^v–**iii^r)

This passage demonstrates that de Serres's attitude toward the power of reason and speech is essentially Platonic and Augustinian, although he has adapted the light of the mind to the Aristotelian building of the structure of knowledge and virtue. The entire edifice of knowledge is held together by the integrity of the human characters who are justified, and some men are more justified than others; that is, spiritual men are "set right" in their judgments by having grasped within themselves more of the eternal power

of God. In these men the City of God is being built by the Word, for spiritual
men teach the Word in their words and enact its power or virtue by stimulating others to seek a correspondence between their minds and the mind of
God. Out of the "most hidden rooms of the mind" de Serres's enlightened
character give the architectural analogy its full architectonic point in what
they do and say

Sidney's Appropriation of the "Philosopher's Book"

In the major passage of the *Defence* preceding his use of the architectonic
metaphor, Sidney's metaphoric terms already persuade the reader to the
philosophical definition about to appear (pp. 74–82). The end of ethical
doctrine is happiness, said Aristotle, and the efficient cause of happiness is
God and virtue, said Jean de Serres (2:250–51). Poesie, aimed at the final end
of learning that is the virtuous action that is happiness, transcends all other
knowledges that depend merely on nature and integrates them in the
service of that exalted end, says Sidney.

The integrity of philosophy and the importance of speech in the practice
of architectonic knowledge occupy de Serres's reflection in several of his
dialogue commentaries besides the Prefatory Letter. His remarks have a
similarly ethical twist. In volume 1 of the *Plato*, de Serres views the argument
of the pseudo-Platonic *Erastae* or *Amatores, siue de Philosophia*, with repeated allusions to architectonic knowledge. The emphasis on the "lovers"
of wisdom sustains the mythic imagination that the *Symposium* states more
fully: to love beauty is to go on the quest for truth. Boldly, de Serres follows
Aristotle to say that the philosopher differs from the practitioners of all the
other arts and sciences because he knows the general reason, the theory of
all the arts. Thus de Serres turns Aristotle's *Metaphysics* into the first or
"primary" architectonic philosophy of the *Ethics*, extended to the economics
of the household and the politics of the state (*Erastae* 1:131).[35] The dialogue
insists on the great difference between architecture—the fabrication of buildings and great physical works—and rule by a true "architect" who governs
"with prudence and understanding" (1:135).[36] The word *architectonic* shows
up repeatedly in this dialogue and in de Serres's commentary.

In volume 2, de Serres considers the contents of the *Philebus* to be Plato's
statement of the ordering principle for the dialogues as a whole. The
Philebus, siue De Voluptate, siue, De summo bono, teaches the doctrine of
proportionality that places God, nature, the mind, the arts and sciences, and
dialectic and rhetoric in relation to one another on the ladder of truly wise
pleasure. The axioms following de Serres's general analysis of this dialogue
convey his theological idea of "the wisdom of God's architecture", incorporate an ethical standard to organize the proportion, and differentiate the arts
and sciences. The emphasis on man's distinctive "ornament" of reason

leads to de Serres's stress on the arts of discourse. He singles out dialectic for high praise. He says that an order of goodness operates in a providentially ruled universe; man's reason or "inborn speech" is, by providential dispensation, akin to divine Wisdom by being copied from it as its image. Again, de Serres's thinking about language emerges in an Augustinian attitude, coupled this time with Aristotelian metaphysics and ethics and with a Platonic vision of the proportions of things that define the production of arts and sciences as "aids and ornaments" to human life (2:8–9).[37]

De Serres's version of the proportionality discussed in the *Philebus* leads him to a remarkably syncretic assertion of an architectonic philosophy of language, an Augustinian philosophy of the recovery of man's divine likeness through "inborn speech." In the ruled universe that de Serres envisions, metaphysics (the organization of knowledge) and ethics are one and the same because the highest Goodness moves through all things in an emanation of light. The overriding end of the life of the mind is an ethical one, for the science of ethics is itself, de Serres says, ἀρχιτεκτονικός, the principal and primary end (2:6).[38] The life of the mind is, however, mysteriously verbal: by working the justice of words, man may discover the grace given to him.

In volume 3 in another dialogue commentary, de Serres presents his rationale for the unity of truth. His concept of the principle of unity is characteristically verbal. Commenting on the *Timaeus*, he provides an extensive analysis of the "making" of the world. At one point he argues unity by referring to the unique *mens architectrex* permeating the universe; the unity of that architectural principle of mind—another grammatically feminine version of the created wisdom who played before God in the morning of the world—stems from the universal, integral Wisdom of "Deus Opifex," God the Artificer, who possesses the knowledge of the causes of all things and articulates them according to his Word (3:5).[39] The full exposition of the verbal articulation of the universe comes, however, in de Serres's commentary on the *Cratylus* and on other dialogues on the arts of language in volume 1.

One scholarly effort of de Serres and Estienne was to reorganize the sequence of Plato's dialogues and to group them in significant subsections or syzygies. The disposition of Plato's extant works in a structure of ideas according to volume and syzygy is as important an avenue to understanding the Platonism of the 1578 edition as the content of the dialogues, commentaries, and glosses.[40] For example, all of the dialogues of volume 2, dedicated to King James, consider ethical and political subjects. The first syzygy of volume 1, dedicated to Queen Elizabeth, presents the religious dialogues—*Euthyphro, Apology, Crito,* and *Phaedo*—and the second syzygy the philosophical ones, including the *Amatores*. The third syzygy collects the *Cratylus, Gorgias,* and *Ion* on the subject of language; de Serres argues an analogical hierarchy of the language arts in Plato's treatment of these three dialogues and identifies three species through them—logic (*Cratylus*), rhetoric (*Gorgias*) and poetic (*Ion*). The focus on religion, philosophy, and speech is also Sidney's.

De Serres uses antithesis as well as analogy and proportion to organize these dialogues (1·378) Augustine had, after all, explained in the *De Ordine*, a treatise on the organization of the arts and sciences, that the harmony of the universe is maintained by a contrast of good and evil; yet God's love of order, which is good, does not imply a love of evil (1.7.18). In the *De Civitate Dei*, Augustine commented further on the mysterious order of antitheses in creation: "As, then, these oppositions of contraries lend beauty to the language, so the beauty of the course of this world is achieved by the opposition of contraries, arranged, as it were, by an eloquence not of words but of things" (11.18, pp. 361–62).[41] The principles of analogy and antithesis, once extended to the scope of knowledge, either justified it in relation to the truth of the Word of God or dramatically set off the difference between good and evil, truth and falsehood, beauty and ugliness. Obviously, this rhetorical patterning of philosophical ideas lent itself to the renaissance composition and the reading of literature in "literary architectonics," and we should not be surprised to see Sidney's following suit with an antithetical aesthetic of the "oblique" and the "right" in the *Defence* (p. 96) as clearly defined as de Serres's exposition of true and false philosophy.[42]

The commentary on the *Cratylus* summarizes de Serres's philosophy of language. First, de Serres identifies logic with plain, straightforward words (*de verbis simplicibus*) and asserts that dialectic, rhetoric, and poetic are three different but related species of logic (1:378). Dialectic pertains to the formation of arguments in speech. Rhetoric devises the diction, copiousness, and ornamentation that makes a speech persuasive. Poetic attends to the modulation of the verses, the measuring out of a latticework or boundary for expression, and the expression of imaginary things that teach and move the soul; taken as a whole, poetic is an art of imitation or *mimesis* (1:378).[43] Words (*verba*) are the *simulacra*, or images and effigies, of things (*res*). At the same time, de Serres explains the "verbal" nature of reality, distinguishing the "icons" of "ideas" and the "first principles" (ἀρχηγόν and *Verba*) that constitute the Nature of things from nature and things so constituted. He says that *Verba* and *Natura* are one, stable, and the same, for *Verba* and *Natura* are the "eternal principles" that God, the "architect and prince" of Nature, established (1:379). Thus de Serres links the *Verba* that constitute the force of things to the First Cause of things.

Then de Serres turns to three well-known scriptural references to the origin of language: the naming of things by Adam; the witness of Moses, "author of the true ἀρχαιολογίας," that there was originally one universal language; and the story of that monument to human pride, the building of a great tower in Babylon, and the multiplication of tongues that resulted (1:379–80). After discussing parallel points on the origin of language in classical thought, de Serres begins a remarkable exposition of the tetragrammaton, the four-lettered name of God in Hebrew, and an analogical exposition of the Hebrew alphabet with respect to classical philosophy (1:381). In this conclusive section of his commentary on the *Cratylus*, he presents a cross-cultural analysis of the universe in the aleph, a metaphysics of letters. The entire passage should be carefully studied with regard to poetic tradition and form, for de Serres not only alludes to Homer and Virgil in his discussion but also to the Kabbalah. He directly analogizes the *archia* or first principles of the Greeks to everything elaborated in the Hebrew alphabet.[44]

The vocabulary and the sense of hierarchy in de Serres's commentary on the *Cratylus* are highly significant in understanding Sidney's view of the movement of creativity from God, the heavenly Maker, to *Natura*, the maker or efficient cause of things, to the poet who speaks with the force of a divine breath that surpasses the workings of constituted nature with the works of a second nature. For the *Verba* are established "by force of nature," and the naming done by the first man Adam plays a part in the identification of things. So, too, Sidney credits Adamic making by the poet in view of the coming of the new Adam, Christ the Word, whose light allows the Christian believer in good faith to participate humanly in the regeneration of all things (*Def.*, pp. 78–79). One reason modern readers of the *Defence* must take care in trying to use deconstructive analysis on the text is the connection between Gnostic and kabbalistic doctrines and Derridean deconstruction as it pursues a course of "negation" of presence and transference of signifiers *ad infinitum*. Deconstruction severs the traces of significance from its metaphysical ground.[45] De Serres, on the other hand, clearly sustains the Hebraic respect for the mystery of divine Presence in his praise of Moses as the author of the true "archeology," the real and unique "first language" (1:379–80) that was what it signified as a system of symbols, not merely of semiotics, until man's building of the tower of Babel fractured language. He also uses his knowledge of Hebraica to Christianize language, including the philosophical language of the "gentiles," that is, the pagans. Words are not merely the images of things; words and the things of nature are one and the same in the divine voicing of the Word through history, and nothing that is true is alien to the Logos but may be appropriated under its rubric.[46] When Sidney follows de Serres's reasoning on this point, he constructs the idea of a poetic language able to create things that are "new," things that do not exist in the nature of the fallen world, things that appear out of the imagination to be handled by the poet for the common good. Sidney's theory of a divine inspiration operating not externally but within the conscience draws on de Serres's refashioning of Hebraic and Orphic ideas into a Calvinist Christian vision of the power of the Word.

In some respects, the commentary on the *Gorgias*, siue *De Rhetorica, Refutandi siue euertandi causa institutus*, extends that on the *Cratylus*. Again the negative interoute of deconstructive criticism may appear to be similar, for de Serres defines rhetoric as "the art of refuting and demolishing." In fact, de Serres draws heavily on Cicero and Quintilian in this commentary to dispute the Socratic identification of rhetoric with sophistry and to establish the "doubleness" of rhetoric—the false art and the true art. With Cicero, Aristotle comes into the picture, also, and Sidney works out his true rhetoric of philosophical eloquence serving ethical and political ends just as de Serres does.[47] This true art of rhetoric accomplishes in theory and in practice a kind of law and justice analogous to the knowledge of medicine—Sidney's "medicine of cherries"—and the "exercise" of its prescriptions (1:442). Since rhetoric is "duplex," true and false, his argument presents the practice of the rhetorical art in the commentary on the *Gorgias* with antithetical reasoning just as he presented, in the commentary on the *Cratylus*, an elaborate hierarchy of words and things through the arguments of etymology and analogy. He also discusses two kinds of images, the *phantastic* and the *eikastic*, in the commentary on the *Ion*. One of the implications of the commentary on the *Gorgias* is the recognition that speech conveys good and bad things through true and false arts of rhetoric (1:443–44).[48]

Finally, de Serres briefly takes up discussion of the *Io, siue De Iliade, vel, De poetico charactere: siue, De poetarum exponendorum ratione*, and the commentary directly illuminates Sidney's *Defence*.[49] De Serres explains how Plato saw God as "the ἀρχηγος and πρωτουργός of poetry," its First Cause, its "Muse" (1:528). The remark needs to be placed in the context of the commentary on the *Cratylus* if one wishes to see its complete orthodoxy. Sidney does not define the poetic art as a *seizure from without* by a divine force. In line with de Serres's Christian reasoning—a course that Scaliger had also observed—Sidney's use of this dialogue "on the poetic character" supports the divine inspiration *within the poet's human mind* by virtue of that original divine gift of the sparks of truth God bestowed on humanity.[50] The poet's "invention" is not a "divine force, far above man's wit" (*Def.*, p. 109), Sidney explains, but the architectonic poetic of "the highest point *of* man's wit" that produces poems "with the *force* of a divine breath"—not *with* a divine breath (*Def.*, p. 79, emphasis mine). The poet's "erected wit" is generative of *verba*, and it balances with Nature—the "maker" made by the "heavenly Maker" (p. 79)—de Serres's *architectrex* and *Opifex*, respectively. Thus the practice of the poetic art remains both similar to and different from Platonic inspiration on the basis of the Christian possession of the truth about God—and Sidney refers to Saint Paul's reference to the Athenians in Acts 17 to transfer the "watchword" against the abuse of philosophy to the understanding of the right use of poetry in the present time when "Christianity hath taken away all the hurtful belief" about the Deity (*Def.*, p. 108). An architectonic, illuminative poetic invention is sown into the nature of the man who practices it, and some men will practice it better than others because of their greater participation in the truth of the Word. De Serres (1:528) and Sidney (p. 111) assert that an orator can be made by his cultivation of learning and skill, but the poet is born: *Orator fit, poeta nascitur.* All the knowledge in the world, if it cannot be enacted in virtue by means of the grace of *synderesis,* is useless. The idea takes us close to the inspired John Milton, too.

De Serres closes his commentary on the *Ion* with a reference to Scaliger's appreciation of the poet's "measures" and "modulations" (1:529), and Sidney's appreciation of "prophetic" verse acknowledges the analogy between the poetics of God who made the world and Daedalean flights of invention in human poetry: "For that same exquisite observing of number and measure in the words, and that high flying liberty of conceit proper to the poet, did seem to have some divine force in it" (*Def.*, p. 77).[51] The poet discovers within his mind and expresses something like a divine force to the degree that his character has, by grace of divine election, recovered the image and likeness of God within. Sidney's Calvinism absorbed the idea of the "seizure by grace" in this "genetic" argument for the goodness of poetry. In this way he Protestantized the architectonics of Italian aesthetics. For just as Jean de Serres's irenic Augustinian theology envisioned nature and grace working spiritual maturity within the human character in the processes of time, Sidney used it to present an Augustinian Daedalus who goes within to Christ's Temple instead of building a labyrinth for Minos or a temple of Apollo. The Cyrus of the audience, not the overreaching Icarus, is the model "child" of the poet.

The key word in Sidney's adaptation of de Serres's argument for architectonic philosophy is obviously "the mistress-knowledge" (p. 82), the poetic analogue of the English Philosopher-Queen. But preceding it is Sidney's etymology of the word ποιητής as "maker" and "builder." How "high and incomparable a title" the poet possesses Sidney demonstrates by marking the limited scope of other sciences (pp. 77–78). What follows is the famous discussion of nature and art in which all other knowledges are shown to have nature as their object; poesie alone has "another nature" as its object in the service of eternal, immutable truth (p. 78). In studying nature, all other arts and sciences examine a *natura naturata,* a fallen and "brazen" artistic product. But the Nature who brought forth the original of that world, the "golden" version, is *natura naturans,* the feminine mastercraftsmanship that expresses God's providential design in human history. The poet is her consort, and with her he generates a new "golden world." Nature is cunning, yet the uttermost cunning of generative Nature, Sidney says, is shown by the poet who "doth grow in effect another nature, in making things either better than nature bringeth forth, or, quite anew" (p. 78). Nature has produced the human mind as our distinguishing characteristic, but if a person uses the mind, the "erected wit," as powerfully as the architectonic and graced poet, the nature of the world as it is might be transformed. Nature may make a man or produce a child—but the one who is a poet will make many other heroic men an abundant posterity for Queen Elizabeth's realm. Nature may bestow a Cyrus upon the world with particular excellence, and art that imitates nature may build a castle in the air. But architectonic poesie and her mastercraftsman bestow upon the world "a Cyrus . . . to make many Cyruses" (p. 79). Readers fulfill some part of this doctrine of man's return to the architectonic and golden first principles of virtue by learning correctly "why and how that maker made him" (p. 79). This is a statement of English religious politics and culture.

The next passage in the *Defence* grounds the heroic identification of the poet-consort and the mistress-knowledge by expressing Sidney's "saucy comparison" of "the highest point of man's wit with the efficacy of nature." The poet-maker is like the "maker" (nature) made by the "heavenly Maker" (God) who "having made man to His own likeness, set him beyond and over all the works of that second nature" (p. 79). Man's likeness to God appears in this complex analogy when "with the force of a divine breath he [the poet] bringeth forth things" that surpass nature. Truly surpassing nature—both *natura naturata* and the original *natura naturans*—is the poet's ability to overcome the effects of the "first accursed fall of Adam" that made the "infected will" impede the human ability to reach the perfection that the "erected wit" teaches (p. 79). Sidney's manipulation of philosophical terms in these analogical images parallels the operations of grace to the work of the poet by uniting the poet's mastercraftsmanship to the philosophical and theological definition of the mistress-knowledge.

The reasoning is metaphoric and complex—and Sidney knows it, for he has identified the poet's "erected wit" made by nature (the *architectrex*) with the philosophical power of the mistress-knowledge: "But these arguments will by few be understood, and by fewer granted. This much (I hope) will be given me, that the Greeks with some probability of reason gave him [the poet] the name above all other names of learning" (p. 79). What makes Sidney's argument so rarely understood and more rarely accepted is its use of de Serres's version of Saint Bonaventure's *apex mentis,* or the "spark of moral discernment," and Saint Augustine's definition of the created light and created wisdom of the inner word. Sidney's phrase, "the highest point of man's wit" (p. 79), translates the *apex mentis* of Saint Bonaventure's metaphysics, the "tip" of the mind or the "erected wit" that gives to knowledge the enlightening and enkindling spark of moral power. The *apex mentis* also crowns the cognitive ladder as one moves from sense perception through the imagination, reason, and understanding to complete intelligence. Paralleling Saint Augustine's "spark" of reason and Saint Jerome's *synderesis scintilla* in de Serres's definition of the "sparks" of truth and virtue in the well-examined life, Sidney's "highest point of man's wit" potentially effects *synderesis*—or what Sidney calls "moving" or the "enabling of judgment" because it fulfills the end of learning (p. 82).[52] Poesie is intellectually and morally efficacious—architectonic—and the presence of the inward light of the mistress-knowledge in the actual language of poetry allows it to do the judgmental work of conscience by inflaming the imaginations of the poet and the reader in the acts of writing and reading.

In two other commentaries Jean de Serres further discusses the architectonic philosophy of the Word. In the commentary on the *Symposium*, or *Convivum, siue De Amore, Metaphysicus siue Theologicus*, he compares the expression of the "naked and simple" dogmatic teachings to the *sententiae* of allegory (3:167). Plato's allegorical mode of philosophizing, says de Serres, "contains many sacred mysteries within it," and allegorical expression is a species of the excellent *eikastic* imagination that so efficaciously moves the spirit (3:167). After comparing the allegory of the Song of Songs to Plato's allegory, de Serres discusses the philosophy of Love, the true and well-grounded philosophy of the divine science and of conscience (3:167–68). He follows an extensive discussion of the "daemons" and the "angels" (3:168–69) with his version of the ladder of love, an exposition of the four degrees and four effects of the ascent of love to absolute Beauty—"that is, to God, in whom consists the true and certain felicity of men" (3:170). Man moves in body and in soul, using his eyes, his spirit, and his reason, through the effects of love—meditation, true desire, and generative action—to the highest good in the highest beauty (3:169–70).[53] He moves by Love and reaches to Beauty and to Goodness as if reaching a universe of golden things. "To that Beauty," therefore, "the Lord and architectonic end [ἀρχιτεκτονικόν τέγος] of our life teaches us to ascend through the intermediation and interpretation of Love" (3:170). In the "shadows" of the allegory, "as the learned and pious reader may judge," are "vestiges of the Truth" who *is* Jesus Christ (3:170), de Serres says, and so, too, Sidney alludes to the possession of the light of Christ as a reason for poets and readers no longer to fear allegorical representation or imagination but to practice a converted ladder of love in their poetic structure and style (*Def.*, pp. 107–8). Twice Sidney defends Love in the manner of de Serres, as I shall shortly explain.

In the commentary on the *Politicus, siue, De regno*, de Serres discusses the providential government of the city of man according to similarly architectonic, "golden," and ethical principles of happiness. That golden world of first principles is the work of the divine "Opifex," and knowledge of it shines even in this world through the "sparks of truth" that have not been extinguished by the darkness of error (2:250–51). Repeatedly, de Serres refers to mankind's "golden" world and "golden age" to establish his political analogy between the rule of God's first principles and this world. Analogy is the means of perceiving in this world the "sparks of truth" that Adam and Eve knew fully in Eden. 61 Later in the commentary, de Serres explains the dignity of statesmanship when it is based on such analogical perception of the truth. Plato saw the art of government and the role of the statesman in a divine sense; and, indeed, in an appropriate *ratio*, "God governs men through a man" (2:252). The statesman essentially rules by means of his discourse, the virtue of his character, and the knowledge of his mind. His "ratio" is the work of proportion-making in both speech and actions. Learned in his judgments, brief and to the point in his speeches, he rules by a "rule" of discovering and demonstrating fundamental causes of things (2:253). In this sense he is the "architect" and "head" on whom the good, not the bad, republic is constituted (2:254). De Serres concludes, therefore, that Plato teaches that virtue is the foundation of the true republic, and Christians understand that there can be no virtue of justice without holiness (2:254).

Jean de Serres's architectonic philosophy saw the full circle of learning sustained by the integrity of conscientious men. The goodness of society and the wisdom of the arts and sciences depended on the exercise of moral judgment—the fleeing from vice and the embracing of virtue. In a Calvinist Protestant context, the exercise of moral judgment depends on grace, too, even though the knowledge of the difference between good and evil exists in all men by virtue of the sparks of truth especially expressed in speech. Thus Sidney's use of de Serres's architectonic epistemology absorbs de Serres's soteriology, also.

First Sidney observes that the androcentric "erected wit" at the height of human nature may envision perfection without "reaching unto it." Then he defends the moving power of poesie precisely as that moment of grace discovered in words that can compel the effeminate "infected will" by enflaming it with the love of well-doing. Some men are more graced than others, and some poets more "right." All of the powers that Sidney assigns to poetry, not philosophy, accrue to the poet's ability to "move" the reader to virtue. Since the moral philosopher with his universals offers merely "the bare rule" and is "hard to be conceived," and since the historian, tied to particulars, is so wanting in precepts that "his example draweth no necessary consequence," the poet emerges as the mastercraftsman. This princely workman accomplishes the *synderesis* of conscience by successfully applying general moral principles to particular circumstances; the success depends on the quality of the application and whether it produces "necessary consequence" (*Def.*, p. 85). The moving power of poesie makes it "well nigh the cause and effect of teaching" (p. 91). Efficacy also establishes the poet's *eikastic* fictions as the best type of de Serres's "brightly burning and wise speech."

The tone of Sidney's use of simple Augustinian language on the doctrine of conscience, however, also shows his triumph over philosophy. He teases the learned Frenchman Jean de Serres who has recapitulated Augustine's doctrine in relation to the Bonaventurian idea of conscience and the semi-Pelagianism of Duns Scotus and the fourteenth-century illuminationists. Sidney parodies the puritanical moral philosophers whom he sees coming toward him "with a sullen gravity . . . rudely clothed for to witness outwardly their contempt of outward things, with books in their hands against glory, whereto they set their names." The philosopher casts a "largess" of "definitions, divisions, and distinctions" (*Def.*, p. 83).

In another passage Sidney teases the "philosopher's book" by countering to it the experiential knowledge of "inward light":

Learned men have learnedly thought that where reason hath so much overmastered passion as that the mind hath a free desire to do well, the inward light each mind hath in itself is as good as a philosopher's book; since in nature we know it is well to do well, and what is well and what is evil, although not in the words of art which philosophers bestow upon us; for out of natural conceit the philosophers drew it. (*Def.*, p. 91)

Human beings "naturally" possess the remnant of reason that enables moral judgment to occur but cannot "move" judgment to action. Thus Philip Sidney's intertextualization of the philosopher's book is an incisive parody of philosophy to say that poesie can accomplish the ends of reason and philosophy better than philosophy can, for poesie allows human beings to know the difference between good and evil. However, like Augustine, Sidney knows that the "inward light"—the spark of reason mentioned in *De Civitate Dei* and the "inward consciousness" mentioned in the essay *De Vera Religione*—lacks motive force. So he explains the motives of poesie: "But to be moved to do that which we know, or to be moved with desire to know, *hoc opus, hic labor est*" (p. 91). The poet's ability to move is so great that his art touches "even those hard-hearted evil men who think virtue a school-name . . . and therefore despise the austere admonitions of the philosopher, and feel not the inward reason they stand upon" (p. 93). These men who lack even Cain's capacity to feel the heat of the "spark" of conscience are, nevertheless, moved by the "good-fellow poet" whose promise of pleasure makes them, like Prometheus, "steal to see the form of goodness." For poetry is like "a medicine of cherries" (p. 93).

The moving work of grace, like the mediating, directive task of the Christian who obeys the divine Architect, is the architectonic poet's contribution to the building of the new world. The poet, therefore, makes pleasing proportions. He causes the reader's "desire to know" and moves the reader to virtue by issuing a verbal imperative in the structure of his poetic measures and the antitheses of his *phantastic* and *eikastic* images—not in scholarly glosses

[A poet] beginneth not with obscure definitions, which must blur the margin with interpretations, and load the memory with doubtfulness; but he cometh to you with words set in delightful proportion, either accompanied with, or prepared for, the well enchanting skill of music; and with a tale forsooth he cometh unto you, with a tale which holdeth children from play, and old men from the chimney corner. And pretending no more, doth intend the winning of the mind from wickedness to virtue. (*Def.*, p. 92)

The moving power of poetic language is no more than the normal conventions of language corrected and set in "musical" order by a good man of regenerate mind. Sidney places poetic efficacy not in "divine inspiration"—nor in some magic of the word itself, nor in the saying of the word—but in the learned and virtuous intent of the poet who decorously arranges his thoughts in "delightful proportion." Surely this is a kabbalistic sentiment, Christianized. As God with a divine breath created Adam, so does the poet, "with the force of a divine breath," bring forth proportions that purify the wit of the natural man and enable his judgment. The good poet is, indeed, "good." He exercises a mastery of passion, nature, and thought by the graced reasoning of his own "inward light" in such a fine measuring of words that the spark of his free desire to do well communicates a spark to the reader, too.[55] As Rosemond Tuve put it, regarding the rhetoric of renaissance poems designed to produce effects in the reader, "Press a button and a spark will ignite the reader's affections."[56]

Sidney's use of the Augustinian analogy of uncreated Light and the created light of the mind expresses one aspect of his larger analogy of man's likeness to God. The focus of the analogy, however, is a correspondence between the divine Word and the poetic word. The tension of analogy allows Sidney, on one hand, to say that he does not compare poetry with divine science because the scope of divine science is "as far beyond any of these [serving sciences] as eternity exceedeth a moment" (p. 84) and, on the other, to evoke the time-eternity paradox: "Now therein of all sciences (I speak still of human, and according to the human conceit) is our poet the monarch" (p. 91). In the analogy of the Word, similarly, verse no more makes a poet than a long gown an advocate, Sidney says; the "right describing note" to know a poet by is "that feigning notable images of virtues, vices, or what else, with that delightful teaching" that moves the reader (p. 81). The making of *eikastic* proportions and the correcting of *phantastic* images are the delightful practice of the ethical architectonic art. This fulfills the end of learning and allows poesie to rule over all the arts and sciences and to "reach" toward the divine realm of the golden world. The art of poetry is a mediator, a measurer of right proportions in the midst of wrong ones, an exercise of the best wits in the limitations of history to make time correspond to eternal truth—a version of the Christian ladder of the Word and the Temple of the Spirit.

The poetic proportions that Sidney recommends obviously are of the "right" *eikastic* sort, not the *phantastic* kind that falsifies knowledge. Besides being visually "true," these images are musical and architectural in the rhetorical traditions of Amphion, Orpheus, and Pythagoras. The poet does not speak words, Sidney explains, as they fall by chance from his mouth; he constructs them in fair measures by "peising each syllable of each word by just proportion according to the dignity of the subject" (pp. 81–82). "Peising" is Sidney's metaphor for analogy or decorum, and he means the word to convey both a rule of style and a judgment of intellectual fit. The poet who "peises" his words builds them in "architectural" measure, for "peising" is a building technique—a way to erect a wall brick by brick, holding it up with a board and removing the board when the proportion can hold itself together. Notice that the construction actually peised out—the latticework of the poet's words and proportions—is not the thing truly being built, the "wall." "Peising," in short, is the stylistic term for the "imaginative ground-plot of a profitable invention" (*Def.*, p. 103). The architectonic building is the profitable invention of the poet's idea that the reader, too, discovers. For the same kind of analogical reason, "peising" signifies more than syllabic quantification; it aims at a correspondence to the intellectual and moral achievement of number, weight, and measure in the universe—some of the first principles explained in the scriptural knowledge of the Word of God. At best, the poet's "peising" of words ought to parallel the emanation of the Logos through the light of the world, the arrival of the "new Song" in time. But to parallel that sublime truth is not to be that truth; so Sidney reminds us that the poet "affirms nothing" (p. 102) and that the construction of "notable images" of virtue and vice is, after all, "feigning" (p. 81). The truth of a poem may be rightly disclosed only in the moral discovery that the poet and the reader act out in their lives. Both the Kabbalah and some aspects of deconstruction are comparable to Sidney's "peising" in technique.

To say that the poetic invention of the *Defence* finds its strongest intellectual source in de Serres's idea of the Christian architectonic philosophy is to say that an ethical and analogical power of language emerges from the "right" state of mind to "enkindle" virtue. Where de Serres notes that there are many "sacred mysteries contained in this philosophy"—for he refers to the allegorical mode of the *Symposium* (3:167) as well as to the integration of knowledge and virtue—Sidney claims the "sacred mysteries of poesy" and argues "that there are many mysteries contained in poetry," which gives men "all knowledge" under "the veil of fables" (*Def.*, p. 121). Where de

Serres discusses Plato's analogical reasoning and warns of right and wrong ways to understand love in the *Symposium* (3:168), and where de Serres celebrates not the heretics' "theater" of "prostituted philosophy" but the Platonism drawn "out of the pure fountains of theology, that is, the Word of God" (3:169), Sidney examines why Plato would "defile the fountain out of which his flowing streams have proceeded," that is, poesie (*Def.*, p. 107).[57]

As Sidney briefly contrasts Plato's enmity for poets with cases in which philosophers were banned from society, he stops himself. The line of reasoning "should requite the objections made against poets with like cavillations against philosophers; as likewise one should do that should bid one read *Phaedrus* or *Symposium* in Plato, or the discourse of love in Plutarch, and see whether any poet do authorize abominable filthiness, as they do" (*Def.*, p. 107). Socrates had been put on trial for supposedly corrupting youth, distracting them from conventional religious practices. De Serres had appended to the axioms following his commentary a condemnation of "a detestable mole in this dialogue," that is, the references to pederasty and to androgyny (3:171). The caveat falls on Aristophanes and suggests that Socrates was contaminated by suspicion, not by actual wrongdoing, while Plato clearly detested such turpitude; the blame for the "mole" falls on Trismegistus and the Egyptians who communicated the monstrosity of the androgyne to the Greeks (3:171).[58] Sidney will counter Plato's objection to poets not by "cavillation" in a vengeful spirit, but by showing that knowledge of the truth of the Word has changed Plato from an "adversary" to a "patron" of poesie.[59] Likewise, Sidney will set up the image of the character of the poet by redefining the androgynous monstrosity as a hierarchical coupling of masculine and feminine prosopopoeias—the poet-statesman who uses and does not abuse the mistress-knowledge—in the temple of the mind and the household of faith.

The four-part refutation in the *Defence*—answers to the charges that poetry is a waste of time, that poets are liars, that poems are sinful fancies, and that Plato banished poets from society—focuses Sidney's creative use of de Serres's arguments to parody the philosophy of Plato. First, Sidney reiterates his main argument, the confirmation of the architectonic poetic art, by asserting that poetry is the learning most conducive to the practice of virtue and no waste of time (pp. 101–2). He has already dismissed critics of poetry on the strength of the axiom that *oratio* is next to *ratio* and that a great blessing bestowed upon mortality is polishing "that blessing of speech" (p. 100). Second, Sidney explains the paradox that the poet "of all writers under the sun . . . is the least liar," for he "affirms nothing" (*Def.*, p. 102). The "feigning" of notable images of virtue and vice in poetic fictions produces a truth independent of the affirmation of this or that in language but directive of the reader's discovery of what should or should not be in his own reading inventiveness (p. 102). Third, Sidney treats the concepts of imitation and imagination under the category of the kind of invention that produces true proportions—that is, *eikastic* images. This refutation answers the name-calling of men like Stephen Gosson who consider poems to be sinful and abusive "fancies."[60]

Borrowing his terms from Plato's *Sophist* and from de Serres's exposition of the language arts, Sidney does not deny that man's wit may be abused by imagination and may abuse it if the poesie of *eikastic* imagination were to be reduced to the function of mere *phantastic* representation (p. 104). The faculty of imagination either "figures forth" good things or abuses the mind by infecting it with unworthy objects—according to the "true" and "false" rhetorics that de Serres had discussed. The enemies of poetry, Sidney says, take up such infected images to "allege herewith that before poets began to be in price our nation had set their hearts' delight upon action, not imagination" (p. 105). Sidney's architectonic poetic arms him, however, with the conviction that true poetry produces the enkindling of virtue. So he focuses the issue of praise and blame on the case of Alexander, who discovered ideal patterns in the reading of Homer and was moved by them more than "by hearing the definition of fortitude" (p. 106). The doing of things fit to be written and the writing of things fit to be done connect, in Sidney's mind, on the ladder of the relation of causes to effects.

The charge that poetry stimulates delight in imagination and not in action is, therefore, "the ordinary doctrine of ignorance" (p. 105). What true learning proves appears in the proof of experience also, as Sidney's *gradatio*, a rhetorical ladder, asserts: "It is manifest that all government of action is to be gotten by knowledge, and knowledge best by gathering many knowledges, which is reading" (p. 105). Knowledge itself—the mind's participation in the "shared" truths sown into it as the "sparks" of virtue that accomplish architectonic ends through religion, conscience, the arts and sciences, and speech—makes the full defence of poesie since poesie demonstrably achieves the end of learning. As an art, poesie is a triumphant "captain" (p. 99); as the product of an art, poetry is "the companion of camps" (p. 105). One does not have to press the point to hear Sidney's implied judgment of poets as the soldierly and rightly politic statesmen.

In Sidney's fourth refutation, however, Plato's idea of the statesman-architect becomes Sidney's weapon against Plato's dismissal of the poet from the true republic. Only after having established through metaphor and etymology the confirmation of the "erected wit" of the poet's mental zodiac, and only after paving the way to the conversion of Plato in the three previous refutations, does Sidney explicitly weigh Plato's judgment against poets. Earlier in the *Defence* Sidney had explained that the wit of the poet who follows the true course of his own invention (p. 80) and does his part "aright" by demonstrating in villains "nothing that is not to be shunned" and in heroes "each thing to be followed" (p. 88) was a truly poetic wit. The erected wit of the inventive poet has been properly educated to produce an intellectually and morally sound poetry—not an art of lies but of true doctrine, not of effeminateness, but of notable stirring of courage; not of abusing man's wit, but of strengthening man's wit." Thin In an art of poesie, therefore, "not banished, but honoured by Plato," who set a watchword against its abuse (p. 108). Sidney's conversion of Plato from "adversary" to "patron" of poetry works simply as an assertion of the architectonic integrity of the life of the mind when exercised by a true and good male character who has mastered the "effeminate" carnality within himself and the feminine order within society (p. 108).

The truth and goodness of the poet's character depend, moreover, on participation in the truth of the Word of God. Thus Sidney argues that Plato condemned poetry merely because poetry was based on religious falsehoods. The classical charges against the abuses of poetry were leveled at poems in which the wrong opinions of the Deity were conveyed. The poets did not originate the abuse, furthermore, but imitated it. Now, however, since "Christianity hath taken away all the hurtful belief" about God, and since men may actively benefit from "the light of Christ" in the exercise of their own minds, there is a moral imperative to practice actively the poetic invention of truth and production of virtue (p. 108). For poesie exercises the rule of the statesman among the arts and sciences and brings the corrective vision of Christian truth into the light of everyday living.

Cato and Chaucer, Agrippa and Spenser, King David and King Arthur all appear by name in Sidney's *Defence* while Saint Augustine and Jean de Serres do not. Yet the fundamentally Augustinian and scholastic reasoning of Jean de Serres's "true and well-grounded philosophy" of Plato informs Sidney's revisionary evaluation of human heroes and history. The absence of explicit reference to Augustine and de Serres strangely confirms their presence and the importance of their contribution to Sidney's views of philosophy and history and of the powers of poetic language—the chief tool of the statesman. Languet cannot have imagined how creatively Sidney's exposition of the power of poetic fiction would press de Serres's inquiry as to how the Queen liked her new *Plato* in giving the inquiry a distinctly English nationality.

In another piece of writing, *In Ecclesiasten Solomonis*, translated into English as *A godlie and learned commentarie upon the excellent book of Solomon called Ecclesiastes, or the Preacher*, Jean de Serres had also articulated the distinction between the "holy" philosophy and profane philosophy.[61] In the 1578 *Plato* de Serres called Plato, with Moses, Homer, and the Fathers, one of "our own," and not "an architect of monstrous opinions." In *A godlie and learned commentarie* he says that philosophy is "a singular gift of God," but "lewd persons do many wayes abuse it" (p. 56). The study of philosophy is not to be put to a stop; but there is a rule for reading Plato and Aristotle just as there is a rule for understanding creation and interpreting history.

> Yet are they in such sort to be read, that they infect not our mindes with their Circean inchauntments: but that severing and shutting out the true use from the abuse, we embrace with sober mindes the true and profitable use of things, in such maner, and so farre as the Lord would have extant in them, that we forsake falshood and vanitie, and in a worde, that in their darknesse wee seeke out the sparkes of the originall truth. And against all these phrensies and errours wee are to set the simplicitie of the worde of God, the which to be the undoubted wisedome we make no doubt at all. . . . Which foundation being layd, wee shall no doubt carrie away most plentifull profite out of humane sciences, as it were out of the spoyles of the Aegyptians. (Pp. 70–71)

With Scripture in place as the rule of faith and the rule of interpretation, human thought may, like Egyptian gold, be constructed on a good foundation and brought out of the darkness into the light.

Through the 1578 *Plato*, a northern humanist synthesis of classical and medieval Christian learning could indeed influence writers and poets of the English Renaissance. Through Sidney's *Defence*, it most certainly did, for Sidney's little treatise both taught the Protestant philosophical ethos and exemplified it.[62] Later Milton would consider the poetic vocation tantamount to a call to prophetic destiny; the poet's knowledge gave him "a sorer burden of mind."[63] If a poet could balance the verisimilitude of his poetic fiction and the antitheses of good and evil in his poetic fables with some stimulation of the reader's discovery of moral truths, poetry might indeed edify the conscience. Through elaborate poetic correspondences, the world as it is might be better seen, and the lost Eden might be remembered—or the new Jerusalem discovered in the making of one's life into a true poem. "Doubtlesse," de Serres had said in *A godlie and learned commentarie*, "before sinne, Adam was not idle in Heden, who is plainly saide to be put by God into the garden for to dresse and keepe it" (p. 217). It is in the same posture of mental cultivation that renaissance poets and readers work out the demonstration of their regeneration after the Fall by the way they toil in the "garden" or city of their lives.

The Lovely Name of Love

Besides transforming much of de Serres's *Plato* into a practical statement of English character, the *Defence* reveals Sidney's labor to establish poetic myth-making on the highest possible plane of renaissance politics and arts debate. Through de Serres's arguments, Sidney primarily defends the combined pleasure and wisdom of poesie against the charges of abuse made by "lewd" English persons who do not know how to read—especially Stephen

Gosson, who dedicated *The School of Abuse* to Sidney in 1579. This "plesaunt inuectiue against Poets, Pipers, Plaiers, Iesters, and such like Caterpillers of a Commonwelth" aims to overthrow their "Bulwarkes." Although Gosson, like Sidney, was an Oxonian, Gosson indicates that "the Schoole which I builde, is narrowe, and at the first blushe appeareth but a dogge hole" (sig. c^v–4^r). Indeed, *The School of Abuse* was too narrow for the zodiac of Sidney's wit and the school of philosophy he attended.

Yet on the "ending end" of learning the two men agreed. Gosson asserts that a man is known by his works. To study without acting is inhuman: "To continue so long without moouinge, to reade so muche without teachings, what differeth it from a dumbe Picture, or a dead body?" (34^v). Sidney's art of reading led also to the governance of action, and to say otherwise was to preach a "doctrine of ignorance" (*Def.*, p. 105). Poetry makes reading a "heart-ravishing knowledge" (*Def.*, p. 76) whose "lofty image" of the "worthies" most inflames the mind with desire to be worthy (p. 98). Far from abusing the wit, writing and reading poetry communicate the force of conscience in the way a medicine of cherries heals a sick man. The poet-architect who builds no narrow school of abuse but imagines, instead, an entire zodiac of the wit as "the house well in model" and constructs the ladder to climb to it practices the living speech of the mistress-knowledge. That "queen" of the arts and sciences stands on the self-knowledge with which poets build the nation on ethically and politically sound foundations. Poets are her lovers, her explorers, and her triumphant captains in England, and neither domestic intrigue nor continental fashion will prevail against them; they stand on the Ladder who is Christ and rebuild the English temple.

Probably the most lyrical use Sidney made of Jean de Serres's scripturally and theologically authorized doctrine of an architectonic philosophy of language comes in his defence of Love. Once again Sidney does his own allegorical mythology in tandem with de Serres's philosophical definitions, and he does so by returning to the ambitious overreaching of Icarus and the possibilities of climbing ladders of power as well as ladders of grace. This time, Icarus appears under the name of Cupid, who has left his level of genre in the "sinful fancies" of "passionate sonnets," according to the accusers of poetry, and "hath ambitiously climbed" to the "heroical." But Cupid is also related to holy Desire.

"Alas, Love, I would thou couldst as well defend thyself as thou canst offend others," Sidney exclaims, beginning with an apology for the flesh accused by carnal minds:

I would those on whom thou dost attend could either put thee away, or yield good reason why they keep thee. But grant love of beauty to be a beastly fault (although it be very hard, since only man, and not beast, hath that gift to discern beauty); grant that lovely name of Love to deserve all hateful reproaches (although even some of my masters the philosophers spent a good deal of their lamp-oil in setting forth the excellency of it); grant, I say, whatsoever they will have granted, that not only love, but lust, but vanity, but (if they list) scurrility, possesseth many leaves of the poets' books; yet think I, when this is granted, they will find their sentence may with good manners put the last words foremost, and not say that poetry abuseth man's wit, but that man's wit abuseth poetry. (*Def.*, pp. 103–4)

Here Sidney wonderfully rewrites the renaissance association of all poetry with love in the long-standing Augustinian-Dantean-Petrarchan tradition of the Platonic ladder of love. Sidney can praise love freely as a good Protestant; the ladder of love has, in effect, been intellectually Protestantized on the strength of Jean de Serres's rehabilitation of the *Symposium* into a Solomonic allegory of love, an Augustinian quest for the Beauty ever ancient and ever new. The sins of the poets or the intellectual limitations of their mythology should not be put on love itself. In the crediting of love as a force of imagination that reaches from the shame of lust to the heights of divinity, we may recognize in the *Defence* the authorization of *eros* that will ring from Shakespeare's stage and will descend like prevenient grace to the fallen Adam and Eve in Milton's *Paradise Lost* so that Eve's love of Adam begins the motion of historical return to communion with God.[64]

Jean de Serres's contribution to Sidney's thought in this respect is the sustained doubling of possibilities throughout his commentaries, which culminates in a doctrine of love. The marginal gloss on *eikastic* and *phantastic* images for the *Sophist* 236 extends to the discussion of imitation and two kinds of production, the divine and the human, in the gloss on the *Sophist* 265. Divine workmanship and artistic productivity show up in nature as the "makings" of God; human production itself divides into two types, the true and the false, the *eikastic* likeness and the *phantastic* distortion. De Serres's subsequent discussion of true and false rhetorics in the *Gorgias* and of true and false imaginations in the *Ion* (1:528) carries out this doubling motif even further, richly informing the sense of Sidney's use of the terms in the third refutation of the *Defence* (p. 104), the discussion whether poems are sinful fancies or fantasies. But the distinction between true and false images, imitations, makings, rhetorics, and imaginations does not stop there. De Serres had also discussed the moving power of true likenesses, εἰϰαςία, in the Prefatory Letter and in the commentary on the *Symposium*. Sidney brings the erotic distinctions home to England.

In the Prefatory Letter, de Serres mentions *eikastic* images with regard to their moving power and their significance in the production of true and false, good and bad, forms of allegory (1:sig. **vi^v). He makes the figurative significance of allegory quite plain: the truth does not stand in the allegories themselves, and certainly Plato does not transform all of the truth into allegory; rather, allegory at its best is useful for teaching the truth efficaciously. Plato's development of symbols and allegory is something he learned from the Egyptians, but the Jews (Moses and the Prophets) and all the erudite Christian doctors have always distinguished between those allegories that pretend to the truth and those that are useful in teaching (1:nig. **vi^v). The discussion gives de Serres the occasion to compare Plato and Aristotle on scientific subjects regarding the use of allegory. "Plato teaches," he says, "Aristotle proves."[65] The commentary on the *Symposium* takes the growing dualism of de Serres's distinctions into a Calvinist philosophy of love by paralleling allegory and the Augustinian definition of two kinds of love. Thus Jean de Serres asserts, "Love, therefore, is duplex, one love being Heavenly and genuinely integral and loving chastely . . . [and] the other common and dishonest, seeking after vile, base things" (3:170).

But he Platonizes further the Augustinian distinction between *caritas* and *cupiditas* by countering the base kind of love with a revised ladder of love and an esoteric teaching influenced by Christian Kabbalah. In discussing the favorite renaissance topic of the "naked truth" (*nuda veritas*) de Serres first speaks of the manner in which the philosophers have clothed many mysteries in allegory and in symbol; he alludes to Plato, but also to Hesiod and Homer—that is, to the accommodation of Orphic doctrines to Stoic doctrines in Cleanthes and then, through Cicero and Cornutus, to Clauserus, to whom Sidney also refers on the subject of the "many mysteries" concealed in poetry (*Def.*, p. 121). As de Serres discusses the philosophers, however, for their validation of the excellencies of allegory and of love (3:167), he adds grist to Sidney's mill. Sidney remarks that "some of my masters the philosophers spent a good deal of their lamp-oil in setting forth the excellency" of love (*Def.*, p. 104). When Sidney distinguishes "beastly" from human love, he also criticizes the philosophers who document how lust, vanity, and scurrility occupy poetry (*Def.*, p. 104). He does not like their "sentence." Likewise, de Serres distinguishes human desire, neither good nor bad in itself, from the kind of love animals exhibit and criticizes the "sentences" of lesser philosophers whose definitions of love are quite different from the ones given by Plato and Socrates (3:168). The lamp-oil the philosophers have spent on love may very well include the long roster of Greek names for love that de Serres lists, beginning with Ficino's amplification of the names for love and arguing the interpretation of Plato's daemons as the Christian's angels and a high metaphysics mediating between divine and mortal nature (3:168–69). Sidney, following de Serres, indicates that the elaborate Platonic theory of nature and of love is an analogy, finally, for the singularly simple Love, the Word of God. De Serres avoids the length of Ficino's commentary in his own, he says, since he simply wants to discuss what is "useful" in this dialogue (3:168). Sidney goes straight to the Savior named Love.

So, too, Sidney's coordination of philosophy, allegory, love, and poesie is relatively succinct as he takes over de Serres's reconstructed Platonic

ladder of love on which erotic desire moves through generation and the
creation of a chain of concord in society up to the architectonic end of love,
which now becomes the *divine* Beauty. Having allowed for the negative
judgment of the love that seeks base things and yet asked for reasons why
love is also excellent, Sidney is free at the end of the *Defence* to say why as he
concludes his treatise. He brings the discussion of love under one name,
then, the "lovely name of Love," back to the discussion of poetic image-
making in which it originated through de Serres's dual definitions. What
Sidney cannot abide, he implies, is *the deadly spirit that is passionless,
incapable of conversion,* unable to move with the power of love.

In commenting on the state of the art of poesie in England, he returns,
therefore, to the theme of vivid speech he had stated at the beginning with
regard to King David's prosopopoeias. These make the reader of the psalms
"see God coming in His majesty." They show David to be a "passionate
lover of that unspeakable and everlasting beauty to be seen by the eyes of the
mind, only cleared by faith" (*Def.,* p. 77). With an appropriately Hebraic-
Christian sense of awe, Sidney fears that "truly now having named him, I
fear me I seem to profane that holy name, applying it to poetry, which is
among us thrown down to so ridiculous an estimation" (*Def.,* p. 77). The
tetragrammaton that Sidney analyzes in his justification of poesie is not the
sacred Hebrew tetragrammaton or even the pentagrammaton YHSVH to
which de Serres and Christian Kabbalists referred the ultimate truth of
language, but a plain English name, "that lovely name of Love" (*Def.,* p.
104).

Of poetry in England Sidney claims the dramatic poems of tragedy and
comedy—the final duality of experience to be represented in imitation—and
then the lyric, the genre of Love, most especially:

Other sort of poetry almost have we none, but that lyrical kind of songs and sonnets:
which, Lord, if He gave us so good minds, how well it might be employed, and with
how heavenly fruit, both private and public, in singing the praises of the immortal
beauty: the immortal goodness of that God who giveth us hands to write and wits to
conceive; of which we might well want words, but never matter; of which we could
turn our eyes to nothing, but we should ever have new-budding occasions. (*Def.,* p.
116)

Sidney's meaning would be simple and not duplex if he stopped at this holy
kind of lyricism. But he presses on, beyond the imitation of David's passionate songs to the heavenly divine Beauty, to incorporate the entire range of de
Serres's ladder—to include what I think is David's earthly line of generation,
too, his erotic love that produced Solomon, and Solomon's allegory of love
in the Song of Songs. Sidney praises passion:

But truly many of such writings come under the banner of unresistible love, if I were a
mistress, would never persuade me they were in love: so coldly they apply fiery

speeches, as men that had rather read lovers' writings . . . than that in truth they feel those passions, which easily (as I think) may be bewrayed by that same forcibleness or *energia* (as the Greeks call it) of the writer. (*Def.*, pp. 116–17)

The dualities with which Sidney is comfortable in the *Defence*—dualities of idea and image, speech and writing, composition and interpretation, symbolic allegory and figurative allegory—have given the treatise its long history of productive and controversial influence, often unacknowledged. For Sidney, the fulcrum of the dualities is sacred and profane love, mixed in historical experience, sorted out by poesie. But the same dualities have more recently divided critics who have not had access to the necessary historical sources to judge the text competently in its cultural context. Now that the recovery of the mistress-knowledge and Sidney's construction of "notable *prosopopoeias*" in his intertextual and sometimes parodic composition have been made clear, the true brilliance of the *Defence* as an English statement should be, too. In his appropriation of the philosopher's book for an allegory of poesie, Sidney accomplished the fullest literary justification of poetry. Centuries of writers would follow suit in Protestant England. The ambivalent definition of poesie as a personification of the poet masked and lifted up in his erected wit by the vigor of invention and as the superior speaker of an epistemological force of conscience and of divine Love provided the necessary sparks for such an enterprise.

Yet some other questions must be answered before we can give Sidney's Solomonic temple-building aesthetics a critical sabbath, putting to rest any doubt of his tremendous formative influence on the production of renaissance poetry. To the extent that Sidney punned on David's failure to build a house and God's building of a house—in the other, genealogical sense of the word—by giving him a line of succession in the wise but libidinous Solomon, Sidney's mistress-knowledge and poet-statesman confront us students of the English Renaissance most acutely with the problem of "desire in language." In theory Sidney locates the epistemology of poesie in the divine and human phenomenon of love; he sees poesie as a reformed ladder of love and beauty, a mediating device between being and nothingness, as Diotima explained to Socrates, and he simultaneously sees divine Love as a Ladder reflected in the changed ladder of a "peised" language. That is, poesie ultimately discloses the high doctrine of creation and redemption in which Christ the Word *is* the Ladder, the *only* mediating power between earth and heaven, and Love. Poetry *as written*—"literature," Derrida calls it—is something else.[66]

In considering the theme of justification reflected in the content and form of book production in the late 1570s and early 1580s and moving from France to England, therefore, one must move from poetic theory to poetic practice and from letters to life. Such a move is the most architectonic gesture of poesie. In doing so, readers discover in Sidney's imagination not so much the absent presence of modern deconstruction, even in the aspect in which it adheres to the knowledge of the Torah and the Kabbalah and imagines the "drama of God" appearing and disappearing, but the Christian theological imagination of the Cross and of the atonement effected singularly in the crucifixion and resurrection of Jesus within desire itself. In the books of Sidney's letters and life, the violence of *écriture* appears in the struggle to make gender and sexuality holy, in the Protestant poet's lay appropriation of the priest's former ritual role as both the presider and the victim in the sacrifices required in a sanctified culture, and, finally, in the acting out of such a paradigm in the self-sacrificial gesture made famous by Sidney's hagiographers, the poet's wounding and subsequent death in the Protestant cause.[67]

To conclude this chapter I shall briefly survey those three features of Sidney's cultural architectonics, beginning with the last one and working back to the first, gender and epistemology, which I shall more fully explore in the next chapter.

The poignancy of Sidney's life and legend, which have recently been completely reevaluated in the celebration of the quadricentenary in 1986 of his death in the Netherlands, is that he carried out the terms of his moral and aesthetic commitment to move well-knowing to well-doing in the chivalric manner. According to Fulke Greville's *Life of Sidney*, Sir Philip was directly obeying the Queen's orders when he went to join his uncle Leicester.[68] Who is playing Minos to Daedalus's son Icarus here? Or David to Uriah, ordering him to the front lines?[69] One aspect of the mythologizing of Sidney in Greville's biography is the Christological model, too. Sidney is the good Son, the obedient Servant, the elect soul who experiences in his prayer and suffering as he lies dying on the cross of his bed the knowledge of the atonement, of which he then becomes an historical emblem in the figure of the Phoenix.[70] The dying Sidney makes his confession of Christian faith, Greville says, "as no book but the heart can truly, and feelingly deliver." In the knowledge of his secret sins, Sidney himself, the poet-priest, leads the assembly around his deathbed, asking no minister to do so. For he is "more properly instructed" by the Spirit who knows the spirit within a man "to apply the eternall Sacrifice of our Saviours Passion and Merits to him" (*Life of Sidney*, pp. 151–52). How different is the image of Sidney's prayer at the moment of death from the image of the Stoic prayer of Sidney's Pamela in the *Arcadia*, and no wonder John Milton satirized the King who supposedly read the written "fiction" of Pamela's pagan prayer on the scaffold.[71]

This imagination of the poet as a living form of the mediating Christ—the Ladder of the Word played out in Sidney's particular history, however Greville adapts it to his political purposes—is not Greville's invention. It is the logical conclusion to be drawn interpretively from Sidney's own poetics, which is ethical, political, and religious. Sidney's application to the poet of the significance of the sixteenth-century Protestant emergence of the priest-hood of everyman is as radical as Sidney's transformation of Jean de Serres's philosopher's book into the defence of poesie. Historically, Sidney's model of the poet who creates, who dies, and who lives again contributes in the seventeenth century to the characterization of man, woman, or text as the projected "victim" of sacrifice.

At the end of the sixteenth century, though, the same Jean de Serres who provided Sidney with the Protestant *Plato* and reinforced the English allegory of Solomon's wisdom in the making of the nation seems to have provided as well a model of the Protestant hero's mimetic office at the new sacrifice of history. This is the biography of the French aristocratic admiral and politician, Coligny, wounded in a failed assassination attempt two days before the Saint Bartholomew's Day Massacre and killed early on the morning of the Massacre. In the English title of the life of Coligny translated by Arthur Golding and published in London by Thomas Vautrollier in 1576, we meet under another name a version of that Cyrus whom Sidney adulated in the *Defence*, the military hero designated by God to make way for his people: *The lyfe of the most godly, valeant, and noble capteine and maintener of the trew Christian religion in Fraunce, Iasper Colignie Shatilion, sometyme great admirall of Fraunce.*

Osborn has suggested in *Young Philip Sidney* that when Coligny was wounded in the assassination attempt perpetrated against him and other Huguenot leaders by the Duke of Guise and his followers, Sidney may have visited the hero at the house on the Rue de Béthisy in Paris to congratulate him on his survival. The attempt was made during celebrations after the wedding on August 17 of the French Catholic Marguerite de Valois, sister to Charles IX and Alençon, and the Huguenot Henry, King of Navarre, for which Sidney was in attendance, and occurred on August 22. While wedding guests were occupied by the performance of a mock battle between the Amazons and the Turks, the assassin Maurevert performed his deed but failed to kill Coligny, who reportedly commented in a laconic fashion, "Bad shot." If Sidney visited the hero, he would have done so on Saturday, August 23. Early on Sunday morning, August 24, and with royal approval, the Duke of Guise went with a company of soldiers to Coligny's house and completed the murder of the Huguenot whom Protestant historians, Jean de Serres among them, have pictured surprised that moment as he knelt in prayer. The Massacre was launched; the rest of the day saw the piling up in the royal courtyard of the bloody bodies of hundreds of Huguenots who were stabbed or put to the sword. As news spread, the Massacre spread from Paris to other French cities, and both domestic and foreign Protestants hid or fled, Sidney included—and Jean de Serres, who took refuge in Lausanne and read and translated Plato.[72]

As difficult as it is from the vantage of a later century to assess accurately the psychological impact of such an event on Sir Philip Sidney, we cannot neglect a certain psychohistory of self-fulfilling prophecy, either. The model of Coligny's Protestant integrity and bravery has to have led by some route to Sidney's defenses of poesie and Love and to his protection of English and Protestant interests in the Netherlands where he, too, became a Protestant martyr. During the 1570s some in the Elizabethan court had advocated Coligny, counterpointing the factions supporting the Queen's liaison with Alençon and engaging the Sidney family, especially Leicester, in power struggles with Cecil and others who finally prevailed. The ultimate competitive challenge to French culture and the greatest self-justification English culture could perform was its production of a native hero like the French one, and in English style. Thus Sir Philip Sidney, not passively caught at home in his prayers but actively riding his horse, was metamorphosed into the emblem of the age in his self-offering.

In Fulke Greville's *Life of Sidney*, such a biographical model established Sir Philip Sidney as the poet who practiced "Architectonical art" (p. 21). In the manufacture of the Sidney legend of the late sixteenth and early seventeenth centuries, similarly, the condition of the poet as the new hero, the priest and victim of the culture being born again, established the standard justification of the English writer from Spenser to Milton. Where Spenser chose the ethical side of this architectonic consideration in his preference for love and governmental service—he calls himself the "priest of Love" in "Colin Clouts Come Home Againe,"— George Herbert and others chose the direct pursuit of pastoral ministry in life and poetic language. John Milton subordinated metaphysics to ethics and brought his increasingly spiritual religion to his poesie (a sacred Muse), bespeaking every degree of the ladder of love from lust and political falsehood to the historical Word of God and the poet's quasi-angelic participation in the Godhead. Not in military violence but in historical developments and in the labor of speech, Milton presided like a priest over a martyrdom similar to that Coligny and Sidney suffered by sword and cannon. He saw himself no less a holy victim in the name of a terrible Love.

How, then, does such a poetic identity manifest itself in poetic language as written? When the literary enterprise itself is conceived by and constructed on the model of the poet as a priest and victim of love, there is hardly room to acknowledge alternative victims and justifications or other agents of sacred power in the culture, or other cultures.

In his poetic practice Sidney provides negative examples of the reconstruction of the temple; positive imaginations are usually left to the reader to invent. The actual history of poesie in operation is a provision of negative and positive possibilities, and the reader must exercise both in the fiction and then make choices in the living. Sidney forms the classical early modern statement of the poet's "balance of experience" in this respect: his poet balances self and other, well-knowing and well-doing, idol and icon. The balance exposes the felt demand of a Pauline paradox—the famous paradox of a wise folly—and the difficulties inherent in a fundamental Pauline question regarding justification: "Knowe ye not that ye are the Temple of God, and the Spirit of God dwelleth in you . . . ? And what agrement hathe the Temple of God with idoles? for ye are the Temple of the living God" (2 Corinthians 6:16, Geneva).

Thus Sidney probes two loves in his sonnet sequence *Astrophil and Stella*. The collection documents the Sidneian value of building an implied temple of characters, living icons and speaking pictures of the divine image and likeness, and in the same breath Astrophil verbally constructs idols and the fearful labyrinth of love in which youths and maidens are vulnerable to a devouring monster. The "peised" or written text of Astrophil is *phantastic*; what Sidney enables us to see through it because of his peising of words and poems is *eikastic*. Likewise, in the "heroical" romance of the *Arcadia* Sidney carries out a similarly historical master-building of character to point the way to a necessary dismantling of disguises and the problem of an absent presence in this supposedly ideal place. He articulates the secular and Stoic mind and its divisions and afflictions as species of our fallen human condition, but with a view toward using them to realize the "politic consideration" of his Christian architectonic art of poesie.

In modern gender studies it is salutary to remember that from the perspective of a properly renaissance literary history, either feminine or masculine representatives of the truth might be sacrificed in its honor to express—to justify?—the culture. Sidney's martyrdom at Zutphen is a leading example of the cost of true discipleship in faithful love and fierce war. Nevertheless, the sacrifice of woman as clearly appears in several renaissance writers, including Sidney and Shakespeare, who often treats the drama of the theme. Sex and death go together in the imagery of this sacrifice for more than the reason informing John Donne's puns on ecstatic losses of consciousness. For instance, Sidney's Pamela reveals in her pagan prayer to her Creator the culturally approved offer to sacrifice herself. To be sure, she asks primarily for deliverance and the avoidance both of her personal destruction and of the loss of her virtue. She says, "But, ô Lord, let never their wickednes have such a hand, but that I may carie a pure minde in a pure bodie" (*Arcadia* 3:3.6, p. 383, ed. Feuillerat). But in the end she adopts the expected position of one who loves, no matter the gender, in her willingness to be sacrificed for the beloved: "(And pausing a while), And ô most gracious Lord (said she) what ever becomes of me, preserve the vertuous *Musidorus*" (3:3.6, p. 383). The question here is, indeed, who is going to be sacrificed for whom or to what end.

Verbal and sexual sacrifice is fundamentally an expression of the Protestant doctrine of the atonement—another type of justification—worked out in the love bond proper to marriage, and it has its antithesis. We know from another version of the *Arcadia* that Sidney conceived a Musidorus who was willing to rape Pamela in their desert flight, and this passage among others purportedly caused the Countess of Pembroke to ask her brother to revise the text and Fulke Greville to accommodate the request.[73] The scandal of Sidney's lusty Astrophil or raping Musidorus or of Spenser's Scudamour in the 1596 version of the ending of Book 3 of *The Faerie Queene* is the failure of the chivalric code and of Christian romance as the medieval mind apparently conceived it. They do not lay down their lives for the beloved. Rather, they may even expect the lady to sacrifice herself to them; or else they take flight from the prospect of rescuing her because it looks impossible. In a Protestant worldview, such a good deed is impossible in terms of human effort; all rescue is providential, and these characters decorously reveal the condition. So we find in the *Old Arcadia* that Musidorus's attempted rape is interrupted providentially and ironically by the arrival of "a Doszen Clownish villeynes" so that one of Pamela's dangers is thwarted by another, and Musidorus's lust turns to "vyolent Rage" against the divinely sent intruders (4:190, ed. Feuillerat).

Next to Sidney's apt perception of a psychological shift from concupiscence to irascibility in this scene, Spenser produces the brilliant designation of Scudamour's despair. The maiden warrior Britomart must rescue Amoret not merely because Amoret is an allegorical extension of Britomart's phantasmic struggle with a thousand monstrous forms of love, but also because Spenser partially anticipates the modern feminist's realization that only woman can rescue herself when she lives in the woods, caves, courts, schools, churches, and palaces of a patriarchal culture.[74] All too often the apparent rescuer is, almost by design of a fallen human history told in fable, the incipient rapist; and even the supposedly sheltering Malacasta fits this image of the unreliability of human nature in Spenser's ingenious gender reversal of the type. Likewise, the womanly power of Sabrina must finally change the victimized Lady of Milton's *Mask*.

Surely readers recognize, therefore, the tremendous ambivalence of Eve in Milton's *Paradise Lost* as Milton probes the mythic model of love's sacrifice. Sanford Budick has explained how Eve has become the priestly and sacrificial victim, and Michael Lieb has considerably clarified the priesthood of Adam—and Milton—in *Paradise Lost*.[75] Together, in their very sexuality, Milton's Adam and Eve constitute the new Protestant religion of love and marriage, the new model of the self-regenerative Phoenix.[76] To the extent that Eve reflects Milton's characterization of his poetic art, his poesie, she also represents some aspect of Milton's sacrifice of himself. The poet is victim as well as cultural priest. Diane Kelsey McColley has associated Eve with Milton's figures for his Muse and with *natura naturans* and the arts of

Eden.[77] This, too, names the poet's generative and regenerative power, which is analogous to the force of the *protoevangelium* in history and in the incarnation of the Word as Milton erects his version of the triumphant chariot of the Cross, the Ladder of the Word, the engine of God.

I am suggesting that Sidney's androgynous figure of the mistress-knowledge and poet-statesman also bequeathed to our literary culture the modern paradigm of the poet's offering of himself or of his poem as a mediator to open the way of divine Presence to the reader or, in an atheistic age, the way of divine Absence, the empty space that the human being must fill.[78] Biographically, Sidney's shift from the chivalric code to the Protestant iconology of the Reformation invited a revision of gender and social roles in subsequent poets, and Spenser, Donne, Herbert, and Vaughan all responded in their lyrics of human love and divine Majesty. The cultural problem Sidney's Protestant theory and practice bestowed upon his fellow poets and centuries of readers and critics is, therefore, as fundamental as his balance of self and other, truth and falsehood, *eikastic* and *phantastic* images, masculinity and femininity, icon and idol. Sidney's *Defence* synthesized in three prosopopoeias (invented, appropriated, and spoken in the "lovely name of Love" but for the significance of his own male, aristocratic ethos) a gendering of knowledge itself.

So the theoretical Sidney gave us a gender analogy and the question of the *degree* to which his true fiction of the intermediacy of the mistress-knowledge as a ladder of the Word may inadvertently submerge us in erotic phantasies, the false philosophy of changed shapes, too. Sidney's androgynous figure for his art—poesie/poet—engages the metamorphoses of allegorical mythology on the intellectual basis of a late medieval and early renaissance gendering of knowledge. The result is a production of gender hierarchies in epistemology, religion, science, and literature. These are visible at first, and then participate invisibly in the construction of a gender-biased critical culture by the end of the seventeenth century. The effect of the duality is a sense of presence and illusion, as Murray Krieger has called the sameness and difference with which metaphor is constructed; and it is also a modern critical inclination either to unite the two or to separate them, but hardly to sustain them in the tensions and multiplicities with which Sidney articulated literary architectonics. Where Sidney imagined a complex relationship between verbal architecture and the living re-creation of character, we have progressively tended to identify the male speaking subject with his technical production of words, with or without the numinous spirit of his mistress floating near. Criticism has almost completely lost that sense of paradox and contradiction in which medieval and renaissance poets saw an experience of the Cross and Resurrection in language and in sexuality. Renaissance poets found the knowledge of the love of God in love poems and in historical fictions as if by design of divine Providence. In our scientific age, our eyes are dazzled with fantasies, that is, with *appearances*, as the Greek etymology tells us, and although the same imagination produces these images, we tend to receive them as mere architecture and not architectonics. This is to prefer even material fragments to spiritual perceptions.

Perhaps the modern Protestant poet and critic Donald Davie has most succinctly stated the inward motivation and the literary outcome of the medieval and renaissance poet's assertion of the bond between decorum and moral architecture in his assessment of the literary history that led to the twentieth-century poet Ezra Pound. A literary civilization, Davie says, is "focused on pleasure." What Dante and the troubadours of love in medieval Provence were excited about in *amor* was a world in which "strenuous intellection—for instance, the constructing or the following of a close argument—affords a pleasure of precisely the same order as love-making or a well-fought tennis match." That such a civilization is based on the principle of pleasure does not commit it to "vulgar hedonism." On the contrary, it commits the civilization to search out a hierarchy of pleasures in which certain activities, such as sodomy and usury, in Pound's estimation, are so low on the scale as to be called "vicious." "From a hierarchy of pleasures it is, then, a short step to a hierarchy of social classes," Davie explains, and, may I add, of the sexes.[79]

Opening up inquiries into existent structures at the same time it searched for decorous sexual balance and class hierarchy, the Renaissance presented a problem to the modern age: the poet (man), whose style observed literary architectonics to stave off effeminacy and to ensure his productivity, inevitably sacrificed the self (masculine), the reader (feminine), or the text (the body, usually feminine) on the altar of his verbal quest for an androgynous virtue and the escape of *his* spirit. Iconology and iconoclasm, true worship in the Spirit and idolatrous fixation, lie very close together in renaissance poetry. The problem is not the mystery the poets seek to join themselves to, but the limits of conceptualization available to their fallen minds.

Another modern British poet, Geoffrey Hill, writing more from the "Catholic" side of what he calls "the spiritual, Platonic old England," clarifies the ethos of atonement. In his sequence of poems called "An Apology for the Revival of Christian Architecture in England," the inaugural poem, "Quaint Mazes," is entitled from Shakespeare's *A Midsummer Night's Dream* and precisely expresses the sense of sacrifice and sanctification with which medieval and early renaissance England was drenched. I quote the second half of the sonnet, from the last line of the octave through the conclusion of the sestet:

Religion of the heart, with trysts and quests

and pangs of consolation, its hawk's hood
twitched off for sweet carnality, again
rejoices in old hymns of servitude,

haunting the sacred well, the hidden shrine.
It is the ravage of the heron wood;
it is the rood blazing upon the green.[80]

Protestant Sidney lived out the new justification of such a religion.

5

Architectonical Art

Because if his purpose had been to leave his memory in books, I am confident, in the right use of Logick, Philosophy, History, and Poësie, nay even in the most ingenuous of Mechanicall Arts, he would have shewed such traits of a searching and judicious spirit; as the professors of every faculty would have striven no less for him, than the seaven Cities did to have *Homer* of their Sept. But the truth is: his end was not writing, even while he wrote; nor his Knowledge moulded for tables, or schooles; but both his wit, and understanding bent upon his heart, to make himself, and others, not in words or opinion, but in life, and action, good and great. In which Architectonical art he was such a Master, with so commending, and yet equall waies amongst men, that wheresoever he went, he was beloved, and obeyed: yea, into what Action so ever he came last at the first, he became first at the last: the whole managing of the business, not by usurpation, or violence but (as it were) by right and acknowledgment, falling in to his hands, as into a naturall Center.

—Fulke Greville, Lord Brooke, *Life of Sidney*

Anthropocentric Sidney and Androgynous Poesie

Although composed between 1609 and 1614 and extant in several manuscripts of different provenance, Fulke Greville's *Life of the Renowned Sr Philip Sidney with the True Interest of England as it then stood in relation to all Forrain Princes: And particularly for suppressing the power of Spain Stated by Him. His principall Actions, Counsels, Designes, and Death. Together with a short Account of the Maximes and Policies used by Queen Elizabeth in her Government* was published posthumously in 1652. Annabel Patterson has aptly suggested that it was printed at that point in order to contribute politically to the resuscitation of the image of a particularly "Puritan" hero.[1] Certainly both domestic and foreign criticism of the English Commonwealth in the wake of the execution of the King in 1649 required some shoring up of different Protestant factions at home, and Greville's preference of Elizabethan to Stuart policies and his observation of the religious politics in Sidney's motivation were useful for shaping public opinion.

But Greville's biography shows us something else, too. In it we may find an anthropocentric image of Sidney fashioned far more rigidly than Sidney's projection of himself in his writings and in his ethical and political choices of courses of action. Greville was not alone in working to ossify the icon of the Protestant soldier-poet, and in almost every case of those who wrote about the dead Sidney his image-making served some vested interest of the writer if only by way of moral identification. His anthropocentrism, as they saw it, helped them to build theirs. Ironically, the very impulse to reify the "saint" in Philip mitigated the Christian radicalism of his doctrine of self-knowledge and the self-examined life, on which there is no closure. As one should expect, the same image-making marks a transition from the epistemology of the sixteenth century, in which many kinds of knowledge, including poetry, were presented in gender analogies, to the more strictly masculinized propositions and logocentrisms of the seventeenth century, which operated on a reified and feminized *Natura* and text-body.

What we find in Greville's *Life of Sidney* is an epideictic definition of his childhood friend's "Architectonical art," but also the mid-seventeenth-century typing of the learned and literary *Elizabethan* hero who tossed off his writings as ink-wasting toys. Greville dismisses the *Arcadia* as an entertainment scribbled for Sidney's friends and inferior to his unbounded spirit. The icon includes praise of Sidney's character and faith, primarily, but not without lengthy considerations of the importance of military endeavor and New World exploration and some reflections on style. Stabilizing an image of Sidney that Alan Hager has called an "exemplary mirage," Greville's icon inevitably slants the presentation of Sidney's literary architectonics as well.[2] In Sidney's architectonics, poetry, like other products of human knowledge and action, represents an overflow of the mind inseparable from moral biography—the life as lived, or poesie. Even though Greville connected poetic style and living mastercraftsmanship, he tended to laud praxis more than gnosis in his rhetorical confirmation of Sidney's character.

Yet the biography is composed early enough in the seventeenth century to sustain two more aptly historical notes. Greville's highest praise for the aristocratic soldier mortally wounded at Zutphen—long before our American Southern poet Allen Tate invented a similar phrase in "Ode for the Confederate Dead"—is that Sidney carried knowledge to the heart, to the "naturall Center" of his own self-knowing management of affairs, and out to the world again. That is, Greville sustains some sense of the dynamism of the "centering" and managing of affairs characteristic of Sidney's "mastery" of self and others, and we may credit such a centripetal power as the source of energy and influence Sidney's poetic theory, practice, and life exercised on the age. Anything that denied the dynamism may appear centered, but was, in fact, literally fixed, mortal, and centrifugal, and Greville's picture of Sidney's death clearly marks the severance of a living spirit, centering and self-examining to the very end, from a decayed and ruptured body.

Thus, while George Gifford, to whom the brief commentary entitled "The Manner of Sidney's Death" is attributed, suppressed the horrors of Sidney's end because of the requirements of decorum, according to Katherine Duncan-Jones's view of Gifford's "pious myth-making," Greville advances rather than suppresses the Christocentric image of Sidney's flesh suffering gangrene and his bones bursting the skin while his spirit triumphs in the fulfillment of an inscrutable divine Providence.[3] Was this conviction, after all, not part of Sir John Harington's skepticism in his most uneulogistic reading of the architectonical art in the mid-nineties, when the *Defence* was first printed? Harington compares the Aristotelian structuring of knowledge in an ethical and political metaphysics not to the order of a sanctioned teleology but to the final end of the "businesse" of the outhouse, the "jakes," in *The Metamorphosis of Ajax*:

Now it is possible that I may be reckoned after these seven, as *sapientum octavus*, because I will write of *A Jakes*, yet I will challenge of right (if the Heralds should appoint us our places) to go before this filthy fellow, for as according to Aristotle, a ryder is an *Architectonicall* science to a sadler, & a sadler to a stirop maker &c. so my discourse must needs be Architectonicall to his, sith I treat of the house it self, and he but part that is to be done in the house, & that no essential part of the businesse: for they say "there be three things that if one neglect to do them, they will do themselves:" one is for a man to make even his reckonings, for who so neglects it will be left even just nothing; an other is to mary his daughters for if the parents bestow them not, they will bestow themselves; the third is that, which the foresaid French man writes of: which if they that omit, their laundress shall finde it done in their linnen.

Perhaps Peter Stallybrass's Bakhtinian discussion of Rabelais clarifies the point. Stallybrass alludes to the class struggle expressed in the grotesque emphasis on orifices of the body and on violation of boundaries versus the aristocratic emphasis on the "head" and rationality or architectural figures of self-containment.[4]

Harington's joke may suggest resistance to the cult of Sidney's heroism or even jealous rivalry; but given the balance of building and unbuilding in Sidney's aesthetics, given his awareness of mortal "clay," the scatalogical joke more likely reflects a skepticism about human wisdom that Sidney himself would have appreciated. After all, Spenser, too, erected images of palaces and churches in *The Faerie Queene* only to prefer to such apparently well-built structures the more difficult task of the development of character. When Red Crosse Knight is in trouble in Lucifera's castle, he escapes through the "priuie Posterne" (1.5.52) or the anus of the house of pride, in whose channels corpses are laid up like so much excrement.

Likewise, the more idealized, anthropocentric typing of the dead Sidney

was fully expressed in the funeral tributes of the two British universities to
him, whom both Oxford and Cambridge claimed in death as one of their
best lights. The social myth-making here is distinctly allegorical mythological and Christian. Again, the sixteenth century statement by virtue of its
syncretism has less containment and more openness in it, more awareness
of life lived and death undergone precisely as a steady crossing of boundaries. The Oxford tribute emphasizes Sidney's double power—with "Ars"
and with "Mars"—as a man who was, in William Camden's opinion, the
glory of the Muses (sig. B2ᵛ) and as a citizen of England (Anglia) who now
sits before the angels in heaven (sig. F4ʳ). The statement not only sanctifies
Sidney but angelifies him in terms of the ancient pun of Pope Saint Gregory, which launched the program to convert the English, as Bede tells the
story. The Cambridge tribute starts immediately with the praise of Sidney's
virtues and his practice of religion (sig. eᵛ) and credits his great learning "in
all philosophy, ancient and new, profane and sacred" (sig. e2ʳ). The
mythological bond erected in this tribute is Sidney's combination of Mercury and Mars. Cambridge gives Sidney its greatest praise of all, however,
when he is identified some seventy pages later as the very type of the
Christian and, later, especially Puritan hero: the true "soldier" whose actions show how he is led by Christ into triumph.[5] Erasmus had explained
the identity of the *miles Christianus* in the *Enchiridion* by arguing the necessity of harmony between the "inward" and the "outward" man whose
self-knowledge paralleled his knowledge of the arts, sciences, technology,
and theology. Sidney, learned and virtuous, contemplative and active,
fulfilled the paradigm in the laudatory opinions of his contemporaries, and
into the seventeenth century he contained the typing of their favorite
dialectics.

The previous four chapters should have conveyed, however, that Sidney
did *not* so type himself. His voice in the *Defence* is both centrifugal and
centripetal, that is, oratorical; it directs multiplicities of elements *toward* and
away from the mistress-knowledge as a project of his own self-knowledge
through speech. But the project, in turn, is a construction of a speaking
picture of English culture, and it includes the strong presence of the
feminine and the problem of trying to rule the feminine *or* the elusively
divine appearances and disappearances of grace. Moreover, Sidney's version of Sophia linked this problem of rule directly to the problem of knowledge. The epistemology of Sidney's intellectually universal poesie, in short,
was the inheritance of a long-standing gender analogy. Sidney's balance of
experience required less self-containment and more overreaching in politics
than Greville's denial of "usurpation" indicates, and his slow death was far
from nonviolent. If the "Architectonical art" described by Greville was a
proportion for Sidney's manhood, and it provided a witty definition of
intellectual and moral masculinity attractive to early modernism, the literary

architectonics imagined in Sidney's moral coupling of the mistress-knowledge and the poet as a triumphant captain and wise reader and writer was something different. It did not articulate simply an anthropocentric iconology; it touched the national making of the "house well in model" in a marital and familial sense that obviously included women and the generation of the future through the education of others.

The critical problem with the anthropocentrism of Sidney's eulogists is that the icon they seek to establish in the image of his character dialectically and necessarily leads to the phantasy of its opposite, too. In centuries of reading the *Defence*, we dismember Orpheus, exercising the dialectical, centrifugal force in which scientific analysis, not the maenads, triumphs over the renaissance impulse to synthesize. We have learned to take Sidney's poetics apart.[6] The Sidneian gender analogy of knowledge followed other sixteenth-century conventions on the arts and sciences and represented a metaphysical unity in feminine metaphors decorously joined to the political practice of masculine rulers. It is in this broader context that Sidney's *Defence* must be read, particularly by modern feminist critics, if a brute stereotyping of all things masculine, logocentric, and phallocentric is to be avoided in favor of a more historically apt cultural critique. We do not need to "save" Sidney according to the distortions of his late sixteenth- and early seventeenth-century reputation among his fellows; but neither do we need to evaluate his work in reaction to their view of him. As anthropocentric as his work is, it always includes images of the feminine in superior and co-equal roles as well as in inferior and subordinate positions.

Richard Halpern has discussed the paradoxical elevation of women in seventeenth-century Puritan views of marriage by way of explaining the presence of a maenad—a female follower of Dionysus—in the subtext of Milton's *Mask*. Halpern sees Milton's construction as a disclosure of class and gender struggle affecting the poet himself in his search for a "helpmeet" and in his consideration of the myth of Orpheus in *Paradise Lost* and, I might add, in "Lycidas." To borrow the figure with regard to Sidney's use of the myth of Orpheus, however, is to enter that other, more rhetorical realm of Orphic legend in which Sidney observes the oratorical tradition and credits Orpheus with the making of harmony.[7] Likewise, the ecstatic destruction of Orpheus is not a figure in the *Defence*; Sidney alludes, rather, to the parallel myth of dismemberment, that of Isis and Osiris, and says that in "the light of Christ" such myths can now be reinterpreted not only in Plutarch's vein, which poses the fragmentation of Osiris only to identify Isis in her regathering function, but as a searching out of religion preferable to atheism (*Def.*, p. 108). Insofar as Sidney works out a gender analogy in his epistemology of poesie, as I think he does, we have to credit the element in his figure of androgyny that does *not* suppress the feminine but even preserves some of its power as a force of integration. Otherwise we read the sixteenth century by the seventeenth.

In this education Sidney would have read Juan Luis Vives, whose Augus-tinian *De Tradendis Disciplinis* and *De Officiis Christiana* repeatedly illus-trated the bond between the architecture of learning and the achievement of integration in character and in society. Vives argued, for instance, that "the leader of an assembly of men cannot be ignorant that he is, as it were, the architect of the whole building, as Aristotle wisely teaches," ordering what ought to be done or not done in the state.[8] Of the statesman-architect he says, in Aristotelian emphasis, that the leader should have at least "a general acquaintance with the contents and aims of the sciences and arts, both those . . . of the hands, and those which solely occupy the mind" (*On Education* 5.3, p. 259). Vives and Sidney and Milton after him were Aristotelian in their judgment of speculative, practical, and productive types of architectonic knowledge—of which rhetoric was one—when they asserted an analogical pattern, or an intellectual and moral decorum, among learning, language, and life. So, too, from Skelton to Milton, before and after the *Defence*, literary achievement may be said to have generalized Sidney's architectonic poetic in the grand conversion of the architecture of learned metaphor to the true poem of a man's character.

At the same time, Sidney's allegory in his adaptation of the universal knowledge of rhetoric to poesie brings some of the questions addressed in contemporary gender studies home to literary architectonics and to English renaissance literature. Does literary architectonics, as a species of rhetoric, suppose gender definitions and hierarchies both in epistemology and in judgments of style? In what sense does Sidney's poetic theory confirm the idea that style is "the man," and in what way has that theory affected English poetry? Without using the word *architectonic*, Rosemond Tuve understood the intellectual brilliance of the architectonic poetic and how to read its tensions and multiplicities when she said that the critical canon of didacticism works best in the reading of renaissance poems if exercised at the same time as the canon of decorum.[9] The sexual and social tension implied in the engendering of self-knowledge appears figuratively in lan-guage; conversely, the gender allegory of language affects the concept of epistemological and social order so that decorum and didacticism cooperate. Thus Sidney's poet, or man of inward light, exercises his androcentric mind by joining powers. *Two* figures, male and female united in an androgynous bond, constitute the power of the poet in Sidney's moral coupling of Lady Poesie and the statesman-architect whose "erected wit" is lifted up in the vigor of invention.[10]

We may not be able to answer but we are compelled to ask whether some knowledges and some modes of verbal expression were "masculine" and others "feminine" in Sidney's opinion. The question inevitably revises critical ways of thinking about speaking, reading, writing, and the sexual nature of literary decorum in the English Renaissance.[11] Is the engendering of thought and of speech merely Sidney's cultural invention of himself and of the standards of civilization at the cost of suppressing woman's identification of herself, or did it contribute something else to English poetry? Mary Jacobus has used a psychoanalytic approach to see gender identity "as instituted by and in language" so that "the production of sexual difference can be viewed as textual, like the production of meaning." Her analysis sorts out the ambiguities of gender objectification and of subject-object interaction in the act of reading.[12] From the standpoint of her analysis, I have judged that Sidney's definition of literary architectonics exemplifies the textual production of sexual difference in the political interest of maintaining a balance of power with his ultimate audience, the Queen; in the process his definition helped to stimulate remarkable poetic productivity. When the presence of a female monarch no longer required that kind of balance of experience, a shift toward male dominance in the hierarchical definition of gender complementarity appeared a fortiori in judgments of style. Old distinctions between verbal "chastity" and "harlotry," between "plain" speech and copious amplification, and between masculine truth and deceptive effeminacy came more fully into play.[13] By the mid-seventeenth century, when Greville's *Life of Sidney* was published, the tense equilibrium of Sidney's moral coupling in the content of the architectonic metaphor was, I think, lost; the feminine prosopopoeia for knowledge had been conceptually rigidified and marginalized, or reduced to specific female characters within a text, or assimilated by the male writer or reader who exerted his power to compose or analyze over a feminized, that is, objectified, verbal architecture. The shift may be figuratively represented in the fact that Shakespeare's Prospero dismissed the phantasy of his "gorgeous palaces" early in the century after marrying Miranda to Ferdinand; but in *Samson Agonistes* Milton's Samson must reject his "sorceress" (1.819), for "thou and I long since are twain" (1.929), *and* destroy "The Edifice" where all the Philistines "were met to see him" (1.1588).[14]

Chapter 1 of this book began with the observation that, not long after Sidney wrote his *Defence*, Pietro Vettori, the Italian commentator on Aristotle's *Ethics*, also synthesized the arts and sciences in Aristotle's doctrine in a royal feminine metaphor, and to this *regina reliquarum* he attributed the greatest power and the highest degree of statesmanship.[15] Earlier renaissance thinkers who had organized knowledge according to Aristotelian standards had often collapsed Aristotle's distinctions between wisdom and science, science and art, and art and craft.[16] Conventionally, they allegorized the arts in feminine gender. John Wilkinson, a mid-century translator of the *Ethiques* from an Italian text, for example, liberally mixed his Aristotle and his Cicero; thus a treatise dedicated to moral philosophy became in English a combination of Greek and Latin ideas of the art of persuasion. Specifically, Wilkinson ignored Aristotle's warning to keep rhetoric separate from political science although related to it. Wilkinson's translation conveyed the conviction that final cause brings to anyone reasoning toward a didactic conclusion. Wilkinson claimed clearly enough that the civil art "that teacheth us to rule Cities is principall and soueraine of all other artes." But rhetoric also was "right noble" in his opinion as it sets in order and fulfills diverse arts "that bee conteined under her." Moreover, "the wealth that foloweth hir science is the welth of man, Because it doth constrain from euyls."[17] Rhetoric, in short, is a feminine power that accomplishes the architectonic end of politics through a persuasive speech restraining men from evil and promoting the good.[18] Wilkinson in another passage similarly ignored Aristotelian distinctions between prudential and sapiential wisdoms in order to make of ethics a kind of metaphysics and of art a kind of philosophic wisdom not unlike Lady Wisdom of the Book of Proverbs.[19]

In the Renaissance of the orator, the Ciceronian idea of philosophical eloquence easily joined the Aristotelian doctrine of the four causes—material, efficient, formal, and final—to substantiate various interpretations of the hierarchy of kinds of knowledge, of the idea of a master science, and of the dominance of ethical and political purpose in the pursuit of learning to define poetry.[20] The interpretations ranged from the specifically didactic exercise of education as the "nurturing" of better citizens in building programs of the state to the teaching of a grand design for eloquence and art. The "new" literacy was to mirror the authority of Holy Scripture and to integrate geometric demonstration with grammar, logic, and rhetoric in words that grounded history in the truths of philosophy, and that species of "first philosophy" made poesie a quasi-secret "schoolmistress" of life.[21]

Sir Thomas Elyot argued the case for learning in the statesman by synthesizing Aristotelian ideas of politics and rhetoric with the oratorical philosophies of Cicero and Quintilian in the same way Wilkinson did. Although Elyot recommended the reading of Aristotle's *Ethics* in Greek, not in English, "for the translations that we yet have be but a rude and gross shadow of the eloquence and wisdom of Aristotle," he produced in his renaissance reading list of "great books" an essentially syncretic interpretation of Aristotle's carefully constructed intellectual hierarchy. Learning, Elyot claimed, is primarily a matter of reading ancient books, and rhetoric and poetry contribute to the education of noble minds. Plato's *Protagoras* had connected poetry to the formation of public virtue (*Protagoras* 325a), and Elyot relates learning to politics and the virtues of citizenship by acknowledging the persuasive power of reading. No man, he says, can apprehend the lesson of the poets unless he has read much and is learned. Only "much reading and vigilant study in every science, specially of that part named moral, which instructeth men in virtue and in politic governance," truly serve the end of understanding. Elyot borrows Quintilian's idea that the statesman-orator should possess "every excellence of mind" and character. In doing so he links Quintilian to Plutarch's view of the proper *ars legendi* much as he had combined Cicero and Aristotle. The practical point of reading is the "fruit" to be gained, and "it is a very gross or obstinate wit that by reading much is not amended."[22] Universal knowledge comes to the mind in a rhetorical and literary mode, in other words, and Elyot presents his education of a good governor as an argument for productive literacy.

In his discussion of dancing, however, Elyot provides another image of prudential wisdom besides reading. His manual is distinctly aimed at the education of noble *men*, but his definition of true nobility is an image of two sexes, not one. In describing the "natural perfection" of a man, Elyot fleshes out his doctrine of hierarchical complementarity or cultural androgyny. A man is "fierce, hardy, strong in opinion, covetous of glory, desirous of knowledge, appetiting by generation to bring forth his semblable," while the "good nature" of a woman is to be "mild, timorous, tractable, benign, of sure remembrance, shamefast." The figure of man and woman dancing in this hierarchical complementarity, in which the masculine is clearly dominant, amplifies for Elyot several virtues; these establish the sign of matrimony, "betokeneth concord," and "set out the figure of very nobility" (*The Governour* 1.21–22, ed. Lehmberg, pp. 77–79). His emphatically masculine educational ideal includes woman at the point of an image of moral coupling and interprets the dance of man and woman as an exercise in prudential wisdom. But reading itself, by Elyot's standards, is a similarly prudential "dance" between the masculine reader and the feminine text for the sake of "amending the wit" of man and engendering moral "fruit." Reading of the feminine text-object tempers the fierce mind of a male subject in much the same way the mildness of the woman dancing with him "knits together" with his fierceness to make the virtue of severity; his desire of knowledge joins with her "sure remembrance" and "procureth sapience" (*The Governour* 1.21–22, ed. Lehmberg, p. 78).

The English humanism represented in Elyot's view of reading does not differ substantially from Vives's argument for Christian composition in the previous generation.[23] For if schoolboys could read pagan classics and gain moral points to form themselves as citizens, Christian writers might actually compose texts by analogy to the supreme truths of divine revelation to transform the reader. Observing the philosophers' use of the poetic fables of Homer to confirm their opinions, Vives argued that Christian writers could cite the oracle of God and teach the arts and sciences under the auspices of an absolute Wisdom, the highest Good and Final Cause of everything both in the world and in human knowledge of the universe (*On Education* 2.4, p. 89). Thus he adopted for the power of composition the architectonic vision of the Wisdom who in Christ the Word, and not a female figure. Vives had glossed the *De Civitate Dei* with a commentary.[24] The revelation of the architectural order of the world by its own divine Architect in the poem of Scripture inspired rhetorical and poetic composition on the best possible models of truth in ways that assimilated and transcended pagan classics. Such composition also assimilated a gender hierarchy in which the male poet was like the creative Word of God and the poem or city being built by him was feminine. Similar educative arguments had inspired Aldus Manutius to put out an anthology of Christian verse at the turn of the sixteenth century; most of the poetry included had been written in Christian antiquity.[25] Fabricius would later follow suit, explicitly stating that Christian schoolboys ought to have the opportunity to compare the fruit of Christian eloquence with pagan parallels.[26]

Another early sixteenth-century treatise by Vives, the *Introductio ad Sapientiam*, articulated the standard humanist program of learning and piety in a series of well-organized moral principles that addressed the presence or the lack of gender differences. Translated into English by Rycharde Morysine and published in London in 1511, *An Introduction to Wysedome* reveals the thoroughly Augustinian interpretation of the interrelationships of wisdom, knowledge, and virtue. Where Plato's architectonic metaphor put the statesman-architect and Aristotle's put the edifice of knowledge, Vives's architectonic metaphor takes both and forms the feminine image of a princess, the intellectual persona both of Proverbs and of Augustine's *City of God*. Accompanying Vives's definition of human wisdom are the principle of self-knowledge, the doctrine of human pilgrimage and liberation in the figure of the ladder of progress, and the assertion of a superior ethical philosophy that cures the mind and controls the tongue. On self-knowledge Vives says, "Wherefore the fyrste grice, that men clymme unto wysedome by, is that so many auncient writers speake of, *se ipsum nosce*, Euery man to knowe himselfe" (sig. B.ii^v). Learning has a distinctly moral purpose in knowing sin and eschewing it and in knowing virtue and attaining it. If learning does not accomplish this final end in the one who possesses knowledge, if "she" does not enable him to achieve this climactic point of moral action in his quest to know, "she leaueth her hoole duetie undone. What other thinge is our lyfe but a certayne peregrination?" (sig. B.v^v). Learning is, in fact, a "she" and the principle of man's pilgrimage; she is the handmaid of a princess: "The quene and princesse of all thyngs moste hyghest, is *Vertue*, unto whom all others serve, as handemaydes their maistresses, yt they doo as by duetie, they are bounden" (sig. B.iii).

Perhaps the most Platonic-Augustinian note of the precepts in *An Intro-duction to Wysedome* is Vives's appreciation of the light of the mind. Com-paring the relative darkness and illumination of different truths interiorizes the gendering of right knowing and right doing to make that moral cou-pling an inward synthesis.

Other erudition is syncere and frutefull, soo that it be applied to his right marke, that is, to *Vertue* and well-doing. There is a diuine Knowlege gyuen of God, wherin all treasures of science and wysedome are layde up, and this in the very and true lyght of mans mynde. All other lernynges, compared unto this, be verye darkenes and chyldyshe trifles. Yet thej be redde for this intent, that our lyght, by com-parynge of the one with the other, may shyne and apere more bryghter. The knowlege of man is sclender, a meruaylous smalle thinge, and that very obscure, and uncertayn; our myndes being tyed and bounde in the prison of this body, be oppressed with great darknes, inso moche, that hard it is, for our wyttes to enter euen into a meane knowlege of thinges. (Sig. D.iiij^v–E.iiij^r)

In sum, Vives's precepts express the intellectual inclination of the human ladder on which "the first steppe is, to knowe thy selfe, and the laste of all, to knowe God" (sig. L.viij^r). Again, reading is an ethical mode of advance in which the reader comes to possess a feminine *Vertue* concomitant with the effective judgment of a conscience that can liberate him from the prison of the body. That light of conscience, that light of self-knowledge, constitutes a man's identity when his assimilation of a power allegorized as feminine is exercised in moral action; his failure to *do* what he knows would unman him.

The *Introductio ad Sapientiam* clarifies the renaissance image of the ar-chitectonic queen and princess of all knowledge in another way. It joins other treatises on education by Vives to address the learning of royal women. Vives composed a collection of pithy statements and their moral explanation for the young princess Mary Tudor. The *Satellitium sive Symbola* was accompanied by a letter to Queen Catherine on the education of Mary and printed in Antwerp in 1530 with the Latin text of the *Introductio ad Sapientiam* and with two epistles on the education of children. The normal pattern of English renaissance education of boys according to the rhetorical models of translation and imitative composition foregrounds Vives's sensi-tive perception of the discrepancies in classical thought on the education of women. For him, common sense and principles of an architectonic philoso-phy dictated that women who were princesses had to be educated. The picture of the feminine exercise of learning and government, in turn, influ-ences the "feminine" metaphor of the architectonic knowledge, the "queen" of knowledge and virtue. As we might expect, the argument for the education of a princess emphasizes her literacy and her grasp of moral philosophy and the tenets of the Christian religion. Grammar, the art of teaching and learning, and the composition of speeches in Latin are the main lessons, and Vives's book list represents the best authors whose works instruct not only in well-knowing but in good living—"non modo bene scire doceant, sed bene viuere" (sig. L.v^r). The list is ancient and modern, for it includes Cicero, Seneca, Plutarch, and Plato's *Dialogues*, especially the *Republic*, and selected writings by Saint Jerome, Saint Ambrose, and Saint Augustine, but also advocates Erasmus's *Institution of a Christian Prince*, the *Enchiridion*, and the *Paraphrases* and Thomas More's *Utopia*. Classical historians stand side by side with Vives's recommendation of the New Testament, and a goodly list of ancient Christian poets—Prudentius, Sidonius, Paulinus, Arator, Prosper, and Iuvencus—precedes the mention of Seneca and Horace.

In *A very fruteful and pleasant boke callyd the Instruction of a Christen woman*, translated from Vives's Latin text by Richard Hyrde, the letter to Catherine of Aragon exposes Vives's mind on the "formacion & bryngyng up of a Christen woman: A matter neuer yet entreated of any man, amonge so great plenty and variete of wyttes and writers."[27] Vives criticizes classical sexism. Xenophon and Aristotle gave only the rules of housekeeping, and Plato, "makyng preceptes of orderyng the comon weale, spake many thynges appertaynyng unto the womans office and dewte."[28] Saints Cyprian, Jerome, Ambrose, and Augustine, similarly, have spoken of "maydes and wydowes, but in suche wyse, that they appere rather to exhorte and counsayle them unto some kynde of lyuynge, than to instructe and teache them" (sig. Aii^r). Both classical and Christian antiquity praise the virtues, particularly chastity, and exhort women to the highest ideals, but Vives will provide a sense of the art of living in his *intellectual* organization of precepts and rules according to the learned pursuit of virtue and "let passe all suche exhortations" (sig. Aii^r).[29] Although the education of women seems especially to require their *moral* likeness to the ethos of the mistress-knowledge, the empiricism of Aristotle appears in Vives's ability to judge the evidence of experience and not to be swayed by antifeminist traditions that would limit the intellectual development of women as well.[30]

He observes, therefore, that some girls are not inclined to learning just as some boys are inept, while others seem to be "borne unto it." For this reason the "dulle" girls should not be discouraged while the apt ones should be "harted and encoraged" the way apt boys are (sig. 5^v). He mounts the argument of experience against the condemnation of learning in women:

I perceiue that lerned women be suspected of many: as who sayth the subtylitie of lerning shuld be a norisshement for the malitioussnes of their nature. Verely I do not alowe in a subtill and a crafty woman such lerning, as shuld teche her disceite, and teche her no good maners and vertues. . . . For if she can fynd in her harte to do naughtyly, hauyng so many preceptes of vertue to kepe her, what shulde we suppose she shuld do, hauyng no knowleg of goodnes at al? And truly if we wold cal the old world to remembrance, and reherse their tyme, we shall fynde no lerned woman that euer was yll, where I coulde brynge forth a hundred good. (Sig. 5^v)

The point gains boldness as Vives refers to the will of a princely father who, in the case of his daughters, wanted them to be learned as well as good and chaste (sig. 8ʳ). In this educational theory, at least, in the century of Queen Mary and Queen Elizabeth, the princess of knowledge and virtue represented by a feminine personification of architectonic knowledge could support the type of feminine philosopher-prince who occupied the throne of England. History suggests that in the cult of Elizabeth the mistress-knowledge was so typed and that the typology helped to generate literary art.[31] But the androgyny that developed for a time, the empowering of the feminine, was soon to pass away with the increased validation of the masculine over the feminine. With the passing of Elizabeth, both court and culture were more open to masculine self-cultivation of power.

Gender and Epistemology

Behind the rhetorical poetics of the sixteenth century, of course, stood the work of the English rhetorician, Thomas Wilson, who had conflated Aristotelian and Ciceronian ideas of persuasion with Augustinian values in his *Arte of Rhetorique* in 1553, and whom Sidney also knew. Cicero had connected eloquence to the fellowship of human life and the maintenance of cities in the *De Inventione* (1.2.3). Wilson implies that language in its very nature is morally and politically architectonic, for well-framed words empower every man who speaks to help produce civilization. At the same time, Wilson's adaptation of Aristotelian moral philosophy to Ciceronian persuasion reveals Augustinian norms; Wilson interprets civic speech in terms of preaching since the building of the Tudor kingdom was also a reformation.[32] The power of the Word lies in the speaker's inventive re-creation of thought and in the audience's participation in the verbal reshaping of ideas in persuasive words. Reasoning beyond Aristotle and Cicero, Wilson comments on the necessity in his own times to reform the mind itself in the name of edifying a fallen human nature. He argues a masculine and semidivine power to frame good social order through words:

Therefore, euen now when man was thus past all hope of amendement, God still tendering his owne workmanshippe stirring vp his faithfull and elect, to perswade with reason all men to societie. And gaue his appointed Ministers knowledge both to see the nature of men, and also graunted them the gift of vtteraunce, that they might with ease win folke at their will and frame them by reason to all good order. (Sig. A. viiʳ [1560], ed. Mair)

Wilson's metaphors recast Aristotle's and Cicero's architectural and geometric analogies for thought into the "rule" of good reason and the pattern of justice, the frame of order.

Wilson's architectonic view of rhetoric in this respect emulates an earlier, feminized view of grammar. The ancient classical debate of an architectural geometry with the alphabet and with grammar was recapitulated in Latin rhetoric and refashioned by renaissance humanists, grammarians, rhetoricians, and poets. The opinion of Philo Judaeus that geometry was the "mother" of all learning, received English notice as early as 1517 when Richard Pace opposed to it the universalizing claim of an art of grammar that composed language. It is self-evident, Pace's speaking image Grammar says, parodying geometric demonstration, that "she" herself is the "foundation of all learning"; for letters lead to syllables, syllables to words and phrases, and words and phrases to complete sentences. Thus Grammar advises her schoolboys to imitate "good architects," much as Cicero had advised his orator, by laying a "good foundation" and having ready at hand a clear understanding of all her rules.[33] She teaches the principles, but the boys do the joining and building of words.

The English geometer Robert Recorde later pointed to a truer source of the analogy between geometry and language in Aristotle's logic and in Quintilian's praise of geometry as the archetype of thought. Logic, rhetoric, and all other parts of philosophy prove nothing without geometry according to Aristotle's testimony, Recorde says, whether by the syllogism, by demonstration, or by similitude: "Yea the faculties of the minde doth hee expresse by Similitude to figures of Geometrye. And in morall phylosophy he thought that iustice coulde not wel be taught, nor yet well executed without proportion geometricall."[34] Aristotle had indeed used geometric method in an analogy in order to develop the syllogism and logical demonstration in the *Posterior Analytics*; he did so, however, to facilitate the expression of the problem of knowledge. The geometric model was a way of proceeding from the known to the unknown. Geometric problem-solving had also worked for Plato's slave-boy as a demonstration of the act of reminiscence by means of which truth is "led out" of the soul and the mind educated (*Meno* 82a–85e). Neither Plato nor Aristotle intended to identify geometry with logical thought; they merely compared them.

Robert Recorde's enthusiasm for geometric science betrays his vulnerability to the renaissance excitement over metaphor as much as it shows a propensity toward literalism in the appropriation of philosophical truth under the aegis of the geometric science. In one respect the excitement is Platonic: Plato had frankly stated that geometry aims at the knowledge of the eternal and draws the soul upward to truth in such a way that geometry creates the spirit of philosophy and raises up what has been allowed to fall down (*Repub.* 7.526–27). Such a "moral" geometry contributed to the renaissance poetic fascination with how the Word "razes" false temples of the mind while "raising" up the true Temple. In another respect the excitement indicates the sexuality of thinking as a process of pursuing knowledge, joining it, and "having" possession of the truth.

Languet appreciated the usefulness of this knowledge, we should recall, but warned Sidney about its dangers for his melancholy temperament. Earlier in the century the artist Albrecht Dürer had portrayed the genius of a feminized *Melancolia* as a goddess surrounded by implements of geometry. The Hebraic and kabbalistic approach to geometry included its erotic relation both to grammar and to hieroglyphics, of course, and even Sir Thomas Elyot knew that the geometric ordering of things in creation, in gender and sexuality, in the making of rational demonstrations and judgments, and in the building of the temple were interrelated. He attaches his awareness of the mixture of wisdom and wantonness in poetry to a Jewish proscription of the reading of certain biblical texts until a certain age of maturity is reached:

And therefore among the Jews, though it were prohibited to children until they came to ripe years to read the books of Genesis, of the Judges, *Cantica Canticorum*, and some part of the book of Ezekiel the Prophet, for that in them was contained some matter which might happen to incense the young mind, wherein were sparks of carnal concupiscence, yet after certain years of men's ages it was lawful for every man to read and diligently study those works. So although I do not approve the lesson of wanton poets to be taught unto all children, yet think I convenient and necessary that, when the mind is become constant and courage assuaged, or that children of their natural disposition be shamefaced and continent, none ancient poet would be excluded from the lesson of such one as desireth to come to the perfection of wisdom. (*The Governour* 1.13, ed. Lehmberg, pp. 49–50)

It falls to John Milton to portray "divinest" Melancholy and his potential consort in "Il Penseroso" and to unify the problems of literature, geometry, astronomy, and sexuality in the conversations between Adam and Raphael in *Paradise Lost*.

Almost always, this excitement over the universal knowledge of geometry was supported in the early sixteenth century by its analogical development in the Latin rhetoricians, affecting the definition of decorum and concepts of style. The renaissance Quintilian resurrected the Aristotelian comparison of logic, rhetoric, and geometry.[35] Although Aristotle had commented that it was not necessary to use fine language to teach geometry, Quintilian turned the axiom around to say that the orator ought to know geometry because there was a direct relation between the well-ordered oration and fine language.[36] Eloquence followed invention and disposition with an intellectual congruence or "fit." The orator ought to study geometry because it provided usefully logical examples for illustrating his points and would help him construct a well-disposed oration. The implication of Quintilian's line of reasoning for renaissance rhetoric was that the rhetorical discovery and expression of ideas, invention and eloquence, might somehow elaborate, figure for figure, a philosophical worldview. Quintilian's catalogue of the figures of speech populated renaissance rhetorical handbooks with ideas; and what the *Institutio Oratoria* contributed to a renaissance sense of style, Cicero's treatises and orations contributed to the association of style with universal knowledge.

Thomas Wilson put the Latin analogy of moral and verbal geometry into the broader context of trivial and quadrivial knowledge using a gender hierarchy in the judgment of the arts and in the judgment of style.[37] In his *Rule of Reason*, for example, Wilson estimates the arts and sciences and divides the tasks of logic and rhetoric. He gives logic an occupation "aboute all matters" while limiting rhetoric to style. Rhetoric is feminized but debased in its identification with verbal "cosmetics": "Rethorique useth gay paincted Sentences" ([London, 1551], sig. B3r). With the same sense of classification, Wilson sees geometry not as a science in the Aristotelian mode but as another name for carpentry, the practical craft that named, too, the medieval concept of the art of architecture. Geometry merely "measures" things thick and broad by line and square (*Rule of Reason* sig. B2r).

In *The Arte of Rhetorique*, however, a Ciceronian influence mixes up aspects of Wilson's classification. By confirming the traditional bond between rhetoric and music, Wilson opens the door to other connections between the trivial arts and the quadrivial sciences that elevate the feminine, even though he has explicitly dismissed arithmetic, geometry, and astronomy from the scope of rhetoric. Men are transformed from wild savages into kind, gentle folk by the harmonizing power of language (cf. Cicero's *De Inventione* 1.2.3). Thus, modifying the debate of Cicero's Antonius and Crassus in the *De Oratore*, Wilson identifies rhetoric as a philosophically universal art at the same time that it is a specialty, an art of words. Moral harmony produces the combination of universality and specialty:

An Orator muste be able to speak fully of all those questions, which by laws and mans ordinaunce are enacted, and appoynted for the use and profite of man, suche as are thought apt for the tongue to set forwarde. . . . Therefore, an Orators profession, is to speake onely all such matters as maie largely be expounded, for mans behoue, and may with muche grace be set out, for all men to heare them. (*Arte of Rhetorique*, p. 1)

Wilson's androgynous rhetoric claims universality on the basis of the moral "grace" and harmony that the orator's rightful possession of ethical and political knowledge gives his language. Cicero's orator aims to stand beside Plato's statesman.[38]

In the actual debate in the *De Oratore*, the question of the use of "language agreeable to the ear and arguments suited to convince" emerges in Cicero's definition of the specialty of the rhetorician. Such language and argumentation are the hallmarks of the orator, and his specialty endows him besides with a "charming variety in many details."[39] To say as much, Cicero's Antonius reviews the person of the orator in relation to those of the soldier, statesman, philosopher, musician, grammarian, and poet. Eager to distinguish the specialty of rhetoric in its charming language, Antonius only reluctantly agrees that it was possible for a natural philosopher, like Empedocles, also to be a poet; simply because Plato was accounted preeminent in geometry and in music was no reason for the moral philosopher and rhetorician to claim those knowledges—unless he truly possessed them as well as the art of persuasion (1.50.217). Antonius compliments those moral philosophers who claim universal knowledge not by some artificial right of dominion but by virtue of the genuine possession of the type of knowledge in question. The arguments of Crassus, however, counter and amplify Antonius's points so that Cicero's conclusive definition of the orator openly embraces the scope of knowledge. In philosophical eloquence, the universal knowledge of all the arts and sciences finds integration in the orator's moral vision in order to create moral harmony through words. Thus Crassus advocates the orator's omniscience in the human realm. The knowable world, human knowledge, and man's duty are interlinked by the single force and harmony of nature; so, too, "the whole content of the liberal and humane sciences is comprised within a single bond of union; since, when we grasp the meaning of the theory that explains the causes and issues of things, we discover that a marvellous agreement and harmony underlies all branches of knowledge" (3.4.23–3.6.22). Crassus cites Plato in this passage, and Cicero's expression of the unity of knowledge shows how he has also joined Aristotelian metaphysics—the theory of causes—with a Platonic and Pythagorean vision of the unity of the operations of the mind. Man's duty in such a universe is fulfilled in the grasping of this "single bond of union," in the exercise of a wise, effective eloquence; for by means of eloquence man upholds the harmony of the world in the harmony of his own knowledge and virtue. As rhetoric is an art, it is a universal art, a master knowledge, which encompasses other sciences, arts, and faculties in ethical and political master-building.

Agreeing with the Augustinian-Ciceronian vision of a morally harmonizing philosophy of rhetoric, Wilson inevitably envisions it as the art of ruling over all other arts and sciences in the construction of figures of speech. Wilson's work is at the source of rhetorical theory in mid-sixteenth-century England. His distinctions between mathematical crafts and the sentences of rhetoric, on one hand, and his telescoping of moral philosophy and the universal, general art of a persuasive philosophy, on the other, contribute to the formulation of a philosophical poetic that is a moral coupling of imaginatively engendered powers exercised by men. Like oratory, poetry is both thoughtful and charming, exact and pleasant, moral and beautiful. Its balancing of those terms makes it, in fact, completely architectonic. Thus Wilson's Ciceronianism finally guided English concepts of poetry away from the division of architectural structure and prudential discovery and toward their fruitful correspondence in architectonic poetic invention.

Sidney versus Puttenham: Master-Building and Suppression of the Feminine

The parallels between Sidney and Puttenham on nature and art have often been observed in literary studies but *not* from the perspective of the gendered architectonic metaphor of poetic mastercraftsmanship. Since Puttenham has become more and more useful to modern theoretical enterprises, it is important to clarify several points of difference between the two renaissance poetic theorists while marking a few similarities. Ultimately their differences address problems of gender appropriation and even social class, with Sidney inevitably taking the side of an older aristocratic sensibility and Puttenham advancing the middle-class cause of *techne*. The best approach to Sidney and Puttenham on the subject of epistemology, however, is through an earlier Italian theorist, namely, Fracastoro, who directly influenced Sidney's *Defence*.

Sidney acknowledges Girolamo Fracastoro for his learning. Indeed, Fracastoro's arguments for the universality of poetic knowledge cover the same Ciceronian ground I have just discussed with regard to the *Defence*, and the Englishman would have found reinforcement in the Italian's ideas. Fracastoro's argument singles out the coupling motif, the making of analogical bonds among the knowledges and in language, as the epistemological essence of architectonics. A natural philosopher, Fracastoro used Cicero to argue the integration of all the arts and sciences in mastercraftsmanship and gave the poet the honors. Observing Cicero's idea of philosophical eloquence, Fracastoro asserted in the *Naugerius*, a treatise on poetic art, that every other artist or scientist limits himself to the purpose set for him in his particular knowledge, but the poet as poet is inspired by no other aim than simply to speak well about anything that proposes itself to him. The poet does this by adapting to his purpose the "ruling, directing, general art" that is rhetoric.[40] A master and judge of speech, the poet is also a philosopher, an historian, and "all the rest," like a "master-builder," Fracastoro says (p. 62).

In the *Turrius*, the companion dialogue to his treatment of poetry, Fracastoro specifies imagination as the architectonic mental faculty, the art of making analogical connections. "For to imagine is nothing," he says, "but to receive the many as many, to compare them in respects in which they are related, and to see how each individual is related to the whole. . . . This [faculty of imagination] mathematicians, architects, and painters especially demonstrate, and those who are concerned with the [fine] arts."[41]

What has puzzled modern interpreters of these companion dialogues, particularly with respect to Sidney's *Defence*, is the apparent contradiction in Fracastoro's definition of the architectonic science.[42] In the *Naugerius* the poet is the "master-builder," but in the *Turrius* the mathematicians and pictorial artists win the prize for their demonstration of an architectonic imagination. Our understanding of the Aristotelian hierarchy of the intellectual virtues in which the knowledge of theory and cause is higher than that of prudence, science, and art shows there is no real contradiction. The argument of the *Turrius* derives its rationale from the "metaphysical" model of architectonics in the *Naugerius*.[43] Although mathematical and pictorial kinds of knowledge may best demonstrate architectonic analogy by elaborating many comparisons, the operative rule of their demonstration *is* the making power identified in the knowledge of theory and causes with the poetic art. The poet both knows the causes of things and is able to produce scientifically the contents, aims, and methods of all arts and sciences in his verbal expression. Thus the poem, the product of the verbal construction of the imagination, possesses a materiality or visible "thingness" as much as a painting or a building, but that is not the glory of the poetic art. The feminine generative power unites with the masculine knowing power of poetic logic, and poetry then glorifies them together as the universal prototype of architectonic thought.[44] This coupled power is, after all, no longer merely feminine or masculine but divine.[45]

By this rule of operation, the poet's *act* of knowledge communicated in his act of making transcends plastic or mathematical reproduction. We have already seen that in a Ciceronian debate over the scope of rhetoric, Antonius and Crassus had come to a similar conclusion (*De Orat.* 1.50.217). What Antonius carefully qualified as acceptable, however, Cicero conclusively defined as the provenance of the orator—the full scope of knowledge expressed in the power of human speech to create moral harmony; Fracastoro transferred this power of the orator to the poet. The poet holds architectonic mastery over renaissance mathematics and fine arts.

Sidney jokes about "figurative speeches" and the "geometry" of Platonic conception (*Def.*, p. 93) but, like Fracastoro, one of the "learned philosophers" who defended poesie, he gives the poet intellectual eminence (p. 110). When Sidney recapitulates the Ciceronian debate between Antonius and Crassus on the subject of style, intellectual universality, and moral effect, he ascribes to poetry the theological power to form the ideas of things and the rhetorical power to compel their political realization. It is typical of Sidney's intellectual bent that he supports the primacy of knowledge—or "truth"—in the poetic art and to this extent restates an implicit gender hierarchy for language. Verbal "charms" have a secondary role to be judged according to their usefulness in conveying the primary intellectual energy of the poem. Yet truth and charms *together* in the universal art of architectonic poesie demonstrate the truly moral invention of thought:

For my part, I do not doubt, when Antonius and Crassus, the great forefathers of Cicero in eloquence, the one (as Cicero testifieth of them) pretended not to know art, the other not to set by it, because with a plain sensibleness they might win credit of popular ears (which credit is the nearest step to persuasion, which persuasion is the chief mark of oratory), I do not doubt (I say) but that they used these knacks very sparingly; which who doth generally use, any man may see doth dance to his own music, and so be noted by the audience more careful to speak curiously than to speak truly. (*Def.*, p. 118)

Although holds that a true poesie art shows learning in the curious part that as well as in theory: it is distinguished from a false learning that "using art to show art, and not to hide art . . . , flieth from nature, and indeed abuseth art" (p. 119). False art, similarly, is merely effeminate and decorative or, alternatively, too manly, hard and doctrinal. True art produces "the planet-like music of poetry" (p. 121), the harmony of genders that the readers, too, may generally seek in their own understanding. Thus Sidney eschews heavily ornamented speech as unnatural at the same time he adapts the teaching, delighting, and moving functions of oratory to poetry; poetic persuasion incorporates the universal harmony of moral truth in "fit" words precisely because it is a two-gendered moral coupling. Cicero's rhetorician built his arguments to persuade not merely as the geometer designed figures or as the architect constructed a habitation, but as the eloquent philosopher made ethical and political harmony with the universe in the characters of his auditors. Sidney's poet, likewise, speaks not merely with the technical charm of the painter's vivid images, or the melodic cadences of the musician, or the measured dispositions of the architect, or the contrasts of the mathematician, or the verbal curiosities of the sophist but with the poet's distinctly universal, particular truth in a speech that can alone parallel nature by recovering the underlying harmony of things for the imagination. Sidney advocates the "plain sensibleness" that can use but conceal art, *not* plain speech. Categorically, Sidney's poet does not "dance to his own music," but in Elyot's sense, he dances with a "woman" named the mistress-knowledge.

In judging the intellectual scope of rhetoric and poetry, Cicero said that the two arts were counterparts in most respects and truly identical in not being restricted in their intellectual claims; both range freely where they will—"quo minus ei liceat eadem illa facultate et copia vagari, qua velit" (*De Orat.* 1.16.69–70). So, too, Sidney's poet practices an art that takes more than the "brazen world" of a fallen nature as its proper object. The poet, "lifted up with the vigour of his own invention, doth grow in effect another nature . . . so as he goeth hand in hand with nature, not enclosed within the narrow warrant of her gifts, but freely ranging only within the zodiac of his own wit" (p. 78). He joins the feminized power of ethical learning to his masculine "erected wit" in self-knowledge, and together they produce decorous poetic language for moving the mind of the reader. Yet Sidney's Christianity required a new definition of "nature" and "wit" beyond the Ciceronian sense of harmony in the cosmos and in the mind. The superiority of the poet is marked in the *Defence* not by Sidney's "partial allegation" of the power of eloquence to uphold the harmony of the world, therefore, but by a recognition that such harmony does not exist in this world.

Sidney uses a *negative* argument to eliminate other sciences as serious contenders for the princely role of mastercraftsmanship (*Def.*, p. 77). Listing precisely what the astronomer, arithmetician, geometrician, and musician do, he especially criticizes the moral philosopher who says, "Follow nature and thou shalt not err" (p. 78). The allusion to Marcus Aurelius prefaces yet another list of comparisons to the lawyer, historian, grammarian, rhetorician, and logician, concluding with references to the physician and metaphysician. Surveying the practitioners of all arts and sciences, Sidney disapproves their intellectual "architecture" and dismisses them all as users of knowledges that "build upon the depth of nature." Only his poet is androgynously generative (p. 78). Invention, in turn, is the specialty of the poet that makes his work like the creative principle of God's world (p. 79). Without *poesis* one may follow nature, Sidney implies, and be damned. With it one may truly read creation and "dance" with it. Poesie is the verbal power of conscience, the decorous mental and social dance that alone penetrates "the secretest cabinet" of the soul to take "naughtiness" away and "plant" goodness (p. 85). As Wilson had put it, when man was past amendment, God "tendered" his own workmanship with the gift of utterance.

When we come to the consideration of Puttenham's treatise, *The Arte of English Poesie*, we inevitably hear echoes of the role of analogy in the arts dispute, but Puttenham seems to have taken the romance out of it. He likes *things*.[46] What the Greeks call analogy, the Latins decorum, the scholastics "decency," and the English "seemelynesse," as Puttenham later names it, "resteth in the discerning part of the minde" (*Arte of English Poesie* 3.23, pp. 269–71); in Horatian terms, decorum appropriately *joins* or *separates* things in true proportions. Aristotle, in his discussion of metaphor in the *Rhetoric*, had singled out the proportional metaphor that depends on the decorous fit of words and things as the most striking kind; but at the same time he recognized that, although metaphor gave style charm and clarity, metaphor could not be taught by one person to another (*Rhet.* 3.2 [1405a]; 3.10 [1411a]). One either "gets" it or does not, and the good metaphor-maker begets it to be gotten. So, too, for Puttenham the poet's manufacture of just correspondences in languages raises the question of poetic inspiration in a Platonic sense, or what we may prefer to call the leap of intuition.[47]

Puttenham's manifold definition of the poetic art at the end of his *Arte of English Poesie* embraces this idea of intuitive perception and transforms both Platonic *furor* and Aristotelian mastery of metaphor (*Poetics* 22 [1159a]) into a highly gendered and visual definition of poetic power, and the gender is masculine. *Puttenham takes Sidney's model away from androgyny and toward a more singularly masculinized epistemology.* Grammar, logic, and rhetoric are not merely "bare Imitations" in which men learn to speak by precept; they are, by means of long and studious observation, arts that work by rupturion and conunncconte naturall, reduced into perfection, and made prompt by use and exercise" (3.25, pp. 311–12). Language as a *product* of a man's mind incorporates language as effected by ecstasy or by nature and achieves a status equal to and *beyond the feminine* or incomplete status of natural things by re-creating and reforming nature. Art may aid nature, or alter nature, or imitate nature's works, or work contrary to nature, "producing effects neither like to hers, nor by participation with her operations, nor by imitation of her paternes" (3.25, p. 310). Thus, in the exercise of the solitary poet and maker, the master of style and metaphor, words produced as the fruit of the poet's "cleare and brighte phantasie and imagination" transcend in Puttenham's valuation all the products of the arts and sciences (3.25, p. 312).

Sidney had said that "where all other arts retain themselves within their subject, and receive, as it were, their being from it, the poet only bringeth his own "stuff," and doth not learn a conceit out of a matter, but maketh matter for a conceit" (*Def.*, p. 79), but not without his mistress. Puttenham argues that in their inventive capacity poets are like creating gods (1.1, p. 20), but he ignores their androgyny and makes them singularly male. When imagination is rightly or decorously or decently ordered in the poet's mind, the products of his intuition bespeak the golden world of unfallen nature, not the brazen world that surrounds mankind (*Def.*, p. 78) and not the darkness of man's own "iron & malitious age" (*Arte of English Poesie* 1.8, p. 36). As Sidney insisted that the mistress-knowledge brought well-knowing into well-doing in the actions of heroic characters who knew the light of Christ, so Puttenham insisted on the decorum of a divine master-building ethos in his view of man's invention, which is distinctly and totally anthropocentric:

Wherefore sure persons as be illuminated with the brightest irradiations of knowledge and of the veritie and due proportion of things, they are called by the learned men not *phantastici* but *euphantasiote*, and of this sorte of phantasie are all good Poets, notable Captaines stratagematique, all cunning artificers and enginers, all Legislators Polititiens and Counsellours of estate, in whose exercises the inuentive part is most employed and is to the sound and true iudgement of man most needful. (1.8, p. 35)

The English poet, a master-builder of society, delivers into the light of reality all the artifices and engines of his time; but he and poesie build—or engender—the good character of himself and of their people more by rules and mechanics than by inspiration.

In this sense style, as Puttenham explained, is truly "the image of man

[*mentis character*] for man is but his minde, and as his minde is tempered
. . . so are his speeches" (3.5, p. 161). Sidney, too, obviously gave poetic
style—the product of the poet's invention in the zodiac of his wit—an
integrating moral purpose, but less mechanically. Sidney explains the use
of contraries, for example, as a scientific and pictorial demonstration that,
by analogy, teaches moral truth in the perceiving of beauty, and his sense
of contraries keeps the feminine in view, too: "Now, as in geometry, the
oblique must be known as well as the right, and in arithmetic the odd as
well as the even, so in the actions of our life who seeth not the filthiness of
evil wanteth a great foil to perceive the beauty of virtue" (*Def.*, p. 96). On
one hand, Sidney merely repeats in this passage a piece of age-old rhetorical advice: the use of contraries and antitheses gives a subject light and
perspicuity. On the other hand, he recognizes in rhetorical method the
same kind of "demonstration of effects" that Leonardo had prized in painting, that Plato had celebrated in the philosophy of beauty and truth, that
Augustine had recognized in the divine poem of creation, and that Aristotle had praised as the intellectual value of antithesis: placing two opposing
conclusions side by side inevitably proves one of them to be false (*Rhet.* 3.9
[1410a]). Sidney's appreciation of antithetical proof reinforced the usefulness of a gendered moral coupling in poetic knowledge, and Puttenham's
idea of the tempered mind pushed literary architectonics toward its more
rigidified aspect in moral architecture.

In the *Rule of Reason*, Thomas Wilson had judged the vagaries of
human memory and connected its lapses to the Fall and an ensuing blindness. Reason is a gift for discerning the oblique and the right, good and
evil:

Manne by nature hath a spark of knowlege, and by the secrete workyng of God,
iudgeth after a sort, and discerneth good from euil. Before the fall of Adam, this
knowlege was perfect, but through offence, darknesse folowed, and the bright light
was taken awaie. Wise men, therefore, consideryng the weakenesse of mannes
witte, and the blyndnesse also, wherein we are all crouned; inuented this arte, to
help us the rather by a naturall order, to find out the truth. (Sig. Bij^v–iij^r)

On the basis of such thinking, Sidney had paired analogy and antithesis
because of the conventional logic of metaphor-making or *translatio*. *Translatio* is a making of correspondences and a "translation" of ideas. Vives
used his knowledge of rhetoric and Greek, for example, to explain that
metaphor was a type of analogy or, in Latin, decorum that the commonly
acknowledged figure of speech, *translatio*, expressed.[48] Vives's knowledge
in this respect was not arcane, for it called attention to the commonplace
that the author of the well-known *Ars Poetica*, Horace, had established as

the classical doctrine of decorum in the suitability of word to subject, image to idea, and art to nature. Latin rhetoricians categorized *translatio* in their manuals of speech, and sixteenth-century rhetoricians meshed the decorum of metaphor with instructions for its use.[49] The instructions follow-ing Ramorch and training mathirical avaniples often essentialize invention in figures of the hunt in ways seventeenth-century writers merely caricature in their emphasis on technique.

The Platonic doctrine of the emanation of light in nature formed various versions of the "ladder" or gradated translations of truth; among them were images of logic and dialectic, of the climactic knowledge of love, of the "chastity" of the mind, and of the mirror. In the sixteenth century, logic was iconologized as a huntswoman who carried the bow of "quaestio" in her right hand and raised the horn of "sonus vox" with her left hand—the hand of argument. She strode between two dogs named "veritas" and "falsitas." She wore the sword of the syllogism and walked swiftly after her quarry—a rabbit named "problema"—as she avoided the "dark wood" of "opinion."[50] Her likeness to the classical goddess of the hunt and of chastity, Artemis or Diana—or to Spenser's Belphoebe, for that matter—seems deliberate. For she is a figure of clarity and of clarification, one who walks the line between nature and art while negotiating both. True thought may be veiled in allegory but is chaste and single-minded. Insofar as poetic invention is like this dialectical invention, it, too, articulates a "chaste" discovery of the truth in the mind that, "right" as a true mirror, produces right translations. But with the mythic evocation of Diana in this image comes also the story of Acteon, who was torn apart for his voyeurism—for looking upon the "naked truth" in an inappropriate or indecorous way.[51] It is the later, seventeenth-century Milton who directs our gaze to the "naked majesty" of Adam and Eve.

In Roger Ascham's treatise *Toxophilus*, a dialogue between the bow-lover and someone called "Philologus," the art of archery not surprisingly parallels the art of writing that was supposed to make memory sure by guaranteeing the quarry of invention. But Ascham criticizes the state of both arts. Purportedly instructing his audience on the shooting of a long bow, the tutor of Queen Elizabeth makes metaphors instead: "In our time now, when euery man is given to know much rather than to live well, very many do write but after such a fashion as very many do shoot."[52] Ascham wants to see a correspondence between the knowledge of the precepts of an art and the knowledge of its exercise. The "hunting" and "shooting" metaphor for invention and eloquence requires that writers bring their discovered ideas to morally persuasive articulation—an eloquence that hits the mark.[53] Ascham insists that the writer perfect knowledge of an art in practice. Archery and writing, arrows and words constitute the four terms of Ascham's *translatio*: inventive eloquence is like hunting deer in a forest with a bow and arrow, for both goodly thoughts and goodly beasts first have to be found and then have to be brought into captivity, dead or alive, on the precise point of an arrow that strikes the object, a word that moves well-knowing to well-doing. Weak wits do not make good hunters—or writers. Likewise, Ascham sustains his emphasis on the practice of precepts in *The Scholemaster* (London, 1570) and distinguishes it visually from mere experience: "Surelie long experience doth proffet moch, but moste, and almost onelie to him (if we meene honest affaires) that is diligentlie before instructed with preceptes of well doinge. For good precepts of learning be the eyes of the minde to looke wiselie before a man, which waie to go right, and which not" (p. 18).

The hunting metaphor for invention appears in George Gascoigne's poetic theory, too. In *Certayne Notes of Instruction* Gascoigne paralleled the rhetorical arts of finding and saying to the Horatian expectation that a poem ought to be both *dulce et utile*. Gascoigne remarks that a poet's invention ought to be "good" and "fine." By saying so he indicates no gap between the process of discovery and the expression of meaning, or invention and eloquence. On the contrary, the assertion that a "fine deuise" will lead "well enough and fast enough" to "pleasant woordes" echoes Horace's view that words are not loath to follow in poetic composition once the "matter" of wisdom has been learned.[54] For Gascoigne, poetic invention legitimately parallels the Horatian sense of the true wisdom of the poet—"Scribendi recte sapere est et principium et fons" (*Ars Poet.* 309). Poetry is a moral philosophical expression, a decorous bringing of knowledge into the light in a useful way. One simply has to "find" a device that propagates significance.

In his poem "Wodsmanship" in *A Hundreth sundrie Flowres*, Gascoigne shows the generative workings of his mind in the search for such a device as the very principle of self-knowledge in the vocation of a poet. The philosophical "hunt" through many moral and political dead ends—philosophy, law, courtly service, and soldiery—has led him to forestry and hunting as to the discovery of his call to letters. Essentially Gascoigne portrays himself in this poem as a lucky man who benefits from patronage. Hunting with Lord Grey of Wilton one day, the woodsman fails to hit any target until, indecorously, he shoots the wrong target, a carrion deer. In this sorry success, he accidentally finds himself. Thus Gascoigne plays on invention to define poetry as the act of discovery that delivers poet and reader to moral wisdom. The discovery is a moment of grace, and "Wodsmanship" concludes with Gascoigne's statement of his realization that he needs to reform his life. The statement hangs on Gascoigne's sexualized view of invention in which the poet who "shoots" the female deer also sucks the milk of her inspiration that will enable him better to hit his poetic mark.[55]

That by the sodaine of his ouerthrowe,
I myght endeuour to amende my parte,
And turne myne eyes that they no more beholde,
Such guylefull marks as seems more than they be, . . .
. . . .
And when I see the milke hang in hir teate,
Me thinkes it sayth, olde babe nowe learne to sucke
Who in thy youth couldst neuer learne the feate
To hitte the whytes whiche liue with all good lucke.
          (139–48, p. 398 in *A Hundreth sundrie Flowres*)

Again, the *translatio* here emphasizes the contrariety rather than the similarity. It is not the capacity of poetic invention actually to *state* an ideal in an eloquent verbal picture that gives invention moral power, but the poet's self-knowledge in a good little fable. The measure of grace is the measure of Gascoigne's understanding of the "hunt" of his poetic vocation. Understanding comes by accidental vision—"And when I see . . . / Me thinkes it sayth. . . ." The fable leads to seeing, but seeing *speaks* and maternally gives suck to—that is, morally instructs—the poet. Obviously, in the interaction of inventing, seeing, speaking, engendering, and nurturing, the poet suggests that there are immoral as well as moral couplings of thoughts and words. The moral ambivalence of style necessitates the rules for true decorum or a proper "fit."

Inevitably, a chaste poetic art that shows forethought for the good of the soul raises the question of love and the sexualized decorum of speech. Puttenham's placement of love poetry among many kinds of poetic expression indicates his high estimation of love and his aim to educate the courtier, but also reveals that love alone does not make poetry (*Arte of English Poesie* 1.22, pp. 59–60). Love is not the universal matrix of knowledge for Puttenham in the way it was for Italian theorists who more closely adhered to the doctrines of Ficino's *Symposium*—or in the way it was for Sidney, who received and modified Jean de Serres's Augustinian and Christian kabbalistic view of "duplex Amor." Puttenham's apparent *ungendering* of knowledge and speech stresses intellectual and moral integrity, a mental chastity that unites all human endeavors in the way light unites the universe. Love, therefore, is one of the many subjects of poetry, including the honor of the gods, the worthy deeds of noble princes, "the memoriall and registry of all great fortunes, the praise of vertue & reproofe of vice, the instruction of morall doctrines, the reuealing of sciences naturall & other profitable Arts," and so forth (1.10, p. 39). All subjects of poetry emphatically share in the educative, re-creative function of moral philosophy.

Thus Puttenham, not Sidney, refashions Diotima's proportion or "ladder" in the *Symposium* in the direction that several modern critics like to ascribe to Sidney. Diotima said that love lies between ignorance and wisdom, earth and heaven, and that poetry, a "making" common to all arts, lies between nonbeing and being (*Symposium* 204b–204d). Puttenham says, rather, that poetry has to be a realized verbal mean between psychological effect and moral vision or it holds no place at all. Because of their shared basis in the one and the many, poetry and love also shared a similar relation to beauty and goodness for the Platonist and for Sidney, who could sustain degrees or steps as well as a dialectic; both poetry and love were forms of "madness" or ecstasy, too. A divine inspiration enraptures the "holy and wondrous and delightful creature" called "poet," who is then able to assume every kind of shape and to imitate all things (*Repub.* 3 [398a]) since he possessed "the madness of the Muses" (*Phaedrus* 245a).

Puttenham develops his sense of poetic proportion in the world, however, by changing the metaphor of the ladder into the decorous *precepts* of a mediating speech over which the poet has control. Invention is the reason poetry may be defined, Puttenham argues, as an art having a "certaine order of rules prescribed by reason and gathered by experience" (1.2, p. 5). Following Plato's idea of dialectical invention, not his idea of ecstatic love or composition, Puttenham epistemologically analogizes poetic invention to the laws of discourse and mathematics, to music, and to vision. As a source of poetry, love has been changed into *either* scientific *or* stolen glances that supply the poet's imagination. Poetic imagination is a perspective glass "whereof there be many tempers and manner of makinges, as the *perspectiues* doe acknowledge, for some be false glasses and shew thinges otherwise than they be in deede, and others right as they be in deede, neither fairer nor fouler, nor greater nor smaller" (1.8, p. 34).

Puttenham's analogy of the perspective glass records the manner in which, through the sixteenth and into the seventeenth centuries, many English poets separated feminine mastercraftsmanship from the architectural model of composition. They conceived and expressed poetic imagination in various epistemological analogies to science and technology, not merely in the old rhetorical analogy that a poem is built like a house. A poem might be composed like the motion of a machine, like the propagation of light, like the anatomy of the body or of the cosmos, or like the workings of a mathematical problem, for example. A severely intellectual self-awareness marked poetic composition and gave poetic fiction the peculiar evanescence of the poet's self-knowledge. Gender distinction gave way to mechanics, the mysterious human body to the new machine. When Spenser defended the fiction of Faeryland against charges that its "famous history" was "th'aboundance of an idle brain," he cited New World exploration as his model of invention, combining the hunt and the mirror in his address to the Queen:

Of Faerie lond yet if he more inquire,
By certaine signes here set in sundry place
He may it find . . .

That no'te without an hound fine footing trace.
And thou, O fairest Princesse vnder sky,
In this faire mirrhour maist behold thy face.

(Proem 4, FQ 2)

Unlike Puttenham and the new technocrats of language and knowledge, Spenser balanced the signifying power of language with New World exploration and with the sense of feminine embodiment of the world that shows up, Stallybrass observes, in Elizabethan cartography.[56] Like Sidney, in other words, Spenser's movement through the zodiac of his wit is gendered with the masculine and the feminine.

In the seventeenth century Ben Jonson appears to keep that feminine force present along with the masculine, but he actually follows Puttenham. Jonson concisely expresses several aspects of the architectonic metaphor in his poetic theory, although the very precision of his definition shows a weakening of the complexity of Sidney's more open concept, a lessening of tensions by moving toward subordination of the feminine.[57] Jonson says, "Poesy is the habit or the Art; nay, rather the Queen of Arts which had her Original from heaven" and to whom court should be paid as to a "Mistresse."[58] The study of poetry "offers to mankind a certain rule and Pattern of living well, and happily; disposing us to all Civil offices of Society" (*Discoveries* 8:636). Jonson did not arrive at the expression of this Platonic idea of poesie's "Original" and of this feminized Aristotelian and medieval metaphor of her status as a "Queen" of the arts and sciences in an intellectual vacuum. As in Sidney's case, his vivid imagery surpasses Vettori's sense of the *regina reliquarum* to distill centuries of thought into the prosopopoeia of a philosophical poetic. Yet how abstract she has become. Jonson's eulogy of the Mistress Poesie and Queen of the arts is really an epitaph on Sidney's mistress-knowledge.

In the actual working out of his poetic theory, Jonson extends the masculinized verbal technology of Puttenham, anticipates the Kantian transcendent ego, and prepares the way for twentieth-century linguistics and structuralism as he admires the manner in which a sentence holds together. Sometimes comparing syntax to a sexual union, he sees in its congruency the model of poetic fable. Other times he decidedly depersonifies the allegorical representation of prosopopoeias in Sidney's literary architectonics and compares the grammatical knitting of words to architecture. The emphasis is on the architectural analogy inherent in master-building, in other words, and not on the moral and personified vision of character-making. "The congruent, and harmonious fitting of parts in a sentence," Jonson said, "hath almost the fastning, and force of knitting, and connexion: As in stones well squar'd, which will rise strong a great way without mortar" (*Discoveries* 8:623). This version of Sidney's "peising" of delightful proportions in words reinforces the architectural motif of poetic composition, making it critically easier to separate invention from imitation and image from idea or person from place.

The Fable is call'd the Imitation of one intire, and perfect Action; whose parts are so joyned . . . as nothing in the structure can be chang'd, or taken away, without impairing, or troubling the whole   As for example; if a man would build a house, he would first appoint a place to build it in, which he would define within certain bounds: So in the Constitution of a *Poeme*, the Action is aym'd at by the *Poet*, which answers *Place* in a building. (*Discoveries* 8:645)

In the actual construction of feminine character in a play, this anthropocentric architecture inevitably satirizes any "woman's" claim to power, any feminine crossing of the boundaries set for her containment. In his metaphoric balancing of the action preferred by the poet with the place that constitutes the poem, Jonson sustains some gender tension in poetic making and emphasizes the joining activity of poetic syntax and analogy. But his metaphors make a metametaphor of the male character who, knowing many things and saying them in conscience, may or may not acknowledge gender imbalances in his speech and know himself—and may, therefore, either rhetorically instruct or logically deceive the reader. Jonson suppresses the feminine or "puts it in its place" and even condemns language that is feminized—that is, copious and dilated, amplified, expansively renegotiating the boundaries the poet has set for it, as Patricia Parker has well demonstrated in the analysis of Jonson's characterization of Ursula the pig-woman in *Bartholomew Fair*.[59]

In fact, Jonson helped to develop the theme of moral architecture to an extreme degree in the poets' absorption in noble or ignoble male character—as if the development would solve the gender tension inherent in literary architectonics by subordinating a feminized architecture or "effeminate" mind to the masculine control of line and structure. In Jonson's well-known tribute to the nobility of the Sidney family, "To Penshurst," the straightforward personification of the Sidney home is a synecdoche taking over the representation of the proven virtue of those whose moral character indwells civilization. Jonson contrasts the nouveau riche and their great houses to a bloodline of great men and the "countrey store" of this house, "rear'd with no man's ruine."

> Now, Penshurst, they that will proportion thee
> With other edifices, when they see
> Those proud ambitious heaps, and nothing else,
> May say their lords have built, but thy lord dwells.
> (ll. 99–102)[60]

The lady of the house, like its lord, is absent upon the royal visitation the poem commemorates—a true reversal of any Sidneian or Spenserian representation, in which houses are always reargrounded in the landscape occupied by characters. Similarly, Jonson's idea of the lady's role is gender-typed and controlled. He specifically praised the high housewifery in which Penshurst's lady is "noble, fruitfull, chaste with all." This praise selects the good wife of Proverbs 31 over the mastercraftswoman of Proverbs 8 as worthy of praise, arranging the subordinate placement of the feminine within a masculine construction of order.

By the time Andrew Marvell writes "Upon Appleton House," the "unproportioned heights" of the buildings made by Italian architects have fallen to a humbler standard of decorum in which art composes "Like Nature, orderly and near." The standard, a morally "better" one according to the judgment of the poet who would imagine Adam alone in "The Garden," reflects an art of living that composes "Paradise's only map."[61] Along with Jonson in his debate with Christopher Wren and Inigo Jones about the makings of city and of theater, Marvell both appreciates the Sidneian architectonic aesthetic and, again, changes its meaning.[62] To great buildings in the material order, these poets opposed the powerful construction of words in search of intellectual and moral discoveries, structure for structure. But they turned aside from the uncontrollable and uncontainable presencing of the feminine mistress-knowledge who could come and go as she willed. Likewise, to the construction of cities, they responded with an engendering of character, but it, too, was by rule.

In a far more prosaic fashion, Milton's friend, Sir Henry Wotton, would express the architectonic principle of the analogy of the arts in his *Elements of Architecture*. Architectural rules "are in truth borrowed, from other Learnings: there being between Arts and Sciences as well as between Men, a kind of good fellowship, and communication of their Principles" (p. 2).[63] One recognizes the adapted title of Euclid's *Elements of Geometry* in Wotton's title, and in the text Wotton observes the Vitruvian paradigm of symmetrical buildings, bodies, and the body-politic. But as Wotton goes on to promise another treatise, one on "moral" architecture, "a second Building or repairing of Nature," it is clear once again that the analogical principle embedded in the architectonic metaphor primarily expressed a moral philosophical significance for Englishmen of the Renaissance (p. 122), and this could be variously interpreted. A "moral" architecture was a rule of practice in the production of all things, whether a schoolboy's mind or a cannon or a poem, and not merely the abstraction of mathematical theory (p. 122). In 1651 Wotton's *Philosophical Survey of Education, or Moral Architecture* was published, going through two other editions by 1672. In his dedicatory epistle he explains his analogy:

But having long since put forth a slight Pamphlet about the Elements of Architecture, which yet hath been entertained with some pardon among my Friends, I was encouraged even at this age, to assay how I could build a Man: For there is a Moral, as well as a Natural or Artifical Compilement, and of better Materials.[64]

Humanist education had cultivated the value of self-knowledge and of moral architecture for well over a century before Wotton wrote. Sidney was neither first nor last to use the metaphoric commonplace when he said that all knowledge, especially poetic learning, was meant to stimulate in human beings as much virtue as our "degenerate souls, made worse by their clayey lodgings" were capable of (*Def.*, p. 82). Spenser had registered acute moral awareness in his architectural figure of the feminine body and the mind of man. The ideal proportions of the human body and soul make the "goodly diapase" of the circle, square, and triangle crowned with the "tower" of the mind in the allegory of Alma's castle where Guyon and Arthur read history; but in misrule the same proportions may become a monster (*FQ* 2.9.1, 22). Milton immortalized Wotton's moral architecture in the essay *Of Education* when he turned the architectonic metaphor into pedagogical *techne* and teleology in a scriptural figure of destruction and edification: the end of learning is "to repair the ruines of our first Parents."[65] Without the power of such renovation, Sidney's gendered and androgynous poesie would be only a serving science, another one of those knowledges a man might accurately practice with a "crooked heart." Yet the universality of the poetry that Milton acknowledged to be both precedent and subsequent to a full course of study has a different quality of feeling to it in its focus on the subjectivity of the poet. Poetry would be diminished in its encyclopedic truth if the character of the poet was not a good one, especially with regard to chastity. In the *Apology for Smectymnuus*, Milton had felt obliged to defend the intellectual integrity of his own poetic art with a genetic argument demonstrating his self-knowledge and therefore defending his character.

The poets in practice and in theory supported the identification of poetry as the rule to achieve virtue, but they nevertheless experienced the discrepancy between an idea of learning aimed at good character and the successful realization of good character in flesh and blood; that sexualized conflict was inherent in language itself. The experience affected the way poetic images were either buildings of inward discovery and moral coupling or merely structures of verbal measure and ruins of the mind. Although numerous renaissance Englishmen, Wotton included, followed earlier Italian precedent in seeing architecture as a learned art, the best poets never envisioned it in their poems without moral qualification, especially when structures were explicitly judged to be feminine. Apparently the constructing of remarkable edifices abroad, the building of great houses at home, and the remaking of London inspired, through the sixteenth and the early seventeenth centuries, a keenly gendered sense of what would last and what would pass away. That sense corresponded to the value judgments of Christianity and of Platonic philosophy on what ought to be built up and what ought to be allowed to decay.

Especially in the last decades of the sixteenth century, when Queen Elizabeth aged without having produced an heir, statesmen-poets elevated character making far above construction programs as a matter of decorum The division between a properly Sidnolan and androgynous poesic and the developing emphasis on a masculinized language that controls the verbal architecture of things is quite apparent We can see the distinction clearly in a philosophical poem written at the end of the century and in Greville's critical biography of Sidney and a poem Greville claims to have written in his youth but one that actually records a seventeenth-century bias.

Nosce Teipsum

Two philosophical poems by Sir John Davies and by Fulke Greville, Lord Brooke, especially describe the intellectual and moral order of architectonic knowledge and may be used to exemplify what happened to Sidney's poetic theory. These writers express the architectonic metaphor in the poetry of statement; they practice not inventive poesie by Sidney's definition but the second sort of poetry, a sharing of "the sweet food of sweetly uttered knowledge" when the poet writes as one whose mind is "wrapped" in the fold of the proposed subject and has not taken "the course of its own invention" (*Def.*, p. 80).

At the turn of the century, Davies taught the philosophical doctrine of Delphi in the "sweet" utterances of poetic measure in "*Nosce Teipsum*, This Oracle Expounded in Two Elegies 1. Of Humane Knowledge 2. Of the Soule of Man, and the Immortality Thereof."[66] A doctrinal compendium, *Nosce Teipsum* summarily gathers up various referends of the architectonic metaphor that informed sixteenth-century poetry. Noteworthy is Davies' conflation of the myth of Prometheus with the architectonic vision. He pictures the poor sparks of human consciousness in their enlightenment by a feminine light of a divinely inspired mastercraftsmanship. The gathering point of knowledge, as we might expect, is the eye of reason, the sparkle of the mind left to man after the Fall; but Davies sees this "Skye-stolne fire" as a power experiencing darkness "Under the ashes" of man's immoral history (11.29–60, pp. 2–3). One must recall that patristic doctrines of conscience depended on the analogizing of Ezekiel's cherubic eyes and sparks in the wheels-within-wheels of the divine chariot-throne to the story of Cain, whom Augustine named the builder of the earthly city. Erasmus, further conflating scriptural and patristic sources with classical myth, analogized Eve's fall and Cain's departure from paradise to Prometheus's theft of knowledge.[67] Assuming this mythological syncretism, Davies, a lawyer, rigidifies the old Vitruvian order of bodies and buildings in his search for the laws of knowledge in the mind.

Ethics and science form his analogical measures of the mind, and he uses them to regulate the cognitive experience of the senses. Davies knows the senses to be limited and vulnerable to distortion:

> How can we hope, that through this Eye and Eare,
> This dying Sparkle, in this cloudy place,
> Can recollect these beames of knowledge cleere,
> Which were infus'd in the first minds by grace.
>
> (11.61–64, p. 3)

We seek to know the motions of each sphere and the strange causes of the ebb and flow of the Nile, Davies says, "But of that clocke within our brests we beare, / The Subtill motions we forget the while." He suitably recommends self-knowledge as a solution, and with it the understanding of time and history, but simultaneously sees the Delphic oracle as the devil's command (11.76–92, p. 4). For the skeptic in Davies, the entire frame of knowledge is untrustworthy; learning, no matter how it may be organized, is a form of darkness that only man's affliction pierces. The whole of man is his eye, and his eye may be dark.

Leaving knowledge, then, Davies in his second elegy treats the soul and its immortality as the hope of man. It is the "center" to which heavenly light might communicate a sense of truth. Man's eyes are the "lights" that shine in the Vitruvian "towre" of his body, but they are not able to look "into this little world" until self-knowledge grants him the "first degree" of true wisdom. When that happens, the heavenly power that gave human nature eyes to view the created world reveals also the gift of "an inward light, / Whereby my Soule, as by a Mirror true, / Of her owne forme may take a perfect sight." The corrective mirror of self-knowledge and inward light expresses succinctly the architectonic work of proportion-making that Jean de Serres, Sidney, Spenser, Puttenham, Milton, and other writers established as the device of a man's regeneration by conscience. But Davies' poem, lengthy as well as philosophical, also narrows down the true philosophy of the architectonic idea into the commonplaces of doctrine.

Davies makes a compendium of knowledge without the benefit of a truly imaginative fiction or narration; he does, however, invent images. He conventionally views the proportion-making of nature in the analogies of art, for example, as the production of harmony by means of which Amphion built Thebes and with which the angels now praise God. His pattern of cognition forms the expected ladder, the *gradatio* from sense to reason, from reason to understanding, from understanding to knowledge, and from knowledge to wisdom. He writes, "So many stayres we must ascend upright / Ere we attain to Wisedomes high degree" (p. 49). So, too, Sidney had made a Platonic ladder for love, poetic composition, and the *ars legendi;*

Spenser straightened out Red Crosse Knight's perplexities by degree; and Shakespeare gave Prince Hal an architectonic progress from degree to degree of justification of rule until he possessed Katherine like a city or a land of cities. Seeking some way to organize the very process of knowing him a unity, Davies ends in the rule of conscience. Although the earth "eclipses" the light of reason that "in instants would like Angels see," the natural "dowrie" of the soul—the "sparks of light"—provides the inner vision of written "characters" and of human character as a judgment of conscience. A feminine nature writes "her lawes" in man's heart:

> Not being blanke, where nought is writ at all,
>   But what the Writer wil, may written be.

> For Nature in Mans heart her lawes doth pen,
>   Prescribing *truth* to *wit*, and *good* to *will*,
>   Which doe accuse, or else excuse all men.
> (P. 50)

Sidney's Astrophil had also heard the Muse tell him to look "in his heart and write" (*A & S* 1.14), for in the heart speaks conscience. George Herbert, another follower of Sidney, would challenge all the winding stairs of knowledge and poetry in "Jordan (I)," similarly, in order to speak immediately from the center of conscience—the only power that rightly might build true poems and true hymns of human character at the same time it erected a scaffolding of inventive metaphors.[68]

Throughout, Davies has been imagining the mistress-knowledge, too; she is the enlightening force of conscience in the soul and is tantamount to the soul herself. She lives there and shines "like the Sunne" into "palace" and "cottage" alike; her "lamp" is the divine oracle of self-knowledge that proportions all other things by a vision of "their perfect end." Her master-craftsmanship appears, finally, "When without hands she doth thus Castles build, / Sees without eyes," and "digests" the world. The "Sparkles" that Davies has imagined multiply, growing "almost infinite" in the world "As fire so spreads as no place holdeth it." Although sin almost quenches them entirely, they have increased with "heavenly light within" to the degree that even those people who strive against their consciences have "some Sparkles in their flinty breasts" (2.21–88, pp. 50–54).

Davies' version of architectonic proportions touches not only the image of man as the measure of all things but also the temple that Herbert will aim to build, for the visionary "wit" can contain what the whole world cannot, according to Davies. So, too, the flinty heart of Henry Vaughan's imagination will "sparkle" with the truths of natural creation and divinely infused rays of light in *Silex Scintillans*. Andrew Marvell would similarly collect all things in the concise image of man's mind—an ocean—that he invents in "The Garden." But Davies had said so before Marvell.

Then what vast body must we make the *mind*,
    Wherein are men, beasts, trees, townes, seas, & lands,
    And yet each thing a proper place doth find,
    And each thing in the true proportion stands.

                    (P. 22)

In fact, a poetry that has been Platonized as greatly as this reaches back to Spenser's vivid image of Merlin's crystal ball (*FQ* 3.2.18–19) and forward to a stylistic change in the expression of metaphor itself, all the way to Kantian idealism.

Philosophical poetry uses the scaffolding or the "cosmetics" or the "garment" of a reduced metaphoric language to express doctrine, but it cannot teach, delight, and move by images, characters, or narrations as truly architectonic metaphor and inventive poetry can (cf. *Def.*, pp. 80–86, 93). In practice, Davies' philosophical poem limits literary architectonics to the presentation of preconceived ideas in well-constructed images; the poem is not an exercise of literary architectonics but a description of it. Puttenham might have considered Davies' poem a good example of verbal carpentry, although the doctrine it expresses is the architectonic one that asked poetry to work even as nature herself works: by generating the discovery of thought. But Puttenham, providing tools for carpentry, probably would not have included Davies' "presencing" of the mistress-knowledge in the house.

In his philosophical poem, "A Treatie of Humane Learning," Fulke Greville also illustrates a shift of style in explaining the architectonic formula. Greville claims that the poem, published posthumously in 1633, the year of publication of Herbert's *The Temple*, was written while he and Sidney were schoolboys together at Shrewsbury.[69] The poem betrays, however, a concern for purified diction and a sense of the limitation of knowledge that reflect a much later development of Sidney's aesthetics. In Greville's mind, the very origin of metaphor may be morally suspect; at least the practice of metaphor reveals, in his estimation, man's intellectual limitations, if not actually showing man's fall to the immorality of a lie. Metaphor, Greville asserts, originates in paucity of language. "Scarcity of words" forced learning "at first to Metaphorike wings, / Because no Language in the earth affords / Sufficient Characters to express all things."[70] In the end to which metaphor, a "matron" of knowledge, has come, the feminized capacity of speech has turned into the ways of the "harlot" (st. 108, p. 43).

Sidney had said something similar on the way "that honey-flowing matron Eloquence had been apparelled, or rather disguised, in a courtesan-like painted affectation." He had even given his point the flavor of nationalism by saying further that "so far-fet words that may seem monsters . . . must seem strangers to any poor Englishman" (*Def.*, p. 117). Both writers allude to a long-standing classical discussion of words and their decorum, as if language itself experienced xenophobia in "translation," that is, in the act of metaphor-making. The proportion between subject and style of expression was matter for the fit articulation of true ideas in some figure of speech and also for the discovery of English words to suit English inventions. Sidney, however, thought classically about similitude and appropriated the classical solution of a wise *ars legendi* and a wise art of poetic composition: not the figures themselves but their proper use or abuse determined the quality of their imitation of the truth. Sidney criticized the diction of the *Shepheardes Calendar (Def.,* p. 112), and he satirized those poets who kept "Nizolian paper-books of their figures and phrases, as by attentive translation . . . [to] devour them whole and make them wholly theirs" (p. 117). He also mocked the verbal "knacks" of the writer who "doth dance to his own music" in curious speech. But "plain sensibleness," not plain speech, persuades artistically in his opinion (p. 118), and he balances his criticism of a "courtesan-like painted affectation" in speech (p. 117) with the earlier praise of his "mistress" (p. 82).

Writing several decades later than Sidney, Greville no longer finds the making of good "translation" or the principle of use and abuse in the reader's art of reading enough to determine metaphoric integrity. He documents the limitations of metaphor in his argument for a literal language; he seeks the "scientific" veracity of an expanded lexicon instead of celebrating the ability of metaphor to express the inexpressible. Plain speech wins the palm in his version of the arts debates, and the explication of Greville's treatment of the architectonic metaphor in "A Treatie of Humane Learning" reveals how doctrinal it had become.

Greville's exposition of the organization of knowledge in the "Treatie" so isolates the architectural figure in a positive manner that the ironic Sidneian bond of a lively proportion between the architectural referend and its metaphysical and ethical reference is practically severed. An active poetic invention, tense with gendered coupling and the struggle for decorum, seems to have given place to the conventional expression of a gender split between word and significance. Philosophical poem that it is, the "Treatie" may have been considered by Sidney as an exercise at "having known" rather than an exercise "to know" (p. 112). Greville reifies the "ground-plot of a profitable invention" so that the poem, instead of being an instrument of the discovery of thought, is an exposed scaffolding on which to hang known doctrine according to Greville's didactic purpose. The text is on its way to becoming an object or a feminized project, a text–body controlled by the writer. Binding together a survey of the arts and sciences in loosely encyclopedic order, the architectural metaphor barely delights, hardly moves, and mostly teaches. Greville's purportedly "poetic" assertions read like a versified redaction of Sidney's lively metaphoric arguments in the *Defence*.

Thus philosophy is nothing but "bookes of Poesie, in Prose compil'd" (st. 29, p. 28).

In principle the soul of man contains the image of divine truth, Greville says, establishing the priority of character in poetry; but then he argues that one may imagine an architectural figure for building the knowledge of the soul into a virtuous, divine similitude (st. 50–75). Thus Greville's metaphor is another version of Pythagorean, Vitruvian, and other classical models of political mastercraftsmanship, too. The spirit of government plays the building role, for it "moulds, and tempers all these serving Arts / . . . in choosing out fit instruments, / To iudge mens inclinations, and their parts." The architectonic motive of government works so "That Bookes, Arts, Natures, may well fitted be, / To hold up this Worlds curious mystery" (st. 79, p. 38). Likewise, the architectural construction of knowledge functions artificially in Greville's poem; architecture is the measuring device to order the arts and sciences—religion, law, physics, political philosophy, the twin forces of music and poetry—but Greville still asserts that poetry, "like a Maker," raises *her* creation on "lines" of truth. She is so materially generative in his poem that military and mechanical "buildings" of all sorts literally proliferate: ships, houses, halls, camps, bulwarks, forts.

Yet the architectural analogy begins to be reduced to a dead metaphor, the cliché of the eighteenth century, when Greville moralizes knowledge in his philosophical theme, and poesie is no longer intellectually generative. When things can be named, they do not need metaphoric description. Greville claims that "Our chief endeauor must be to effect / A sound foundation." At the same time, Greville tries to sustain a christian-kabbolistic principle. We must take care not to try to name metaphorically what is unnameable, to "ouerbuilde our states, / In searching secrets of the Deity."

In Greville's poem the sexual tension with which Sidney's mistress-knowledge mediated human and divine knowledge is gone. The combination of straightforward teaching and direct address to the reader further isolates Greville's effort to express the architectonic idea; he erects merely the scaffolding of thought until, finally, antithetically, he turns his architectural analogue against the idea of any literal building in this world, whether cities, machines, thoughts, or the verbal structures of poems:

> Lastly, we must not to the world erect
> Theaters, nor plant our Paradise in dust,
> Nor build up Babels for the Diuels elect;
> Make temples of our hearts to God we must;
> And then as Godlesse wisedomes follies be
> So are his heights our true Philosophie. . . .
> . . . .

> Thus are true Learnings in the humble heart
> A Spirituall worke, raising Gods image, rased
> By our transgressions, a well-framed art,
>   (St. 144–50, pp. 50–51)

By the time we finish reading this poem, Greville's condemnation of human efforts to build either systematic theology and philosophy *or* an earthly paradise reflects directly on the building of metaphor in poetry, too. Metaphor-making must now also be a spiritual work and not merely an enterprise of proportions in language that would make of learning a tower of Babel or an Eden that, having its genesis in dust, returns to dust. Poetry must be able, if necessary, to tear down false constructions of the mind and imagination by means of the poet's language.

In the *Defence*, Sidney warned of the necessity to bend "matter and manner" the right way; even if English is a "mingled language" or one that "wants grammar," it would be "a piece of the Tower of Babylon's curse, that a man should be put to school to learn his mother-tongue." His hope for the language, a hope best fulfilled by poetry, was "the uttering sweetly and properly the conceits of the mind" that is the end of speech (*Def.*, p. 119). But Sidney was more interested in arousing and building good conceits in the minds of readers than in tearing down false ones; Greville bends all toward neoclassicism, and Sidney did not.

Several passages in his *Life of Sidney* reveal Greville's astuteness as a critic, no matter how we judge him as a poet.[71] To begin with, Greville appropriately compares his limited poetic achievement and his character to the heroic quality of his friend Sidney's art and life. In speaking of *Ironia* as the figure managing diplomacy and courtesy in talk—an artless ease—so that it might truly be called "that hypocriticall figure . . . wherin men commonly (to keep aboue their workes) seem to make toies of the utmost they can doe" (p. 176)—Greville actually refers to his own authorial modesty. But he presses on to contrast his work to the kind of *ironia* Sidney used in "tossing off" the *Arcadia*. Sidney's fine courtesy, often read by critics as a gentleman's *sprezzatura*, contained the other, deeper rationale that Greville morally cherished: Sidney did not place much stock in human endeavor, Greville explains, even while he labored hard and well in various forms of it. As Greville goes on to contrast his poetry with Sidney's, however, the emphasis changes. Greville does not claim for his own "creeping Genius" those "witty Fictions" and "delicate Images" that overabundantly furnished Sidney's language with "Images of wit" to exercise the fancy of people. For his poetry Greville claims, rather, the "Images of Life" that he has addressed to those members of the audience who are already "weatherbeaten in the Sea of this World" (pp. 244–46).

The contrast between "witty Fictions" and "Images of Life" marks a distinction between verisimilitude and similitude and, once again, raises the problematical question of renaissance poetic theory: what is the relation of poetic imitation to truth? Yet, from our longer historical view, Greville's contrast of witty fictions and images of life can appear as two sides of the same coin that Sidney defined in the *Defence* when he identified poetic invention as an exercise truly "to know" as well as an art of "making" speaking pictures. The effort of the mind truly to know underwrote the ossification of older linguistic and noetic structures, including the architectural analogy for the organization of the arts and sciences. Literary architectonics promoted the expression of knowledge in analogies as fresh, as gendered in androgynous tension, and as scientifically precise as the individually unique characters who composed them.

That Greville understood how Sidney had poetically licensed the richly proportioned movement from apt judgments of the mind to precise expressions of speech to the virtuous actions of human characters clearly shows in the high tribute he paid Sir Philip, "in whom the life of true worth did (by way of example) far exceed the pictures of it in any moral Precepts." Greville judges that if his own creation—that is, his own nature both as a man and as a poet producing poems—had been equal to Sidney's, it would have been as easy for him "to have followed his patern in the practice of reall virtue, as to engage my self into this *Characteristicall* kind of Poesie," the metaphor-making by which Sidney enabled "free-born spirits" to undertake the greatest affairs of state (pp. 2–3). Ironically, Greville rightly practices a lesser writer's form of self-knowledge to say that he is not, in short, an architectonic poet. For the "Architectonical art" of poesie works out a certain kind of poetic artifice or fiction, but has its formal definition and its final cause in the "making" of human character; out of an expanding encyclopedia, the architectonic poet leaves book-knowledge behind in the practice of an integral understanding, a wisdom-discipline in action, a metaphysical mistress-knowledge.

To Fulke Greville, the word *character* in the description of the origin of metaphoric language in "A Treatie of Humane Learning" signified the conventional marking or impression that shapes a letter of the alphabet. His sense of *"Characteristicall* poetry" simultaneously referred, however, to the entire system of meaning that interconnected all existent things in the universe, each one having a character and all analogically summed up in the measure of human nature.[72] Man's character was the image and likeness of God the Maker stamped or imprinted on the human soul. The idea of English renaissance literary architectonics expresses a stylistic continuum that leads the analogy of the arts and sciences into the poetry of character and toward the poetics of written characters and verbal hieroglyphs. "Style" in this respect is not merely "the man" revealed in his craft and technically producing a "well-framed art." Style now explicitly engages masculine sexual energy in the effort to find decorous intellectual correspondences for the complex state of knowledge in poetic speech. And style now joins such correspondences to the integration of all things in conscience, the inward light of the centered mind, as Milton will put it, to enable character to stand and not to fall. If some poets proceed immediately to the ethical point of knowledge and stay there to shape language according to its moral end in eroticized utterance, other poets like Donne, Herbert, and Vaughan nevertheless sustain the "building" and "sparks" of the mind and of Nature in tension with the gender-ambivalent work of conscience in their more "metaphysical" poetry—but that is the subject of other essays in practical criticism of the texts literary architectonics helped to inspire.

Greville's architectural exhortation on the need to purify metaphoric diction and to build the inward image of the mind paradoxically testifies to the historical recession of the metaphor of "architectural" proportion-making and to the appearance of a metaphor of character that was, indeed, sufficiently inventive to express all things. As we carry Sidney's idea of poesie into the seventeenth century, however, the different emphases that poets and critics made of *aspects* of Sidney's aesthetics require our careful sorting out of the kind and degree of influence involved. There are no easy generalizations except that rule of anachronism. We should not "read" Sidney's sixteenth-century treatise according even to the best lights of those who historically followed Sidney. But we may read many to come after him by his light.

The English poet's rule of architectonic knowledge proves more than philosophy ever could that the architecture of human thought, art, science, politics, history, religion, and the fine arts was only as good as the makings of the very self—that quaking image of inexpressible divinity represented in two sexes, not one. When the poems exhort each reader to "know thyself," the exhortation takes the shape of little models of thought and little icons of human character in various figures of speech. Admittedly, Aristotle's advice in the *Rhetoric* that "nobody uses fine language when teaching geometry" (3.1 [1404a]) has undergone quite a transformation to become the poet's rule, the intuitive leap of an encyclopedic geometry, a speaking picture, and a moral architecture. But the sexual sense of intellectual decorum involved in this poetic invention—the "style" of a poet's well-tempered mind—was also his triumph as a mastercraftsman. The rule proved that renaissance poets might not be exiled from the English nation *because* a renovated Christian Plato did not allow it. As a result, renaissance poets often mock Platonic idealism in poetic words while their teaching of Platonic "idea" in moving images triumphs in the name of the Word.

Milton's narrator explains the ambivalence, for instance, when he imagines the disrupted moral coupling of history in the conflated myths of Noah,

Deucalion, and Janus. History is a process of building up and tearing down and building up. We live "Betwixt the world destroy'd and world restor'd" (*PL* 12.3) and try to say all of it through the measure of our character—like the Adam who, feeling compelled to tell "My Story" (8.205) in juxtaposition to the great myths of creation and of the battle in heaven, inevitably tells the story of his seeing and loving Eve, trying to "contain" her who, for him, seemed to contain all things, and he wanted nothing else (8.473).

For poets of the English Renaissance, such *copia* or "plenty" is a way to juxtapose the masks of human character—its so-called "image and likeness to God"—to its many moral failures and constant hopes. Without such juxtaposition the renaissance poet could not excoriate intellectual vanity and simultaneously express the paradox of learned folly and fortunate Fall that Erasmian humanism celebrated as the surest human likeness to Christ, the beautiful truth revealed, Erasmus suggests in *The Praise of Folly*, in the breaking open of the Silenus. Thus the complex ironies of plain truth balance the loud claims made on "plain speech" to constitute the greatest mythopoesis of all in this rhetorical age: the assertion of artless art, an art like Nature herself. In ornate figures of speech a "plain sensibleness" by Sidney's definition establishes the much-needed awareness that men draw straight lines with crooked hearts and that the poet has the "call" to correct such knowledge in conscience. Catching the sense of divine mystery "at two removes," as George Herbert queried, the poet praises the Word neither by capturing God in plainness nor by containing the Spirit in words but by praising, dispraising, and struggling with the conventions of what best contains things in human nature. Language itself is the new order of mediation between earth and heaven.

Literary architectonics addresses these balances and contraries; it does not privilege one side over the other but orchestrates the multiplicity. Thus, in style, literary architectonics seeks the proportionate "fit" of words and character to the contents, scopes, methods, and objects of the variety of arts and sciences that renaissance epistemology promoted. Skelton the priest anticipated such a design in his allegories of politics, religion, and poetry. So, too, in Spenser, for example, the gendered rhetoric of likeness and unlikeness, similitude and contrariety, often organizes the intellectual decorum of style in relation to some didactic principle, moral discovery, or affective comfort along sexual, political, and religious lines. In structure—truly the large-scale manifestation of style—literary architectonics aims to generate verbal artifacts through which a poet has set forward an integration of thought in the morally effective image of a "speaking picture" of himself or others. In rhetorical form—the aspect most often confused with structure in modern studies—literary architectonics requires a visionary departure from the architectural platform of style and from the structure of "speaking pictures" to produce the significance of prosopopoeias larger or smaller than life in the reader's experience—all the way to the two divine icons of *Paradise Lost*. The engendering of moral architecture in the reading and writing of this poetry communit aims the prudential and decorous exercise of an open, overseeing, inventive mistress-knowledge, or the poet reduces himself to a parody of Prometheus the thief or Acteon the voyeur or Cain the murderer and fugitive or Orpheus the impotent and dismembered bard or Satan the disfigured voyager.

In Milton, the poet of architectonical art was compelled to journey developmentally from Adam the uxorious and Samson the self-destructive to seek spiritual integration with the mistress-knowledge as his Muse; he made her as invisible as celestial Light and identified his blind self with the spirit of Christ the Word. Saint Augustine's dismissal of the idea of an androgynous prelapsarian Adam because such a likeness to God would have implied divine androgyny did not make Milton's task easy. But in the validation of the feminine form of wisdom in the Solomonic characterization of Sophia and in Sidney's appropriation of that allegorical figure for his art of poesie, Milton found a "readie and easy way" to travel.

The very thought of the achievement of intellectual unity implies the recovery of the vision of a lost paradise as the supreme act of mythopoesis; but the moral success that proves the truth of the fable, or poetic fiction, hangs in the balance of the correspondences the poet decorously or indecorously composes. Similarly, the main character in the poem and the reader "make" correspondences in self-knowledge that leave the poem finished in art but unfinished in moral discovery. The recovery of paradise—and its corollary discovery of the divine similitude in human character—is inherently ambivalent on the moral plane that ensures the intellectual integrity of the pursuit of poetry. As the poet writes, so will the reader read, but readers of different genders, class, and times will find different moral selves in the glass of the poem.

Renaissance poets use images of architecture in structural ways while denigrating their own verbal master-building in comparison to the architectonic truth of the human mind and character. What grows up on the former ground of the medieval castle of the mind is the dynamic image in the seventeenth century of the prophetic "engine" of the created universe, the new temple-building of the spiritually enlightened heart, and the vision of the divine Mercy-Seat or chariot-throne of the Word operative in conscience.[73] Adapted from Jean de Serres's philosophy and transforming it, what Sidney's theory of literary architectonics shows us through the figure of the mistress-knowledge is, therefore, paralleled by the practical compositions of renaissance poets. We find in their poems not the rigidification of historical, religious, social, sexual, or literary models, but the intelligent awareness that oversees differences among human possibilities and experiences. The mistress-knowledge oversees *différance*.

Certainly much more work remains to be done on the subject of renaissance style and the historical-critical judgment of it. In part the historical data recovered in this book are a response to the combined nonsense and perception of Yvor Winters in his historical essay on renaissance poetry and how the lyric could contain and communicate moral doctrine, "The 16th Century Lyric in England: A Critical and Historical Reinterpretation," written fifty years ago. Winters astutely praises George Gascoigne and Fulke Greville for their style of metaphoric clarity but mistakenly thinks Sidney and Spenser to be poets of "ingenuity" who love the specialty of rhetoric for its own sake; he does not see their love of rhetoric as a universal knowledge having an intellectual purpose.[74] In part the exposition of Sidney's architectonics also challenges historiographical opinions of the eighteenth century that have provoked the reactions of modern philosophical criticism and critical theory. The critic, scholar, and "professor" of literature, in their fascination with textuality and authorship and their widespread use of modern computer technology, more and more resemble the "professional" editor, printer, and coffee-house journalist of the eighteenth century.

Perhaps one example will illustrate my point regarding the "fetishizing" of the text. In 1749 when Bishop Thomas Newton published the first variorum edition of *Paradise Lost*, he took a razor to Patrick Hume's first annotated edition of the poem published in 1695. Newton felt that "certainly next to a good writer, a good critic holds the second rank in the republic of letters" (sig. a2^r), and he cut away what he thought to be superfluous in Hume's commentary. The description of his procedure for notes, corrections of former editions, discussion of variant readings, and efforts to establish the "true genuine text" of Milton is a good thumbnail sketch of textual and historical criticism (sig. a4^v). What is this cutting away to make true and pure but a form of sacralization? If Newton transferred the poet's obligation to develop encyclopedic learning to the critic, he merely imitated the manner in which Milton's recording of the charge of "ostentation of learning" made against him in *The Reason of Church Government* would be picked up, unacknowledged, by Addison and, subsequently, by T. S. Eliot as if they were making an original charge against Milton.

Meantime, after Newton's transfer of the poet's learning to the critic, later readers of *Paradise Lost* felt free to tamper with the text, as if the poem were an object in nature to be refashioned strictly according to the reader's desire and sensibility. Within two centuries of its publication *Paradise Lost* was cast into rhyme and into Latin, reshaped as a drama and as an oratorio, and divided into four abridgments suitable for Lenten reading. Today we subject it, and other renaissance texts, to post-Saussurian linguistic theory and to other critical theories that, if judged in themselves, must be seen in their contingency upon the poetic text and in the embedded knowledge-metaphors in their proposed methodologies. The poems of the Renaissance are writ large enough in their feminized "art" to take the analytical treatment we give to a feminized *Natura*, too. In the age of the "Gaia hypothesis," however, perhaps a feminist critique ought to begin to assert a new synthesis over analysis. Composed rhetorically, the poems demand our subjective projections. Yet, like nature, they also constitute an historical "other ness" (*naturata*) or object, and an elusively subjective (*naturans*) textual reality seen through the veil of the text. This combination encourages the poet's manipulation of style and the reader's ingenuity on the very topic of the containment and uncontainability of knowledge.

Preceding critics, Bacon rejected the rigidity of an older kind of geometric comparison for the definition of some ruling knowledge, but he still pursued the intention of setting up one universal science. He feminized nature and placed divine power in man.[75] Kepler, too, articulated a similarly integrative search for intellectual universality in astronomy when he sought the proportion between physics and the quadrivial sciences in order to show how the fruits of different disciplines may flow from the head of one argument. He produced, at the same time, a hypothetical model of the universe in his famous series of many-sided solids.[76] If history has relegated Kepler's cosmological paradigm to the dustbin while it has assimilated Bacon's idea of nature and of experimental knowledge, it has also judged Bacon for his moral faults and thanked Kepler for his optics while continuing to ponder Milton.

Less than fifteen years ago, Robert L. Sinsheimer, writing of "The Presumptions of Science" in an issue of *Daedalus* dedicated to the limits of scientific inquiry, asked, like Milton's Adam, whether there was a "forbidden" knowledge and whether we, in our "singleminded pursuit of new knowledge," would defeat ourselves and the "human, social enterprise."[77] His voice echoes the architectonic poets of the Renaissance on the darker side of the relation of knowledge to virtue. The darker side inevitably belongs to the moral ambivalence of human character and to the construction of gender allegories as the knowing mind *chooses* its language, its learning, and the actions of its body in the making of self and society.

Epilogue

Literary History, Sidney's *Defence*, and Criticism after Kant

Then would he add certain praises, by telling what a peerless beast the horse was . . . that if I had not been a piece of a logician before I came to him, I think he would have persuaded me to have wished myself a horse. But thus much at least with his no few words he drave into me, that self-love is better than any gilding to make that seem gorgeous wherein ourselves be parties. . . . And yet I must say that, as I have more just cause to make a pitiful defence of poor poetry, which from almost the highest estimation of learning is fallen to be the laughing-stock of children, so have I need to bring some more available proofs: since the former is by no man barred of his deserved credit, the silly latter hath had even the names of the philosophers used to the defacing of it, with great danger of civil war among the Muses.
> —Sir Philip Sidney, *The Defence of Poesie*, pp. 73–74

Pure reason is so perfect a unity that if its principle were insufficient for the solution of even a single one of all the questions to which it itself gives birth we should have no alternative but to reject the principle. . . . I have to deal with nothing save reason itself and its pure thinking; and to obtain complete knowledge of these, there is no need to go far afield, since I come upon them in my own self.
> —Immanuel Kant, Preface to the First Edition,
> *Critique of Pure Reason*

For architecture, the abolishment of the tectonic scaffolding would be equivalent to self-destruction. . . . Every architectonic whole is a perfect unity.
> —Heinrich Wölfflin, *The Principles of Art History: The Problem of the Development of Style in Later Art*, 7th ed.

In simple historical order, the eighteenth century and Immanuel Kant's composition of an "Architectonic of Pure Reason" at the end of the *Critique of Pure Reason* occur after the sixteenth and seventeenth centuries. Yet modern critical reliance on Kantian themes and definitions has

225

apparently allowed literary scholarship to ignore Sir Philip Sidney's Aristotelian statement of a renaissance theory of literary architectonics.
Likewise, the confusion of Kant's thinking with the architectonic metaphor
in the philosophy of Aristotle has utterly obscured the revisionary Augus
tinian Platonism of Sidney's mistress-knowledge with concepts of Kantian
self-consciousness—the transcendent ego, *not* Sidneian self-knowledge [1]

At least one nineteenth-century interpreter of Kant found his thought
to be both seminal and terminal; that is, Kantian philosophy captured the
zeitgeist of eighteenth-century love of rational order but simultaneously
presided over the demise of the Enlightenment.[2] So, too, the efforts of
romantic poets and critics first to validate and then to institutionalize literary knowledge were variously funded by Kantian thought or by Hegel's
adaptation of it to affect modern aesthetics and, inevitably, to bring literary
theory into conjunction with the philosophical discussion of the problems
of reason, religious belief, morality, and values. Where Kant insisted in the
Preface to the Second Edition of the *Critique of Pure Reason* that he had
found it "necessary to deny *knowledge,* in order to make room for *faith*"—
because "the dogmatism of metaphysics, that is, the preconception that it
is possible to make headway in metaphysics without a previous criticism of
pure reason, is the source of all that unbelief, always very undogmatic,
which wars against morality" (trans. Smith, p. 29)—Hegel developed his
philosophy of Spirit. According to J. N. Findlay, Hegel's thought developed in his experience of the ethos of his Protestant family, in his
combination of Kant's self-consciousness with Fichte's transcendent ego,
and in his attraction to Aristotle's thinking on thinking, as well as through
the mysticism of Meister Eckhart and Jakob Boehme. And according to
William K. Wimsatt, Jr., and Cleanth Brooks in *Literary Criticism: A Short
History,* Kant's *Critique of Judgment* and "Kantian *a priorism*" are the source
of all modern literary formalism, including that of twentieth-century New
Criticism.[3] Thus, on the foundation of religious and aesthetic inquiries
made in the last two centuries, we have arrived in contemporary literary
study at our intense interrogation of the transcendent ego, the central self,
the speaking subject, and the problem of text and meaning, linguistic structure and spiritual absence or presence.

This discussion has led to a politics of critical language in our current
theoretical debates in which it is fashionable, usually, to "blame" Kant. I
come neither to blame Kant nor to bury Aristotle, but to discuss their
ghosts in whatever way is necessary to bring Sir Philip Sidney's literary
architectonics into the light. What implications does Sidney's *Defence of
Poesie* have for the elaboration of English letters in the past four centuries?
How can we consciously put our modern methods of reading, historiciz-
ing, and critiquing into perspective with his self-knowledge, that is, with
his appropriation of Sophia?

We seem to have avoided the Sidneian meaning of ἀρχιτεκτονική precisely because, falling between Aristotle's meaning in the *Nicomachean Ethics* and Kant's meaning in the *Critique of Pure Reason,* it has defied easy philosophical categorization. Sidney's mistress-knowledge compounds the difficulty; the figure is *sui generis* to the modern systematic judgment and has probably been marginalized because it is a metaphor and not "purely" a political statement or "purely" a logical truth.[4] The word *architectonic* has appeared in literary studies of the twentieth century in merely one sense, and this reference to *architectonic form,* as I shall shortly explain, has occurred by way of adaptation from the terminology of art history; this, in turn, borrowed the principles and system-making Kant located in science to justify the knowledge of art history. Critical principles, theories, and methods conduct today's debate between ways of knowing and claims to truth, and one kind of knowledge usually borrows the structure or terminology of another knowledge to advance its own cause; but by doing so the borrower defines itself metaphorically. To distinguish Sidney's theory from various philosophies, we need to look directly at texts and sort out the metaphors that pass for critical principles. We need to look at history, beginning with New Critics and working backward from Kant to Cudworth to de Serres to Sidney and then forward again.

Even to express a preference for an historical approach puts us on the scene of debate that New Critics entered, too, in the name of aesthetics. One aim of New Criticism was to constitute an internally consistent, if complex, set of principles for the scientific knowledge of the truth of a text. Nevertheless, in their *Literary Criticism: A Short History,* William K. Wimsatt, Jr., and Cleanth Brooks also produced a "history," but not without limiting the results with several pointed qualifications. They openly acknowledge that their history cannot escape "being written from a point of view," that it cannot be a "direct history," and that it is "the history of one kind of thinking about values, and hence it could not have been written . . . at random" (p. vii). Besides supporting the New Critical idea of the poem, this *Short History* continues at various points to express disdain for history and things historical and things that *are* "random" or nonsystematic (see p. 532). For Wimsatt and Brooks, Sidney's *Defence,* for example, is an "epitome," a rhapsody of critical notes insofar as it recites a selection of these in a kind of miscellany. What saves the *Defence* in New Critical judgment is the elaboration of an Aristotelian "idea" of the didactic and the moral (p. 726) and its cultivation of some system, namely, the "truth of correspondence" rather than the "truth of coherence," which they closely relate to "the tensions of values and emotions" in I. A. Richards's "poetics of tension" (pp. 748–49; *vide* pp. 610–34). These features make the *Defence* in Wimsatt's and Brooks's opinion "an early landmark in the progress of English literary self-consciousness and literary history" (pp. 169–70). In considering historically whether or not and how much Sidney read Greek, which Aristotle he knew, whether Ficino's Plato was Sidney's Plato, and what transmutation some of the Italian critical ideas Sidney selected may have undergone in his English mind, Wimsatt and Brooks say, "But it all matters little. Sidney wrote not a pedant's encyclopedia, but a gentleman's essay" (p. 169). Historical documentation is pedantry for them, and the aristocratic Sidney possesses some of the a priori authority of the Kantian subject.

Yet without better historical knowledge, literary scholarship has continued to suppress Sidney's view of architectonics; of its encyclopedic learning; of its intellectual accuracy; of its imagination of political and social hierarchy; and of its gender reference, on one level, to the poet's relation to the Queen, and its religious reference, on another level, to the sovereignty of conscience as a type of Solomonic wisdom. Knowing the aggregate of historical data and asking the theoretical questions that bring the sophistication of the *Defence* into the light is not pedantry; it is the recovery of Sidney's own historicism wonderfully integrated with the poetics of his image of the mistress-knowledge. Indeed, the mistress-knowledge in Sidney's *Defence of Poesie* is so lively a figure that she is disturbing enough to have been denied her presence in traditional New Critical studies, and this denial has been historically equivalent to the reduction of the Muse to the phantasmic status of a mere "apposition." Likewise, she has been integral enough to have been ignored as well in contemporary critical theories that demand an act of faith in various forms of systematic analysis even though the tools of our modern theories are refined enough to have discovered her.

The problem is that New Criticism itself is not purely aesthetic or Kantian. New Criticism has knowingly associated Sidney's poetics in general with Aristotle, if not in particular with classical and medieval notions of architectonics, and observed the difference between Sidney's *Defence* and Shelley's *Defence* by saying that it is as profound as the difference between Aristotle and Kant (*Literary Criticism*, pp. 422–23). The most contemporary genealogy of theories—New Criticism, structuralism, poststructuralism, and deconstruction, especially—protests too much reaction for or against the Enlightenment, perhaps, to be trusted in the interpretation of Sidney's architectonic poesie. From the point of view of this study of the mistress-knowledge, furthermore, other modern critical theories express glimpses of that lost "body" of the mistress-knowledge and her vital powers without naming her as Sidney did. Phenomenology, Marxist and psychoanalytic theory, dialogism, and feminism and gender study inevitably participate in the chaos of today's critical systems-making. The language of polemicism invariably breeds more and more mergers of critical terms whose origins, ironically, are often in renaissance arts treatises and critical theories, and whose boundaries of definition have been neither historically nor philosophically determined. From the point of view of the history of critical theory, therefore, our thinking today looks very much like a hall of mirrors in which it is extremely difficult to judge "the thing itself" (if it exists at all, the deconstructionist might say) from its many reflections (which the New Historicist would be pleased to list). And from the point of view of theory, it is only fair to ask what historical criticism has actually provided by way of illumination.

Looking Backward: Kant's Hecuba or Sidney's Sophia?

The thrust of my argument in this Epilogue is, simply enough, to place in the historical light of Sidney's architectonics the late twentieth-century characterization of New Criticism as a pure formalism in the Kantian mode. This reveals the confusion to which New Criticism brought itself by adapting the Kantian ideas of system and antihistoricism to its own critical purpose. When so much has been made even a little clearer, we should be able to see the difference between the operations of renaissance poems as products of literary architectonics and the expectations of any critical theory in which history has been separated from linguistic structures or teleology from *techne*.

In the Preface to the Second Edition of the *Kritik der reinen Vernunft* in 1787, Kant made it quite clear that his treatise on pure reason was a treatise on method aimed at revolutionizing the procedure that had prevailed in metaphysics by conforming it to the example set by the geometers and physicists in the Newtonian synthesis. As a treatise on method, the *Critique of Pure Reason* is not a system of the science itself.[5] Along the way, Kant establishes the primacy of the thinking subject since "nothing in a priori knowledge can be ascribed to objects save what the thinking subject derives from itself." Transformations in the history of human reason have occurred—in mathematics, for example—because, he says, "the happy thought of a single man" brought about the revolution (trans. Smith, pp. 25, 19). If we can know a priori of things, however, "only what we ourselves put into them," he says, "pure reason, so far as the principles of its knowledge are concerned, is a quite separate, self-subsistent unity, in which, as in an organised body, every member exists for every other, and all for the sake of each, so that no principle can safely be taken in *any one* relation, unless it has been investigated in the *entirety* of its relations to the whole employment of pure reason" (trans. Smith, pp. 23, 25–26). Such logical purity is fundamentally different from Sidneian metaphor-making, and if we have any epistemological doubts, we need only hear Kant's defense of logical science and rejection of the analogy-making on which renaissance epistemology and poetry thrived. "We do not enlarge but disfigure sciences," Kant states, "if we allow them to trespass upon one another's territory" (trans. Smith, p. 18).

Kant's treatise on method leads to his statement of the germ of his system however in the "Architectonic." In order to untangle a few of the current anamorphoses in criticism, I shall begin with Kant's statement of his plan and methodology, leaving Smith's twentieth-century translation and going back to Meiklejohn's nineteenth-century one:

> By the term *Architectonic* I mean the art of constructing a system. Without systematic unity, our knowledge cannot become science; it will be an aggregate, and not a system. Thus Architectonic is the doctrine of the scientific in cognition, and therefore necessarily forms part of our Methodology.
>
> Reason cannot permit our knowledge to remain in an unconnected and rhapsodic state, but requires that the sum of our cognitions should constitute a system. It is thus alone that they can advance the ends of reason. By a system I mean the unity of various cognitions under one idea. This idea is the conception—given by reason—of the form of a whole, in so far as the conception determines *a priori* not only the limits of its content, but the place which each of its parts is to occupy. The scientific idea contains, therefore, the end, and the form of the whole which is in accordance with that end. The unity of that end, to which all the parts of the system relate, and through which all have a relation to each other, communicates unity to the whole system, so that the absence of any part can be immediately detected from our knowledge of the rest; and it determines *a priori* the limits of the system, thus excluding all contingent or arbitrary additions. The whole is thus an organism (*articulatio*), and not an aggregate (*coacervatio*); it may grow from within (*per intussusceptionem*), but it cannot increase by external additions (*per appositionem*). It is thus like an animal body. (Trans. Meiklejohn, pp. 503–4)

After making this statement, Kant goes on to explain the necessity of a schema, or a content and arrangement of parts determined a priori by the principle that the aim of the system describes, to execute the system. A schema that is not projected in accordance with an idea provides merely technical unity, not architectonical unity (p. 504).[6] In this way Kant's system links the end of reason or *teleologia rationis humanae* to principles, ideas, science, and philosophizing (pp. 504–7) and splits them from *techne*, which he associates with the empirical, the contingent, and the arbitrary (pp. 504, 512) as distinct from the rational. He also distinguishes historical cognition (*cognitio ex datis*) from rational cognition (*cognitio ex principiis*).[7] Identifying philosophy as "the system of all philosophical cognition" (p. 507), Kant defines the philosopher not as one who knows philosophy but as one who philosophizes and whose legislative power "resides in the mind of every man."[8] Teleologically, the ultimate end of reason allows Kant's identification of "Moral Philosophy" and "Metaphysic" as practiced by an ideal teacher. But the "ideal teacher" does not exist.[9]

This "Architectonic" is obviously highly self-contained in Kant's precise and consistent networking of definitions, but the end result in literary studies of positive *and* negative reactions to Kant's revision of metaphysics, ethics, and aesthetics in the nineteenth and twentieth centuries has been the invisibility of Sidney's metaphor of the mistress-knowledge.

The historical invisibility of this metaphor, which Kant might have considered a most *impure* Metaphysic/Moral Philosophy in its "admixture of foreign elements" (p. 509), has been accompanied in literary criticism first by an overestimation of the visible structural or architectural metaphor, and then by the possibility of splitting the aesthetics of the will from the technical production of a design.[10] The severance of the first principles, or *archia*, from history conceived as a mere aggregate or rhapsody throws historical discourse into a state of either discord or felicity, insofar as it constitutes nothing more than a miscellany of recitations selected from an unscientifically known whole, and not the whole.[11] The potential division of teleology from technique, similarly, supports a literary critical aesthetic literalism that identifies significance with perceivable structure and also a literary critical bravery that asserts human joy in the face of historical and textual indeterminacy.[12] *Archia*, *techne*, and *teleologia*—these are the encircled terms whose unity in Kant's architectonic of scientific system and whose potential division in his view of the rhapsodic nature of historical knowledge have engendered numerous spectral presences in modern criticism.

We will not have succeeded in the exposition of Sidney's metaphors in the *Defence*, it seems, without having recognized these presences in our modern critical judgments and detached ourselves from either their rigidifications or their oppositions. Even in this book, to partake of the debate at all is to run the risk of participating in one or more of the dialectics we have made of Kant. The reading of Sidney requires us to consult a more distant past than the eighteenth or nineteenth century, for classical and Christian antiquity as it was reformed in the sixteenth century communicated much of Sidney's matter to him, and to discover the presences he felt as best we can. Similarly, to read the architectonic concept of the times called Renaissance, we have to sustain *archia*, *techne*, and *teleologia* in our purview at once, neither enclosing them in a system nor severing them, but balancing them.

Looking backward from our modern vantage, we ought to examine, for instance, Ralph Cudworth's late seventeenth-century English adaptation of architectonics in his version of Plato precisely because Cudworth's argument precedes Kant's "Architectonic."[13] In his *True Intellectual System of the Universe Wherein All the Reason and Philosophy of Atheism Is Confuted and Its Impossibility Demonstrated*, Cudworth places his Platonic view of the Nous or intellect, which was properly the Demiurgus or "architectonic framer" of the world, *above* "the self-moving Psyche" or "universal mundane soul . . .

and the immediate, or proper cause of all that motion, which is in the world," yet *beneath* the higher hypostasis of "the most simple and most absolutely perfect Being, which he calls τὸ ἕν, in opposition to that multiplicity, which speaks something of imperfection in it, and τ᾽ ἀγαθόν, goodness itself, as being above mind and understanding" (2:4.23, pp. 300–301, 1820 ed.). Here Cudworth is working out a trinitarian view of God on the basis of Platonism; earlier he had done his etymological work by listing the pagan philosophical interpretation of the Demiurgus as the opifex, the architect, or maker of the world; of the Ἀρχηγέτης as the prince and chief ruler of the universe; of the Ἀρχὴ Ἀρχῶν as the "Principle of principles"; and of the supreme and eternal Being, "'Ἀρχή, καὶ τέλος, καὶ μέσον ἁπάντων, the beginning, and end and middle of all things" (2:4.14, pp. 11–12; cf. 2:4.23, pp. 302–3). Later, discussing Plotinus, Cudworth expatiates on the second hypostasis: "Neither is it fit to attribute the architecture of the world to the first God, but rather to account him the father of that god, who is the artificer. . . . He therefore is properly called the demiurgus, as the contriving architect, or artificer, in whom the archetypal world is contained, and the first paradigm, or pattern of the whole universe" (3:4.35, p. 107).

As Cudworth continues to the third hypostasis, we find in his Platonism the figure that the earlier Renaissance associated with Urania, with Sidney's mistress-knowledge, and with Milton's celestial Muse or Holy Spirit partly under kabbalistic influence:

> The third is a kind of moveable deity . . . as Plotinus speaks. . . . That which moveth about mind, or intellect, the light or effulgency thereof, and its print or signature, which always dependeth upon it, and acteth according to it. This is that, which reduces both the fecundity of the first simple good, and also the immoveable wisdom and architectonic contrivance of the second into act or energy. (3:4.35, p. 107)

What moves architectonic well-knowing into well-doing closely parallels Sidney's mistress-knowledge.

Behind Cudworth's reasoning on the three hypostases lies his knowledge of patristic theology, through which he sets Athanasius, Cyril, and Augustine against Arius and associates the third hypostasis with the Holy Spirit (3:4.35, p. 119). But some philosophers merge the second and third hypostases. Tagathon, the supreme good and first hypostasis, Demiurgus, the second hypostasis, and Psyche, the third hypostasis, are a generation within the divine Being as well as a gradation and do not simply mirror the imperfect generation of a grandfather to a father to a grandson, Cudworth explains (3:4.35, pp. 114–15). Since Psyche is "the offspring of the highest mind," it, too, is "consubstantial with it" (3:4.35, pp. 97–98). But since the controversy in the *Timaeus* over whether the third hypostasis is eternal is generally decided by envisioning a *double* Psyche—ἐγκόσμιον and ὑπερκόσμιον, that is, a mundane and a supramundane soul named by

Plotinus as an earthly and heavenly Venus—we find some philosophers, such as Ficino and Proclus, sometimes calling the higher Psyche by the name of the Demiurgus or the architectonic framer of the world, the architect, the Word (3:4.35, pp. 93, 98–99).[14]

Where all of this leads in Cudworth's four volumes is not only to the philosophical defense of the divine existence against atheists but also, somewhat tangentially, to the steadfast resistance of seeing the feminine in *any* superior position in the Christian understanding of the three hypostases. Cudworth names Psyche a "grandson" even while rejecting the simple model of generation for the divine procession. Plotinus, he explains, saw Psyche or the mundane soul of the world, however, as πρεσβυτέραν καὶ ἀδελφὴν, "the elder *sister* of our human souls." This is an opinion, Cudworth says,

which as it rankly savours of philosophic pride and arrogancy, thus to think so magnificently of themselves, and to equalize in a manner their own souls with that mundane soul; so was it a monstrous degradation of that third hypostasis of their trinity, and little other than an absolute creaturizing of the same. If our human soul be ὁμοειδής, if the same kind or species with the third hypostasis of the trinity; then is it not only ὁμότιμος, of like honour and dignity, but also, in the language of the Christian church, ὁμοούσιος, coessential with our human souls (as our Saviour Christ, according to the Arians in Athanasius, is said to be . . . coessential with us men). From whence it will follow, that either that must be a creature, or else our human souls are Divine. (3:4.35, p. 127)

In Cudworth's view, following Saint Augustine, this is a foundation for creature-worship or idolatry and must be completely rejected.

Elsewhere in his *True Intellectual System*, Cudworth addresses the gendering of gods and goddesses in paganism and outlines the Christian Platonist's way to resist androgyny in figures of the godhead, particularly with regard to the identification of Christ the Word as the Demiurgus. He sees all of the gods and goddesses of the pagan pantheon as "metonymically and catachrestically" called by divine names; they are mere adjuncts of the supreme Being (1:4.13, p. 472), or they are the personifications of dead men, heroes, animated stars, elements, and things of nature (1:4.13, pp. 464ff.).[15] In doing his exegesis of Proclus's hymn to Jove as first, last, and middle, and both a man and an immortal maid, therefore, Cudworth dismisses the figure of divine androgyny as "the strangest" expression of all and "nothing but a poetic description of ἀρρενόθηλυς, male and female together," which was a common figure among pagan mystical theologians. In calling God ἀρρενόθηλυς, male and female together, they emphatically signified "the divine fecundity, or the generative and creative power of the Deity;—that God was able from himself alone to produce all things"—that is, to create out of nothing else (2:4.17, p. 89).

Proclus's thinking in this respect reflects Orphic theology, and Sidney, we must remember, appeals to the many traditions surrounding Orpheus the poet at several points in the *Defence*. He especially pulls in the Orphic authority at the end of the *Defence* when he cites Clauserus, who in citing Cornutus, who knew Cicero's testimony to Orpheus in Cleanthes' second book of the nature of the gods where he accommodates the fables of Orpheus, Musaeus, Hesiod, and Homer to the Stoics (*Def.*, p. 121). Sidney here invokes the "mystery" in the arcane and mystical allegorical tradition of the poet.

So, too, next to Ficino's authorization of the chaste androgyne in response to the elevation of a feminine Psyche to the level of the masculine Demiurgus, we must remember Jean de Serres's Protestant rejection of the ἀρρενοθῆλυ or "man-woman" of pagan philosophy in the commentary on the *Symposium* as an aspect of his validation of married love and generation (*Plato* 3:171). Sidney, like Milton after him, is poetically much friendlier toward the imagination of androgyny and the crossing of gender boundaries than the theologians. Cudworth disputes the Epicureans and Atomists who saw the world as an inept system of irregular things such as Centaurs, Scyllas, and Chimeras. His argument against the Epicureans is the classical Augustinian refutation—the confirmation of divine Providence that Calvin also proposed in the *Institutes of the Christian Religion*. When Sidney alludes to the creative power of the poet, "lifted up with the vigour of his own invention," he pulls his audience into this theological context; for the poet "doth grow in effect another nature, in making things either better than nature bringeth forth, or, quite anew, forms such as never were in nature, as the Heroes, Demigods, Cyclops, Chimeras, Furies and such like" (*Def.*, p. 78). A problem Cudworth finds in the Epicurean assertion of such inept forms is that they do not literally exist at the present time. Why have they not continued or why do they not propagate now by generation, "or at least why it should not happen, that, in some ages or countries, there were either all Androgyna, of both sexes, or else no animal but of one sex, male or female only; or, lastly, none of any sex at all?" (3:5, pp. 290–91).

Sidney's assertion of a type of androgyny in the poet may have followed the Orphic tradition not as a matter of literal doctrine, but as *an allegory of the divine fecundity of a superior Love that creates out of nothing*. So, too, Sidney's Calvinism would reinforce his assertion of the doctrine of divine Providence *against* the Epicurean inept forms. For him neither "Heroes" nor "Chimeras" come from the nature that God made, and the poet inventing such forms is clearly *not* imitating nature but acting as a second nature. Thus the androgyny of Sidney's poet types his Christian orthodoxy, his morally effective ability to bring forth things *better* than a fallen nature through words that develop on the paradigm of the Word, the *Logos* who is the paradigm of all created things. The poet's skill shows in his ability to manufacture things that never existed in nature as the means through which human distortions of the truth can be corrected according to the revealed standard of the Word.

In reading Sidney's Aristotelian and Platonic architectonics backward from Kant and then from Cudworth, I do not mean to commit an anachronism. On the contrary, chronological reversal of historical evidence from 1781 to 1678 to 1595 is meant only to trace a widening circle of the influence of renaissance learning as applied to poetry *and* to philosophy and theology in the span of two centuries with influences into a third and fourth, our own. Cudworth's *True Intellectual System* precedes Kant's "Architectonic" as a logical plan, methodology, and system by a century. De Serres's architectonic philosophy of language precedes Cudworth by another century. One may wish to argue that *the* philosophy of the Renaissance in general, which was given to the presentation of cognitive arguments in vivid images in prose treatises, was supremely the philosophizing of the English Renaissance in particular. That is, the great poems of the English Renaissance *are* its philosophy.

In a strange coincidence that some historian of philosophy might clarify, though, the philosophical defense of religious belief against atheism by the seventeenth-century English Platonist may have influenced Kant. For Cudworth's *True Intellectual System* was translated into Latin by Laurence Mosheim and published in Germany in 1733 as *Systema Intellectuale Hujus Universi*. According to Werkmeister, Kant was interested in the humanities when he first entered the university in 1740 but soon transferred to mathematics and physics, then to philosophy. Kant's first publication of a treatise in 1747 addressed the problem of "living forces" stemming from the philosophies of Leibniz and Descartes, and Kant aimed to repudiate Leibniz, Wolff, Hermann, Bernoulli, Bulfinger, and others. Werkmeister explains Kant's questioning of a plurality of worlds, divine creation, and the problem of space: "But if such worlds were possible, 'it is also probable that God had actually created them somewhere.' Such worlds, however, could have no relation to ours, and the question would arise 'why God has separated one world from the other when the combination of them would have given his creation (seinem Werke) a greater perfection' " (*Kant: The Architectonic*, p. 3). In this early work it appears that Kant saw God as the "workmaster" or architectonic framer of creation. Werkmeister sees the problems raised in it as the problem Kant reserved for "the project of a meditation" later and the problem of space that Kant solved in the dawning of a "great light" on him in 1769, which was presented in the inaugural dissertation of 1770 and, from there, in the *Critique of Pure Reason* in which his "Architectonic" is fully expressed.

The task of following the chronology of philosophy from 1678 to 1781 belongs to other scholars. Perhaps it is sufficient here to note that when

modern criticism tries to read renaissance texts according to the positions
developed by Kant against earlier philosophers and developed by later
nineteenth- and twentieth-century philosophers and literary theorists
against Kant or in modification of Kant, it is simply asking for intellectual
distortion of those renaissance texts by the most blatant form of anachi-
ronism This chronology is more interesting than mere anachronism if
Cudworth knew Sidney's treatise or read Milton or used de Serres's *Plato*,
or all three of the above, for *his* philosophy makes a documented transition
from the Renaissance to the Enlightenment to romanticism. What we do
know certainly is that Coleridge read Cudworth and the other Cambridge
Platonists. Coleridge's annotated copy of the *True Intellectual System* is in
the British Museum, and Wimsatt and Brooks find the usual nineteenth-
century borrowing of literary terms from Kant's *Critique of Judgment* to have
little bearing on Coleridge's aesthetics. The relation to Kant is "a vaguer
one" lying "in the direction . . . of Kant's general epistemology and ontology in the *Critique of Pure Reason*" (*Literary Criticism*, p. 309).

At the end of the *Critique of Pure Reason*, Kant's "Architectonic of Pure
Reason" lauded "system" and dismissed the "mere rhapsody" of diverse
modes of knowledge. It also subordinated historical knowledge (*cognitio ex
datis*) to philosophy (*cognitio ex principiis*). At the beginning of the *Critique of
Pure Reason*, however, in the Preface to the 1781 edition, Kant addressed not
his plan but his subject, and he did so metaphorically. The subject is
metaphysics, and Kant's ending in an architectonic plan is all of a piece with
his beginning, in which he sees metaphysics as an "arena" of "endless
contests," that is, the scene of power struggles, because it employs principles that transcend the limits of "experience," and these cannot be tested by
that criterion (trans. Meiklejohn, p. xvii). Apparently sympathetic, Kant
then presents the medieval and renaissance feminized image of metaphysics
before he condemns "her government under the administration of the
dogmatists" as an historical event of "absolute *despotism*."

The figure of speech Kant especially chooses is Greek—that is, "Trojan"
and Latin, since he draws it from Ovid's *Metamorphoses* in a neat parody of
the allegorical mythology of the Renaissance and its open-ended classicism:

Time was, when she was the queen of all the sciences; and, if we take the will for the
deed, she certainly deserves, so far as regards the high-importance of her subject-
matter, this title of honour. Now it is the fashion of the time to heap contempt and
scorn upon her; and the matron mourns, forlorn and forsaken, like Hecuba.
(Pp. xvii–xviii)

Citing Ovid, then, Kant does some allegorical mythology of his own. He
allegorizes the downfall of metaphysics in the distraught image of the
Queen of Troy who, in Ovid's words, says she had been "lately on the

pinnacle of fame, strong in my many sons, my daughters, and my husband, now, exiled, penniless, torn from the tombs of my loved ones" (*Metamorphoses* 13.508–10).[16] Kant's aim is to remodel metaphysics, and his use of and then stripping away of the feminine image with a preference for the Architectonic of system is not, I think, an accident of metaphor; it is, rather, one of the few instances in which Kant is gripped by the metaphoric statement of a truth of the past essentially lost to him but preserved in poetic analogies.[17]

Here Queen Hecuba bespeaks her grief over the ruins of Troy in the manner in which Kant wants his reader to perceive Queen Metaphysics ruling over all the intellectual ruins, the mere rhapsody or aggregate of knowledge. *His* metaphysics is no queen and will rule over no ruins, no aggregate, but will philosophize systematically according to the end of reason, which will produce unity of the whole in relation to all of its parts. His metaphysics is no personification, but essentially the purity of moral philosophy, which distinguishes the role of the ideal teacher from those of the mathematician, the natural philosopher, and the logician, who are merely artists. They are engaged in the arrangement and formation of conceptions. One alone, the ideal teacher, is the philosopher who uses all of them "as instruments for the advancement of the essential aims of human reason . . . but he nowhere exists" (p. 508). But the ruins are gone, too, and what stands where Hecuba, the fragments and ashes of Troy, the potential of "new Troy," and man himself in his transcendent ego might stand is nothing but an invisible, incorporeal system.[18]

If a somewhat cheeky renaissance character could have spoken back to Kant, one wonders, would the speech be Hamlet's question, "What's Hecuba to him, or he to Hecuba / That he should weep for her?" (*Hamlet* 2.2.559–60). Kant is on the side of the Greeks of late eighteenth-century German classicism, as it were. Although he anticipates transcendentals that English romantics would envision, his Greece is not one with which the English renaissance imagination could be mythically at home. Its wellspring is the myth of fallen Troy, which fed an historical definition of English identity in the sixteenth century when Hecuba—and metaphysics—meant something.[19]

From the historical vantage of a renaissance definition of architectonic knowledge in Fracastoro and in Sidney, similarly, the "Architectonic" of Kant is neither a personified mystery of the integration of knowledge nor an "architecture" of thought. It is an *abstract unity* of cognitions under one idea, and it separates "nature" and "freedom."[20] In Kant's moral philosophy well-doing is finally based not on the security of knowledge but in the courageous freedom of the will. Although Kant recognizes in his Preface to the Second Edition of the *Critique* that its results seem to be "merely negative, warning us that we must never venture with speculative reason beyond the limits of experience," in fact, he claims, such a teaching has a positive use in narrowing the proper limits of reason and acknowledging that principles venturing beyond those limits actually belong to sensibility, not reason (*Critique of Pure Reason*, trans. Smith, p. 26). Kantian metaphysics at its purest is useful in *preventing* error, or *censoring*, more than in extending knowledge (*Critique of Pure Reason*, trans. Meiklejohn, p. 514). Kantian ethics presides over internal power struggles insofar as the whole interest of reason is centered on three questions—What can I know? What ought I do? What may I hope? (pp. 483–88)—but without the guidance of a metaphysical foundation in religion, which is too much to have expected of the true nature of metaphysics (p. 513).

Yet Kant seems to extend a kindly hand to this other, battered metaphysics "as a beloved one who has been for a time estranged" and whose questions nevertheless "relate to the highest aims of humanity, and reason must always labour either to attain to settled views in regard to these, or to destroy those which others have already established" (p. 514). The ethos of Kantian metaphysics is to prevent, censor, or destroy since it sees attainment of "settled views" as highly unlikely or even impossible. Kant's "Architectonic," consequently, is a systematic development of rational negation to "defend" against wrong. It is unlike Jean de Serres's, Sidney's, and Cudworth's equal proposition of known and revealed goodness.[21]

We may contrast Sidney's literary architectonics and Kant's architectonic plan and methodology on several points. Sidney's poetic model, first of all, is agriculturally organic and technical at once, and in ways that Kant's "organism," which grows from within "like an animal body" but *cannot grow by addition,* is not. Sidney's model is Aristotelian and Platonic; he imagines it in spirited human bodies and well-constructed houses rather concretely, but not as contained or self-enclosed systems. It is also Ovidian. Both bodies and houses (or poems) exist in relation to other bodies and to other houses and natural landscape, *et cetera,* with flexible boundaries of exchange that include metamorphoses, gender-shifts, appearance and disappearance, and annihilation and rebirth. Hybrid growth by addition is just as possible as growth from within, since Sidney's mythos approximates the fragmentation and integration of Isis and Osiris. Moreover, Sidney's architectonic is not merely Aristotelian; its moral philosophy, its privileging of self-knowledge acted out in the political sphere, and its view of language are particularly Platonic in the northern Protestant manner of the historian and theologian Jean de Serres. De Serres's thinking is an historical aggregate of Christian-Platonic-Aristotelian-Augustinian-scholastic-Calvinistic cognitions. Kant's Architectonic could no more abide this mixture of foreign elements than "pure" Kantian aesthetics can abide, even in Shakespeare's self-conscious parody of his own art, the "tragical-comical-historical-pastoral" of the "poem unlimited" (*Hamlet* 2.2.417–19).

Second, Kant's Architectonic elevates reason "to a scientific and clear self-knowledge" (p. 514) while Sidney's yokes him, it seems, to an historical "mistress" who complicates the exercise of his self-knowledge and commits him to the earthly condition of intermediacy between paradise lost and paradise regained. Kant's metaphysical system wants to check the tendency of reason toward dialectic and to escape the arena of endless contests (*Critique of Pure Reason*, p. 514); Sidney's rhetorical and political metaphysics revels in debate because the "highest point of man's wit" offers an authority by which to make final judgments (*Def.*, p. 79). Kant is in love with system for its own sake, one of his commentators remarks, and his "Architectonic" has about it the pleasure of a game.[22] As Kant subordinates history to philosophy, he marks the subordination with a shift from the noun to the verb. "Philosophy—unless it be done in an historical manner—cannot be learned," he says. "We can at most learn to *philosophize*" (*Critique of Pure Reason*, p. 507). Sidney thoroughly enjoys the play of wit and simultaneously unites the aims of *both* philosophy and history in "poesie," to which he subordinates both. Kant's Architectonic proposes carrying out "the Copernican revolution" and means, at least, to carry out the Newtonian revolution in physics. Sidney lived between revolutions of that sort and bespeaks visions they do not. The Renaissance in which Sidney lived may not be as clearly bounded in our historical concepts as it once was, but that is because we know more history, not less.[23] As Hiram Haydn has explained, that Renaissance was an age caught between two "edifices" of thought, the scholastic synthesis of the thirteenth-century philosophers and the scientific synthesis of the "architects" of the Newtonian vision to come.[24] Sidney's *Defence* falls characteristically into this condition of intermediacy.[25] This intermediacy, though, accounts for the originality of Sidney's poetics and the significance of the *Defence* in the development of literary criticism in English literature.

In the third place, Kant's Architectonic by definition dismisses the rhapsodic or the aggregate for its "disorganization," which disturbs for him a teleological rationale. Sidney sees no need to defend the "gathering" of knowledges, which is "reading," against "the ordinary doctrine of ignorance" (*Def.*, p. 105). He overwhelmingly asserts a teleology in the poesie that mediates *between* the historian's empiricism and the philosopher's intuition of first truths and *above* them in moving power. So, too, Sidney affirms the "rhapsody" of the miscellany not by itself, which would constitute the historian's collection of "mouse-eaten" records, but in relation to significant interpretation.[26]

Most of all, in the "gathering" of many knowledges that Sidney defines as reading, which, in turn, affects the "government of action" (*Def.*, p. 105), he almost musically takes the aggregate and the rhapsodic in his *own* selection of ideas from classical, medieval, and renaissance lore, and

metaphorically articulates their integration as an evanescent personification. He personifies in the feminine allegorical figure what neither fits into
systems nor depends totally on the making of them. This figure is not
random but sovereign; she is a wonderfully *impure* transcendent mask in
relation to the male poet's struggle in language to search out and unravel the
structure of everything known. As Kant turns from a metaphysics that
cannot test its own principles by the criterion of "experience," he "unsexes"
his language and his system; Sidney expresses the self-knowing man's
vision of the mistress-knowledge precisely as what *is known* "by the balance
of experience" in gender and in politics as an ethical proof of superiority and
cannot be subordinated to merely human rationality. This is Sophia in
operation. Sidney observes the general thrust of renaissance philosophy
toward subordinating metaphysics to ethics and politics and converting
both to rhetoric, but he nevertheless does not split these powers of knowledge. Sidney's Protestantism does not allow him to locate the freedom with
which the poet ranges in "the zodiac of his own wit" completely within the
pale of the exercise of the will (*Def.*, p. 78). Unlike Kant, Sidney cannot "take
the will for the deed" since he sees "infected will" curtailing the reach of
"erected wit." The moral balance that Sidney envisions is one of conscience,
which always arbitrates between that "infected will" and the possibility of
regeneration. And a graced conscience has the power to affirm and to
negate. Where Kant constructs a system able to negate, Sidney unveils a
presence, a mask and a voice, of the mistress-knowledge who is able to
affirm or to deny.

Having "read" Sidney's mistress-knowledge, I experience some horror,
some Hecuban grief, when I can put Wimsatt and Brooks's summary of
Kant's aesthetic next to Leitch's summary of Derrida's "deconstructive
man" and his nihilism. This juxtaposition, *not* the juxtaposition of Sidney's
literary architectonics and Kant's systematic Architectonic, properly exposes an historical relationship, that is, the relationship in our anamorphic
blurring of differences. It is possible that *critical* reduction of the queen of the
arts and sciences is another example of centuries of antifeminism. Even
though the feminine image has been distorted in masculine projections of
culture, sometimes the image still radiates a truth that would be utterly lost if
the image were simply stripped away.[27] Until the loss of the positive
feminine image in the cultural articulation of philosophy, history, and letters
is sufficiently redressed, perhaps all our cultures will mark the spiritual
dislocation of a world in which gender, language, poetry, philosophy,
science, politics, and religion irresponsibly oppress. Here are Wimsatt and
Brooks:

Kant's idea of beauty was severe; it related (so far as human making was concerned)
almost exclusively to the formal, decorative, and abstract: to Greek designs, foliation
on wallpaper, arabesques (things which 'mean nothing in themselves'), music without words. The 'charms' of direct sensuous pleasure might fuse with beauty, and

beauty *might* be combined with perfect natural forms and purposive human artifacts (the good, the ideal), but in neither of these cases was beauty pure. Beauty allied to the good was not 'free beauty' (*pulchritudo vaga*) but dependent beauty (*pulchritudo adhaerens*). The two might help *us* by being together, but strictly speaking neither helped the other. It is worth noting that here was a system which conceived of Homer and Shakespeare as less aesthetically pure than wallpaper. (*Literary Criticism*, p. 372)

In *Writing and Difference*, Derrida posed two ideas of interpretation and chose what he considered to be affirmation of play in Nietzschean fashion over negation and nostalgia in Rousseauistic thinking.[28] He claimed to have done so "in order to pass beyond man and humanism, the name of man being the name of that being who, throughout the history of metaphysics or of ontotheology—in other words, throughout his entire history—has dreamed of full presence, the reassuring foundation, the origin and end of play."[29] Leitch explains,

As prophet, Derrida presents to us deconstructive man—who accepts in joy and affirmation the play of the world and the innocence of becoming, who affirms the world of signs and the activity of interpretation, who neither pesters the world for truth nor indulges the dream of origins, who traces around the center the free play of signifiers and the tendential productions of structure, who writes off man and humanism, who denounces the old logocentric wizardry and passes joyously beyond. Cold and remorseless, deconstructive man assaults the old sensibility and subverts traditional foundations. Semiology, a recent formation of the logocentric era, is savaged: deconstruction offers us an affront of joy and affirmation.[30]

The diction is important since there is a vast difference between the expected syntactical structure, "an affront *to*," and the Derridean statement, in Leitch's view, of "an affront *of* joy and affirmation." Since the Derridean turn from logocentrism is, in part, a turn from the complicity of logocentrism with phallocentrism in the thinking of Lacan, the feminist may wish to hail deconstruction as an avenue of liberation.[31] Insofar as deconstruction tears down oppressive structures of the patriarchy, I suppose one may. But in the face of history this woman scholar remains skeptical of "deconstructive man." I must prefer the positive and real historical presence of the mistress-knowledge, even in her partially appropriated power and suppression, to the subversions at which deconstructive man plays. For she has so often been one of the dreams of full presence in his view, which he must destroy or relinquish as a negation of him if he cannot have it. Woman's *experience*, "though noon auctoritee," of the theories of men in history, bespeaks that "wo" and says that such skepticism is justified.

Wölfflin, Jaeger, and German Architectonic Culture

In renaissance poetry, the sexualized sense of intellectual decorum was the triumph of style in the poet's well-tempered mind. "Style is the man," the axiom goes, and in Sidney's case style represents an "Architectonical art" of mastery. Modern consideration of style has, however, recapitulated Kantian aesthetics in the name of the poetry and painting debate of the Renaissance. Missing Sidney's view of architectonics has meant that we have, after all, been missing his metaphor, too.

In the early twentieth century the German art historian Heinrich Wölfflin shifted the Kantian identification of architectonics with a nontechnical systems-building to the technical description of different styles in architecture and painting. Thus he reliteralized the architectonic metaphor of philosophy, stripping it of metaphysical, ethical and political, and logical significance for the sake of the etymological reference, *architecture*. Since the objects of Wölfflin's effort to classify styles were the products of the plastic arts, we may see his reversion to the literal as a return to *techne* and a protest of the Kantian departure from it in the definition of science. Since the products Wölfflin used for his examples were sixteenth- and seventeenth-century artworks, *The Principles of Art History* helped to introduce still other mirror-distortions into the definition of renaissance art forms in general and, by extension, into the discussion of poems and paintings of all periods.[32] Thus we find Wölfflin carrying out the Kantian program of determining a "science" in art historical study more or less because it may be elaborated according to principles. And we find that in mid-twentieth-century literary studies, formalists have borrowed the word *architectonic* from art history to indicate the unity and self-containment of a poem or other literary work as an internal system of meanings.[33] Under the developing authority, then, of New Criticism and its view of structure and style, a spate of literary essays assumes the unity and closure of "architectonic form" in a given literary text well into the 1960s; in the 1980s psychoanalytic criticism has picked up the theme.[34]

In effect Wölfflin had borrowed the word *architectonic* back from nineteenth-century philosophy, collapsed the vehicle and tenor of the metaphor as if it were a logical identity, and returned it to architecture as a principle of unity that could, in turn, become a metaphor for the organization of a painting. His five formulas of change in renaissance art—from the linear to the painterly, from plane to recession, from closed to open form, from multiplicity to unity, and from absolute to relative clarity—measured the structural or so-called architectonic values of painting (pp. 14–15). Wölfflin states explicitly that "every architectonic whole is a perfect unity," self-contained, proportionate, and clearly exemplified in architecture. Tectonic forms are frozen forms (pp. 185–86; cf. pp. 132, 166).

Subsequently, when modern literary critics populated mid-twentieth-century essays with discussions of poetic style and architectonic form, they actually translated Wölfflin's concern with structural design—an appropriate concern in pictorial arts—into standards of literary unity. It was as if the ancient Horatian axiom that a poem is like a painting, *ut pictura poesis*, authorized a new critical doctrine, *ut architectura poesis*. Implicit in the literal application of the architectural vehicle of the architectonic metaphor as a literary critical standard was the judgment that a poet's craft was inferior if the poem was not somehow self-contained, but superior if a multiplicity of ideas was somehow "frozen" together in an image. Lost in the identification of referent and reference—the archetypal misinterpretation of the logical similitude of metaphor that Horace's *ut* signified—was the tension between thought and expression; invention and eloquence; subject and object; speaker, text, and reader, which the disposition of things in words requires more than pictorial art usually does.

I am, of course, using some of the vocabulary of New Criticism, particularly that of I. A. Richards's *Principles of Literary Criticism*, which may share the platform with Wölfflin's *Principles of Art History*. Like art history, this literary criticism sought to be authorized as a type of knowledge; it might even approximate a science because it operated systematically on the exercise of regular principles. So, too, *The Well Wrought Urn* celebrated "frozen" form. In contrast, by similarly Kantian standards, literary history ran the risk of tending toward the intellectually aggregate, which might never determine meaning conclusively. Worse still, criticism poorly practiced tended toward the rhapsodic or nonsystematic, the impressionistic, and did not deserve to be called criticism.

But the problem of the elaboration of a split between *techne* and teleology, historical diversity and philosophical unity, has not been resolved by New Criticism, which actually made some effort to keep both possibilities within view, or by recent reactions against New Criticism. The emphasis on the textual artifact in structuralism a fortiori has established *techne*; deconstruction has seen its way beyond teleology in the quest simply for "differánce." Thus the literary complaint of the historical scholar also derives from a technical perception of metaphor and an awareness of its multiplying differences. The literal adoption of the etymological referent of a philosophical metaphor has severely rigidified our twentieth-century understanding of the significances of architectonic knowledge in the English Renaissance, falsifying it in the process. As a consequence, the ontology of renaissance poetry as a powerful species of architectonic philosophy in the renaissance analogy of the arts and sciences has been seriously obscured. If renaissance poetry is, indeed, a type of architectonic philosophy, it is as mythic and dynamic as thought, not literal and static, even when a poet may use the static images of an architectural building of words to express the character-making interest of the thought process. In the images of renaissance poetry, reason and sensibility are not divorced.

One may conjecture that New Criticism was especially able to take hold of the interpretation of renaissance texts in their apparent architectonic form because the pictorial and architectural analogy is everywhere in renaissance poetry. It contributes, for instance, to Sir Thomas Wyatt's spatial setting in the narrative frame for his translation of Aretino's version of the penitential psalms, to Spenser's disposition of core allegorical episodes in *The Faerie Queene*, and to Milton's arrangement of the parts of the *Ode on the Morning of Christ's Nativity*. Nevertheless, the poet's metaphoric proportion making among the arts and sciences—his inventive intellectual and moral building of ideas in images—exceeds the merely spatial imitation of nature. Poets such as Sidney and Spenser credited the epistemological analogy when they pressed the philosophical superiority of poetry to painting and architecture in their English recapitulations of the renaissance *dispute dell'arti*. Sidney's "speaking picture," a definition of poetry supported by Italian critical theory of the Renaissance, is an analogue that he introduces self-consciously—"to speak metaphorically" (*Def.*, pp. 79–80). So, too, Spenser's "Poet's wit, that passeth Painter far" envisioned universal truth in the metaphors made of words (*FQ* III, Proem 2). Both statements argue not so much the comparison of poesie to the pictorial art as the superiority of poesie in the scheme of knowledge.[35]

Yet, given the great importance of the literary criticism of Coleridge, Shelley, and Arnold in creating the premises of early twentieth-century criticism—in conjunction with conflicting demands from historiography and philosophy that also reach into the twentieth century—we may expect that the line leading from Kant to New Criticism and, from there, by many indirections, perhaps, to structuralism, poststructuralism, and deconstruction is fraught with complexity. Wimsatt and Brooks's *Literary Criticism: A Short History* presents that complexity through the New Critical vision of the poem that is stated best, I think, in a paraphrase of Robert Penn Warren's "Pure and Impure Poetry" (p. 647). So, too, the New Critical definition of the task of criticism draws from but modifies I. A. Richards's semantic theory. "The greatest poems reveal an organic structure of parts intricately related to each other," and this view of poetic excellence requires that "a principal task of criticism—perhaps *the* task of criticism—is to make explicit to the reader the implicit manifold of meanings" (p. 652). As Wimsatt and Brooks go on to cite Plotinus on the description of either "organic unity" and "internal differentiation" or the "*absence* of internal *differentiation*" and to cite Saint Augustine on the preference for totality, unity, and integrity in the judgment of beauty (p. 653, emphasis mine), critical readers of the 1990s may indeed hear in their vocabulary of 1957 anticipations of the debates now surrounding Miller's and Derrida's deconstruction. For deconstruction speaks of technical brilliance, difference, and absence.

Or we may hear their Kantian appreciation for a text that develops from within like systems formed by "certain worms" or a germ (*Critique of Pure Reason*, p. 503). Seeing a tension between history and the elaboration of principles and rules in *Literary Criticism: A Short History* also gives priority to the "critical idea" and resists "encyclopedism" and conversation (pp. vii–viii). Thus it resonates back to Kant's preference for a schema *with* an idea rather than a merely technical or empirical unity. Is this a Kantian metaphysics, based on the coherence, internal tensions, and system of Newtonian physics, being used to control "the ravages a lawless speculative reason would infallibly commit" without such a force of moral containment (*Critique of Pure Reason*, p. 514)? When Wimsatt and Brooks say that "metaphor is the union of history and philosophy which was the main premise of Sidney's *Defence*" (p. 749), I could not agree more; indeed, I have tried to carry out the analysis that justifies such a remark. But the same reading has produced copious historical evidence of the "name" and origin of that feminine metaphor, which the "values" history of New Criticism omitted, but not "at random" (p. viii).

The problem is that New Critics, in the effort to record some aspects of the real historical placement of Sidney's *Defence* between Aristotle and Kant, absorbed elements from both philosophers selectively so as to construct methods of formalist textual interpretation that have some boundaries. Theirs is an assumption of sufficient historical knowledge to put histories aside as an ever-growing aggregate or as material that might be adduced only as an external addition (*per appositionem*). The formalism of Sidney's literary architectonics is something else. Its "aggregate" encyclopedism is not that of mathematical principles and inert matter as in Newtonian physics, but that of a living, embodied spiritual organism. Although the emerging impulses of early modern mechanics can be felt in the Sidneian theme of "engineering" the world, Sidney's mistress-knowledge in the native wit or *ingenium* of the poet still articulates the elusive spiritual presence and is no mere apposition.

Werner Jaeger's discussion of Greek philosophical organicism and its corollary aesthetic instinct to analogize seems initially to help explain Sidney's view of the intellectual universality of the poet and allegory of poesie. Jaeger's twentieth-century study of *Paideia* and Sidney's sixteenth-century rewriting of classical education, literacy, and heroism as a Christian "cyropaedia" would thus share a culture of architectonics.[36] In Jaeger's view, Greek organicism is the wellspring of *paideia*, or acculturation and the Greek commitment to education; the Greek educational process, like Sidney's humanistic educational process aimed at reading in order to govern action, is founded on an anthropology that places the essential quality of a human being in his political character (*Paideia* 1:xxvi). The principles of form that construct architectonic qualities in a poem do so not because the structural values of painting, sculpture, or architecture have been imitated, Jaeger explains, but because there are analogous standards in language and its structure (1:xx–xxi). Behind Jaeger's vision of architectonic qualities based on analogous standards is, of course, the Kantian view that "human reason is by nature architectonic." Yet Jaeger simultaneously recognizes and iden-tifies in Greek culture themes that Erasmian humanism also selected from the classics in the renaissance cultivation of a Christianized philosophical quest. Jaeger speaks of the aristocratic or "highminded man" in whose character the pursuit of *arete*, or excellence, was securely linked to an "ennobled self-love," a φιλαυτία on the strength of whose energy a man would reach out "towards the highest arete" and take possession of the beautiful, sometimes through self-sacrifice (1:10–13). Erasmus had satirized *philautia* in *The Praise of Folly*, but not without praising its other face in the dialectic of Christ's incarnation and self-sacrifice, and we have already seen how Sidney carried out this cultural commitment in his life and works. Sidney's architectonics was not Kantian, but his *paideia* was classical-Christian in his imitation of this sort of Greek excellence.

It is now a commonplace that modern German scholarship has institu-tionally defined the structure and content of thought in various ways that have profoundly affected twentieth-century academic life and the profes-sion of the humanities in America. The Greek educational process was, indeed, understood as *bildung*, the plastic formation of the man according to a guiding pattern, the *idea* or *typos*, present to the imagination (*Paideia* 1:xxiii). Like Kant, Jaeger explains a certain shift in Greek education as a movement from process to content, from a verb to a noun. Richard McKeon, a prominent modern exponent of Aristotle and architectonics in the Chicago school, has similarly explained the shift from medieval disciplines to renais-sance subject matters. *Paideia* grew "to include the objective side, the con-tent . . . just as our word *culture* or the Latin *cultura*, having once meant the process of education, came to mean the state of being educated," Jaeger said, "and then the content of education, and finally the whole intellectual and spiritual world revealed by education, into which any individual, ac-cording to his nationality or social position is born. The historical process by which the world of culture is built up culminates when the ideal of culture is consciously formulated" (1:303). In New Historical terms one might express this shift toward reification as one that needs to be conceptually reversed in its connection to historical process so that history can be understood as something else besides a building of rigid formulations of culture. McKeon's appeal for new interdisciplinary ways of knowing rather than bodies of knowledge in the history of the liberal arts is similar.

Jaeger's explanation of architectonics and of the shift in definitions of culture is dispassionate. Contemporary Marxist theorists are not, however, dispassionate in their considerations of literary education and literary criti-cism. Modern critical theorists blame the building up of a world of culture, which they attribute to a Western humanism that has come to rest in a "state" instead of carrying out a process of change and has, therefore, constituted a form of oppression. Thus Terry Eagleton, for example, strikes out at the abuses of class, political status, and the literary profession itself when he locates the advent of literary criticism in the eighteenth century in a struggle against the absolutist state: "Within that repressive regime, in the seventeenth and eighteenth centuries, the European bourgeoisie begins to carve out for itself a distinct discursive space, one of rational judgement and enlightened critique rather than of the brutal ukases of an authoritarian politics."[37] Then in carrying out the thesis of his book, Eagleton asserts that criticism today lacks all substantive function. He does not index Kant in this book, but the echoes of Kant resonate in Eagleton's reaction *against* aspects of the Kantian aesthetic in ways that are worth exploring.

For instance, midbook Eagleton lands with particular force on Matthew Arnold and "Culture and Anarchy" as a primary source of our modern critical woes. He says Arnold's desire for a criticism so objective and non-partisan that it transcended "all particular social classes and interests" led to a "Criticism" or "Culture" that had "absolutely nothing to say" and "no effectiveness whatsoever" (pp. 60–61). Eagleton's parody of Arnold's definition of culture rings with Kantian values of totality, negation, and purity, which Eagleton sees in Arnold—and with the mathematical abstraction, I might add, of Newtonian worldviews:

Culture is the negation of all particular claims in the name of the totality—a totality which is therefore purely void because it is no more than a totalization of negated moments. In order to preserve its effectiveness, criticism must divorce itself so radically from the region into which it intervenes that it consumes itself in its own luminous purity and so has no effectiveness whatsoever. (P. 61)

Thus Eagleton opposes the Kantian preference for totality over the aggregate of history, which he sees embedded in Arnold's definition of culture. Likewise, Eagleton strips the Arnoldian-Kantian logic that produces "purity" at the price of negation. The Marxist critique, in short, contrasts a particular definition of history to the development of criticism in the direction of a fundamentally Kantian deconstruction.

If one returns to Arnold's text, one finds several passages revealing its resonance with Kant and its apparent rejection of some Kantian ideas.[38] Arnold, like Kant, lauds Socratic self-knowledge but, unlike Socrates or Sidney, indicates that he does not wish "to see men of culture asking to be entrusted with power" (p. 407); yet neither is culture anything "so intellectual as curiosity" (p. 408). It is this sort of canceling out of knowledge *and* power that I think Eagleton rightly protests. History enters the protest when Arnold sees the origin of culture in the love of perfection, as if one possesses a preconceived idea of what that perfection is. Arnold's culture expresses, it seems, a Kantian law of development that reflects Newtonian physics, for Arnold sees culture as *"a study of perfection,"* that is, the pursuit of completeness. He argues that "it moves by a force, not merely or primarily of the scientific passion for pure knowledge, but also of the moral and social passion for doing good" (pp. 409 10). At the same time Arnold espouses Newtonian "force" and tries to make it ethics, however, analogizing it on the authority of Kant to moral power; he also resists aspects of Kant "Culture is always assigning to system-makers and systems a smaller share in the bent of human destiny than their friends like" (p. 424). From the perspective of this remark, one might truly see the historical umbrage Eagleton takes from Arnold's criticism, for Marxism, too, is a making of systems. The argument between the dead but influential Arnold and the living and astute Eagleton is ideological, but *both* reflect the influence of Kant in forms of appropriation or reaction. Sidney's version of self-knowledge, which also develops from the Socratic model but is not limited to that, is mixed up in this debate insofar as Arnold may have drawn on Sidney. It is true that, like Sidney, Arnold put culture into a "like spirit" with poetry and with religion and associated both with the Greeks (p. 416).

The problem of the definition of culture in terms of the relation between the pursuit of knowledge and the love of the good expressed in action is still with us. Here in the United States, Frank Lentricchia appeals to Dewey's pragmatism and to Kenneth Burke's rhetorical and cultural analyses on similar Marxist grounds, which seek to fashion literary education and criticism into instruments of social change.[39] But from a longer view of history, one that reaches deeper than the eighteenth century and the origins of American educational theory, Lentricchia sounds remarkably like a renaissance humanist. English renaissance humanism was, after all, a literary movement and an educational program that not only sought social and political change but evidently achieved some change in the Reformation and in the establishment of a certain Tudor nationalism and English identity, for better or for worse. The perennial Western question of the relation between well-knowing and well-doing catches us in the circularities of the mirrors of *our* culture and criticism. It seems to me that one effect of this modern ideological disputation is a continuation of the dialectic. The scholar who tries to enter this discourse with a contribution to knowledge—especially knowledge of an historical sort—inevitably has to address the critical atmosphere in which dialectical voices demand some accommodation to their theories.

Sir Philip Sidney reenters this apparently eclectic assortment of writers on Greek, nineteenth-century, and contemporary European-American "cultures" by virtue of the fact that tensions of theory and practice, gnosis and praxis, appear also in modern studies of renaissance rhetoric. In *Rhetoric, Prudence, and Skepticism in the Renaissance*, Victoria Kahn recovers "various conventions of writing and interpretation within a given period" as a description of "the literary competence necessary for the readers of this period." She does so, I think, in order to redeem humanism for modern critical theory of the pragmatic kind.[40]

Kahn argues that the central assumption of renaissance humanism is that "reading is a form of prudence or deliberative rhetoric." The text is valuable "insofar as it educates the reader in an activity of discrimination and thereby educates the faculty of practical reason or prudential judgment which is essential to the active life." Citing a passage of the *Defence* as her epigraph, Kahn privileges praxis over gnosis in Sidney's version of the humanists' rhetorical enterprise (p. 9), and such is indeed the thrust of that passage. As we have seen, that passage is not, however, an accurate assessment of the balance of powers in the *Defence* as a whole. Sidney criticizes the historian as well as the philosopher and subordinates both to the poet in the same breath he insists on the relation of well-doing to well-knowing, that is, on the critically invisible image of the mistress-knowledge.

Rhetoric, Prudence, and Skepticism in the Renaissance is definitely the contribution to "historical poetics" that its author wanted it to be (p. 11), for there is no question that the book adds to our historical knowledge of humanist rhetoric, the Quattrocento, and the Erasmian view of prudence and faith, which are Kahn's main subjects. Sidney is not her main subject, and apart from her citation of the *Defence* in an epigraph, Kahn spends only a few pages on his critical treatise when she characterizes Sidney's view of reading as a "substitute for rather than a means to action" and assesses Sidney's defense as a movement from consideration of the power of poetry to consideration of the playfulness of power (pp. 188–90). Critically, Kahn's position partially reflects Margaret V. Ferguson's view of Sidney's "retreat to the 'aesthetic' position."[41] But Kahn does more; she performs the historical scholar's and critic's service of placing all of these assertions in the light of a reaction to the formalism rooted in Kantian philosophy.[42]

First, Kahn says that Sidney's "retreat" is instructive about "our own twentieth-century notions of poetry, our bias against the persuasive powers of literature" (p. 189), that is, the self-imposed limitations of our formalism. Then she deftly links the formalist understanding of Sidney's emphasis on the activity of reading to an anticipation of "the Kantian notion of the noncognitive aesthetic judgment," and quite accurately rejects that linkage. She is on her way to recovering the balance that Sidney proposed through his rhetoric. Sidney's emphasis on the *activity* of reading, Kahn explains,

finally uncovers the rhetorical and practical moment that the Kantian notion of aesthetics seeks to suppress: the fact that even arguments for the aesthetic effects of poetry are governed by rhetorical considerations, that the aesthetic experience has a claim on us only because it engages the mind in an activity that is ultimately conducive to ethical action. Thus even Kant writes in the *Kritik der Urteilskraft* (par. 29; see also par. 59) that aesthetic judgment is "purposive in reference to moral feeling." (Pp. 189–90)

It seems to me that Kahn's analysis has, at this point, undone some of the mirror reflections of our critical thinking.[43] She succeeds in seeing Sidney in his historical context through her clarification of Kant's aesthetics in juxtaposition to her analysis of Sidney's rhetorical operations. Kahn uses the in her critique, Kritik der Urteilskraft, to do so.

For my purposes, though, the point must be developed and qualified by the Kritik der reinen Vernunft on the Kantian Architectonic, since its definitions most obscure Sidney's philosophical poetics. Missing from Kahn's analysis of Sidney's participation in the humanist emphasis on praxis is any mention of his ἀρχιτεκτονική. Thus, when Kahn observes that the conflict between philosophy and rhetoric articulated by renaissance humanists continues into the twentieth century (p. 190), her earlier rejection of the connection between a formalist understanding of Sidney's idea of reading and Kantian noncognitive aesthetic judgment leads her straight past renaissance epistemology to that of deconstruction. This, I think, Kahn has not completely resolved with regard to Sidney. Yet she sharply characterizes the historical difference between the modern deconstructionist and the renaissance humanist rhetorician, taking us back to the position of the pragmatists:

The deconstructive critic tends to view rhetoric in terms of the epistemological consequences of figurative language. Action, accordingly, is a subset of cognition, performative language is subject to the same epistemological critique as constative language. The early humanists, however, tended to be unconcerned with the epistemological problems of figurative language. . . . While the deconstructive notion of undecidability has similarities with the formalist critic's skeptical approach to meaning, that is, with the traditional analogy between epistemological skepticism and the hypothetical nature of fictional discourse, for the humanist, as we have seen, the skeptical or hypothetical dimension of the text exemplifies the condition of the possibility of action. In this respect the humanists are more like Dewey than Derrida. (P. 191)

I thoroughly admire this distinction, for it helps me to distinguish Sidney's literary architectonics both from New Critical formalism and from deconstructive criticism. At the same time, though, the missing piece is still Sidney's balancing of theory, practice, and aesthetic delight in his view of architectonic *knowledge* as precisely the kind of knowledge that transcends the limitations of arts and sciences. The recovery of this view may qualify Kahn's circumvention of the question of metaphysics in her discussion of epistemology and in her subordination of gnosis to praxis. Although early humanists were not concerned with the epistemological problems of figurative language, later humanists, and certainly the humanist-poets of the English Renaissance, were very much concerned with questions of truth and fiction, the potential "lie" in eloquence, the breaking up of the organization of knowledge and the addition of new knowledges, and the changed status of allegory.[44] Kahn's sorting out of Kant in this respect helps point out my direction: the disentangling of anamorphic parallels in Aristotle, Sidney, and Kant.

Trials of Faith

It is not difficult to see, from one historical perspective, how various aspects of our current debate on culture and criticism recapitulate aspects of the renaissance critical struggle to balance dialectical invention, imitation, and imagination. By no means has literary history to date resolved the deep paralleling of idea and image, argument and icon, that characterizes the syncretic impulses of renaissance philosophy. Nearly twenty years ago Forrest G. Robinson, in *The Shape of Things Known: Sidney's Apology in Its Philosophical Tradition,* discussed the linearity of Sidney's argumentation and extended Sidney's revision of the Greek organic point of view in the vision of "visual epistemology." His book contributed a great deal to the historical understanding of Sidney's Augustinian Platonism and of the Ramistic and diagrammatic nature of Sidney's definition of poetic imitation as a speaking picture. By neglecting the allegorical nature and the femininity of Sidney's personification of the poetic art and also the androgynous balancing of knowledge and virtue in the epistemology of the *Defence,* however, Robinson inadvertently undercut his own argument.[45] He neglected the moral faith with which Sidney, like other renaissance theorists, counterbalanced the architecture of poetic imitation with the imaginative power to invent character not only *in* the text but *through* the text in the actual lives of the composer and the interpreter of poetic language.

This rhetorically moving power to make or engender character focused the debates of renaissance critical theory on idea and image, or the role of fiction or imitation in a renaissance notion of architectonic art. It pushed imitation into the territory of judgments of conscience, as I have already suggested in chapters 2 and 4. Thus the judgment of conscience as it affirms and denies imagined actions is the "rule" of writing and reading par excellence for Sidney, too. We do not have to wait for Hamlet at the turn of the seventeenth century to earmark the play of conscience as the verbally unspoken word (until the end of act 2) but the *res,* "the thing / Wherein I'll catch the conscience of the King" (2.2.632–34), that has been operative since act 1, scene 1. Conscience is the sum of the philosophical tradition that Sidney intertextualized in his *Defence* by recomposing the past to catch his Queen in a mirror for magistrates called the mistress-knowledge. Conscience is the special gnosis of the Renaissance. In the poet's appropriation of its political aspect from the feminine image, he informed his own ethical aspect, his self-knowledge. But the appropriation did not occur without the record of her struggle and her passage through history first being inscribed

in numerous renaissance texts. The projection of this gnosis, this conscience, into praxis and technology engages allegory as a form of thinking.

Sidney's allegorical imagining of architectonic knowledge whereu in the
historical intermediacy of other features of his *Defence*. Allegory for the
fifteenth century Florentalla Mirandola was an empirically ordered rule lug
of correspondences that he could wonder at in its reflection of the mysterious wholeness and knowability of the cosmos itself in the *Heptaplus*. By the
time Sir Francis Bacon wrote his *Novum Organum,* however, the advancement of learning depended not on the augmentation of the symbolic correspondences but on the replacement of the fictions of poetic invention, which
are "merely" allegorical, with the inventions of scientific models of reality.
Through Bacon an audience was being readied, at that point, for the
"paradigms" of Thomas Kuhn and *The Structure of Scientific Revolutions.* [46]

But if it is true that, for the Sidneian poet, the "mind's eye" of conscience
was the moral vision of self-knowledge transcendentally orchestrating all
other knowledges, we must look at the entirety of the *Defence* as an allegorical construction of meaning. In her book, *Trials of Desire: Renaissance Defenses of Poetry,* Margaret V. Ferguson has done so by way of her knowledge
of literary forms—the "genre" of apology and the courtly masking that
characterized the figurative role of allegory in the judgment of renaissance
rhetoric—and by way of deconstruction (pp. 137–62). She situates Sidney's
Defence in the genre of apology as a special class of writings, a class "speaking away from" some accusatory discourse and justifying the speaker
through his construction of a fable of himself, a didactic allegory of the ego
(pp. 2–4). Her aesthetic handling of the text is grounded on the recognition
of irony in Socratic apology, in which the friends of poetry have a vested
interest in accusing the philosopher of the corruption of youth in matters of
religion, and extends through Plutarch's notion of reading to Puttenham's
presentation of the doubleness inherent in "the courtier," a nickname for
allegory as a rhetorically extended metaphor. In general, Ferguson's treatment of the *Defence* as a "quasi-autobiographical allegory" astutely liberates
it from the wrong-minded judgment of generations of editors and critics
who found the treatise to be merely derivative in ideas. Her reading also has
the analytical perspicuity to avoid the either-or pitfall of Stanley Fish's
"affective stylistics," which would obliterate the ego of the speaking subject
in the name of his altruistic desire to promote virtue. Rather, Ferguson
presents Sidney's arts treatise as a dialogic defense in the Bakhtinian mode.
Sidney's allegory engages the reader's self-recognition through the
speaker's mask so as to criticize the lack of self-knowledge and to promote
self-examination (pp. 155–59). I could not agree more, but on the historical
grounds of the regularly contradictory operations of renaissance rhetoric in
the midst of any debate, not on the grounds of a modern theory of dialogics.

When Ferguson defines what she means by desire, the subtext of her essay as a contribution to our current debates over literary criticism surpasses its status as an essay in the historical criticism of a renaissance genre. In Ferguson's synthesis of histories, desire expresses the intention to escape the scene of trial and defense that is created "by the literary artist's or critic's status as a member of the body politic" (p. 17). The *Defence* is, therefore, by generic necessity as an "apology," the very model of literary criticism that is, in turn, a construction of and subverting of significances. This deconstruction reflects our particular historical and political condition, I think, more than Sidney's. In other words, this reading of Sidney specifically mirrors our critical selves *to us* as *we* write critical theory and practice literary interpretation.

Within this sense of aesthetic play, however, knowledge of the text interrupts Ferguson's deconstruction with a brief reminder of Sidney's "other foundation," that is, his metaphysical ethics of Christian Platonism. This Ferguson does not work out on its own terms, although she glances at definitions of Sidney's Protestant poetics, because her interest is not either theological or similarly historical research (p. 156). Her interest is in the adaptation of Sidney's aesthetic theory to the requirements of a deconstructive model. For example, she explains that "the epistemological barrier" that seems to exist "between Sidney's intention (desire) and his discourse" is not "impenetrable" because "lack of cognitive certainty need not entail lack of moral awareness." Sidney's text "offers the reader a choice not between error and truth but between error and recognition of the inevitability of error in the self" (p. 155). This conclusion is interestingly compatible with *one* reading of Sidney's Protestantism—that which would assign his Calvinism only to the sure determination of a man's knowledge of his own depravity—but there *are* other readings.

In my view, for instance, Sidney's self-knowing man reflected a certain kind of Christian Platonism in his Calvinistic Protestantism, and self-knowledge included within its range of experience not only the judgment of the self in error but the assertion of the self in virtue, which could provide experiential evidence of spiritual regeneration and its power. Ferguson takes the examination of Sidney's ironies in this respect not in the direction of a graced conscience, to which renaissance thinkers attributed the power to affirm *and* to deny, but in the direction of Kantian metaphysics and moral philosophy whose essential power is that of preventing error. Thus Sidney, in her view, re-creates the argument between idealism and pragmatism and resolves it in irony; the moral judgment that Ferguson makes on Sidney when she states the irony of his allegory is analogous to the judgment Eagleton makes on Arnold for his "totalization of negated moments" (*Function of Criticism*, p. 61). Sidney's tension neutralizes his terms since the altruistic foundation of the *Defence* in Christianity and Platonism inevitably has "an egotistical dimension" (*Trials of Desire*, p. 159). The Protestant humanism inherent in Sidney's sense of subjectivity, however, regards such a dimension differently. In other words, Ferguson's essay is a critical tour de force absolutely peppered with textual insights on the way to her discovery of modern difficulties in balancing Sidney's theory (gnosis, science, art, reading) with desire (delight, pleasure, aesthetics) and with rhetorical practice (pragmatism, pleas for power, virtue, moral awareness, self-knowledge). Behind Ferguson's extremely interesting interpretation stand, however, two powerfully inspiring but historically anachronistic minds for the reading of Sidney: Kant and Freud.

Ferguson indexes Kant only once, and that in her discussion of Sidney's *Defence* when she is advancing her argument about the nature of literary criticism per se against formalism: "It is an irony of literary history that those who rely on Kantian, Aristotelian, or other theories of aesthetic formalism to fence off a sphere for innocent art (and innocent criticism) simply repeat a defensive strategy which Sidney himself employs in a dialectical and self-reflexive way" (p. 140). Thus Ferguson logically observes the reaction of contemporary literary theory against New Criticism and other formalist views that uphold the "science" of literary inquiry according to the systematic elaboration of "principles" that Kant recommended for true "philosophizing." She does not observe, because it is assumed, *her own* extension of Kant's other sphere of influence, namely, the role of the will to act in spite of the lack of a grounding knowledge of first principles for guidance. Ferguson's Sidney is a most modern hero in the scene of defense from which he wishes to escape; his combined desire to be good and to have experiential knowledge of the freedom and error of his own ways, at least in the pursuit of power, makes him the critical predecessor of the Derridean or deconstructive man who is "guilty" of literary interpretation but willing to make the "turn," to desire to escape the scene of trial through an aesthetic retreat into play. But Ferguson, who leaves Sidney standing before his court with his inner contradictions, knows that something remains to be said and outside the boundaries of the essay on Sidney takes up the burden of guilt with Freud.

In discussing allegory, Ferguson commented on the political necessity of dissembling when the aristocratic Elizabethan author challenged a court "in which the Queen played the role of chief judge" (p. 138). She located the duplicities of the rhetorician in the duplicities of language itself in Sidney's perception, marking how Sidney self-consciously defends himself for crossing the boundary between "the language of play" and "the language of power," that is, poetry and oratory (p. 140). Beyond the boundary of the chapter on Sidney, then, Ferguson takes us into a scene of modern trial and defense, for we locate our seat of power not in metaphysics, religion, history, or physics but in the judgments of psychoanalysis.

Ferguson compares Sidney and Freud in order to include Freud's thinking within the circle of her critique of criticism. Criticism is thus an act of cultural interpretation determined by the difficulties of membership in the body politic. Sidneian self-knowledge may be seen to parallel what Freud called recognition in his elaboration of defensive strategies for psychoanalysis. In front of the fictions of novelists—the extreme form of play, one that escapes the Kantian demand to define a science by principles—Freud presents himself as an allied claimant of the power of imagination. But "somewhere in the textual court sits an imagined version of the censoring and judging agency Freud called the superego" (p. 165), Ferguson remarks. From the outset of her argument, Ferguson had taken up the perennially defensive posture of literary criticism under the umbrella of the psychoanalytic practice of interpretation (pp. 12–17). In the Conclusion to her book, she draws this analogy: "The novelist is for Freud what the historian or philosopher is for Sidney" (p. 165). Freud practices, as Sidney did, double strategies of "attack and courtship" (p. 165) in face of his potential critics. In other words, Ferguson dismantles Freud's defense of psychoanalysis as a science of nature on the grounds, first, of its lack of the Kantian requirement for the Architectonic, or systems-making of knowledge, on which the principles of science depend, and, second, on the demonstrable *formal* similarity between Freud's discourse in its structures of defense and the discourse of literary criticism as the verbal structure of defense per se. Psychoanalytic interpretation, we may deduce from Ferguson's analysis, is a duplicity of language and a doubling in power motives. It seeks the good of the other (client, object) only in relation simultaneously to the ego interests of the speaking self (doctor, subject). But looking this condition squarely in the eye, then, Ferguson seems to defend *both* literary criticism and psychoanalytic interpretation as she historically contextualizes their strange freedom: the will to act within the scene of trial by speaking attack and courtship. But their trial is finally that of Ferguson and all critics.

As an essay on criticism, Ferguson's "Pleas for Power" is brilliant. As a literary-*historical* interpretation of Sidney's *Defence,* however, the essay presents historical distortions that may finally weaken its critical value. It matters which Socrates and Plato we read to read Sidney; my argument is that we have to read Jean de Serres's 1578 edition of *Plato* and not rely on Havelock or Derrida (*Trials of Desire,* pp. 7–8). When we read Jean de Serres *and* Sidney, similarly, we find an architectonic philosophy stated, particularly with regard to the operations of language, that shatters the "epistemological barrier" on the grounds of a theological faith. Modern literary theorists and critics allude to first philosophy and faith, especially in reference to renaissance skepticism, but do not like to examine their grounds openly because moderns are supposed to eschew the metaphysics or the fideism of the past and its ideologies.

Historically, though, such deliberate silence is a form of politics and, with regard to culture, race, and gender, may be a form of oppression by erasing the memory. The sociologist Philip Rieff, in his book *The Triumph of the Therapeutic: Uses of Faith after Freud*, has amply demonstrated how the nineteenth century replaced the religious prophecy of earlier ages with relentless privelegy and how modern churches and believers in the West are now engaged in a struggle to survive by adapting their authorities to therapeutic models.[47] But the fact that we in the late twentieth century are only *now* criticizing psychoanalysis does not mean we have to deny historical differences in our effort to understand critically the theological views embedded in Sidney's formulation of poetics. On the contrary, the present ability to criticize may actually shape *new* alliances in which, for instance, theological suppositions may become the advocates of woman's cause in this world. If Margaret Ferguson has made the first (political) gesture in this direction as she places Freud in the position of trial, I would like to strike the second (ethical and mystical) one as a reclamation of marginalized spiritual authority, but without having been compelled to carry out the New Critical disdain for history. Rather, I would like to see history recovered put to good use in the discovery of modern alternatives, including feminism and faith.

One such alternative is obviously the operative definition of conscience. Jean de Serres advocated conscience in an irenic posture of sixteenth-century Calvinism with a presupposition of the powers of the grace, election, justification, and assurance at work in it. Without grace, conscience as developed in the thinking of Saints Jerome and Augustine possessed merely a negative function; it was the inner voice or forum telling someone what not to do. With grace, the same conscience could move one toward praxis, either not to do or to do, either to eschew evil or to perform the good. In Luther the negations of conscience were properly understood to be horrible forces analogous to the Furies chasing Orestes, and he actually used that mythological language to describe its pain in a fashion compatible with the Freudian or psychoanalytic exposition of the oedipal complex and the superego. But Luther's inauguration of the Reformation was characteristically the announcement of grace, not works, as the source of justification. Fundamentally similar, though more intellectualized, sixteenth-century Calvinism constructed a definition of conscience with which Sidney marked his Anglicized notion of "inward light."

The historical differences among Freud's superego, de Serres's conscientious architectonic speech, and Sidney's voicing of a light both seen, however dimly, and feminized as a *comforting* presence are as historically profound as the differences between atheism and belief, Judaism and Christianity, and science and art. Such differences return us to the ironies of Sidney's pleas for power, to his aestheticism, and to his resolution of idealism and pragmatism—that is, to the apparent contradictions in his rhetoric—not merely as the evidence of a division in the speaking subject but also as the evidence of the nature of the division and its relation to a still centering self. Such historical differences return us to the nature of Sidney's articulation of the negating and affirming roles assigned to conscience in the very living of life. Sidney locates that role positively and substantively, it seems to me, in the vital bond between well-knowing and well-doing, and he expresses this bond in his most lively figurative coupling of the knowledge of a man's self with the mistress-knowledge. Yes, Sidney eroticizes conscience, but not in Freud's way or with Freud's attitudes toward the primal scene and the superego. In *The Defence of Poesie* sexuality is clearly inscribed in Sidney's textual proposal for conscientious speech, and it is the allegory of self-knowledge in time funded by Augustinian-Platonic doctrines of a lovely Love that energizes the Sidneian proposition of poetic generativity and gender.

Although Ferguson's critical and my historicist enterprises separate us, the scene of another trial going on in literary criticism, namely, the trial of feminism, may actually unite my "conscience" to her "politics." The arena shaped by male cultural history and by male critical standards is not that of metaphysics à la Kant, but that of theory and literary practice in the academy and whether or not women scholars have intellectual authority. Presumably the doubling of attack and courtship that Ferguson has marked as the character of literary criticism in general—and English literary criticism in particular in its descent from Sidney's *Defence*—will also appear in the language of women scholars and critics who perform their cultural critique in order to make the world a better place and, egoistically, to serve the cause of the advancement of women.

Ferguson produces, in this respect, a most satisfying diagnosis of our critical condition, and I should like to borrow it. If a patriarchal critical culture has required linear argumentation of me pro forma, in the course of which I have contested both men and women thinkers and qualified several "reading women" as scholars and critics; if feminist "contests" serve a patriarchal purpose as a mode of dividing and conquering; and if the inherited practice of literary criticism in its doubling of attack and courtship particularly marginalizes or silences the scholarly contributions of women, then I, too, not only "desire to escape," as Ferguson puts it, but say that I and women thinkers in general are in the process of escaping. We are on our way *to* a positive freedom, not merely *in* a negative flight, and the definition of freedom we are expressing is our own, not that bounded by patriarchal institutions. The history that has tried to exclude women has failed; it has slowly taught us to know ourselves. In literary criticism and history earlier in this century in England and in America, and in renaissance studies particularly, the positive achievements of women scholars need no apology. The list is growing of those women scholars in renaissance studies whose achievements are often historical-minded—that is, *cognitio ex datis*—and neither circumscribed nor daunted by the systematic theorizing claimed in gender politics as the intellectual "building" territory of men.

Long live Hecuba and her various children; let the "engineers" remember their origin and put down their weapons before her *ingenium*. The interpretation of Sidney and of the Renaissance that either stops or starts with Kant's mock-Hecubean metaphysics runs the risk of missing the manner in which the *regina reliquarum* of the Renaissance truly does participate, in the form of Sidney's mistress-knowledge, in the English recapitulation of the Troy myth and its limitations for the sake of understanding the Tudor national identity. As scholarly women in particular, we have a vested interest in remembering history; not to remember contributes too often to the sacrifice of daughters, the abandonment of spouses, and the utter desecration of the community.

This book ends, therefore, with a coda. The figure of the mistress-knowledge appears and disappears in history almost according to the alchemist's axiom, *solve et coagula*, "dissolve and conjoin." The recovery of the figure presents modern readers of the texts of the English Renaissance with, perhaps, the problem of the possible discovery of a lost "original" integrity. In the Reformation, the subject of human integrity or the so-called central self was certainly in doubt, as all renaissance skeptics perceived, but it was also established in the paradox of faith.

The integrity imagined in renaissance literary characters, including the figure of the mistress-knowledge as a species of allegorical *eikastic* personification, is never seen by the writer as a positive achievement of human labor; rather, it is a gift of grace. Protestant poets portray the gap between the content of their rational discoveries of false selves and human malaise and their radical faith and hope that, in the end, the true human self will be reconstituted in its original integrity, its likeness to the only true Icon of God, Jesus the Christ. This apparently contradictory set of convictions— human malaise exposed through history and divine intervention disclosed in it—establishes a major moral-psychological paradox in renaissance texts alien to the modern secular mind. Modernist and postmodernist thinkers are likely to reify fragmentation; the lack of integration, and certainly a profound skepticism if not utter cynicism, is the new essentialism of the modern mind that judges redemption and recovery of lost integrity impossible. From our perspective, it is a naive religious optimism that has posited any such hope, and such optimism has cruelly drugged history seeking its own revolution. From a renaissance perspective, however, the paradox of sin and grace is based on a soteriological continuum through the Middle Ages and into the Reformation, which requires an Augustinian vision of the uses of time and history. Time is *for* the moral and spiritual recovery of the image of the Image both in biography, which is the lifetime of the individual, and in history, which is the biography of races, cultures, nations, and genders. Nietzsche asks moderns to "dance with the fragments." Renaissance poets ask readers to know themselves. These are related but fundamentally different moral imperatives, as different as the death of God and the seeking of an elusive but self-revealing presence.

One of the benefits of perceiving the difference is insight enough to speak not of the central or centered self with regard to renaissance humanism but of the *centering* self. The moral-psychological paradox of a human identity located between sin and grace obviously poses human character in a state of division, a condition of being off-balance and nonintegral. To create images that approximate integration, however, is not to assert that one has arrived finally and conclusively at integrity. It is to give oneself models for striving through time, for balancing and losing balance and regaining it. Thus this paradox belongs to the list of other renaissance paradoxes—those of *eikastic* and *phantastic* images, of time and eternity, and of the losing of one's life and the gaining of one's life in the work of salvation. If the relation between sin and grace is the working out of salvation in time (election, justification, sanctification, with a subspecies in the quest for assurance), the relation of time and eternity positively necessitates the simultaneous viewing of the limitations and the possibilities of human authors and of fictive characters. The religious doctrine of the Reformation bravely asserts the power of regenerate reason to build the world *in face of* the historical evidence of the ruination caused in time by fallen minds, even in the construction of their best devices.

With regard to Sidney, in particular, the dualities of these paradoxes have a forcefully simultaneous expression. An earlier phase of the study of Sidney's Protestant poetics has shown its effects in his thinking about our fragmentation and multiplicity—the condition of "our degenerate souls, made worse by their clayey lodgings" (*Def.*, p. 82), which logically assigns poetry, the artifact of fallen minds, a limited function—but a fuller view of Sidney's thought must credit as well his assertion of the power of poesie in the graced "light of Christ" that allows a rereading of classical mythology and philosophy and aligns poetics with wisdom and conscience because "Christianity hath taken away all the hurtful belief" (*Def.*, p. 108).

When we speak of Protestant and Puritan iconoclasm, therefore, we are acknowledging how renaissance thinkers used a Christian humanist perspective to recognize the fallacies inherent in "self-fashioning," as Stephen Greenblatt has shown, even when Sir Thomas More, Sir Thomas Wyatt, and Shakespeare rigorously took on the burden of living in time and temporally fashioned themselves as literary characters. Greenblatt suggests an atheistic or a secular motive for such performance, which I see as theatrical and theistic. The most literate renaissance characters "mask" gods and goddesses; one puts on and takes off the images of the self because one is thrust onto the stage of time and must do one's best to play one's part. Wearing and changing historical costumes does not imply that there is not, simultaneously, an actor struggling to center the self. The proximate real name of that actor in history was conscientiously understood to be the ultimate judgment of God that would be revealed only at the end of time, and renaissance writers are quite skilled in satirizing any persona that thinks of itself as having arrived at the full revelation of the truth of the naked self while still dressed in some costume. Puritan thinking in particular tore down any public, ritual, and communal idols and often tacitly made up new icons of the Puritan self or saint. Sidney's handling of prosopopoeia reflects such a development in an early and brilliant phase well before Milton specialized in the joint projection of iconology and iconoclasm, and before American Puritans adapted this dualism to their historical situation. The central self that modern critical theory debunks is much more an artifact of nineteenth-century interpretations of renaissance idealization of "man" than it is a product of renaissance and reformation humanism or poetic theory.

The latter is truly Augustinian as it addresses the phenomenon of lost integrity in the Fall and the possibility of recovery in the process of history. Inevitably Augustine phrases the issue with reference to sexuality and gender. Early in the *Confessions* Augustine describes his own intellectual errors as parallels to sins of concupiscence and ire; his analogy follows, therefore, the Platonic definition of the threefold powers of the soul—the rational, the concupiscent, and the irascible. First, he concluded that "in goodness there was unity, but in evil disunion of some kind" as he posed the unity of goodness in a sexless monad and the disunion in the dyad that leads to violence and lust; but "I did not know what I was saying, because no one had taught me, and I had not yet found out for myself, that evil is not a substance and man's mind is not the supreme good that does not vary" (*Conf.* 4.15, trans. Pine-Coffin, p. 86). So he qualifies his point:

Crimes against other men are committed when the emotions, which spur us to action, are corrupt and rise in revolt without control. Sins of self-indulgence are committed when the soul fails to govern the impulses from which it derives bodily pleasure. In the same way, if the rational mind is corrupt, mistaken ideas and false beliefs will poison life. In those days my mind was corrupt. I did not know that if I was to share in the truth, it must be illuminated by another light, because the mind itself is not the essence of truth. (*Conf.* 4.15, trans. Pine-Coffin, p. 86)

By recognizing that the mind itself is not the essence of truth, Augustine acknowledged what we moderns call the proliferation of ideologies; but for him the existence of a Truth with whom the mind might be brought into correspondence also remained a possibility. We tend to see nothing but ideologies.

As he underwent conversion, Augustine received the light, according to his own testimony, and it operated morally as the corrective force of a graced conscience in sorting out the exercise of the rational, concupiscent, and irascible powers of the soul. As I indicated in chapter 4 with regard to Jean de Serres's Augustinianism, Saint Jerome defined Christian conscience as the *fourth* power of the soul, the power of *scintilla synderesis*, revising the Platonic doctrine of these three powers. In Augustine's case, later in the *Confessions* he singles out the practical means of the recovery of unity or integrity of the soul in the context of his own story of sin and grace when he has been illuminated in his mind by a light other than that of his own making. In one of the most famous passages of the *Confessions*, he addresses the personal sin that most impeded his conversion process as he discusses his struggle for chastity as the hallmark of the integrity of the soul—our central self:

Give me the grace to do as you command, and command me to do what you will! You command us to control our bodily desires. And, as we are told, when I knew that no man can be master of himself, except of God's bounty, I was wise enough already to know whence the gift came. *Truly it is by continence that we are made as one and regain that unity of self which we lost* by falling apart in the search for a variety of pleasures. (*Conf.* 10.29, trans. Pine-Coffin, p. 233, emphasis mine)

In making such an assertion, Augustine recapitulates a standard doctrine of patristic humanism on the nature of the virtue of chastity or virginity, clarifying for us the question of desire raised subsequently by renaissance poets. Physically, virginity lost is lost forever; but morally, chastity practiced and virginity "recovered" are fundamentally the conditions of philosophical and spiritual integrity—the conditions of heaven where, as the Sadducees learned from Christ, there is no need for marriage. In time and history, however, chastity practiced is symbolized either by a literally physical continence or by holy matrimony.

Obviously, the Protestant Reformation reversed the emphasis of the monastic centuries and preferred the way of marriage, the chaste union of the sexes. The Reformers' preference brings the subject of the central self being raised in contemporary studies out of the domain of some singularly male ego—the topos of Adam alone in the Garden—and distinctly into the historical domain of relationship between the genders. Masculine and feminine in its very statement as an ideal, the *centering* self of the couple becomes an historical approximation of the only true Self, the incarnate and anointed One. The union of Sidney's mistress-knowledge and architect-poet constitutes an image of the head and body of Christ, the only real Icon of God, who will be revealed at the end of time and who reveals, all in all, the union of the human and the divine. Such a perception of original unity is probably one reason Mary Nyquist has recently drawn on Phyllis Trible's earlier feminism in *God and the Rhetoric of Sexuality* (1978) to point out areas that now need to be qualified further. In her essay "The genesis of gendered subjectivity in the divorce tracts and in *Paradise Lost*" in the collection of essays she has coedited with Margaret Ferguson called *Re-Membering Milton*, Nyquist credits Trible's exegesis of the Yahwist and priestly stories of creation as a source of new orthodoxy among feminists, who take it as a standard for positioning their commentaries outside the traditions of masculinist interpretation. The is concerned though that even this rethinking makes it too easy to adopt a view of Genesis as a text "inaugurating a transhistorically homogeneous patriarchal culture" that, in turn, has validated the reading of direct, unmediated influence between Genesis and Milton's stereotypical portrayal of gender in his Adam and Eve.[48] Sidney's expression of a centering self, a dynamism in time between sin and grace and a moral dynamism between the masculine and the feminine, certainly influenced Milton's poetics and may enter into the discussion of subjectivity by way of presenting some needed historical qualifiers.

Particularly with regard to the lost figure of the mistress-knowledge that this book has aimed to recover historically, contemporary gender studies of the so-called central self must take great care not to sabotage the feminist project of recovering lost images in the same breath they seek to debunk the so-called humanist project of the central self. In challenging this humanism, Ferguson, Quilligan, and Vickers in the introduction to their collection of essays, *Rewriting the Renaissance*, have already recognized the degree to which it is historically articulated as male ego. To extend the dismantling of the so-called central self to the male aristocratic Sidney in simple terms is not hard to do, but I have tried to suggest ways in which it is profitable to recognize that Sidney was more sophisticated and complex in regard to gender and desire than we have given him credit for and merits a less simple approach. That is, while I would not see him or his discourse in the *Defence* as merely a divided subject, he appears to have known himself as one still centering, as the Reformation insisted—a soul not yet in heaven but working out salvation in time. To extend the debunking of the central self to the image of the feminine he ambivalently constructed in the figure of the mistress-knowledge is quite another project, however, and one that may be self-defeating for women scholars now. Nyquist opens her essay on "gendered subjectivity" by speaking of "third-wave feminism" and "postfeminist feminism," which are to be associated with "a variety of attacks mounted against Western bourgeois or liberal feminism" and with the problem of "the historically determinate and class-inflected nature of the discourse of 'equal rights' " (p. 99). Certainly Marxist feminism must proceed in this direction and would emphasize that even the positive features of the image of the mistress-knowledge could be negatively used by men in history—and were—to oppress masses of women in the sixteenth and seventeenth centuries and in modern times through traditional religious, educational, and economic structures. But women may also positively reclaim in this image a spirituality, which arises in splendidly literary form in renaissance poetry, in Sidney's poetics, and in his searching out of his own subjectivity, by articulating a power of conscience that briefly exerted a positive influence in the history of woman. Her protest need not be merely woman's *negation* of man's centrality but her insistence on also occupying the human center and redefining it, her refusal to be pushed out, and her empowered voicing of a centering self. Since the mistress-knowledge is an *eikastic* image expressing that renaissance desire for lost integrity in a prosopopoeia of the moral and intellectual leadings of grace, who are we moderns to deny her centripetal attractiveness for renaissance thinkers because our times put up serious obstacles to our "faith" that integration or integrity is possible in language, sexuality, religion, or politics? The testimony of the Renaissance is, rather, as Sidney's Dorus puts it, "a certain dawning . . . of some possibilities of comfort" or assurance "from a huge darkness of sorrowes" and "such a light" as to help "the miserable caitife . . . better remember the light, of which he is depriued" (*Arcadia* [1590], ed. Feuillerat, 1:2.2, 153).

In the late sixteenth century, Sidney's vision of conscience was still fairly incarnate because of his commitment to poesie and had not yet become the militant assertion of moral judgment detached from divine and human presences to which Protestantism would be reduced in the advance of secularism. The argument of the mistress-knowledge is but one aspect of a larger cultural history we continue to probe and to understand.

Like a portrait in a renaissance tapestry that has survived the past four centuries, the image of the mistress-knowledge reclaimed from history is composed of many threads still whole enough to let us perceive her face as one of the faces of what our civilization has called "God"—even the name, Martin Buber once said, "that lies in the dust and bears . . . the whole burden." For the great images of "God" fashioned by human beings, Buber asserted in *The Eclipse of God*, were born not of fantasy but of "real encounters with real divine power and glory."[49] For this reason Buber rejected Kant's proposition that "God" is not a substantial subject outside ourselves, "but only a moral condition within us" and the source of moral obligation (p. 16). As a conversation among multiple, divided, and unresolved selves, let "God" be dead, for such a "God" is merely one of many idols and masks. But if our literary ancestors found, in masking even these images, an experience of the living and mysterious presence external to human nature nevertheless rhapsodically entering into our psyches and language in feminine as well as masculine forms, perhaps we moderns have reason to continue to listen to their testimony to their experience.

The argument of the mistress-knowledge is more portraiture and storytelling than syllogism. In the telling, since it is true that her narrative design has been obscured in literary-critical history, it is true as well that we must witness the gaps, the unravelings with which her image in time descends to us and hear her kind of Solomonic comfort as an echo. But the loosened threads and silences in this effort to recall the image of Sophia can also tell us moderns, perhaps, about the difficulties of restoring any true image of the Image. We are in conflict about logocentrism and gender now; but long before Lacan, Derrida, and Kristeva expressed the terms of the conflict, long before Milton struggled with Arianism and his creaturely identification with a feminized celestial Spirit and Sidney with "her" appearances, and long before the Venerable Bede worried over Arian tendencies in English religion, Saint Athanasius, the theologian of orthodoxy in the original Arian controversy, articulated in his treatise *De Incarnatione Verbi Dei* the terms in which Western history would conceive the retrieval of what was lost in the original Fall:

What then was God to do? or what was to be done save the renewing of that which was in God's image. . . ? For by men's means it was impossible, since they are but made after the image; nor by angels either, for not even they are (God's) images. Whence the Word of God came . . . to create afresh. . . . For as, when the likeness painted on a panel has been effaced by stains from without, he whose likeness it is must needs come once more to enable the portrait to be renewed on the same wood . . . ; in the same way . . . the Image . . . came to our region to renew . . . and find . . . one lost.[50]

The Christian humanism of the Renaissance disturbs our modern sensibilities both because of its incarnationism and because of the nightmares perpetrated under its name. But Athanasius, like Stephen Dedalus, strove to awake from those nightmares of history as a monstrous defacing of the prophetic dream in which "the Word was made human that we might be made God" (*Incarnation of the Word* 54.3, p. 65), and Sir Philip Sidney recognized the desire for such divine humanity in the mistress-knowledge poesie.

Abbreviations

CCSL	*Corpus Christianorum Series Latina* (Turnhout, Belgium: Brepols, 1954-present), 250 vols. (incomplete)
CI	*Critical Inquiry*
CL	*Comparative Literature*
CLS	*Comparative Literature Studies*
DR	*Dalhousie Review*
EETS	*Early English Text Society*
ELH	[A Journal of English Literary History]
ELR	*English Literary Renaissance*
EM	*English Miscellany*
ES	*English Studies*
JAAC	*Journal of Aesthetics and Art Criticism*
JEGP	*Journal of English and Germanic Philology*
JMRS	*Journal of Medieval and Renaissance Studies*
JWCI	*Journal of the Warburg and Courtauld Institutes*
MLQ	*Modern Language Quarterly*
MLR	*Modern Language Review*
MP	*Modern Philology*
NLH	*New Literary History*
NM	*Neuphilologische Mitteilungen*
PG	*Patrologia Graeca*, ed. J.–P. Migne (Paris, 1857-87), 161 vols.
PL	*Patrologia Latina*, ed. J.–P. Migne (Paris, 1844-64), 221 vols.
PMLA	*Publications of the Modern Language Association of America*
PQ	*Philological Quarterly*
RES	*Review of English Studies*
SEL	*Studies in English Literature 1500–1900*
SN	*Sidney Newsletter*
SP	*Studies in Philology*
UISLL	*University of Illinois Studies in Language and Literature*
UTSE	*University of Texas Studies in English*
UTQ	*University of Toronto Quarterly*
YES	*Yearbook of English Studies*

Notes

Preface

1. *A Woorke concerning the trewnesse of the Christian Religion . . . Against Atheists, Epicures, Paynims, Jewes, Mahumelists, und uther Infidels*, trans. Sir Philip Sidney and Arthur Golding, in *The Complete Works of Sir Philip Sidney*, ed. Albert Feuillerat, 4 vols. (Cambridge: Cambridge Univ. Press, 1912), 3:249–50.

2. The Platonism of Jean de Serres and Sidney's connection to de Serres and to his Platonism have been sleeping giants in literary history. J. E. Sandys in *The History of Classical Scholarship*, 3 vols. (Cambridge: Cambridge Univ. Press, 1906–8), 2:175–76, remarks that de Serres's edition of *Plato* held ground for two centuries as the main edition, and my cursory examination of listings in the British Library supports the point with editions of the *Ion* "cum Serrani interpretatione" (1782), the *Phaedo* "annotatibus Serrani" (1825), and *Platonis . . . Scripta Omnia*, Greek and Latin (1826). Languet's letter to Sidney on the politics of this edition of *Plato* published in 1578 is dated September 24, 1579, and printed in *Epistolae Politicae et Historicae ad Philippum Sydnaeum Equitem Anglum* (Leyden, 1646), p. 394. William A. Ringler called attention to Sidney's knowledge of de Serres's *Plato* in a note in *The Poems of Sir Philip Sidney* (Oxford: Clarendon, 1962), observing the influence of commentaries on the *Symposium* and the *Ion* on the *Defence* (p. 468 n.6). James M. Osborn, *Young Philip Sidney 1572–1577* (New Haven: Yale Univ. Press, 1972), pp. 56–73, discusses Jean de Serres as the French Protestant historian who describes the corruption of the French court at the time of the wedding of the Catholic Marguerite de Valois to the Huguenot Henry of Navarre (at which Sidney was present), who records the events leading to the Saint Bartholomew's Day Massacre on August 24, 1572 (which caused Sidney, Languet, and other Protestants to flee Paris and during which Peter Ramus was killed), and who makes a Protestant hero of the wounded Coligny (whom Sidney may have visited, Osborn says [p. 65]), assassinated early on the morning of the Massacre. The histories were quickly translated into English by T. Timme, and the biography of Coligny by Arthur Golding between 1573 and 1576. In their edition of Sidney's *Miscellaneous Prose* (Oxford: Clarendon, 1973), Duncan-Jones and van Dorsten mention Sidney's reception of the gift of de Serres's *Plato* in 1579, and in my dissertation (University of Wisconsin—Madison, 1977) I discuss the influence of several of de Serres's commentaries in the *Plato* on the *Defence*, arguing at some length (1:184–208) that Sidney took his architectonic philosophy of language from Jean de Serres. Finally, S. K. Heninger, Jr., in "Sidney and Serranus' *Plato*," *ELR* 13 (1983): 146–61, followed through on Ringler's suggestion, translating the commentary on the *Ion*, examining its influence on Sidney's *Defence*, and developing the biographical material on Jean de Serres in several informative notes. This book should further amplify the importance of de Serres's *Plato* in the study of Sidney and other English renaissance poets.

3. Cf. G. W. F. Hegel, *Introduction to the Lectures on the History of Philosophy*, trans. T. M. Knox and A. V. Miller (Oxford: Clarendon, 1985), p. 65, on "the series of shapes which thinking takes" as "the superficial mode in which the history of philosophy appears." Hegel

also discusses self-knowledge and the effort of the spirit to externalize itself in shapes and images (objects), which is a development both differentiating the self and bringing it home. "This being at home with self, this coming to itself, may be called the supreme aim of the spirit," he says, and "to be at home with oneself in the negative of oneself is also the freedom of man" (p. 79). Martin Heidegger, a disciple of Hegel, says in "The Anaximander Fragment," in Early Greek Thinking: The Dawn of Western Philosophy, trans. David Farrell Krell and Frank A. Capuzzi (New York: Harper and Row, 1975), pp. 13–58, that thinking is "poeticizing" (p. 19).

4. Such recovery of an image is a scholarly enterprise of feminism advocated by Margaret W. Ferguson, Maureen Quilligan, and Nancy J. Vickers, eds., *Rewriting the Renaissance: The Discourses of Sexual Difference in Early Modern Europe* (Chicago: Univ. of Chicago Press, 1986), pp. xxi–xxii, because it places in the foreground phenomena and documents that have been overlooked or relegated to the margins of scholarly discourse.

5. Neither A. E. Malloch, "Architectonic Knowledge in Sidney's *Apologie*," *ELH* 20 (1953): 181–85, nor Josephine A. Roberts, *Architectonic Knowledge in the* New Arcadia *(1590): Sidney's Use of the Heroic Journey*, ed. Dr. James Hogg, *Elizabethan and Renaissance Studies*, vol. 69 (Salzburg: Institut für Englische Sprache und Literatur, Universität Salzburg, 1978), acknowledges the feminine personification, although both treat the theme of self-knowledge. That theme has become a commonplace in criticism, and so has the suppression of the mistress-knowledge.

6. See W. A. Ringler, Jr., "Sir Philip Sidney: The Myth and the Man," in *Sir Philip Sidney: 1586 and the Creation of a Legend*, ed. Jan van Dorsten, Dominic Baker-Smith, and Arthur F. Kinney (Leiden: E. J. Brill, 1986), pp. 3–15.

7. *English Literature in the Sixteenth Century* (Oxford: Clarendon, 1954), pp. 1–2, 42–44, 318–25, 343–46.

8. John Addington Symonds, *Sir Philip Sidney* (London: Macmillan, 1886), p. 200. For a superb overview of the rise, fall, and revival of Sidney's literary reputation, see Dennis Kay, "Sidney—A Critical Heritage," in *Sir Philip Sidney: An Anthology of Modern Criticism*, ed. Dennis Kay (Oxford: Clarendon, 1987), pp. 3–41.

9. I. A. Richards, *Principles of Literary Criticism* (1925; reprint, New York: Harcourt, Brace, Jovanovich, 1985); Kenneth Orne Myrick, *Sir Philip Sidney As a Literary Craftsman* (Cambridge, Mass.: Harvard Univ. Press, 1935); William K. Wimsatt and Cleanth Brooks, *Literary Criticism: A Short History* (New York: Knopf, 1957), pp. 169–70. One of the sanest introductions to the problem of Sidney's reputation and critical evaluation remains that of A. C. Hamilton, "Sidney in Life, Legend, and in His Works," in *Sir Philip Sidney: A Study of His Life and Works* (Cambridge: Cambridge Univ. Press, 1977), pp. 1–16: "The movements in current thought to which he was exposed did not lead him to endorse any personal or independent position, in part because he sought instead a synthesis in which opposing points of view were balanced; in part because he had a unifying, rather than a unified, sensibility; and in chief part because he was of an introspective nature which separated him from the world even while he was deeply engaged in it" (p. 13).

10. See Terry Eagleton, *Literary Theory: An Introduction* (Minneapolis: Univ. of Minnesota Press, 1983), pp. 15, 18, 19, 29, 31–49, and cf. the historical scholarship of D. J. Palmer in *The Rise of English Studies: An Account of the Study of English Language and Literature from Its Origins to the Making of the Oxford English School* (New York: Oxford Univ. Press, 1965), pp. 18–19, from which I quote Dale. Curiously, the historical context of Eagleton's argument is remarkably similar to Palmer's, and Eagleton calls his first chapter "The Rise of English" but nowhere cites Palmer. See Palmer, p. 1, on the sixteenth-century point of departure, and see Jerome McGann, *Social Values and Poetic Acts: The Historical Judgment of Literary Work* (Cambridge, Mass.: Harvard Univ. Press, 1988), p. 73, for the cited remark on Sidney. Gerald Graff, *Professing Literature: An Institutional History* (Chicago: Univ. of Chicago Press, 1987), has offered an American version of the rise of English, beginning with the Yale Report of 1828,

the same year as Dale's lecture in London, and Graff does not allude to Palmer's institutional history either.

11. See Jacques Derrida, *Of Grammatology*, trans. Gayatri Chakravorty Spivak (Baltimore: Johns Hopkins Univ. Press, 1976), pp. 6, 18–19, 141–43. Also see Vincent B. Leitch, "The Subversion of Foundations," in *Deconstructive Criticism: An Advanced Introduction* (New York: Columbia Univ. Press, 1983), pp. 24–38, 39–42. Leitch comments that the apparent opposition to traditional hermeneutics in deconstruction may historically mirror an ancient division between Talmudic and Hellenistic modes of examining a text and Gnostic and kabbalistic modes, with deconstruction deriving from the latter (p. 246). But see Betty Roitman's use of deconstructive analysis in her discussion of the Kabbalah, "Sacred Language and Open Text," in *Midrash and Literature*, ed. Geoffrey Hartman and Sanford Budick (New Haven: Yale Univ. Press, 1986), pp. 159–75, in which Roitman poses a final paradox that qualifies indeterminacy by making it compatible with the truth of meaning: "All is determined and yet all is open. This system of thought claims to calculate the metaphysical probability of a radically new act, 'and poses the dialectic of the unpredictable and the absolute" (p. 174). Pico della Mirandola knew the Kabbalah, which is wisdom literature in the Jewish mystical tradition, and Dorothy Connell, *Sir Philip Sidney, the Maker's Mind* (Oxford: Clarendon, 1977), pp. 1–2, suggests that Sidney's knowledge of Pico has not been sufficiently studied. Johannes Reuchlin's *De Arte Cabalistica* would have been published in Latin in 1517, and it is not impossible that Sidney knew it.

12. "Sir Philip Sidney: Pleas for Power," in *Trials of Desire: Renaissance Defenses of Poetry* (New Haven: Yale Univ. Press, 1983), pp. 137–62, 227–34.

13. *The Winter's Tale* 2.1.98 and 5.3.125–28.

14. The definition of intertextuality on which I rely is Julia Kristeva's as described by Jonathan Culler, *Structuralist Poetics: Structuralism, Linguistics, and the Study of Literature* (Ithaca: Cornell Univ. Press, 1975), pp. 139–40. Culler explains Kristeva's *vraisemblance* and its inclination toward parody.

15. See Julia Kristeva, *Desire in Language: A Semiotic Approach to Literature and Art*, ed. Leon S. Roudiez, trans. Thomas Gora et al. (New York: Columbia Univ. Press, 1980), pp. 49–50, on the feminizing and then theologizing of the "other" and its subsequent masculine incorporation into the "same" thing as the self.

16. *Desire in Language*, pp. x–xi. Cf. the longer and earlier French version of this book, *Polylogue* (Paris: Editions du Seuil, 1977), pp. 204–8, on Augustine.

17. *Paideia: The Ideals of Greek Culture*, 2d ed., 3 vols. (New York: Oxford Univ. Press, 1939–44), 1:xxi.

18. See Alan Sinfield, *Literature in Protestant England 1560–1660* (London: Croom Helm, 1983), pp. 23–27, on the design of the *Defence* "to justify literature to the ardent protestant," and cf. F. J. Levy, "Philip Sidney Reconsidered," *ELR* 2 (1972): 5–18, on Sidney's willingness to serve Elizabeth only in her readiness to do God's will.

19. These are mythological identifications and literary parallels extracted from the Oxford and Cambridge funeral miscellanies for Sidney and especially from one of the "Astrophil" elegies for him, "An Epitaph upon the right Honourable sir Philip Sidney knight," which may be found in *Spenser, Poetical Works*, ed. J. C. Smith and E. de Selincourt (London: Oxford Univ. Press, 1912), p. 559. On the miscellanies, see especially Dominic Baker-Smith, "Sidney's Death and the Poets," in *Sir Philip Sidney: 1586*, ed. Jan van Dorsten et al., pp. 83–103.

20. In *"Astrophil and Stella*: A Radical Reading," in *Spenser Studies* (Pittsburgh: Univ. of Pittsburgh Press, 1982), 3:139–91, Thomas P. Roche, Jr., calls Astrophil a "negative example" and comments on Sidney's brilliance in having him end in despair "because he never learns from his experience. The reader is meant to supply the Christian context that will make sense of the insufficiencies of Astrophil's insights into his predicament" (pp. 142–43).

21. See, for example, Heiko A. Oberman, *"Die Gelehrten die Verkehrten*: Popular Response to Learned Culture in the Renaissance and Reformation," in *Religion & Culture in the Renais-*

sance and Reformation, ed. Steven Ozment, *Sixteenth-Century Essays & Studies* 11 (1989): 43–62, on the manner in which a "learned culture" had such an impact on the populace that literacy grew by leaps and bounds and confidence in the contribution of learning to Church and society developed alongside suspicion of scholars (p. 46).

22. See C. L. Greenslade, *The English Reformers and the Fathers of the Church* (Oxford: Clarendon, 1960), and "The Authority of the Tradition of the Early Church in Early Anglican Thought," *Tradition im Luthertum und Anglikanismus*, *Oecumenica* (1971): 9–33. Also see William P. Haaugaard, "Renaissance Patristic Scholarship and Theology in Sixteenth-Century England," *Sixteenth-Century Journal* 10 (1979): 37–60, and Henry Chadwick, "Tradition, Fathers, and Councils," in *The Study of Anglicanism*, ed. Stephen Sykes and John Booty (Philadelphia: Fortress, 1988), pp. 91–105.

23. Steven Ozment, "Luther and the Late Middle Ages: The Formation of Reformation Thought," in *Transition and Revolution: Problems and Issues of European Renaissance and Reformation History*, ed. Robert Kingdon (Minneapolis: Burgess Pub. Co., 1974), pp. 109–29.

24. See especially Merry E. Wiesner, "Beyond Women and the Family: Towards a Gender Analysis of the Reformation," *Sixteenth-Century Journal* 18 (1987): 311–21, and Allison P. Coudert, "The Myth of the Improved Status of Protestant Women: The Case of the Witchcraze," in *The Politics of Gender in Early Modern Europe*, ed. Jean R. Brink et al., *Sixteenth-Century Essays & Studies* 12 (1989): 61–90. On du Plessis Mornay and androgyny, see Robert Kimbrough, *Shakespeare and the Art of Humankindness: The Essay Toward Androgyny* (Atlantic Highlands, N. J.: The Humanities Press, 1990), pp. 41–43.

25. *Sir Philip Sidney and the Poetics of Protestantism* (Minneapolis: Univ. of Minnesota Press, 1978). See also Diane Borstein, *The Countess of Pembroke's Translation of Philippe de Mornay's Discourse of Life and Death* (Detroit: Medieval and Renaissance Monographs, 1983).

26. "Moving and Teaching: Sidney's *Defence of Poesie* as a Protestant Poetic," *JMRS* 2 (1972): 259–78; see pp. 267–68.

27. *The Shape of Things Known: Sidney's Apology in Its Philosophical Tradition* (Cambridge, Mass.: Harvard Univ. Press, 1972).

28. *Protestant Poetics and the Seventeenth-Century Religious Lyric* (Princeton, N.J.: Princeton Univ. Press, 1979).

29. Eugene Rice, *The Renaissance Idea of Wisdom* (Cambridge, Mass.: Harvard Univ. Press, 1958), p. 209, and Antonio V. Romualdez, "Towards a History of the Renaissance Idea of Wisdom," *Studies in the Renaissance* 11 (1964): 133–54.

30. Annabel Patterson, *Censorship and Interpretation: The Conditions of Writing and Reading in Early Modern England* (Madison: Univ. of Wisconsin Press, 1984), pp. 5–7; by way of isolating her particular subject, Patterson focuses on the hermeneutics of censorship in secular texts in which, she says, it can be more cogently interrogated than in biblical hermeneutics (p. 7). I do not think we can make such a division except in the scholarly necessity of trying to narrow down one's material. See also Patricia Parker, *Literary Fat Ladies: Rhetoric, Gender, Property* (London: Methuen, 1987), pp. 8–17, 26–35.

31. See "Literature in the Reader: Affective Stylistics," *NLH* 2 (1970): 126–27, and S. K. Heninger, Jr.'s quarrel with it in *Touches of Sweet Harmony: Pythagorean Cosmology and Renaissance Poetics* (San Marino, Calif.: Huntington Library, 1974), p. x, and my praise and qualification of *Touches of Sweet Harmony* in a review-article, *Shakespeare Studies* 10 (1977): 357–65. Most recently Heninger has returned to the problem of the informed reader and the idea of the poet as maker in *Sidney and Spenser: The Poet as Maker* (University Park: Pennsylvania State Univ. Press, 1989), p. 53; but in discussing Sidney's "poetics of making," Heninger suggests a sympathy with Derrida and Barthes, too (p. xi), and Iser (p. 31); see also pp. 507–8 n.32, on the "artifact." The numinosity of the mistress-knowledge poesie challenges and counterpoints the idea of the poem as a technological machine.

32. Maureen Quilligan calls the *Defence* an oration "written to be read" in comparing it to Milton's *Areopagitica* in *Milton's Spenser: The Politics of Reading* (Ithaca: Cornell Univ. Press,

1983), pp. 31–36. One of the most apt, although brief, readings of the *Defence* as a "public oration" engaging the reader in an instructive process of judgment is Victoria Kahn's in *Rhetoric, Prudence, and Skepticism in the Renaissance* (Ithaca, N.Y.: Cornell Univ. Press, 1985), pp. 188–90, which I shall discuss more fully in the Epilogue.

33. The quotation is from one of the Sidney elegies in *Spenser, Poetical Works*, p. 560.

Chapter 1

1. On Sidney's *energia*, see Quintilian *Institutio Oratoria* 3.8.89, trans. H. E. Butler (Cambridge, Mass.: Harvard Univ. Press, 1920–21); Neil Rudenstine, *Sidney's Poetic Development* (Cambridge, Mass.: Harvard Univ. Press, 1967), chapter 10; Annabel M. Patterson, *Hermogenes and the Renaissance: Seven Ideas of Style* (Princeton, N.J.: Princeton Univ. Press, 1970), pp. 129–36; and Forrest Robinson, *The Shape of Things Known: Sidney's Apology in Its Philosophical Tradition* (Cambridge, Mass.: Harvard Univ. Press, 1972), pp. 130–31. Robinson also provides a bibliographical note on *energia* (pp. 130–31) and disagrees with Rudenstine (p. 169).

2. See Elder Olson, "The Poetic Method of Aristotle: Its Powers and Limitations," in *Aristotle's 'Poetics' and English Literature* (Chicago: Univ. of Chicago Press, 1965), pp. 175–91, and Richard P. McKeon, "Literary Criticism and the Concept of Imitation in Antiquity," *MP* 24 (1963): 1–35. Also see Bernard Weinberg, *History of Literary Criticism in the Italian Renaissance*, 2 vols. (Chicago: Univ. of Chicago Press, 1961), 2:799–813.

3. Here is the passage in full:

Videri autem posset illius, quae summam potestam habet. & maxime tamquam regina reliquarum est. Huiuscemodi autem facultas ciuilis perspicitur esse: quas enim opus est scientia esse in ciuitatibus. & quales singulos perdiscere, & quatenus, haes statuit. Videmus autem & facultates eas, quae maximo in honore sunt, sub jac esse, ceu artem ducis exercitus, disciplinam domesticam, artem dicendi.

Public speaking is characteristically the "domestic" discipline. Besides the *Commentarii in X Libros Aristotelis, De Moribus ad Nicomachum* (Florence, 1584), from the first page of which this passage is cited, Vettori also composed the *Commentarii, In Primum Librum Aristotelis de Arte Poetarum* (1st ed., Florence, 1560; 2d ed., Florence, 1573), which Weinberg discusses extensively in his *History of Literary Criticism* 1:461–66 and considers the only major commentary at midcentury (1:475) before the great commentaries of the seventies.

4. I shall discuss this confusion and its origin in the Epilogue; here it is sufficient illustration to observe the problem in mid-twentieth-century literary studies of renaissance texts, especially Milton. For example, see Alexander Sackton's essay, "Architectonic Structure in *Paradise Regained*," *UTSE* 33 (1954): 33–45, in which Sackton suppressed the problem of "architectural metaphor," the "preconceived plan," and the " 'architectonic' quality" of the poem in relation to "building construction" and the balance of parts by taking the general sense of the term as applied to literature to be clear enough.

5. I am borrowing from Barbara Johnson's lucid discussion of deconstruction and sexual difference in her book, *The Critical Difference: Essays in the Contemporary Rhetoric of Reading* (Baltimore: Johns Hopkins Univ. Press, 1980), pp. ix–xii, 3–12. But on the "double science" and "double writing" of Western hierarchical terms, see Jacques Derrida, *Dissemination*, trans. Barbara Johnson (Chicago: Univ. of Chicago Press, 1981), pp. 4–7.

6. *Libri Septem* (Lyons, 1561) 3.48, p. 126:

Prosopopoeia verò duplex est. Primus modus, vbi ficta persona introducitur, vt Fama a Virgilio, & Fames ab Ouidio. Haec non est figura, sed pars argumenti poetici. hanc fictionem appellat Quintilianus ἰδεῶν: vt Dirarum, & Irae, & Furoris. . . . Alterum genus Prosopopoeiae, vbi non persona fingitur eo modo, sed orationis attributione. quae adeò pertinet ad διατύπωσιν, vt supra eius partem secerimus Sermocinationem.

7. Cf. Margaret Ferguson's note on Sidney's allusion to David's prosopopoeias as "sometimes" the personification of "inanimate objects" and sometimes the "giving voice to an absent or imaginary person" (p. 229 n.21). The note addresses Ferguson's remarks in her essay, "Plea for Power," in *Trials of Desire: Renaissance Defenses of Poetry* (New Haven: Yale Univ. Press, 1983), pp. 137–62, at the point at which she refers to the section in which Sidney coins the figure of the mistress-knowledge. See my Preface and n.12. Ferguson *deletes* the figure in her quotation, replacing it with her interpretative word *wisdom*, which is also mine, though with a different sense. Ferguson uses Puttenham's limited definition of prosopopoeia (*Arte of English Poesie* 3:19), which postdates Sidney's *Defence*, and I use Scaliger's and Quintilian's definitions, which antedate the text. Ferguson's *wisdom* is also an epistemological standard:

> By the trope of *prosopopeia* [sic] ("counterfeit in personation") Sidney makes poetry's rivals each voice its own claim to be the best guide to wisdom, "which stands . . . in the knowledge of man's self in the ethic and politic consideration, with the end of well-doing and not of well-knowing only." (P. 142)

Scaliger's definition of the second mode of personification quite amply explains the nature of division in Sidney's disputation as a type of quite conscious sermocination, or conversation either with oneself or with others or both; this kind of discourse has the feeling of a dialogue about it, and that, no doubt, accounts for Ferguson's use of Bakhtin's "dialogics" to examine the *Defence*. In this respect see also Jonathan Crewe, *Hidden Designs: The Critical Profession and Renaissance Literature* (New York: Methuen, 1986), in which he asserts the adequate supply of definitions of *poesis* in renaissance works, including *poesis* as vaticination, as "making," as personifying, and as "representing that which is normally mute, absent, or unconceived (*prosopopoeia*)," with which I tend to agree (p. 17). I do not agree with his remarks "*contra* historicism" on the same page, however, in which he splits "the historical period or its particular ensemble of significations and cultural-political strategies" from the phenomenon of *poesis* as the object of criticism.

8. Again, see Ferguson's discussion (pp. 160–61), which makes splendid associations between the "letter" and the *Defence*, and her notes on the subject in *Trials of Desire* (pp. 233–34 nn.63–67). The suggestion of Erasmus's *Prosopopoeia* as a model is one of my "historicist" observations.

9. See the *Nicomachean Ethics* 1.1.4 and 1.2.4 (1094a), trans. H. Rackham, Loeb Edition (London: William Heinemann, 1926), pp. 3–5. Aristotle's first use of the word is plural and genitive regarding the fact that "the ends of the master arts [ἀρχιτεκτονικῶν τέλη] are to be desired more than all those of the arts subordinate to them" (1.1.4). Cf. *Nicomachean Ethics* 1.3 (1095a); 1.6 (1097). Sidney turns Aristotle's bridle-making and the trades concerned with harness into the making of a "good saddle" (*Def.*, p. 83). The nominative plural form of the noun is feminine, too, and is ἀρχιτεκτονικαί.

10. *The First & Chief Groundes of Architecture by John Shute, Paynter and Archytecte* was first printed by Thomas Marshe in 1563. I have seen the facsimile of the first edition with an introduction by Lawrence Weaver of the Reform Club (London: Country Life, 1912 [Limited/ 20]), sig. A.ij^v of the letter to the reader, in which Shute commends the learning that makes men "most like immortall Goddes." Only five copies of Shute's work are extant, including those copies in the Bodleian, the University Library at Cambridge, and Trinity College Library, Dublin. Joseph Ames and William Herbert in their *Typographical Antiquities; or, The History of Printing in England*, 4 vols. (London: W. Miller, 1810–19), note the edition of 1579 as having a colophon of 1580; Maunsell in his *Catalogue* of 1595 notes an edition of 1584 in reference to John Evelyn's comment on Shute, "our country-man whose book being printed in 1584 (and one of the first that was published of architecture in the English tongue)." There is no entry in the Stationers' Register for the edition of 1579–80, which was probably a reprint of the 1563 edition. Shute suitably dedicated his volume to Queen Elizabeth, referring to his

service to the Duke of Northumberland and his trip around Italy in 1550 or thereabouts to look at the monuments (sig. A.ij^r). I am indebted to Professor Mario Valmarana of the University of Virginia School of Architecture for this information.

11. See Catherine Barnes, "The Hidden Persuader: The Complex Speaking Voice of Sidney's *Defence* of Poetry," *PMLA* 86 (1971): 422–27; Robert M. Strozier, "Poetic Conception in Sir Philip Sidney's *An Apology for Poetry*," *YES* 2 (1972): 49–60; Martin Raitiere, "The Unity of Sidney's *Apology for Poetry*," *SEL 1500–1900* 21 (1981): 37–57; and A. Leigh DeNeef, "Rereading Sidney's Apology," *JMRS* 10 (1982): 155–92. Barnes especially addresses the irony and the beguiling psychology of the opening of the *Defence* rather than its logical argumentation; see Ferguson's view of Pugliano in *Trials of Desire*, pp. 138, 151–55, 228 n.5, 230 n.37, 231 n.42. Strozier discusses Sidney's conception of phenomena and the relation of nature and art as a strategy for unity of thought and structure. The integrating metaphor is missing from discussion.

12. Here I could not agree more with Margaret Ferguson's discussion of the commonplace critical judgment of a division between style and content in the *Defence* (*Trials of Desire*, p. 138); but I do not find the same kind of choice between error and the inevitability of error obtaining in the *exordium* and the *peroratio* as she does (p. 155), partly because she is reading Sidney's allegory for "difference" and I am reading it for similarity; likewise Ferguson's allegory is a principle of duplicity and an ironic doubling while mine is a sustained pattern of analogies and antitheses that takes the theme of horsemanship and poetry all the way through the text.

13. *Life of Sidney* (1652), pp. 20–21. A. K. Taylor has written a dissertation on the subject of *ménage* entitled "The *Ménage* of Love and Authority: Studies in Sidney and Shakespeare" (Ph.D. diss., University of Texas, 1969) in which she examines the metaphor as a symbol of the rational mind controlling passion. Sidney has incorporated this Platonic notion of the dominance of the will over the body into his Aristotelian architectonic hierarchy, which puts the trade of harness-making under horsemanship and horsemanship under military science, and so forth, all the way to the mastercraftsmanship of politics at the top, both in the *Defence* and in a subsequence of sonnets in *Astrophil and Stella*.

14. Consider the title of the Norwich Manuscript of the *Defence*, "A Treatise of Horseman Shipp."

15. Here Margaret Ferguson's discussion of the *Defence* as a "quasi-autobiographical" allegory in the rhetorical mode is useful for its insights into Sidney's political motivations; nevertheless, the rhetorical allegory that my reading will develop in chapter 2 out of the traditional allegory of Sophia and Conscience still results in a different interpretation. Ferguson's Freudian reading of Sidney's courtly and duplicitous allegory depends on motives hidden in Sidney's speech stylistically and constructed toward the manipulation of the reader, particularly if one of the readers imagined by Sidney is the Queen herself; my reading of the rhetorical kind of allegory in which the figure of the Queen is quite openly presented in the type of the mistress-knowledge suggests instead that Sidney is hardly veiled at all. His plea for power, then, is not hidden but quite overt as a standard piece of courtly flattery having a dangerous tone of parody. When this rhetorical allegory is combined with the more philosophical and symbolic kind, moreover, the flattery and parody tend to disappear in Sidney's high motives to persuade his Queen to a certain kind of goodness. Ferguson makes the astute comment that in the *Letter* to the Queen Sidney assumes the role of "orator-teacher" to the Queen (*Trials of Desire*, p. 160), and it may be useful to incorporate some awareness of that function in interpretations of the *Defence*, too.

16. *ELH* 20 (1953): 181–85; cf. Duncan-Jones and van Dorsten, *Miscellaneous Prose*, p. 193 nn.82.28–83.9; and Forrest Robinson, ed., *An Apology for Poetry* (Indianapolis: Bobbs-Merrill, 1970), p. 23. At stake is the understanding that Aristotle did not separate the architectonic organization of the arts and sciences from the architectonic achievement of virtue but sought to integrate them. Ronald Levao, *Renaissance Minds and Their Fictions: Cusanus, Sidney, Shake-*

speare (Berkeley: Univ. of California Press, 1985), p. 140, also faults Malloch's understanding of the subject-object relation in poetry and the way, in Sidney's estimation, it produces "many Circes" (*Defense*, p. 70).

17. The *Defense of Poesy* (Boston: Ginn, 1890), pp. xxiv–xxxii. Cook rightly discusses the mediating role of poetry in Sidney's view and explains how Sidney gradually gives ethics a divine sanction through religion and then gives poetry the moving power to fulfill that ethics: "We can thus understand how Sidney the Puritan was also Sidney the poet, and how religion and creative poetry were to him almost as sisters." Disagreeing with Cook, Murray Bundy in his introduction to Ruth Kelso's translation of *Naugerius, siue De Poetica Dialogus*, UISLL, vol. 9, no. 3 (1924), p. 10 n.1, says that "Sidney aims to show not that poetry is the architectonic science but that it is a prince in relation to the other serving sciences." On Sidney and Fracastoro, see chapter 5, pp. 319–21. Geoffrey Shepherd, ed., *An Apology for Poetry* (London: Thomas Nelson and Sons, 1965; Manchester: Manchester Univ. Press, 1973), compliments Cook's notes (p. xi) and concurs on the definition of architectonic poetry in his own superb introduction and notes (pp. 30–31, 167–68).

18. See Madeleine K. Doran, *Endeavors of Art: A Study of Form in Elizabethan Drama* (Madison: Univ. of Wisconsin Press, 1954), pp. 54–61, and Edward W. Tayler, *Nature and Art in Renaissance Literature* (New York: Columbia Univ. Press, 1964), pp. 30–31, 48–49. The critical interpretation of Sidney's Platonism, to which much of this book is dedicated, has often stumbled on difficulties associated with verisimilitude and its concept of proportionality or likeness. See Mark Roberts, "The Pill and the Cherries: Sidney and the Neo-Classical Tradition," *Essays in Criticism* 16 (1966): 22–32, on the ambiguity of "delight" aimed at moral edification, and compare the discussion of wisdom and pleasure in Plato's *Philebus*, for example. Cf. Duncan-Jones and van Dorsten on the Protestant view of the "inward light" in Sidney's idea that poetry can make a "better" nature by diminishing the opposition between wit and will (*Miscellaneous Prose*, p. 198 nn.91.3ff.). Also see Virginia Hyman, "Sidney's Definition of Poetry," *SEL 1500–1900* 10 (1970): 49–62, on the partial influence of Plato and the ladder of becoming on the *Defence*, on Sidney's rejection of the identification of the poet with divinity, and on the generativity of the poet's ideas.

19. Cf. Louis Adrian Montrose's discussion of the New Historicism and of Spenser's handling of his subject-sovereign relationship to Queen Elizabeth in "The Elizabethan Subject and the Spenserian Text," in *Literary Theory/Renaissance Texts*, ed. Patricia Parker and David Quint (Baltimore: Johns Hopkins Univ. Press, 1986), pp. 303–40, especially pp. 303–18. "Every representation of power is also an appropriation of power" (p. 331). For a definition of *appropriation*, see Robert Weimann, " 'Appropriation' and Modern History in Renaissance Prose Narrative," *NLH* 14 (1983): 459–95. Sidney's moral coupling of poesie and the poet constitutes what Patricia Parker calls a "copular" or "anagogic" metaphor that transcends syntax and logic in "Anagogic Metaphor: Breaking Down the Wall of Partition," in *Centre and Labyrinth: Essays in Honor of Northrop Frye*, ed. Eleanor Cooke et al. (Toronto: Univ. of Toronto Press, 1983), pp. 38–58.

20. The early advice of Sir Henry Sidney, Philip's father, to his son at Shrewsbury marks this educational practice of reading for sense, matter, vocabulary, judgment, and virtue ("A Very Godly Letter" [ca. 1566; London: T. Dawson, 1591; Oxford, 1929], sig. A2ᵛ-A3ʳ). Cf. W. H. Woodward, *Studies in Education During the Age of the Renaissance 1400–1600* (Cambridge: Cambridge Univ. Press, 1924), and the early chapters of Donald Lemen Clark, *Milton at Saint Paul's School* (New York: Columbia Univ. Press, 1948), on the humanist program of learning and piety and the humanist practice of seeking virtuous action out of knowledge. Joel Altman discusses renaissance education in the art of rhetorical antithesis in *The Tudor Play of Mind* (Berkeley: Univ. of California Press, 1978). The letter to Robert is in *The Complete Works of Sir Philip Sidney*, ed. Albert Feuillerat, 4 vols. (Cambridge: Cambridge Univ. Press, 1912), 3:124–33; the letter to Ned Denny is reprinted in James M. Osborn, *Young Philip Sidney 1572–1577* (New Haven: Yale Univ. Press, 1972), pp. 537–40 on the pursuit of knowledge through read-

ing. For a discussion of the question of gender in reading, see Elizabeth A. Flynn and Patrocinio P. Schweickart, eds., *Gender and Reading: Essays on Readers, Texts, and Contexts* (Baltimore: Johns Hopkins Univ. Press, 1986). See especially pp. 35–45 of Schweickart's essay, "Reading Ourselves: Toward a Feminist Theory of Reading" (pp. 31–62).

21. For the appearance of Cyrus in Holy Scripture and his role in the rebuilding of the Temple, see Isaiah 44:28 and Daniel 9:21–27, especially the gloss on the numerology of the years taken up in leaving captivity and reconstructing in the Geneva Bible of 1560 (p. 363) and, in the Apocrypha included in the Geneva Bible, 1 Esdras 5:55–63 and 6:17–23. Saint Paul uses the metaphor of edification and temple-building without mentioning Cyrus in 1 Corinthians 3:9–17 in the philosophical context of his paradoxical definitions of Christian folly and wisdom.

22. See Annabel Patterson, *Censorship and Interpretation: The Conditions of Writing and Reading in Early Modern England* (Madison: Univ. of Wisconsin Press, 1984), pp. 25–29, on the "disguised discourse" of the *Arcadia*, on Sidney's involvement in parliamentary debates on censorship, and on the relationship between the *Defence* and *Arcadia* regarding literature and the sociopolitical experience (p. 28). Patterson aims her argument at the use made of the *Arcadia* in seventeenth-century politics, and her comments on the role of Greville's *Life of Sidney*, composed around 1610 or 1612 but printed in 1652, are equally illuminating (pp. 24–25). Arthur Kinney, "Sir Philip Sidney and the Uses of History," in *The Historical Renaissance: New Essays on Tudor and Stuart Literature and Culture*, ed. Heather Dubrow and Richard Strier (Chicago: Univ. of Chicago Press, 1988), pp. 293–314, briefly mentions Sidney's "citation of Xenophon's *Cyropaedia* as a new *paideia*" in the *Defence* and largely clarifies the application of the model of Cyrus to the development of the past and present in the *Arcadia*. Kinney concludes that Sidney's fictional use of history had a great deal to do with the revival of interest in history and the transformation of the historian's concept of his function.

23. Bercker's translation was published in London in 1567; see p. 25 on Bercker's earlier translation of Saint Basil's *ars legendi*.

24. See Terry Eagleton's parody of this axiom of the circumferenceless circle in his discussion of Matthew Arnold in *The Function of Criticism from the Spectator to Post-Structuralism* (London: Verso Editions, 1984), pp. 61–62, and cf. the usage made of Menander's axiom by Peter Ramus in the Renaissance discussed on pp. 48–51 of this chapter.

25. The critical argument over Sidney's knowledge and appreciation of du Bartas, like the debate over Sidney's use of Plato, centers on what Sidney thought about "divine" poetry. See E. K. Gregory, Jr., "Du Bartas, Sidney, and Spenser," *CLS* 7 (1970): 437–49, and Alan Sinfield, "Sidney and du Bartas," *CL* 27 (1975): 8–20. Du Bartas expresses theologically several doctrines of the architectonic metaphor; the *Diuine Weekes* begins with a prayer to the "great Architect of wonders, / Whose mighty Voyce speakes in the midst of Thunders" and goes on to speak of the world as "this Frame; wherein / (As in a Glasse) God's glorious face is seen" (trans. Joshua Sylvester [London, 1621], pp. 1–3). The particular items out of which du Bartas makes metaphors are also architectonic analogues, for he compares the world to a school, a pair of stairs, a sumptuous hall, a wealthy shop, a bridge, a cloud, a stage, and "a Book in Folio" in which "Each Creature is a Page; and each Effect, / A faire Character" (pp. 4–5). Finally du Bartas compares the construction of this "Book" to architectural construction in order to contrast to God's architectonic creation out of nothing. The architect building a stately palace for a prince may examine various edifices selectively and out of thirty models "digest" one house, but the divine Author did not settle "on some fantastik fore-conceited Plot: / Much less did he an elder World erect, / By form whereof, he might his Frame erect" (p. 5). God "invents" purely, and by analogy so must the architectonic poet invent purely. Cf. Derrida's discussion of Hegel, Novalis, Mallarmé, the encyclopedia, the "Book," and "literature" in *Dissemination*, trans. Johnson, pp. 50–55. Although he appeals to some medieval and renaissance ideas, Derrida steadfastly assesses them in a post-eighteenth-century fashion.

26. Cf. Aristotle's *Nicomachean Ethics* 10.9 (1179b–1181b) on the necessity of law in the

nurture and education of the young and of society at large; also cf. *Rhetoric* 1.1 (1355a); 1.2 (1356a). Cf. the *Defence*, p. 118, and Cicero's *De Oratore* 1.50.218, trans. E. W. Sutton and H. Rackham (London: William Heinemann, 1942). "Drawing men by the ears" is a rhetorical commonplace that Sidney leases in his picture of Hercules led by the ears by Limphnir (*Defence*, pp. 92, 115).

27. Martin Heidegger, "The Anaximander Fragment," in *Early Greek Thinking. The Dawn of Western Philosophy*, trans. David Farrell Krell and Frank A. Capuzzi (New York: Harper and Row, 1975), p. 19. Like other classical treatises on education, Plutarch's essay on the nurture and education of children, which inaugurates his *Moralia* and which Sir Thomas Elyot translated in 1533, had a celebrated textual history in the Renaissance; this included Leonardo Bruni's translation in the late fifteenth century. Numerous Latin versions and reprints of Bruni followed. A multilingual edition coupled the essay with Isocrates and with a compendium of Christian ethics: *Libelli Aliquot Formandis, tum Inuentutis Moribus tam Linguae Graecae, Latinae, Gallicae & Germanicae Utilissimi* was printed by John Cherpontus for Eustathius Vignon in 1581 in parallel columns, and it contained Plutarch's *Libellus de Puerorum Educatione*, Isocrates' orations *Ad Demonicum* and *Ad Nicoclem*, and a kind of catechism, the *Ethices Christianae*, which distinguishes the philosopher's definition of virtue and its origins in human nature from Christian recognition of God alone as the source of all good and the proper seat of all virtue. I cannot prove that Sidney knew this edition, but its thinking is, in any case, compatible with his. Plutarch is discussed in terms of Cicero's statement that man produces himself and his republic from within his own potentialities; so parents ought to educate their sons in letters and in the liberal arts and sciences—especially those of language, which are so necessary in times when it is easy to experience the confusion of Babel (sig. A.ij^r). The orations of Isocrates concern, respectively, a general and a particular persuasion to the service of the republic (sig. A.iii^v), and the catechism comes to Cherpontus from a disciple of Lambert Daneau in Geneva (sig. A.iiij^r). According to Thomas Zouch, *Memoirs of the Life and Writings of Sir Philip Sidney* (York, Eng.: Thomas Wilson, 1808), p. 306, Daneau met and admired Sidney. The pertinent essays of Plutarch on the *ars legendi* are "Of the Nouriture and Education of Children" (pp. 1–16); "Reading and Hearing of Poemes and Poets" (pp. 17–50); and "Of Hearing" (pp. 50–54). I cite Philemon Holland's translation of Plutarch's *The Philosophie, commonlie called, the Morals* (London, 1603). For a good overview of our contemporary revival in reading, see Elizabeth Freund, *Return of the Reader: Reader-Response Criticism* (New York: Methuen, 1987).

28. Cf. Ferguson's similar discussion of Plutarch in Sidney's *Defence* (*Trials of Desire*, pp. 140–41, 147–79). Ferguson notes that Sidney uses a "Christian metaphysical frame for turning around the moralist's charge against poetry" (p. 147), but she does not pursue discussion of Sidney's Christian aesthetics. Likewise Ferguson indicates that Sidney "adopts Plutarch's notion of a strong reader but rejects his faith in the moral authority of philosophy" (p. 149). She argues Sidney's borrowing of two defensive strategies for the reader from Plutarch: the "aesthetic shield" and "critical faculties" (p. 149).

29. See S. K. Heninger, Jr., *Sidney and Spenser: The Poet As Maker* (University Park: Pennsylvania State Univ. Press, 1989), pp. 171–77; Heninger gives a full reading to Sidney's Plutarch but neglects Saint Basil.

30. "Address to Young Men," in *The Letters*, trans. Roy J. DeFerrari (Cambridge, Mass.: Harvard Univ. Press, 1934), 4:365–435. Saint Basil's letter, usually known in renaissance editions as *De legendis libris saecularibus* or *De institutis iuvenum* or *De legendis libris*, was printed as early as 1470 and went through numerous publications by humanists, often in Leonardo Bruni Aretinus's Latin. Bruni's epistle to Coluccio Salutati was published with it, "In magni Basilii librum ad juvenes," and the texts often accompanied Plutarch's *De liberis educandis* and the educational treatise by Vergerius, *De ingenuis moribus & liberalibus studiis adolescentiae*. See Luzi Schucan, "Das Nachleben von Basilius Magnus 'Ad Adolescentes,'" *Travaux d'Humanisme et Renaissance*, 133 (Geneva: Librairie Droz, 1973), for a survey of the

provenance of the text and for an extensive bibliography. The modern translator Roy J. DeFerrari refers to Jacks's *Saint Basil and Greek Literature* (p. 42) to mention twenty-four easily traceable references to Plutarch in the letter (p. 367). The British Library has a copy of letters, *Basilii Magni, et Gregorii Nazanzeni, Theologorum, Epistolae Graecae*, ed. V. Opsopoeus (Haganoa, 1528), that is stamped with the names of Lord and Lady Burghley, William and Myldred Cicyll, and with her autograph, but *Ad Adolescentes* does not appear to be among these letters. See F. M. Padelford, *Essays on the Study and Use of Poetry by Plutarch and Basil the Great* (New York: H. Holt, 1902), and H. D. Betz, *Plutarch's Theological Writings and Early Christian Literature* (Leiden: Brill, 1975).

31. *Ad Adolescentes* 2.383; 4.391; on the analogy of the bee, see Pliny *Natural History* 11.10.22–24, and Plutarch's "Reading and Hearing of Poemes and Poets," in *Philosophie*, trans. Holland, p. 43, and Isocrates *Ad Demonicum* 52; Saint John Chrysostom and Saint Gregory Nazianzus also use this commonplace. Judith Dundas has beautifully exposed this critical analogy for art—and its counterpart, the weaving of the spider—in her book, *The Spider and the Bee: The Artistry of Spenser's Faerie Queene* (Urbana: Univ. of Illinois Press, 1985), to discuss two kinds of poetic form; see especially pp. 1–33.

32. I disagree here with S. K. Heninger's strict adherence to merely *one* of Sidney's statements in the *Defence* in which he apparently rejects the doctrine of divine inspiration in poesie ("Sidney and Serranus' *Plato*," *ELR* 13 [1983]: 146–61). For a fuller discussion, see chapter 4, pp. 238–46 and nn. 28–40. The proper renaissance aesthetic context in which to read the analogy of the three kinds of poets and Sidney's triangulation of the inventive poet, nature, and God as "makers" is described by John Steadman, *The Lamb and the Elephant: Ideal Imitation and the Context of Renaissance Allegory* (San Marino, Calif.: Huntington Library, 1974), pp. xix–xxiv, on the identification of poesie as a "divine Science"; Steadman has qualifications about assuming that all renaissance poets in practice "consciously subordinated poetics to the ends of theology or moral philosophy" (p. xviii). Throughout the *Defence* Sidney appeals several times to the analogy between human poesis and the mysterious science of divine making out of nothing. Because Sidney's treatise is more a metaphoric discourse than a linear or sequential presentation of logical predications, one must read it by juxtaposing passages with other passages.

33. In *The Rule of Reason* (London, 1551) cf. Thomas Wilson's classification of geometry not as a science in the Aristotelian sense but as the practical craft of carpentry and measuring while logic is occupied "aboute all matters" and rhetoric feminized and reduced to the "gay paincted sentences" or verbal cosmetics of style (sig. B2^r-B3^r). Also cf. Puttenham's distinction of the poet's inventive art from the way nature makes and even from the artificial craft of "the carpenter that builds a house" (3.25), in *The Arte of English Poesie* (London, 1589) in facsimile, ed. Baxter Hathaway (Kent, Ohio: Kent State Univ. Press, 1970). For one view of how Sidney's faith affects his theory of inspiration, see Andrew D. Weiner, "Moving and Teaching: Sidney's *Defence of Poesie* as a Protestant Poetic," *JMRS* 2 (1972): 259–78.

34. "To the moste Vertvouvs and Noble Qvene Elisabet," sig. ∴ii^r–∴iii^v, in *The Bible and Holy Scriptures Conteyned in the Olde and Newe Testament* (Geneva: Rouland Hall, 1560) in facsimile, ed. Lloyd E. Berry (Madison: Univ. of Wisconsin Press, 1969).

35. A summary of the history of the ladder may be found in the *Dictionnaire de spiritualité*, s.v. "Échelle spirituelle," in an article by Émile Bertaud and André Rayez (4:62–86). The scriptural analogues were primarily developed by Origen in his commentary on the Song of Songs with respect to the concept of spiritual ascent implied in the *Symposium*. Origen's purgative, illuminative, and unitive degrees entered medieval theology, as did Saint John Climacus's *Ladder of Divine Ascent*, and almost every important theologian or monastic writer mentions the idea of the ascent, often in reference to Origen's commentary on the Song of Songs. The fact that Jean de Serres interprets the Platonic allegory of love in the *Symposium* with reference to the Song of Songs also shows the influence to be a relatively standard one. See Saint Jerome's letter "To Furia" 54.6, in *The Principal Works of Saint Jerome*, trans. W. H.

Freemantle, vol. 6 of *A Select Library of Nicene and Post-Nicene Fathers of the Christian Church*, 2d ser. (1892; reprint, Grand Rapids, Mich.: Eerdmans, 1979), p. 104, on how the Christian life is the true Jacob's ladder on which the angels ascend and descend, and cf. Saint Gregory of Nyssa on the ladder of beatitudes (PL 44:1254), 1488, 1494). Most of all see Saint Augustine's identification of Christ as both the mountain that the Christian climbs and the ladder for climbing (PL 37:1397, 1000). C. A. Patrides discusses the ladder as a topos in *Premises and Motifs in Renaissance Thought and Literature* (Princeton, N.J.: Princeton Univ. Press, 1982), pp. 31–51.

36. See Saint Bonaventure's view in the *Itinerarium* 1.3-5; 2.1; 4.2, trans. José de Vinck (*The Works of Bonaventure*, 3 vols. [Paterson, N.J.: St. Anthony Guild Press, 1960]), on the divine craftsmanship of mirror and ladder and on the soul's conformation to heavenly Jerusalem. Bonaventure had exclaimed that "Christ is our ladder, our ladder and our vehicle." Self-knowledge, epistemology, and soteriology gather together in the figure, for

> it was impossible for men to rise completely from the pit of the senses to the true seeing of themselves, and, within themselves, [to the seeing] of the Eternal Truth [Verbum] until that Truth, assuming human nature in the Person of Christ, became unto them a ladder, restoring the first ladder broken by Adam. (1:36)

The doctrine of the ladder is analogical in its very form: Christ makes proportions between God and men; Christ mediates. "And so all ascension to the knowledge of God is perilous unless one has the humility of Christ crucified," Luther says in "De Assumptione Beatae Mariae Virginis" (*Werke*, 63 vols. [Weimar: Herman Böhlaus, 1886], 4:647; cf. 16:114.144–45 [pub. 1899]). See Andrew Louth on distinguishing Platonic doctrine from more strictly Christian doctrine: in the Platonic framework the soul's search for God is naturally seen as a return, an ascent to God, while the Christian framework of the Incarnation poses the idea of the ladder as God's descent into the world to give human beings the possibility of a communion with divinity that is not open to us by nature (*The Origins of the Christian Mystical Tradition: From Plato to Denys* [Oxford: Clarendon, 1981], pp. 98–158 and xiv, respectively).

37. See T. H. L. Parker, *John Calvin: A Biography* (Philadelphia: Westminster, 1975), on Calvin's view of the Church as a visible form; Calvin essentially rejected the argument of hierarchy and institution in favor of an activity corresponding to the "being" of the Church, that is, in favor of the proclamation of the Gospel and the administration of the sacraments (p. 35). See Calvin's *Commentary on Genesis* with respect to Christ the Mediator and Ladder and on the way the metaphor of the ladder reveals a vision in which form and content are closely related so as to straighten out any perplexity in interpretation in *Calvin: Commentaries*, ed. Joseph Haroutunian (Philadelphia: Westminster, 1958), pp. 146–48.

38. *Institutes of the Christian Religion*, ed. John T. McNeill, trans. Ford Lewis Battles, 2 vols. (Philadelphia: Westminster, 1960), 1:2.9.2, p. 425. See also Calvin's *Commentary on the Gospel According to Saint John*, trans. William Pringle (Grand Rapids, Mich.: Eerdmans, 1956), 1:80–81.

39. Parker says that Calvin's influence on England came largely through the *Institutes* and the sympathies of individual divines (*John Calvin*, p. 144), but the Geneva Bible clearly communicated many doctrines sympathetically as well. Cf. R. T. Kendall, *Calvin and English Calvinism to 1649* (Oxford: Oxford Univ. Press, 1979), on the strong influence of Beza. Also see T. F. Torrance, "Knowledge of God and Speech about Him According to John Calvin," in *Regards Contemporains sur Jean Calvin* (Strasbourg: Presses Universitaires de France, 1964), pp. 140–60, on Calvin's great indebtedness to the thought of the Greek Fathers and not merely to Saint Augustine (p. 141) and his concern with the epistemology of the late medieval world and the thinking of John Major, Ockham, Duns Scotus, and others.

40. The *locus classicus* in the Renaissance is Cardinal Bembo's discussion of the "ladder" in Castiglione's *Courtier*. It is important to remember, however, that the ladder of love was also a ladder of truth when Diotima explained it in the *Symposium* 204b–d, and the combination has

special application to poetry: as love is intermediate between ignorance and wisdom, so poetry, a "making" common to all the arts, is proportionate or intermediate between being and nonbeing.

41. See John M. Steadman, " 'Meaning' and 'Name': Some Renaissance Interpretations of Urania," *NM* 64 (1963): 209–32. Also see Panofsky on the Neoplatonism of Ficino and Pico regarding the "two" Venuses, Urania, and naked truth in *Studies in Iconology: Humanistic Themes in the Art of the Renaissance* (New York: Harper and Row, 1939), pp. 129–55, and Katherine Duncan-Jones, "Sidney's Urania," *RES*, n.s., 17 (1966): 123–32. Mary Wroth's *Urania* is dated to 1621, and much has been written about it of late. See especially Margaret Patterson Hannay, "Mary Sidney: Lady Wroth," in *Women Writers of the Renaissance and Reformation*, ed. Katherine M. Wilson (Athens: Univ. of Georgia Press, 1987), pp. 548–65, which includes the publication of several Pamphilia poems and a selective bibliography. I cite *Spenser, Poetical Works*, ed. J. C. Smith and E. de Selincourt (London: Oxford Univ. Press, 1912), and John Milton, *Complete Poems and Major Prose*, ed. Merritt Y. Hughes (Indianapolis: Bobbs-Merrill, 1967).

42. For Proverbs 8:30, the Vulgate suggests mutual composition with the phrase *cuncta componens*; the Douay-Rheims has Wisdom say, "I was with him forming all things"; the King James reads, "Then I was by him as one brought up with him." Cf. Saint Augustine *Confessions* 12.15. Although the primary collection of kabbalistic material, the *Zohar*, was not printed until editions came out of Mantua and Cremona in 1588–90, after Sidney died, Johannes Reuchlin's Latin commentary on the Kabbalah, *De Arte Cabalistica*, was published early in the sixteenth century (Hagenau, 1517). Through the work of John Scotus Erigena, Raymond Lull, Nicholas of Cusa, and Pico della Mirandola, similarly, certain kabbalistic ideas would have reached Sidney. On the Wisdom of Solomon and its complexities in Hebrew and kabbalistic tradition see, in this order, three different books by Gershom G. Scholem: *Kabbalah* (Jerusalem: Keter Publishing House, 1974), p. 9; *On the Kabbalah and Its Symbolism*, trans. Ralph Mannheim (London: Routledge and Kegan Paul, 1965), pp. 41–42; and *Origins of the Kabbalah*, ed. R. J. Z. Werblowsky, trans. Allan Arkush (Princeton, N.J.: The Jewish Publication Society and Princeton Univ. Press, 1987), pp. 91–92, 132–38, 169–73, 430–54. In many circles, Scholem observes, this Wisdom was considered to be the Torah itself, the Word of God, the form of expression of divine power, and such a view helps explain the parallelism between rabbinic exegesis of Scripture and Hebraic handling of Greek philosophical speculation on the *logos* (*Kabbalah*, p. 9). Solomon's Wisdom functions as daughter and bride and as the house or "quarry" of the cosmos and of the Torah (Proverbs 9:1), as Scholem explains (*Origins of the Kabbalah*, pp. 134–36). The Genevan translators of the Bible are, of course, explaining Proverbs from a Johannine point of view that registers an Orphic and Hellenic idea of Eros as well as a Christian Platonic notion of Logos, according to G. Quispel, "God is Eros," in *Early Christian Literature and the Classical Intellectual Tradition* (Paris: Éditions Beauchesne, 1979), pp. 189–205; see especially p. 198 on wisdom and pp. 203–5 on love.

43. L. Staley Johnson, "Elizabeth, Bride and Queen: A Study of Spenser's April Eclogue and the Metaphors of English Protestantism," *Spenser Studies* 2 (1981): 75–91, has examined Protestant eulogies of Elizabeth in Old Testament terms as a female Solomon. But such a metaphor is metonymic for Lady Wisdom. Three essays on the Kabbalah further open the discussion on the Christian word of God and Hokhmah, the second emanation of the ten emanations of the *sefirot* and one often identified with the logos of Platonic philosophy. In Christian Platonism the Word of God or Logos is the Architect of the universe, the Demiurge, or second hypostasis sometimes identified with "the chief worker," who is, in turn, sometimes identified with the third and feminized hypostasis. See Joseph Dan, "Midrash and the Dawn of Kabbalah," pp. 127–40, especially pp. 133–34; Moshe Idel, "Infinities of Torah in the Kabbalah," pp. 141–58, especially pp. 143–51; and Betty Roitman, "Sacred Language and Open Text," pp. 159–78, in *Midrash and Literature*, ed. Geoffrey Hartman and Sanford Budick (New Haven: Yale Univ. Press, 1986). Idel comments on similarities between kabbalistic

semiotics and some aspects of deconstruction, noting Jacques Derrida's comment from *La Dissemination* that the Kabbalah and its combinatory letters are a science of an interior, superior logic (p. 149). Roitman also uses some comparisons to deconstructive analysis, but her sense of significance prevails, and I prefer her approach. She explains, for example, how equivalences and coherences gather around foci of signification so that apparently "empty" terms are invested with meaning through contexts (p. 160). Regarding the analogies among levels of emanation, she remarks that "the architecture of the kabbalistic universe is crucial" (p. 166). Roitman points out that the feminine and masculine demonstrative pronouns, *zot* and *zeh*, designate the emanations of God closest to the world and indicate, respectively, Providence and the revelation of a saving God (p. 168). The closest emanations, similarly, have to do with the seat, receptacle, house, or temple open to the Presence (pp. 166, 168) and pose the possibility of a mystical wedding or union (p. 168). The emanations, or *sefirot*, also possess a unitive drive, and Roitman concludes her discussion of anagogy and indeterminacy by explaining that in the Kabbalah indeterminacy and "truth of meaning" are compatible (p. 174). Through the allegory of wisdom in Scripture, the Apocrypha, patristic thought, and renaissance Christian Hebraica as well as in Christian Platonism, Sidney is able to express his figure of poesie.

44. *De Optime Genere Oratorum* 2.5, in *De Inventione, De Optime Genere Oratorum, and Topica*, trans. H. M. Hubbell (London: William Heinemann, 1949). Cicero extends his architectural analogy to the comparison of orators and painters. See Paul Oskar Kristeller on the bond between rhetoric and moral philosophy in "The Moral Thought of Renaissance Humanism," in *Renaissance Thought II* (New York: Harper and Row, 1965), pp. 20–68.

45. In Edmund Faral, ed., *Les Arts poétiques au XIIe et du XIIIe siècles. Recherches et documents sur la technique littéraire du Moyen Âge* (Paris: Librairie Ancienne Edouard Champion, 1923), pp. 198–99. See J. W. H. Atkins, *English Literary Criticism; The Medieval Phase* (Cambridge: Cambridge Univ. Press, 1934; Gloucester, Mass.: Peter Smith, 1961), pp. 91–100.

46. *Rhetor, vel duorum dierum Oratio, De Natura, Artem & Exercitatione Rhetorica* (London: Henry Bynnemen, 1577), passim. Harvey's title bespeaks a standard renaissance appeal to the Stoic formula for knowledge: intelligent nature, precepts or rules, good imitation, and exercise. Sturm also refers to this pattern in his *Scholae in Libros IIII Hermogenis de Inventione* (Strasbourg, 1570), sig. a.iiij, and Sidney mentions "art, imitation, and exercise" in the *Defence* (p. 112). Sidney's brother, Robert, purportedly studied with Sturm; see Osborn, *Young Philip Sidney*, p. 502. See also Annabel M. Patterson, *Hermogenes and the Renaissance*, pp. iii–xiv, 17, 33, 37–41.

47. Dame Frances Yates notes general English unfamiliarity with the word *architect* in the late sixteenth century in her book, *Theater of the World* (Chicago: Univ. of Chicago Press, 1969), p. 21; she observes Doctor John Dee's use of the word in 1570 but neglects Sidney's English coinage, "architector" (*Defence*, p. 85), and the frequency of the Latin word *architectus* in texts available to Englishmen. See Marc Girouard, *Robert Smythson and the Architecture of the Elizabethan Era* (South Brunswick, N.J.: Barnes, 1967), pp. 29–31, on rare English examples of the word from 1563 to 1580. On self-knowledge see John of Salisbury *Polycraticus* 7.7, ed. C. C. J. Webb (Oxford: Oxford Univ. Press, 1909), and *Metalogicon* 4.40, trans. Daniel D. McGarry (Berkeley: Univ. of California Press, 1962). For a listing of medieval references to the saying of the Delphic oracle, see Hugh of St. Victor's *Didascalicon*, trans. and ed. Jerome Taylor (New York: Columbia Univ. Press, 1961), pp. 46, 177; for renaissance usage, see S. K. Heninger, Jr., *Touches of Sweet Harmony: Pythagorean Cosmology and Renaissance Poetics* (San Marino, Calif.: Huntington Library, 1974), pp. 263–65, 337–38.

48. According to Walter Ong, S.J., in *Ramus, Method, and the Decay of Dialogue* (Cambridge, Mass.: Harvard Univ. Press, 1958), p. 89, Peter Ramus's *Dialectiae* (1555) and *Scholae in Liberales Artes* (1569) establish a "method" for knowledge that connects words spatially to geometric patterns; Ramus lectured on mathematics, especially Euclid, in Paris in 1566, and he

enlisted Plato and Aristotle as sponsors of his view of *dispositio* or judgment or "method" (p. 257).

49. *Commentariorum de Religione Christiana, Libri Quatuor . . . Eiusdem Vita a Theophilo Banosius* (Frankfurt: Andreas Wechel, 1576). Gabriel Harvey refers to Ramus in the *Rhetor*, sig. L.ʳ.

50. See Osborn, *Young Philip Sidney*, pp. 320–21, 424–25, on the correspondence between de Banos and Sidney and on Sidney's embarrassment at de Banos's praise. The most philosophically developed study of Sidney's Ramism is Forrest Robinson's *Shape of Things Known*. This book has evoked controversy over Robinson's definition of "visual epistemology" and the minimizing of verbal forms; see John Mulryan's review-article, "Sir Philip and the Scholars," *Cithara* 13 (1974): 76–82, and Lawrence C. Wolfley, "Sidney's Visual-Didactic Poetic: Some Complexities and Limitations," *JMRS* 6 (1976): 217–41.

51. Ramus's further application in *Commentariorum de Religione Christiana* of the complex analogy touches on the holiness of the Church as the City of God—"Civitas autem Dei, singulis aetatibus prophetam, apostolum, martyrem veraeque pietatis exemplum aliquod habuit"—and on the Christian republic (1.20–21, pp. 77–78). Donald K. McKim, "The Function of Ramism in William Perkins' Theology," *The Sixteenth-Century Journal* 16 (1985): 503–17, asserts sympathy between Ramus's bond between ethics and theology as an art of living well and the English Calvinist's emphasis on living blessedly because so encouraged by plain-style preaching. Although Sidney antedates Perkins, one can trace in Sidney's application of doctrines—or his imagery of ideas according to a demand for "plain sensibleness" (*Defence*, p. 118)—an Augustinian, Calvinistic, and Ramistic expectation.

52. Revelation 4; Saint Jerome *Commentariorum in Ezechielem* (PL 25:22).

53. See Saint Augustine *De Doctrina Christiana* 2.39; and *Contra Academicos* 3.17.37. In the *Soliloquies* 1.49; 2.18–20, Saint Augustine discussed the usefulness of geometry for the knowledge of God and for self-knowledge. Ramus's Augustinian sense of the "signs" of things that correspond to the "signs" of words in Scripture ought to be compared to Giordano Bruno's *De Compendiosa Architectura, & Complimentis Artis Lullii* (Paris, 1582) with respect to Sidney; Sidney's use of a mental vision of architectural rather than abstract geometric space for literary purposes may qualify his Ramism and indicate Bruno's influence. See G. F. Waller, " 'This Matching of Contraries': Bruno, Calvin, and the Sidney Circle," *Neophilologus* 56 (1972): 331–43.

54. Cf. Vettori's effort to get around the absence of an organizing preface in Aristotle's *Poetics*. In his *Commentarii, In Primum Librum Aristotelis de Arte Poetarum*, 2d ed., p. 1, Vettori explains that an *exordium* is placed before the explication of the precepts of an art to instruct the reader and to show briefly the author's plan; a *proemium*, on the other hand, is a fuller development used by orators to pursue their causes. Vettori tactfully considers Aristotle's opening an *exordium*; Sidney's opening is decidedly a *proemium*. On this subject see Richard P. McKeon's "Rhetoric and Poetic in the Philosophy of Aristotle," in *Aristotle's 'Poetics' and English Literature*, ed. Elder Olson (Chicago: Univ. of Chicago Press, 1965). Also see McKeon's essay, "The New Rhetoric as an Architectonic and Productive Art," *Center Magazine* 13 (1980): 41–53, on the usefulness of architectonic knowledge in constructing systems, including the system of eloquence and wisdom known as renaissance *belles lettres*.

55. *Nicomachean Ethics* 1.1.4–1.2.4.

56. Trans. Philip Wicksteed and Francis Cornford (London: William Heinemann, 1929).

57. See Weinberg, *History of Literary Criticism* 1:26–28.

58. *Compact Oxford English Dictionary*, s.v. "architectonical."

59. *A New Discourse of a Stale Subject, Called the Metamorphosis of Ajax*, ed. Elizabeth S. Donno (New York: Columbia Univ. Press, 1962), pp. 64–65. See T. G. A. Nelson, "Sir John Harington as a Critic of Sir Philip Sidney," *SP* 67 (1970): 41–56. Kenneth Myrick, *Sir Philip Sidney as a Literary Craftsman* (Cambridge, Mass.: Harvard Univ. Press, 1935; Lincoln: Univ. of

Nebraska Press, 1965), pp. 93–97, discusses Sidney's knowledge of Greek language and literature with the conclusion that Sidney learned most of his Greek words, including *architectonic*,
from Aristotle's *Nicomachean Ethics*; but see chapter 4 on Jean de Serres's frequent use of this
Greek word in the 1578 *Plato*, pp. 244–48, 258, and n. 47 of this chapter.

60. See Madeleine Doran, "Imagery in *Richard II* and *Henry IV*," *MLR* 37 (1942): 113–22.

61. For Heninger, *Touches of Sweet Harmony: Pythagorean Cosmology and Renaissance Poetics*
(Princeton, N.J.: Princeton Univ. Press, 1979), pp. 53–69, on the importance of the canonical
books of Solomon to renaissance sermon literature and allegory and on their contribution to a
temple-building motif to poetry. One should also note a Jungian view of the literary role of
architecture in Bettina Knapp, *Archetype, Architecture, and the Writer* (Bloomington: Indiana
Univ. Press, 1986).

62. *Compact Oxford English Dictionary*, s.v. "architectonic." See *John Milton, Complete
Poems and Major Prose*, ed. Merritt Y. Hughes, p. 231n, for the classical parallels to the bee
simile, for the Vatican analogy, and for the reference to the "apian" monarchy.

63. *The True Intellectual System of the Universe Wherein All the Reason and Philosophy of
Atheism Is Confuted and Its Impossibility Demonstrated* (1678) 3:4.36. Cudworth was the son of a
theologian whose lifetime overlapped that of William Perkins, and Cudworth himself was in
the chair of Hebrew and theology at Christ College, Cambridge. The history of his *True
Intellectual System* merits attention because of its links to nineteenth-century romanticism and
to twentieth-century literary criticism and critical theory. In 1733 Cudworth's work was translated into Latin by Johannes Laurentius Mosheimius and published in Germany under the
title *Systema Intellectuale Huius Universi, seu de Veris Naturae Rerum Originibus Commentarii*.
Cudworth's *True Intellectual System* is loaded with architectonic considerations, as I shall
explain in the Epilogue, and its publication in Latin in the eighteenth century in Germany
would have made Cudworth's scriptural, philosophical, apocryphal, and kabbalistic knowledge available to Immanuel Kant, whose first publication was an examination of the problem
of the plurality of worlds, of extension, and of space in 1741. This evolved into the *Critique of
Pure Reason* by 1781, in which Kant expressed his "Architectonic of Pure Reason" as the third
chapter of his conclusive "Transcendental Doctrine of Method." Moreover, Cudworth's *True
Intellectual System* was republished in England in the early nineteenth century, in four volumes introduced by Thomas Birch in 1820 and later, in 1845, with the notes of Mosheim. I am
using Birch's edition (London: J. F. Dore, 1820) but have consulted the 1678 edition in the
Memorial Library, University of Wisconsin. Professor Philip Harth of the University of Wisconsin Department of English and Institute for Research in the Humanities has informed me
that Coleridge had read the Cambridge Platonists in general and that his copiously annotated
copy of *The True Intellectual System* is in the British Library and may be examined in the North
Reading Room. I shall return to this subject in the Epilogue, particularly with a view toward
any connection between Cudworth's work and the *Plato* of Jean de Serres, which Sidney
knew. My reasoning here is not an anachronistic reading of Sidney by Cudworth but a
projection forward to the dilemmas a line of thought from Cudworth to Kant or to Coleridge
or to both presents to the twentieth-century scholar trying to distinguish Sidneian architectonics from Kantian kinds in modern critical theory.

64. Shepherd glosses "ground-plot" as "what the rhetoricians called 'the seat of argument' . . . where material is hidden and whence it is sought in the process of 'invention'"
(*Apology for Poetry*, p. 201 n. 25f.). Duncan-Jones and van Dorsten gloss it with respect to the
art of memory as "an imaginary map . . . on which the 'inventions' are 'placed' in such a way
that the reader may fetch them back for his own use" (*Miscellaneous Prose*, p. 204 n. 103.15–
16). Forrest Robinson devotes a chapter, "Sidney's *Apology*: From Foreconceit to Ground-
Plot" (*Shape of Things Known*, pp. 97–136), to the relationship between "ground-plot" and
"method" and mathematical science; Robinson uses John Dee's actual ground-plot, or diagram of the mathematical sciences, which accompanies the Preface to Billingsley's *Euclid*, and
aptly comments on the structure of the arts and sciences (p. 126). I refer to Dee's use of the

renaissance commonplace of "the learned architect" in Alberti and Vasari to clarify the term further. Panofsky, too, has explained that the true interest of the Vitruvius that Alberti appropriated was proportion ("The History of the Theory of Human Proportions as a Reflection of the History of Styles," in *Meaning in the Visual Arts* [Chicago: Univ. of Chicago Press, 1955], pp. 55–107). Panofsky observes the use of Vitruvian analogies in the Middle Ages; the adaptation of their value to metaphysics and the unity of the liberal arts in the Renaissance; and the connection of perspective to optics and to mathematics (pp. 88–92). Two essays by Father Ong state the broader issues: "System, Space, and Intellect in Renaissance Symbolism," *Bibliothèque d'humanisme et renaissance* 18 (1956), and "From Allegory to Diagram in the Renaissance Mind," *JAAC* 17 (1959). See Yates, *Theater of the World*, pp. 20–41.

65. See n. 10 of this chapter, pp. 409–10.

66. See Osborn, *Young Philip Sidney*, pp. 136–37.

67. The "visual epistemology" explained by Forrest Robinson belongs in the category of method and has distinct roots in philosophies of language and art. See n.36 of chapter 2, pp. 454–55, regarding renaissance method and *katalepsis*, Sturm's use of Hermogenes' rhetoric and Ramus's use of Sturm, with whom Robert Sidney purportedly studied, and see n.46 on Sturm and Gabriel Harvey, p. 427.

68. William and Martha Kneale, *The Development of Logic* (Oxford: Clarendon, 1968), explain in their analysis of the relation of logic to the new mathematics and the rise of physics that synthetic geometry remained the model of "systems-building" when logic itself was no longer regarded as a tool of discovery (p. 309). Renaissance thinkers made numerous analogies of the arts and sciences to "geometry" as the archetype of thought for grammar, logic, rhetoric, and poetry and for the more obviously "geometric" sciences of perspective, optics, and astronomical physics. On the difference between rational memory arts and magical ones and on theoretical and practical geometries, see Walter Ong, S.J., "Memory as Art," in *Rhetoric, Romance, and Technology* (Ithaca, N.Y.: Cornell Univ. Press, 1971), pp. 104–12. Father Ong distinguishes printed words deployed in abstract geometrical space from iconographic images set in architectural space.

69. *Gorgias* 504–8, 517–19, in *Collected Dialogues,* ed. Edith Hamilton and Huntington Cairns (Princeton, N.J.: Princeton Univ. Press, 1961).

70. *De Optime Genere Oratorum* 2.5, in *De Inventione,* trans. Hubbell.

71. See A. E. Taylor, *Plato, the Man, and His Work,* 3d ed., rev. (London: Methuen, 1929), pp. 98–99, on Plato's definition of statesmanship and on the master knowledge—an absolute knowing of moral principles simply acted out in the communication of the learning of goodness from man to man—and compare the definition of dichotomous dialectic in the *Phaedrus* (277b–c) and Sidney's reference (*Defence*, p. 107). See also Charles L. Griswold, Jr., *Self-Knowledge in Plato's Phaedrus* (New Haven: Yale Univ. Press, 1986).

72. In Feuillerat, ed., *Complete Works* 3:124–33; the letter to Languet is translated in *The Correspondence of Sir Philip Sidney and Hubert Languet,* ed. and trans. Stewart A. Pears (London: W. Pickering, 1845), pp. 28–29. Cf. Elizabeth S. Donno, "Old Mouse-Eaten Records: History in Sidney's 'Apology,'" *SP* 72 (1975): 275–98.

73. Various editions of Plutarch were in print when Sidney wrote the *Defence,* including Estienne's Greek and Latin edition of Plutarch's *Opera* and a Latin text of several *Opuscula,* published in 1572; in the third volume of the *Opuscula,* Nicolaus Saguntius's translation of the "De Ciuile Institutione" contains the story about the "duobus architectis" (p. 55) and Pindar's comparison of the architect and the governor (p. 66). Sidney mentions the desire to obtain Amyot's Plutarch, *Les Oeuvres Morales* (Paris, 1572), in letters to Languet in December 1573 and early in 1574 (Osborn, *Young Philip Sidney,* pp. 121, 135). The *Defence* shows traces of influence from Amyot's Preface, which was included in Thomas North's translation of the *Lives* in 1579; in general, Amyot's recollection in *Les Oeuvres Morales* of the Platonic commonplace of the philosopher-king (sig. a.ij), his advocacy of the profession of letters, and his recommendation of royal conferences with those savants who know all the liberal arts and

literature (sig. aiij) would have appealed to Sidney. Nevertheless, a fourth source of Plutarch may have been the Latin version by Hermann Cruserius, *Ethica, siue Moralia* (Basel, 1573). See Robert Aulotte, "Amyot et Plutarque: La Tradition des Moralia au xvi⁵ siecle." *Travaux d Humanisme et Renaissance,* 69 (Geneva: Librairie Droz, 1965); M. Hearny, "The Defence of Poesie and Amyot's Preface in North's *Plutarch*," *SP* 30 (1933): 535–50; and Donno, "Old Mouse-Eaten Records," p. 293.

74. In the prefatory letter to the *Poetices Libri Septem* (Lyons, 1561), sig. a.iiᵛ, Scaliger later explains why all other knowledges are inferior to philosophy when he argues that philosophical principles can lead to beatitude through poetry.

75. Scaliger discusses in this section the "figures of definition" that he considers to be "quasi-analogical." *Tractatio* belongs to the same class as Quintilian's "deformationis," Scaliger says, and then he gives his own analogy: "id quod architecti modulum, vulgus Italicum adhuc magis diminutiua voce dicunt, *Modellum*. ad cuius lineaturas atque dimensiones totius operis ratio dirigitur" (3.33, p. 122).

76. The Greco-Latin correspondences of terms, particularly *image* and *icon*, carry with them the theological interest of Protestantism that we shall see, for example, in Jean de Serres's concern to distinguish the "true likeness" from falsehood and in Sidney's concern to distinguish *eikastic* and *phantastic* images. The theology of the Greek Fathers restored to renaissance poetic theorists the divine aspect of their art simply by making a parallel between the effects of the good poem on the reader and the effects of the "true Image," Christ, on the restoration of all those characters who are made "according to the image."

77. See Herbert Musurillo, S.J., *Symbolism and the Christian Imagination* (Baltimore, Md.: Helicon, 1962), pp. 3–5.

78. The example Scaliger uses is Herodotus: "Tum siquis Herodoti suauitates pedibus fecerit numerosas: efficiet is historicum poetam. . . . Poetae finem esse, docere cum delectatione: Poesim vero esse politiae partem, quae sub legis latore, quanquam alia facie atque colore, continetur" (7.2, p. 347). Cf. Jerome J. McGann's discussion, *Social Values and Poetic Acts: The Historical Judgment of Literary Work* (Cambridge, Mass.: Harvard Univ. Press, 1988), pp. 64–72.

79. In the *Della poetica* of 1553, published in Florence in the *Lezzioni* of 1590, Benedetto Varchi explained, for example, that the rational faculties are the greater part of the civil art and that poetry uses them all to bring man to happiness by moving him to amend his life; thus the poet works with architectonic scope and is much more like the philosopher than the painter, the sculptor, or the orator (pp. 571–92). But in the 1570s, Lodovico Castelvetro disputed the architectonic scope of poetry: he argued that poetry was primarily an act of imitation "perfect and worthy of praise without depending on extraordinary or even moderate knowledge of the sciences and arts" (*The Poetics of Aristotle Translated and Annotated* [1571], in *Literary Criticism, Plato to Dryden*, ed. Allen Gilbert [New York: American Book Co., 1940; Detroit: Wayne State Univ. Press, 1962], p. 357). In his *Della difesa della "Commedia" di Dante* (1587), Jacopo Mazzoni agreed that poetry was a "fabricating" art but asked whether it treated the law of the making of images "politically" or whether it "built up" and formed the image "esthetically" (*Literary Criticism*, ed. Gilbert, p. 397). See Robert L. Montgomery, ed. and trans., *Giacopo Mazzoni's On the Defense of the Comedy of Dante* (Tallahassee: Florida State Univ. Press, 1983).

80. James Westfall Thompson, trans., *The Frankfurt Book Fair* (Chicago: Caxton Club, 1911), pp. 56–57 on Frankfurt as a cultural watering hole, and p. 62 on the elephant, a classical symbol of wisdom.

81. Henri Estienne *Francofordiense Emporium* (Geneva, 1574), pp. 23–26, in *The Frankfurt Book Fair*, pp. 170–71.

82. Much of Sidney's peroration paraphrases Conrad Clauserus's translation, *De Natura Deorum Gentilium* (Basel, 1543), of Cornutus, the first-century Stoic pedagogue. See Shepherd's discussion in his edition of the *Apology* (*Apology for Poetry*, p. 236 nn. 37ff.), and note the common use of the axiomatic oath "by Hesiod and Homer" in Plutarch and in Saint

Basil as well. Also see Jean de Serres's use of it in commenting on the *Symposium* in the *Platonis Opera* 3:167. The Orphic tradition is blended in with this reference simply because Cleanthes, on whom Cornutus drew, accommodated the fables of Orpheus, Musaeus, Hesiod, and Homer to Stoicism in the second book on the nature of the gods. Sidney's allusion to this complex tradition in his conclusion once again situates the intermediacy of poesie between divine truth and human knowledge; she may be acknowledged as a power of the imagination without violating Sidney's religious orthodoxy. Robert Lamberton has recently published *Hesiod* (New Haven: Yale Univ. Press, 1988), but I have not examined it. Cf. Hegel's citation of the conventional appeal to Hesiod and Homer in his discussion of the mediation of consciousness by art in *Introduction to the Lectures on the History of Philosophy*, trans. T. M. Knox and A. V. Miller (Oxford: Clarendon, 1985), p. 32.

83. *An Apology to Smectymnuus*, ed. Frederick L. Taft, in *Complete Prose Works of John Milton*, ed. Don M. Wolfe, 8 vols. (New Haven: Yale Univ. Press, 1953–83), 1:890.

84. In *La Défense et illustration de la langue française et oeuvres poétiques diverses (extraits)*, ed. Yvonne Wendel-Bellenger (Paris: Librairie Larousse, 1972), p. 159. My reference is merely a passing allusion in comparison to Margaret Ferguson's deconstruction of du Bellay's treatise in *Trials of Desire*, pp. 18–53. Especially note Ferguson's mentioning of du Bellay's association of invention with divinity, the encyclopedia, *copia*, and *energeia* (p. 34) as du Bellay develops "the idea of a transportation of literary power into a myth of progress that has a geographical as well as a historical dimension" (p. 35). This is a remarkable essay, and because I am not "defending" Sidney I can thoroughly appreciate it.

85. Cf. this reading of Spenser's use of du Bellay to Thomas Greene's in *The Light in Troy: Imitation and Discovery in Renaissance Poetry* (New Haven: Yale Univ. Press, 1982), p. 272; see also Greene's discussion of du Bellay's *Defense* (pp. 188–93) and of his architectural themes (pp. 220–32, 238–41). Greene's apt historical contextualization of the quest for a "fixed linguistic ground" and of the renaissance treatment of Hebrew as a "natural language" (p. 6) should be contrasted to Derrida's use of the Kabbalah, *Dissemination*, trans. Johnson, pp. 340–49.

86. *Confessions* 12.15; cf. Saint Paul, Galatians 4:26.

87. In the introduction to her edition of *The Book of the City of Ladies* (London: Pan Books, 1983), Marina Warner says that Christine "did not intend that her City of Ladies rival the City of God, but that her political vision be understood as participating in a Christian tradition of political philosophy" (p. xxvi). Christine herself says that she writes her book to contest the antifeminist lies of numerous male authorities (1.1.1, pp. 3–5). But see Susan Schibanoff's essay, "Taking the Gold out of Egypt: The Art of Reading as a Woman," in *Gender and Reading*, ed. Flynn and Schweickart, pp. 83–106, for the way Christine first "immasculates" herself and learns how to read as a man, a patristic exegete, and then progresses to reading like a woman by reentering old texts from new critical directions (p. 91).

88. *Discourse on Method*, trans. F. D. Sutcliffe (Harmondsworth, Middlesex, Eng.: Penguin, 1968), "Discourse 2," pp. 35–37.

89. Ed. James Strachey (New York: Norton, 1961), pp. 16–20.

90. *The Arte of English Poesie* 3.25, ed. Baxter Hathaway, p. 313.

91. In Hesiod, Prometheus remains a crafty thief punished by Zeus (*Works and Days* 40ff.; *Theogony* 535ff.), but Aeschylus's *Prometheus Unbound* images him as an heroic victim reconciled with Zeus and a giver of gifts to humankind. Boccaccio comments on Prometheus and the price humanity pays for consciousness in *Genealogy of the Gentile Gods* 4.44; 12.70; and Ficino allegorizes him in the commentary on Plato's *Philebus*, a dialogue that credits Prometheus with the gift of recognizing "intermediate" things between the one and the many so that all the arts and sciences may be learned as avenues to a unitive truth (16c). Plato also comments on Prometheus by way of explaining human self-governance after divine guidance had ceased (*Politicus* 274c). Werner Jaeger associates Plato's idea in the *Laws* that the proper duty of the state is to mold character, not to advance knowledge in itself, with the mythic status of Prometheus in Greek thought in *Paideia: The Ideals of Greek Culture*, 2d ed., 3 vols.

(New York: Oxford Univ. Press, 1939–44), 3:228. In the *Metamorphoses* 1.75–80, Ovid developed the Promethean themes of the molding of men out of the divine seed or spark of fire and the golden age. This Promethean making of men out of fire, clay, and spittle Saint Augustine acknowledges in *De Civitate Dei* 10.0. Erasmus links the allegory of Prometheus to the paradise myth, Eve's sin, and the ejection from Eden in the *Enchiridion* on the subject of interpreting parables (upon Christ [he] does take Wisdom, AVII, LVIVia), asking in lodging that Eve is, of course, "ourselves," or the carnal and effeminate man within. In a letter of November 1499 to John Sixtin, Erasmus relates his further connection of a Promethean theme to the story of Cain and why Cain's offering was less pleasing to God than Abel's: Cain bribed an angel at the gate of Eden to give him some of the seed of paradise (Letter 116, in *Erasmi Epistolae*, ed. P. S. and H. M. Allen, 12 vols. [Oxford: Oxford Univ. Press, 1906–58], 1:268–71). D. C. Allen reports in *The Legend of Noah: Renaissance Rationalism in Art, Science, and Letters* (Urbana: Univ. of Illinois Press, 1949), p. 83, that renaissance commentators thought Noah was known to the pagans under the name of Prometheus. For Augustine, of course, Cain is the founder of the earthly city and the originator of various arts, sciences, and technologies (*De Civitate Dei* 15.1–8). God's instruction to Cain about his sin parallels the instruction to Eve about her concupiscence, for the husband is to rule the wife as the soul rules the flesh; but Cain did not receive this advice in the spirit of amendment while Eve did, for the flesh is to be healed, not to be abandoned to destruction (*De Civitate Dei* 15.7). For a feminist critical effort to recover the literary work of women from the historical judgment of Eve, see Elaine V. Beilin, *Redeeming Eve: Women Writers of the English Renaissance* (Princeton, N.J.: Princeton Univ. Press, 1987).

92. Cf. Beth Wynne Fisken, "Mary Sidney's *Psalmes*: Education and Wisdom," in *Silent But for the Word: Tudor Women as Patrons, Translators, and Writers of Religious Works*, ed. Margaret Patterson Hannay (Kent, Ohio: Kent State Univ. Press, 1985), pp. 166–83, on displays of verbal wit ("Wisdom in Words") distinct from simplicity (the "Word of Wisdom").

93. See du Bartas, *Diuine Weekes*, pp. 4–5, and n. 25 of this chapter; John Donne, "Expostulation IX," in *Devotions upon Emergent Occasions* (Ann Arbor: Univ. of Michigan Press, 1959), pp. 60–61; and John Milton, *Areopagitica*, ed. Ernest Sirluck, in *Complete Prose Works*, ed. Wolfe, 2:492–93. Cf. Jacques Derrida, *Of Grammatology*, trans. Spivak, pp. 6–26, on the end of the book and the beginning of writing, and *Dissemination*, trans. Johnson, pp. 183–86, on Plato's *Philebus*, the book, logos, literature, and truth. I appreciate the clarity of Johnson's introductory remark: "The Book, the Preface, and the Encyclopedia are all structures of unification and totalization. Dissemination, on the other hand, is what subverts all such recuperative gestures of mastery. It is what foils the attempt to progress in an orderly way toward meaning or knowledge, what breaks the circuit of intentions or expectations through some ungovernable excess or loss" (p. xxxii).

Chapter 2

1. *Allegorical Imagery: Some Mediaeval Books and Their Posterity* (Princeton, N.J.: Princeton Univ. Press, 1966), p. 21. Also see Tuve's comments in *Elizabethan and Metaphysical Imagery: Renaissance Poetic and Twentieth-Century Critics* (Chicago: Univ. of Chicago Press, 1947), pp. 105–9, 133–37.

2. *The Language of Allegory: Defining the Genre* (Ithaca: Cornell Univ. Press, 1979), p. 26; see also pp. 19–21 on the Christian addition of historical dimension and narrative extension to the rhetorical significance of the trope and pp. 156–57 on the "potential sacralizing power in language" always presupposed in allegory.

3. See Elaine Showalter, "Women's Time, Women's Space: Writing the History of Feminist Criticism," in *Feminist Issues in Literary Scholarship*, ed. Shari Benstock (Bloomington: Indiana Univ. Press, 1987), pp. 30–44, especially p. 30 on "heresy" not quite having become "orthodoxy" but nevertheless having had a strong impact on the academy in a short time, and

pp. 36–37 on French criticism and Kristeva's rejection of the label "feminist" as a liberal anachronism.

4. In the politics of criticism, this is a dangerous religious version of a secular process Annette Kolodny once called "Dancing through a Minefield: Some Observations on the Theory, Practice, and Politics of a Feminist Literary Criticism." See especially pp. 151–54 of Kolodny's essay in *The New Feminist Criticism*, ed. Elaine Showalter (New York: Pantheon, 1985), pp. 144–67.

5. The best statement of a reason to avoid literary theories and methodologies developed by male "masters"—some of whom have even aimed to authorize feminism itself, as in Jonathan Culler's discussion of "reading like a woman" in his book *On Deconstruction*—and to read liberally and widely, thinking for oneself, is Nina Auerbach's essay, "Engorging the Patriarchy," in *Feminist Issues in Literary Scholarship*, pp. 150–59, which was originally published in 1984–85. Auerbach defies the neatness and institutionalization of theory and prefers the messiness of experience. She states that she does not want "to abandon the energy, the achievements, of patriarchal culture" any more than she wants "to be abandoned by these things" (p. 157). In the process of saying so, Auerbach rejects a differentiation of the voices of women and men to the extent that it is a caricature and challenges Lawrence Lipking's strange position that, on one hand, affirms how women are not a subspecies of men and, on the other, reduces the voice of women to love, need, and craving, not form. Against this kind of invasion and appropriation of women by men, therefore, Auerbach argues that women scholars should leave an "inviolate female tradition" and read, rather, through "a feminist prism" while freely invading the patriarchal culture (pp. 157–58). Cf. Culler, *On Deconstruction: Theory and Criticism after Structuralism* (Ithaca, N.Y.: Cornell Univ. Press, 1982), and Lipking, *Abandoned Women and Poetic Tradition* (Chicago: Univ. of Chicago Press, 1988), in which the article to which Auerbach refers, "Aristotle's Sister: A Poetics of Abandonment," *Critical Inquiry* 10 (1983), is reprinted as chapter 7, pp. 209–28. Lipking mentions Auerbach only in one footnote, and that in reference to Swinburne (pp. 254–55), but his prefatory remark that poetry about abandoned women "often envisions a community of sexes" may suggest that Lipking has benefited somewhat from Auerbach's observations. Such poetry "does not regard gender as a prison or mystery but as a set of terms through which human beings discover what separates them—and sometimes brings them together" (Lipking, p. xxiii).

6. See Ernest B. Gilman, *Iconoclasm and Poetry in the English Reformation: Down Went Dagon* (Chicago: Univ. of Chicago Press, 1986), p. 2, on "the meaning of iconoclasm to a body of deeply iconic Renaissance Poetry."

7. *Poetic Presence and Illusion: Essays in Critical History and Theory* (Baltimore: Johns Hopkins Univ. Press, 1979), p. 7.

8. *The Veil of Allegory: Some Notes toward a Theory of Allegorical Rhetoric in the Renaissance* (Chicago: Univ. of Chicago Press, 1969), especially p. 184, where Murrin notes that while Sidney belonged to "the oratorical camp," he nevertheless possessed "his own unique point of view" and includes both ends of the argument on the poet's divinization: "The manner in which he talks about the word *vates* and the poetic genius, for example, convinces his audience that poetry is divinely inspired, despite his explicit denial of the idea later on." Murrin attributes this inclusion not to an unconscious division of the argument in Sidney but to the "transitional character" of the period. Epitomizing the transition, Sidney was original in his inclusion of the allegorists and the orators, and in this respect his "theories anticipate the metaphysical poets" and the romantics "who likewise exalted the poetic genius and yet received many notions common to allegorical criticism" (p. 185). I agree.

9. *The Lamb and the Elephant: Ideal Imitation and the Context of Renaissance Allegory* (San Marino, Calif.: Huntington Library, 1974), p. xiv. Fletcher's book, *Allegory: The Theory of a Symbolic Mode* (Ithaca, N.Y.: Cornell Univ. Press, 1964), outlines a phenomenological view that has been most useful to me, however, in my reconstruction of the mistress-knowledge. Leonard Barkan, *Nature's Work of Art: The Human Body as Image of the World* (New Haven:

Yale Univ. Press, 1975), has studied the particular allegory of the world and the body in Sidney's *Astrophil and Stella* and in Spenser's *Faerie Queene*; see especially chapter 3, "The Human Body, Esthetics, and the Constructions of Man," pp. 116–74. Although full of insights on poetry, the body politic, and the Church, this book emphasizes structure and systems-making and suppresses both the numinosity and the femininity of Sidney's particular allegory of poesie. Val Mahini's historical interpretation is important.

10. See Murrin's comments on the further confusion brought to twentieth-century studies of allegory as allegory was further separated from myth and associated with moral *exempla* by Samuel Johnson and, later, by Coleridge (*Veil*, pp. 197–98). Hazard Adams has made this development the thesis of his book, *Philosophy of the Literary Symbolic* (Tallahassee: Florida State Univ. Press, 1983), a study of the critical movements of the last two hundred years that have marginalized the symbolic in favor of a reductive version of allegory—that is, allegory merely as a continued and duplicitous metaphor rather than allegory as a symbolic mode. See also Andrew D. Weiner, "Moving and Teaching: Sidney's *Defence of Poesie* as a Protestant Poetic," *JMRS* 2 (1972): 259–78. In a few succinct and well-focused pages, Weiner identifies the necessity of the imagination (p. 272) as the *locus* of the poet's moving power, explains the ease with which renaissance readers would have grasped Sidney's joint application of reading allegorically and figuratively as a fact of Protestant *artes legendi* (pp. 272–77), and observes that the "speaking picture" or mimetic image of poetry is not the whole of poesie (p. 276). In these matters I not only agree but go on to apply the case regarding the mistress-knowledge, and that is where I diverge. Weiner simply does not include her in his arguments; but she is the generative type of the imagination that is the *locus* of the poet's moving power according to Weiner's first point, on which he quotes Puttenham (p. 272). That is, she produces images both of chimeras and monsters that do not exist in nature and of the beautiful, good, and true in her technical or mimetic role but also conscientiously distinguishes them in her teleological role. See the Epilogue, pp. 374–76, on Cudworth's handling of Urania and the celestial Venus in terms of the third hypostasis of the Trinity, or the feminized wisdom of the Hellenized books of wisdom in Holy Scripture and the relation of the figure to the Holy Spirit.

11. See Richard P. McKeon, "Rhetoric and Poetic in the Philosophy of Aristotle," in *Aristotle's 'Poetics' and English Literature*, ed. Elder Olson (Chicago: Univ. of Chicago Press, 1965), pp. 201–36. McKeon explains how renaissance metaphysics was first adulterated with logic, then analogized to politics, and finally translated through ethics and politics to the realistic, practical ends of rhetoric (p. 204).

12. *De Officiis* 1.43.153: "If wisdom is the most important of the virtues, as it certainly is, it necessarily follows that that duty which is connected with the social obligation is the most important duty. And service is better than mere theoretical knowledge, for the study and knowledge of the universe would somehow be lame and defective, were no practical results to follow" (trans. W. Miller [London: William Heinemann, 1913], p. 157).

13. See chapter 3, pp. 100–109, on Sidney's intertextualization of Augustine and Boethius.

14. One may conjecture about the continuity of this kind of power struggle among types of knowledge *after* the Renaissance as physics, then history, psychoanalysis, and criticism compete for the designation of the superior, organizing knowledge.

15. See Richard P. McKeon, "The Transformation of the Liberal Arts in the Renaissance," in *Developments in the Early Renaissance*, ed. Bernard S. Levy (Albany, N.Y.: State Univ. Press, 1972), pp. 158–223, especially pp. 188–89 on the development of the liberal arts in Christian thought through the Middle Ages and the Renaissance.

16. The moral plane is implicit here. See Ian Breward's introduction to his edition, *The Work of William Perkins* (Appleford, Eng.: Sutton Courtenay, 1970), for a discussion of the manner in which conflict is the sign of grace; there is no faith without the sort of knowledge of discernment that conscience provides in the ability of its inwardness to go even against reason (pp. 30–31, 64).

17. In Breward, ed., *Work*, pp. 27–31, 64.

18. Urania is linked to "remembrance" or memory in an Augustinian sense in the opening pages of the *Arcadia*; see my comments in the Preface of this book, pp. xiii–xv. In his poem published in 1595, the year the *Defence* was published, Spenser allegorized the Countess of Pembroke as "Vrania, sister vnto Astrofell, / In whose braue mynd, as in a golden cofer, / All heauenly gifts and riches locked are" (*Poetical Works* ll. 487-89, p. 541).

19. *The Geneva Bible, a Facsimile of the 1560 Edition*, introduction by Lloyd E. Berry (Madison: Univ. of Wisconsin Press, 1969), p. 419.

20. On the *Arcadia*, see Patterson's view of the conflicts and contradictory political uses made of Sidney's text in the seventeenth century in her chapter, " 'Under Pretty Tales': Intention in Sidney's *Arcadia*," in *Censorship and Interpretation*, pp. 24–43. See also Steve Davies and William B. Hunter, "Milton's Urania: 'The meaning not the Name I call,' " *SEL 1500–1900* 28 (1988): 95–111.

21. See *Herodotus* 3.60, trans. A. D. Godley, 4 vols. (London: William Heinemann, 1921), 4:87–88. Sidney mentions Herodotus twice in the *Defence*—once asserting that Herodotus "entitled his History by the name of the Nine muses" and usurped the passionate description of passionate actions and long orations from the poets (*Misc. Prose*, ed. Katherine Duncan-Jones and Jan van Dorsten, p. 75) and once paralleling Herodotus and Justin the historian on the difference between a feigned and a true example (p. 90). Sir Francis Bacon echoes the distinction, asserting in the *Advancement of Learning* that poetry is but "feigned history" (2.4.1-2, in G. W. Kitchin's edition [London: J. M. Dent & Sons, 1973]). Herodotus himself did not put the names of the Muses in his history, but his history was put to all the uses their names suggest; see Werner Jaeger, *Paideia: The Ideals of Greek Culture*, 2d ed., 3 vols. (New York: Oxford Univ. Press, 1939–44), 1:383–84. Cf. Jerome McGann's discussion of the relevance and irrelevance of Herodotus in modern critical assumptions of an infinite capacity to "divine" texts in *Social Values and Poetic Acts: The Historical Judgment of Literary Work* (Cambridge, Mass.: Harvard Univ. Press, 1988), pp. 64–72.

22. See Carolyn G. Heilbrun, *Toward a Recognition of Androgyny* (1964; reprint, New York: Norton, 1982), and cf. Robert Kimbrough's suggestion that the layered playing of sexual roles in Shakespeare's plays, for example, reveals an "ungendering" of human identity rather than an intensification of sexual stereotypes or androgynous bonding, in "Androgyny Seen through Shakespeare's Disguise," *SQ* 33 (1982): 17–33. Subsequent feminist inquiries have challenged the nature (female)/culture (male) analogy and looked to gender, cognitive perception, and language. See Mary Crawford and Roger Chaffin, "The Reader's Construction of Meaning: Cognitive Research on Gender and Comprehension," in *Gender and Reading: Essays on Readers, Texts, and Contexts*, ed. Elizabeth A. Flynn and Patrocinio P. Schweickart (Baltimore: Johns Hopkins Univ. Press, 1986), pp. 3–30. The renaissance gendering of *both* nature and art as "feminine" things to be controlled and refashioned by masculine forces of mind invites the critical effort to sort out gender differences and dominations in the definition of style. With regard to Sidney's androgynous figure, especially note Patricia Parker's discussion of Ben Jonson's *Bartholomew Fair*, in the context of which she aptly connects Dionysius's remark about the puppets having "neither male nor female" among them both to the biblical prophecy that in the Apocalypse "or final Recognition Scene of history there will be neither male nor female, whatever the more hierarchical relation of the sexes in the meantime" and to Sidney's defence of a poetry that "neither affirmeth" nor "denieth" and therefore does not lie (*Literary Fat Ladies: Rhetoric, Gender, Property* [London: Methuen, 1987], pp. 25–26). See also Catherine R. Stimpson, *Where the Meanings Are: Feminism and Cultural Spaces* (New York: Methuen, 1988), for the argument that gender difference can be the basis of balance, not merely division.

23. *The Discarded Image: An Introduction to Medieval and Renaissance Literature* (Cambridge: Cambridge Univ. Press, 1970), pp. 185–97. We should add to Lewis's observation in this respect a recent distinction between feminist criticism and gynocriticism that Carolyn Heilbrun and Catherine R. Stimpson drew in their essay, "Theories of Feminist Criticism," in

Feminist Literary Criticism: Explorations in Theory, ed. Josephine Donovan (Lexington: Univ. of Kentucky Press, 1976), pp. 64, 68, 72, when they remarked that feminist criticism looks for the sins and errors of the past and gynocriticism seeks the grace of the imagination. In chapter 1, The Mistress-Knowledge," I search for a new consciousness within the text" (p. 84).

24. See J. W. H. Atkins, *English Literary Criticism: The Medieval Phase* (Cambridge: Cambridge Univ. Press, 1934; Gloucester, Mass.: Peter Smith, 1961), pp. 30–31.

25. "Speke Parott" (11.202–3), in *John Skelton, The Complete English Poems*, ed. John Scattergood (New Haven: Yale Univ. Press, 1983). On the political background of Skelton's use of metaphor, see John Chalker, "The Literary Seriousness of Skelton's *Speke Parrot*," *Neophilologus* 44 (1960): 839–47. See also Richard Halpern's comments on Skelton's "disturbance" of historical species of critical assessments of his transitional status and on the "political topography" that informs his writing ("John Skelton and the Poetics of Primitive Accumulation," in *Literary Theory/Renaissance Texts*, ed. Patricia Parker and David Quint [Baltimore: Johns Hopkins Univ. Press, 1986], pp. 225, 230–31).

26. 1.13, ed. S. E. Lehmberg (London: J. M. Dent and Sons, 1962). Cf. Quintilian *Institutio Oratoria* 1.10.1, "Orbis ille doctrinae quam Graeci ἐγκύκλιον παιδείαν vocant" (trans. H. E. Butler [Cambridge, Mass.: Harvard Univ. Press, 1943]).

27. See A. C. Hamilton's synthesis of Sidney's life, legend, and writings in *Sir Philip Sidney: A Study of His Life and Works* (Cambridge: Cambridge Univ. Press, 1977) on Sidney's sense of the confines of life (p. 9) and his commitment to the life of self-examination (pp. 32–35). Fulke Greville, Lord Brooke, makes much of Sidney's profession of reformed Christianity and his interest in the Protestant League in the biography *The Life of the Renowmed Sir Philip Sidney with the True Intent of England as It Then Stood in Relation to All Forrain Princes* (London, 1652), pp. 3, 21, 41–51. Martin Raitiere, in his recent study of Sidney's politics, *Faire Bitts: Sir Philip Sidney and Renaissance Political Theory* (Pittsburgh: Duquesne Univ. Press, 1984), qualifies Sidney's actual support of the League and comments that from a Calvinist perspective, "no act of Sidney's was more egregious than his decision to commit a fiction" (p. 17). Cf. Alan Sinfield's view of allegorical mythology, poetic fiction, and Sidney's negotiation of classical pagan literature and Protestantism in "The Cultural Politics of *The Defence of Poetry*," in *Sir Philip Sidney and the Interpretation of Renaissance Culture*, ed. Gary F. Waller and Michael D. Moore (Totowa, N.J.: Barnes & Noble, 1984), pp. 124–43.

28. In her special use of Bakhtin's theory of the dialogic, Margaret Ferguson reads Sidney's *Defence* as a plea for power in such a dialectic of escape from the imprisoning limitations of language in *Trials of Desire* (pp. 137–62). Ferguson acknowledges Ramistic method (p. 144) and refers to the *Defence* as Sidney's own register of the crisis of interpretation in which the abuse of poetry is analogous to the abuse of God's Word (p.147) but does not develop the argument. In Ferguson's discussion of the strategies of Sidney's irony a few pages later, she departs from the historical context in which Sidney asserts a positive value and positive significance in his language.

29. See John M. Ellis, *Against Deconstruction* (Princeton, N.J.: Princeton Univ. Press, 1989), pp. 113–22, on the deconstructive definitions of textuality and the role of the reader.

30. See, in this order, Jacques Derrida, *Positions*, trans. Alan Bass (Chicago: Univ. of Chicago Press, 1981), p. 26; *Writing and Difference*, trans. Alan Bass (Chicago: Univ. of Chicago Press, 1978), p. 280; *Of Grammatology*, trans. Spivak, p. 50; and John Ellis, *Against Deconstruction*, pp. 50–66, in which Ellis argues that Derrida has confused "the process of meaning with the analysis of that process" as he appropriates Saussure (p. 55). Cf. John Steadman's historical approach to the problem of interpretation in *The Lamb and the Elephant*; he remarks on the affinities of renaissance theories of mimesis with the medieval tradition (p. xiv) and attempts the differentiation of often overlapping renaissance definitions of invention, imitation, imagination, and inspiration. Steadman sees the *icon* or *eidolon* as a constructed image (p. xl) and recognizes the claims both of fifteenth- and sixteenth-century Italians and of Sidney and other English apologists "for the transcendental inspiration and

vision of the artist" and poet as "familiar *topoi* in Renaissance polemics and critical theory" (p. 150). See also Wolfgang Iser, *The Act of Reading: A Theory of Aesthetic Response* (1976; trans. by author and pub. Baltimore: Johns Hopkins Univ. Press, 1978), pp. 107–52. Of particular interest is Iser's discussion of "building images" (pp. 140–41), which leads again to modern semiotics and Kantian "schemata" and away from Sidney's architectonics as a renaissance "making" of character through rhetoric. In the variety of deconstructions possible, we almost always confront the debate between Kantian idealism and a Hegelian phenomenology of reading. See also Jonathan Culler, *On Deconstruction*, and Art Berman, *From the New Criticism to Deconstruction: The Reception of Structuralism and Post-Structuralism* (Champaign: Univ. of Illinois Press, 1988).

31. See especially McGann's essay, "The Monks and the Giants: Textual and Bibliographical Studies and the Interpretation of Literary Works," in *The Beauty of Inflections: Literary Investigations in Historical Method and Theory* (Oxford: Oxford Univ. Press, 1985), pp. 69–110, and his brief discussion of Sidney's "Aristotelian" doctrine of imitation in the introduction to his collection of essays, *Historical Studies and Literary Criticism* (Madison: Univ. of Wisconsin Press, 1985), pp. 12–13, in which McGann attributes a "traditional" view of referentiality, moral essences, and history to Sidney's concept of history. I shall comment on this view shortly.

32. Cf. Thomas Greene's discussion of Sidney's Daedalus and classical literature in *The Light in Troy: Imitation and Discovery in Renaissance Poetry* (New Haven: Yale Univ. Press, 1982), p. 270. Earlier Greene quotes Palmieri (on reading and writing, letters and liberal studies, as the preeminent guides and "true mistresses" of every worthy discipline that have been forgotten for eight hundred years) in the context of his careful discussion of the "leap" the Renaissance made in appropriating the classical past for itself (p. 35). Greene singles out Petrarch and his personal copy of the *Aeneid* as a special source of the transmission of "the hermeneutic sedimentation of fourteen centuries." Beyond ruins and constructions, I think the Christian humanism of the Renaissance also saw a hope in history that depended on the kind of collective memory or history that Augustine described in his biographical adaptation of the *Aeneid* to his quest through memory in the *Confessions*. See also Camille Bennett, "The Conversion of Vergil: The *Aeneid* in Augustine's *Confessions*," *Revue des Études Augustiniennes* 34 (1988): 47–69.

33. *Renaissance Self-Fashioning from More to Shakespeare* (Chicago: Univ. of Chicago Press, 1982), p. 2. Greenblatt takes Augustine's remark as a moral principle applicable to the interpretation of renaissance literary composition but severs the principle from its significance in Augustine's larger philosophical and theological enterprise.

34. *The Aspiring Mind of the Elizabethan Younger Generation* (Durham, N.C.: Duke University Press, 1966), pp. 53–54. In discussing the cult of honor in this generation Esler links it to the invisible world of the Christian heaven and the Platonic ideal realm and comments on the great reality of this invisible world in the Elizabethan imagination (pp. 116–17).

35. Robert Kimbrough observed Sidney's emphasis on exercise in this formula of "art, imitation, and exercise" in his book, *Sir Philip Sidney* (New York: Twayne, 1971), pp. 19–37, as an aspect of the renaissance pragmatism that pursued specific, concrete ends of knowledge.

36. One can locate an important contemporary source of the axiom in Johannes Sturm's *Scholae in Libros IIII Hermogenis de Inventione* (Strasbourg, 1570) in which Sturm states that the mastery of an art, like the art of oratory, requires an intelligent nature, knowledge of the precepts, exercise, and imitation. He relates imitation to invention and to a "gathering of timber" (sig. a.iiij). He sees exercise as the means by which precepts learned and "percepts" grasped come together. Stoicism defined art, according to Neal Gilbert in *Renaissance Concepts of Method* (New York: Columbia Univ. Press, 1960), pp. 11–12, as a system of grasping sense perceptions, which may then be exercised together toward some end in life. That is, Stoicism saw art empirically, technically, and teleologically. Gilbert explains, "As originally conceived, this was an epistemological doctrine, for *katalepsis*, literally a 'grasping', was a

Stoic technical term for a sense impression conveying the truth so powerfully as to defy shaking by reasoning." This definition was ubiquitous in classical writings of Cicero, Quintilian, Lucian, and Hermogenes, and these writings were favored by renaissance humanists such as Sturm. Often, however, renaissance humanism confused the system of phantasy sense impressions or percepts or rules and then reconciled them with the effect of creating another view of art, a hybrid of the Stoic view with, for example, the Aristotelian rules and with the Platonic notion of art as the exercise of forethought for the good of the soul. One view of the source of this joint persuasiveness would attribute it to Peter Ramus's influence on Sidney's thinking. See Pierre Duhamel, "The Logic and Rhetoric of Peter Ramus," *MP* 46 (1949): 163–71, on the effect of logical exercise implied by Peter Ramus's treatment of the syllogism:

> One of the more or less explicit assumptions of the Ramistic dialectic was the inevitability of the mind's assent to a true proposition, once it was presented to the mind. This had the effect of making all true propositions postulates, i.e., a proposition whose truth is so patent that the mind cannot refuse assent. Investigation by means of the syllogism became almost superfluous. (P. 169)

37. The fullest survey of renaissance poetic theory is Bernard Weinberg's *History of Literary Criticism in the Italian Renaissance*, 2 vols. (Chicago: Univ. of Chicago Press, 1961). In his essay, "From Aristotle to Pseudo-Aristotle," in *Aristotle's 'Poetics' and English Literature*, ed. Olson, pp. 192–200, Weinberg describes the development of renaissance poetic theory as a piecemeal, fragmentary event. Our modern efforts to define a scientific literary theory seem to reflect a similarly piecemeal effort that Paisley Livingston judges to be lacking in scientific rigor, confused and vague, lacking in consensus, and given to "framework relativism" (*Literary Knowledge: Humanistic Inquiry and the Philosophy of Science* [Ithaca, N.Y.: Cornell Univ. Press, 1988], pp. 9, 15, 33). Yet even such relativism is preferable to the "naive empiricism" from which literary disciplines so often suffer (p. 33). Of particular value is Livingston's taxonomy of substantive theory, formal theory, theory as art or fun, and theory as social action (pp. 10–31) as a prelude to his advocacy of theory as epistemology.

38. See Aristotle's distinction between speculative and productive knowledge and of both from the highest or metaphysical activity of the mind in the *Metaphysics* (12.9 [1074b–1075a], trans. Hugh Tredennick [London: William Heinemann, 1933–35]), and Aristotle's discussion of the intellectual virtues of wisdom, prudence, science, and art in the *Nicomachean Ethics* 6.3.1–6.12.5 (1139b–1144a). The impact of Aristotle's definitions of the intellectual virtues and his predication of an architectonic knowledge in the *Nicomachean Ethics* 1.1 (1094a) on renaissance theorists of various arts and sciences varied in accordance with their knowledge and love of Aristotle. One finds his definitions put to different uses in the placement of a given knowledge in the structure of knowledge in arts treatises as diverse, for example, as Cennini's *Libro dell'Arte* early in the fifteenth century (on science versus craft); Leon Battista Alberti's association of painting with mathematical science in the *Della Pittura* also in the early fifteenth century (regarding the sciences of geometry and perspective versus *historia*); and Leonardo's claim to all of natural philosophy and the moral effects of demonstration for the pictorial and plastic arts in the *Paragone* in the sixteenth century. These treatises were the context of the painting and poetry debates of the sixteenth century, and it is not surprising that a similarly Aristotelian hierarchy of knowledges—a hierarchy that "privileges" the speculative and theoretical we would say today—appears in English arts treatises of the sixteenth century as well, such as Thomas Wilson's *Arte of Rhetorique* and *Rule of Reason*, Robert Recorde's geometry *The Pathway to Knowledge*, and others, at the same time as it values the practical.

39. See Jonathan Culler, *Structuralist Poetics: Structuralism, Linguistics, and the Study of Literature* (Ithaca, N.Y.: Cornell Univ. Press, 1975), p. 128.

40. On "histories" rather than "History," see the work of Frank Lentricchia, *After the New*

Criticism (Chicago: Univ. of Chicago Press, 1980), pp. xiii–xiv, and Michael McCanles, "The Authentic Discourse of the Renaissance," *Diacritics* 10 (1980): 77–87.

41. See F. J. Levy, "Sir Philip Sidney and the Idea of History," *Bibliothèque d'humanisme et renaissance* 26 (1964): 608–17; Elizabeth S. Donno, "Old Mouse-Eaten Records: History in Sidney's Apology," *SP* 72 (1975): 275–98; and David Norbrook, *Poetry and Politics in the English Renaissance* (Boston: Routledge and Kegan Paul, 1984), for three different views of Sidney's use of history. Levy's later essay, "Sir Philip Sidney Reconsidered," *ELR* 2 (1972): 5–18, examines Sidney's choice, as a man of action, both to seek the role of the statesman while playing the part of the courtier in the unfolding of Elizabethan history and to commit himself to a support of the Protestant League that added public "failure" to his private temperament of pessimism and melancholy. I see one qualification to the argument of Jerome J. McGann's brief discussion of Sidney's "Aristotelian" doctrine of imitation in the introduction to his edition of essays, *Historical Studies and Literary Criticism*, pp. 12–13, in which he attributes a "traditional" view of referentiality, moral essences, and history to Sidney's concept. The Platonic Augustinianism of Sidney's sense of tension between the building of history and the lively invention of character through poetic composition and reading suggests that Sidney saw the dilemma in giving history an essentialist reference and in giving poetry the status of known truth and did neither.

42. For an amplification see Ronald Levao's discussion of Sidney's ambivalent use of the word *vates* in *Renaissance Minds and Their Fictions: Cusanus, Sidney, Shakespeare* (Berkeley: Univ. of California Press, 1985), pp. 137–38. Levao contributes a great deal of philosophical precision to the discussion of Sidney's poetic theory by comparing it to those of Italian critics (pp. 103–33) but misses the further precision that would come from study of Sidney's use of the 1578 *Plato* and its Calvinist interests.

43. See Greene, *The Light in Troy*, pp. 11–19. I part ways with Greene as he follows Derrida on the drift of the *verbum* from the *res*, the slippage of significance, and the questioning of "Latinitas" in Dante and in other redactors of the *Aeneid* and the matter of Troy.

44. See Herbert Weisinger, "Renaissance Theories of the Revivals of the Fine Arts," *Italica* 20 (1943); John White, *The Birth and Rebirth of Pictorial Space* (London: Faber and Faber, 1957); Paul Oskar Kristeller, "The Modern System of the Arts," in *Renaissance Thought II* (New York: Harper and Row, 1965), pp. 163–227; Rensselaer Lee, *Ut Pictura Poesis: The Humanistic Theory of Painting* (New York: Norton, 1967); Michael Baxandall, *Giotto and the Orators: Humanist Observers of Painting in Italy and the Discovery of Pictorial Composition 1350–1450* (Oxford: Clarendon, 1971); and Erwin Panofsky, "Perspective as Symbolic Form," in private translation from *Vörtrage de Bibliothek Warburg*, 1921–25, and *Life and Art of Albrecht Dürer* (Princeton, N.J.: Princeton Univ. Press, 1955), p. 261.

45. Compare Leon Battista Alberti's rhetorical and moral sense of "history" in relation to painting: the artist practiced a "sensate wisdom" that made him like God (*Della Pittura*, trans. John R. Spencer [London: Routledge and Kegan Paul, 1956], p. 64), and see Lee's discussion of the learned painter in *Ut Pictura Poesis*, pp. 1–30.

46. *Methodus Historica, Duodecim Eiusdem Argumenti Scriptorum, Tam Veterum Quam Recentiorum, Commentariis Adaucta* (Basel, 1576); twelve treatises accompany the *Methodus ac Facilem Historiarum Cognitionem* of 1566, and another edition of 1579 added five more treatises. See Leonard F. Dean, "Bodin's *Methodus* in England before 1625," *SP* 39 (1942): 160–66. Also see Eric Cochrane, *Historians and Historiography in the Italian Renaissance* (Chicago: Univ. of Chicago Press, 1981). The sixth treatise in the 1576 *Methodus* is Johannes Antoninus Viperanus's "De Scribendi Historia," which typically asserts that history is a "mirror" in which one might see everything; the orator persuades, the poet makes similitudes (*effingere*), but the historian exemplifies the precepts of philosophy (p. 851). Several other treatises discuss the writing of history or the rules for writing it. Sidney mentioned Bodin's *Methodus* in a letter to his brother Robert, available in *The Complete Works*, ed. Albert Feuillerat, 4 vols. (Cambridge:

Cambridge Univ. Press, 1912), 3:130. Saint Augustine compared the historical order of the ages to the parts of a poem in *De Vera Religione* 22.42–43. His clarity about one difference in his similitude, however, suggests that Augustine considered the fixed referentiality of history a reality only incompletely known by the human mind that labors within it. Anyone can read all of a poem, which is read for us to judge it, he says; but no one can know all of history: we are parts of the endless order because of our being, and the source of history is made up of the labors of those who will be judged.

47. *The Civil Wars*, ed. Laurence Michel, 2 vols. (New Haven: Yale Univ. Press, 1958), in the prefatory letter to Sidney's sister, the Countess of Pembroke (1:68). Cf. Greene, *The Light in Troy*, pp. 6, 272, on Daniel.

48. See Katherine R. Firth, *The Apocalyptic Tradition in Reformation Britain 1530–1645* (Oxford: Oxford Univ. Press, 1979), pp. 4–6, 109–10, and C. A. Patrides and Joseph Wittreich, eds., *The Apocalypse in English Renaissance Thought and Literature* (Ithaca, N.Y.: Cornell Univ. Press, 1984). See also Murrin's discussion, "Allegory and Prophecy in the Ancient World," in *Veil*, pp. 21–53, and cf. Paisley Livingston's association of theory with "sacred matter" and its observation by envoys sent to watch religious rituals ("From Prophecy to Inquiry," in *Literary Knowledge*, pp. 10ff.).

49. See Hegel's discussion of the relation of philosophy to religion in the *Introduction to the Lectures on the History of Philosophy*, trans. Knox and Miller, pp. 124–25, in which Hegel asserts that they have a common subject matter in what is absolutely true, but philosophy is pure thinking while religion incorporates the play of imagination in mythology. Although Hegel is usually identified as the philosopher of the secular divinization of man, his discussion of Christ, the Spirit, and his own Lutheran faith (pp. 126–36) is more nuanced than such a representation suggests. Regarding religion and philosophy, Hegel tries to avoid a "false peace" (p. 145). Regarding religion and art, Hegel argues that the spirit has a peculiar form in religion that is sensuously perceptible in the forms of art, since art portrays Divinity, "and in poetry, in which likewise a sensuous presentation constitutes the essence of the exposition. We may say, generally speaking, that this mode of spirit's formation is imagination" (p. 137). Sidney's effort to interrelate and yet distinguish religion, philosophy, history, and poesie reflects a similar but earlier post-Reformation faith. Livingston emphasizes a corollary point about Hegel's aesthetics and the judgment of ends and means: once a literary text is not pursued as an end in itself but a means to something, it has uncertain value (*Literary Knowledge*, p. 259). In this respect Sidney's view of poetic imagination anticipates the Hegelian assessment of value, for renaissance art characteristically places its technical perfection and aesthetic pleasure at the service of a higher end; poesie is more important than poetry.

50. See McGann, *Social Values and Poetic Acts*, pp. 74–75, on the need to use both grammatological and documentary modes of analysis in looking at the discourse of a poem. The documentary mode associated with history confronts poetic discourse as "a particular deed of language" taking place according to "certain particular rules and possibilities" with "particular ends in view," all of which change "with time and circumstances." Thus, McGann explains, "The reading of the performative dimension of the poetic event has to seek the same kind of concreteness and specificity which grammatological readings have always insisted upon. The horizon of concreteness in the performative dimension is social and historical." This is a strong contemporary statement of what justifies literary history, in my view, and I prefer it as a standard for reading the "voices" of absent presences through the renaissance writer's use of prosopopoeia to the "grammatological" and utterly boundless view of Jonathan Goldberg in *Voice Terminal Echo: Post-Modernism and English Renaissance Texts* (New York: Methuen, 1986). I would prefer to read "echo" in the Renaissance as John Hollander does in *The Figure of Echo: A Mode of Allusion in Milton and After* (Berkeley: Univ. of California Press, 1981), especially pp. 29, 63 on a resonance returning to its origin in the Word of God.

51. In the *Poetices Libri Septem* (Lyons, 1561) 3.33, p. 122. Scaliger is here discussing figures of definition, which he considers "quasi-analogical." Sidney seems to have gotten his notion

of models or paradigms from this sort of rhetorical discussion, which is itself an architectural analogy. *Tractatio,* according to Scaliger, is a figure of definition related to Quintilian's "deformationis," and then Scaliger gives his own comparison: "id quod architecti modulum, vulgus Italicum adhuc magis diminutiua voce dicunt, *Modellum."* He follows a similar path with "image" or "icon." See the discussion in chapter 1, pp. 65–67. Scaliger's definition of prosopopoeia, similarly, presents it as both the introduction of a fictive persona in a disputation and a figure that *consciously* divides a disputation by presenting different "voices" or perspectives on a subject (*Poetics* 3.48, p. 126). See chapter 1, p. 4.

52. See William K. Wimsatt, Jr., and Cleanth Brooks, *Literary Criticism: A Short History* (New York: Knopf, 1957), p. 423, on the difference between Sidney's *Defence* and Shelley's *Defence* being "as deep as the difference between Aristotle and Kant." Also see their remarks on pp. 490–91 as Wimsatt and Brooks propose for criticism the Kantian origins of formalism, and see Livingston, *Literary Knowledge,* pp. 27–29, for a caricature of the modern critical attitude that "something happened after Kant." Livingston aptly comments that the dichotomies drawn in modern assessments of the Enlightenment and its contraries are "too tidy to be trusted" (p. 1). Culler had suggested in *Structuralist Poetics,* p. viii, that French structuralism would help to "revitalize criticism and free it from an exclusively interpretive role" and contribute toward developing "a programme which would justify it as a mode of knowledge." Livingston's book moves in that direction by trying to relate literary theory to developments in the social and natural sciences and developing a notion of literary theory that is epistemological (p. 17).

53. Aristotle etymologically explained the architectonic knowledges with regard to *archia;* the architectonic arts are especially called "beginnings" or "first" because they are *directing* principles (*Metaphysics* 5.1 [1013a]) characterized by knowledge of final cause (*Metaphysics* 1.1 [981a–b]).

54. Richards's book was first published in 1925, and in it he performed his own analogy of the arts as he sorted out psychology, painting, sculpture, and poetry with regard to form and one's responses to form.

55. See Culler's *Structuralist Poetics,* pp. 96ff., on linguistic metaphors in criticism. Structuralism poses its question of analogy as an inquiry into whether the individual literary work is like a language or whether literature as a whole is like a language. The analogy of the arts and sciences in the renaissance *dispute dell'arti* opened up the definition of poetics to much broader cognitive and epistemological comparisons; for if the Middle Ages analogized music and then poetry to grammar, that analogy continued with some force into the Renaissance, and Sidney's mistress-knowledge absorbs the role of grammar but extends the possibilities of poesie to any number of kinds of knowledge; and that is why cognitive and epistemological concerns are central to the understanding of the *Defence* and why "intellectual decorum" is a feature of literary architectonics.

56. Aristotle placed the character of architectonic knowledge or mastercraftsmanship precisely in the possession of the knowledge of final cause: "Master craftsmen are superior in wisdom not because they can do things, but because they possess a theory and know the cause" (*Metaphysics* 1.1 [981a–b]). Kant promised a Copernican revolution in metaphysics but did not achieve it, with the result that his architectonic is the elaboration of a rationale but not truly a theory and a knowledge of causes in Aristotle's sense.

57. See, for example, Murray Krieger's counterpointing of "presence and illusion" in his study of metaphor in his book already cited, *Poetic Presence and Illusion.* Krieger tries to keep the double sense operative; acknowledges that his notions seem "derived from the post-Kantian tradition," which is hardly fashionable "in these post-Hegelian and post-Nietzschean days" (p. xii); and looks wisely at "the concept of poetic imagination in the Renaissance as it relates to metaphysical claims on the one hand and to a philosophy of language on the other" (p. 3). In short, Krieger's thinking makes a strong case against deconstruction regarding renaissance theory and renaissance poetic texts. Krieger amplifies the case by noting that "the

disappearance of God" is emphatic in Derrida and in Paul de Man: "Verbal meanings seem to follow God out of experience, the one abandoning our language as the other abandons our world" (p. 172), and he sees both existential senses of absence as "a lingering Heideggerean impulse" from the post-Heggelian perspective that may cite Terry Eagleton's caricature of phenomenology in The Function of Criticism from the Spectator to Post-Structuralism (London: Verso Editions, 1984) as a theory of reading that provided a kind of phenomenology converted the literary work into a subject in its own right, offering the epistemology of reading itself, that erotic coupling or merging of subject and object everywhere absent in social reality" (p. 93).

58. Martin Heidegger, "The Anaximander Fragment," in Early Greek Thinking: The Dawn of Western Philosophy, trans. David Farrell Krell and Frank A. Capuzzi (New York: Harper and Row, 1975), pp. 13–58. Heidegger sees presence—"the Being of beings"—"gathered in the ultimacy of its destiny" thus disappearing with its truth still veiled. "The history of Being is gathered in this departure" (p. 18), he says, and "thinking of Being is the original way of poeticizing" (p. 19).

59. Heidegger says that "Hegel is the only Western thinker who has thoughtfully experienced the history of thought" ("Anaximander Fragment," p. 14) and remarks that "the eschatology of Being" or its gathering in departure is to be thought in the way the phenomenology of spirit is to be thought, that is, "from within the history of Being" (p. 18), and not theologically. "The phenomenology of spirit itself constitutes a phase in the eschatology of Being, when Being gathers itself in the ultimacy of its essence, hitherto determined through metaphysics, as the absolute subjectivity of the unconditioned will to will" (p. 18).

60. Vincent B. Leitch, Deconstructive Criticism: An Advanced Introduction (New York: Columbia Univ. Press, 1983), traces Derrida's movement away from the phenomenology of Husserl and Heidegger in his deconstructive counter-readings of their metaphysics of presence (pp. 39–40), which begins with Derrida's La Voix et la Phenomene (1967), trans. David B. Allison as Speech and Phenomena: And Other Essays on Husserl's Theory of Signs (Evanston: Northwestern Univ. Press, 1973). Cf. Jonathan Culler's discussion of Derrida's criticism of the "metaphysics of presence" in structuralism in Structuralist Poetics (pp. 19–20, 132–33, 244–45).

61. "Anaximander Fragment," pp. 17–19. I cite Heidegger here only to emphasize his parallels to Kant's critique of history later, in my Epilogue.

62. Leitch says that Derrida has kept referencing Husserl and Heidegger throughout his entire critical enterprise (Deconstructive Criticism, p. 40). Leitch also describes the deconstruction of Joseph Riddel as one that evolved out of formalism through phenomenology to a position between Derrida and Heidegger, for which triangulation J. Hillis Miller criticized Riddel (p. 89).

63. Wimsatt and Brooks, Literary Criticism, p. 170. On deconstruction and New Criticism see Rudolphe Gasche, "Deconstruction as Criticism," Glyph 6 (1979): 177–216. Deconstruction supposedly gives up the project of "interpreting" texts, but its linguistic and philosophical inquiry into the verbal operations of texts has actually lent it, in practice, to the methodical use of a generation of younger critics and scholars precisely for the work of interpretation or "readings" of texts.

64. See Terry Eagleton's caricature of "the Yale school" in Function of Criticism, pp. 92, 100–102.

65. René Wellek, A History of Modern Criticism: 1750–1950, 4 vols. (London: Jonathan Cape, 1955), 1:6, makes the remark with regard to neoclassicism as a fusion of Aristotle and Horace that underwent little change in three centuries, from the sixteenth-century Sidney to the eighteenth-century Dr. Johnson:

> This fact alone establishes something that many literary historians are reluctant to recognize: the deep gulf between theory and practice throughout the history of literature. . . .

> Literary styles had undergone profound revolutions during these three centuries, but no new or different theory of literature was ever formulated. The metaphysicals . . . wrote poetry totally different in structure and local detail from that of Spenser.

Obviously, in trying to work out Sidney's definition of literary architectonics in its evolution out of renaissance knowledge and also in its influence well into the seventeenth century, I see certain continuities both in theory and in style that Wellek does not allow.

Similarly, while I respect John Steadman's informed and learned judgment in resisting the making of large-scale generalizations about renaissance aesthetic theories or texts (*The Lamb and the Elephant*, p. xiv), I think Sidney's *Defence* is an exception because of its quite measurable formative influence on major poems of the English Renaissance and because focusing on its theory narrows the channels of transmission quite a bit. Cf. Murrin's comments on renaissance views of allegory and their continuation in metaphysical poetry and, by other names, in the poetry of the romantics (*Veil*, pp. 197–98).

66. In *Deconstructive Criticism* Vincent B. Leitch also explains that Derrida in *De la grammatologie* sees Saussure's semiology as "a final gasp of Western philosophy, that is, of a metaphysical system that spans from Plato to Aristotle to Heidegger and Levi-Strauss," namely, logocentrism (p. 24).

67. See Steadman, *The Lamb and the Elephant*, on the "divine science" (pp. xix–xxiv), and for the caveat that we may not assume that all renaissance poets in practice "consciously subordinated poetics to the ends of theology or moral philosophy" (p. xviii). Within the Renaissance I would especially look at the complex development of rhetoric. The bibliography on rhetoric is extensive, but from it I would single out the following as especially significant: W. S. Howell, *Logic and Rhetoric in England 1500–1700* (New York: Russell and Russell, 1956); Lisa Jardine, "The Place of Dialectic Teaching in Sixteenth-Century Cambridge," *Studies in the Renaissance* 22 (1974): 31–62; Richard A. Lanham, *Motives of Eloquence: Literary Rhetoric in the Renaissance* (New Haven: Yale Univ. Press, 1976); and William J. Kennedy, *Rhetorical Norms in Renaissance Literature* (New Haven: Yale Univ. Press, 1978). Two essays give an historical summary: Richard J. McKeon, "Rhetoric in the Middle Ages," *Speculum* 17 (1942): 1–32, and Walter Ong, S.J., "Tudor Writings on Rhetoric, Poetic, and Literary Theory," in *Rhetoric, Romance, and Technology* (Ithaca, N.Y.: Cornell Univ. Press, 1971), pp. 48–103. A new and most provocative book is Patricia Parker's *Literary Fat Ladies*, in which the first chapter, "Literary Fat Ladies and the Generation of the Text," pp. 8–35, moves from Saint Augustine's sense of dilating a text and Erasmus's view of *copia* through Derrida, and the second chapter, "The Metaphorical Plot," pp. 36–53, is a superb tracing of the origins of metaphor in "place" or "topics" and its complicated historical course toward indeterminacy. See also the collection of essays by Yale critics, *Rhetoric and Form: Deconstruction at Yale*, ed. Robert Con Davis and Ronald Schliefer (Norman: Univ. of Oklahoma Press, 1988).

68. See Kathleen M. Davies, "The Sacred Condition of Equality—How Original Were Puritan Doctrines of Marriage?" *Social History* 5 (1977): 563–80; John K. Yost, "The Value of Married Life for the Social Order in the Early English Renaissance," *Societas* 6 (1976): 25–39; Steven Ozment, *When Fathers Ruled: Family Life in Reformation Europe* (Cambridge, Mass.: Harvard Univ. Press, 1986); and James G. Turner, *One Flesh: Paradisal Marriage and Sexual Relations in the Age of Milton* (Oxford: Clarendon, 1987).

69. In this I find myself partly agreeing with Lawrence Lipking on "otherness" and the manner in which it is perceived but may break down as an hypothesis and partly disagreeing with his reluctance to receive certain feminine archetypes into purview *without* skepticism (*Abandoned Women and Poetic Tradition*, pp. xxiff.).

70. *Rewriting the Renaissance: The Discourses of Sexual Difference in Early Modern Europe* (Chicago: Univ. of Chicago Press, 1986), p. xxi.

71. For studies of Sidney and power see Louis Adrian Montrose, " 'Shaping Fantasies': Figurations of Gender and Power in Elizabethan Culture," *Representations* 1 (1983): 61–94, and

In Mirrors More Than One: Elizabeth I and the Figurations of Power (Chicago: Univ. of Chicago Press, 1986).

72. Cf. Thomas M. Greene, *The Vulnerable Text: Essays on Renaissance Literature* (New York: Columbia Univ. Press, 1986); Jon Stratton, *The Virgin Text: Fiction, Sexuality, Ideology* (Norman: Univ. of Oklahoma Press, 1986); and Mary Jacobus, *Reading Woman: Essays in Feminist Criticism* (New York: Columbia Univ. Press, 1986), particularly pp. 3–35 and her discussion of the symbolic value of Judith's chastity in the overcoming of Holofernes as a recurrent incident in literary and pictorial art.

73. Linda Woodbridge, *Women and the English Renaissance: Literature and the Nature of Womankind, 1540–1620* (Urbana: Univ. of Illinois Press, 1986), has widely documented the historical sources of the feminist and antifeminist debate, which she finds rooted in "patristic misogyny" that was "perfectly compatible with Aristotelian notions of women's innate imperfection" (p. 15). The mixture of classical and Judeo-Christian sources was useful to *both* defenses of and attacks on women (p. 15; cf. p. 17 n.1). However, in the same way that Chaucer's Wife of Bath was able to "resource" Scripture and the Fathers, especially Saint Jerome's treatise advocating virginity, *Ad Jovinianum*, I think women's history can gain from looking at patristic sources on virginity from the perspective of power, not male definition. Another way to put this point is simply to say, with Judith Newton in "Making—and Remaking—History: Another Look at Patriarchy," in *Feminist Issues in Literary Scholarship*, ed. Benstock, pp. 124–40, that there is a "tendency in feminist criticism toward tragic essentialism in regard to male domination" (p. 125).

74. See Nina Baym, "The Madwoman and Her Languages: Why I Don't Do Feminist Criticism," in *Feminist Issues in Literary Scholarship*, ed. Benstock, pp. 45–61, especially pp. 54–56 on Lacan, Freud, and feminists.

75. *Critique et vérité* (Paris: (Éditions du Seuil, 1966), p. 79.

76. *Structuralist Poetics*, p. 255. Culler says that the possibility of looking at literature through a linguistic model "helped to justify the idea to abandon literary history and biographical criticism" and has been "eminently salutary" in "securing for the French some of the benefits of Anglo-American 'New Criticism.' "

77. Jacobus, *Reading Woman*, p. 4.

78. See Steadman on the boundaries of the Renaissance, especially its end, in *The Lamb and the Elephant*, pp. 213–31.

79. See McGann's reminder (in *Social Values and Poetic Acts*, pp. 14–16) that Nietzsche, in his role as a philologist, dismissed philology. McGann argues that while one should not revive "the historicist program," one should and must "reincorporate its work into literary studies" (p. 16). Cf. Nietzsche's remark, in the notes included by Walter Kaufman, ed., *The Portable Nietzsche* (New York: Viking, 1954), p. 75, that "one hardly dares to speak any more of the will to power: it was different in Athens."

80. *The Idea of History* (Oxford: Clarendon, 1946; Oxford: Oxford Univ. Press, 1956) was composed during the crucial prewar years of the thirties. Cf. Ernst Cassirer, "Fundamental Forms and Tendencies of Historical Knowledge," part 3 of *The Problem of Knowledge: Philosophy, Science, and History Since Hegel* (New Haven: Yale Univ. Press, 1950), pp. 217–325. Cassirer observes that the questioning of historicism has grown more and more severe since Nietzsche's publication of *Unzeitgemässen Betrachtungen* in 1874, but that it would be a mistake "to believe, however, that historical thinking as such was discovered, and its specific value to knowledge first realized by Herder and romanticism" (p. 216). Interestingly he notes Herder's late eighteenth-century perception of the heart of nature and the heart of history in the man of feeling as Herder sought to compose a history of the human spirit. "All that had happened in the past became an allegory, for only in allegory could the nature of man be grasped and expressed" (p. 220).

81. *PMLA* 102 (1987): 292–303. But see Christine Froula's response to Pechter's thinking about the poem as an historical artifact and the problems of the definition of poetic inspira-

tion, spirit, and numinosity in "Pechter's Specter: Milton's Bogey Writ Small," *CI* 11 (1984): 171–78, and Pechter's remarks in the same issue, "When Pechter Reads Froula, Pretending She's Eve Reading Milton; or, New Feminist Is But Old Priest Writ Large," pp. 163–70.

82. *English Literature in the Sixteenth Century* (Oxford: Clarendon, 1954), p. 346.

83. In *Literary Theory/Renaissance Texts*, ed. Parker and Quint, pp. 373–96.

84. *Mnemosyne: The Parallel between Literature and the Visual Arts* (Princeton, N.J.: Princeton Univ. Press, 1974), pp. 18–27.

85. See especially "The Modern System of the Arts," in *Renaissance Thought II*, pp. 163–227, and in the same volume, "The Moral Thought of Renaissance Humanism," pp. 20–68.

86. *The Art of Poetry*, trans. Denise Folliot (New York: Pantheon, 1958), pp. 78–79. Cf. Barkan's discussion of Sidney's allegory of the body in *Astrophil and Stella* as the transformation of the body into "a complete machine" (*Nature's Work of Art*, p. 184). Barkan rightly assesses "the allegorical heterocosm" in Spenser and in other poets who distill "a total experience or world view into a complex poetic machine," quoting Saint Gregory the Great in his *Commentary on the Song of Songs* on how the allegory of the soul is proposed by God in the manner of a machine raising the soul to God (pp. 206–7). The Gregorian view is sympathetic, strange to say, with the Hegelian view in which "the spiritual animal kingdom" and the "beautiful soul" are both forms of "defective selfhood." See Donald Philip Verene, *Hegel's Recollection: A Study of the Images of the Phenomenology of Spirit* (Albany, N.Y.: State Univ. Press of New York, 1985), who sees the first defect coming at the end of reason and leading to "the self-absorbed high mindedness" of the Stoic and the skeptic and the vices of German romanticism, the nineteenth-century empire builder, the American business executive, and the Nazi (p. 93) and to the problem of the uses of technology (p. 96), and the second defect arising in romanticism, particularly in Novalis, in the end of the spirit. The idea of the beautiful soul contests philosophy from the side of the subject; it is morally and intellectually dangerous because it is "a degenerate version of the relation of self-consciousness to the absolute" (p. 101).

87. *Elizabethan and Metaphysical Imagery*, p. 147.

88. *Shifting Gears: Technology, Literature, and Culture in Modernist America* (Chapel Hill: Univ. of North Carolina Press, 1987), pp. 130ff. Also see Strother B. Purdy, "Technopoetics: Seeing What Literature Has to Do with the Machine," *CI* 11 (1984): 130–40.

89. *About the House* (New York: Random House, 1965), pp. 3–4. Auden's comments on poetry as a game of knowledge may be found in his essay, "Squares and Oblongs," in *Poets at Work*, ed. Charles D. Abbott (New York: Harcourt, Brace, and World, 1948), pp. 171–81.

90. The fullest precise discussion of the implications of Protestant thinking for English renaissance poetics as a whole is Barbara Lewalski's opening chapter in *Protestant Poetics and the Seventeenth-Century Religious Lyric* (Princeton, N.J.: Princeton Univ. Press, 1979), pp. 3–27.

91. "Patriarchal Territories: The Body Enclosed," in *Rewriting the Renaissance*, pp. 123–42. See also Stanley Stewart's *The Enclosed Garden: The Tradition and the Image in Seventeenth-Century Poetry* (Madison: Univ. of Wisconsin Press, 1966), pp. 3–30, in which Stewart discusses the Elizabethan and Stuart poets' paraphrases of Solomon's Song of Songs, and pp. 31–59, in which Stewart quite rightly establishes the primary sense of the *hortus conclusus* with regard to a contained and unopened space, that is, with regard to a virginal femininity. Stewart explains that "the value of chastity reflects a view of history which is at the core of the Canticles tradition" and doubles the image of the eternal and the temporal, of Mary and Eve, of the wise Solomon and the sinful Solomon (pp. 33–35). In developing the troubles of the temporal version, modern literary theories tend to underplay the doubling that Stewart and others have carefully and correctly denoted.

92. *Hidden Designs: The Critical Profession and Renaissance Literature* (New York: Methuen, 1986), pp. 73–74. See also the review of recent criticism of renaissance texts by Donald Cheney (*SEL 1500–1900* 28 [1988]: 149–91) in which he questions the fascination of Crewe and other

critics with logocentric anxieties and challenges the apparent replacement of Sidney with Puttenham in contemporary examinations of patterns of meaning and of censored desire.

93. *The Faerie Queene*, Book 1, stanza 4 of the Proem.

Chapter 4

1. *William Temple's Analysis of Sir Philip Sidney's Apology for Poetry*, ed. and trans. John Webster (Binghamton, N.Y.: Center for Medieval & Early Renaissance Studies, 1984). The idea that Sidney's metaphoric discourse in the *Defence* is *not* a conscious art of accounting for poetic fiction also persists in modern criticism; see, for example, D. H. Craig, " 'A Hybrid Growth': Sidney's Theory of Poetry in *An Apology for Poetry*," *ELR* 10 (1980): 183–201.

2. In *The Pursuit of Signs* (Ithaca, N.Y.: Cornell Univ. Press, 1981), p. 109, Jonathan Culler discusses the problem of intertextuality as a critical concept developed by Barthes and Kristeva, asking what distinguishes intertextuality from source studies of a traditional kind and from the examination of pre-texts and presuppositions convenient to the critic's interpretation. See also Culler's *Structuralist Poetics: Structuralism, Linguistics, and the Study of Literature* (Ithaca, N.Y.: Cornell Univ. Press, 1975), pp. 139–60, and especially Kristeva's *Desire in Language: A Semiotic Approach to Literature and Art* (New York: Columbia Univ. Press, 1980), pp. 52–54 on blazon and citation, and pp. 76–85 on "epic monologism," carnival, Socratic dialogue, and Menippean discourse. Cf. Martin Raitiere, *Faire Bitts: Sir Philip Sidney and Renaissance Political Theory* (Pittsburgh, Pa.: Duquesne Univ. Press, 1984), p. 17, on the judgment of Calvinism that making a "fiction" is an egregious wrong, on Sidney's part or on anyone else's. I disagree insofar as the human construction of images for cognitive purposes is unavoidable by even Calvinist standards; these asked for an avoidance of the fashioning of religious idols and for wise use, not abuse, of icons *as* icons, and Sidney advocates a similar policy. See also Maureen Quilligan on the *Defence* as an oration "written to be read" in *Milton's Spenser: The Politics of Reading* (Ithaca, N.Y.: Cornell Univ. Press, 1983), pp. 31–36.

3. *Institutes of the Christian Religion* 2.2.11, ed. John T. McNeill and trans. Ford Lewis Battles, 2 vols. (Philadelphia: Westminster, 1960), 1:268–69.

4. See *Temple's Analysis*, ed. Webster, p. 12, on Temple's division of the *Defence* into confirmation and refutation, and see M. H. Partee, "Anti-Platonism in Sidney's *Defence*," *EM* 22 (1971): 7–29, on the resemblance between Sidney's poet and Plato's philosopher.

5. Cf. Joseph Fargnoli, "Patterns of Imagination in Sir Philip Sidney's *Defence of Poesie*," *Massachusetts Studies in English* 8 (1982): 36–42.

6. Cf. Margaret W. Ferguson, *Trials of Desire: Renaissance Defenses of Poetry* (New Haven: Yale Univ. Press, 1983), on Joachim du Bellay and "The Exile's Defense of His Native Language," pp. 18–53.

7. *De Inventione, De Optime Genere Oratorum, and Topica*, trans. H. M. Hubbell (London: William Heinemann, 1949).

8. One might be tempted to see "intersubjectivity" at work here, but I think Kristeva's comments on the origin of Menippean discourse as social discourse (*Desire in Language*, pp. 82–84ff.) in the carnivalesque, which is "anti-christian and antirationalist" (p. 79), rule out the identification of the *Defence* as a kind of Menippean statement. One should compare, though, Kristeva's comments on Socratic dialogism as a destruction of the person because the subjects are "nonpersons" hidden by the discourse constituting them (pp. 80–81). Cf. Ferguson's dialogic argument that Sidney is not a "blunderer" but a "counterfeiter" (*Trials of Desire*, 1p. 138). The more ordinary classical source of Cicero's invention of confirmation and the renaissance source of Scaliger's definition of prosopopoeia as a means to divide a disputation through question and answer achieve the same purpose, on Sidney's part, quite consciously, and support an even more "cogent" oratorical case for poetry in the *Defence* than dialogism.

9. On the medieval tradition of the personifications of learning and language, see W. H.

Stahl, Richard Johnson, and E. L. Burge, eds., *Martianus Capella and the Seven Liberal Arts*, 2 vols. (New York: Columbia Univ. Press, 1971, 1977).

10. See Linda Woodbridge, *Women and the English Renaissance: Literature and the Nature of Womankind, 1540–1620* (Urbana: Univ. of Illinois Press, 1986), p. 25, for the discussion of the *Defence* as a judicial oration in Quintilian's sense, mixing confirmation and refutation or divided into five parts. Woodbridge also notes that the judicial oration is aimed at attack and defense. Cf. Ferguson, *Trials of Desire*, passim, whose Freudian argument of accusation and defense seems to observe five parts.

11. See Kenneth Myrick, *Sir Philip Sidney as a Literary Craftsman*, 2d ed. (Cambridge, Mass.: Harvard Univ. Press, 1935; Lincoln: Univ. of Nebraska Press, 1965), pp. 84–109, and cf. Katherine Duncan-Jones and Jan van Dorsten, eds., *Miscellaneous Prose of Sir Philip Sidney* (Oxford: Clarendon, 1973), pp. 74–80. Geoffrey Shepherd, ed., *An Apology for Poetry* (London: Thomas Nelson and Sons, 1965; Manchester: Manchester Univ. Press, 1973), sees three sections and seven parts within them (pp. 12–17), although he notes the "highly artificial form" and "clear, intelligible line of argument" throughout (p. 12). Robert Kimbrough, ed., *Sir Philip Sidney, Selected Prose and Poetry*, 2d ed. (Madison: Univ. of Wisconsin Press, 1983), p. 100, differs on where the divisions into seven parts fall but keeps the conventional seven-part division; at the same time, Kimbrough observes that "even with the division . . . the art of the whole is so graceful and complete that it tends to hide the very art of its creation" (p. 100). Robinson, ed., *An Apology* (Indianapolis: Bobbs-Merrill, 1970), remarks that "Sidney erected his treatise on the foundation of the classical oration," and that publication in 1595 "marks the advent of neoclassicism in England" (p. xviii). Robert M. Strozier, "Poetic Conception in Sir Philip Sidney's *An Apology for Poetry*," *YES* 2 (1972): 49–60, argues the case for unity of thought and structure in Sidney's text, and O. B. Hardison, Jr., "The Two Voices of Sidney's *Apology for Poetry*," *ELR* 2 (1972): 83–99, disputes Myrick's view of the seven-part division of the *Defence* and suggests that Sidney independently formulated the structure of his "oration" according to "two voices," one of humanistic poetic theory and the other of incipient neoclassicism. See Thomas Wilson's definitions of the seven parts in *The Arte of Rhetorique* (1560), ed. G. H. Mair (Oxford: Clarendon, 1909), p. 7. Webster, "Oration and Method in Sidney's *Apology: A Contemporary Account*," *MP* 79 (1981): 1–15, also contrasts Temple's two-part division with editorial seven-part divisions.

12. See Dorothy Connell's illuminating remarks on Sidney, Erasmus, and the defense of poesie and praise of folly in her book, *Sir Philip Sidney, the Maker's Mind* (Oxford: Clarendon, 1977), pp. 5–6, 38–39. Also see Elliott M. Simon, "Sidney's *Old Arcadia*: In Praise of Folly," *Sixteenth-Century Journal* 17 (1986): 285–302.

13. The *Enchiridion Militis Christiani* (Antwerp, 1503). Erasmus explains in his letter to Martin Dorp that *The Praise of Folly* performs as a kind of literary joke the same serious doctrine of the Christian life discussed in the *Enchiridion*; pleasure invites the reader to reflect (in *Christian Humanism and the Reformation: Selected Writings of Desiderius Erasmus*, ed. and trans. John C. Olin [New York: Harper and Row, 1965], pp. 59, 65). Cf. Kristeva on the ambivalence of Menippean discourse, which is serious and comic at once and therefore politically and socially disturbing as it frees speech from historical constraints (*Desire in Language*, pp. 82–84). Again the problem of definition here is dialogism that, Kristeva says, does battle against philosophy and religious metaphysics. In my view Erasmus certainly does battle against false religion and philosophy but ultimately with a higher religious purpose revealed in his *serio ludere*, his paradox of the wise folly of Christ, and Sidney does likewise.

14. I refer to the copy of the *Letter* printed in Duncan-Jones and van Dorsten, *Miscellaneous Prose*, pp. 46–57. Sidney's metaphors for the Queen's mystical marriage to her people are Solomonic; they may also show some kabbalistic influence or even understanding. See Gershom G. Scholem, *On the Kabbalah and Its Symbolism* (London: Routledge and Kegan Paul, 1965), pp. 132–39. Especially see Maureen Quilligan, "Sidney and His Queen," in *The Historical Renaissance: New Essays on Tudor and Stuart Literature and Culture*, ed. Heather Dubrow

and Richard Strier (Chicago: Univ. of Chicago Press, 1988), pp. 171–96, for a superb discussion of the *Letter*, Sidney's political posture in *Astrophil and Stella*, and the argument of Greville's biography on Sidney's relation to the Queen.

15. Bishop Kroomun's letter to Henry VIII, the *Ren001poponia Rritummion Majooio* (1400), nnn another contemporary example of the instruction of royalty discussed by Carole Levin, "John Foxe and the Responsibilities of Queenship," in *Women in the Middle Ages and the Renaissance: Literary and Historical Perspectives*, ed. Mary Beth Rose (Syracuse, N.Y.: Syracuse Univ. Press, 1986), pp. 113–33. Levin observes that Foxe, unlike the later Puritan Reformers, praised and warned Elizabeth at the beginning of her reign about the difficulties of a woman governing England and "was never openly willing to criticize this queen" (p. 129).

16. *Confessions*, trans. William Watts, 2 vols. (London, 1631; London: William Heinemann, 1912), 2:843–46. Where I cite other translations such as those by J. K. Ryan (New York: Doubleday, 1960) or by R. S. Pine-Coffin (Harmondsworth, Middlesex, Eng.: Penguin, 1961), I indicate accordingly.

17. The best overview of the development of the liberal arts from the Middle Ages to the eighteenth century is Richard McKeon's essay, "The Transformation of the Liberal Arts in the Renaissance," in *Developments in the Early Renaissance*, ed. Bernard S. Levy (Albany, N.Y.: State Univ. Press, 1972), pp. 158–223.

18. See Robert J. O'Connell, S.J., *Art and the Christian Intelligence in Saint Augustine* (Oxford: Basil Blackwell, 1978), pp. 28–49.

19. *Philosophiae Consolationis* 1.1.29, trans. "I.T." (1609); rev. H. F. Stewart (Cambridge, Mass.: Harvard Univ. Press, 1918). Much of my discussion of Boethius is informed with the insights of Pearl Kibre, Richard McKeon, and Winthrop Wetherbee expressed at a conference, "Boethius and the Liberal Arts," held at the Newberry Library, Chicago, October 5–6, 1973. Especially important in the published collection of conference essays is Myra L. Uhlfelder's essay, "The Role of the Liberal Arts in Boethius' *Consolatio*," in *Boethius and the Liberal Arts*, ed. Michael Masi, Utah Studies in Literature and Linguistics, vol. 18 (Las Vegas: Peter Lang, 1981), pp. 17–34. Cf. the description of the Muses as prostitutes to the babbling harlot who is Lady Wisdom's antitype in Proverbs 7:10–11 (Geneva Bible, p. 269^r) and to Sidney's conditional phrase on the disgraceful productivity of English poetry, "as if all the Muses were got with child to bring forth bastard poets" and "without any commission they do post over the banks of the Helicon, till they make their readers more weary than post-horses" (*Defence*, p. 111).

20. In the course of her development after Boethius had imagined her, Lady Philosophy became a favorite subject in medieval iconography. Sometimes she is pictured with a particular knowledge as her spokesman or handmaiden, her most effective means of communication; astronomy or grammar or dialectic was portrayed at particular moments by particular authors, for instance, as Lady Philosophy's most expressive *disciplina* or way of knowing. Thus particular knowledges, almost identified with her but not quite, were elevated to the status of a general or universal knowledge by means of the close association with a ruling philosophy. Iconographic representation of Lady Philosophy in the early renaissance book Reisch's *Margarita Philosophica*, which went through multiple publications between 1496 and 1535, shows how commonplace her image was. One edition pictures her as the root of all learning, for out of her body rises a tree trunk branching into the seven arts and sciences while she sits enthroned in a crowd of men and women. Her representation in another edition surrounds her with seven handmaidens as the seven arts and with symbols of the Holy Trinity to indicate that she is the mediation of human and divine knowledge, intermediate to the divine Person of Truth, aided by the theology of the Fathers of the Church, and directing all the arts and sciences. In an edition published in Basel in 1517, Lady Philosophy merges with the tree; the more theological integration of her image is in an edition published in Basel in 1535, both at the Folger Shakespeare Library. See especially Henry Chadwick, *Boethius: The Consolations of Music, Logic, Theology, and Philosophy* (Oxford: Clarendon, 1981), notably pp. 225–27 on

Lady Philosophy. See M. Thérèse d'Alverny, "La Sagesse et ses sept filles. Recherches sur les allégories de la philosophie et des arts libéraux du IXe au XIIe siècle," in *Mélanges dédiés a la memoire de Félix Grat* (Paris, 1946). See also David Wagner, *The Seven Liberal Arts in the Middle Ages* (Bloomington: Indiana Univ. Press, 1983).

21. For the Queen's translation see *Queen Elizabeth's Englishings*, ed. Caroline Pemberton, *EETS* O.S. 113 (London: Kegan Paul, Trench, Trübner & Co., 1899), pp. 1–120. Using Camden's notes, the editor assigns the translation to 1593 (p. vii). On renaissance antecedents to this sort of comfort literature, see Michael H. Means, *The Consolatio Genre in Medieval English Literature* (Gainesville: Univ. of Florida Press, 1972).

22. Compare Pico's discussion of the way God, the master-builder, fabricated the house of this world and then took man, a creature of indeterminate form, and placed him at the midpoint of the world to this androcentric concept of a text (*On the Dignity of Man*, trans. Charles Glenn Wallis [New York: Bobbs-Merrill, 1965], pp. 3–5). Pico knew the Kabbalah.

23. *Hamlet* 2.2.246–61, in *The Complete Works of Shakespeare*, ed. Hardin Craig (Glenview, Ill.: Scott, Foresman, 1951).

24. See S. L. Greenslade, *The English Reformers and the Fathers of the Church* (Oxford: Clarendon, 1960); Hughes Oliphant Old, *The Patristic Roots of Reformed Worship* (Zurich, 1975); and William P. Haaugaard, "Renaissance Patristic Scholarship and Theology in Sixteenth-Century England," *Sixteenth-Century Journal* 10 (1979): 37–60.

25. For studies of the general patristic context in which to place Augustine's thought, see Edwin Hatch, *The Influence of Greek Ideas on Christianity* (New York: Harper and Row, 1957; Gloucester, Mass.: Peter Smith, 1970); Werner Jaeger, *Early Christianity & Greek Paideia* (Cambridge, Mass.: Harvard Univ. Press, 1961; New York: Oxford Univ. Press, 1977); Henry Chadwick, *Early Christian Thought and the Classical Tradition* (Oxford: Clarendon, 1966); William R. Schoedel and Robert L. Wilken, eds., *Early Christian Literature and the Classical Intellectual Tradition* (Paris: Éditions Beauchesne, 1979); Andrew Louth, *The Origins of the Christian Mystical Tradition: From Plato to Denys* (Oxford: Clarendon, 1981); and Maurice Testard, *Chrétiens latins des premiers siècles: La littérature et la vie* (Paris: Société d'Édition, 1981).

26. In "The Transformation of the Liberal Arts," Richard P. McKeon has observed that Augustine adapted Plato's threefold philosophy (physics, logic, ethics) to the triune God of Christianity and put the liberal arts to hermeneutic, demonstrative, and persuasive uses (p. 163).

27. Besides affecting the ethical judgments of individuals in their personal journey back to God, Augustine's incorporation of the seven liberal arts into the seven gifts of the Holy Spirit in the *De Doctrina Christiana* (2.7–9) influenced the moral philosophical interpretation of Christian society and the building of the Christian state (see the translation by D. W. Robertson, Jr. [New York: Bobbs-Merrill, 1958]). Where possible I refer to this English translation of Augustine, after having checked it against Migne's *PL* or the *CCSL*, and I record title, book number, and section in my text. See Père M. D. Chenu's comments in "The Symbolist Mentality," in *Nature, Man, and Society in the Twelfth Century*, ed. and trans. Jerome Taylor and Lester K. Little (Chicago: Univ. of Chicago Press, 1968), p. 119. See *De Civitate Dei* 14.28; *De Trinitate* 14.15; and *De Doctrina Christiana* 1.39; 2.38 on the superiority of the love of God and of fraternal charity to knowledge; see *Enchiridion* 2 on the true wisdom of piety and worship.

28. The ten-volume edition of Saint Augustine (Paris: Claude Chevallon, 1531–32) autographed by Archbishop Cranmer is in the British Library. Vol. 2, *Epistolae*, shows marginal annotations on Augustine's answer to Marcellinus on the law, the Gospel, the republic, and the Christian prince (4^v–6^r); to Valentinus on free will (31^v–32^v); to Vincentius on the correction of heretics (32^v–37^v); and on other letters. Vol. 10 contains Cranmer's underlining of passages of the commentary on Saint John's Gospel, notably the section on the bread of life (John 6) and on the spirit and the flesh. In Augustine's commentary on the epistles of John,

Cranmer makes marginal notes on the questioning of heretics; where Augustine asks whether or not Jesus is the Christ, for example, Cranmer notes, in Latin, "Against the Donatists." The comment suggests Cranmer's familiarity with the ancient controversy and the use of Augustine's arguments in contemporary debate on the sacraments (10.1??).

29. *Platonic de Republica vel de Iusto*, Libri Decem (Paris, 1544), sig. Aii', translation mine. Ronald Levao, *Renaissance Minds and Their Fictions: Cusanus, Sidney, Shakespeare* (Berkeley. Univ. of California Press, 1985), uses Ficinian Neoplatonism to address tensions in Sidney's *Defence* (pp. 103–33), but see chapter 4 on Sidney's use of de Serres's *Plato* of 1578. Cf. Hegel's view of the evolution of Christian history toward the establishment of the ideal state in the opinion of Alexander Kojève, *Introduction to the Reading of Hegel*, ed. Allan Bloom, trans. James H. Nichols, Jr. (Ithaca, N.Y.: Cornell Univ. Press, 1969), pp. 66–67.

30. *Symposium* (1469), ed. and trans. Sears Reynolds Jayne, University of Missouri Studies, vol. 1, no. 19 (Columbia: Univ. of Missouri Press, 1944), p. 58.

31. Frederick Copleston, S.J., reminds us in *A History of Philosophy* (1950; reprint, New York: Doubleday, 1962) that Augustine did not elaborate a theory of knowledge as a methodological propaedeutic to metaphysics; he searched rather for the good that is a personal God and for the happiness to be gained in loving the truth that is a living Wisdom, and epistemological questions were useful in the articulation of those ends (2:1.4, p. 67). See Marcia Colish, *The Mirror of Language: A Study in the Medieval Theory of Knowledge* (New Haven: Yale Univ. Press, 1968).

32. *De Vera Religione* 49.98, in *Augustine: Earlier Writings*, trans. John H. S. Burleigh (Philadelphia: Westminster, 1953).

33. See also *De Doctrina Christiana* 2.40 (trans. Robertson). Cf. *De Doctrina Christiana* 2.12 on faith and the cleansed understanding, and Cicero's *De Officiis* 1.43–44 on the superiority of wisdom among the virtues and the superiority of social obligation among moral duties: "And service is better than mere theoretical knowledge, for the study and knowledge of the universe would somehow be lame and defective, were no practical results to follow" (trans. W. Miller [London: Heinemann, 1913]). Thus Cicero ranks justice above wisdom; Augustine unites wisdom and love in the person of the Word; and Sidney seeks the moral end of learning. See Webster, *Temple's Analysis*, p. 28, on Sidney's idea of poesie as a "messianic vehicle."

34. See *De Doctrina Christiana* 1.11; cf. 2.32; 2.39 on dialectic. Cf. Hegel's view of religion as impure philosophy because it uses images and myths in *Introduction to the Lectures on History of Philosophy*, trans. T. M. Knox and A. V. Miller (Oxford: Clarendon, 1985), pp. 125–30.

35. For Augustine, love is the motive of intellectual search, the standard of judgment in practical life, and the end of man's journey through time; see *De Trinitate* 7.3; *De Doctrina Christiana* 3.10–12; 1.22–40. In *De Trinitate* 12, Augustine distinguishes knowledge from wisdom; later he explains that the mind knows and loves itself by virtue of the image of God in it and in order to cleave to that image. "And when its cleaving to him has become absolute, it will be one spirit with him" (*De Trinitate* 14.20, in *Augustine: Later Works*, trans. John Burnaby [Philadelphia: Westminster, 1955], p. 118).

36. Augustine attributes ideas of universal disorder to lack of self-knowledge; the lack can be overcome by reflection and by liberal studies (*De Ordine* 1.1 in *CCSL* 29 [1970]). *De Ordine* 2.7 to the end gives a full account of the authority, reason, and order of study. By no means do the hermeneutical value of grammar, the demonstrative power of dialectic, and the persuasive role of rhetoric indicate that Augustine ignored the quadrivial sciences, the fine arts, or natural history. He did give all the arts and sciences an extraordinarily verbal cast. Unchangeable truth is "the law of all the arts and the art of the omnipotent artificer," the Word of God. In the *Republic* 7 (522c–534a), Socrates had established number, plane geometry, solid geometry, astronomy, harmony, and dialectic as an order of study; in the *Philebus* 66a–d, Plato provides another hierarchy of knowledge, wisdom, and pleasure by using the rule of the one and the many.

37. See *De Doctrina Christiana* 2.16 and compare *De Ordine* 2.9–11 on reason and authority; *De Civitate Dei* 12.18 on Scripture and Plato; *De Trinitate* 11 on the parallel of memory, thought, and voluntary attention to measure, number, and weight; and *De Vera Religione* 29–30 on the use to be made of the knowledge of nature and on the pleasure of symmetry. In *De Vera Religione* 32.59–33.61 Augustine compares the art of the Artificer to the role of beauty, intelligibility, and unity that workmen observe in building an arch. In *De Vera Religione* 31.66, Augustine discusses the truth of the Word: "If falsehood springs from things which imitate unity not insofar as they imitate it, but insofar as they cannot achieve it, the truth which does achieve it, and is identical with it, is unity and manifest unity as it is in reality. Hence it is rightly called unity's Word and Light" (trans. Burleigh). Cf. *De Civitate Dei* 22.24 on the blessings of the heavenly kingdom where the spirit of man may drink the wisdom of God at the fountainhead, in contrast to the blessings of speech, knowledge, and nature that give solace to the wretched in the present. Augustinian architectonics underwrites renaissance "justification."

38. *De Ordine* 2.20; cf. *De Doctrina Christiana* 2.39. Augustine mentions history as a specially useful knowledge to have. Cf. *Soliloquies* 1.13, in *Augustine: Earlier Writings*, trans. Burleigh, pp. 73–74.

39. See, for example, Augustine's discussion of the cases of Theodosius and of Alypius in *De Civitate Dei* 5.26 and *Confessions* 6.10, respectively, with regard to their roles as statesmen.

40. Persuasion to the truth helps one avoid the danger of coming too late to the divine Beauty, ever ancient and ever new, because of the vagaries of an unguided search (*Confessions* 10.27). The search—the philosophical quest—implements learning and charity in the work of Christian rhetoric but operates, too, as special reminiscence. By remembering, understanding, and loving, human nature may accomplish the various tasks of knowledge; by remembering, understanding, and loving God in the chaste mind of the City of God, however, human nature performs the work—and knows the joy—of the only wisdom truly possible, that is, the worship of God that is the recovery of the paradise within. The thinking that recalls the trinity of memory, understanding, and will, in which the human likeness to the Holy Trinity resides, is a temporal process; see *De Trinitate* 10 on self-knowledge, and 11–13 on the trinity of sense, imagination, and faith, and cf. *De Vera Religione* 22.42–43 on change, temporality, and transiency in poetry and history. See *De Trinitate* 14.15 (trans. Burnaby) on the only human wisdom possible, that is, the worship of God.

41. See chapter 4, pp. 237, 247–48. Also see *De Trinitate* 13; 15.15; 15.20; 15.24–26; 15.30–32; 15.44 on the inward word and human likeness to divine Wisdom. Cf. *De Civitate Dei* 22.24; and Peter Brown, *Augustine of Hippo* (Berkeley: Univ. of California Press, 1967), pp. 325–29, on human love and on Augustine's transformation of classical ethics.

42. See the *Soliloquies* 2.20.35, and *The Greatness of the Soul* 2.20.34. Also see Peter Brown, *Augustine*, pp. 88–114, on Platonism and philosophy.

43. The antithesis is particularly evident in Augustine's treatment of the liberal arts as knowledges subordinate to the divine Character of Christ, the only Architect of the world, the only Teacher of wisdom in the soul, and the only sure Love. See *De Trinitate* 9, 10 (trans. Burnaby) on self-knowledge and self-love, and cf. *Confessions* 10.8.

44. Augustine makes the foolishness of the city of man and its products explicit in his treatment of Rome. In mind and in body, he says, Rome was never a true republic because true justice never had a place in it; the fact is, "true justice has no existence save in that republic whose founder and ruler is Christ" (*De Civitate Dei* 2.21 [trans. Marcus Dods (Edinburgh: T. & T. Clark, 1871–72; New York: Modern Library, 1950)]). In the absence of justice, human kingdoms are nothing but great robberies (4.4). The Augustinian antithesis sets up, therefore, a philosophical disjuncture between the two cities but implies, at the same time, a philosophical correspondence through the work of history. Justice, or justification, is the way the earthly city may, through history, be made congruent to Christ's design and finally merge with the heavenly City.

45. See *De Vera Religione* 22.42–43 on the order of history and the order of parts of a poem; we temporally read and judge the poem, but are read and judged by God since history is made up of our labors.

46. *On the Usefulness of Belief* 15.33 in *Augustine: Earlier Writings*, trans. Burleigh. For a contemporary study of "signo" in the Renaissance, see Richard Waswo, *Language and Meaning in the Renaissance* (Princeton, N.J.: Princeton Univ. Press, 1987). See Jacques Derrida, *Of Grammatology*, trans. Spivak, pp. 10–15, 49–52 on signs and signifiers, and p. 61 on the trace, and *Dissemination*, trans. Johnson, pp. 48–50 on encyclopedism and the *logos spermatikos*, and pp. 80–84 on *logos* and the return to the father.

47. Socrates argues the superiority of the eye and uses it analogically to discuss intellectual "ratio" and the proportions of visibles to invisibles in the "light" of the mind in the *Republic* 6 (508). Compare the law of contradiction stated in Aristotle's *Metaphysics* 4.3 (1005b) with the discussion of contradictories in the essay *On Interpretation* 6 (17a ff.) and with the statement of the principle in *Posterior Analytics* 1.11 (77a). In the *Metaphysics* 12.9 (1074b–1075a) Aristotle says that the activity of the mind must be self-thinking: "Mind thinks itself, if it is that which is best; and its thinking is a thinking of thinking." He then distinguishes the productive sciences from the speculative to say that in speculative knowledge the act of thinking will be one with the object of thought (trans. Hugh Tredennick [London: William Heinemann, 1933–35]).

48. *Republic* 6 (511b), trans. Paul Shorey, in *Collected Dialogues*, ed. Hamilton and Cairns; Socrates explains that dialectic treats its assumptions not as "absolute beginnings but literally as hypotheses, underpinnings, footings, and springboards." Cf. *Metaphysics* 1.1.12–17 (982a) and *Nicomachean Ethics* 1.1 (1094a); 6.3.1–6.12.5 (1139b–1144a), trans. Rackham, on the intellectual virtues of wisdom, prudence, science, art, and the "immediate perceptions of intelligence" (6.11.4 [1143b]). Aristotle concludes by saying that wisdom produces happiness not as medicine produces health but as healthiness produces health; but since wisdom is a part of virtue as a whole, only its possession, that is, its practice, makes a person happy (6.12.5 [1144a]).

49. On Plato's trip to Egypt see Cicero *De Finibus* 5.29.87; Plutarch *Moralia* 5.10; Diogenes Laertius 3.6; Saint Clement of Alexandria *Stromata* 1.66.3; and Origen *Contra Celsum* 4.40. Saint Basil uses the commonplace in *Ad Adolescentes* 3.3 before discussing pagan poetry.

50. See Pico della Mirandola (*Heptaplus* Proem 2) on different "worlds" that exchange natures and names in a mutual containment—the principle from which flows the science of allegorical interpretation: "The early Fathers could not properly represent some thing by the images of others unless trained . . . in the hidden alliances and affinities of all natures" (trans. Douglas Carmichael [Indianapolis: Bobbs-Merrill, 1965]), pp. 78–79. Saint Augustine had allegorically compared the Exodus from Egypt to the Christian use of pagan learning in the *De Doctrina Christiana* 2.40–41, and Saint Thomas More followed suit when, as chancellor of England, he insisted on having Greek in the Oxford curriculum so that the mind could rise from natural to supernatural things on a "ladder" of philosophy and the liberal arts (*Selected Letters*, ed. Elizabeth F. Rogers [New Haven: Yale Univ. Press, 1961], pp. 98–99). Sir Francis Bacon's remark almost a century later makes a good contrast, for Bacon observes the opposition to natural philosophy posed by "the immoderate zeal" of religion in the *New Organon* 1.89, ed. Fulton H. Anderson (Indianapolis: Bobbs-Merrill, 1960).

51. Besides comparing the divine folly of Christ to that of Socrates in *The Praise of Folly*, Erasmus expanded on the similitude of the *sileni Alcibiades* in the *Adagia* of 1515. In the *Antibarbarorum* (1488?), Erasmus defended pagan learning on the basis of patristic thought by arguing that, although no one discipline is Christianity, all refer to Christianity (Basel: Froben, 1520), pp. 103–10. He concluded with the commonplace that the learning of the "gentiles" is like spoils from Egypt (p. 114). The *locus classicus* for Egyptian gold is Saint Augustine's *De Doctrina Christiana* 2.40 on interpretation of Scripture.

52. In the *First Apology* 44, Justin says that Plato followed Moses, who was more ancient

than all the Greeks; in the *Second Apology* 9–10, he compares Christ and Socrates. Cf. Derrida, *Dissemination,* trans. Johnson, p. 50, on the deconstructionist dismissal of the *logos spermatikos* of the philosophers.

53. In the epistle dedicatory to Robert, Earl of Leicester, Sir Philip Sidney's uncle, line 8 and lines 332–50, ed. John Frederick Nims (1567; New York: Macmillan, 1965), pp. 405, 415. Cf. Leonard Barkan, *The Gods Made Flesh: Metamorphosis and the Pursuit of Paganism* (New Haven: Yale Univ. Press, 1986).

54. Strephon and Claius, hearing Musidorus speak in Greek "which was their naturall language," become tender-hearted toward him (*Arcadia,* Feuillerat ed., 1:1.1. p. 9). On the versions of the *Arcadia* and Greville's relation to its production and Protestant politics, see Victor Skretkowicz, "Building Sidney's Reputation: Texts and Editions of the *Arcadia,*" in *Sir Philip Sidney: 1586 and the Creation of a Legend,* ed. Jan van Dorsten, Dominic Baker-Smith, and Arthur F. Kinney (Leiden: E. J. Brill, 1986), pp. 111–24.

55. On the *Old Arcadia"* see P. Jeffrey Ford, "Philosophy, History, and Sidney's *Old Arcadia,*" *CL* 26 (1974): 32–50, and Margaret E. Dana, "The Providential Plot of the *Old Arcadia,*" *SEL 1500–1900* 17 (1977): 39–57. On the circling and to-and-fro structure of the *Arcadia* supported by its rhetoric and related both to its Greek tragic peripeteia and conflict and to its Christianity, see John Carey, "Structure and Rhetoric in Sidney's *Arcadia,*" in *Sir Philip Sidney: An Anthology of Modern Criticism,* ed. Dennis Kay (Oxford: Clarendon, 1987), pp. 245–64, especially pp. 249–50. For a view of Sidney's interweaving of sources in the *Arcadia* similar to my intertextual reading of the *Defence* as a text showing Christian ambivalence toward classical and contemporary sources, see A. C. Hamilton, "Sidney's *Arcadia* as Prose Fiction: Its Relation to Its Sources," in *Sidney in Retrospect: Selections from* ELR, ed. Arthur Kinney et al. (Amherst, Mass.: Univ. of Massachusetts Press, 1988), pp. 119–50.

56. *Poetic Presence and Illusion: Essays in Critical History and Theory* (Baltimore: Johns Hopkins Univ. Press, 1979), pp. 4–12, 28. See especially chapter 1 on the duplicity of metaphor (pp. 3–27). For a different view see Stephen Greenblatt, *Representing the Renaissance* (Berkeley: Univ. of California Press, 1988).

57. A Latin translation of Herodotus, *Herodoti Halicarnassei Historiographie Libri VIII,* which was the work of Lorenzo Valla, was published in Lyons in 1542, but Sidney probably knew Estienne's work on this historian and Scaliger's reference in the *Poetices Libri Septem* (Lyons, 1561) to Herodotus as the "poet" who made history in order to teach and to delight (7.1, p. 347). Cf. Jerome McGann's discussion of Herodotus's lines of force and counterforce—that is, his celebration of Greek nationalism and power on one side, and a moral warning about potential ruination on the other (*Social Values and Poetic Acts: The Historical Judgment of Literary Work* [Cambridge, Mass.: Harvard Univ. Press, 1988], pp. 68–69). As usual, the Renaissance joined this interpretive history to sound documentation.

58. I have looked at a seventeenth-century edition, *Herodoti Halicarnassei Historiarum Libri IX* (London, 1679), sig. Ooo–Qqq 4ᵛ. Estienne had met Sidney in Heidelberg, in Strasbourg, and in Vienna; he documents these meetings in his dedication of a Greek New Testament to Sidney (1576), which John Buxton has partially translated in *Sir Philip Sidney and the English Renaissance* (London: Macmillan, 1954), pp. 57–58. Estienne refers to a volume of Greek maxims he had given Sidney earlier with the remark that in the New Testament the young Englishman will find even wiser maxims pronounced "by the lips of Him who is Prince and Founder of Wisdom to all mankind." Later Estienne gave Sidney another book, *Herodiani, Histor. Lib. VIII* (1581), which was annotated by Angelo Politiano; Estienne's comments on historiography reflect the "mirror" tradition of "sweet and useful" historical poetry (sig. ijᵛ).

59. *L'Introduction au traite de la conformité des merveilles anciennes avec les modernes. Ou, traite preparatif a l'apologie pour Herodote* (1566), which was published in English translation as *A world of wonders: or an introduction to a treatise teaching the conformities of ancient and modern wonders: or a preparative treatise to the apologie for Herodotus* (London, 1607).

60. See Aristotle *Rhetoric* 3.2–4 (1405a–1407a); *Poetics* 20 (1470b), especially on the "pro-

portional" kind of metaphor (trans. W. Rhys Roberts and Ingram Bywater, ed. Friedrich Solmsen [New York: Random House, 1954]).

61. See Ioan Kelly's essay, "Did Women Have a Renaissance?" in Women, History, and Theory (Chicago: Univ. of Chicago Press, 1984) pp. 19–50 and the effort to refine responses to Kelly's questions in Women in the Middle Ages and the Renaissance, ed. Mary Beth Rose (Syracuse, N.Y.: Syracuse Univ. Press, 1986), in this volume see especially Merry E. Wiesner, "Women's Defense of Their Public Role," pp. 1–28, in which the author argues that a deepening split between private and public lives increasingly restricted women to lives of domesticity.

62. See A. E. Taylor, Plato, the Man, and His Work, 3d ed., rev. (London: Methuen, 1929), pp. 98–99.

63. See Aristotle's Metaphysics 6.1 (1025b–1026a) and compare the Topica 1.4 (105b) in which propositions are divided according to their ethical, logical, or physical status—that is, in a Platonic fashion. Aristotle relates metaphysics, as the investigation of causes and first principles, to wisdom (Metaphysics 1.1.17 [981b–982a]). In the Charmides Socrates is not so sure whether knowledge and wisdom are the same. Cf. Nicomachean Ethics 1.2 (1094a); Politics 1.1–2 (1252a); and Rhetoric 1.2 (1355b). Richard McKeon adumbrated Aristotle's view of the architectonic arts during a conference on Boethius and the liberal arts at the Newberry Library, Chicago, October 5–6, 1973; see McKeon's essay, "The New Rhetoric as an Architectonic and Productive Art," Center Magazine 13 (1980): 41–53, especially pp. 42–43.

64. On the history of the word and the place of the architect, see N. Pevsner, "The Term 'Architect' in the Middle Ages," Speculum 17 (1942): 549–62.

65. Leon Battista Alberti is the chief exponent of the idea of the learned architect in his adaptation of Vitruvius in the De Re Aedificatoria (Florence, 1485), which was cited by Doctor John Dee in the Preface to Billingsley's Euclid (London, 1570) in the same year that Palladio's Quattro Libri dell' Architettura was published in Venice (1570). On the Vitruvian and Palladian traditions in England, see Frederick Hard's introduction to the facsimile edition of Sir Henry Wotton's Elements of Architecture (London, 1624; Charlottesville: Univ. Press of Virginia, 1968).

66. On "metascience" see Robert Klein, "Les Humanistes et la science," Bibliothèque d'humanisme et renaissance 23 (1961): 7–16.

67. Varchi closes his lecture on virtù with references to Michelangelo and the fact that the perfection of art is found in its exercise and its doctrine (Lezzioni [1590], p. 204). See Thomas M. Greene, "The End of Discourse in Machiavelli's 'Prince,' " in Concepts of Closure, Yale French Studies, vol. 67 (New Haven: Yale Univ. Press, 1984), pp. 57–71, for a discussion of the meaning of the word virtù in Machiavelli's treatise.

68. Omnia Divini Platonis Opera (Venice, 1556), pp. 136–37. See Michael Levey, Early Renaissance (Harmondsworth, Middlesex, Eng.: Penguin, 1967), pp. 41–44, and Cecil H. Clough, "Federigo de Montefeltro's Private Study in His Ducal Palace of Gubbio," Apollo 86 (1967): 278–87.

69. The Courtier, trans. Thomas Hoby, ed. W. E. Henley (London: David Nutt, 1900), pp. 29–30.

70. On the analogy of the statesman's "building" of the good society in his speech, see Plato's discussion of the human response to the "workmanship" of the world in Timaeus 47b–c, where the purpose of sight, speech, and hearing is defined as the imitation of the absolutely unerring course of God and the regulation of our vagaries. Cf. Saint Augustine De Civitate Dei 22.24 on man's erect form having been created to look heavenward, his hands to write, and his tongue to speak, and Petrarch's use of a parallel passage in the Confessions (10.8) to exhort himself not to the admiration of the mountains but to the admiration of the mind that knows itself (The Ascent of Mount Ventoux, trans. Hans Nachod, in The Renaissance Philosophy of Man, ed. Ernst Cassirer et al. [Chicago: Univ. of Chicago Press, 1948], p. 44). Cf. Thomas M. Greene's different handling of Petrarch and the question of hermeneutics in The

Light in Troy: Imitation and Discovery in Renaissance Poetry (New Haven: Yale Univ. Press, 1982) as Greene probes the "Copernican leap" with which Petrarch and other renaissance figures thought they knew the classical past. Greene focuses his argument not on the Augustinian strain in Petrarch but on Petrarch's possession of a manuscript of the *Aeneid*. Augustine, however, rewrote the *Aeneid* in his criticism of his own love of the text in the *Confessions* and in his reconstruction of the myth of rebuilding the burnt-out city of man by attending to one's pilgrimage to the City of God. Greene decidedly emphasizes the problems of cultural ruins and historical fragments, which I see as more of a "romantic" than a "renaissance" notion (*Light in Troy*, pp. 29–37). The problem is historically compounded, of course, by the fact that Rousseau's development of autobiography incorporated not only Augustine's *Confessions* but also Petrarch's use of it in *The Ascent of Mount Ventoux*. The problem is an old critical problem: the funding of twentieth-century critical views and methods by romanticism, the tenets of which are then mistakenly used to understand the texts of the Renaissance that romantics applauded in reaction to eighteenth-century rationalism, which had, in turn, ossified many of the lively, open-ended propositions of the Renaissance.

71. Richard Haydocke, translator of Giovanni Paolo Lomazzo's treatise on the pictorial and plastic arts in 1598, expanded the idea in praise of Thomas Bodley. Haydocke compares the library to a temple of the Muses to whom he makes the offering of his book *A Tracte Containing the Arts of Curious Paintings, Caruinge, Building Written First in Italian by Jo. Paul Lomatius, Painter of Milan and Englyshed by R. H. Student in Physik* (Oxford, 1598), sig. ij. He is not afraid to dovetail the place of his book in that temple of the mind to the place "which wee see the silly Sparrowes and Swallowes haue in the greatest Churches." The core of the Bodleian Library that Haydocke praised, after all, had been Duke Humfrey's remarkable collection of humanistic texts. See the catalogue, *Duke Humfrey and English Humanism in the Fifteenth Century* (Oxford: Bodleian Library, 1970).

72. *Philebus* 16–18; other "proportions" discussed in this dialogue concern the arts of building and music, number and dialectic (57–58), and the analogical measure of beauty, intelligence, arts and sciences, and pleasure (66).

73. Madeleine Doran has sketched out the sources of the Amphion and Orpheus stories in "Yet Am I Inland Bred," *SQ* 15 (1964): 99–114.

74. *Ars Poetica* 391ff., trans. H. R. Fairclough (London: William Heinemann, 1926). On the syncretic nature of classical poetic theory in renaissance criticism, see Marvin Herrick, *The Fusion of Horatian and Aristotelian Literary Criticism 1531–1555* (Urbana: Univ. of Illinois Press, 1946). Thomas Drant, who sought Sidney's attention, had translated *Horace, his arte of poetrie* in 1567.

75. *Protreptikos, Exhortation to the Greeks* 1.4–5, trans. G. W. Butterworth (London: William Heinemann, 1919). A Greek edition of Clement's works was dedicated to Cosimo Medici and printed in Florence in 1550, followed by a Latin translation by Gentian Hervet, *Omnia Quae Quidem Extant Opera* (Florence: L. Torrentinus, 1551); the translation contains the *Protreptikos*, or *Exhortation*, the *Paedagogus*, and the *Stromata*, or commentary on the "Christian philosophy," along with a prefatory letter to Cosimo on the use of his Greek copy (sig. *ii). See D. C. Allen, *The Legend of Noah: Renaissance Rationalism in Art, Science, and Letters* (Urbana: Univ. of Illinois Press, 1949), on the way renaissance commentators conflated the story of Noah with the stories of Deucalion, Prometheus, Janus, Saturn, and other mythic figures of change and origin (p. 83).

76. Cf. Clement *Exhortation* 1: "See how mighty is the new song! It has made men out of stones and men out of wild beasts" (trans. Butterworth).

77. Irene Samuel, "The Influence of Plato on Sir Philip Sidney's *Defence of Poesy*," *MLQ* 1 (1940): 708–23, first presented the case for Sidney's Platonism; Michael Krouse reinstated Aristotle's sense of form and function with Plato's sense of the ethical effects of poetry in "Sidney's *Defence of Poesie*," *CL* 6 (1954): 138–47; and M. H. Partee demonstrated Sidney's extraordinary knowledge of Plato by the number and weight of suggestions in "Sir Philip

Sidney and the Renaissance Knowledge of Plato," *ES* 51 (1970): 49–62. S. K. Heninger, Jr., traced some of Sidney's debt to Plato to de Serres's 1578 edition in "Sidney and Serranus' *Plato*," *ELR* 13 (1983): 146–61, and I shall broaden and deepen Heninger's argument of influ- ence, particularly on the subject of inspiration.

79. See Terry Comito, "The Lady in a Landscape and the Poetics of Elizabethan Pastoral," *UTQ* 41 (1971–72): 200–18, on Urania's formation of perishable beauty. See especially Josephine A. Roberts, *Architectonic Knowledge in the New Arcadia (1590): Sidney's Use of the Heroic Journey*, ed. Dr. James Hogg, *Elizabethan and Renaissance Studies*, vol. 69 (Salzburg: Institut für Englische Sprache und Literatur, Universität Salzburg, 1978). Roberts applies the Aristotelian definition of architectonic knowledge in ethics and politics to the theme of the training of young princes and to Sidney's image of Hercules.

79. See Myron Turner, "The Disfigured Face of Nature: Image and Metaphor in the Revised *Arcadia*," *ELR* 2 (1972): 116–35.

80. See Thomas P. Roche, Jr., "*Astrophil and Stella*: A Radical Reading," in *Spenser Studies* (Pittsburgh: Univ. of Pittsburgh Press, 1982), 3:139–91, on Astrophil's moral dilemma and Sidney's imaginative construction of his antiheroic journey of love, especially p. 143.

81. See Saint Jerome *Against Jovinianus* 2.37 for the identification of the Amazon with lust, and compare Jerome's letter 107 in which he praises, on the contrary, the Christian warrior woman or "bellatrix" ("To Laeta" 107.9) in *The Principal Works of Saint Jerome*, trans W. H. Freemantle, vol. 6 of *A Select Library of Nicene and Post-Nicene Fathers of the Christian Church*, 2d ser. (1982; reprint, Grand Rapids, Mich.: Eerdmans, 1979). Cf. the fate of Artegal at the hands of the Amazon Radigune in *The Faerie Queene* (5.5.12–17) and the narrator's comment on the place versus the lust of women (5.5.25–27).

82. James Nohrnberg has collected many of the classical and Christian commonplaces on the labyrinth in *The Analogy of the* Fairie Queene (Princeton, N.J.: Princeton Univ. Press, 1978), pp. 136–39, and he cites two sources—W. H. Matthews, *Mazes and Labyrinths* (London: Longmans, Green and Co., 1922), and John Steadman, "Spenser's Errour and the Renaissance Allegorical Tradition," *NM* 62 (1961): 22–38—for further reference.

83. Although she is writing about the seventeenth-century American Puritans, Ann Kibbey's discussion of Calvinistic theology and its special kind of iconology—the living Puritan icon of the self—expresses the hidden aspect of Puritan iconoclasm that Sidney seems to have observed somewhat, too. Kibbey's analysis in "Iconoclastic Materialism," in *The Interpretation of Material Shapes in Puritanism: A Study of Rhetoric, Prejudice, and Violence* (Cambridge: Cambridge Univ. Press, 1986), pp. 42–64, makes interesting observations on the Puritan use of aural figures of speech. Decades earlier, Sidney's centering of his own self and self-knowledge among the "characters" he creates in his three prosopopoeias and the "voices" of authors of many other texts suggests the movement of his speech and his art toward the moral values of a Calvinistic aesthetic.

84. I am paraphrasing Professor John Freccero, Harris Visiting Professor at the University of Chicago, in the announcement of a comparative literature seminar entitled "Inventing the Self: Augustine, Dante, Petrarch" in the autumn of 1988 as he referred to Stephen Greenblatt's book, *Renaissance Self-Fashioning from More to Shakespeare* (Chicago: Univ. of Chicago Press, 1980). Except with regard to *Astrophil and Stella* 45, and that only in passing, Greenblatt does not mention Sidney or his *Defence* in this book.

85. In *Trials of Desire*, Margaret Ferguson compares Tasso to Freud in *Civilization and Its Discontents* as she discusses, in Kenneth Burke's terms, "the court of conscience." Thus Freud commented that the superego stirs up conscience in face of external frustrations, and the price paid for advances in civilization is the heightening of a sense of guilt, which means a loss of happiness, and Tasso's guilty attitude in his defense of poetry corresponds (pp. 109–10). In the chapter on Sidney, however, Ferguson postpones the Freudian comparison, letting Sidney's Protestant self-examination control her points, until she takes up Freud's defense of himself and psychoanalysis in the Appendix of her book by comparing his position before

novelists to Sidney's position before the philosopher and the historian. By probing the rhetoric of defense in Freud's speech, Ferguson deals a blow to the authority of psychoanalysis as another form of "fiction" in which the practitioner seeks his own good despite claims to be seeking the good of the audience or client.

86. *The Aeneid* 4.340–61, 395–96; 6.67–68, 84–85, 458–64, 752–892, trans. Frank O. Copley (Indianapolis: Bobbs-Merrill, 1965). Cf. Lipking, *Abandoned Women and Poetic Tradition* (Chicago: Univ. of Chicago Press, 1988), pp. 3–4, on how the abandoned woman subverts the rule of action and gives the reader pause. Lipking does not write specifically about Dido, but he develops the myth of Ariadne, the woman abandoned by Theseus, the heroic slayer of the Minotaur in Daedalus's labyrinth, in the chapter called "Ariadne at the Wedding: Abandoned Women and the Poetic Tradition," pp. 1–31. Jonathan Crewe, in his extensive "antiromantic" exposé of aristocratic intrigue in *Hidden Designs: The Critical Profession and Renaissance Literature* (New York. Methuen, 1986), pp. 71–88, examines the relationship between Sidney and Penelope Devereux Rich in *Astrophil and Stella* as a public confession aimed at using shared "secrets" to gain power. This reading, in its eagerness to prove the historicism of a certain kind of politics, credits but does not treat any other possible motive in Sidney's writing or life, especially that of religion. On Aeneas's "obeying God's commandment to leave Dido" and the "excellence" of Aeneas carrying Anchises, see the *Defence*, pp. 98, 92.

87. *The Aeneid* 6.31–33 (trans. Copley).

88. *The Confessions* 1.13, trans. Rex Warner (New York: New American Library, 1963), pp. 30–31.

89. *The Ascent of Mount Ventoux*, trans. Nachod, p. 44. See Greene, *The Light in Troy*, pp. 35–37, 81–103, 104–26.

90. These events are summarized in James M. Osborn, *Young Philip Sidney 1572–1577* (New Haven: Yale Univ. Press, 1972), pp. 500–506. But one can find an earlier expression of the moral impetus in Sidney's response in the letter Sir Henry Sidney wrote to his son while he was a student at Shrewsbury:

> Study & endeuour your selfe to be vertuously occupied, so shall you make such an habite of well doing in you, as you shall not know how to do euill though you would: Remember my Sonne the Noble bloud you are discended of by your mothers side, & thinke that only by vertuous life and good action, you may be an ornament to that ylustre family, and other wise through vice & sloth you may be accompted *Labes generis,* a spot of your kin, one of the greatest cursses that can happen to man.

The letter may be found reprinted and entitled *A Very Godly letter made by the right Honourable Sir Henry Sidney . . . vnto Phillip Sidney his Sonne* (ca. 1566; London: T. Dawson, 1591; Oxford, 1929), sig. A3ᵛ. The postscript of Sidney's mother warns her son to keep before the eyes of his mind "these excellent counsailes of my Lord your deere Father."

91. Cf. Patricia Parker's discussion of the relation between fiction and error in the mode of romance and in the labyrinths of Spenser's *Faerie Queene* in her book *Inescapable Romance: Studies in the Poetics of a Mode* (Princeton, N.J.: Princeton Univ. Press, 1979), pp. 53–113. Angus Fletcher, *The Prophetic Moment: An Essay on Spenser* (Chicago: Univ. of Chicago Press, 1971), especially observed the design of *The Faerie Queene* as both temple and labyrinth. Both Parker and Fletcher credit Northrop Frye for the observation.

Chapter 4

1. The bibliography of Jean de Serres is amply supplied by S. K. Heninger, Jr., "Sidney and Serranus' *Plato*," *ELR* 13 (1983): 146–61, so I will not repeat it here.

2. See Ernst Robert Curtius, "The Book as Symbol," in *European Literature in the Latin Middle Ages*, trans. Willard R. Trask (New York: Harper and Row, 1953), pp. 302–47, especially p. 317 on Pythagoras as a man transformed into a book and Boethius's personification of

theoria and *praxis* in Lady Philosophy, who bears their letters on her robe, and p. 319 on the biblical injunction to write on the heart and the image of parchments of the alphabet nailed to the wall like Christ to the Cross. Cf. Jacques Derrida, *Dissemination*, trans. Barbara Johnson (Chicago: Univ. of Chicago Press, 1981), p. 9, for a rejection of "the form of the 'book'" that can no longer settle writing processes which, "in *practically* questioning that form, must also dismantle it." Derrida also investigates the hierarchical opposition between writing and speech and applies "the name 'work' or 'practice' to that which disorganizes the philosophical opposition *praxis/theoria*" (p. 4). The English renaissance Protestant's pursuit of justification takes a different approach to these problems, obviously, and where Derrida calls everything that lies outside classical oppositions "matter" and observes that it no longer assumes "any reassuring form" as a referent, a presence, or a "totalizing principle" (pp. 4–5), writers such as Sidney identify themselves as people of the Book, inspired, transcendent, variegated, and believing. Two different but historically apt studies of philosophy and belief in Sidney's making of literature or fiction in the *Arcadia* do not dispute Derrida but offer, nevertheless, readings that counterpoint his hermeneutics: Andrew D. Weiner expresses the extreme fideism of Sidney's fiction in *Sir Philip Sidney and the Poetics of Protestantism: A Study of Contexts* (Minneapolis: Univ. of Minnesota Press, 1978), pp. 47–50, 184–85, and Arthur F. Kinney, "*Primus inter pares*: Sir Philip Sidney, the *Arcadia*, and the Poetic Uses of Philosophy," in his book, *Humanist Poetics: Thought, Rhetoric, and Fiction in Sixteenth-Century England* (Amherst: Univ. of Massachusetts Press, 1986), pp. 230–91, argues that the *Arcadia* juxtaposes "the cruelty and anguish of a corrupted world" and "a splendid image of another existence where, philosophically informed and poetically conceived, art can still cultivate and learning still civilize" (p. 290).

3. Cf. Haggai 2:8, in the translation of the Geneva Bible: "And I will moue all nacions, and the desire of all nacions shal come, and I will fil this House with glorie, saith the Lord of hostes." Greville's remark may be found in *The Life of the Renowned Sr Philip Sidney* (London: Henry Seile, 1652), p. 21, in facsimile edition introduced by Warren W. Wooden (Delmar, N.Y.: Scholars' Facsimiles and Reprints, 1984).

4. *Miscellaneous Prose of Sir Philip Sidney* (Oxford: Clarendon, 1973), pp. 5–6.

5. Heninger traces de Serres's studies in philosophy and theology, assigning the composition of the commentaries on Plato and the translation of the *Dialogues* into Latin to a period of asylum in Lausanne in retreat from the Saint Bartholomew's Day Massacre in "Sidney and Serranus' Plato," pp. 148–50.

6. See Heninger, p. 148 n.10, for a translation of Languet's letter.

7. *Literary Theory: An Introduction* (Minneapolis: Univ. of Minnesota Press, 1983), pp. 19, 29.

8. See, for example, Leonardo's *Paragone, a Comparison of the Arts*, trans. Irma A. Richter (New York: Oxford Univ. Press, 1949), pp. 26–27, 56. Leonardo argued the supremacy of painting to poetry because painting combined speculation and experience, thought and sense, in the production of an "external creation" of work of art "far superior in dignity to the contemplation of the science which precedes it" while poetry produced only written characters drawn from the darkness of the mind's eye (p. 50). Poets had only the "effects of demonstrations," but painters had the "demonstrations of the effects" in the real light of day (p. 56). See pp. 70–71 on the supremacy of the eye itself.

9. The Italian version of Leon Battista Alberti's *Della Pittura* (1436) has been translated by John R. Spencer (London: Routledge and Kegan Paul, 1956); the Latin version, *On Painting and on Sculpture*, by Cecil Grayson (London: Phaidon, 1972). Cf. Lodovico Dolce's mid-sixteenth-century differentiation of painting and poetry according to the norms of nature and moral philosophy by elaborating the Platonic contrasts of beauty and ugliness and of good and evil in the *Dialogo della Pittura* of 1557, in Dolce's *"Aretino" and Venetian Art Theory of the Cinquecento*, trans. Mark W. Roskill (New York: New York Univ. Press, 1968), pp. 102–3; see also pp. 112–13, 148–49. Dolce actually modeled aesthetic pleasure on the moral pleasure to be

gained from reading literature; one may return to a good painting to "read" it as one returns again and again to a good poem. For a contemporary discussion of the significance of perspective, see Murray Roston, *Renaissance Perspectives in Literature and the Visual Arts* (Princeton, N.J.: Princeton Univ. Press, 1987).

10. Paolo Lomazzo's *Trattato dell'arte de la pittura* was published in Milan in 1584, and Richard Haydocke's translation, *A Tracte Containing the Artes of Curious Paintinge, Caruinge, Building*, was published in London in 1598; the reference is to 3.1, pp. 94–95. See Wylie Sypher, *Four Stages of Renaissance Style: Transformations in Art and Literature 1400–1700* (New York: Doubleday, 1955). Nicholas Hilliard, the court miniaturist, records a conversation with Sidney in which perspective, the art of limning, and control of "color"—whether in paint or in words—were discussed; see *A Treatise Concerning the Art of Limning*, introduction by Philip Norman (Oxford: Walpole Society, 1912), 1:1–54, and see A. C. Judson, *Sidney's Appearances* (Bloomington: Indiana Univ. Press, 1958), pp. 21–22.

11. *Theater of the World* (Chicago: Univ. of Chicago Press, 1969), p. 36; the entire chapter on Dee and Vitruvius, pp. 20–41, should be consulted. See Leonard Barkan's *Nature's Work of Art: The Human Body as Image of the World* (New Haven: Yale Univ. Press, 1975), pp. 140–43, for a superb discussion of the body, the Church, the cosmos, and *discordia concors*, but Barkan does not explore this Vitruvian commonplace with regard to the philosophical organization of all the arts and sciences and the poetics of conscience in the mistress-knowledge. See S. K. Heninger, Jr., *Sidney and Spenser: The Poet As Maker* (University Park: Pennsylvania State Univ. Press, 1989), pp. 68–73, for a parallel discussion of architecture and other arts in Dee's estimation, with the emphasis on music. Heninger draws on Alberti and Ficino, available to Dee, and on Sir Henry Wotton's idea of architectural symmetry as "harmonie in Sight" and refers to the heavenly *opifex* followed by the earthly architect (pp. 71–72). The Platonic tradition subordinates the *architrex* to the *opifex*, later rendering that subordination in a gender hierarchy.

12. See Robert Recorde's *The Pathway to Knowledge* (1551), sig. iii^r; Robert Greene's *Friar Bacon and Friar Bungay* (1589); and Shakespeare's *Twelfth Night*.

13. Agrippa's treatise, *De incertitudine et vanitate omnium scientiarum & artium liber . . . atque excellentia Verbi Dei declamatio* (Antwerp, 1530), was "Englished" by James Sanford and printed in London in 1569 and again in 1575 with an epigraph from Ecclesiastes 1, "All is but moste vaine Vanitie. . . ." See A. C. Hamilton, "Sidney and Agrippa," *RES* 7 (1956): 151–57.

14. See Roger Bacon *Opus Majus*, trans. R. B. Burke (Philadelphia: Univ. of Pennsylvania Press, 1928), pp. 238–39, for the similitude of the infusion of grace and the propagation of light. The best history of optics in the Renaissance is Stephen M. Straker's dissertation, "Kepler's Optics: A Study in the Development of Seventeenth-Century Natural Philosophy" (Ph.D. diss., Indiana University, 1970).

15. Jean de Serres was a member of the circle of the Genevan theologian Lambert Daneau and shared his enthusiasm for Aristotle and for scholasticism without relinquishing a love of Plato; see Oliver Fatio, *Méthode et Théologie: Lambert Daneau et les débuts de la scholastique reformée* (Geneva: Librairie Droz, 1976), pp. 16, 100–104. Daneau's *Physice Christiana* (Geneva, 1579) contains a prefatory poem by Jean de Serres. See also John Patrick Donnelly, S.J., "Calvinist Thomism," *Viator* 7:441–55. Fatio observes that Daneau's first work on the Fathers was on Tertullian and Cyprian (*Méthode*, p. 102). In his Prolegomena to Augustine's *De Haeresibus* (Geneva, 1576) and to Lombard's *Sententiae* (Geneva, 1580), Daneau also discusses the orthodoxy of the faith of the Fathers and his preference for early scholastic writers who emphasized the Word of God.

16. See Oliver Fatio, *Nihil Pulchrius Ordine. Contribution a l'étude de l'établissement de la discipline ecclésiastique aux Pays-Bas ou Lambert Daneau aux Pays-Bas 1581–1583* (Leiden: Brill, 1971).

17. According to Thomas Zouch, *Memoirs of the Life and Writings of Sir Philip Sidney* (York, Eng.: Thomas Wilson, 1808), p. 306, Daneau met and admired Sidney.

18. A mélange of political and religious concerns involved this belle-édition in the establishment of Calvinist irenicism in the England of the late 1570s and 1580s. In scholarly quality, Estienne and de Serres intended their work to surpass the *Plato* of Ficino; they took pains to explain their scholarly principles; to emend textual problems in their dual-language edition (Greek and Latin); and to gloss and annotate the contents. Translations of de Serres's Latin are my own.

19. In the *Paraclesis* that prefaces his Greek-Latin New Testament of 1516, Erasmus asks, "What else is the philosophy of Christ, which He himself calls a rebirth, than the restoration of human nature originally well formed?" (*Christian Humanism and the Reformation: Selected Writings of Desiderius Erasmus*, ed. and trans. John C. Olin [New York: Harper and Row, 1965], p. 100). See Georges Chantraine, *"Mystère" et "philosophie du Christ" selon Erasmus. Étude de la lettre a P. Volz et de la "Ratio verae theologiae"* (Namur, Belgium: J. Duculot, 1971), and Margaret Mann Phillips, *Erasmus and the Northern Renaissance*, rev. ed. (Suffolk, Eng.: Boydell, 1981), pp. 36–65. Cf. the patrology in Calvin's *Institutes of the Christian Religion*, ed. John T. McNeill, trans. Ford Lewis Battles, 2 vols. (Philadelphia: Westminster, 1960), 2:1591–1634. See also the Calvinist patristic florilegium published by Jean Crespin, *Bibliotheca Studii Theologici, ex Plerisque Doctorum Prisci Seculi Monumentis Collecta* (Geneva, 1565), which was largely Augustinian in emphasis; in three parts this text reprints the Augustinian florilegium published in 1537 by Piscatorius, then texts of Eusebius and Jerome, then Peter Lombard's *Sentences* and the sayings of the Fathers—Augustine, Jerome, Tertullian, Cyprian, Origen, Irenaeus, Athanasius, Cyril, Lactantius, Ambrose, and Bernard. These sayings are organized under Calvinist theological headings with cautions on the harmony or disharmony of various opinions with the theology of Geneva.

20. J. E. Sandys, *A History of Classical Scholarship*, 2d ed., 3 vols. (Cambridge: Cambridge Univ. Press, 1906–8), 2:175–76. See the article on Jean de Serres in the *Nouvelle Biographie Générale*, ed. Jean C. F. Hoefer, 46 vols. (Paris: Firmin Didot Frères, Fils, 1854–77), 43:795–97 (hereafter cited as *NBG*); also see August Renouard, *Annales de l'imprimerie des Estienne ou histoire de la famille des Estienne*, 2d ed. (Paris: Paul Renouard, 1843), pp. 145–46. The *NBG* essayist reports that Estienne was nearly broken financially by printing the *Plato* when he did and that Lanir praised the summaries for their Platonic doctrine while Dacier criticized the translation for having more style than exactness (*NBG* 43:797). Johann Alberti Fabricius (*Bibliothecae Graecae*, 14 vols. [Hamburg: Liebezeit, 1716]) reports Leone Allatio's judgment that the *Plato* of 1578 was faithful to Socratic thought and to Ficino, and Claudius Fleury's view, on the contrary, that the text was a traduction of Ficino, not faithful in its abandonment of the allegories and mysteries, and that the scholastic analysis deformed Plato; Fleury found it not surprising that the man who wrote an "inventive" history of France would give Plato such an estimation (2:35–36). Jean de Serres was a member of the Protestant party that believed moderation more advantageous than violence in the pursuit of reformation. His commentaries in the *Plato* exhibit an orthodox Christian humanism that would persuade readers to the learning and the good sense of the Calvinist version of Christianity.

21. See Rupert E. Davies, *The Problem of Authority in the Continental Reformers* (London: Epworth, 1946), and compare Calvin's reference to the "holy fathers" in the letter to Cardinal Sadoleto, "On Reform," in *John Calvin, a Selection of His Writings*, ed. John Dillenberger (New York: Doubleday, 1971), p. 93. See especially Saint Clement of Alexandria *Stromata* 4.21 (*PG* 8:1339–46); Saint Basil *Ad Adolescentes*; and Saint Gregory Nazianzus *First Theological Oration*, available in *Christology of the Later Fathers*, ed. E. R. Hardy (Philadelphia: Westminster, 1954), pp. 128–34. Because of his fine rhetorical style, Gregory and his *Theological Orations* were well known and much appreciated in the Renaissance. See also Saint Gregory of Nyssa *The Life of Moses* 2.305–20, and Saint Clement *Stromata* 1.22–26. The doctrines of Saint Clement and the Cappadocians especially undergird de Serres's view of the propaedeutic nature of learning.

22. In the preface to the 1560 edition of the *Institutes*, Calvin explained his text as a

"Christian philosophy," an aid to believers seeking "the sum of what God meant to teach us in his Word" (1:6); see McNeill's note on Calvin and double emphasis on self-knowledge and the knowledge of God (1:6–7). Also see Charles Partee, *Calvin and Classical Philosophy* (Leiden: Brill, 1977): "These reformers seek not only a proper and faithful understanding of the Scriptures and patristic theology, but also a better and freer use of classical thought which does not jeopardize the revealed truth of God . . . as an example of the fact that God has not left himself without witness even among the pagans" (p. 4).

23. *Prescription against Heretics* 7, in *The Ante-Nicene Christian Library*, ed. Alexander Roberts and James Donaldson, 9 vols. (1868; reprint, Grand Rapids, Mich.: Eerdmans, 1978), 3:246. Saint Jerome, too, posed the question of the relationship between Christian truth and classical thought and rhetoric; especially in Letter 22, *Ad Eustochium*, he reports how he was accused during a nightmare of being a Ciceronian rather than a Christian (*Jerome: Select Letters*, trans. F. A. Wright [London: William Heinemann, 1954], p. 125). Jerome's interroga tive style on the subject of rhetoric and Christian belief parallels Tertullian's style; both writers refer to Saint Paul's similar interrogatives on the communion of light and darkness and the difference between the temple of idols and the living temple in 2 Corinthians 6:14–16. Cf. Calvin's *Institutes* (Books 1 and 2, passim) on the knowledge of God the Creator and God the Redeemer. Acts 17:22–31 is one of Calvin's favorite allusions (e.g., *Institutes* 1.5.1–14; 3.3.7), although he clearly upholds the primacy of Scripture against the philosophers, all of whom have partaken, in some way, of superstition (1.8.2). Ford Lewis Battles lists at least ten allusions to 2 Corinthians 6:16 on the "living Temple" in his index of biblical references in the *Institutes* (2:1583).

24. Philosophy "shares" in the primary truths that God has distributed in the nature of things and has made accessible to the human mind (sig. **iʳ, ***iiʳ), de Serres says. In *The First Apology, The Second Apology*, and *The Dialogue with Trypho* Justin developed the idea of λογὸς σπερματικός, the "spermatic word" or the "seeds of truth"; expressed a sense of the special role of the elect Christian "philosophers" among men; and set a standard for the reconciliation of philosophical contradictions (see *The First Apology* and *The Second Apology*, in *The Ante-Nicene Christian Library* 1:163–93). Justin's idea of the spermatic word is primarily a theory of distribution and a ladder of proportion that implies measure, degree, and partici- pation in the nature of the truth that is known fully in the Logos; see the *Second Apology* 8.78. See also the *Second Apology* 13.82–83 on the way each man "speaks well" in proportion to his possession of the spermatic word and on how contradiction on the more important points indicates a lack of possession of the heavenly wisdom. Cf. *First Apology* 44 and *Second Apology* 10.79. Joachim Peronius edited a Latin version of Justin's *Opera Omnia* (Paris, 1551), and John Lang produced another translation from Greek into Latin, *Operum Quae Extant Omnium* (Basel, 1565), reflecting aspects of reformation polemicism.

25. In the *Ante-Nicene Fathers*, American Edition, ed. A. Cleveland Coxe (1884; reprint, Grand Rapids, Mich.: Eerdmans, 1981). Cf. 4.33 on the judgment of the spiritual man against heretics and false prophets and on his "true knowledge," and 4.37–38 on free will and on the developmental or maturation theory of human nature in the prelapsarian state.

26. *Divini Irenaei, Graeci Scriptoris Eruditissimi, Episcopi Lugdunensis, Libri Quinque Adver- sus Portentosas Haereses Valentini & Aliorum* (Geneva, 1569). In the letter to Grindal, des Gallars refers to mutual concerns over Anabaptism and the persecuted church; see Patrick Collinson, *Archbishop Grindal 1519–1583: The Struggle for a Reformed Church* (London: Jonathan Cape, 1979), pp. 130–34, on the background of Grindal's and des Gallars's relation- ship. Irenaeus became famous in the Reformation for his comments on oral and written tradition and his discussion of the "canon" of the books of the New Testament. Des Gallars's letter to the reader, "De instituto huius operis & de utilitate colligende ex lectione veterum doctorum," refers to the consensus of faith and the unity of Scripture and tradition and to Irenaeus's careful description of heresies as means to combat the contemporary revival of old, monstrous errors and false doctrines of Satan (sig. **iʳ); to the usefulness of the Fathers in

distinguishing noxious from salvific doctrines (sig. **ii^r); and to Irenaeus's rule of faith that fits everything to the divine legislator, Christ the Word, *ad praescriptum Verbi,* anything else having to be censured or emended (sig. **iii^v).

27. De fi.... .... opinion of a intillai ... the .... quantil. of truth, stems from the argument that God has impressed his own image in man and that the development of that likeness is the .... of Christ that presides over the human mind and dwells in the inner man, teaching each person according to what he is capable of receiving because of good or bad will; cf. *De Trinitate* 15.15 (*CCSL* 50A: 497–98). See *De Civitate Dei* 15.1–8 on Cain and the building of cities and differences between the heavenly and the earthly cities and *De Civitate Dei* 22–24 (*CCSL* 48:846–48) on the development of knowledge and the arts and sciences from the spark. The *locus classicus* for Augustine's idea of the *scintilla rationis* is *De Civitate Dei* 22.24 (*PL* 41:789): "non in eo tamen penitus exstincta est quaedam valut scintilla rationis, in qua factus est ad imaginem Dei." In *De Spiritu et Anima* cap. 10 (*PL* 40:785), the definition is more strongly stated with regard to the "eye" of the soul: "Dicitur spiritus mens rationalis, ubi quadam scintilla tanquam oculus animae, ad quem pertinent imago et cognitio Dei." However, the Benedictine editors of *PL* place *De Spiritu et Anima* in an appendix on the testimony of Erasmus that it was gathered from various sources, including Boethius, Cassiodorus, Isidore, Bede, Alcuin, Hugo of St. Victor, Bernard, Isaac of Stella, and Vincent of Beauvais. Also see Augustine's *Retractiones* 1.9.6 (*PL* 32:598).

28. See n.31 and see Saint Jerome *Commentariorum in Ezechielem* (*PL* 25:22). See also Etienne Gilson, *The Spirit of Medieval Philosophy*, trans. A. H. C. Donnes (New York: Charles Scribner's Sons, 1936), chapter 17, "Intention, Conscience, and Obligation," pp. 343–63, and the notes on synderesis, pp. 476–78; also see the article s.v. "syndérèse" in the *Dictionnaire de Théologie Catholique*, ed. A. Vacant et al. (Paris: Librairie Letouzey et Ane, 1941), 14:2992–96. The fullest discussion to date in English is Timothy Potts's *Conscience in Medieval Philosophy* (Cambridge: Cambridge Univ. Press, 1980), which also provides a partial translation of Saint Jerome's comments (pp. 79–80) and those of several scholastic philosophers.

29. See Frederick Copleston, S.J., *History of Philosophy*, 8 vols. (New York: Doubleday, 1962), 2:1, 319, and see Potts, *Conscience in Medieval Philosophy*, pp. 32–44, 110–21; Bonaventure makes most of his comments on conscience in his *Commentary on Peter Lombard's Sentences* 2.39, and asks whether conscience, the law of the mind, belongs to desire and whether it can be extinguished or corrupted by sin. On conscience as the "erected" ladder or "highest point of man's wit," see Bonaventure *Itinerarium* 1.6, in *The Works of Bonaventure*, trans. José de Vinck, 5 vols. (Paterson, N.J.: St. Anthony Guild Press, 1960), 1:11. The Latin text confirms the translation: "sensus, imaginatio; ratio, intellectus; intelligentia, et apex mentis, seu synderesis scintilla. Hos gradus in nobis habemus plantatos per naturam, deformatos per culpam, reformatos per gratiam; purgandos per iustitiam, exercendos per scientiam, perficiendos per sapientiam" (*Obras de San Buenaventura*, ed. Leon Amores, O.F.M., et al., 2d ed. [Madrid: Biblioteca de Autores Cristianos, 1955], p. 568).

30. In the *Itinerarium* 1.5; 3.5, Bonaventure speaks of the ascent of the mind on a metaphysical ladder that reaches from the creatures to Christ the Word in the metaphoric terms of the "mirror" through which and in which the mind rejoins the Holy Trinity in light. See Copleston, *History of Philosophy* 2:1, 322. Cf. Aquinas *Quaestiones Disputatae* 16.1–3; 17.1–4, in the *Opera Omnia*, 22 vols. (Rome, 1882–1972), 22:501–28, and Duns Scotus *Quaestiones in secundum librum sententiarum*, in *Opera Omnia*, ed. Lucas Wadding (Paris: Vives, 1893), pp. 407ff. See Charles R. S. Harris, *Duns Scotus*, 2 vols. (Oxford: Clarendon, 1927).

31. See Calvin, *Institutes* 1.15.1–8 on self-knowledge, fear of punishment, image and likeness to God, and power of moral choice; cf. 3.2.20–22 on anguish of conscience and on "right" fear; and see 2.14.18–19 on good conscience and its consolations, the accomplishment of good works being a confirmation of "call" or election. Also see R. T. Kendall, *Calvin and English Calvinism to 1649* (Oxford: Oxford Univ. Press, 1979), pp. 20–22, on conversion. See Ian

Breward, ed., *The Work of William Perkins* (Appleford, Eng.: Sutton Courtenay, 1970), pp. 30–33, 43, 53–99, on Perkins's view of conscience, spiritual direction, and assurance. The *Compact Oxford English Dictionary*, s.v. "synderesis," lists theatrical use of the word by Ben Jonson and Tourneur et al.

32. The thesis of R. T. Kendall's book, *Calvin and English Calvinism to 1649*—that English Calvinism followed Theodore Beza more than John Calvin and, through the work of William Perkins and others, emphasized the great difference between the regenerate and the reprobate—may qualify this assertion. If English Calvinists were concerned with "fear and trembling" over whether they were regenerate or not, there was little room for the expression of an optimistic spirit; all the attention would necessarily go toward discerning one's regeneration, comforting spiritual affliction, gaining assurance, and preparing for faith prior to regeneration. See especially Kendall's discussion of Richard Hooker, pp. 125–38, and cf. Hooker's comments about Calvin's rule to judge "doctrine and discipline by" in "A Preface to Them That Seek . . . the Reformation of the Laws in Order Ecclesiastical in the Church of England," in *Of the Laws of Ecclesiastical Polity*, ed. Christopher Morris (London: J. M. Dent & Sons, 1907; New York: Dutton, 1969), p. 91. Morris cites a comment on Calvin's alleging of Scripture being more forceful than ten thousand "musty doctors" (p. 91).

33. See Jane Donawerth, *Shakespeare and the Sixteenth-Century Study of Language* (Urbana: Univ. of Illinois Press, 1984), pp. 3–8, for a summary of renaissance conflicts about language.

34. Calvin had challenged Augustine's view in the *De Trinitate* on the soul's reflection of the Trinity residing in the powers of understanding, will, and memory (*Institutes* 1.15.4) and followed a Greek patristic emphasis on the image and likeness of God in man being dependent on man's reformation, after the Fall, according to the image of the new man, Christ. De Serres dovetails Augustinian and Greek views in his theology of the image. Cf. de Serres's view of the image of God impressed in the soul according to the truth of the Word of God and of the soul imprisoned and held by chains in the body (sig. **.ii^r) to Calvin's view of the "house of clay," the "ruins" and the utter disaster in which the image of God resides (*Institutes* 1.15.2, 4, 6, 8). One may also compare Calvin to Jerome on the corrective power of the "eagle-like" conscience in the spirit of a man versus the cast-down conscience of someone who lacks shame and insight (*Commentariorum in Ezechielem* [PL 25:22]; Potts, *Conscience in Medieval Philosophy*, pp. 78–79).

35. Compare Sidney's comment about the moral philosophers who plainly set down how virtue "extendeth itself out of the limits of a man's own little world to the government of families and maintaining of public societies" (*Defence*, p. 83) to de Serres's point: "Indeed, the peculiar and proper office to which philosophy is oriented is the teaching of the reasons for making life rightly and honestly, that is, the manner in which single men ought to govern themselves and their families and, finally, the fashion in which the republic may rightly be administered" (*Erastae* 1:131). Cf. *Timaeus* 47b–c; *De Civitate Dei* 22.24; and *De Trinitate* 15.15 with this Aristotelian passage in de Serres.

36. A marginal gloss carefully links the encyclopedia of knowledges, through which the mind ranges, to the pursuit of the architectonic end of learning, for the question under consideration by Socrates in his analogy to the architect is the difference between the work of the hands and the work "cum prudentio & cognitione." "Nam in hac arte, fabri operam quinque aut ad summa sex minarum pretio redimeres: architectum vero, ne infinitarum quidem drachmarum mercede" (1:135).

37. The reference is to the *Philebus* 66b–d, and de Serres has made it correspondent both to Aristotle and to Augustine; the passage as quoted in my text is actually a combination of de Serres's axioms seven through ten (2:8–9). Since the *Philebus* comes first in the second volume of the *Plato*, dedicated to James VI, the ethical and political extension of architectonic doctrine is important.

38. This conflation of ethics and metaphysics deserves comparison with Immanuel Kant's "Architectonic of Pure Reason," in the *Critique of Pure Reason*, the first edition of which was

published in 1781, two hundred years after the publication of Jean de Serres's *Plato* and the composition of Sidney's *Defence*. See my Epilogue, pp. 238–41, 254–58.

39. "Sicuti & unica est mens architectrix nihilominus tamen distinxit Opifex rerum illarum naturas; est vt Universo constantiorem, robur singularibus fluuiam atque caducum tribuerit naturam" (3·5)

40. Cf. de Serres's comments on the care with which he and Estienne put together the edition, sig. ***.ii^r in the Prefatory Letter, and the explanation forwarded in the commentary on the *Cratylus* that Plato orders his dialogues cumulatively in series or families (1:378). The implication is that the structure of Plato's book reflects the structure of thought.

41. *The City of God* (11.18), trans. Marcus Dods (New York: Modern Library, 1950), pp. 361–62.

42. Cf. the fourth-century Christian *rhetor*, Lactantius, in *Libri Septem Divinarum Institutionum Adversus Gentes*, in *Opera* (Lyons, 1548), on the cultivation of ethical, philosophical, and religious antitheses in Christian discourse. This thinking and its structure are adapted by Sidney and also by Milton in his "Commonplace Book," ed. Ruth Mohl, in *Complete Prose Works of John Milton*, ed. Don M. Wolfe et al., 8 vols. (New Haven: Yale Univ. Press, 1953–83), 1:363–64, 369, 374. In her superb notes Mohl lists the titles of Lactantius's "seven books," illustrating the point in his statements, for instance, "Of False Wisdom" and "Of True Wisdom" (1:363).

43. The statement deserves emphasis because of obvious parallels to Sidney's theory of imagination, of modulation, and of teaching and moving, as I shall explain further in this chapter, and because of several parallels to Scaliger's theory, as I have explained in chapter 1, pp. 41–42.

44. In this, Jean de Serres continues the effort to persuade Christian humanists to take the Kabbalah seriously, which was begun by Pico della Mirandola and executed in great part by Johannes Reuchlin in his *De Arte Cabalistica* published in 1517. This has been printed in facsimile as *On the Art of the Kabbalah*, trans. Martin and Sarah Goodman and introduced by G. Lloyd Jones (New York: Abaris Books, 1983). Jones discusses the reception accorded Reuchlin's Christian Kabbalah by Martin Luther, Erasmus, and John Colet, marking some Catholic and Protestant differences and suggesting that reception was relatively cool in England until Doctor John Dee appropriated Reuchlin's explanation of the angelic hierarchies in his book, *Philosophia Moysaica* (pp. 22–27). Dame Frances A. Yates, *The Occult Philosophy in the Elizabethan Age* (London: Routledge and Kegan Paul, 1979), discusses Doctor John Dee as a "Christian Cabalist" (pp. 79–93). Clearly, Jean de Serres contributed a discussion of kabbalistic principles to Sidney's thought through the commentary on the *Symposium*, which I shall discuss momentarily, and his treatment of allegory, love, and angelology (3:168–69). Of the angels, he says, "These species said to be Love, therefore, are, namely Daemons, not God, that is, beings mediating between divine and mortal nature" (3:168).

45. See Moshe Idel's comments in "Infinities of Torah in Kabbalah," in *Midrash and Literature*, ed. Geoffrey H. Hartman and Sanford Budick (New Haven: Yale Univ. Press, 1986), pp. 149–50, on Abulafia, Pico, Lull, Mallarmé, Derrida, and Umberto Eco with regard to the *ars combinatoria* and Orphic infinities of meaning. Derrida refers to the combinatory logic in *Dissemination*, pp. 343–44, 348–50, cross-referencing the number, dot, spark, and seed and exploring the "square of the world" (the labyrinth, the serpent of the eternal return, and sperm); he does not relate his ideogram to the Cross as the Christian kabbalists did but follows either classical thought (Empedocles, Pythagoras) or Hegel and mentions the polysemy revolving around the Torah (pp. 344–45).

46. Cf. Reuchlin's *De Verbo Mirifico* or "wonder-working word," and Yates's discussion of it in *The Occult Philosophy*, pp. 23–24; Reuchlin transforms the sacred tetragrammaton into a pentagrammaton by inserting an "S" among the four holy letters "YHVH" to make the name of Jesus (Joshua) "YHSVH." It is this Word, in Scripture and in history, that summons the power of angels and performs wonders. *De Verbo Mirifico* was published in Germany in 1494 and in Lyons in 1552.

47. De Serres alludes to the argument of Crassus and Antonius in Cicero's *De Oratore*—the same passage that appears in Fracastoro's and Sidney's references—to interpret Plato's damnation of false rhetoric and his praise of a true art of rhetoric that "represents nature" (1:441). Sidney speaks of a style "fittest to nature" that "doth according to art, though not by art" (*Defence*, pp. 118–19). See chapter 5, pp. 300–9, on Cicero, Fracastoro, and Sidney.

48. "Duplex itaque est Rhetorica: una vera & fructuosa: altera, Adulterina & damnosa" (1:444, axiom 7). The reasoning is Plato's in the *Gorgias*, but the antithetical emphasis is de Serres's.

49. S. K. Heninger, Jr., has translated this short commentary and analyzed aspects of its pertinence to Sidney's *Defence*. Heninger observes the parallels between de Serres's and Sidney's ideas of the double mode of imagination, *eikastic* and *phantastic*; the similar definition of three kinds of poetry—the theological or divine, the philosophical, and the inventive; and the corresponding use of the poetic theory of Julius Scaliger. In the light of de Serres's opening gambit on *furor poeticus* or "divine frenzy," Heninger says that "Sidney rejected the notion of divine inspiration, largely because his puritanical view of man would not allow even a poet to be raised so near the status of God" ("Sidney and Serranus' *Plato*," pp. 156–57). I think the influence of Jean de Serres's commentaries on Sidney goes beyond but includes the *Ion* and is deeper, broader, and more philosophically precise. Sidney testifies to a new definition of poetic inspiration in which poesie may be practiced truly the way the spiritual man or the Puritan icon of the redeemed self may come close, indeed, to God. Cf. Ann Kibbey's discussion of the living Puritan icon of the self in seventeenth-century American Puritan discourse in "Iconoclastic Materialism," in *The Interpretation of Material Shapes in Puritanism: A Study of Rhetoric, Prejudice, and Violence* (Cambridge: Cambridge Univ. Press, 1986), pp. 42–64.

50. Compare Scaliger's view in *Poetices Libri Septem* (Lyons, 1561) that poetry leads to "beatitude." See also Debora K. Shuger's study, *Sacred Rhetoric: The Christian Grand Style in the English Renaissance* (Princeton, N.J.: Princeton Univ. Press, 1988), pp. 231–32, 235–40.

51. Cf. Scaliger's analogy of the arts in the *Poetices* in which he compares the "toga" and "arms" of the statue as ornaments to the rhythm, or number, figures, and word-pictures of poetry (2.1, p. 55). Scaliger goes on to make a geometric and architectural analogy to the poet's "music" or rhythm: "Sicuti apud Geometram regula rectam lineam ducemus: at eam sumptam architectus praeponet, apponet, transponet, eriget, deprimet, circulo, semicirculo, ouali accommodabit. Erit igitur Mensura praescriptio tractus. Rhythmus autem praescriptionis temperamentum" (2.2, p. 56). Elsewhere in the *Poetices* Scaliger discusses the architect's *modellum*, or little model, and compares it to the poet's use of *tractatio* (3.33, p. 122). See my discussion in chapter 1, pp. 59–69, on Sidney's "house well in model."

52. Cf. Ronald Levao, "Sidney's Feigned *Apology*," *PMLA* 94 (1979): 223–33, on Sidney's ambiguities, play, and outright contradictions. Levao is almost certainly correct that Sidney views the imagination as the faculty "that creates fictions, the faculty that creates another nature and so reveals our divinity to ourselves," but he is incorrect in his assertion that there is no clear transition from the mind's operations to its "transcendental source" and in his denial that the " 'highest point of man's wit' " is an *apex mentis* "directly sparked by the divine." Poetry is fiction; but poesie can convey exactly that spark to those who are capable of receiving it in Jean de Serres's and in Sidney's opinion. The reader must make the transition from knowing to doing, from fiction to action, and poesie presides over that transition as a form of grace. Thus Levao argues that the *Defence* is a demonstration, not a justification of wit, and the argument, which is true in great part, nevertheless perpetrates yet another omission of recognition of the mistress-knowledge.

53. De Serres makes almost the same comment on the moving power of *eikastic* images in the Prefatory Letter, sig. **.vi^v. The commentary on the two kinds of images in the discussion of the *Ion* (1:528) parallels the view of true and false reasoning in de Serres's and Estienne's marginal gloss on *eikastic* and *phantastic* proportionality in its original Platonic source, *Sophist* 236 (1:235), and also parallels the discussion of true and false speech in the commentary on the

"two" rhetorics in the *Gorgias* (1:444). Appearing also in Sidney's refutation in the *Defence* (p. 104), the moral dualism of de Serres's idea of language extends to divine and human workmanship in nature and in art. Cf. Saint Augustine's similar combination of antithesis and *gradatio* in his definition of the four phases of the Christian's life in the *Enchiridion* 118 and of the end, the love of God, that makes lust diminish in the *Enchiridion* 121. Augustine spoke of love and the eternity and so on and so on" in *Confessions* 1.1, 10.27–37.

54. De Serres's commentary on the *Politicus* has great significance for Sidney's view of the poet-statesman's production of the "golden world" (2:251). See Harry Levin's discussion of the theme in the Renaissance in *The Myth of the Golden Age in the Renaissance* (Bloomington: Indiana Univ. Press, 1969) and a recent collection of essays by Harry Berger, Jr., *Second World and Green World: Studies in Renaissance Fiction-Making*, ed. John Patrick Lynch (Berkeley: Univ. of California Press, 1988).

55. Cf. Cicero *De Oratore* 1.16, on orators and poets being alike because they are not restricted intellectually and may range freely where they will to gather their *copia*. Also cf. Horace's dismissal of the wildeyed poet from the city of man while the true poet receives praise for morally building up the city by use of his intelligence (*Ars Poetica* 396–401). A mid-sixteenth-century example of the overlap of definitions of art, science, wisdom, wit, invention, and imagination is Alessandro Lionardi's view of "wit" both as invention and as amplification in the *Dialogi della inventione poetica* (Venice, 1554). On this subject see William Crane, *Wit and Rhetoric in the Renaissance* (New York: Columbia Univ. Press, 1937), and two studies by Murray W. Bundy: *Theory of Imagination in Classical and Medieval Thought, UISLL*, vol. 12, nos. 2–3 (1927), and " 'Invention' and 'Imagination' in the Renaissance," *JEGP* 24 (1930): 535–45.

56. *Elizabethan and Metaphysical Imagery: Renaissance Poetic and Twentieth-Century Critics* (Chicago: Univ. of Chicago Press, 1947), p. 187. Tuve is discussing rhetorical efficacy and the safeguard of decorum.

57. On the topos of prostitution with regard to philosophy or poetry, see Uhlfelder, "The Role of the Liberal Arts in Boethius' *Consolatio*," in *Boethius and the Liberal Arts*, ed. Michael Masi, Utah Studies in Literature and Linguistics, vol. 18 (Las Vegas: Peter Lang, 1981), p. 17, on Boethian use of the phrase *scenicas meretriculas* and on stock harlots who brought young men to financial or moral ruin.

58. Cf. Sidney's discussion of Plutarch's discourse on Isis and Osiris with respect to Egyptian knowledge (p. 108). In the 1603 translation of Plutarch's *Philosophie*, Holland writes a long summary in which he identifies Osiris with the Nile and Isis with "that nature which preserveth and governeth the world" (p. 1287).

59. *Defence*, p. 108. In line of reasoning, Sidney follows Scaliger, as indicated, but in refusing to overthrow "the authority" of Plato, Sidney sympathizes with de Serres's admiration for the wise man. Cf. M. H. Partee, "Anti-Platonism in Sidney's *Defence*," *EM* 22 (1971): 7–29, on the resemblance between Sidney's poet and Plato's philosopher.

60. On the influence of Gosson's *School of Abuse* on the *Defence*, see Katherine Duncan-Jones and Jan van Dorsten, eds., *Miscellaneous Prose of Sir Philip Sidney* (Oxford: Clarendon, 1973), p. 62, and cf. Arthur F. Kinney, "Parody and Its Implications in Sidney's *Defence of Poesie*," *SEL 1500–1900* 12 (1972): 1–19. See also Peter C. Herman's essay, "Do as I say, Not as I Do: *The Apology for Poetry* and Sir Philip Sidney's Letters to Edward Denny and Robert Sidney," in *SN* 10 (1989), and cf. the discussion of these letters and reading in chapter 1, pp. 20ff., on the ambivalence of Cyrus. Herman points out that Sidney does not particularly advocate the reading of poetry in his letters to Denny and his brother Robert.

61. Though turned into English by John Stockwood (London, 1585), *Joannis Serrani in Ecclesiasten Solomonis* was originally published in Geneva in 1579 by Peter Santandreanus; see the preface, passim, ¶ iiiij^r–¶ vij^v. On the commentary and seventeenth-century typology in relation to Platonic allegory in the *Symposium*, see Barbara Lewalski, *Protestant Poetics and the Seventeenth-Century Religious Lyric* (Princeton, N.J.: Princeton Univ. Press, 1979), pp. 57–58.

62. Cf. Ronald Levao's argument on Sidney's justification of poetry and demonstration of it in the *Defence* in "Sidney's Feigned *Apology.*" Levao also sees the ambivalence in Sidney's handling of poetic inspiration and metaphysics; yet he seems to deny that, in Protestant soteriology, imagination is a faculty capable of being graced, too.

63. In the preface to Book 2, *The Reason of Church Government*, ed. Ralph A. Haug, in *Complete Prose Works of John Milton*, ed. Don M. Wolfe et al., 8 vols. (New Haven: Yale Univ. Press, 1953–83), 1:801.

64. See James G. Turner, *One Flesh: Paradisal Marriage and Sexual Relations in the Age of Milton* (Oxford: Clarendon, 1987).

65. "Plato docet, Aristoteles probat" (1:**.vi^v). In his effort to interrelate the two philosophers, de Serres states this axiom in his Prefatory Letter after explaining Platonic allegory and before observing that Moses and the Prophets possessed all of these doctrines. Cf. my account of Scaliger's discussion of the usefulness of prosopopoeia in teaching (in chapter 1, p. 4, and pp. 407–8 nn.6, 7).

66. See *Dissemination*, pp. 3–4, questioning literature, and pp. 187–96, on the Platonic idea of the book as mimesis of thinking, not thinking, for example.

67. See *Of Grammatology*, pp. 101–40, on the violence of writing, and *Dissemination*, pp. 344–45, on the drama of God and the polysemy of the Torah as the possibility of a "new" Torah arising out of the other. Derrida expatiates on Hegel's and Heidegger's sense of the hieroglyphic in this book; he also plays with Plato's notion of the "seeds" of words in an elaborate pun on dissemination and insemination, sowing and sewing (*Dissemination*, p. 304, for instance), and it is useful to examine a renaissance Plato's play with the same idea in the French philosopher Jean de Serres, whose work may have fed the mainstream of French philosophy long enough even to affect a modern French philosopher such as Derrida. In his Prefatory Letter, de Serres conflates Justin's idea of *logos spermatikos* with Augustine's and Jerome's notions of the *scintilla rationis* and *synderesis scintilla*. Sparks are the "seeds" of fire, and all three versions of the patristic "dissemination" of the Word in things and in language and culture derive from Plato's *semina* in Jean de Serres's acknowledgment of it, too (1:sig. **. iii.^{r}). The difference between Derrida and de Serres seems to be the logical one between a modern technical interest in the mechanics of semination and dissemination of words and the French Protestant's interest in sparks of conscience moving through words, the arts and sciences, and all of culture. De Serres definitely links his *scintillae* and seed-sowing to language and speech in his praise of the light of the Word that shines in the darkness in the arts of "right speaking, arguing, and proclaiming" (*bene loquendi, disserendi, dicendi*), and in renaissance printing, *disserendi* offers itself, as well, as *differendi* (1:sig. **. ii.^{v}). Etymologically, *disserendi* indicates the sowing of seed or the act of arguing, dissertating. From a Christian perspective, Sidney's self-sacrifice is a form of sowing his own body, as Christ's death was, in the larger project of the Word's regeneration of the fallen world.

68. *Life of Sidney*, pp. 88–89; Greville describes an "Imperiall Mandate . . . carrying with it in the one hand grace, the other thunder." He also refers to "the secret influence of destinie" in Sidney's having disarmed "that part, where God (it seems) had resolved to strike him" in his wounding at Zutphen (p.143).

69. See 2 Samuel 11–12, Geneva for the story of David's sin.

70. See for example, *The Phoenix Nest*.

71. *Eikonoklastes*, in *Complete Prose Works of John Milton*, ed. Wolfe et al., 3:362–63.

72. Osborn, *Young Philip Sidney 1572–1577* (New Haven: Yale Univ. Press, 1972), pp. 56–73. Osborn describes the conditions and disposition of the English fugitives from Paris, asserting that the possibility "that Sidney may have been forced to ride pillion to view Coligny's mangled body and other gory scenes" is not as "unlikely" as it seems (p. 70).

73. See Victor Skretkowicz, "Building Sidney's Reputation: Texts and Editions of the *Arcadia*," in *Sir Philip Sidney: 1586 and the Creation of a Legend*, ed. Jan van Dorsten, Dominic Baker-Smith, and Arthur F. Kinney (Leiden: Brill, 1986), pp. 111–24.

74. See Lauren Silberman, "Singing Unsung Heroines: Androgynous Discourse in Book 3 of *The Faerie Queene*," in *Rewriting the Renaissance: The Discourses of Sexual Difference in Early Modern Europe*, ed. Margaret W. Ferguson, Maureen Quilligan, and Nancy Vickers (Chicago: Univ. of Chicago Press, 1986), pp. 259–71.

75. See Budick's chapter, "*Paradise Lost*: Reason, Interpretation, Sacrifice," in *The Dividing Muse: Images of Sacred Disjunction in Milton's Poetry* (New Haven: Yale Univ. Press, 1985), pp. 100–121, for a superb discussion of Milton's search for temple sanctuary, love, the "architectural significance" of Milton's construction of Adam and Eve's alternative scene after Eden, and the Christian consciousness of the Son's model of self-sacrifice. See Lieb's full exposition of Milton's reconstruction of the "spirituall architecture" of the inward temple in his "sacral poetics" in *Poetics of the Holy: A Reading of Paradise Lost* (Chapel Hill: Univ. of North Carolina Press, 1981).

76. See my forthcoming essay, "Sidney, Milton, and the Phoenix," in a collection of essays on Milton edited by Margo Swiss and David Kent.

77. "Eve and the Arts of Eden," in *Milton and the Idea of Woman*, ed. Julia M. Walker (Urbana: Univ. of Illinois Press, 1988), pp. 100–119.

78. Cf. Weiner, *Sir Philip Sidney and the Poetics of Protestantism*. Although Weiner makes too strict a separation between Urania and Christ in discussing whether Strephon and Claius in the *Arcadia* run her race or his, for instance, Weiner does identify their view of Urania's attributes as "a kind of combination of those of celestial Venus and Christ" (pp. 140–41). Elsewhere in his discussion, Weiner also expresses the role of the poet's "play" in indirectly serving Presence, in a rule actually paraphrasing the neo-Pelagianism informing the Reformation: "If only, Sidney suggests, we try to observe the rules of the game, we will not go unconsoled," Weiner aptly remarks, and "For Sidney, God's game may be a hard one, but it is the only one in town" (p. 185). Also cf. Murray Krieger, *Poetic Presence and Illusion: Essays in Critical History and Theory* (Baltimore: Johns Hopkins Univ. Press, 1979), p. 25, on searching out in renaissance poems "a method by which each confronts the emptiness of words as signifiers—their distance from their signifieds—and, having thus confronted that emptiness and that distance, converts itself into an invocation of presence that becomes itself a verbal presence."

79. *Ezra Pound* (Chicago: Univ. of Chicago Press, 1975), pp. 103–4, 113, 115–16.

80. Geoffrey Hill in *Tenebrae* (London: André Deutsch, 1978), p. 22.

Chapter 5

1. Any references to Fulke Greville, *The Life of the Renowned Sr Philip Sidney*, in this chapter are to the facsimile reproduction, introduced by Warren W. Wooden (Delmar, N.Y.: Scholars' Facsimiles & Reprints, 1984). The passage in the epigraph is on pp. 20–21. For Patterson's observation see "Under . . . Pretty Tales: Intention in Sidney's *Arcadia*," in *Censorship and Interpretation: The Condition of Writing and Reading in Early Modern England* (Madison: Univ. of Wisconsin Press, 1984), pp. 24–25.

2. "The Exemplary Mirage: Fabrication of Sir Philip Sidney's Biographical Image and the Sidney Reader," *ELH* 48 (1981): 1–16.

3. In the *Life of Sidney*, Greville reports that Sidney sought spiritual profit in the pains he suffered as a "sensible natured man" under the surgeons' hands "yet one to whom a stronger Spirit had given power above himself, either to do, or suffer" (p. 146). Greville also reports how "the very shoulder-bones of this delicate Patient" were "worn through the skin" and "many other symptoms of decay" including the "noisom savor about him," that is, the odor of the gangrene, were manifest (p. 149). Gifford's essay and Duncan-Jones's comment on it may be found in *Miscellaneous Prose of Sir Philip Sidney*, ed. Katherine Duncan-Jones and Jan van Dorsten (Oxford: Clarendon, 1973), pp. 161–65.

4. *A New Discourse of a Stale Subject, Called the Metamorphosis of Ajax*, ed. Elizabeth S.

Donno (New York: Columbia Univ. Press, 1962), pp. 64–65. See my chapter 1, p. 54, and p. 430 n.59. I am in debt to the Rev. Thomas Arthur for pointing this passage out to me. For Stallybrass's comments see "Patriarchal Territories: The Body Enclosed," in *Rewriting the Renaissance: The Discourses of Sexual Difference in Early Modern Europe*, ed. Margaret W. Ferguson, Maureen Quilligan, and Nancy J. Vickers (Chicago: Univ. of Chicago Press, 1986), p. 124.

5. *Exequiae Illustrissimi Equitis, D. Philippi Sidnaei* (Oxford, 1587) and *Academiae Cantabrigiensis Lachrymae Tumulo Nobilissimi Equitis, D. Philippi Sidnei Sacratae* (London, 1587). Dominic Baker-Smith, " 'Great Expectation': Sidney's Death and the Poets," in *Sir Philip Sidney: 1586 and the Creation of a Legend*, ed. Jan van Dorsten, Dominic Baker-Smith, and Arthur F. Kinney (Leiden: Brill, 1986), pp. 83–103, places these commemorative volumes in a larger historical perspective.

6. A book that may inaugurate a different but equally modern and psychological approach to the positive side of the Orpheus legend used in the Renaissance may be Barbara L. Estrin's *The Raven and the Lark: Lost Children in the Literature of the English Renaissance* (London: Associated Univ. Presses, 1985) not because Estrin considers Orpheus but because her recognition of the plot of lost and found, rendered and restored, reveals the theological model of forgiveness of original sin in the image of the wholeness of the child.

7. "Puritanism and Maenadism in *A Mask*," in *Rewriting the Renaissance*, ed. Ferguson et al., pp. 88–105. Cf. Thomas Wilson, *Wilson's Arte of Rhetorique, 1560*, ed. G. H. Mair (Oxford: Clarendon, 1909), p. 47:

> Now againe, the same Poets doe declare that Orpheus the Musition and Minstrell, did stirre and make soft with his pleasaunt melodie, the most harde Rockes and stones. And what is their meaning herein? Assuredly nothing els, but that a wise and well spoken man, did call backe harde harted men, such as liued abrode like beastes from open whoredom, & brought them to liue after the most holy lawes of Matrimonie. Thus we see plainly, that such a one as hath no mind of mariage, seemeth to be no man but rather a stone, an enemie of nature, a rebell to God himselfe, seeking through his owne folly, his last ende and destruction.

8. *On Education, a Translation of the De Tradendis Disciplinis* 5.3, ed. Foster Watson (Cambridge: Cambridge Univ. Press, 1913). Sidney's headmaster at Shrewsbury, Thomas Ashton, used portions of Cicero and Vives to aid his students in their Latin, and Sidney accompanied Ashton and the rhetorician Thomas Wilson to Oxford on a visit in 1566. These associations provide some of the historical sources of Sidney's interpretation of an architectonic rhetoric in the feminine metaphor of learned rule in the *Defence*. See the discussion of Sidney's biography in the introduction to *The Poems of Sir Philip Sidney*, ed. William A. Ringler (Oxford: Clarendon, 1962), pp. xvii–xviii.

9. *Elizabethan and Metaphysical Imagery: Renaissance Poetic and Twentieth-Century Critics* (Chicago: Univ. of Chicago Press, 1947), p. 45.

10. See Louis Adrian Montrose, " 'Shaping Fantasies': Figurations of Gender and Power in Elizabethan Culture," *Representations* 1 (1983): 61–94, and especially his comments in "*A Midsummer Night's Dream* and the Shaping Fantasies of Elizabethan Culture: Gender, Power, Form," in which Montrose comments on Shakespeare's imaging of a "boy's transition from the female-centered world of his childhood to the male-centered world of his youth" as a form of transition from "matriarchy to patriarchy" (p. 74); on Shakespeare's Aristotelian and phallocentric identification of the mother as a "container" for her son, not a "maker" (p. 75); and on the interplay between "sexual politics in the Elizabethan family and sexual politics in the Elizabethan monarchy, for the woman to whom *all* Elizabethan men were vulnerable was Queen Elizabeth herself" (p. 77), in *Rewriting the Renaissance*, pp. 65–87. Montrose's idea that patriarchal norms are artistically asserted because of the vulnerability of men in Elizabeth's reign is most provocative with regard to this play since *A Midsummer Night's*

Dream shows the influence of Sidney's idea of poetic fiction and the creative power of poetic imagination. The androgynous speaking picture of Sidney's *Defence* may appear in Shakespeare's play, however, in ways that Montrose tends to tilt one way or the other in his view of the sexual power struggle.

11. For two general perspectives, see Alice Jardine, *Men in Feminism* (New York: Methuen, 1987), and Catherine R. Stimpson, *Where the Meanings Are. Feminism and Cultural Spaces* (New York: Methuen, 1988), for the argument that gender difference can be the basis of balance, not merely division.

12. "Reading Woman (Reading)," in *Reading Woman: Essays in Feminist Criticism* (New York: Columbia Univ. Press, 1986), p. 40. See also Toril Moi, *Sexual/Textual Politics* (London: Methuen, 1985), and Gayatri Chakravorty Spivak, *In Other Worlds: Essays in Cultural Politics* (New York: Methuen, 1987).

13. Patricia Parker discusses this development of *copia* as a feminine figure linked to rhetorical dilation and to the generation of the text in *Literary Fat Ladies: Rhetoric, Gender, Property* (London: Methuen, 1987), pp. 3–4, 8–35.

14. See John Guillory, "Dalila's House: *Samson Agonistes* and the Sexual Division of Labor," in *Rewriting the Renaissance*, pp. 106–22; Guillory observes the tragedy of Samson in his refusal of Dalila's offer to take him home to her house, and this is the tragedy of divorce that reinforces the sacrifice of woman and the "egregious exercises of restraint" that signify a man's "patriarchal 'standing' " (pp. 107, 117). Guillory does not examine the parallel self-destruction in Samson's authoritative and patriarchal destruction of the temple of the Philistines. See also the essay by Mary Nyquist, "Textual Overlapping and Dalilah's Harlot-Lap," in *Literary Theory/Renaissance Texts*, ed. Patricia Parker and David Quint (Baltimore: Johns Hopkins Univ. Press, 1986), pp. 341–72.

15. Pietro Vettori *Commentarii in X Libros Aristotelis, De Moribus ad Nicomachum* (Florence, 1584), p. 1.

16. See also Victoria Kahn, "Humanism and the Resistance to Theory," in *Literary Theory/Renaissance Texts*, ed. Parker and Quint, pp. 383, 393 n.27, on the telescoping of Aristotle's definitions of *sophia* and *techne*.

17. *The Ethiques of Aristotle, that is to saye, preceptes of good behaoure and perfighte honestie, now newly translated into English* (London, 1547), sig. A.iii^v–A.iiii^r. Cf. Aristotle's *Rhetoric* 1.1 (1354b); 1.4 (1359b). Leonardo Bruni's Latin translation of Aristotle's *Ethics* was at Oxford as early as 1439 with other items in Duke Humfrey's gift; the text was printed at Oxford by Theodoric Rood in 1479.

18. For Cicero's view of the universality of rhetoric, see the *De Oratore* 1.3, trans. E. W. Sutton and H. Rackham (London: William Heinemann, 1942). Cf. Aristotle's *Rhetoric* 3.1 (1403b–1404a); Cicero's *De Oratore* 1.31.142–43; and Quintilian's *Institutio Oratoria* 3.3.1–15. In the *De Inventione* 1.5.6, Cicero treats rhetoric as a department of politics.

19. Wilkinson defines *sapience*, Aristotle's philosophic wisdom, as an "advaunsing or ioiyng of artificers that hath obtayned scyence. And when it is said of one that he is wyse in his art, ther is shewed the goodnes and gretnes of his art" (sig. F.v^r). Earlier in the text Wilkinson compares geometry and rhetoric in their respective "demonstracions" and "argumentes semblables" (sig. A.iiii^v) but loses the distinction between the instrumental nature of a practical faculty, or craft, and the "necessary" knowledge of science; the loss of this distinction suggests the Ciceronian influence of a "wise eloquence" that unites a charming craft having particular scope with a universal science that generally knows the truth.

20. The fullest exposition of Aristotle's doctrine of causes may be found in the *Physics* 194b; cf. *Metaphysics* 1.3 (983); 5.2 (1013a–1014a). Aristotle compared poetry to rhetoric on the basis of style (*Rhetoric* 3.1 [1404a]), and the warning not to make the practical faculties of rhetoric and dialectic into sciences extends to poetic, too, but in complicated ways. The complication derives from Aristotle's definition of formal cause in logic and the impossibility of a "metaphysical logic," for Aristotle had broken up the old ontology of word and thing, and

formal cause was meant to restore the bond between the ground of knowing and the ground of being; see Werner Jaeger, *Aristotle, Fundamentals of the History of His Development*, trans. Richard Robinson, 2d ed. (Oxford: Clarendon, 1948), p. 370. The Italian poetic theorists sustained confusion on this matter so that the organic unity of a poem (*Poetics* 1459a) and the Aristotelian emphasis on action (*Poetics* 1450a) were taken up by the consideration of character and moral purpose; see Weinberg, *History of Literary Criticism in the Italian Renaissance*, 2 vols. (Chicago: Univ. of Chicago Press, 1961), 1:140–41. Since a poem is composed of imitation and harmony, it is both a "word" and a musical "thing" (*Poetics* 1448b) and is treated by Aristotle under the category of material cause while rhetoric is treated under the category of efficient cause; see Richard P. McKeon, "Rhetoric and Poetic in the Philosophy of Aristotle," in *Aristotle's 'Poetics' and English Literature*, ed. Elder Olson (Chicago: Univ. of Chicago Press, 1965), pp. 209–10.

21. See Giraldi's comment of 1547, for example, as quoted in Weinberg, *History of Literary Criticism* 1:140 n.40: "quasi occulta maestra della uita."

22. *Institutio Oratoria* Preface; 1.1. See S. E. Lehmberg, *Sir Thomas Elyot: Tudor Humanist* (Austin: Univ. of Texas Press, 1960), for a full bibliography of Elyot's works. For the passages cited and on the subject of reading, see *The Governour* 1.11–13, ed. S. E. Lehmberg (London: J. M. Dent and Sons, 1962), pp. 39, 50; and cf. Plutarch, "The Education or Bringing up of Children," which Elyot translated in 1533.

23. See Constance Jordan, "Feminism and the Humanists: The Case for Sir Thomas Elyot's *Defense of Good Women*," in *Rewriting the Renaissance*, pp. 242–58. Jordan argues Elyot's greater validation of the excellency of women in the political and historical spheres, suggesting that Elyot presented "a model of femininity more aggressively political" than Vives did (p. 258).

24. I have looked at two later editions: the *De Civitate Dei Libri XXII* (Basel, 1570) and the translation by John Healey, *Of the Cities of God, with the comments of Iu. L. Vives* (London, 1610). Vives subtitled the second book of his *De Disciplinis* in Augustinian fashion: *Libri de Tradendis Disciplinis siue de Doctrina Christiana* (Antwerp, 1531), fol. 79–160. He considers the work of "authores misti" in "historias & fabulas" as a species of oratory and philosophy, with philology, and refers to Augustine's *City of God* (fol. 108ᵛ), to Erasmus's *Adagia*, and then, in another context, to Plutarch's essay on the poets and to Saint Basil's essay on reading secular literature and to Aristotle's art of poetry (fol. 110ʳ). Vives's humanism unabashedly mixes ancient and contemporary sources.

25. Manutius's three-volume work consists of a collection of Prudentius's poems; an anthology, *Christianae Poetae*; and a Greek and Latin edition of the *Carmini* of Saint Gregory Nazianzus, all published between 1501 and 1504.

26. Fabricius's anthology, *Poetarum Veterum Ecclesiasticorum Opera Christiana* (Basel, 1562), is based on the argument that poets are not only for the theater and for the "gentiles" but for Christians, since the Holy Scriptures are largely composed of poetry and since various Fathers have witnessed to the value of the arts in the life of the Church (sig. a2ᵛ; p. 8).

27. *A very fruteful and pleasant boke callyd the Instruction of a Christen woman, made fyrste in latyne, by the right famous clerk mayster Lewes Vives, and tourned oute of latyne into Englysshe by Richard Hyrde* (London: Th. Berthelet, 1541), sig. Aiiʳ.

28. Cf. Jean Bethke Elshtain's similarly critical remarks on Plato's antifeminism in "Feminist Discourse and Its Discontents: Language, Power, and Meaning," *Signs: Journal of Women in Culture and Society* 7 (1982): 606.

29. See Susan Schibanoff's interesting discussion of Father Ong's view of the way oral cultures constantly "re-read" their texts; she applies the principle of "structural amnesia," or selectivity for the sake of social equilibrium, to the way written cultures like those of the Fathers and the renaissance recoverers of patristic exegesis reread Christian doctrine in "Taking the Gold Out of Egypt," in *Gender and Reading: Essays on Readers, Texts, and Contexts*, ed. Elizabeth A. Flynn and Patrocinio P. Schweickart (Baltimore: Johns Hopkins Univ. Press,

1986), pp. 89–91. Vives here seems to be correcting the patristic emphasis on chastity in women to describe a curriculum to meet the present renaissance need to educate *some* women.

30. Perhaps her arise I am looking more at the intellectual than the pragmatic, I give more feminist credit to Vives than Carole Levin ("John Foxe and the Responsibilities of Queenship," in *Women in the Middle Ages and the Renaissance,* ed. Mary Beth Rose [Syracuse, N.Y.: Syracuse Univ. Press, 1986], pp. 113–34), who holds the qualified view that "even though Vives wrote in favor of a humanist education for women, he also condemned women for playing a role in public life" (p. 116).

31. See, for example, Robin Headlam Wells, *Spenser's* Faerie Queene *and the Cult of Elizabeth* (London: Croom Helm, 1983), pp. 58–61, on Spenser's architectural conceit and Elizabeth's body in the house of Alma. See also Louis Adrian Montrose, "The Elizabethan Subject and the Spenserian Text," in *Literary Theory/Renaissance Texts,* ed. Parker and Quint, pp. 303–40, especially the bibliographical n.14 on p. 335. From a different perspective, that of androgyny, Leah S. Marcus in "Shakespeare's Comic Heroines, Elizabeth I, and the Political Uses of Androgyny," in *Women in the Middle Ages and the Renaissance,* ed. Rose, pp. 135–53, has also studied the literary typing of the Queen.

32. In "A Prologue to the Reader," Wilson discusses his own travail over his book while he was visiting Rome and was interrogated for his religious views. In his preface he explains how eloquence is a gift of God to "repair" mankind that, "being destitute of God's grace," did not know itself (*Arte of Rhetorique,* ed. Mair, sig. A. vi^v). See also John N. Wall, Jr., "Godly and Fruitful Lessons: The English Bible, Erasmus' Paraphrases, and the Book of Homilies," in *The Godly Kingdom of Tudor England: Great Books of the English Reformation,* ed. John E. Booty et al. (Wilton, Conn.: Morehouse-Barlow Co., 1981), pp. 47–135. Patricia Parker has quite specifically discussed the development of sexist bias and male linearity in the language of rhetoric in the sixteenth century in her sixth chapter, "Motivated Rhetorics: Gender, Order, Rule," in *Literary Fat Ladies,* pp. 97–125. I am indebted to her idea of the *copula* and *sequitur* and feminine suppression in the construction of social order through speech.

33. *De Fructu Qui Ex Doctrina Percipitur,* or "The Benefit of a Liberal Education," ed. and trans. Frank Manley and Richard Sylvester (New York: Frederick Ungar, 1967), p. 107. Cf. Jorge Luis Borges, "The Aleph," in *A Personal Anthology,* ed. and trans. Anthony Kerrigan (New York: Grove, 1967), and de Serres's commentary on Plato's *Cratylus* in the 1578 *Plato* (1:378–83).

34. *The pathway to knowledge containing the first principles of geometrie as they may moste aptly be applied to practice* (London, 1551), sig. iv. Recorde is like his contemporaries in interpreting Aristotle, for Aristotle's notion of the "mean" in the definition of virtue is quasi-mathematical (*Nicomachean Ethics* 2.6 [1106b–1107a]). The idea of justice is not easily accommodated to the mean, for distributive justice is a kind of geometric proportion or equality of ratios (5.3 [1131a]), and corrective justice is a kind of arithmetical progression (5.4 [1131b]). Similarly, there is no true excess or deficiency of justice; its "mean" is an extreme point of excellence and rightness, an absolute (2.6 [1107a]; 5.5 [1133b–1134a]). Cf. Sir Thomas Elyot's discussion of distributive justice in *The Governour* 3.1–7.

35. See Aristotle's *Posterior Analytics* 1.1–10 (71a–76b); 1.15 (79a). Aristotle compares and contrasts geometry and dialectic, especially with respect to "first principles" or ἀρχάς such as the law of contradiction and intuitive knowledge (1.2 [72a]). William and Martha Kneale, *The Development of Logic* (Oxford: Clarendon, 1968), pp. 2ff., comment on the significance of geometry as a deductive system according to which other knowledges could be patterned— from the Greeks through Spinoza's *Ethica more geometrica demonstrata.* Aristotle refers to the dilemma of the *Meno* in *Posterior Analytics* 1.1 (71a).

36. *Institutio Oratoria* 1.10.34–49. Quintilian advocates the enthymeme as the strongest rhetorical proof because it is a type of geometric demonstration; he also refers to a "geometric" process of thought to validate rhetoric. Aristotle makes the remark about teaching geometry in the *Rhetoric* 3.1 (1404a), and Robert Recorde apologizes to his reader for the manner in which

he has rearranged geometry by putting the conclusions before the theorems in order to teach the causes through the effects (*The Pathway to Knowledge* 2, sig. aiij^r).

37. Wilson considers eloquence to be an "apt" framing of words and sentences together, and he cites "Tully" to say that "finding" reason out and "framing" it (invention and disposition) is the part of a wise man, but only an orator has the gift to "set forthe . . . wisedome" (*Arte of Rhetorique*, pp. 160–61).

38. Cf. Plato's discussion of geometry as an absolutely necessary knowledge for the statesman who is both a soldier and a philosopher; geometry, although a pure knowledge, is "spoken" by its adepts as if all their works were directed toward action (*Republic* 7.526–27). See Osborn, *Young Philip Sidney*, pp. 136–37, on Languet's view of the practicality of geometry, which does not differ too much from Wilson's. See also Dorothy Koenigsberger, *Renaissance Man and Creative Thinking: A History of Concepts of Harmony 1400–1700* (Sussex, Eng.: Harvester, 1979), especially pp. 213–65, "Universality and the Bringing Together of Disciplines."

39. *De Oratore* 1.50.218 (trans. Sutton and Rackham).

40. *Naugerius, siue de Poetica Dialogus*, trans. Ruth Kelso, *UISLL*, vol. 9, no. 3 (1924), pp. 51, 62. Navagero answers the question on the different natures of the philosopher and the poet by overturning the distinction: as the poet is a philosopher, he knows; as he is a poet, he writes well (p. 73). Thus the *scientia* of the natural philosopher and the *locutio* of the rhetorician—the contrast discussed by Antonius and Crassus in Cicero's *De Oratore* 1.50—may be united in the poet.

41. *Turrius, siue de Intellectione*, as quoted by Murray Bundy, "Fracastoro and the Imagination," *PQ* 20 (1941): 48–52.

42. My argument qualifies Bundy's view that Fracastoro failed to relate the penetrating analysis of the "architectonic" imagination in the *Turrius* to the poetic theory of the *Naugerius* and to the conception of the poet. The argument of connection between these two texts has to move in the other direction; that is, the architectonic and philosophical capacity of the poet is the model on which the architectonic capacity of the productive "scientist" may be founded.

43. Fracastoro's main intention in the *Naugerius* seems to have been to keep each art and science distinctly defined, in Aristotelian fashion, while he worked out the scope in which all arts and sciences might be joined in the person who practiced universal knowledge. The poet is the "architect" par excellence not only because he may be a philosopher as he knows, a painter as he describes, a rhetorician as he writes, and so forth, and not merely because he can fabricate "subnotions" into chimeras and castles, but especially because he gathers many knowledges together and arranges them in instructive and delightful expressions—a proportion of major significance (*Turrius*, as quoted in Bundy, "Fracastoro," p. 53).

44. Evelyn Fox Keller further illuminates the problem of subjective and objective assignations to different arts and sciences and to the genders of their practitioners in her essay, "Feminism and Science," *Signs* 7 (1982): 589–602.

45. Cf. other Italian theorists. Jacopo Mazzoni, for example, had related the poetic fiction produced by imitation to the truth of scientific logic by also linking "image" to "idea," Aristotelian mimesis to Platonic form. Mazzoni concluded in this fashion that poetry was the re-creative faculty of the civil science, statesmanship (*Literary Criticism, Plato to Dryden*, trans. Allen Gilbert [New York: American Book Co., 1940; Detroit: Wayne State Univ. Press, 1962], pp. 355–56). Tasso went further even than Fracastoro's scientific poetics and Mazzoni's political poetics when discussing the relation of poetry to theology. He examined the intelligible, dialectical aspect of the *eikastic* representations of the imagination rather than the visible aspect, and so left the debate with the pictorial arts far behind. If the poet is a maker of images, Tasso explains, this is not to say that he is a maker of idols, like the sophist in his verbal fantasies, but

a maker of images in the guise of a speaking picture, and in this like to the divine theologian who forms the ideas of things and commands that they be realized, and if dialectic and metaphysic, which were the divine philosophy of the Gentiles, have such conformity that they were by the ancients thought of as the same, it is not strange that the poet should be almost the same as the theologian and the dialectician. (*Discorsi*; Gilbert, *Literary Criticism*, p. 476)

Tasso refers to two other commonplaces in the renaissance arts debates that also appear in Sidney's *Defence*. Using the Horatian argument of profit and pleasure, Tasso says that profit is chiefly considered

with respect to that art which is as it were architect of all others. Therefore, it is the statesman's duty to consider what poetry and what delight should be prohibited, since pleasure, which should correspond to that honey with which the lip of the cup is smeared when medicine is given to children, should not produce the effect of injurious poison and should not keep the mind occupied in vain reading. (P. 468)

Later Tasso identifies "art" with "wisdom" (p. 471). In other words, Tasso turned poetic imagination into the principle of transcendent reason, the wisdom discipline that understands the causes of the arts and sciences. His use of the proportionality of visibles to invisibles appropriately reinterpreted Plato's analogy of the sun as the model of cognition in Book 6 of the *Republic*. What the poet gives his reader to see by way of images and figures in the light of the poetic fiction is a vision that the reader must creatively realize in life. It is the likeness of the divine mind itself, beyond the natural cosmos, that poetry re-creates intellectually in its images and morally in its effect on human character.

46. I shall cite Puttenham, *The Arte of English Poesie*, in facsimile, ed. Baxter Hathaway (Kent, Ohio: Kent State Univ. Press, 1970).

47. For a recent treatment see Derek Attridge, "Puttenham's Perplexity: Nature, Art, and the Supplement in Renaissance Poetic Theory," in *Literary Theory/Renaissance Texts*, ed. Parker and Quint, pp. 257–79. See especially pp. 271–72 on whether art can restore the "true self" lost in the Fall, and p. 279 n.23 on the way art might replace religion as an avenue of grace if Sidney's logic were followed. I have argued that such a companioning of art and religion is, of course, precisely what Sidney intended. Attridge says that decorum is the most important rule in Puttenham but is, in effect, no rule because it names the aspect of the poet's art that is "not reducible to rule" and is "natural" (p. 266). On the preference of Puttenham to Sidney in New Historicism, see Jonathan Crewe, *Hidden Designs: The Critical Profession and Renaissance Literature* (New York: Methuen, 1986), pp. 21–34, 70–71, 129.

48. In the *De Censura Veri Liber Prior* published with the *De Disciplinis Libri XX* and the *De Tradendis Disciplinis* (Antwerp, 1531), fol. 48ʳ: "Sunt que gradu aliq transeunt ad res etiam alias signandas, ideo metaphora nominatur, siue translatio. . . . ideo & hoc analogum appellemus, quasi proportionale."

49. See Wilson's *Arte of Rhetorique* (ed. Mair): a metaphor is "an alteration of a worde, from the proper and naturall meaning, to that which is not proper, and yet greeth thereunto by some likeness, that appereth to be in it" (pp. 172–73). Wilson argues that no oration persuades efficaciously "without the helpe of wordes altered and translated," and then explains "the diuersitie of translations" as those from the mind to the body, from the creature without reason to the creature with reason, from the living to those without life, or vice versa. "In obseruing the worke of Nature in all seuerall substances wee may finde translations at will, then the which nothing is more profitable for any one, that mindeth by his utteraunce to stirre the hartes of men, either one waie or other" (p. 173). Cf. Henry Peacham *The Garden of Eloquence* (London, 1577), sig. B.ij.ᵛ, on the special usefulness of visual metaphors "because the mind and the sight so much resemble one another." For a recent study of late sixteenth- and early seventeenth-century poetic observation, see Elizabeth Cook, *Seeing through Words: The Scope of Late Renaissance Poetry* (New Haven: Yale Univ. Press, 1986).

50. See Gregorius Reisch *Margarita Philosophica* (Basel, 1535), p. 120.

51. See James Nohrnberg's collection of examples of punishment for skeptophilia in renaissance texts in *The Analogy of* The Faerie Queene (Princeton, N.J.: Princeton Univ. Press, 1976), p. 774.

52. In the prefatory letter, "To All Gentle Men and Yomen of Englande," in *Toxophilus*, ed. W. W. Wright (Cambridge: Cambridge Univ. Press, 1904), p. xv. *Toxophilus* was published in 1545 and reprinted in 1571 and 1589.

53. Compare Sir Thomas Wyatt's analogy of invention and desire in "Whoso list to hunt" and see Goldblatt's reading of Wyatt's paraphrases in "Power, Sexuality, Inwardness in Wyatt's Poetry," in *Renaissance Self-Fashioning* (Chicago: Univ. of Chicago Press, 1980), pp. 115–56. See also Anne Ferry, *The 'Inward' Language: Sonnets of Wyatt, Sidney, and Donne* (Chicago: Univ. of Chicago Press, 1983).

54. *Certayne Notes of Instruction* (1575), sig. L.ij, in facsimile edition of *A Hundreth sundrie Flowres* (London, 1573), the two having been printed together (Yorkshire: Scolar Press, 1970).

55. Cf. Yvor Winters's reading of this poem in "The 16th Century Lyric in England: A Critical and Historical Reinterpretation," *Poetry* 53 (1939): 258–72, 320–35; 54 (1939): 35–51.

56. "Patriarchal Territories: The Body Enclosed," in *Rewriting the Renaissance*, pp. 123–44. Especially see Jonathan Crewe's essay, "The Hegemonic Theater of George Puttenham," *ELR* 16 (1986): 71–85, and his development of Puttenham's political sensitivity to the role of art in establishing social order in *Hidden Designs*, pp. 19–34. Crewe places Puttenham's work in relation to Wilson's and to the constructive rhetorical myths of Orpheus and Amphion (p. 24) and rightly compares Puttenham's "reductive" treatment of tragedy to Sidney's (p. 31).

57. See Woodbridge on the renaissance linking of husband-domination by the wife to the satire of feminine shrewishness (*Women and the English Renaissance*, pp. 191–93). Woodbridge has presented the textual evidence for much of Ben Jonson's subordination of the feminine in his plays.

58. *Timber, or Discoveries* (London, 1641), in *Ben Jonson, the Poems, the Prose Works*, ed. C. H. Herford Percy and Evelyn Simpson, 11 vols. (Oxford: Clarendon, 1925–52), 8:636. Study of the tensions in literary architectonics may qualify the standard literary association of Ben Jonson with "plain style." See Wesley Trimpi, *Ben Jonson's Poems: A Study of the Plain Style* (Stanford: Stanford Univ. Press, 1962) and Annabel M. Patterson's critique of Trimpi's view of the three styles in her book, *Hermogenes and the Renaissance: Seven Ideas of Style* (Princeton, N.J.: Princeton Univ. Press, 1970), p. 29 n.36. From a different perspective, Stanley Fish makes a similar comment in "Authors-Readers: Jonson's Community of the Same," in *Lyric Poetry: Beyond New Criticism*, ed. Chaviva Hosek and Patricia Parker (Ithaca, N.Y.: Cornell Univ. Press, 1985), p. 143.

59. *Literary Fat Ladies*, pp. 24–26.

60. *The Poems of Ben Jonson*, ed. Ian Donaldson (New York: Oxford Univ. Press, 1975), p. 91; see Don E. Wayne, *Penshurst: The Semiotics of Place and the Poetics of History* (Madison: Univ. of Wisconsin Press, 1984), on "the book of Sidney" represented by the house and on the history of myth and the myth of history (pp. 79–80).

61. For the text of Marvell, see *Poems & Letters*, ed. H. M. Margoliouth, 2d ed., 2 vols. (Oxford: Oxford Univ. Press, 1952), 1:59–83.

62. See D. J. Gordon, "Poet and Architect: The Intellectual Setting of the Quarrel between Ben Jonson and Inigo Jones," *JWCI* 12 (1949): 152–78; reprinted in *The Renaissance Imagination*, ed. Stephen Orgel (Berkeley: Univ. of California Press, 1975), pp. 77–101.

63. (London, 1624), in facsimile, ed. Frederick Hard (Charlottesville: Univ. of Virginia Press, 1968).

64. *Philosophical Survey*, 3d ed., in *Reliquiae Wottonianae* (London: T. Roycroft, 1572), pp. 75, 72 (printer's error). On American use of the concept of the "architectural" nurturing of children through education, see David MacLeod, *Building Character in the American Boy: The Boy Scouts, YMCA, and Their Forerunners, 1870–1920* (Madison: Univ. of Wisconsin Press, 1983).

65. *Of Education,* ed. Allan Abbott, in *The Works of John Milton,* ed. Frank Allen Patterson, 18 vols. (New York: Columbia Univ. Press, 1931), 4:277. Cf. Calvin *Institutes* 1.1.1 on the "miserable ruin" caused by the first man.

66. Cf. Jean de Serres's *Platonis Opera* 2.164–65 on self-knowledge; *Nosce Teipsum* was published in 1599 with a dedication to Queen Elizabeth; it was sufficiently popular to go through several editions in the early seventeenth century; and I am citing the one published in London in 1619. Cf. Sidney's remarks on the oracular in the *Defence* with regard to both Delphos and the Sibyl (p. 77).

67. See chapter 1, n. 91.

68. F. E. Hutchinson, in the introduction to his edition of *The Works of George Herbert* (Oxford: Clarendon, 1941), p. xxv, remarks that Herbert's early amatory sonnets are imitative of Sidney; but see Arnold Stein's comment on Herbert's criticism of rhetoric to master the rhetoric of sincerity and his tone of cultivated naivete, in *George Herbert's Lyrics* (Baltimore: Johns Hopkins Univ. Press, 1968), pp. 1–44, and especially see Louis Martz's discussion of Herbert and Sidney in *The Poetry of Meditation* (New Haven: Yale Univ. Press, 1954), pp. 259–82. Martz found Sidney's translation of the Psalms, not only Sidney's sonnets, to have directly affected the "music" of Herbert's *Temple* (p. 273). Cf. Rosemond Tuve, *A Reading of George Herbert* (Chicago: Univ. of Chicago Press, 1952), on how

> imaginative logic, this functioning of the mind as it "sees resemblances" has results for poetry which excite us by their power, not by their newness. What his connexions do is to reawaken into new life whole complexes of meaning, deeper, more ancient, and more inclusive than the meanings any single man's experience can provide, and by the same token we cannot follow where he leads with minds too innocent. (P. 63)

To Tuve should go the credit for recognizing that Herbert's claim to plain speech in "Jordan (I)" is not a rejection of the Neoplatonic love poetry of the Cambridge Spenserians but an effort to express divine love as well as human love, as Sidney also desired. See also Barbara Lewalski's borrowing of George Herbert's question, "Is there in truth no beautie?" for her discussion of Protestant poetics in general in *Protestant Poetics and the Seventeenth-Century Religious Lyric* (Princeton, N.J.: Princeton Univ. Press, 1979), pp. 3–27, and the chapter on Herbert ("Artful Psalms from the Temple of the Heart," pp. 283–316). Diana Benet has furthered the discussion in *Secretary of Praise: The Poetic Vocation of George Herbert* (Columbia: Univ. of Missouri Press, 1984), and Richard Todd, *The Opacity of Signs: Acts of Interpretation in George Herbert's* The Temple (Columbia: Univ. of Missouri Press, 1986), has shown the complexity of Herbert's exegesis.

69. *In Certaine Learned and Elegant Workes . . . Written in His Youth, and Familiar Exercises with Sir Philip Sidney* (London, 1633), pp. 23–52.

70. Donald Davie, in *Purity of Diction in English Verse* (New York: Schocken, 1967), lists Greville among those who produced a "strength of statement" to be found "in chaste or pure diction, because it goes together with economy in metaphor" (p. 68). Cf. Yvor Winters, "The 16th Century Lyric in England: A Critical and Historical Reinterpretation."

71. See J. G. Nichols's comparison of poems by Sidney and Greville in *The Poetry of Sir Philip Sidney* (Liverpool: Liverpool Univ. Press, 1974), pp. 49–50, and compare Donald Davie's remark that the poet who tries for pure diction and its strength "will never have his reader's love, but he may have his esteem" (*Purity of Diction,* p. 68). Also see Hardin Craig's evaluation in *The Literature of the English Renaissance* (New York: Oxford Univ. Press, 1950; New York: Collier Books, 1962), p. 131.

72. See Richard Haydocke's translation of Lomazzo's arts treatise (*A Tracte Containing the Artes*), for example, on the development of the characters of writing as a form of painting in black and white to preserve the time and to contain all the ideas and similitudes of the arts and sciences because of the weak power of "memorative corporall" (pp. 2–3), and compare the broader use of the term *character* in Francis Bacon's idea in *The Advancement of Learning,* ed.

G. W. Kitchin (London: J. M. Dent and Sons, 1915), that in divine philosophy, natural philosophy, and human philosophy, all things are "stamped with the triple character of the power of God, the difference of nature, and the use of man" (2.5.2, p. 85).

73. See, for example, Thomas Morton, bishop of Durham, *Ezekiel's Wheels: A Treatise Concerning Divine Providence Very Seasonable for All Ages* (London: J. G. for Richard Royston, 1653), especially the preface, sig. A2r–A4r, and the first section of Morton's treatise, pp. 17–39.

74. Reprinted by Paul Alpers, ed., *Elizabethan Poetry: Modern Essays in Criticism* (New York: Oxford Univ. Press, 1967), pp. 93–125. Cf. the remarks of Jonathan Crewe on Winters and the British sense of the literary essay in *Hidden Designs*, p. 15.

75. *The Advancement of Learning* 2.5.2. Cf. Bacon's discussion of the division of knowledge and the ladder of the intellect in the *New Organon*, "The Plan of the Great Instauration." On Bacon's influence see Charles Whitney, *Francis Bacon and Modernity* (New Haven: Yale Univ. Press, 1986).

76. *Astronomia Nova* (1609), reprinted in *Gesämmelte Werke* (Munich: C. H. Beck'sche Verlagsbuchhandlung, 1937), 3:35.

77. *Daedalus* 107 (1978): 23–35.

Epilogue

1. See, for example, the characterization of the difference between Sidney's and Shelley's *Defences* in William K. Wimsatt, Jr., and Cleanth Brooks, *Literary Criticism: A Short History* (New York: Knopf, 1957), p. 423: the difference between the two *Defences* "lies as deep as the difference between Aristotle and Kant." This analogy is made despite an earlier effort in the same book to credit both Platonic and Aristotelian themes in Sidney's *Defence* (pp. 167–72). But compare Frank Lentricchia's characterization of Sidney's "neo-Aristotelianism" on the status of history as "intransigent, irrational particularity" and of art's trafficking "in the realm of the universal" in *Criticism and Social Change* (Chicago: Univ. of Chicago Press, 1983), p. 59. Lentricchia makes the remark parenthetically before he explicitly refers to Wimsatt's critical history and Kenneth Burke's social and political view of the comedy of history distinct from the moral view of "any number of Christianized Renaissance neo-Aristotelians" (pp. 63–66) and before he discusses Burke's revision of Kantian essentialism (p. 68). Lentricchia's characterization of Sidney's view of history and of art strikes me as Kantian and neither particularly Aristotelian *nor* truly Sidneian. A much better sorting out is done by Jerome J. McGann, *Social Values and Poetic Acts: The Historical Judgment of Literary Work* (Cambridge, Mass.: Harvard Univ. Press, 1988), pp. 73–74, when he observes Sidney's use of an Aristotelian argument to defend poetry from Platonic criticism; confirms the theological nature of Sidney's "ideological ground"; compares Sidney's "light of Christ" to Coleridge's "sacramentalism"; and contrasts both, not to Kant's assertion of values, but to Kant's placement of the "fundament of the aesthetic moment" in metaphysics and not theology.

2. Edward Caird, *The Critical Philosophy of Immanuel Kant*, 2 vols. (Glasgow: James Maclehose and Sons, 1889), vol. 1, chap. 2, pp. 45–51. Throughout the Epilogue, rather than use an original German edition, I draw on two English translations of Kant's *Critique of Pure Reason* to suggest the manner in which Kantian thinking infused nineteenth- and twentieth-century English and American developments in reading literature and in constructing a view of literary knowledge and literary forms: the translation of Norman Kemp Smith (London: Macmillan, 1929) and that of J. M. D. Meiklejohn (London: George Bell and Sons, 1876).

3. See J. N. Findlay, *Hegel: A Re-Examination* (London: Allen and Unwin, 1958), pp. 28–29, 48–55, and Wimsatt and Brooks, *Literary Criticism*, pp. 490–91.

4. See William Temple's discussion of Sidney's argument at the point at which Sidney compares metaphysics, natural philosophy, and the poetic art in *William Temple's Analysis of Sir Philip Sidney's Apology for Poetry*, ed. and trans. John Webster (Binghamton, N. Y.: Center for

Medieval and Early Renaissance Studies, 1984), pp. 76–77. Temple interprets Sidney's use of the word *metaphysics*, saying that for Sidney it is made up of "abstract notions" and that from its name he supposes "both that the 'supernatural' is an alien of and that metaphysics is concerned with the contemplation of nature" in its especially deep and hidden aspects. He faults Sidney for not distinguishing metaphysics and natural philosophy sufficiently, since natural philosophy is made up of abstract notions and "the universals of theory" (p. 76). But later Temple explains that metaphysics and natural philosophy meet in the "forms" of things and that "the wisdom of Aristotle's metaphysics" is "not a single and a singular art anyway, but rather it is like a sort of chaos, made up from the disciplines of many arts" (p. 77). Temple goes on, then, to comment on the method with which Sidney has put the special knowledge in order with regard to the organization of the arts and sciences. In the discussion of the ends of the "serving sciences" versus the "ending end" of the highest knowledge, Temple simply comments that Sidney embellishes his analogy of the arts with regard to the poetic art from the definition of "Architectonic" (p. 93). He, too, ignores the feminized metaphor of the mistress-knowledge.

5. See the *Critique*, trans. Meiklejohn, pp. 503–4. The word *system* is the source of many difficulties in modern criticism. Cf. Ferdinand de Saussure's definition of *language* as "a self-contained whole and a principle of classification" (p. 9) and "a system of signs in which the only essential thing is the union of meanings and sound-images" (p. 15) in the *Course in General Linguistics*, trans. Wade Baskin (1959; reprint, New York: McGraw-Hill, 1966), with Culler's remarks that the possibility of looking at literature through a linguistic model "helped to justify the idea to abandon literary history and biographical criticism" and has been "eminently salutary" in "securing for the French some of the benefits of Anglo-American 'New Criticism' " (*Structuralist Poetics: Structuralism, Linguistics, and the Study of Literature* [Ithaca, N.Y.: Cornell Univ. Press, 1975], p. 255). Culler discusses Roland Barthes's sense of system in Racinian tragedy noting that to analyze the text as a system, one must determine the functional oppositions and grasp the "centre" of the system, which functions as a principle of inclusion and exclusion (pp. 98–99). See also Livingston's effort to use the social-science definition of *system* developed by Richard S. Rudner in the definition of literary theory epistemologically; "the concept of 'system' is not synonymous with general notions of 'orderliness' or of 'fitting together' " given the word loosely in literary circles, but imposes, rather, "a rigorous set of formal requirements upon the builder of a theory" (*Literary Knowledge: Humanistic Inquiry and the Philosophy of Science* [Ithaca, N.Y.: Cornell Univ. Press, 1989], p. 14). From the historical vantage of Sidney's literary architectonics, which includes a self-referential critique of master-building of all sorts, including its own, the problem is that modern theories of criticism or "systems" do, indeed, represent a kind of "building."

6. Yirmiahu Yovel's comments in *Kant and the Philosophy of History* (Princeton, N.J.: Princeton Univ. Press, 1980) will help to clarify insofar as Yovel explains the way Kant's philosophical system expounds "the self-development of reason" from which it gets its "organizing schema" and unites all into an "organic whole" that cannot, however, emerge all at once because of the finitude of human reason (p. 228):

> Kant adds that "at the present time" it is already possible to devise the whole architectonic human knowledge; but this is only because the history of philosophy, which is now coming to an end, has the same organic form as the final system that brings it to light. In other words, *the structure of the history of philosophy is inherently the same as that of the system of philosophy, although it must be concealed and become distorted in the process of its development.* This proto-Hegelian view is complemented by other texts, which add the elements of *opposition* and *revolution* to the dynamics of the history of philosophy. To say that the development of reason is gradual does not mean that it is continuous. Instead it is characterized by periods of accumulation, contradiction, collapse, and radical innovation. It is true *in principle* that there can be no "polemic" and no "antithetic" in the field of reason . . . but such contradictions are inevitable in the *history* of philosophy—which is, as we shall see, the historicized form of the architectonic, where its single components emerge disjointedly and

in seeming opposition to one another. Hence the great controversies in the history of philosophy have their origin in the nature of pure reason. (Pp. 228–29)

7. Cf. Jacques Derrida, *Of Grammatology*, trans. Gayatri Chakravorty Spivak (Baltimore: Johns Hopkins Univ. Press, 1976), pp. 65–67, on Kant's development of unity and on the subject of Saussure's linguistics:

> Origin of the experience of space and time, this writing of difference, this fabric of the trace, permits the difference between space and time to be articulated, to appear as such, in the unity of an experience. . . . The concepts of *present, past,* and *future,* everything in the concepts of time and history which implies evidence of them—the metaphysical concept of time in general—cannot adequately describe the structure of the trace.

Derrida goes on to connect the trace to "différance" and the presence-absence of the trace with play, turning away from Kant's systems-making and totalization:

> All dualisms, all theories of the immortality of the soul or of the spirit, as well as all monisms, spiritualist or materialist, dialectical or vulgar, are the unique theme of a metaphysics whose entire history was compelled to strive toward the reduction of the trace. The subordination of the trace to the full presence summed up in the logos, the humbling of writing beneath a speech dreaming its plenitude, such are the gestures required by an onto-theology determining the archeological and eschatological meaning of being as presence, as parousia, as life without différance: another name for death, historical metonymy where God's name holds death in check. (*Of Grammatology*, p. 71)

8. W. H. Werkmeister, *Kant: The Architectonic and Development of His Philosophy* (London: Open Court Pub. Co., 1980), p. 101, reminds us that integration and synthesis, which alone constitute experience, are essential to Kant:

> In his view, it was not sufficient to bring the manifold of sense perceptions under the unity of concepts and to view nature as appearance in space and time in strict conformity with laws . . . ; his conception of the architectonic of reason led him to a unitary conception of philosophy as an all-embracing system of principles and laws. (P. 101)

Werkmeister's thesis, however, is that Kant's unity has been misinterpreted, that the architectonic indicates the unity not of "a preconceived or static system" but of "a problem-determined development in his thinking" (Introduction, unpaginated).

9. In the *Critique of Pure Reason* (trans. Meiklejohn), Kant distinguishes the philosopher from the historian of philosophy and the historian; he distinguishes the "ideal teacher" or type of the philosopher from the mathematician, the natural philosopher, and the logician, since these knowers are "artists engaged in the arrangement and formation of conceptions" (p. 508). His identification of the metaphysician and the moral philosopher has recently been reevaluated by William James Booth in *Interpreting the World: Kant's Philosophy of History and Politics* (Toronto: Univ. of Toronto Press, 1986). Booth takes Kant out of the usual association with German idealism and with Hegel and Marx and their "essentially optimistic" view of history and associates him with more skeptical positions on history and politics: "In a sort of moral Cartesianism, Kant clings to the idea of a finite but autonomous self, and his critique of the historical optimist and the revolutionary makers of heavenly kingdoms on earth flows from that single point" (p. xxiv). Citing Kant's view of the failure of metaphysics to succeed in "building a tower which should reach to the heavens" and the metaphysical provision of materials sufficient "only for a dwelling-house," Booth argues that Kant's *Critique* can be read as the most radical skeptical argument (pp. 16–17):

> In this sense, the value of the *Critique* is purely negative. It is a discipline limiting the claims of reason, and it has the modest task of calling the mind back from its pleasant, but fruitless, dreams. It teaches us that our knowledge is a plane with a horizon or, to use the constructive

metaphor more appropriate to a theory that emphasizes the role of spontaneity in experience, it invites us to consider the materials available for building our edifice, and the height
to which the building may rise. . . . The structure can be high enough. Kant wrote, for our
business here on earth, our practical purposes, but not of sufficient height to allow us certain
knowledge of the suprasensible. Kant's Copernican revolution places man at the centre of its
appraisal of nature but at the same time limits and undermines his pretensions. It tells man
that the world is his, his property, the edifice that he has constructed, but it also tells him
that the world is all that is the case. Where determination by laws of nature comes to an
end, all *explanation* comes to an end as well. Nothing is left by defence." (Pp. 17–18)

10. The phrase "the aesthetics of the will" is my way of condensing Werkmeister's careful
working out of the argument in Kant's three *Critiques* (on *Pure Reason, Practical Reason,* and
Judgment) and associating his purposiveness, which is subjectively aesthetic, and teleological
with regard to nature and natural beauty (p. 100), with natural science and with morals (pp.
101–48). Werkmeister sees Kant's *Critique of Practical Reason* as an aspect of the *Critique of Pure
Reason* partly because Kant is trying to work out his architectonic in which *all* systems of
philosophy finally interrelate and synthesize. Kant sees the morally responsible will as "nothing other than practical reason" (p. 132), Werkmeister says, and the will is "a law of duty, or
moral restraint," which implies the ultimate unity of the realm of nature and the realm of
freedom. "Therein lies its [the conception of a basic law of practical reason] systematic importance for the architectonic of Kant's philosophy" (*Kant: The Architectonic,* p. 133). See also René
Wellek, *A History of Modern Criticism: 1750–1950,* 4 vols. (London: Jonathan Cape, 1955), vol. 1,
The Later Eighteenth Century, on Kant's isolation of the aesthetic realm, on one hand, from the
realm of science, morality, and utility and his definition of aesthetic pleasure as "disinterested
satisfaction" (p. 229), and Kant's view of the "purposeless purposiveness" of art and nature as
organisms, on the other, so that art possesses "the possibility of bridging the gulf between
necessity and freedom, the world of deterministic nature and the world of moral action" (p.
231). Wellek considers a "deep dualism" basic to Kant's philosophy. Cf. Derrida, *Of Grammatology,* p. 71.

11. Cf. Wimsatt and Brooks's identification of Sidney's *Defence* as a "brilliant epitome" of
Italian criticism—that is, a miscellany of ideas (*Literary Criticism,* p. 167). Contrast it to Sidney's
preference of the "exercise to know" over the "exercise as having known" (*Defence,* p. 112).
Wimsatt and Brooks go on to say, "The pre-Platonic directness of this apology—as if the
rhapsode Ion were speaking—was perhaps possible only because it came before the great vogue
of Aristotle's *Poetics*" (p. 167, emphasis mine). But see S. K. Heninger, Jr., *Sidney and Spenser:
The Poet As Maker* (University Park: Pennsylvania State Univ. Press, 1989), p. 231, on Sidney's
syncretic use of Aristotle.

12. I am condensing in this sentence several different conclusions of Roland Barthes in
structuralist analysis and of Jacques Derrida in his confrontation of the limits of structuralism
and his move to deconstruction, particularly in his book *L'écriture et la différence* (Paris: Seuil,
1967). Some trace a critical development from Kant to Abrams and from Hegel to Derrida; others
see a merger; and still others say deconstruction develops out of New Criticism, which evolves
out of Kantian formalism. Aristotle etymologically explained the architectonic knowledges with
regard to *archia*: the architectonic arts especially are called "beginnings" because they are
directing principles (*Metaphysics* 5.1 [1013a]).

13. For pertinent bibliographic references, see chapter 1, p. 58, and n.63.

14. Cf. Cudworth's *True Intellectual System* (2:4.23, pp. 295–96) on the one God "self-made"
and producing other things while we human beings can merely produce images of ourselves
and whatever else we wish by interposing a looking glass. The same God is "all will," nor is
there anything in him that he does not will, nor is his being before his will; "but his will is
himself, or he himself is the first will," Cudworth remarks (2:4.23, p. 299).

15. See Patricia Parker's discussion of *catachresis* as an "abusive" form of metaphor because

"unmaidenly" in the estimation of renaissance rhetoricians, in *Literary Fat Ladies: Rhetoric, Gender, Property* (London: Methuen, 1987), p. 108.

16. Trans. Frank Justus Miller, 2 vols. (London: William Heinemann, 1916), 2:265. Cf. Richard Lanham's discussion of the two different strategies, the "serious" and the "rhetorical," of speaking in the Renaissance—both underwritten by Plato and Ovid, in *The Motives of Eloquence: Literary Rhetoric in the Renaissance* (New Haven: Yale Univ. Press, 1976), pp. 36–64. Kant strips away the Ovidian allegorization, it appears, but silently keeps the central self of Platonic or philosophical discourse.

17. Kant alludes to Alexander Pope, too. See Booth's discussion of Kant's comparison of metaphysics to Hecuba, *Interpreting the World*, pp. 3–4, and Werkmeister, *Kant: The Architectonic*, pp. 10–11, on Pope.

18. Yovel's comments in *Kant and the Philosophy of History* are most helpful here. He points out that Kant's praxis is a principle of totalization and that his special imperative to act toward promoting the highest good in the world is an historical imperative (pp. 6–7); that the history of religion latent in Kant's history of reason is a moral totality (p. 7); and that Kant's model of the history of philosophy in the "Architectonic" in the *Critique of Pure Reason* and his theory of revolution "bear a striking resemblance to those of Hegel" (p. 9).

19. See Greene, *The Light in Troy: Imitation and Discovery in Renaissance Poetry* (New Haven: Yale Univ. Press, 1982), pp. 19–27, on our loss not of *what* but *how* metaphor means something in the classical, medieval, and renaissance past; cf. Livingston's caricature of those who still follow Husserl and phenomenology in a definition of philosophy as queen *and* handmaiden of the sciences "in a tangled hierarchy" (*Literary Knowledge*, p. 124).

20. See Booth, *Interpreting the World*, pp. 16–51, on negation in Kant, and Werkmeister, *Kant: The Architectonic*, pp. 96–97, on the "Architectonic," nature, and freedom, and pp. 129–31.

21. According to J. E. Sandys, *A History of Classical Scholarship*, 2d ed., 3 vols. (Cambridge: Cambridge Univ. Press, 1906–8), 2:175–76, de Serres's *Plato* was the edition used for two centuries after its publication in 1578. This makes it the likely edition used by Ralph Cudworth in his *True Intellectual System*, but I have noticed only Cudworth's allusions to Ficino.

22. Norman Kemp Smith, *A Commentary on Kant's "Critique of Pure Reason,"* 2d ed. (1923; reprint, New York: Humanities Press, 1962), pp. xxii–xxiii:

> To the general plan, based upon professedly logical principles, Kant . . . has given the title, architectonic; and he carries it out with a thoroughness to which all other considerations, and even at times those of sound reasoning, are made to give way. Indeed, he clings to it with the unreasoning affection which not infrequently attaches to a favorite hobby.

Cf. Werkmeister, *Kant: The Architectonic*, pp. 73–75, for some disagreement with Smith, whose notion of the *Critique* not as a unified system in fact but as a record of Kant's efforts to work out manifold problems in making such a system is the one Werkmeister's book develops.

23. See Steadman, *The Lamb and the Elephant: Ideal Imitation and the Context of Renaissance Allegory* (San Marino, Calif.: Huntington Library, 1974), p. 213ff., on the problem of periodization of the Renaissance.

24. *The Counter Renaissance* (New York: Charles Scribner, 1950), p. 28.

25. See Murrin, *The Veil of Allegory: Some Notes toward a Theory of Allegorical Rhetoric in the Renaissance* (Chicago: Univ. of Chicago Press, 1969), on Sidney's "middle position" (pp. 184–89). Murrin carefully distinguishes moral, political, philosophical, and theological levels of allegory before he notes Sidney's claim to *and* denial of inspiration (pp. 169–72) and reads Sidney's position as one between allegorists and prophets and the incipient neoclassicists, the orators shifting from divine truth to poetic genius. I see Sidney's middle position in yet another sense with regard to the epistemological mediation of the arts and sciences.

26. See Elizabeth S. Donno, " 'Old Mouse-Eaten Records': History in Sidney's *Apology*," *SP*

72 (1975): 275–98, and cf. David Norbrook's view in *Poetry and Politics in the English Renaissance* (Boston: Routledge and Kegan Paul, 1984) that Sidney's use of Aristotle to find poetry more philosophical than history indicates an "autonomy," a "freedom from subjection to empirical fact," and "a detachment from traditional ideas and the free exploration of alternatives" (p. 94). Norbrook's summary is fine as long as it is contextualized by renaissance sources on historiography, in Puttenham's "art and the poetic idea according with modern theories of the free exploration of alternatives" in the freedom of poetry from history. See chapter 3, pp. 178–79, 191 nn. 58–59 of this book for an example of extraordinary "allegorical" freedom in Estienne's interpretation of Herodotus.

27. Thus Sidney's figure of mistress-knowledge, as a prosopopoeia, is a distinct figure made to work in Sidney's apparent allegorical veiling; but in fact his appropriation of her powers moves us toward his notion of regenerated poetic genius, and her role politically and epistemologically is quite unveiled elsewhere in the *Defence*. With regard to the appearance of the veiled presence of Sophia in antiquity, only recently have theologians taken it up in the study of gnosticism and the goddess because of the heretical nature of the subject. See especially Pheme Perkins, "Sophia and the Mother-Father: The Gnostic Goddess," in *The Book of the Goddess Past and Present: An Introduction to Her Religion*, ed. Carl Olson (New York: Crossroad, 1987), pp. 97–109. Perkins's essay is particularly useful in its comments on Irenaeus, whose treatment of Valentinian and the "queen of heaven" would have been readily available in renaissance patrology.

28. On Kant, Newton, and Rousseau, see Werkmeister, *Kant: The Architectonic*, pp. 14–15.

29. *Writing and Difference*, trans. Alan Bass (Chicago: Univ. of Chicago Press, 1978), p. 292.

30. Vincent B. Leitch, *Deconstructive Criticism: An Advanced Introduction* (New York: Columbia Univ. Press, 1983), p. 38; cf. Leitch on Derrida's criticism of Jacques Lacan, pp. 29–32.

31. See Jacques Lacan, *Feminine Sexuality*, ed. Juliet Mitchell and Jacqueline Rose, trans. Jacqueline Rose (New York: Norton, 1985), especially "God and the *Jouissance* of The Woman," on the idea that, contrary to Freud, it is the man who takes on the woman since he is a "speaking being" and the making of love is "poetry" (p. 143), and "A Love Letter," on the sexual relation in knowledge and the subversion of knowledge (*connaissance*) and the relation between the idea of God (Other) and "that Other which, if she existed, the woman might be" (p. 153). In his presentation of the Seminar of January 21, 1975, Lacan again asserts that he speaks of *a* woman, since "*the* woman does not exist" (p. 167) and in the sexual relation "a woman is a symptom" for man, warding off the unconscious and ensuring the consistency of his relation with the phallic term. On courtly love, the sweet dreams of philosophy, and the dream of neurosis, see "A Love Letter," pp. 156–57. In "God and the *Jouissance* of The Woman," Lacan considers women, mystics, and the idea that there is a *jouissance* that goes beyond the phallus (pp. 145–47). Page du Bois astutely presents the case for the limitations of psychoanalysis in the first chapter of her book, "To Historicize Psychoanalysis," in *Sowing the Body: Psychoanalysis and Ancient Representations of Women* (Chicago: Univ. of Chicago Press, 1988), pp. 7–36, and is especially fine in the assessment of Lacan.

32. *The Principles of Art History: The Problem of the Development of Style in Later Art*, 7th ed. (1929), trans. M. D. Hottinger (1932; reprint, New York: Dover, 1950). The critical discrimination needed to sort this out is one that Madeleine Doran expressed at the beginning of *Endeavors of Art: A Study of Form in Elizabethan Drama* (Madison: Univ. of Wisconsin Press, 1954), p. 5, with regard to terminology: the presence of ideas in verbal forms of art may work with structural parallels to techniques of pictorial composition, but ideas complicate the judgment of the artistry and the significance of words such as *imitation, verisimilitude,* and *decorum*. E. H. Gombrich notes the aesthetic hybridization of renaissance arts debates that Wölfflin's system of classification further complicated by standardizing Alberti's and Vasari's use of Vitruvius's classifications of styles; see Gombrich's "Norm and Form: The Stylistic Categories of Art History and Their Origins in Renaissance Ideals," in *Norm and Form: Studies in the Art of the Renaissance*, 2d ed. (London: Phaidon, 1971), pp. 81–98. Gombrich makes similar comments on

the caprice of classification with respect to mannerism (pp. 99–106). The first edition of Vasari's *Lives of the Artists* had appeared in Florence in 1550; the second, expanded edition in 1568.

33. The confusion of *architectural* and *architectonic* in studies of Milton is frequent. See, for example, my discussion, p. 407 n.4. R. W. Condee has also collapsed the terms of the metaphor in his study as a critical expression of an idea (*Structure in Milton's Poetry: From the Foundation to the Pinnacle* [University Park: Pennsylvania State Univ. Press, 1974]). Judith Dundas has looked at Elizabethan architecture and *The Faerie Queene* (*DR* 45 [1966]: 470–78).

34. For example, John D. Walker, "The Architectonics of George Herbert's *The Temple*," *ELH* 29 (1962): 289–305, tries to force the analogy with the Hebraic Temple but inevitably leaves the architectural structure behind when he interprets the poems themselves. Roy Daniells, "A Happy Rural Seat," in *Paradise Lost, A Tercentenary Tribute*, ed. Balachandra Rajan (Toronto: Univ. of Toronto Press, 1969), considers the geographical architecture of Milton's Eden only to come round to a consideration of the encyclopedia of knowledges that Adam and the reader discover through self knowledge or the lack of it (p. 15). Also see *PMLA* 103 (1988): 998 for the description of a panel of papers on the "edifice complex" and "arch-expressed desire" and so forth in nineteenth-century literature.

35. See Joseph B. Dallett, "Ideas of Sight in *The Faerie Queene*," *ELH* 27 (1960): 87–121, for a more sophisticated grasp of Spenser's visual language than the literalizing of architectural metaphors.

36. *Paideia: The Ideals of Greek Culture*, trans. Gilbert Highet, 2d ed., 3 vols. (New York: Oxford Univ. Press, 1939–44), 1:xx–xxi.

37. *The Function of Criticism from the Spectator to Post-Structuralism* (Thetford, Eng.: Thetford Press, 1984), p. 9.

38. Eagleton is, of course, parodying with the title of his book the title of an essay by Arnold, "The Function of Criticism at the Present Time." My references are to Arnold's "Culture and Anarchy," in *Poetry and Criticism of Matthew Arnold*, ed. A. Dwight Culler (New Haven: Yale Univ. Press, 1961), pp. 407–75. Cf. Arnold's remark in a third essay, "Literature and Science," that literature is a "large word" encompassing all that is printed in a book, including Newton's *Principia* and Euclid's *Elements* (p. 385), to the structuralist reading of most things as "texts" and to the New Historical interest in reading literary culture through other discursive practices besides, formally speaking, literary texts.

39. This is the thesis of the entire book *Criticism and Social Change*.

40. (Ithaca, N.Y.: Cornell Univ. Press, 1985), p. 11.

41. Kahn, *Rhetoric*, pp. 188–90.

42. Kahn, *Rhetoric*, p. 189; see also Kahn's observation of the apparent contradiction in her use of Sidney (pp. 236–37 n.11) as she refers to the discussion of that doubting of the persuasiveness of poetry in Ferguson, *Trials of Desire: Renaissance Defenses of Poetry* (New Haven: Yale Univ. Press, 1983), pp. 137–62. Kahn sees Sidney as her subtext.

43. Kahn, *Rhetoric*, does so with reference to Terry Eagleton's discussion of the analogies between formalism, skepticism, and Anglo-American deconstruction in *Literary Theory: An Introduction* (Minneapolis: Univ. of Minnesota Press, 1983), pp. 143–47.

44. Kahn does discuss the *locus classicus* of an ethical definition of architectonics, Aristotle's *Nicomachean Ethics*, looking primarily at the Aristotelian placement of prudence in his hierarchy of the intellectual virtues in Book 6 and moving most skillfully from Aristotle to Cicero to the Quattrocento humanists, pp. 30–37, and to another citation of Sidney, p. 41. She very clearly works out this historical argument regarding phronesis—which is something I must admit, in fairness, I have not done in my more Platonic "leap of intuition" to Sidney's association of that power of practical reason with the mistress-knowledge. We are obviously working with some of the same texts and sources but asking different questions.

45. The best discussion I know of this problem in English renaissance poetic handling of allegory, poetry, and prophecy is Michael Murrin's book *The Veil of Allegory*, especially pp. 167–77 on Sidney and on "the end of allegory." Also see Steadman, *The Lamb and the Elephant*,

p. 75, on the frequent use of *prosopopoeiae*, like Reason and Dame Philosophy, in allegory and on their proper distinction from *allegoria*.

46. *The Structure of Scientific Revolutions*, 2d ed., enlarged, *Encyclopedia of Unified Science*, vol. 2, no. 2 (Chicago: Univ. of Chicago Press, 1970).

47. (Chicago: Univ. of Chicago Press, 1967). See especially the conclusion, pp. 232–62.

48. (New York: Methuen, 1967), pp. 99–127, passim, especially p. 101.

49. (New York: Harper and Row, 1952), pp. 8, 14–18. Buber's book arose out of lectures he gave at Yale, Princeton, Columbia, and Chicago in November and December 1951.

50. *The Incarnation of the Word* 13.7–8; 14.1–2, in *Select Writings and Letters of Athanasius, Bishop of Alexandria*, ed. Archibald Robertson, vol. 4 of *A Select Library of Nicene and Post-Nicene Fathers of the Christian Church*, ed. Philip Schaff and Henry Wace (1891; reprint, Grand Rapids, Mich.: Eerdmans, 1978), p. 43.

Index

Greek Words and Phrases
(variant forms reflect parent texts)

Ἀρρενοθήλυ, 234

Ἀῤῥενόθηλυς, 233

Ἀρχάς, 326 n.35
Ἀρχαιολογίας, 154
Ἄρχων, 9
Ἀρχή, 5

Ἀρχὴ Ἀρχῶν, 232

Ἀρχηγέτης, 232

Ἀρχηγόν, 154

Ἀρχηγός, 156

"'Ἀρχή, καὶ τέλος, καὶ μέσον ἁπάντων," 232
Ἀρχιτεκτονικαί, 272 n.9
Ἀρχιτεκτονική, xii-xiv, xix, xxi, xxii, 4, 6,
  17, 227, 250
Ἀρχιτεκτονικην, 133, 151
Ἀρχιτεκτονικόν τέγος, 159
Ἀρχιτεκτονικός, 153
Ἀρχιτεκτονικῶν τέλη, 272 n.9

Γνωςτόν, 151

Διατύπωσιν, 271 n.6

Ἐγκόσμιον, 232
Εἰκαςία, 169
Ἐγκύκλιον παιδείαν, 290 n.26
Θεοῦ, 151
Ἰδεῶν, 3, 271 n.6

Λογὸς σπερματικός, 315 n.24

Μισόμουσοι, 58

Ὁμοειδής, 233
Ὁμοούσιος, 233
Ὁμότιμος, 233

Ποιητής, 157
Πρεσβυτέραν καὶ ἀδελφὴν, 233
Πρωτουργός, 156

Τ' ἀγαθὸν, 232

Τὸ γνωςτὸν τοῦ Θεοῦ ἐν αὐτοῖς ἐφανερώθη,
  151
Τὸ ἕν, 232

Ὑπερκόσμιον, 232

Φιλαυτία, 246

General Index

Abel, 286 n.91
Abulafia, 318 n.45
Academy, Florentine, 117
Accommodation, rule of (*see also* Reading;
  Interpretation), 16, 19–20, 106, 167
Achilles, 12, 15–16
Acteon, 204, 222
Action (*see also* Government), xi, xiii, xxiv,
  12, 41–44, 190, 208–9, 274 n.20, 278 n.37,
  292 n.37, 294 n.41, 311 nn.86, 90; 319 n.52,
  325 n.20, 327 n.38, 334 n.10; private and
  public government of, 12–16, 104–7, 159,
  161, 181, 249, 251
Adam, xxvi, 36–37, 46, 67, 88, 126, 127,
  154–55, 158, 160, 162, 167, 169, 177, 203,
  221, 222, 224, 261–62, 278 n.37, 322 n.75,
  337 n.34; and naming things, xiv, 154–55

339